THE GLASGOW EDITION OF
THE WORKS OF ADAM SMITH

THE GLASGOW EDITION OF THE WORKS AND CORRESPONDENCE OF ADAM SMITH

Commissioned by the University of Glasgow to celebrate the bicentenary of the Wealth of Nations

I

THE THEORY OF MORAL SENTIMENTS
Edited by D. D. RAPHAEL *and* A. L. MACFIE

II

AN INQUIRY INTO THE NATURE AND CAUSES OF THE WEALTH OF NATIONS
Edited by R. H. CAMPBELL *and* A. S. SKINNER; *textual editor* W. B. TODD

III

ESSAYS ON PHILOSOPHICAL SUBJECTS
(and Miscellaneous Pieces)
Edited by W. P. D. WIGHTMAN

IV

LECTURES ON RHETORIC AND BELLES LETTRES
Edited by J. C. BRYCE
This volume includes the *Considerations concerning the First Formation of Languages*

V

LECTURES ON JURISPRUDENCE
Edited by R. L. MEEK, D. D. RAPHAEL, *and* P. G. STEIN
This volume includes two reports of Smith's course together with the 'Early Draft' of part of the *Wealth of Nations*

VI

CORRESPONDENCE OF ADAM SMITH
Edited by E. C. MOSSNER *and* I. S. ROSS

Associated volumes:

ESSAYS ON ADAM SMITH
Edited by A. S. SKINNER *and* T. WILSON

LIFE OF ADAM SMITH
By I. S. ROSS

The Correspondence of
ADAM SMITH

EDITED BY

ERNEST CAMPBELL MOSSNER
AND
IAN SIMPSON ROSS

OXFORD
AT THE CLARENDON PRESS
1977

Oxford University Press, Walton Street, Oxford, OX2 6DP

OXFORD LONDON GLASGOW NEW YORK
TORONTO MELBOURNE WELLINGTON CAPE TOWN
IBADAN NAIROBI DAR ES SALAAM LUSAKA ADDIS ABABA
KUALA LUMPUR SINGAPORE JAKARTA HONG KONG TOKYO
DELHI BOMBAY CALCUTTA MADRAS KARACHI

ISBN 0 19 828185 4

*Printed in Great Britain
at the University Press, Oxford
by Vivian Ridler
Printer to the University*

To
Carolyn

Preface

IN 1965 the senior editor of this volume was invited by the Adam Smith Committee of Glasgow University to write a life of Smith. Professor Mossner saw that an indispensable preliminary was an edition of the correspondence, and he prevailed on the Committee to sponsor this project, also to ask the junior editor to collaborate with him. No complete collection of the correspondence was in print, though John Rae's *Life of Adam Smith* (1895, reprinted 1965) and W. R. Scott's *Adam Smith as Student and Professor* (1937) presented the letters known to the respective authors. A few other letters had appeared in periodicals. The lack of a collected edition is all the more surprising in that no extensive correspondence is involved. Our tabulation is as follows:

from Smith (published): 131	to Smith (published): 98
(unpublished): 48	(unpublished): 27
(missing): 53	(missing): 40
232	165

In view of these numbers, we decided to print Smith's letters and those addressed to him whose contents provided significant information about Smith, or the lives of acquaintances in his career. The remainder of the letters to Smith have been calendared (Nos. 16, 62, 211, 255, 271, 279, and 285). Certain texts were not fully available to us: Letter 220 dated September 1782 (noted in a Caxton Head Catalogue); Letter 231 addressed to William Strahan, dated 6 October 1783 (sold at the Parke-Bernet Galleries, New York, on 22 October 1963); also Letter 257 addressed to Thomas Cadell, dated 14 March 1786 (sold at Sotheby's on 27 October 1959). It is to be hoped that their owners will make them accessible to the scholarly world, also that the missing letters or some of them, at least, will be found.

To be sure, Adam Smith for the most part was a perfunctory, dilatory correspondent. When addressing him, David Hume could resort to bold remonstrance: 'I can write as seldom and as short as you' (Letter 90, January 1766); or, again, 'I am as Lazy a Correspondent as you; yet my Anxiety about you makes me write' (Letter 149, 8 February 1776). Another good friend, James Hutton, the vigorous extrovert geologist, affected to see in Smith's absorption in his studies the characteristics of a Laputan: 'I send you this flap in the ear to inform you that november is begun and there is little danger of frost till after the new year; so if you have anything to do with what is without you may conduct yourself accordingly; if it is otherwise and you are made up for sleep and vision, let me know when I should waken you again' (Letter 301, undated).

Another difficulty about editing the correspondence is that Smith himself was not in favour of such enterprises, as he indicated clearly to William Strahan in connection with a proposal to bring out a volume of Hume's letters: 'Many things would be published not fit to see the light to the great mortification of all those who wish well to his memory' (Letter 181, 2 December 1776). Such a feeling no doubt caused Smith to give instructions to his executors Joseph Black and James Hutton to commit his papers to the flames in the last week of his life.

Yet, if much has been irretrievably lost, and if some of what remains is brief, the range of correspondence published here reflects the preoccupations and activities of Smith's life, and in opposition to his wish to veil private life, there can be quoted his statement in the *Lectures on Rhetoric and Belles Lettres*: 'The smallest circumstances, the most minute transactions of a great man, are sought after with eagerness' (Monday 17 January). We recall, too, the pleasure he took himself in knowing such details as that Milton wore latchets in his shoes (BLJ v. 19, n. 1). Among the many topics covered in the correspondence that go beyond the level of shoe latchets is the revision of the *Theory of Moral Sentiments* (Letter 40, and its enclosure), as well as source material for a part of *The Wealth of Nations* (Letters 115–20). On the biographical side, letters published here for the first time show Smith's solicitude for a pupil (45–9), and solve a murder mystery (97–8). The appendices contain some printed letters addressed to Smith on matters of political economy, also documents associated with the American problem and the customs service.

Concerning the division of editorial responsibilities, Professor Mossner undertook to edit the letters from Smith, and the other editor dealt with letters to Smith. Sad to say ill health forced Professor Mossner to relinquish his share in the book in 1971, but he handed over accurate texts of the Smith letters and the basis for their annotation.

Acknowledgement is made here of the permission readily given by the Clarendon Press to quote from the notes to Hume's letters to Smith printed in J. Y. T. Greig's edition of *The Letters of David Hume* (1932, reprinted 1969), and in *New Letters of David Hume*, edited by Raymond Klibansky and Ernest C. Mossner (1954, reprinted 1969). A similar acknowledgement is made of permission from Glasgow University to quote from the notes to the Smith correspondence presented in W. R. Scott, *Adam Smith as Student and Professor* (Glasgow University Publications xlvi, 1937); from the University of Chicago Press and the Syndics of Cambridge University Press to draw facts and identifications from the notes to the Burke–Smith letters printed in the *Burke Correspondence*, edited by Thomas W. Copeland and others (from 1958).

Errors that remain in the text and notes are the responsibility of the junior editor, who wishes to pay every tribute of affection and respect to his colleague for his care in establishing sound principles for the edition, and for his patience and skill in solving knotty problems.

The format adopted for the edition required numbering and arranging each letter in chronological sequence, with the exception of No. 297 and following, these being letters whose dates are conjectural. After the number of each letter comes a brief citation of the address, when known, as well as the manuscript or printed source. The provenance and date of each letter are to be found in the top right-hand corner of the text, silently normalized to place, day, month, and year. Editors' conjectures are placed within square brackets, and three dots indicate a cut by a previous editor, empty square brackets indicate a torn or otherwise damaged manuscript.

As for editorial rules, the original spelling, punctuation, and capitalization are all retained, except that in conformity with modern practice capitals are used after periods closing sentences, on the very rare occasions when writers do not observe this convention. Ampersands and contractions are expanded, except for contractions in signatures. The original accentuation of French words in the letters is preserved, except that the grave accent is normalized to the acute where modern practice requires this, as in Abbé. The guiding principle in all of this has been expressed by Dr. Johnson, who 'did not take to' Smith but would have hugged him for his love of rhyme: 'An author's language Sir, is a characteristical part of his composition, and is also characteristical of the age in which he writes. Besides, Sir, when the language is changed we are not sure that the sense is the same' (BLJ iv. 315).

It is a pleasure to close this preface by recording the names of the institutions and people who gave us help. Research support was received from the Universities of Texas and British Columbia (1969, 1970), also the Canada Council (1969). The staff at the libraries of these Universities, also at Glasgow University Library, the National Library of Scotland, and the Scottish Record Office, were particularly helpful. Attention was drawn to important manuscript and printed sources by Mr. Edward Carson, librarian of H.M. Customs and Excise Department; Mr. C. P. Finlayson of Edinburgh University Library; Dr. J. D. Fleeman of Pembroke College, Oxford; Lady Edith Haden-Guest of Glasgow University; Dr. T. I. Rae of the National Library of Scotland; and the late Professor Jacob Viner of Princeton University. To the great advantage of the edition in terms of accuracy and clarity, the text and notes were carefully scrutinized by Professor D. D. Raphael of Imperial College, London, and Mr. Andrew S. Skinner, the efficient and knowledgeable secretary of the Adam Smith Committee.

Warm and special thanks go to Miss Moira McKeachie, who drove the

editors across Scotland in 1965 when they first pursued Smith letters; to
Mr. Antony Grinkus of Vancouver, who acted as research assistant to the
project in 1971; to Professor David Stevens of Whitman College, who
prepared Appendix B; to Mrs. Magda Chichini Pavitt for research help
in 1973; to Miss Jane Douglas of Vancouver, who typed drafts of the
edition; and to Mrs. Carolyn Mossner, whose good sense and good humour
sustained the enterprise in difficult times.

I. S. R.

Vancouver, British Columbia
July 1974

Acknowledgements

FOR permission to publish letters in this volume, acknowledgement is gratefully made to the following individuals and institutions: James Abbey, Esq., Edinburgh; Messrs. George Allen & Unwin Ltd.; the Master and Fellows of Balliol College, Oxford; the Bentham Committee, University College, London; Sir James Hunter Blair of Blairquhan; the Trustees of the Bodleian Library, Oxford; the Trustees of the Boston Public Library (items in the Mellen Chamberlain Collection and the Virginia and Richard Ehrlich Autograph Collection); the British Library Board (now vested with ownership of the former Library Departments of the British Museum); Columbia University Library (Seligman Collection); Earl Fitzwilliam and Earl Fitzwilliam Wentworth Estates Company, also the City Librarian, Sheffield: Wentworth Woodhouse Muniments; Edinburgh University Library; Harvard University Library: Houghton Library and the Vanderblue Collection of Smithiana, Kress Library of Business and Economics; the Historical Society of Pennsylvania; the Trustees of the Henry E. Huntington Library and Art Gallery, San Marino, California; Mrs. Donald F. Hyde, Somerville, New Jersey: Mary and Donald F. Hyde Collection; the Most Hon. the Marquess of Lansdowne; Lehigh University Library: Honeyman Collection; Lincoln Savings and Loan Association, Los Angeles: Mr. Roy Crocker, President; the Hon. Mrs. John Mildmay-White and her Trustees, Baring Brothers & Co. Ltd., London; the Trustees of the National Library of Scotland: Manuscript Department and Mrs. P. G. C. Somervell Deposit; New York Public Library: Manuscript Division and Henry W. and Albert A. Berg Collection; Mr. M. Nitta, Managing Director, Yushudo Booksellers Ltd., Tokyo; the James M. and Marie-Louise Osborn Collection, Yale University Library; the Pierpont Morgan Library, New York City; the Royal Society of Edinburgh; the Scottish Record Office; the Syndics of Cambridge University Press; the Rt. Hon. Viscount Thurso of Ulbster; University of Illinois Library; University of London: Goldsmith Library; University of Michigan: William L. Clements Library; University of Tokyo; the Editorial Committee of the Yale Editions of the Private Papers of James Boswell; and Yale University Library.

Contents

Abbreviations

(i) Smith's Works

Corr.	*Correspondence*
EPS	*Essays on Philosophical Subjects (which include)*
Ancient Logics	'History of the Ancient Logics and Meta-physics'
Ancient Physics	'History of the Ancient Physics'
Astronomy	'History of Astronomy'
English and Italian Verses	'Of the Affinity between certain English and Italian Verses'
External Senses	'Of the External Senses'
Imitative Arts	'Of the Nature of the Imitation which takes place in what are called the Imitative Arts'
Music, Dancing, and Poetry	'Of the Affinity between Music, Dancing, and Poetry'
Stewart	Dugald Stewart, 'Account of the Life and Writings of Adam Smith, LL.D.'
LJ (A)	*Lectures on Jurisprudence* (Lothian version)
LJ (B)	*Lectures on Jurisprudence* (Cannan version)
LRBL	*Lectures on Rhetoric and Belles Lettres*
TMS	*The Theory of Moral Sentiments*
WN	*The Wealth of Nations*

(ii) Other Works, Institutions, etc.

Bentham Corr.	*The Correspondence of Jeremy Bentham*, ed. Timothy L. S. Sprigge *et al.* University of London: Athlone Press, 1968–
BLJ	*Boswell's Life of Johnson*, ed. G. Birkbeck Hill, revsd. and enlgd. by L. F. Powell, 6 vols. Oxford, 1934–65
BM	British Museum
Bonar	James Bonar, *A Catalogue of the Library of Adam Smith*, 2nd edn. London, 1932
Burke Corr.	*The Correspondence of Edmund Burke*, ed. Thomas W. Copeland *et al.*, Cambridge University Press and Chicago University Press, 1958–
Brougham	Henry Peter Brougham, *Lives of Men of Letters and Science . . . in the time of George III*, 2 vols. London, 1845–6

Carlyle	*The Autobiography of Dr Alexander Carlyle of Inveresk 1722–1805*, ed. John Hill Burton, new edn. Edinburgh, 1910
DNB	*Dictionary of National Biography*
EUL	Edinburgh University Library
Fay	C. R. Fay, *Adam Smith and the Scotland of His Day*, Cambridge University Press, 1956
Fraser, *Scotts of Buccleuch*	Sir William Fraser, *The Scotts of Buccleuch*, 2 vols. Edinburgh, 1878
Geo. III Corr.	*The Correspondence of George III 1760–1783*, ed. Sir John Fortescue, 6 vols. London, 1927–8
GUA	Glasgow University Archives
GUL	Glasgow University Library
Hamilton	Henry Hamilton, *An Economic History of Scotland in the Eighteenth Century*, Oxford, 1963
HL	*The Letters of David Hume*, ed. J. Y. T. Greig, 2 vols. Oxford, 1932
HP	*The History of Parliament: The House of Commons 1754–1790*, ed. Sir Lewis Namier and John Brooke, 3 vols. H.M.S.O., 1964
Hume, *Phil. Wks.*	*The Philosophical Works of David Hume*, ed. T. H. Green and T. H. Grose, 4 vols. London, 1874–5
Mizuta	Hiroshi Mizuta, *Adam Smith's Library: A Supplement to Bonar's Catalogue with a Check-list of the whole Library*, Cambridge University Press, 1967
NHL	*New Letters of David Hume*, ed. Raymond Klibansky and Ernest C. Mossner, Oxford, 1954
NLS	National Library of Scotland
NYPL	New York Public Library
Rae	John Rae, *Life of Adam Smith*, London, 1895 (reprinted Augustus M. Kelley, New York, 1965, with an Introduction 'Guide to Rae's "Life of Smith"' by Jacob Viner)
Ramsay of Ochtertyre	*Scotland and Scotsmen in the Eighteenth Century from the MSS. of John Ramsay, Esq. of Ochtertyre*, ed. Alexander Allardyce, 2 vols. Edinburgh, 1888
RSE	Royal Society of Edinburgh

Scott

W. R. Scott, *Adam Smith as Student and Professor*, Glasgow University Publications, xlvi, 1937

Sinclair, *Corr.*

The Correspondence of . . . Sir John Sinclair, 2 vols. Edinburgh 1831

Small

John Small, 'Biographical Sketch of Adam Ferguson', RSE *Transactions* xxiii (1864), 599–665

SRO

Scottish Record Office, H.M. General Register House, Edinburgh

Thomson

John Thomson, *Life, Lectures and Writings of William Cullen*, vol. i, Edinburgh, 1832

Walpole, *Corr.*

The Correspondence of Horace Walpole, 4th Earl of Orford, ed. W. S. Lewis *et al.*, Yale Edition, Yale University Press, New Haven, 1937–

Life and Works of Adam Smith

1720   Adam Smith Sr. md. Margaret Douglas of Strathenry

1723   *c.* 25 Jan. Adam Smith Sr. died; 5 June, Adam Smith baptized in Kirkcaldy

*c.*1732–7   attended Kirkcaldy Burgh School

1737–40   attended Glasgow University; taught by Francis Hutcheson; grad. M.A. with distinction

1740–6   at Balliol College, Oxford, as Snell Exhibitioner (£40 p.a.); matric. 7 July 1740; nominated to Warner Exhibition (£8. 5s. p.a.) 2 Nov. 1742; visited Adderbury on holidays, home of John 2nd Duke of Argyll; left Balliol *c.* 15 Aug. 1746; resigned Snell Exhibition 4 Feb. 1749.

1746–8   lived with his mother in Kirkcaldy

1748–51   lectured at Edinburgh on rhetoric and belles lettres, also jurisprudence, under the patronage of Henry Home of Kames, James Oswald of Dunnikier, and Robert Craigie of Glendoick

1751   9 Jan. elected Professor of Logic at Glasgow; admitted 16 Jan. then went back to Edinburgh to complete lecture course; from Oct. taught logic at Glasgow, also jurisprudence and politics.

1752   22 Apr. elected Professor of Moral Philosophy at Glasgow; became member of the Glasgow Literary Society, also Philosophical Society, Edinburgh

1754   member of the Select Society, Edinburgh

1755	lectured on economic ideas to a Club organized by Andrew Cochrane, Provost of Glasgow	articles in *Edinburgh Review*: 'A Dictionary of the English Language by Samuel Johnson' (No. 1, Jan. 1755); 'A Letter to the Authors of the Edinburgh Review' (No. 2, July 1755)
1758	Quaestor for Glasgow University Library, served until 1760	
1759	visited Inveraray, home of Archibald 3rd Duke of Argyll	TMS ed. 1
1760	chosen Dean of Arts, served until 1763; summer jaunt for health reasons to England; visited the home of Lord Shelburne at High Wycombe	
1761	Vice-rector of Glasgow University, served until 1763; in London on University business, late Aug.–early Oct.	'Considerations concerning the First Formation of Languages, and the Different Genius of Original and Compounded Languages,' *The Philological Miscellany* i (1761) 440–79 TMS ed. 2
1762	3 May made a Burgess of Glasgow; 21 Oct. nominated Glasgow LL.D.	
1763	8 Nov. gave notice of resignation of his Chair; resigned 14 Feb. 1764, from Paris	
1764	Jan. left Glasgow for London, *en route* to France as travelling tutor to Henry Scott, 3rd Duke of Buccleuch; arrived in Paris 13 Feb. and remained ten days, then left for Toulouse; joined there by the Duke's brother, the Hon. Hew Campbell Scott	
1765	in Toulouse until Sept., at work on an early draft of WN; toured the south of France Sept.–Oct.; in Geneva Oct.–Dec. and met Voltaire; went to Paris Dec.	
1766	in Paris until Oct., on friendly terms with the La Rochefoucauld circle, Mme de Boufflers, the *philosophes*, and the Quesnai circle; 19 Oct. Hon. Hew Campbell Scott died of a fever;	

Smith and the Duke of Buccleuch returned to England, landing at Dover on 1 Nov.; Smith was given a pension of £300 p.a. for life from the Buccleuch estates

1766   Nov.–Mar. 1767 in London: assisted Charles Townshend with taxation projects; carried out research on the history of colonies for Lord Shelburne; elected Fellow of the Royal Society 21 May (admitted 27 May 1773)

1767   TMS ed. 3

May–Apr. 1773 lived in Kirkcaldy with his mother, working on WN; made a Burgess of Edinburgh, June 1770

1773   May–Apr. 1776 in London, working on WN; elected member of The Club which Joshua Reynolds had founded as a forum for Dr. Johnson

1774   TMS ed. 4

1776   9 Mar. publication of WN; May–Dec. in Kirkcaldy, visited Hume in Edinburgh during his last illness   WN

1777   Jan.–beginning of Oct. in London   'Letter to Strahan' (9 Nov. 1776) on the death of Hume, *Scots Magazine* xxxi (Jan. 1777), 5–7

Oct.–Jan. 1778 in Kirkcaldy and Edinburgh   ? composed 'Thoughts on the State of the Contest with America'

1778   30 Jan. gazetted Commissioner of Customs for Scotland (£500 p.a.) and of Salt Duties (£100 p.a.); settled in Panmure House, Canongate, Edinburgh, with his mother and as housekeeper his cousin Janet Douglas; adopted as his heir David Douglas (later Lord Reston), a nephew's son; resumed membership of the Poker Club; gave Sunday suppers for friends among the literati and distinguished visitors   WN ed. 2 (early in the year)

1781		TMS ed. 5
1782	in London, attended dinners of The Club; returned to Scotland early in July	
1783	founder member of the Royal Society of Edinburgh; served as one of the presidents of its literary class	
1784	Apr. accompanied Edmund Burke to Glasgow for his installation as Lord Rector of the University; his mother died on 23 May	WN ed. 3 ('Additions and Corrections' to eds. 1 and 2 were printed separately)
1786	Apr.–May in London: consulted Dr. John Hunter about his health	WN ed. 4
1787	Mar.–Aug. in London, probably for health reasons; said to have been consulted by the Government of Pitt the Younger; 15 Nov. elected Lord Rector of Glasgow University, and served until 1789	
1788	sometime after Sept. Janet Douglas died	
1789		WN ed. 5
1790	May 17 July, Adam Smith died in Panmure House; buried in the Canongate kirkyard.	TMS ed. 6 (revised and enlarged)

Posthumous Publications

1795	EPS, ed. Joseph Black and James Hutton
1896	LJ (B), ed. Edwin Cannan
1933	'Smiths Thoughts on the State of the Contest with America, February 1778', ed. G. H. Guttridge, *American Historical Review* xxxviii. 714–20
1963	LRBL, ed. John M. Lothian
1977	LJ (A), ed. Ronald Meek, D. D. Raphael, and Peter Stein

List of Letters

1. *To* WILLIAM SMITH[1]

Address: To William Smith, at the Duke of Argyles house in Brutin Street, London[2]
MS., GUL Gen. 1035/126; Scott 232.

Oxford, 24 Aug. 1740

Sir

I yesterday receiv'd your letter with a bill of sixteen pounds inclos'd, for which I humbly thank you, but more for the good advice you were pleased to give me: I am indeed affraid that my expences at college must necessarily amount to a much greater sum this year than at any time hereafter; because of the extraordinary and most extravagant fees we are obligd to pay the College and University on our admittance;[3] it will be his own fault if anyone should endanger his health at Oxford by excessive Study, our only business here being to go to prayers twice a day, and to lecture twice a week.[4] I am, dear Sir

Your most Oblig'd Servant
Adam Smith

2. *To* his Mother[1]

Address: To Mrs Smith at Kirkaldy[2]
MS., GUL Gen. 1464/6; unpubl.

[Oxford, 1740–6]

Dear Mother I have but just time to tell you that I am well. I received a letter from Mr Miller[3] today but have not time to answer it. I shall have the Box you mention provided against next week. I have not yet received the money

A Smith

[1] William Smith (d. 1753), secretary to John 2nd Duke of Argyll; he was Adam Smith's cousin, also his tutor and curator, i.e. guardian.

[2] The Duke's town house in Bruton Street, just off Berkeley Square.

[3] Smith was a Snell Exhibitioner at Balliol; matriculated 7 July 1740.

[4] Smith's first but by no means last sharp comment on Oxford education; cf. WN V.i.f.8: 'In the university of Oxford, the greater part of the publick professors have for these many years, given up altogether even the pretence of teaching.'

[1] Margaret Douglas Smith (1694–1784), dau. of Robert Douglas of Strathenry, M.P. for Fife in the Scottish Parliament 1703–6. She married Adam Smith, W.S., in 1720. After serving as private secretary to Hugh, Earl of Loudoun from 1705, he was made Clerk of the Courts Martial and Councils of War in Scotland (1707), then Comptroller of Customs at Kirkcaldy, a Fife seaport, from 1714. He died on 25 Jan. 1723. Adam Smith, the man of letters, was baptized on 5 June 1723.

[2] Place of Smith's birth and early education. His mother continued to live there after the father's death.

[3] Not traced.

3. *To* his Mother

Address: To Mrs Smith at Kirkaldy
MS., GUL Gen. 1035/127; Scott 232.

Adderbury,[1] 23 Oct. 1741

Dear Mother

I have been these fourteen days last past here at Adderbury with Mr Smith;[2] the Place is agreeable enough, and there is a great deal of good company in the town.

In my last Letter I desir'd you to send me some Stocking's, the sooner you send 'em the better; I have taken this opportunity to write, to you, and to give my service to all friends, tho' as you see, I have not very much to say,

     I am Dear Mother, your most Affectionate son,

Adam Smith

4. *To* his Mother

Address: To Mrs Smith at Kirkaldy
MS., GUL Gen. 1035/128; Scott 233.

[Oxford,] 12 May [1742][1]

Dear Mother

I take this opportunity of writing to you, by a Gentleman of my acquaintance who sets out for Scotland tomorrow. The Certificate of my age which I mentioned in my last Letter's, will not be necessary so soon as I then expected; if you have not sent it already, it will come in full time if you give it to Mr Smith[2] when he returns from Scotland. I told you in my last to inform Mr Smith that one of the £40 Exhibitions[3] would shortly be vacant, in case that he intended to make interest for any of his friends: 'Twill not however be vacant so soon as I expected. The Gentleman who carry's this to Edinburgh (one Mr Preston)[4] I have been very much oblig'd to; he will probably be at Kirkaldy and will wait upon you before he leaves Scotland.

     I am Dear Mother, Yours etc.

A S

---

[1] Adderbury House, some eighteen miles north of Oxford, was owned by the Duke of Argyll; it was formerly a residence of the Earl of Rochester (1647–80).
[2] William Smith; see Letter 1.

[1] The date is indicated by the fact that the 'Mr Preston' referred to it in the letter did not resign his Snell Exhibition until 1743.
[2] Very likely the William Smith of Letter 1.   [3] On the Snell Foundation.
[4] John Preston (*c.* 1718–81), ygr. son of Sir George Preston, Bt., of Valleyfield, who resigned his Snell Exhibition in 1743 and entered the Church of England. The next vacancy occurred in 1747.

5. *To* his Mother

Brougham, ii. 216; Rae 25.

Oxford, 29 Nov. 1743

I am just recovered of a violent fit of laziness, which has confined me to my elbow-chair these three months.[1]

6. *To* his Mother

Brougham, ii. 216; Rae 25.[1]

Oxford, 2 July 1744

I am quite inexcusable for not writing to you oftener. I think of you every day, but always defer writing till the post is just going, and then sometimes business or company, but oftener laziness, hinders me. Tar water is a remedy very much in vogue here at present for almost all diseases.[2] It has perfectly cured me of an inveterate scurvy and shaking in the head.[3] I wish you'd try it. I fancy it might be of service to you.

7. *To* [DR THEOPHILUS LEIGH][1]

MS., Balliol College, Oxford; Scott 137.

Edinburgh, 4 Feb. 1748/9[2]

I Adam Smith one of the Exhibitioners on Mr Snells foundation in Baliol College in Oxford do hereby resign into the hands of the Revd Dr

[1] Only an excerpt from this letter seems to have survived.

[1] Another excerpt.
[2] George Berkeley's *Philosophical Reflexions and Inquiries Concerning the Virtues of Tar-Water* (later prefixed by the title *Siris*) was first published in London in April 1744, and caused an immediate sensation. A correspondent of the Archbishop of York commented in June: 'it is impossible to write a letter now without tincturing the ink with tar-water. This is the common topic of discourse, both among the rich and poor, high and low; and the Bishop of Cloyne has made it as fashionable as going to Vauxhall or Ranelagh.' The Archbishop replied that he thought it a defect in Berkeley's recommendation that he had made it a 'catholicon' (*Letters from . . . Dr. Thomas Herring to William Duncombe*, London, 1777).
[3] The first of many references to Smith's illnesses.

[1] The Revd. Dr. Theophilus Leigh, elected Master of Balliol 1726; remembered for his Jacobite sympathies; Vice-Chancellor of Oxford University 1738–41.
[2] Smith dated this document '1748/9', presumably recollecting that England followed the Old Style practice of beginning the year on 25 Mar. Scotland had adopted the New Style rule of beginning the year on 1 Jan. in 1600. England and Scotland conformed to the New Style (Gregorian) calendar from 1752 as a result of the Act 24 Geo. II c.23 (1751).

Leigh Master of the said college all rights and title which I have to an Exhibition on the said foundation[3] as witness my hand

Adam Smith

8. *To* [ROBERT SIMSON][1]

MS., GUA; unpubl.

Edinburgh, 10 Jan. 1751

Sir

I have just received the favor of yours.[2] And must begg leave by your hands to return my sincere thanks to the gentlemen of your Society for the [favour] they have done me by electing me to supply the vacant proffesor-ship to declare my acceptance of their favor, and to assure them that it shall be my chief study to render myselfe a useful member of their Society.

I shall do my endeavour to get to Glasgow on Tuesday night, if some-thing extraordinary does not prevent it. I shall, however, be under a necessity of returning in a day or in two days thereafter to Edinburgh. And cannot even be very certain if that absence will be consented to by my friends here.[3] I am with great esteem dear Sir

most faithfully yours
A Smith

9. *To* WILLIAM CULLEN[1]

Thomson i. 605; Rae 44.

Edinburgh, 3 Sept. 1751

Dear Sir

I received yours this moment. I am very glad that Mr Craigie has at last

---

[3] Smith had left Oxford at the end of the '4th Quarter', i.e. in Aug. 1746.

[1] This letter was meant for the Clerk of Senate, then Robert Simson (1687–1768), Professor of Mathematics at Glasgow (1711–61), the celebrated 'restorer of ancient geometry'. Smith paid tribute to him in the 6th edition of TMS (1790): 'The two greatest mathematicians that I ever had the honour to be known to, and, I believe, the two greatest that have ever lived in my time, Dr Robert Simson of Glasgow, and Dr Matthew Stewart of Edinburgh, never seemed to feel even the slightest uneasiness from the neglect with which the ignorance of the public received some of their most valuable works' (III. ii).

[2] Senate directed its Clerk on 9 Jan. 1751 to write to Smith, acquainting him with his election as Professor of Logic and desiring him to be in Glasgow, 'as soon as his affairs can allow him' to be admitted to his chair (Scott 138). See Letter 304.

[3] Presumably an allusion to Smith's commitment to give lectures on rhetoric and jurisprudence in Edinburgh (1748–51) sponsored by Henry Home, Robert Craigie of Glendoick, and James Oswald of Dunnikier.

[1] William Cullen (1710–90) medical scientist and teacher: educ. at Glasgow University and Edinburgh (under Alexander Monro, *Primus*, 1734–6); in practice at Hamilton, 1736–44; removed to Glasgow, 1744 and from 1746 lectured there on Medicine, Materia Medica, Botany, and Chemistry; Professor of Medicine, Glasgow 1751; jt. Professor of

resolved to go to Lisbon.[2] I make no doubt but he will soon receive all the benefit he expects, or can wish, from a warmer climate. I shall, with great pleasure, do what I can to relieve him of the burden of his class. You mention Natural Jurisprudence and Politics as the parts of his lectures, which it would be most agreeable for me to take upon me to teach.[3] I shall willingly undertake both. I should be glad to know when he sets out for Lisbon, because, if it is not before the 1st of October, I would endeavour to see him before he goes, that I might receive his advice about the plan I ought to follow. I would pay great deference to it in every thing, and would follow it implicitly in this, as I shall consider myself as standing in his place and representing him. If he goes before that time, I wish he would leave some directions for me, either with you or with Mr Leechman,[4] were it only by word of mouth.

I am, dear Doctor, most faithfully yours

A. Smith

10. *To* WILLIAN CULLEN

Thomson, *Life of Cullen* i. 606; Rae 45-6.

Edinburgh, Tuesday, Nov. 1751

Dear Sir,

I did not write to you on Saturday, as I promised, because I was every moment expecting Mr. Home to town.[1] He is not, however, yet come.

I should prefer David Hume to any man for a colleague; but I am afraid the public would not be of my opinion; and the interest of the society will oblige us to have some regard to the opinion of the public.[2] If the event,

Chemistry, Edinburgh 1755, sole Professor 1756; Professor of the Practice of Physic, Edinburgh 1773. His most famous patient, David Hume; his most distinguished pupils, William Hunter the anatomist and Joseph Black the chemist.

[2] Thomas Craigie (d. at Lisbon, 27 Nov. 1751), Professor of Moral Philosophy and successor to Francis Hutcheson.

[3] Francis Hutcheson had taught jurisprudence and government as part of the moral philosophy course which Smith took at Glasgow.

[4] William Leechman (1706–85) graduated in 1724 from Edinburgh and about 1727 became tutor to William Mure of Caldwell. He was ordained in 1736 and became Professor of Divinity at Glasgow in 1743. In 1761 he became Principal, having served as Vice-Rector from 1756. Among his writings was an introduction to Hutcheson's *System of Moral Philosophy* (1755) drawing attention to its empirical bias.

[1] Henry Home of Kames (1696–1782) lawyer, man of letters, and promoter of economic development; advocate 1723; Lord of Session (civil judge) 1752; Lord Commissioner of Justiciary (criminal judge) 1763; his chief works were *Historical Law-Tracts* (1758), *Principles of Equity* (1760), *Elements of Criticism* (1762), *Sketches of the History of Man* (1774), and *The Gentleman Farmer* (1776).

[2] David Hume (1711–76) philosopher and historian. In 1744–5 he was an unsuccessful candidate for the Chair of Moral Philosophy at Edinburgh. He also failed to get Smith's vacant Chair of Logic at Glasgow. As Smith intimates, the Senate was alarmed at the thought of Hume becoming a professor because of the views attributed to him on religion.

however, we are afraid of should happen, we can see how the public receives it. From the particular knowledge I have of Mr. Elliot's[3] sentiments, I am pretty certain Mr. Lindsay must have proposed it to him, not he to Lindsay.[4] I am for ever obliged to you for your concern for my interest in that affair.

When I saw you at Edinburgh, you talked to me of the Principal's proposing to retire.[5] I gave little attention to it at that time but, upon further consideration, should be glad to listen to any proposal of that kind. The reasons of my changing my opinion I shall tell you at meeting. I need not recommend secrecy to you upon this head. Be so good as to thank the Principal in my name for his kindness in mentioning me to the Duke [of Argyll].[6] I waited on him at his levee at Edinburgh, where I was introduced to him by Mr. Lind;[7] but it seems he had forgot.

I can tell you nothing particular about your own affair, more than what I wrote you last, till I see Mr. Home, whom I expect every moment.[8] I am, most dear Sir, ever yours,

A. Smith

11. *To* JAMES OSWALD[1]

Memorials of . . . James Oswald of Dunnikier, ed. by his grandson (1825) 124; Rae 103–4.

Glasgow, 19 Jan. 1752 N.S.

Sir,

This will be delivered to you by Mr. William Johnstone,[2] son to Sir

[3] Gilbert Elliot (1722–77) of Minto, 3rd Bt.; educ. Edinburgh and Leyden; advocate 1743; M.P. 1748–77; Lord of Admiralty 1754–61; Lord of Treasury 1761–70; Privy Councillor 1762; Keeper of the Signet 1766–d. One of Hume's closest friends.

[4] Hercules Lindesay (d. 1761), promoted LL.D. 1746 at Glasgow after teaching law there for several years; appointed Professor of Civil Law 1750. Possibly Lindesay prevailed on Elliot to get Hume to apply for Smith's Chair, somewhat against Hume's judgement.

[5] Neil Campbell (d. 1761), Minister of Renfrew, admitted to the office of Principal of Glasgow University 1728; taught Divinity. In 1752 he became paralysed and was unable thereafter to take part in University business.

[6] Archibald Campbell, 3rd Duke of Argyll (1682–1761).　　　　[7] Unidentified.

[8] Henry Home wanted Cullen to move to Edinburgh, and helped to arrange rewards for his experimental work with processes of bleaching and purifying salt.

[1] James Oswald (1715–69) of Dunnikier, Fife; educ. Edinburgh, Lincoln's Inn, and Leyden; advocate 1738; M.P. 1741–68; Commissioner of the Navy 1745–7; Lord of Trade 1751–9; Lord of Treasury 1759–63; Privy Councillor 1763; Joint Vice-Treasurer of Ireland 1763–7. A fellow-townsman of Smith's, Oswald was an early and intimate friend of Smith, Henry Home, and David Hume. Horace Walpole reckoned him among the thirty best speakers in the House of Commons, where his knowledge of economic affairs led him to become the principal spokesman for the Board of Trade.

[2] William Johnstone (1729–1805) 2nd son of Sir James Johnstone of Westerhall; Bt.; advocate 1751; M.P. for Cromarty 1768–74, and Shrewsbury 1775–1805. He became

James Johnstone of Westerhall, a young gentleman whom I have known intimately these four years, and of whose discretion, good temper, sincerity, and honour, I have had, during all that time, frequent proofs. You will find in him too, if you come to know him better, some qualities which, from real and unaffected modesty, he does not at first discover; a refinement and depth of observation, and an accuracy of judgment, joined to a natural delicacy of sentiment, as much improved as study, and the narrow sphere of acquaintance which this country affords, can improve it. He had, first when I knew him, a good deal of vivacity and humour, but he has studied them away. He is an advocate; and, though I am sensible of the folly of prophesying with regard to the future fortune of so young a man, yet I could almost venture to foretell, that, if he lives, he will be eminent in that profession. He has, I think, every quality that ought to forward, and not one that should obstruct his progress, modesy and sincerity excepted, and these, it is to be hoped, experience and a better sense of things may, in part, cure him of. I do not, I assure you, exaggerate knowingly, but could pawn my honour upon the truth of every article. You will find him, I imagine, a young gentleman of solid, substantial (not flashy) abilities and worth. Private business obliges him to spend some time at London. He would beg to be allowed the privilege of waiting on you sometimes, to receive your advice how he may employ his time there in the manner that will tend most to his real and lasting improvement.

I am very sensible how much I presume upon your indulgence, in giving you this trouble; but, as it is to serve and comply with a person for whom I have the most entire friendship, I know you will excuse me, though guilty of an indiscretion; at least, if you do not, you will not judge others as you would desire to be judged yourself; for I am very sure a like motive would carry you to be guilty of a greater.

I would have waited on you when you was last in Scotland, had the College allowed me three days' vacation; and it gave me real uneasiness that I should be in the same country with you, and not have the pleasure of seeing you. Believe it, no man can more rejoice at your late success,[3] or at whatever else tends to your honour and prosperity, than does,

> Sir,
> Your ever obliged,
> and very humble servant,
> Adam Smith

fabulously wealthy and took the name of Pulteney in 1767, when his wife succeeded to the estates of the Earl of Bath; see Letter 132 addressed to William Pulteney, dated 3 Sept. 1772, for Smith's testimony to his kindness.

[3] Towards the end of 1751 Oswald ʲoined the Pelham Administration.

12. *From* DAVID HUME

MS., RSE ii. 25; HL i.167–9.

24 Sept. 1752

Dear Sir

I confess, I was once of the same Opinion with you, and thought that the best Period to begin an English History was about Henry the 7th.[1] But you will please to observe, that the Change, which then happen'd in public Affairs, was very insensible, and did not display its Influence till many Years afterwards. Twas under James that the House of Commons began first to raise their Head, and then the Quarrel betwixt Privilege and Prerogative commenc'd. The Government, no longer opprest by the enormous Authority of the Crown, display'd its Genius; and the Factions, which then arose, having an Influence on our present Affairs, form the most curious, interesting, and instructive Part of our History. The preceding Events or Causes may easily be shown in a Reflection or Review, which may be artfully inserted in the Body of the Work and the whole, by that means, be render'd more compact and uniform. I confess, that the Subject appears to me very fine; and I enter upon it with great Ardour and Pleasure. You need not doubt of my Perseverance.[2]

I am just now diverted for a Moment by correcting my Essays moral and political, for a new Edition.[3] If any thing occur to you to be inserted or retrench'd, I shall be obligd to you for the Hint. In case you shou'd not have the last Edition[4] by you, I shall send you a Copy of it. In that Edition, I was engag'd to act contrary to my Judgement in retaining the 6th and 7th Essays,[5] which I had resolv'd to throw out, as too frivolous for the rest, and not very agreeable neither even in that trifling manner: But Millar, my Bookseller,[6] made such Protestations against it, and told me how much he had heard them praisd by the best Judges; that the Bowels of a Parent melted, and I preserv'd them alive.

---

[1] Smith has much to say about history and historians in LRBL, especially nos. 16–20, but he does not express there the opinion ascribed to him by Hume.

[2] Hume commenced his *History of England* with the reigns of James I and Charles I (vol. i, published in 1754), dealt with the period from the Restoration of the Monarchy in 1660 to the Revolution of 1688 (vol. ii, 1757), turned back to the Tudors (vols. iii, iv, 1759), and then concluded with the period from Julius Caesar to the accession of Henry VII (vols. v, vi, 1762).

[3] Published in 1753 as vol. i of *Essays and Treatises on Several Subjects*.

[4] 1748.

[5] *Of Love and Marriage* and *Of the Study of History*: they were dropped after 1760.

[6] Andrew Millar (1707–68), born in Edinburgh, moved to London to become the most famous bookseller (publisher) of his time: 'I respect Millar, Sir,' said Dr. Johnson, 'he has raised the price of literature' (BLJ i. 288). Millar began publishing Hume's writings in 1748, and he published TMS: see Letter 31 from Hume, dated 12 Apr. 1759. His other leading authors were Johnson, Thomson, Fielding, and Robertson.

All the rest of Bolingbroke's Works went to the Press last Week, as Millar informs me.[7] I confess my Curiosity is not much rais'd.

I had almost lost your Letter by its being wrong directed. I receiv'd it late; which was the Reason why you got not sooner a Copy of Joannes Magnus.[8] Direct to me in Riddal's Land, Lawn Market.[9] I am Dear Sir Yours sincerely

David Hume

13. *From* DAVID HUME

MS., in possession of Maggs Bros. (1932); HL i. 176.

Edinburgh, Jack's Land,[1] 26 May 1753

My Dear Sir

I was very sorry to hear by Mr Leechman[2] that you had been ill of late. I am afraid the Fatigues of your Class have exhausted you too much, and that you require more Leizure and Rest than you allow yourself.[3] However,

---

[7] *Letters on the Study and Use of History* (priv. ptd. before Bolingbroke's death) published under the editorship of David Mallet in 1752, together with other pieces, in two volumes. Johnson expressed himself in violent terms about the posthumous publication of Bolingbroke's works, calling him 'a scoundrel, for charging a blunderbuss against religion and morality; a coward, because he had not resolution to fire it off himself, but left half a crown to a beggarly Scotchman, to draw the trigger after his death!' (BLJ i. 268) Smith's scruples over undertaking to publish the *Dialogues concerning Natural Religion* after Hume's death may have arisen from the response to Mallet's publication; see J. H. Burton's *Hume* (Edinburgh, 1846), ii. 491, and, below, Letter 157 from Hume, dated 3 May 1776.

[8] Possibly *Gothorum Suionumque historia, ex probatissimis monumentis collecta* by Joannes Magnus, Archbishop of Uppsala (1st ed. Rome, 1554), or *Orationes duae, quarum altera est de praestantia Academiae Parisiensis, altera de philosophia eleganter et Latine tractanda*, by Joannes Magnus (Carnutis) (Paris, 1584). Neither book, however, is listed in the catalogue of Smith's library. Could *Magnus* be an error for *Major*? Smith had a copy of *Historia Maioris Britanniae tam Angliae quam Scotiae per Joannem Maiorem* ([Paris], 1521).

[9] Hume secured a house in Riddle's Land, on the south side of the Lawnmarket, Edinburgh, about May 1752; see HL i.170.

[1] Beyond the Netherbow and in the Canongate, near the Tolbooth. Hume removed from Riddle's Land to the 'very small' house in Jack's Land at Whitsunday 1753 and stayed nine years, mostly spent on writing his *History of England*.

[2] See Letter 3, n. 4. Hume probably knew Leechman from their time together at Edinburgh University.

[3] The college session extended from 10 Oct. to 10 June. From Monday to Friday Smith taught the Moral Philosophy public class of at most 90 students between 7.30 a.m. and 8.30 a.m. He then held at noon an hour's examination on the morning lecture for a third of his students. His private class of about 20 students met three times a week from 11 a.m. to noon. He was accessible to his students and diligent in preparing lectures. John Millar reported that his course consisted of four parts: Natural Theology, Ethics, Jurisprudence, and Political Economy. This and other information about Smith as a professor was presented by Dugald Stewart in his 'Account of the Life and Writings of Adam Smith' (RSE *Transactions*, iii (1794), pt. 1. 55–137 (reissued with additions, Dugald Stewart, *Biographical*

the good Season and the Vacation now approaches; and I hope you intend, both for Exercise and Relaxation, to take a Jaunt to this Place. I have many things to communicate to you. Were you not my Friend, you wou'd envy my robust Constitution. My Application has been and is continual; and yet I preserve entire Health. I am now beginning the Long Parliament; which, considering the great Number of Volumes I peruse, and my scrupulous method of composing, I regard as a very great Advance[4] I think you shou'd settle in this Town during the Vacation; where there always is some good Company; and you know, that I can supply you with Books, as much as you please.

I beg to hear from you at your Leizure; and am

Your affectionate Friend and humble Servant

David Hume.

14. From DAVID HUME

MS., Houghton Library, Harvard University, T.P. 2050.50.2; NHL 35–7.

Edinburgh, 27 Feb. 1754

Dear Sir[1]

I am writing kind of circular Letters, recommending Mr Blacklock's[2] Poems[3] [to][4] all my Acquaintance, but especially to those, whose Approbation[5] wou'd contribute most to recommend them [to] the World. They are, indeed, many of them very elegant, and wou'd have deserv'd much Esteem, had [t]hey come from a Man plac'd in the most favorable Circumstances. What a Prodigy are they, when considerd as the Production of a man, so cruelly dealt with, both by Nature [and] Fortune? When you add to this, that the Author is a Man of the best Dispositions, that I have ever known, and tho' of great Frugality, is plac'd in the most cruel Indigence, you will

Memoirs of Smith, Robertson, and Reid, 1811, 3–152; *Works of Smith*, ed. Stewart (1811), v. 403–552; *Works of Stewart*, ed. Hamilton (1858), x. 5–98). See, also, Rae 51–7, and Scott 69–71); text in Glasgow edn. EPS.

    [4] *History of England* (1754), i, ch. 10.

    [1] No addressee: Klibansky and Mossner conjecture Adam Smith in view of Letters 13 and 19 from Hume, dated 26 May 1753 and 17 Dec. 1754.
    [2] Thomas Blacklock (1721–91), poet, schoolmaster, clergyman; son of a bricklayer in Annan, Dumfriesshire; blinded by smallpox at six months; sent to an Edinburgh grammar school when twenty to learn Latin, and then to the University to study Greek and Divinity; ordained, 1762; Minister of Kirkcudbright, 1762–4; D.D. from Marischal College, Aberdeen, 1767; broke with David Hume in that year and accepted patronage from James Beattie; befriended Robert Burns and Walter Scott in his last years, his praise preventing Burns from emigrating to the West Indies in 1786.
    [3] *Poems on Several Occasions* (Edinburgh, 1754); other editions appeared in 1746, 1756, 1793 (posthumous, ed. by Henry Mackenzie). Blacklock was hailed as the Scottish Pindar.   [4] The left edge of the MS. first sheet is torn.
    [5] Among the other recipients of Hume's circular letter were John Clephane, Robert Dodsley, the Abbé Le Blanc, John Stewart, John Wilkes, and Joseph Spence.

certainly think his Case more deserving of Pity and Regard than any you have almost met with. Mr Foulis[6] has Copies to dispose of, which I have sent him; and which he will disperse without expecting any Profit. I must entreat you, not only to take a Copy yourself, but also to take a few more and [dis]pose of among your Acquaintance. I trust at least to have half a dozen disposd of by your [me]ans. I have sold off about fifty in a few days. The Price is three Shillings. That you may [rec]ommend them with a safer Conscience, please read the Ode to a young Gentleman going to the Coast of Guinea, that on Refinements in metaphysical Philosophy, that to a Lady on the Death of her Son; the Wish, an Elegy; the Soliloquy. I am much mistaken, if you do not find all these [v]ery laudable Performances; and such as wou'd be esteem'd an Ornament to Dodesley's Miscellanies [o]r even to better Collections.[7]

We expected to have seen you in Town about this time; but have been dissappointed. I am [v]ery glad your Health has been so well confirmd this Winter, as I hear it has been. My Compliments to Mr and Mrs Betham.[8] If that Lady can be engag'd to have an Esteem of Mr Blacklock's Productions, she wou'd be of great Service in dispersing them. Tho born blin[d], he is not insensible to that Passion, which we foolish People are apt to receive first by th[e] Eyes; and unless a man were both blind and deaf, I do not know how he cou'd be altogether secure of Impressions from Mrs Betham. I am Dear Sir

Yours sincerely
David Hume.

15. *From* ALEXANDER WEDDERBURN[1]

MS., GUL Gen. 1035/135; Scott 233–5.

Balliol College, Oxford, 20 Mar. [1754][2]

Dear Smith

I should endeavour to make my way to you by an Apology for not having

---

[6] Andrew (1712–75) or Robert Foulis (1707–76), booksellers and printers to Glasgow University. Robert started business as a bookseller in 1739, as publisher in 1741, and printer in 1742, joined by Andrew in 1746. Their books were famous for beauty and accuracy, the typefaces being designed by Alexander Wilson, e.g. the editions of Homer (1756–8) and Milton (1770). Robert founded an Academy of the Fine Arts in 1754 which trained David Allan and James Tassie.

[7] Robert Dodsley (1703–64), poet, dramatist, bookseller; well known for collections of old plays and contemporary poetry.

[8] The Bethams were Glasgow friends of Smith. Mr. Betham was an original member of the Glasgow Literary Society (HL i. 213).

[1] Alexander Wedderburn (1733–1805) lawyer and politician; advocate 1754; Inner Temple 1753; called to the English Bar 1757, after a quarrel with Lord President Craigie in the Court of Session; M.P. 1761–80; Solicitor-Gen. 1771–8; Attorney-Gen. 1778–80; Privy Councillor 1780; Lord Chief Justice of the Common Pleas 1780–93; cr. Baron

[*Continuation of footnote 1 and footnote 2 overleaf*

wrote during so long a period as we have been absent from each other, were I not perfectly satisfied That It must be unnecessary. Though I have not heard once from you since we parted, I make very little Doubt that I have been frequently in your Thoughts. I judge so, because amidst all the variety of Objects which have since I may rather say distracted than interested me I have always in my Best Hours of Reflexion, had my Thoughts turned towards you. If you judge by the same Rule, you will not infer from my Silence either Neglect or Forgetfulness; you may very possibly conclude That I have been Giddy, Idle and dissipated and I am afraid with great Truth. The only Merit I can pretend is the being sensible of my Follies, even whilst I was most engaged in them and The having at length made my Escape from Them. You have inquired I dare say sometimes, about me and have very likely been Told, that I was perfectly Idle and followed nothing but pleasure. I have not studied enough to be able to contradict This intirely but I have paid some Attention to the Courts of Law here and have even read a little of My Lord Coke.[3] My acquaintance at London was grown so large and was so much more Engaging than my Business That I could not well carry on both in the same place. I have had Resolution enough to leave Town and am now at your Old habitation Oxford where the Acquaintances I have found are so totally different from those I have left that my Studies run no risk of being much interrupted. It has occurred to me since I came here That on the plan I should wish to pursue, I could make one of the Scotch Exhibitions very serviceable to me. I make no Ceremony in mentioning it To you nor no preamble but That I believe it would be an Advantage to me and That you would be of the same opinion If I had time to lay all the Circumstances before you. One of Them Dr Smith's[4] must be vacant, soon in course there is another which will in all probability be vacant as the Gentleman[5] is Thought to be in the utmost Hazard, I am sufficiently qualified by my Standing and should have some Friends at Glasgow. Do you Think I should have any Difficulty in

Loughborough 1780; Lord Chancellor 1783–1801; cr. Earl of Rosslyn 1801. Wedderburn was loyal to his friends among the Scottish *literati*, for example, Hume and Smith, but as a rising politician was not overscrupulous in changing alliances. He vehemently supported the British Government's position against that of the American colonists, but grew increasingly critical of North's conduct of the American war. He then briefly joined Fox, and finally received the Great Seal from Pitt. On being informed of his death, George III is alleged to have said: 'Then he has not left a greater knave behind him in my dominions' (John, Lord Campbell, *Lives of the Chancellors* (1868), viii. 203).

[2] The conjectured date fits the facts concerning tenure of a Snell Exhibition (Scott 233).

[3] Sir Edward Coke (1552–1634) Lord Chief Justice: *Institutes of the Laws of England* (1628–44)—the first part is known as *Coke upon Littleton*, i.e. a commentary on Sir Thomas Littleton's treatise on tenures, the principal authority on English real property law.

[4] John Smith (*fl.* 1766) educ. Glasgow and Balliol; M.A. 1751; D.Med. 1757; vacated Snell Exhibition 1755; elected Savilian Professor of Geometry, Oxford 1766.

[5] Not identified.

getting The Nomination? It is a Thing I would rather wish to be offered than to ask and that at any rate I would not seem to take too much pains upon nor ask with the least chance of a Disappointment. I have not mentioned this to any one but yourself, nor shall I till I hear from you. If It is necessary to prevent a preengagement to take any Step in it, you can best judge; only I should wish to be as little mentioned in it as possible and especially while my Father[6] is not acquainted with my Intentions. I know you don't love College Business but This I hope can scarcely be an Affair of any Trouble. Believe me My Dear Smith with the same Affection as ever Your Sincere Friend

Alexr Wedderburn

Shall I hear from you soon.

16. *From* ADAM SMITH, Collector of Customs at Alloa[1]

MS., GUL Gen. 1464/10; Scott 235.

Alloa, 27 Aug. 1754

[Replies to his cousin, Professor Adam Smith, who has asked him to make inquiries on behalf of a friend wishing to purchase an office. Reckons his collectorship is worth 'above 200 Pounds per ann.' and does not think he would resign it 'under ten years purchase'.[2] Has addressed a memorial to the Duke of Argyll about some of his own affairs. Recommends that his cousin take a jaunt into Ayrshire, 'it will be good for your health and amuse you'.]

17. *From* ADAM FERGUSON[1]

Small 603.

Groningen, Oct. 1754

[Ferguson requests Smith to address a reply to him at Rotterdam[2]] without any clerical titles, for I am a downright layman.

---

[6] Peter Wedderburn (d. 1756) advocate 1715; Assessor of the City of Edinburgh; Secretary to the Court of Excise; Lord of Session, as Lord Chesterhall 1755.

[1] Born in Aberdeen, 1711, and known to have a wife and four children by 1752.

[2] In 1752 this Adam Smith received £30 a year as Collector of Customs and a similar sum as a Collector of the Salt Duty. He would possibly have some smaller offices. While it is understood that the actual income of a Collector at this time was double the official salary, Smith was suggesting initially a stiff price for his office.

[1] Adam Ferguson (1723–1816) clergyman, professor, pioneer sociologist; educ. Perth and St. Andrews University; Gaelic speaker; chaplain to the Black Watch, said to have served at Fontenoy 1745, resigned his commission 1754; Hume's successor as Keeper of the Advocate's Library 1757; Professor of Natural Philosophy, Edinburgh 1759, of Moral Philosophy 1764, of Mathematics 1785; Secretary to the Conciliation Commission sent

[*Continuation of footnote 1 and footnote 2 overleaf*

18. *From* ADAM FERGUSON

Address: To Mr Adam Smith, Professor of Philosophy in the College of Glasgow, North Brittain
MS., University of Illinois Libr.; unpubl.

Leipzig, 1 Dec. 1754

Dear Sir

I wrote last from Groninguen[1] and told you of Mr. Gordons[2] Intention of passing the Winter at this place. The impressions he had got of Groninguen upon the Road woud have made him constantly Dissatisfied at that place, for people sometimes think meanly of themselves at an University of little repute, as in a Coat that is out of Fashion; otherwise I am not well qualified to Judge of the Superiority of this University.[3] There are a great Variety of Professors, and all who have got the Degree of Master of Arts here may advertise a College upon any Branch they please, they have scarcely any Vacations. The publick lectures are in German and Strangers are Obliged to have private lessons in Latin for themselves which make the fees very high. Mr. Gordon attends three in Company with Mr. Abercrombie.[4] The Civil Law, The Law of Nature and Nations, and Modern History, which are rather too many at once, at least they would be so to one who could give application to books and pursue a Point steadily, but that habit is seldom acquired by People in Mr. Gordons Way; he likes very well to hear about matters of Study but what is called Poring, is not much to his mind. I have no trouble in advising him against Irregularitys, and the whole remittances are very safely entrusted to his own management so that you may call me a very happy Governour, provided you will always keep in mind how far the happiness of a Governour mounts. This is not a place of Conversation to me, there may be agreeable people but I have

---

to Philadelphia 1778. His most important book was *An Essay on the History of Civil Society* (1767). Its publication led to charges that he had plagiarized Smith's ideas, and this was alleged to have caused a coolness between the two men (Carlyle 299). Priority in time of the *Essay* over WN caused Marx to regard Ferguson as Smith's 'teacher', e.g. in the matter of the disadvantages of the division of labour (*Capital* I.xiv.5). Ferguson was reconciled to Smith during the latter's final illness. His other chief works were *The History of the Progress and Termination of the Roman Republic* (1783) and *Principles of Moral and Political Science* (1792). With Hume, Smith, John Millar, Robertson, and Kames, Ferguson was one of the leaders of what has become known as the Scottish school of sociological historians: see the references cited in Ian Ross, *Lord Kames and the Scotland of his Day* (Oxford, 1972), 186 n. 2; also David Kettler, *Ferguson* (Ohio State U.P. 1965).

[2] Rotterdam's University was frequented by Scots studying Roman law.

[1] Dutch University attended by Scots studying Roman law.
[2] Not identified but as this letter suggests, he was a young man of good family, known to Smith, who had a relative ('your Mr. Gordon') in Smith's charge at Glasgow.
[3] The most famous professor of this period was the philosopher and theologian Christian August Crusius (1715–75).   [4] Not identified.

not yet been able to find them out or relish much through the Medium of bad Latin and bad French. I am already of opinion that Learning is very frequent here, but have not met with any Glimmering of Taste, or very elegant Reflexions: but you must consider me as a stranger who may know more hereafter.

A Gentleman passed some days ago in his way from Paris to Berlin, and told some Storys of Mr. Fontenelle[5]: one that he was in Company with a Lady who happend to drop her Fan, he put himself immediatly in motion to take it up, but she prevented him, for he is a hundred years old, upon which he said; Plut a Dieu que Je n'avois que quatre Vingt Ans. Another Lady who it seems had removed lately to his neighbourhood made him a Visit and told him; she expected to see him often for that reason; he replyed that wont be my reason, that will only be my Pretence. I wish you may relish these Bons mots, that come so far as Germany, if not you may make reflections upon the length of time it may take to turn a Frenchman Sour. I saw lately some Smart letters in Manuscript that Passed between Voltaire, and a Church Man of Dignitee in France on account of his Infidelity. They say he is Constantly Complaining of his Health and threatning to Die. A Lady here tells me she saw him in his way from Berlin,[6] and that he caressed one of her Children and said he woud be fond of him even if he had been begotten by Maupertuis.[7] We Lodge here with a Frenchman, who is a little Foolish, for the sake of learning his Language; he has taught French in this Place for some years, he has translated some of Mr. Humes Works into French and has the Title of secretary to the King of Poland, all which is very fine in a Landlord.[8] The King when he has a mind to Flatter a Man cannot give A Title of Nobility but makes many Secretarys and members of the Privy Council.[9] The Nobility waste away here to Nothing; for all the Sons share alike in the Estate and Title; all ranks almost have Voluminous Titles, if you was a Professor at Leipzig instead of Glasgow I shoud have directed my Letter, To his Excellency

[5] Bernard Le Bovier de Fontenelle (1657–1757), Secretary to the Academy of Sciences, 1697, later its President and historian; his best-known works: *Entretiens sur la pluralité des mondes* (1686), and *Histoire des oracles* (1687); he also compiled a collection of entertaining stories, *Lettres galantes du chevalier d'Her* (1685).

[6] Voltaire was in Berlin, 1750–3, as a pensioner of Frederick the Great. He parted from the King after quarrelling with Maupertuis.

[7] Pierre Moreau de Maupertuis (1698–1759), mathematician. He was made President of the Berlin Academy. Many found him bad-tempered, and Voltaire satirized him in *Micromégas*. Smith lent Maupertuis's works to a correspondent in 1762; see Letter 63 from Thomas Wallace, dated 4 Jan. 1762.

[8] Eléazar de Mauvillon (1712–79), native of Provence, became a Protestant and went to live in Leipzig 1743; published his translation of Hume's *Political Discourses* (1753); wrote historical works, e.g. *Histoire de Gustave-Adolphe* (1764). He is said to have been a hard and opinionated man who made his family suffer.

[9] Frederic August (1696–1763), Elector of Saxony, became King of Poland 1734, took Maria Theresa's side in the Second Silesian war 1744–5, and was vanquished by Frederick of Prussia, thereafter lived in exile.

The most learned & Celebrated &c. I should be sorry to have written all this Idleness to a Man who is not well and I hope to hear you don't Complain this Winter. Make my Compliments to Mrs. Smith[10] Miss Douglass[11] and other Friends at Glasgow. If Mr. Bagwell and Mr. Reid[12] be at Glasgow my Compliments to Both. I woud write to them if I was quite sure of their being there. Mr. Gordon Joins me in Good Wishes. I am Dear Sir Your most affectionate

> humble Servant
> Adam Ferguson

My Compliments to your Mr. Gordon

19. *From* DAVID HUME

Address: To Mr Adam Smith Professor of Philosophy at Glasgow
MS., RSE ii. 26; HL i. 212–13.

> Edinburgh, 17 Dec. 1754

Dear Sir,

I told you, that I intended to apply to the Faculty for Redress; and if refusd, to throw up the Library. I was assur'd that two of the Curators[1] intended before the Faculty to declare their Willingness to redress me, after which there cou'd be no Difficulty to gain a Victory over the other two. But before the day came, the Dean[2] prevaild on them to change their Resolution, and joind them himself with all his Interest. I saw it then impossible to succeed, and accordingly retracted my Application: But being equally unwilling to lose the Use of the Books and to bear an Indignity; I retain the Office, but have given Blacklock, our blind Poet, a Bond of Annuity for the Sallary. I have now put it out of these malicious Fellows power to offer me any Indignity; while my Motives for remaining in this

---

[10] Adam Smith's mother.
[11] Janet Douglas (d. 1788), Smith's cousin and housekeeper.
[12] Not traced.

---

[1] On 4 Apr. 1754 Hume, as Keeper of the Advocates' Library, bought a number of books, among them the *Contes* of La Fontaine, *L'Écumoire* by Crébillon *fils*, and *L'histoire amoureuse des Gaules* by Roger de Rabutin, comte de Bussy (generally known as Bussy-Rabutin). When the Curators made their general inspection in June, some of them objected to these three books as indecent, and after long deliberation they ordered them to be removed from the shelves (NLS, MS. Register of the Curators and Keeper). At the same time, they ordained that no more books should be bought for the Library on the authority of the Keeper alone (Draft minute in Hume's handwriting, Hume MSS., RSE) Hume wanted the books re-instated (HL i. 211) and believed two of the Curators, Peter Wedderburn, later Lord Chesterhall, and Thomas Miller of Glenlee (1717–89), were favourably disposed towards him. The other two were James Burnet (later Lord Monboddo) and Sir David Dalrymple (later Lord Hailes).
[2] Robert Dundas of Arniston the Younger (1713–87), educ. Edinburgh and Utrecht; Solicitor-Gen. 1742–6; Dean of the Faculty, 1746; Lord Advocate, 1754; M.P. 1756–60; Lord President of the Court of Session 1760–d.

Office are so apparent. I shou'd be glad that you approve of my Conduct: I own I am satisfy'd with myself.

Pray tell me, and tell me ingenuously, What Success has my History met with among the Judges with you, I mean Dr Cullen, Mr Betham,[3] Mrs Betham, Mr Leechman, Mr Muirhead,[4] Mr Crawford,[5] etc? Dare I presume, that it has been found worthy of Examination, and that its Beauties are found to overballance its Defects? I am very desirous to know my Errors, and I dare swear you think me tolerably docile, to be so veterane an Author. I cannot indeed hope soon to have an Opportunity of correcting my Errors; this Impression is so very numerous.[6] The Sale indeed has been very great in Edinburgh; but how it goes on at London, we have not been precisely inform'd.[7] In all Cases, I am desirous of storing up Instruction, and as you are now idle (I mean, have nothing but your Class to teach: Which to you is comparative Idleness) I will insist upon hearing from you.[8]

Pray tell Mr Crawford, that I sent a Copy to Lord Cathcart,[9] as he desird.

I am Dear Sir
Yours sincerely
David Hume

20. *From* DAVID HUME

Address: To Mr Adam Smith Professor at Glasgow
MS., RSE ii. 27; HL i. 216–17.

Edinburgh, 9 Jan. 1755

Dear Sir

I beg you to make my Compliments to the Society,[1] and to take the

---

³ See Letter 14, n. 8.

⁴ George Muirhead (1715–73), Professor of Oriental Languages, Glasgow, 1753; of Humanity, 1754–73. With James Moore he supervised the edition of Homer printed by the Foulis brothers in 1747.

⁵ Probably Patrick Crawford of Auchenames (d. 1778), elder bro. of Ronald Crawford, WS, and father of John ('Fish') Crawford, both of whom were friends of Hume. Patrick Crawford was M.P. for Renfrewshire in 1761, having previously been M.P. for Ayrshire in 1741 and 1747.

⁶ 2,000 copies (Mossner, *Life of Hume*, Austin, 1954, 303).

⁷ In Edinburgh about 450 'in five weeks', Hume to the Earl of Balcarres (HL i. 214, 17 Dec. 1754); in London—'Mr Millar told me, that in a twelve-month he sold only forty five Copies' (Hume, *My Own Life*).

⁸ No communication from Smith to Hume about his *History* seems to have survived, but Smith studied the work carefully and described Hume as 'by far the most illustrious philosopher and historian of the present age' (WN V.i.g.3).

⁹ Charles, 9th Baron Cathcart (1721–76), A.D.C. to Duke of Cumberland at Fontenoy; Lord High Commissioner to the General Assembly of the Kirk of Scotland, 1755–63 and 1773–6; Ambassador at St. Petersburg, 1768–71.

¹ The Literary Society of Glasgow, founded by Smith and others connected with the University. Hume, Sir John Dalrymple, and the Foulis brothers were among the members:

Fault on Yourself, If I have not executed my Duty, and sent them this time my Anniversary Paper. Had I got a Week's warning, I shou'd have been able to have supply'd them; I shou'd willingly have sent some Sheets of the History of the Commonwealth or Protectorship; but they are all of them out of my hand at present, and I have not been able to recall them.

I think you are extremely in the right, that the Parliaments Bigotry has nothing in common with Hiero's Generosity.[2] They were themselves violent Persecutors at home to the utmost of their Power. Besides, the Hugonots in France were not persecuted; they were really seditious, turbulent People, whom their King was not able to reduce to Obedience. The French Persecutions did not begin till sixty Years after.

Your Objection to the Irish Massacre[3] is just; but falls not on the Execution but the Subject. Had I been to describe the Massacre of Paris, I should not have fallen into that Fault: But in the Irish Massacre no single eminent Man fell, or by a remarkable Death. If the Elocution of that whole Chapter be blameable, it is because my Conception labord with too great an Idea of my Subject, which is there the most important. But that Misfortune is not unusual. I am Dear Sir

Yours most sincerely

David Hume.

21. *To* [DR. GEORGE STONE][1]

MS., GUA/MS./B/Snell 15626 (draft unsigned); unpubl.

[Glasgow, 14 Feb. 1755][2]

My Lord

I am commanded by the University to whom your Graces Letter of the 25th January was communicated, to inform your Grace, that they had, before they received the honor of this last application been solicited by several persons of the greatest distinction in this country particularly by the Earl of Glasgow the Present Rector of the University[3] to allow Mr Anderson to stay abroad another year with Mr Campbell; that, however,

---

see D. D. McElroy, *Scotland's Age of Improvement: A Survey of Eighteenth-Century Clubs and Societies* (Washington State University Press, Pullman, 1969).

   [2] ? Hiero (Hieron) II, Tyrant of Syracuse, 270–216 B.C. See Theocritus xvi, and Polybius, i.8.viii.

   [3] Hume gave an account of the Irish Massacre of 1641 in vol. i, ch. vi, of his *History*.

   [1] On 13 Feb. a University meeting heard a letter from the 'Primate of Ireland' to which this letter is a reply; the dignitary in question was Dr. George Stone (?1708–64), Archbishop of Armagh and Primate of all Ireland: see Scott 188 n. 1.

   [2] The reference to the 'University meeting of yesterday', i.e. 13 Feb. (Scott 188), suggests the draft letter was written on the 14th.

   [3] John Boyle, Earl of Glasgow, Lord Rector of the University 1754–5.

upon account of some inconveniencies, which they foresaw might follow from complying with this request, both to the University and to Mr Anderson,[4] they excused themselves from granting it. All the members of the Society being personally known to that Noble Lord made confident that He would pardon want of complaisance in this particular and not impute it to any failure of regard to him by whose condescension in allowing himselfe to be placed at the head of the University [they] think [themselves] highly honoured and obliged. They hoped too that the neighbourhood of that Nobleman and of the other Persons of Distinction who sollicited them to the same purpose, would afford the University many opportunities of expressing the high esteem which it has for that friendship. The Great Distance which separates us from your Grace giving us but few opportunities of expressing the very great veneration which we have for your Graces person, Character and station we cannot avoid even in so small a matter embracing any occasion to assure your grace that no distance can render us insensible of what is due to all of these. Mr Anderson has by order of the University meeting of yesterday obtain'd leave of absence till the 4th. Oct. 1756 which is the whole time desired by Mr Campbell. Be pleased [to] give me leave to assure you that tho' unknown, I have the honour to be with the highest regard Your Graces

Most Obedient and most humble Servant

The principal[5] whose indisposition puts it out of his power to write, heartily concurrs in granting the allowance and desires that his most humble compliments should be offered to your Grace

22. *From* DAVID HUME

MS., RSE ii. 26; HL i. 245–6.

[Mar. 1757][1]

Dear Smith

I have got down a few Copies of my Dissertations[2] lately publish'd at London; and shall send you one by the first Glasgow Waggon. I beg of you

---

[4] John Anderson (1726–96), Professor of Oriental Languages, 1754–6, and of Natural Philosophy from 1757. Known as 'Jolly Jack Phosphorus', Anderson was a talented but quarrelsome man, sometimes given to beating students and directing polemic against his colleagues. He stressed the teaching of applied science, and Anderson's College was founded after his death to incorporate some of his ideas. His papers are at Strathclyde University, which is perhaps the fullest realization of his schemes. The 'Mr Campbell' to whom he acted as a travelling tutor has not been identified.

[5] Principal Neil Campbell.

[1] MS. torn, but the date is suggested by the reference to the London production of *Douglas*.

[2] *Four Dissertations*, viz. 'The National History of Religion', 'Of the Passions', 'Of Tragedy', 'Of the Standard of Taste', published 7 Feb. 1757.

to do me the Favor of accepting this Trifle. You have read all the Dissertations in Manuscript; but you will find that on the natural History of Religion somewhat amended in point of Prudence. I do not apprehend, that it will much encrease the Clamour against me.[3]

The Dedication to John Hume you have probably seen:[4] For I find it has been inserted in some of the weekly Papers, both here and in London. Some of my Friends thought it was indiscreet in me to make myself responsible to the Public for the Productions of another: But the Author had lain under such singular and unaccountable Obstructions in his Road to Fame; that I thought it incumbent on his Wellwishers to go as much out of the common Road to assist him. I believe the Composition of the Dedication will be esteemd very prudent; and not inelegant.

I can now give you the Satisfaction of hearing, that the Play, tho' not near so well acted in Covent Garden as in this Place,[5] is likely to be very successful: Its great intrinsic Merit breaks thro all Obstacles. When it shall be printed (which will be soon) I am perswaded it will be esteem'd the best; and by French Critics, the only Tragedy of our Language. This Encouragement will, no doubt, engage the Author to go on in the same Carrier. He meets with great Countenance in London: And I hope will soon be render'd independant in his Fortune.

Did you ever hear of such Madness and Folly as our Clergy have lately fallen into? For my Part, I expect that the next Assembly will very solemnly pronounce the Sentence of Excommunication[6] against me: But I do not apprehend it to be a Matter of any Consequence. What do you think?

I am somewhat idle at present; and somewhat undetermin'd as to my next Undertaking. Shall I go backwards or forwards in my History? I think you us'd to tell me, that you approvd more of my going backwards. The other woud be the more popular Subject; but I am afraid, that I shall not find Materials sufficient to ascertain the Truth; at least, without settling in London: Which I own, I have some Reluctance to. I am settled here

---

[3] By William Warburton and others (Mossner, *Life of Hume*, 321–6). For changes in the text of 'The Natural History of Religion', see Mossner 619: phrases are altered that might have led to a charge of blasphemy.

[4] The dedication was published separately. It was addressed to 'The Reverend Mr Home, Author of Douglas, a Tragedy'. John Home (1722–1808), educ. at Leith and Edinburgh University; Minister of Athelstaneford 1746–57; dramatist: *Douglas* (1757), *Agis* (1758), *Siege of Aquileia* (1769), *The Fatal Discovery* (1769), *Alonzo* (1773), *Alfred* (1778); private secretary to Lord Bute and tutor to the Prince of Wales, later George III, from whom he received a pension; settled at Edinburgh, 1779. Home published a *History of the Rebellion of 1745* (1802) in part based on his own experiences, including capture by the Highlanders at Falkirk in 1746.

[5] Produced at Edinburgh by West Digges, 14 Dec. 1756, and by Rich at Covent Garden, 14 Mar. 1757, with Peg Woffington as Lady Randolph.

[6] Threatened against Hume in 1756. The object of attack by the Highflyers in 1757 was Hume's great friend the Revd. Alexander Carlyle.

very much to my Mind; and wou'd not wish, at my Years, to change the Place of my abode.

I have just now receivd a copy of Douglas from London: It will instantly be put in the Press. I hope to be able to send you a Copy in the same Parcel [with the Dissertations].[7]

I am Dear Sir [   ]

Pray why did we not see you this Winter? We shall excuse you for no other Reason but because we hope you were busy. But you must not only have Industry: You must also have Perseverance.

23. *To* [GILBERT ELLIOT]

MS., Kress Libr., Harvard University; unpubl.

Glasgow College, 7 Sept. 1757

Dear Sir

I take the liberty to write to you at the desire of a very old friend to sollicit a favour of you which I am by no means sure but it may be improper for you to grant, and which I am afraid it is still more improper for me to ask. Mr. John Currie,[1] a Gentleman who I understand has been recommended to you by John Hume, is an old Schoolfellow of mine and a very worthy Clergyman of more learning than is common. He has had the imprudence to make a love marriage with a young Lady, a cousin of mine for whom I have always had a very high regard, but who had not a single shilling to her fortune. He is at present only helper to his father and as their family is encreasing you may believe their circumstances are far from being easy. One Preston[2] the Minister of Mankinch dyed about ten days ago; The presentation is in the Gift of the Crown. Could you with any propriety apply for it to this worthy man? I am sensible how little title I have to ask anything of this kind of you, but the urgency of this Gentlemans situation has forced me to get over all scruples. I am sure if I could tell his case fully to Mrs. Murray[3] she would heartily join me in the Application.

I have no news of any consequence with regard to your friends in this country. Your English friends are here in the highest degree of Popularity and reputation. The Lincolnshire mobs provoke our severest indignation for opposing the militia, and we hope to hear that the ringleaders are all to

---

[7] MS. torn.

[1] William Currie (1722–70), ordained 1750, son of John Currie (d. 1765), whom he succeeded as Minister of Kinglassie, Fife. He married Jean Douglas (d. 1768) on 9 May 1755.

[2] George Preston, Minister of Markinch, Fife, d. 24 Aug. 1757.

[3] Elliot md. on 15 Dec. 1746 Agnes, dau. and heiress of Hugh Dalrymple Murray Kynynmound of Melgund, Forfar, and Lochgelly and Kynynmound, Fife.

be hanged.[4] I heartily beg your Pardon for my forwardness in making this application and am notwithstanding with the greatest respect as well as affection your most Obedient

humble Servant
Adam Smith

24. *To* [LORD MILTON][1]

MS., NLS SB 88 (1757); unpubl.

Glasgow, Oct. 1757

My Lord

Tho' I have not the honour to be known to your Lordship, I am obliged to take the Liberty to write to you at the very earnest desire of my friend Mr. Wilkie.[2] As soon as we received your Lordships Letter I carried it to Mr. Clow[3] who assured me that he was yet entirely disengaged, expressed the highest opinion of Mr. Wilkie and desired to be made acquainted with him, but seemed to regard your Letter rather as a permission to go on to make friends to Mr. Wilkie than a direct recommendation. Mr. Leechman to whom I showd it immediately after, assured me that he should be extremely sorry if he was obliged to prefer Mr. Buchanan[4] to Mr. Wilkie, that one was much more conspicuous than the other, but that however he could in the mean time give the new proposal no direct encouragement, that My Lord Buchan[5] had two letters from him in which he had expressed

---

[4] The Militia Act, effective 1 May 1757, authorized raising militia in the English countries, also training on Sundays, but made no provision for funds. In August a mob rose at Stowe, Lincs., and demanded money and a barrel of ale from an aged clergyman. On being refused they broke his windows and demonstrated in Lincoln, asking for the return of the militia lists and money from each constable. Participants said they would sacrifice their lives for King and country but 'would not be obliged to quit home for sixpence a day to serve in the militia' (*Scots Mag.*, xix, 1757, 430). Scotland was not allowed to have a militia after the '45 Rising, and patriotic Scots seeking to change this state of affairs were indignant at anti-militia feeling in England. Together with most of the *literati*, Smith was a member of the Poker Club formed in 1762 to stir up the question of a Scottish militia, the country having been aroused about its defenceless state in 1759 on the appearance of Thurot off the Scottish coast (Rae 135–6).

[1] The subject of academic patronage and allusions to the Duke of Argyll suggest that this letter was addressed to Andrew Fletcher (1692–1766) Lord Milton, nephew of Fletcher of Saltoun; judge and politician; Lord Justice-Clerk 1735–48; Keeper of the Signet 1746; chief associate of the 3rd Duke of Argyll in the management of Scotland.

[2] William Wilkie (1721–72), the 'Scottish Homer'; poet, clergyman, and professor; educ. Edinburgh University; published *The Epigoniad* (1757) based on *Iliad* iv; Professor of Natural Philosophy, St. Andrews, 1759. See Mossner, *The Forgotten Hume*, (New York, 1943), ch. 4.

[3] James Clow, Smith's successor as Professor of Logic at Glasgow.

[4] In the event, James Buchanan was elected Professor of Oriental Languages 1757.

[5] Henry David Erskine (1710–67) 10th Earl of Buchan, fa. of David Stewart Erskine (1742–1829), 11th Earl, dilettante; former student of Smith.

himselfe in favour of Mr. Buchanan, But that in these letters he had made
his promise rowl entirely upon the Duke of Argylls recommending him. He
seemed heartily to wish however that our scheme might succeed and that
his Grace would provide for Mr. Buchanan in some other way. Mr.
Anderson[6] assured me that he would give a considerable sum of money
that Mr. Wilkie should succeed, but that he had promised the rector[7] to
vote for Mr. Buchanan in the second Place upon the Rectors agreeing to
vote for him in the first. Mr. Lindsey[8] expressed the highest regard for
Mr. Wilkie, approved of the scheme of his friends, but was hindered from
doing any thing to forward it by an old personal friendship with Mr.
Buchanan. Mr. Simson I have not spoke to myselfe but hear from Dr.
Black[9] that he thinks himselfe not absolutely engaged to Mr. Buchanan.
These with the four who recommended Mr. Wilkie to your Lordship are
all the members of our society at present in Scotland. Six of them make a
majority. If his Grace could be induced to recommend it himselfe either
to Mr. Clow or to Mr. Simson or what would be still better, to both, I am
persuaded it would succeed very easily. Mr. Clow will, I imagine, regard
the Distinction as a very great honour and will exert himselfe to the utmost
to second his Graces recommendation. As soon as a majority goes into it,
I am sure that the whole society will declare their approbation of it and
rejoice at its success. I cannot express to your Lordship how much the
Public, both here and at Edinburgh, is interested in Mr. Wilkies success.
Your Lordship, I hope, will have the thanks of the whole country in general,
and of our society in Particular for your generous patronage of a man whom
we regard as undoubtedly the first Poet as well as one of the most eminent
Philosophers of the Present age. If his Grace should decline writing himselfe, a letter from your Lordship in his name to the two Gentlemen I mentioned above and to any others you thought proper, would I am persuaded
be sufficient. The other however would still be surer. Whatever it may
appear proper to do in this affair I begg it may be done soon for the sake
of the whole society that all appearance of Discord may be at an end among
us, of which at least some of us are very heartily tired. I can make no other
apology for troubling your Lordship with so long a letter but that it is to
serve a man for whom you have expressed some esteem, and who has the
utmost gratitude for the Protection you have already afforded him, as well

---

[6] John Anderson, Professor of Natural Philosophy.

[7] Patrick Boyle (d. 1761), Lord Shewalton, son of the 1st Earl of Glasgow; advocate
1712; Lord of Session 1746.

[8] Hercules Lindesay, Professor of Civil Law.

[9] Joseph Black (1728–99), Professor of Medicine. He had embarked by 1756 on his
fundamental research into latent heat which laid the foundations of thermal science and
stimulated Watt's improvements in the steam engine. From 1766 to 1797 Black taught
Medicine and Chemistry at Edinburgh. Smith 'never knew a man with less nonsense in
him' (Rae 336) and called on him to be his literary executor.

as the highest admiration for your character in respect. I am with the greatest respect

Your Lordships most
Obedient and most humble
Servant
Adam Smith

I had forgot Mr. Hamilton.[10] I do not know his inclinations. Mr. Wilkie is an excellent Hebreist.

Docketed: Professor Adam Smith, Glasgow, Oct. 1757.

25. *From* DAVID HUME

MS., RSE ii. 29; HL i. 279–80.

8 June 1758

Dear Smith

I sit down to write to you along with Johnstone,[1] and as we have been talking over the Matter, it is probable we shall employ the same Arguments. As he is the younger Lawyer, I leave him to open the Case; and suppose that you have read his Letter first. We are certain, that the Settlement of you here and of Ferguson[2] at Glasgow[3] woud be perfectly easy by Lord Miltons Interest. The Prospect of prevailing with Abercrombie[4] is also very good: For the same Statesman, by his Influence over the Town Council, cou'd oblige him[5] either to attend, which he never woud do, or dispose of the Office for the Money which he gave for it. The only real Difficulty is then with you. Pray then consider, that this is perhaps the only Opportunity we shall ever have of getting you to Town: I dare swear, that you think the Difference of Place is worth paying something for; and yet it will really cost you nothing. You made above 100 Pound a Year by your Class when it this Place, tho' you had not the Character of Professor: We cannot suppose that it will be less than 130 after you are settled. John Stevenson;[6] and it is John Stevenson, makes near 150; as we were inform'd upon Enquiry. Here is 100 Pounds a Year for 8 Years Purchase; which is

---

[10] Thomas Hamilton, Professor of Medicine.

[1] William Johnstone: see Letter 11, n. 2.

[2] Adam Ferguson.   [3] In Smith's Chair of Moral Philosophy.

[4] George Abercromby of Tullibody (d. 1800), fa. of Gen. Ralph Abercromby; Professor of the Law of Nature and Nations at Edinburgh since 1735. This Chair was worth £300 at times, but was usually treated as a sinecure. Hume and Johnstone wanted Smith to buy Abercromby out.

[5] Abercromby.

[6] Professor of Logic in Edinburgh, 1730–74. Stevenson replaced Aristotle with Locke in his course, and his lectures on Rhetoric and Literary Criticism made a deep impression on his students.

a cheap Purchase, even considerd as the way of a Bargain. We flatter our-selves that you rate our Company as something; and the Prospect of settling Ferguson will be an additional Inducement. For tho' we think of making him take up the Project if you refuse it, yet it is uncertain whether he will consent; and it is attended in his Case with many very obvious Objections.[7] I beseech you therefore to weigh all these Motives over again; The altera-tion of these Circumstances merit that you shoud put the matter again in Deliberation.[8] I had a Letter from Miss Hepburn,[9] where she regrets very much, that you are settled at Glasgow, and that we had the Chance of seeing you so seldom. I am

> Dear Smith
> Yours sincerely
> David Hume.

P.S.
Lord Milton can with his Finger, stop the foul Mouths of all the Roarers against Heresy.

26. *To* WILLIAM JOHNSTONE

MS., Pierpont Morgan Libr., New York; Scott 236.

Glasgow, 19 Aug. 1758

Dear Johnstoune
I am much obliged to you for your attention in mentioning me to Mr. Elliot:[1] I have the greatest desire to see him but have been looking in the map and find Minto[2] above three score mortal miles from Glasgow the nearest way that I can go to it. This abates my ardor a good deal. However I shall take the affair ad avisandum.

I send you enclosed a portion of a letter I received last night from Cap-tain Gordon;[3] it is of an early date, but it had come under cover to another Gentleman who was out of the way. It is [n]ot what I expected. I had told him that we might make a demand upon him for one or two hundred pounds, and tho he gives me here an unlimited commision we must not

---

[7] Ferguson had no training in law.

[8] No evidence has come to hand about Smith considering Hume's proposal, but Abercromby demitted his Chair in this year to Robert Bruce, his son-in-law. Bruce passed it on to the philosopher James Balfour of Pilrig in 1764, and Balfour in his turn gave way to Allan Maconochie in 1779, for the sum of £1,522 18s. 2d.

[9] The Miss Hepburns of Keith were good friends of John Home the dramatists, and he is said to have obtained from one of them the idea of *Douglas*.

[1] Gilbert Elliot.   [2] Minto, Roxburgh.

[3] ? Hon. William Russell Gordon (1736–1816), 2nd s. of William, 2nd Earl of Aberdeen; educ. Glasgow University 1748; Cornet 11th Dragoons 1756, Captain 1759.

abuse Generosity, but confine our demand to a sum within the largest of
the two; and the more within it the better. Show this letter to John Hume[4]
and if you can too to James Russel;[5] and let me know by next post if
possible what sum will be wanted from him.[6] I ever am,

Dear Johnstoune

ever yours

Adam Smith

27. *From* GILBERT ELLIOT

MS., GUL Gen. 1035/136; Scott 239-40.

London, 14 Nov. 1758

Dear Sir

   I have of late had a good deal of conversation with Lord Fitsmorris[1]
about the education of his Brother[2] who is now at Eaton, and I believe about
fifteen or sixteen years of age: He thinks his Brother too young to go abroad,
and as he left Oxford himself about two years ago, has no sort of inclination
to send him to that University: After stating to him as well as I coud the
nature of our Universitys and the advantage I thought his Brother might
draw from being put under your direction, he came to a resolution of
adviseing his Father Lord Shelburn[3] to follow that course: his Lordship
has agreed to it, and I have undertaken to open it to you, and to learn as
soon as possible whether it be agreeable to you to undertake the charge:
Lord Shelburn has an immence estate, and can afford if he pleases to settle
ten thousand a year upon his second Son without at all hurting Lord
Fitsmorris, he tells me he will not spare money, but did not wish the boy
shoud be indulged in too great an expence, which I am afraid has hitherto

---

  [4] John Home the dramatist.
  [5] James Russel (d.1773), Edinburgh surgeon and later Professor of Natural Philosophy.
  [6] Scott speculates (236, n. 3) that the project mentioned in this letter was the establishment of the Glasgow Academy of Art.

  [1] Sir William Petty, Viscount Fitzmaurice (1737–1805), 2nd Earl of Shelburne (from
1761) and 1st Marquess of Lansdowne (from 1784); soldier and statesman; educ. Oxford;
fought at Minden, 1759 (rose to General, 1783); M.P. 1760–1; succeeded his father, 1761,
and took his seat in the House of Lords: 1st Lord of Trade, 1763; Secretary of State,
Southern Dept., 1766–8; opposed government policy towards the Americans, 1768–82;
Secretary of State for Home affairs, 1782; 1st Lord of Treasury, 1782–3, when independence was conceded to the Americans. A man of great intelligence, he was an aristocratic
forerunner of the 'philosophical radicals' and the patron of Priestley, Bentham, and Price.
  [2] Hon. Thomas Petty-Fitzmaurice (1742–93) of Llewenny Hall, Denb., Wales; educ.
Eton; matriculated at Glasgow, 1759; St. Mary Hall, Oxford, 1761; called to the English
Bar, 1768; M.P. 1762–80. In 1779, he set up as a linen merchant and established a bleaching factory at Llewenny, Wales, because his Irish estates were unproductive. He was
reported to have lived on 'the most intimate terms with Johnson, Hawkesworth and
Garrick' (*Gentleman's Magazine*, 1793, 1053).
  [3] John Petty (1706–61), 1st Earl of Shelburne.

been the case: He proposes that he shoud be in your house and intirely under your direction, and to give you for his board and the inspection of his education a hundred pound a year, or more if it shoud be thought proper. I understand he is a very good school Scholar, very lively, and tolerably ungovernable, but probably will not give you much trouble, as you will have the total charge and direction without any controul. If you have no objection to taking him into your house, he will come to you immediately, as Lord Fitsmorris tells me he may probably take that opportunity of runing over Scotland, paying a visit to Lord Dunmore,[4] and puting his Brother upon a proper foot: I think myself that a young man of this rank coming to your University may of be of advantage to it, especially as I find every thinking man here begins to discover the very absurd constitution of the English Universitys, without knowing what to do better: It is indeed possible, that Oxford may a little recover itself, by having lately established there, a Professor for the common, constitutional law of the Kingdom,[5] and also admitted Masters for some of the exercises, which two last articles have some connection at least with the occupations of ordinary life, and I can hardly say so much for the usual academical Institutions; little adapted for the improvement of young men either of rank or liberal views: I have very little doubt, but you might even draw a good many of the youth of this part of the world to pass a winter or two at Glasgow, notwithstanding the distance and disadvantage of the dialect, provided that to your real advantages you were to add the best Masters for the exercises, and also for acquiring the french language; an accomplishment indispensably necessary, and which cannot be acquired either at Eaton or Westminster, tho' all children male and female bred in their Fathers houses are regularly taught both to speak and write french with tolerable facility. Pray let me have your answer as soon as possible; is your book in the press, or will it be there soon?[6] belive Dear Sir

Yours very faithfully
Gilb: Elliot

[4] John Murray (1730–1809) 4th Earl of Dunmore; soldier, administrator. and politician; page of honour to Prince Charles 1745; British army career 1753–8; Governor of New York 1769, of Virginia 1774–6, of the Bahamas 1787–96; representative peer of Scotland 1761–8, 1776, 1780, 1784.

[5] By a will dated 29 Dec. 1755, Charles Viner left his money to endow a Professor, Fellows, and Scholars in English Common Law at Oxford. The first Vinerian Professor was William Blackstone (1723–80), whose lectures between 1758 and 1766 attracted widespread attention and formed the basis for his *Commentaries on the Law of England* (1st edn., 1765–9).

[6] The reference is to TMS. The book was in circulation by 12 Apr. 1759, when Hume thanked Smith for a copy (see Letter No. 31), and by 26 Apr. the London publisher had 'no Sort of doubt of this Impression being gone tho' it will not be published till next Week' (see Letter 33 from Andrew Millar).

28. *To* LORD FITZMAURICE[1]

Address: To Lord Fitzmaurice at the Earl of Shelburnes house Hanover Square, London.
MS., Bowood Libr., Marquess of Lansdowne; Scott 241–2.

Glasgow College, 21 Feb. 1759

My Lord,

I give you the trouble of This Letter, tho I have nothing particular to inform you of besides what I told you in my last, that Mr Fitzmaurice[2] attends all his classes with the most exact punctuality and gives more application to his studies than could reasonably be expected. I find him perfectly tractable and docile in every respect and I heartily wish that we may give the same satisfaction to him which he gives to all of us. I find he is so far advanced in the Greek language that it will not be difficult to carry him on and if he continues to be as regular as at present, I believe, I can promise, that against this time twelve-month he will be able to read it with ease. He masters all that he is about at present so easily that I intend in about a month hence he should begin to learn Algebra and Arithmetic with the Proffessor of Mathematics.

This country is so barren of all sorts of transactions that can interest anybody that lives at a distance from it that little entertainment is to be expected from any correspondence on this Side the tweed. Our epistles to our friends at the capital commonly consist more in enquiries than in information. I must therefore put your Lordship in mind of the promise you was so good as to make to me of some times letting me hear from you of what passes in the Great World, either at home or abroad. I hear there is no faction in parliament, which I am glad of. For tho' a little faction now and then gives spirit to the nation the continuance of it obstructs all public business and puts it out of the power of [the] best Minister to do much good. Even Sir Robert Walpoles administration would, I imagine have been better had it not been for the violence of the opposition that was made to him, which in its beginnings had no great foundation. There is at present so little noise made about our own affairs that the Portuguese Conspiracy takes up a good part of the attention of this part of the world. I see this day in the newspapers an abstract of the evidence or rather of the facts for which these unhappy noblemen have been condemned.[3] In the end of it they found a great deal upon the presumptions of law which were against them which, as no other evidence is particularly specified,

---

[1] Sir William Petty, Viscount Fitzmaurice, later 2nd Earl of Shelburne.

[2] Hon. Thomas Petty-Fitzmaurice, bro. of Viscount Fitzmaurice.

[3] The conspiracy of 3 Sept. 1758 was crushed by the Marquis de Pombal, Prime Minister, with singular ferocity: the Duke of Aveiro and Marquis of Tavora were broken alive on the wheel: the Duke's sons and a son-in-law were strangled; and Tavora's wife was beheaded.

makes me fear that this horrid execution has been a little precipitate. For want of some thing else to write to your Lordship I am obliged to talk to you of subjects you must not only know much better than I, but which you must be quite sick of.

I am with the greatest regard
Your Lordships most Obedient and most Humble Servant,
Adam Smith

29. *To* LORD SHELBURNE[1]

MS., Bowood Libr., Marquess of Lansdowne; Scott 243–4.

Glasgow, 10 Mar. 1759

My Lord

I have been very much out of my Duty in having so long neglected to write to your Lordship who have trusted me with so very important a charge as the Education of Mr Fitzmaurice. I waited till I could say something to your Lordship with regard to what I expected of him which might be depended upon, and I can now venture to assure your Lordship that the fault ought to be laid to my charge if he does not turn out at least an uncommonly good Scholar. There is not a poor boy in the college who is supported by charity and studies for bread that is more punctual in his attendance upon every part of College discipline. He attends different Masters for Greek, Latin and Philosophy five hours a day, and is besides employ'd with me at home between two and three hours, in going over the subjects of those different lectures.[2] He reads too every day some thing by himself and a good deal on Saturdays and Sundays when he has most leisure. He has never yet missed a Single hour, except two days that he was ill of a very voilent Cholic, occasioned by cold and I suspect by the want of his usual exercise, which, I find, was very violent at Eton, and for which he has at present no leisure. It was with the greatest difficulty that I could keep him at home for those two days. He is perfectly sober, eats no supper, or what is next to none, a roasted apple or some such trifle and drinks scarce any thing but water. There is the more merit in this part of his conduct as it is the effect of Resolution not of habit: for I find he had been accustomed to a different way of living at Eton: But your Lordships and My Lady Shelburnes[3] good advice has, I understand, produced this change. I can assure your Lordship that I have conversed with him for these two months with the greatest intimacy and that I find him every way

[1] 1st Earl of Shelburne.

[2] The strict regimen at Glasgow is to be contrasted with the laxity at Oxford; see Letter 1 addressed to William Smith, dated 24 Aug. 1740, and Letter 27 from Gilbert Elliot, dated 14 Nov. 1758.

[3] Lady Mary, dau. of Hon. William Fitzmaurice of Gullane, Co. Kerry, Ireland. She married her cousin, Hon. John Fitzmaurice (later 1st Earl of Shelburne) in 1734.

agreeable; full of spirit and sensibility; two qualities which are very rarely joined together. I have a great deal more to say to your Lordship, but an unexpected call obliges me to conclude this letter abruptly. I shall write to your Lordship again by next at greater length. I had delayed writing so long that I was ashamed to delay it any longer, so snatched the first quarter of an hour which business of this [?kind] afforded me to scrawl this Letter

I am with the greatest respect

Your Lordships most Obedient and most humble Servant

Adam Smith

30. *To* LORD SHELBURNE

MS., Bowood Libr., Marquess of Lansdowne; Scott 243–5.

Glasgow College, 4 Apr. 1759.

My Lord

I did myselfe the honour to write to your Lordship some time ago and promised to write more distinctly by next post. It was not in my Power to keep my word. A slight indisposition which has hung about me ever since, joined to a multiplicity of business which several accidents have conspired to bring upon me, have kept me either so exhausted or so hurried that till this moment I have not had one hour in which I had both leisure and spirits to sit down to write to your Lordship.

I have nothing to add to what I said to your Lordship in my Last letter concerning Mr Fitzmaurices behaviour here. It has hitherto been altogether unexceptionable.

With regard to the Plan which I would propose for his education while he continues here; he will finish his Philosophical studies next winter; and as My Lord Fitzmaurice[1] seemed to propose that he should stay here another year after that, I would propose that it should be employed in perfecting himselfe in Philosophy and the Languages, but chiefly and principally in the Study of Law and history. In that year I would advise him to attend the Lectures of the Professor of Civil Law:[2] for tho' the civil law has no authority in the English courts, the study of it is an admirable preparation for the Study of the English Law. The civil Law is digested into a more regular System than the English Law has yet been, and tho' the Principles of the former are in many respects different from those of the latter, yet there are many principles common to both, and one who has studied the civil law at least knows what a System of law is, what parts it consist of, and how these ought to be arranged: so that when he afterwards comes to study the law of any other country which is not so well digested, he carries at least the Idea of a System in his head and knows to what part of it he ought to refer every thing that he reads. While he

---

[1] Later 2nd Earl of Shelburne.   [2] Hercules Lindesay.

attends the lectures of the Proffessor of Civil Law, I shall read with him myselfe an institute of the feudal law, which is the foundation of the present laws and Government of all European Nations.[3]

In order to have him immediately under my own eye I have hurried him a little in his Philosophical studies. I have made him pass the logic class, which ought regularly to have been his first study, and brought him at once into my own, the moral Philosophy. He attends however the lectures of the Proffessor of Logic[4] one hour a day. This, with two hours that he attends upon my Lectures, with one hour which he gives to the Professor of Mathematics,[5] one hour to the Proffessor of Greek[6] and another to that of Latin,[7] makes his hours which he attends every day except Saturday and Sunday to be six in all. He has never yet missed a single hour, and in the evening and the morning goes over very regularly with me the business of those different classes. I chuse rather to oppress him with business for this first winter: It keeps him constantly employed and leaves no time for Idleness. The oppression too is not so great as it may seem. The Study of Greek and latin is not at all new to him: Logic requires little attention so that moral philosophy and mathematicks are the only studies which take up much of his time. The great vigour both of mind and body with which he seems to be peculiarly blessed makes every thing easy to him. We have one holiday in the month which he has hitherto constantly chosen of his own accord to employ rather in learning something which he had missed by being too late in coming to the College, than in diversion.

The College breaks up in the beginning of June and does not sit down again till the beginning of October. During this interval I propose that he should learn french and Dancing and fencing and that besides he should read with me the best greek, latin and french Authors on Moral Philosophy for two or three hours every morning, so that he will not be idle in the vacation. The Proffessor of Mathematics too proposes to teach him Euclid at that time as he was too late to learn it in the Class. That Gentleman, who is now turned seventy but preserves all the gaiety and vigour of youth, takes more pains upon Mr Fitzmaurice than I ever knew him to do upon any Person, and generally gives him a private lecture twice or thrice a week. This is purely the effect of personal liking, for no other consideration is capable of making Mr Simson give up his ease.

I make Mr Fitzmaurice pay all his own accounts after he has summed and examin'd them along with me. He gives me a receipt for whatever money he receives: in the receipt he marks the purpose for which it is to be applyed and preserves the account as his voucher, marking upon the

[3] See LJ for elaboration of Smith's ideas on law. Possibly the 'institute on feudal law' was Sir Thomas Craig's *Jus Feudale*, 1603, which was used in the Dutch Universities as an authoritative legal source.

[4] James Clow.   [5] Robert Simson.   [6] James Moor.
[7] George Muirhead.

back of it the day when it was payed. These shall all be transmitted to your Lordship when there is occasion: But as My Lord Fitzmaurice left fifty Pounds here I shall have no occasion to make any demand for some time.

Your Lordship may depend upon the most religious complyance with whatever commands you shall please to lay upon me with regard to the conduct or Education of Mr Fitzmaurice.

I have been lately made to flatter myselfe with the Pleasure and Honour of seeing your Lordship in Scotland this summer. It would give the greatest satisfaction both to Mr Fitzmaurice and me. Your Lordship would then see with your own eyes in what manner he was employed and could judge better how far it was necessary either to increase or diminish the quantity of work which is now imposed upon him.

We are no Strangers in this country to the very noble and generous work which your Lordship has been employed in in Ireland. We have in Scotland some noblemen whose estates extend from the east to the west sea, who call themselves improvers, and are called so by their countrymen, when they cultivate two or three hundred acres round their own family seat while they allow all the rest of their country to lie waste, almost uninhabited and entirely unimproved, not worth a shilling the hundred acres, without thinking themselves answerable to God, their country and their Posterity for so shameful as well as so foolish a neglect. Your Lordship, I hear, is not of that opinion, and tho' you are not negligent either of the elegance or magnificence of your country Villas, you do not think that any attention of that kind dispenses with the more noble and important duty of attempting to introduce arts, industry and independency into a miserable country, which has hitherto been a stranger to them all. Nothing, I have often imagined, would give more pleasure to Sir William Petty,[8] your Lordship's ever honoured ancestor, than to see his representative pursuing a Plan so suitable to his own Ideas which are generally equally wise and public spirited.

Believe me to be with the greatest respect

My Lord
Your Lordships most
Obliged and most obedient
Humble Servant,
Adam Smith

[8] Sir William Petty (1623–87), political economist and founder of 'political arithmetic' (statistics); friend of Hobbes; Professor of Anatomy, Oxford, 1651; carried out for the Commonwealth the 'Down Survey,' the first systematic survey of Ireland; superintended redistribution of lands in Ireland; knighted and made F.R.S., 1662; his economic treatises, published 1662–90, rejected the mercantilist identification of wealth and money, holding that wealth resided in labour and land. While he refers here to Petty in a respectful way, Smith was sceptical about 'political arithmetic' and wrote in WN he had 'no great faith in [it]' (IV.v.6.30); see, also, Letter 249 addressed to George Chalmers, dated 10 Nov. 1785.

31. *From* DAVID HUME

MS., NLS Acc. 776 (Robertson Papers); NHL 51–5.

Lisle Street, Leicester Fields, 12 Apr. 1759

Dear Smith

I give you thanks for the agreeable Present of your Theory[1] Wedderburn[2] and I made Presents of our Copies to such of our Acquaintance as we thought good Judges, and proper to spread the Reputation of the Book. I sent one to the Duke of Argyle,[3] to Lord Lyttleton,[4] Horace Walpole,[5] Soames Jennyns,[6] and Burke,[7] an Irish Gentleman, who wrote lately a very pretty Treatise on the Sublime. Millar desird my Permission to send one in your Name to Dr Warburton.[8] I have delayd writing to you till I cou'd tell you something of the Success of the Book, and coud prognosticate with some Probability whether it shoud be finally damnd to Oblivion, or shoud be registerd in the Temple of Immortality. Tho' it has been publishd only a few Weeks, I think there appear already such strong Symptoms, that I can almost venture to fortell its Fate. It is in short this— — But I have been interrupted in my Letter by a foolish impertinent Visit of one who has lately come from Scotland. He tells me, that the University of Glasgow intend to declare Rouets Office Vacant upon his going abroad with Lord Hope.[9] I question not but you will have our Friend, Ferguson,

---

[1] TMS which Millar had just brought out; see Letter 33 from Andrew Millar, dated 26 Apr. 1759.

[2] Alexander Wedderburn.

[3] Archibald Campbell, 3rd Duke of Argyll.

[4] Sir George, afterwards Lord, Lyttleton (1709–73); politician, patron, and man of letters; Lord of Treasury 1744–54; Chancellor of Exchequer 1756; author of *Dialogues of the Dead* (1760), and *History of the Life of Henry the Second* (1767–71).

[5] Horace Walpole (1717–97) of Strawberry Hill, Mdx., 3rd s. of Sir Robert Walpole; 4th Earl of Orford, 1791; dilettante memorialist and famous letter writer, also remembered for his 'Gothic' novel, *The Castle of Otranto* (1764); educ. Eton and Cambridge; on the Grand Tour with Thomas Gray, 1739–41; M.P. 1741–68; played a conspicuous part in the Hume–Rousseau quarrel of 1766.

[6] Soame Jenyns (1704–87), M.P. 1742–60; author of *Free Enquiry into the Nature and Origin of Evil* (1757) and *View of the Internal Evidence of the Christian Religion* (1777).

[7] Edmund Burke (1729–97), author and statesman, by this time had written a *Vindication of Natural Society* (1756) and *A Philosophical Enquiry into the Origin of Our Ideas of the Sublime and Beautiful* (1757). See Letter 38 from Edmund Burke dated 10 Sept. 1759.

[8] William Warburton (1698–1779), churchman (Dean of Bristol 1757; Bp. of Gloucester 1759–79) and controversialist; castigated by Hume in *My Own Life*; 'I found by Dr Warburton's Railing that [my] Books were beginning to be esteemed in good Company', and again, '. . . the illiberal Petulance, Arrogance, and Scurrility which distinguishes the Warburtonian School'. See E. C. Mossner, 'Hume's *Four Dissertations*', *Modern Philogy* xlviii (1950) 37–57, and A. W. Evans, *Warburton and the Warburtonians* (London, 1932).

[9] William Rouet (Rouat, Ruet), Professor of Oriental Languages, Glasgow, 1751; Professor of Church History 1752; travelling tutor to Lord Hope (d. 1765) 1759; resigned from Glasgow University, 1762, amid controversy; see Letter 59 from Lord Erroll, dated 27 Oct. 1761, and Scott 190–5.

in your Eye, in case another Project for procuring him a Place in the
University of Edinburgh shou'd fail. Ferguson has very much polishd
and improved his Treatise on Refinement,[10] and with some Amendments
it will make an admirable Book, and discovers an elegant and a singular
Genius. The Epigoniad, I hope, will do; but it is somewhat up-hill Work.
As I doubt not but you consult the Reviews sometimes at present, you will
see in the critical Review a Letter upon that Poem; and I desire you to
employ your Conjectures in finding out the Author. Let me see a Sample
of your Skill in knowing hands by your guessing at the Person.[11] I am
afraid of Lord Kaims's Law Tracts.[12] A man might as well think of making
a fine Sauce by a Mixture of Wormwood and Aloes as an agreeable Composition by joining Metaphysics and Scotch Law. However, the Book, I
believe, has Merit; tho' few People will take the Pains of diving into it.
But to return to your Book, and its Success in this Town, I must tell you
— — A Plague of Interruptions! I orderd myself to be deny'd; and yet
here is one that has broke in upon me again. He is a man of Letters, and we
have had a good deal of literary Conversation. You told me, that you was
curious of literary Anecdotes, and therefore I shall inform you of a few,
that have come to my Knowledge. I believe I have mentiond to you already
Helvetius's Book de l'Esprit.[13] It is worth your Reading, not for its
Philosophy, which I do not highly value, but for its agreeable Composition.
I had a Letter from him a few days ago, wherein he tells me that my Name
was much oftener in the Manuscript, but that the Censor of Books at Paris
oblig'd him to strike it out.[14] Voltaire[15] has lately publishd a small Work
calld *Candide, ou L'optimisme*. It is full of Sprightliness and Impiety, and
is indeed a Satyre upon Providence, under Pretext of criticizing the
Leibnitian System. I shall give you a Detail of it— —But what is all this
to my Book? say you.——My Dear Mr Smith, have Patience: Compose
yourself to Tranquillity: Show yourself a Philosopher in Practice as well
as Profession: Think on the Emptiness, and Rashness, and Futility of the
common Judgements of Men: How little they are regulatd by Reason in
any Subject, much more in philosophical Subjects, which so far exceed

[10] No work of Ferguson's by this title was published, but the reference may be to an
early draft or part of *An Essay on the History of Civil Society*.

[11] Hume wrote this letter, see *Critical Review*, Apr. 1759, reprinted. Hume, *Phil. Wks.*
iv. 425–37.

[12] *Historical Law-Tracts*, 2 vols. (Edinburgh, 1758).

[13] Claude-Adrien Helvétius (1715–71), philosopher, author of *De l'esprit* (1758), which
was condemned by the Parlement of Paris and burnt, 10 Feb. 1762.

[14] Dated 1 Apr. 1759; MS., RSE v. 50: 'Votre nom honore mon livre, et je l'aurois cité
plus souvent, si la sévérité du censeur me l'eût permis.' The censor was Chrétien-Guillaume
de Lamoignon de Malesherbes (1721–94), who carried out his duties with restraint, seeing
to it, for example, that the *Encyclopédie* was published despite its subversive tendencies.

[15] François-Marie Arouet (1694–1778), under the pen name of Voltaire, the great
French man of letters whose *Candide* had just appeared. Smith met him at Ferney and
was his lifelong admirer.

the Comprehension of the Vulgar. *Non si quid improba Roma, Elevet, accedas examenque improbum in illa, Perpendas trutina, nec te quaesiveris extra.*[16] A wise man's Kingdom is his own Breast: Or, if he ever looks farther, it will only be to the Judgement of a select few, who are free from Prejudices, and capable of examining his Work. Nothing indeed can be a stronger Presumption of Falshood than the Approbation of the Multitude; and Phocion, you know, always suspected himself of some Blunder, when he was attended with the Applauses of the Populace.

Supposing, therefore, that you have duely prepard yourself for the worst by all these Reflections; I proceed to tell you the melancholy News, that your Book has been very unfortunate: For the Public seem disposd to applaud it extremely. It was lookd for by the foolish People with some Impatience; and the Mob of Literati are beginning already to be very loud in its Praises. Three Bishops calld yesterday at Millar's Shop in order to buy Copies, and to ask Questions about the Author: The Bishop of Peterborough[17] said he had passd the Evening in a Company, where he heard it extolld above all Books in the World. You may conclude what Opinion true Philosophers will entertain of it, when these Retainers to Superstition praise it so highly. The Duke of Argyle is more decisive than he uses to be in its Favour: I suppose he either considers it as an Exotic, or thinks the Author will be serviceable to him in the Glasgow Elections. Lord Lyttleton says, that Robertson[18] and Smith and Bower[19] are the Glories of English Literature. Oswald[20] protests he does not know whether he has reap'd more Instruction or Entertainment from it: But you may easily judge what Reliance can be put on his Judgement, who has been engagd all his Life in public Business and who never sees any Faults in his Friends. Millar exults and brags that two thirds of the Edition are already sold, and that he is now sure of Success. You see what a Son of the Earth that is, to value Books only by the Profit they bring him. In that View, I believe it may prove a very good Book.

[16] Persius, *Sat.* I, 5–7;

> . . . non, si quid turbida Roma
> elevet, accedas examenque improbum in illa
> castiges trutina, nec te quaesiveris extra.

[If confused Rome makes light of anything, do not go up and correct the deceitful tongue in that balance of theirs, or look to anyone beside yourself.]

[17] Richard Terrick (1710–77), Bishop of Peterborough 1757–64, and of London 1764–77.

[18] William Robertson (1721–93), historian, Church statesman, and university administrator; had just published his *History of Scotland* (1759); to come were his *History of Charles V* (1769) and *History of America* (1771), also an unfinished *History of India* (1791). He was principal of Edinburgh University, from 1762, and Moderator of the General Assembly of the Church of Scotland, from 1763, for most of the remainder of his life.

[19] Archibald Bower (1686–1766) pamphleteer and author of a *History of the Popes* (1748–66); a protégé of Lyttleton's.

[20] James Oswald of Dunnikier.

Charles Townshend,[21] who passes for the cleverest Fellow in England, is so taken with the Performance, that he said to Oswald he wou'd put the Duke of Buccleugh under the Authors Care, and woud endeavour to make it worth his while to accept of that Charge.[22] As soon as I heard this, I calld on him twice with a View of talking with him about the Matter, and of convincing him of the Propriety of sending that young Nobleman to Glasgow: For I coud not hope, that he coud offer you any Terms, which woud tempt you to renounce your Professorship: But I missd him. Mr Townsend passes for being a little uncertain in his Resolutions; so perhaps you need not build much on this Sally.

In recompense for so many mortifying things, which nothing but Truth coud have extorted from me, and which I coud easily have multiply'd to a greater Number; I doubt not but you are so good a Christian as to return good for evil and to flatter my Vanity, by telling me, that all the Godly in Scotland abuse me for my Account of John Knox and the Reformation etc. I suppose you are glad to see my Paper end, and that I am obligd to conclude with

Your humble Servant
David Hume

32. *From* LORD SHELBURNE

MS., GUL Gen. 1035/138; Scott 245–8.

Dublin, 26 Apr. 1759

Sir

I have lately received your letter of the 4th inst; your former of the 10th of March, came also to my hands in due time. I can not sufficiently express my Satisfaction at the account you give me of my Son, now under your care; the description you make of him, convinces me of your power of looking into him, so does the Scheme you chalk out for the prosecution of his Studies, convince me of your judgment; Every thing confirms that you merit that Character which made me wish so much that you should take the Charge of him upon you, and, if I mistake you not, I shall make you much amends by assuring you, that the more I reflect on the Situation

---

[21] The Hon. Charles Townshend (1725–67) of Adderbury, Oxon.; statesman; his troubled personality is now believed to have been affected by an epileptic tendency; M.P. 1747–d.; Lord of Admiralty 1754; Treasurer of the Chamber 1756; Secretary-at-War 1761–2; President of the Board of Trade 1763; Paymaster-General 1765; Chancellor of the Exchequer 1766–d.; md. Lady Dalkeith, 1755, and became stepfather of her children: the later 3rd Duke of Buccleuch, the Hon. Hew Campbell Scott, and Lady Frances Scott.

[22] This came about in 1764–6, when Smith was made tutor of Henry Scott (1746–1812), 3rd Duke of Buccleuch, and, from 1810, 5th Duke of Queensbury. The Duke took no direct part in public life other than becoming the first President, 1783, of the Royal Society of Edinburgh. His extensive estates, however, gave him a considerable electoral interest.

he is in, the more I am happy; so much so, and so satisfied both of your Ability and Inclination to do him Service, that I must refuse the request you make, that I shou'd point out what I wish to have done, I can point out nothing, I can only approve of what you mean to do. The great fault I find with Oxford and Cambridge, is that Boys sent thither instead of being the Governed, become the Governors of the Colleges, and that Birth and Fortune there are more respected than Literary Merit; I flatter'd myself that it was not so at Glasgow, and your commendation of my Son's conformity to the Discipline of the place he is in, persuades me that you think as I do, that no greater Service can be done in leading to Manhood, than to confirm Youth, by long practice, in the habit of Obedience; a power of adopting the Will of another, will make one Master of one's own. Oeconomy seems likewise to have a just place in your attention; No fortune is able to do without it, nor can any man be Charitable, Generous or Just who neglects it, it will make a man happy under Slender Circumstances, and make him Shine if his Income be Affluent. Your Pupil comes into the World a sort of an Adventurer, intitl'd to nothing, and will, if I may venture to prophesy concerning him, have more in proportion as his own wants are few. I wish him train'd to Need little, not for the purpose of Accumulating, but in order to enable him to Give more. The Building which is to be rais'd by Him, on the foundation that I am laying, is what I can not hope to see, and what I trust, and do believe, I shall not be troubled about, when my power to interpose shall cease; I wish him therefore to be convinc'd, that it is His happiness and not my own, that I have in view. I wish him to become an honest and a Benevolent man; I wish him Punctual and Sober; a lover of Method, and so skill'd in Figures and the businesses of Life, as by Assisting me in my latter days, he may make me rejoice at my Labours in his early ones.

Perhaps it is not yet the Season of procuring for him some Instruction to mend his hand-writing, but it is what he will want, and what he is capable of receiving, for when he writes with care, he does it in a manner that makes me think him capable of writing well. His Genius I *have* thought, Open to everything, his perception of Images and of Lines express'd on paper, was in the earliest part of his life, quick and clear; this makes me hope that the Study of Euclid, which you intend for him, will be of profit and not above his reach, it is, in my mind, a far better teacher of Reasoning than Logic is. If his Idleness and Volatility can be overcome, Mathematicks in general I fancy will be agreeable to him, and from a turn that he has to Mechanicks, the Experimental parts of Natural Philosophy will I am sure be a great delight to him. I mention these things, only to convince you that I have him and his future happiness at heart, and if he shall not turn out such as his Talents are equal to, be assur'd that I shall not be the more doubtful of, or the less thankful for your Endeavours.

The time of my Son's stay at Glasgow, is by no means limited as you seem to think from what his Elder brother told you; I wish him to stay so long as You, Sir, can endure him under your Eye, and so long as he shall continue worthy of your Attention; for my part, having no view to anything but his Improvement, nor any use to make of him until he shall be perfect in those things which I only know how to Admire, but not how to Teach, I shall rejoice at the length of his Absence from me, being much of opinion that great Evils arise by suffering Boys to become Men too soon. A knowledge in the Civil Law, is the best foundation he can have to introduce him to that of his own Country, the Study of it may make him Wise, but it is upon Your Precepts and Example in Morality, that I depend for making him Happy.

I can hardly flatter myself with the hope of seeing Scotland this Summer, but I think of a jaunt thither with much pleasure.

You make me very vain by approving so much my endeavours to make a part of this Country happier than I found it, if I succeed I shall make myself so; I shall be glad that Good is done how little hand soever I may have in doing it, in the present case a very Slender share of praise is to fall to my Lot, the truth is, that my Property is so scatter'd, and my Avocations from Every place so frequent, that I cou'd only have Imagin'd the Work you have heard of, but cou'd not possibly have brought it to a likelyhood of perfection, were it not for the great and able aid I received from my friend Dr. Henry.[1] This Gentleman has had his Education in your University, tho' a Native of this Country; it is an honour to Glasgow to have train'd up one of a Spirit so Great and so Disinterested as his in doing good to Mankind; the burthen of my late work has been borne by him, and so ought the praise, if any it shall deserve; it is a pleasure to me to give this just Character of him, to one of your merit; your pupil will be glad, I hope, to hear that his friend Dr. Henry continues both to deserve and acquire the Esteem of Everybody; I pray you to assure him of my Love, and to believe me to be with much Esteem, Sir

Your Much Oblig'd
and Very humble Servant
Shelburne

[1] ? William Henry (d. 1768), Dean of Killaloe 1761–8; chaplain to Archbishop Josiah Hort; D.D. Dublin 1750; F.R.S. 1755.

33. *From* ANDREW MILLAR

MS., GUL Gen. 1035/137; Scott 238.

London, 26 Apr. 1759

Presented of Mr Smiths Theory of Moral Sentiments in half binding.

Earl of Bute[1]—Earl of Hardwicke[2]—Dr Markham[3]—Mr Selwyn[4]—Earl of Shelburne—Lord Mansfield[5]—Mr Hume—Lord Lyttelton—Dr Warburton—Mr Elliot—Mr Wedderburn—Mr Jennings[6]—Duke of Argyle—Mr Walpole—Mr Burke—Dr Birch[7]—Charles Townshend Esq.—Mr Solicitor General[8]—

Dear Sir

I received the errata which are printed, and I made 1/2 Sheet of Contents, which makes the whole book 34 Sheets a Cheap 6s: volume bound especially considering the Matter which I am sure is excellent.

The above 18 copys have been delivered by the order of Messrs Hume, Wedderburn and John Dalrymple.[9] I think of 2 more to the Authors of the Reviews,[10] which will make £20. I Propose 10 of them in a Present to you, and the other is to be charged 2, the price to Booksellers taking a number, as they were only delivered to the Persons in blue Papers and

[1] John Stuart (1713–92), 3rd Earl of Bute, politician; given charge of education of Prince George, later George III; Secretary of State 1761; First Lord of Treasury 1762; head of Administration during signing of Treaty of Paris, 1763, but lost his popularity; resigned 1765; procured pensions or places for Johnson, John Home, and William Robertson.

[2] Philip Yorke (1690–1764), 1st Earl of Hardwicke, Lord Chancellor 1737–56, distinguished for his equity decisions; responsible for legislation directed at 'pacifying' the Highlands after the 1745 Rising.

[3] William Markham (1719–1807), clergyman and scholar; Headmaster of Westminster School 1753–65, rose to be Archbishop of York 1777; intimate friend of Burke.

[4] George Augustus Selwyn (1719–91), wit and politician; M.P. 1747–80.

[5] Hon. William Murray (1705–94) of Ken Wood, Middlesex; 4th son of 5th Viscount Stormont; educ. Perth, Westminster, Christ Church, Oxford; called to the English Bar 1730; M.P. 1742–56; Solicitor-General 1742–5; Attorney-Gen. 1754–6; Privy Councillor 1756; Lord Chief Justice, King's Bench 1756–88; Lord Mansfield 1756; Earl of Mansfield, Notts., 1792; Lord Mansfield's decisions are celebrated for their eloquence and legal insight, particularly as related to the law merchant. He was the friend of Alexander Pope.

[6] Soame Jenyns.

[7] Thomas Birch (1705–66), historical scholar and divine; Secretary of the Royal Society 1752–65.

[8] The Hon. Charles Yorke (1722–70) of Tittenhanger, Herts.; 2nd son of 1st Earl of Hardwicke; educ. Cambridge; called to the English Bar 1746; M.P. 1747–70; Solicitor-General 1756–61; Attorney-Gen. 1762–3, 1765–6; Lord Chancellor (for 3 days, before committing suicide) 1770. He was the friend of Montesquieu.

[9] Sir John Dalrymple (1726–1810) of Cranstoun, 4th Bt.; historian and Exchequer judge; educ. Edinburgh and Cambridge; advocate 1748; Baron of Scottish Exchequer Court 1776–1807; discovered the art of making soap from herrings; *Essay Towards a General History of Feudal Property in Great Britain* (1757); *Memoirs of Great Britain and Ireland, 1683–92* (1771). [10] *Monthly Review* and *Critical Review*.

boards. So the 3d of the differences is to be by Kincaid and Bell[11] paid you and the other 2.3ds of the copy right by me.

Mr Rose at Kew[12] whom Rouet knows well took 25 copys to dispose amongst his friends, that I have no Sort of doubt of this Impression being Soon gone tho' it will not be published till next Week, before which I shall Ship Mr Kincaid which I hope will Sail next week with convoy.[13] Mrs Millar[14] desired to Join with me in our kind remembrance of your Mother, yourself and all friends and I am

Dear Sir
Yours most sincerely
And. Millar

34. *From* WILLIAM ROBERTSON

Address: To Mr Adam Smith, Professor of Moral Philosophy, Glasgow
MS., GUL Gen. 1035/139; Scott 238–9.

Edinburgh, 14 June [1759]

My Dear Sir

Our friend John Home arrived here from London two days ago. Tho' I dare say you have heard of the good reception of the *Theory* from [m]any different people, I must acquaint you with the intelligence Home brings. He assures me that it is in the hands of all persons of the best fashion; that it meets with great approbation both on account of the matter and stile; and that it is impossible for any book on so serious a subject to be received in a more gracious manner. It comforts the English a good deal to hear that you were bred at Oxford, they claim some part of you on that account. Home joins with me in insisting that your next work shall be on some subject less abstruse. I still wish you would think on the History of Philosophy.[1] I write this in great haste, as Johnstone[2] is waiting me that we may go to walk. When shall we see you in town. I ever am

Yours most faithfully
William Robertson

[11] Alexander Kincaid (1734–77) and John Bell (?1736–1806), Edinburgh booksellers; cited along with Millar as publishers on title-page of TMS ed. 1.

[12] William Rose (1719–86), educator and translator of Sallust; educ. Marischal Coll., Aberdeen; conducted a school at Kew and, from 1758, at Chiswick; co-founder, with Ralph Griffiths, of the *Monthly Review*.

[13] The syntax is obscure; Smith means that he will ship copies of the TMS to Kincaid, and that he hopes the ship will sail next week in a convoy.

[14] Mrs. Jane Millar (d. 1788), after Millar's death she remarried Sir Archibald Grant of Monymusk.

[1] In the 1750s, Smith read to the Literary Club of Glasgow papers on 'Taste, Composition and the History of Philosophy' which he had previously delivered while a lecturer on rhetoric in Edinburgh (R. Duncan, *Notes and Documents Illustrative of the Literary History of Glasgow* (Maitland Club, Glasgow, 1831, 16). See EPS for 'The History of Ancient Logics and Metaphysics', 'The History of Astronomy', and 'The History of the Ancient Physics', the extant parts of the work Robertson desired.   [2] William Johnstone.

35. *To* LORD SHELBURNE

MS., Bowood Libr., Marquess of Lansdowne; Scott 248–9.

Glasgow College, 23 July 1759

My Lord

It must give everybody the greatest pleasure to serve your Lordship, when you express so agreeably your satisfaction with every attempt of this kind, and I must return your Lordship the thanks of the University for your goodness in recommending it as a proper place of Education for the Children of your friend Sir John Colthurst.[1]

The expense of board in the common boarding houses is from five to eight Pounds per quarter for each person. The expense of washing is not included in this; the ordinary rate of which is at 1 sh. 10D per Dozen. The expence of Masters fees will probably amount to eight or ten Guineas for each Person. There are, besides, some other College dues which, however, will not upon the whole amount to twenty shillings per annum for each Person. Their linnen ought to be sent from Ireland where it is both cheaper and better than here. A suit of plain Cloaths of the finest cloth may be had for about five Pounds. These are all the necessary expenses which any Gentlemans son has occasion to be at while he attends upon this University. What the unnecessary expenses may be, it is impossible for me to determine. These will depend upon the young gentlemen themselves, upon the habits they have been bred up in and the injunctions that are laid upon them. Your Lordship may depend upon every attention which it can be in my power to give to whoever has the honour of being so nearly connected with your Lordships family: and I shall endeavour to settle them in such a manner that I can have as exact an account of their conduct as if they were in my own house. If I am not mistaken Mr Fitzmaurice shewed me some time last winter two letters that had been written by these two young gentlemen to your Lordship. I was greatly pleased with them as marking the sobriety, modesty and innocence of their manners; so that I have no fear of the behaviour of those who appear to have been so properly educated.

With regard to Mr Fitzmaurice his conduct is in every respect as regular as ever. I was obliged to go into Edinburgh about a month ago, when I carried him along with me. This relaxation, which lasted about a fortnight, had no other effect than to serve as a short vacation to him. The day after he returned he began the same course of life which he had practised before without being at all dissipated by the amusements of Edinburgh. While he

[1] Sir John Conway Colthurst (d. 1775), 1st Bt.; Irish M.P. 1751–75; md. Lady Charlotte Fitzmaurice, 3rd dau. of 1st Earl of Kerry, cousin of 1st Earl of Shelburne. His two eldest sons were John, 2nd Bt. (d. 1787, as the result of a duel), and Nicholas, 3rd Bt. (d. 1795), who became an M.P.

was there, indeed, he entered fully into them and I think did not miss any one public diversion, which led him into a little more expence than I expected. As this, however, is all the vacation which he will have, I did not grudge it him nor think it necessary to check him.

I will begg your Lordship to offer my complements, tho' unknown to Dr Henry. I was no stranger to his character before the very honourable and generous mention which your Lordship was pleased to make of him in your letter to me. Mr Fitzmaurice shewed me last winter a letter from him which gave me an impression of his character which exactly corresponded with what your Lordship was pleased to say of him. I am with the greatest respect My Lord,

> Your Lordships
> Most Obedient and
> Most humble Servant
> Adam Smith

36. *From* DAVID HUME

MS., RSE ii. 30; HL i. 311–14.

London, 28 July 1759

Dear Sir

Your Friend, Mr Wilson,[1] calld on me two or three days ago when I was abroad, and he left your Letter: I did not see him till to day. He seems a very modest, sensible, ingenious Man. Before I saw him, I spoke to A. Millar about him, and found him very much dispos'd to serve him. I proposd particularly to Mr Millar, that it was worthy of so eminent a Bookseller as he to make a compleat elegant Set of the Classics, which might set up his Name equal to the Alduses, Stevens, or Elzivirs; and that Mr Wilson was the properest Person in the World to assist him in such a Project. He confest to me, that he had sometimes thought of it; but that his great Difficulty was to find a Man of Letters, who cou'd correct the Press. I mentioned the Matter to Wilson, who said he had a Man of Letters in his Eye; one Lyon,[2] a nonjuring Clergyman at Glasgow. He is probably known to you, or at least may be so: I wou'd desire your Opinion of him.

Mr Wilson told me of his Machines, which seem very ingenious, and deserve much Encouragement. I shall soon see them.

I am very well acquainted with Bourke,[3] who was much taken with your Book. He got your Direction from me with a View of writing to you, and

---

[1] Alexander Wilson, M.D. (1733–86), educ. at St Andrews, practiced medicine in London, then became a type-founder; appointed in that capacity to Glasgow University, 1748; Professor of Practical Astronomy, and Observer, Glasgow, 1760; awarded the gold medal of the Royal Society of Sciences, Copenhagen, 1772, for a dissertation on sun-spots. He founded the types for the Foulis Press, Glasgow, his Greek founts being unsurpassed.

[2] ? Revd. James Lyon.   [3] Edmund Burke: see his Letter 38, dated 10 Sept. 1759.

thanking you for your Present: For I made it pass in your Name. I wonder he has not done it: He is now in Ireland. I am not acquainted with Jennyns;[4] but he spoke very highly of the Book to Oswald, who is his Brother in the Board of Trade. Millar show'd me a few days ago a Letter from Lord Fitzmaurice;[5] where he tells him, that he had carryd over a few Copies to the Hague for Presents. Mr Yorke[6] was much taken with it as well as several others who had read it.

I am told that you are preparing a new Edition,[7] and propose to make some Additions and Alterations, in order to obviate Objections. I shall use the Freedom to propose one, which, if it appears to be of any Weight, you may have in your Eye. I wish you had more particularly and fully prov'd, that all kinds of Sympathy are necessarily Agreeable. This is the Hinge of your System, and yet you only mention the Matter cursorily in p. 20. Now it woud appear that there is a disagreeable Sympathy, as well as an agreeable: And indeed, as the Sympathetic Passion is a reflex Image of the principal, it must partake of its Qualities, and be painful where that is so. Indeed, *when we converse with a man with whom we can entirely sympathize*, that is, where there is a warm and intimate Friendship, the cordial openness of such a Commerce overpowers the Pain of a disagreeable Sympathy, and renders the whole Movement agreeable. But in ordinary Cases, this cannot have place. An ill-humord Fellow; a man tir'd and disgusted with every thing, always *ennuié*; sickly, complaining, embarass'd; such a one throws an evident Damp on Company, which I suppose wou'd be accounted for by Sympathy; and yet is disagreeable.

It is always thought a difficult Problem to account for the Pleasure, receivd from the Tears and Grief and Sympathy of Tragedy; which woud not be the Case, if all Sympathy was agreeable. An Hospital woud be a more entertaining Place than a Ball. I am afraid that in p. 99 and 111 this Proposition has escapd you, or rather is interwove with your Reasonings in that place. You say expressly, *it is painful to go along with Grief and we always enter into it with Reluctance*. It will probably be requisite for you to modify or explain this Sentiment, and reconcile it to your System.

My Dear Mr Smith; You must not be so much engross'd with your own Book, as never to mention mine.[8] The Whigs, I am told, are anew in a Rage against me; tho' they know not how to vent themselves: For they are constrain'd to allow all my Facts. You have probably seen Hurd's Abuse of me.[9] He is of the Warburtonian School; and consequently very insolent

---

[4] Soame Jenyns.   [5] See Letter 27, n. 1.   [6] ? Hon. Charles Yorke.
[7] TMS ed. 2, 1761: for Smith's revisions, see Letter 40 addressed to Gilbert Elliot, dated 10 Oct. 1759.   [8] *History of England: The Tudors*, 2 vols. 1759.
[9] See the postscript to Richard Hurd's *Moral and Political Dialogues*, ed. 1, 1759: 'For having undertaken to conjure up the spirit of absolute power, he [Hume] judged it necessary to the charm, to reverse the order of things, and to evoke this frightful spectre by writing (as witches use to say their prayers) *backwards*. . . . Accordingly, while one half

and very scurrilous; but I shall never reply a word to him. If my past Writings do not sufficiently prove me to be no Jacobite, ten Volumes in folio never would.

I signd yesterday an Agreement with Mr Millar; where I mention that I proposed to write the History of England from the Beginning till the Accession of Henry the VII; and he engages to give me 1400 Pounds for the Copy. This is the first previous Agreement ever I made with a Bookseller. I shall execute this Work at Leizure, without fatiguing myself by such ardent Application as I have hitherto employd. It is chiefly as a Ressource against Idleness, that I shall undertake this Work: For as to Money, I have enough: And as to Reputation, what I have wrote already will be sufficient, if it be good: If not, it is not likely I shall now write better. I found it impracticable (at least fancy'd so) to write the History since the Revolution. I am in doubt whether I shall stay here and execute the Work; or return to Scotland, and only come up here to consult the Manuscripts. I have several Inducements on both Sides. Scotland suits my Fortune best, and is the Seat of my principal Friendships; but it is too narrow a Place for me, and it mortifies me that I sometimes hurt my Friends. Pray write me your Judgement soon. Are the Bigots much in Arms on account of this last Volume? Robertson's Book[10] has great Merit; but it was visible that he profited here by the Animosity against me. I suppose the Case was the same with you. I am

Dear Smith
Yours sincerely
David Hume.

37. *To* LORD SHELBURNE

MS., Bowood Libr., Marquess of Lansdowne; Scott 249–50.

Glasgow College, 31 Aug. 1759

My Lord

I wrote to your Lordship about a month ago and directed my Letter to Hanover Square that My Lady Shelburne might see it as it passed to Ireland. In that Letter I gave your Lordship a full detail of the different Articles of expence incurred at Glasgow. I shall not at present repeat them; as your Lordship must undoubtedly by this time have received it. What you Lordship seems chiefly anxious about, the care that is to be taken of the Morals of the two young people you are so good as to recommend to our

---

of his pains is laid out in exposing the absurdities of *reformed religion*, the other half is suitably employed in discrediting the cause of *civil liberty*.' Later eds. omitted the postscript and presented a footnote in which Hurd gave some qualified praise to the first part of Hume's *History* (*Julius Caesar to Henry VII*) as distinguished from the other parts.

[10] William Robertson's *History of Scotland* (1759).

care, is undoubtedly of far the greatest importance.[1] What I would advise for this purpose is either first, that the Tutor, of whom your Lordship gives so advantageous a character, should, if at all convenient, come along with them: or, secondly, that a Tutor should be appointed them here; or, last of all, they that should be boarded in some of the Proffessors houses who are in the Practise of taking Boarders. The first expedient I look upon as incomparably the Best, nothing being equal to established Authority for the government of young people. The objection against the second, is not only the expence that would attend it which would probably be considerable (as not only a fee of at least twenty or thirty Pounds a year must probably be paid to such a tutor, but to have the proper use of him, he must be boarded along with them) but likewise the extreme difficulty of finding a good one: I think, however, this might be taken care of. The objection against the third expedient is likewise its expensiveness, the board taken by the Proffessors being ten pounds per quarter for each Person. Your Lordship will judge which of these is the most proper expedient.

Your Lordship makes me very vain when you mention the satisfaction you have had in reading the book I lately published, and the engagements you think I have come under to the Public. I can, however, assure your Lordship that I have come under no engagements which I look upon as so sacred as those by which I am bound as a member of this University to do every[thing] in my Power to serve the young people who are sent here to study, such especially as are particularly recommended to my care. I shall expect, whenever they are settled, that your Lordships friends will look upon my house as their home, and that they will have recourse to me in every Difficulty that they meet with in the Prosecution of their studies, and that I shall never regard any application of this kind as an interruption of business, but as the most agreeable and useful business in which I can be engaged.

I shall soon have occasion for a remittance from your Lordship. The fifty Pounds left here by Lord Fitzmaurice are now spent, and I am now about thirty Pounds in advance. I shall send your Lordship upon the sitting down of the College a full account of every article of the former years expence. The chief articles have been fees to different Masters, two suits of Cloaths, a suit of mourning and a summer suit of fustian, Books and some other necessaries. His allowance for Pocket is a guinea per month. I am with the greatest respect

My Lord

Your Lordships most Obliged, most Obedient and

most humble Servant

Adam Smith

[1] Sons of Sir John Colthurst; see Letter 35.

38. *From* EDMUND BURKE

MS., James M. and Marie-Louise Osborn Collection, Yale University Libr.;
Burke Corr. i. 129–30.

Wimple Street, Cavendish Square,
Westminster, 10 Sept. 1759

Sir

I am quite ashamed that the first Letter I have the honour of writing to you should be an apology for my conduct. It ought to be entirely taken up with my thanks to you for the satisfaction I received from your very agreeable and instructive work, but I cannot do that pleasing act of Justice without apologising at the same time for not having done it much earlier. When I received the Theory of Moral Sentiments from Mr Hume, I ran through it with great eagerness; I was immediately after hurried out of Town, and involved ever since in a Variety of troublesome affairs.[1] My resolution was to defer my acknowledgements until I had read your book with proper care and attention; to do otherwise with so well studied a piece would be to treat it with great injustice. It was indeed an attention extremely well bestowed and abundantly repaid. I am not only pleased with the ingenuity of your Theory; I am convinced of its solidity and Truth; and I do not know that it ever cost me less trouble to admit so many things to which I had been a stranger before.[2] I have ever thought that the old Systems of morality were too contracted and that this Science could never stand well upon any narrower Basis than the whole of Human Nature. All the writers who have treated this Subject before you were like those Gothic Architects who were fond of turning great Vaults upon a single slender Pillar; There is art in this, and there is a degree of ingenuity without doubt; but it is not sensible, and it cannot long be pleasing. A theory like yours founded on the Nature of man, which is always the same, will last, when those that are founded on his opinions, which are always changing, will and must be forgotten. I own I am particularly pleased with those easy and happy illustrations from common Life and manners in which your work abounds more than any other that I know by far. They are indeed the fittest to explain those natural movements of the mind with which every Science relating to our Nature ought to begin. But one sees, that nothing

[1] See Letter 36 from Hume, dated 28 July 1759; Hume thought Burke was in Ireland at this time but there is no other evidence of this.

[2] Burke's review of the book in the *Annual Register* for 1759 praises particularly Smith's originality: 'this author has struck out a new, and at the same time a perfectly natural road of speculation on this subject . . . We conceive, that here the theory is in all its essential parts just, and founded on truth and nature. The author seeks for the foundation of the just, the fit, the proper, the decent, in our most common and most allowed passions; and making approbation and disapprobation the tests of virtue and vice, and shewing that those are founded on sympathy, he raises from this simple truth, one of the most beautiful fabrics of moral theory, that has perhaps ever appeared.'

is less used, than what lies directly in our way. Philosophers therefore very frequently miss a thousand things that might be of infinite advantage, though the rude Swain treads daily on them with his clouted Shoon.[3] It seems to require that infantine simplicity which despises nothing, to make a good Philosopher, as well as to make a good Christian. Besides so much powerful reasoning as your Book contains, there is so much elegant Painting of the manners and passions, that it is highly valuable even on that account. The stile is every where lively and elegant, and what is, I think equally important in a work of that kind, it is well varied; it is often sublime too, particularly in that fine Picture of the Stoic Philosophy towards the end of your first part which is dressed out in all the grandeur and Pomp that becomes that magnificent delusion. I have mentioned something of what affected me as Beauties in your work. I will take the Liberty to mention too what appeared to me as a sort of Fault. You are in some few Places, what Mr Locke is in most of his writings, rather a little too diffuse. This is however a fault of the generous kind, and infinitely preferable to the dry sterile manner, which those of dull imaginations are apt to fall into. To another I should apologise for a freedom of this Nature.

My delay on this occasion may I am afraid make it improper for me to ask any favour from you. But there is one, I have too much at heart not to sacrifice any propriety to attain it. It is, that whenever you come to Town, I may have the honour of being made personally known to you.[4] I shall take the Liberty of putting this office on our friend Mr. Hume who has already so much obliged me by giving me your Book. I am Sir with the truest esteem for your Work and your Character

your most obliged and
obedient Servant
Edm. Burke.

39. *To* CHARLES TOWNSHEND

Rae 148.

College of Glasgow, 17 Sept. 1759

Sir,

It gives me great concern that the first letter I ever have done myself the honour to write to you should be upon so melancholy an occasion. As your Brother[1] was generally known here, he is universally regretted, and your

---

[3] *Comus*, ll. 634–5. Burke uses the quotation in a similar way in his *Speech on Conciliation with the Colonies* (*Works*, Bohn edn. i. 489).

[4] Smith and Burke do not appear to have met until 1777.

[1] Col. Roger Townshend, youngest brother of George and Charles, killed in July 1759 by a cannon-shot from Fort Ticonderoga (*Scots Mag.*, xxi. Sept. 1759, 501).

friends are sorry that, amidst the public rejoicings and prosperity, your family should have occasion to be in mourning. Everybody here remembers you with the greatest admiration and affection, and nothing that concerns you is indifferent to them, and there are more people who sympathise with you than you are aware of. It would be the greatest pedantry to offer any topics of consolation to you who are naturally so firm and so manly. As your Brother dyed in the service of his country, you have the best and the noblest consolation: That since it has pleased God to deprive you of the satisfaction you might have expected from the continuance of his life, it has at least been so ordered that the manner of his death does you honour.

You left Scotland so much sooner than you proposed, when I had the pleasure of seeing you at Glasgow, that I had not an opportunity of making you a visit at Dalkieth, as I intended, before you should return to London.

I sent about a fortnight ago the books which you ordered for the Duke of Buccleugh to Mr. Campbell at Edinburgh. I paid for them, according to your orders, as soon as they were ready. I send you enclosed a list of them, with the prices discharged on the back. You will compare with the books when they arrive. Mr. Campbell will further them to London.[2] I should have wrote to you of this a fortnight ago, but my natural dilatoriness prevented me.

I ever am, with the greatest esteem and regard, your most obliged and most obedient humble servant,

Adam Smith

40. *To* [GILBERT ELLIOT]

MS., NLS Minto Collection; unpubl.

Glasgow, 10 Oct. 1759

Dear Sir

I know not what apology to make for having so long delayed to write to you. I thought myselfe infinitely obliged to you for the objection which you made to a Part of my system,[1] and immediately began to write a philosophical letter to you to show that the consequence which you seemed

---

[2] See Letters 41 and 44 addressed to Archibald Campbell, dated 24 Oct. 1759 and 9 Jan. 1760.

[1] Elliot had philosophical interests, e.g. Hume assigned him in 1751 the task of strengthening the part of Cleanthes, the empirical theist, in *Dialogues Concerning Natural Religion* (HL i. 150–8). Professor David Raphael communicates the following note: 'From the evidence of this letter and its enclosure, we can infer the general drift of Elliot's objection: if moral judgement on our own actions were a reflection of the approval and disapproval of society, then it would be impossible for a man to form a moral judgement which he knows is contrary to popular opinion. The second and longer of the amendments which Smith enclosed with this letter answers the objection by developing Smith's theory of the impartial spectator.'

to fear would follow from it, had no necessary connection with it. Upon second thoughts, however, I thought it would be better to alter the 2d Section of the 3d part of my book[2] so as to obviate that objection and to send you this alteration. This cost me more time and thought than you could well imagine the composition of three sheets of Paper would stand me; for nothing is more difficult than to insert something into the middle of what is already composed and to connect it cleverly at both ends. Before you read it I will begg of you to read over the first paragraphs of the second Section of the third part, then pass over the three next paragraphs, and read the sixth and seventh till you come to the paragraph at the bottom of page 260 which begins with the word, *Unfortunately*; instead of that paragraph insert the second of those additions which you will receive by this Post under another cover. I will be greatly obliged to you if you will send me your opinion of it. You will observe that it is intended both to confirm my Doctrine that our judgements concerning our own conduct have always a reference to the sentiments of some other being, and to shew that, notwithstanding this, real magnanimity and conscious virtue can support itselfe under the disapprobation of all mankind. I should be glad to know how far you think I have made out both; if you do not think it quite satisfactory I can make it still a great deal plainer, by a great number of new illustrations. I would likewise beg of you to read what I say upon Mandevilles system and then consider whether upon the whole I do not make Virtue sufficiently independent of popular opinion.

I think, I have made it sufficiently plain that our judgements concerning the conduct of others are founded in Sympathy. But it would seem very odd if we judged of our own conduct by one principle and of that of other men by another.

You will find too in the Papers I have sent you an answer to an objection of D. Humes.[3] I think I have entirely discomfitted him.

I am now about publishing a new edition of my Book[4] and would be greatly obliged to you for any criticisms you could make upon it. If you see Colonel Clerk I should be glad to know his opinion and would wish you to communicate the papers I have sent you to him.[5] I am fully sensible

[2] TMS ed. 1, April 1759: Part III, Section ii, of that edition is entitled 'In what manner our own judgments refer to what ought to be the judgment of others: And of the origin of general rules'.

[3] See Letter 36 from Hume, dated 28 July 1759: 'I wish you had more particularly and fully prov'd, that all kinds of Sympathy are necessarily Agreeable.' For Smith's answer, see the TMS note for insertion below (Glasgow TMS, I.iii.1.9).

[4] TMS ed. 2, in print by 30 Dec. 1760: see Letter 54 addressed to Strahan on that date. The ed. is dated 1761.

[5] Robert Clerk (?1724–97), educ. Edinburgh University, c. 1737–40; entered army, Col. 1762, Maj. Gen. 1772, Lt. Gen. 1793. He became a protégé of Lord Shelburne: Carlyle of Inveresk (473) called him 'truly the greatest siccatore in the world'; and Hume, 'that Meteor' (NHL 87). Adam Ferguson represented Clerk as opposed to Smith's doctrine of sympathy: see *Journal of the History of Ideas* xxi (1960) 222–32.

how much trouble I am giving you by all this. I know, however, your friendship will excuse it.

Boscawens Victory gave everybody here the greatest satisfaction.[6] We look upon it as a preventative of the threatened invasion, about the event of which few people seem very anxious. I thought myself equally honoured and obliged by the letter you was so good as to write to me upon it.[7]

The only news here relates to elections. Mr. Crawfurd has lost the town of Air. Sir Adam Ferguson and Lord Loudoun have got the better of him there. Your friend Mr. Muir of Caldwell is in some danger from Mr. Cunningham of Craigen[d]s. The head court of the Shire was held yesterday in which everything was carried for Mr. Muir, and all the new votes, that were made to oppose him, rejected. The decision of that affair will depend, I hear, on the Duke of Argylle.[8] I ever am Dear Sir

> Your most obliged and
> most obedient humble Servt
> Adam Smith

[6] In 1758–9 the French collected troops and flat-bottomed boats for an invasion of Britain. When de la Clue ventured out of Toulon with his fleet he was caught off Lagos and defeated on 18 August 1759 by Admiral Hon. Edward Boscawen (1711–61), known as Wry-necked Dick or Old Dreadnought to his sailors. In November Conflans was defeated by Hawke at Quiberon Bay, which finally ended the invasion threat.

[7] Not traced: perhaps the letter in which Elliot advanced his 'objection' to TMS: dated, very likely, early in September, as it would take two to three weeks for news of Boscawen's victory to reach London.

[8] Parliamentary affairs at this date in some areas of Scotland were at a critical phase. Management had been firmly in the hands of the 3rd Duke of Argyll, to whom Elliot owed his seat in Selkirkshire, but Elliot also had links with Bute whose star was rising in view of his influence over the Prince of Wales and the imminence of George II's death. The manager of Bute's affairs in Scotland was William Mure of Caldwell (1718–76), M.P. for Renfrewshire 1742–61. In 1759 Mure supported as candidate for Ayr burghs, Patrick Craufurd of Auchenames (c. 1704–78), thus opposing the wishes of Argyll and John Campbell, 4th Earl of Loudoun (1705–82), who had been superseded the year before as Commander-in-Chief in America. In consequence, Mure was opposed in Renfrewshire by the Earl of Glencairn, who supported as candidate William Cuninghame of Craigends, son of a former Member. At the Michaelmas head court—when the list of voters for Renfrewshire was established on the basis of property ownership—the roll stood as follows: 13 freeholders for Mure; 6 for Cuninghame; and 7 neutral, waiting for Argyll's instructions. Mure wrote to Bute on 16 Oct.: 'I had the good fortune to out-number my opponents by more than two to one, so we kept off the roll the whole of Glencairn's new creations and are preparing to stand a law suit in defence of our proceedings' (Bute MSS., HP i. 493). In 1760 Argyll backed Mure, then a place was found for him as a Baron of the Exchequer Court of Scotland, and Craufurd was forced on the county. In Ayr in 1759 Argyll supported Sir Adam Fergusson (1733–1812), son of Lord Kilkerran, but when Bute came to power in 1760, Argyll compromised with him and sought to get Fergusson to withdraw. The Ayr council were angered by the Argyll–Bute deal and refused to replace Fergusson, but in 1761 the election went to Alexander Wedderburn, a supporter of Bute.

[*MS. Draft Amendments* for Edition 2 of TMS, 1761][9]

Page 99. Line 12.[10] After the following Sentence: *But it is painful to go along with grief, and we always enter into it with reluctance:*

Make a reference and insert the following note at the bottom of the page.

Note.

It has been objected to me that as I found the Sentiment of Approbation, which is always agreable, upon Sympathy, it is inconsistent with my System to allow of any disagreeable Sympathy. I answer that in the sentiment of approbation, there are two things to be taken notice of; first, the Sympathetic passion of the Spectator; and, secondly, the emotion which arises from his observing the perfect coincidence between this sympathetic passion in himself and the original passion in the person principally concerned. This last emotion, in which the Sentiment of approbation properly Consists, is always agreable and delightful. The other may either be agreable or disagreable, according to the nature of the original passion, whose features it must always, in some measure, retain. Two Sounds, I suppose, may, each of them taken singly, be austere, and yet, if they are perfect concords, the perception of this harmony and coincidence may be agreable.

page 260. At the bottom.[11]

⁹ The draft amendments are in the hand of the amanuensis who produced the MS. of the 'Early Draft of the *Wealth of Nations*' (Scott 386–7). The same hand is found in GUL University Records, vol. 30, pp. 166–84, Minutes of University Meeting of 13 Aug. 1762, 'Report of the Committee on the Rector's and Principal's Powers' (see Scott 203–5, for the text). The document accompanying the letter of 10 Oct. 1759 is presumably a copy of a draft prepared for the printer. The text of this was subsequently altered before publication; see notes 2 and 3. The draft amendments are written on three double folio sheets, the kind Smith customarily used. The water-mark is the same as that of the fragment on Justice (GUL, MS., Gen. 1035/227).

¹⁰ The first draft amendment relates to a paragraph which in edition 1 was Part I, Section iv, Chapter 1, § 9. In ed. 2 this became Part I, Section iii, Chapter 1, § 9, and that is how it remained in ed. 6 (Glasgow edn., I.iii.1.9). In ed. 2 the footnote was added pretty well as in the draft amendment, but with slight revision. The final sentence of the note was deleted in ed. 6, 1790.

¹¹ Like the first draft amendment, this one received a slight revision here and there, but in addition it received very ample supplementation towards the end when it was actually printed in the second edition. Smith in his letter asks Elliot to pass over paragraphs 3–5 in Part III, Section ii. Two of these deleted paragraphs are in fact reproduced, with slight revision, in the second and third paragraphs of the amendment. In the sixth edition, and consequently in the Glasgow edition, the first two paragraphs of the amendment are printed at III.1.6–7. The third paragraph of the amendment was deleted in ed. 6. Paragraphs 4–7 of the amendment ('The Great Judge . . . disadvantageous Judgement') were replaced in ed. 6, at III.1. §§ 31–2, by a revised and condensed statement of their thought. The 8th and 9th paragraphs of the amendment, and part of the 10th paragraph ('It is only . . . inequality of our sentiments') are at III.3. §§ 1–3. The remainder of the 10th paragraph of the amendment was amplified in ed. 2, and the amplification appears in ed. 6 at III.3. §§ 4–5, 7–9, 11. The 11th paragraph of the amendment was amplified in ed. 2,

Instead of the erased passage in this and the following page insert what follows into the Text.

When I endeavour to examine my own conduct, when I endeavour to pass sentence upon it and either to approve or condemn it, it is evident that, in all such cases, I divide myself, as it were, into two persons, and that I, the examiner and Judge, represent a different character from that other I, the person whose conduct is examined into and judged of. The first is the Spectator whose sentiments with regard to my own conduct I endeavour to enter into, by placing myself in his Situation, and by considering how it would appear to me when seen from that particular point of view. The second is the Agent, the person whom I properly call myself, and of whose conduct, under the Character of a Spectator, I was endeavouring to form some oppinion. The first is the Judge; the Second, the pannel. But that the Judge should, in every respect, be the same with the pannel, is as impossible, as that the cause should, in every respect, be the same with the effect.

To be amiable and to be meritorious, that is, to deserve Love and to deserve reward, are the great Characters of virtue, and to be odious and punishable, of vice. But all these characters have an immediate reference to the sentiments of others. Virtue is not said to be amiable or to be meritorious, because it is the object of its own Love or of its own gratitude; but because it excites those sentiments in other men. The consciousness that it is the object of such favourable regards is the source of that inward tranquillity and self satisfaction with which it is naturally attended, as the Suspicion of the contrary gives occasion to the torments of vice. What so great happiness as to be beloved, and to know that we deserve to be beloved? What so great misery as to be hated, and to know that we deserve to be hated?

Man is considered as a moral, because he is regarded as an accountable being. But an Accountable being, as the word expresses, is a being that must give an Account of its actions to some other, and that, consequently, must regulate them according to the good liking of this other. Man is accountable to God and his fellow creatures. But tho' he is, no doubt, principally accountable to God, in the order of time, he must necessarily conceive himself as accountable to his fellow creatures, before he can form any idea of the Deity, or of the rules by which that Divine Being will judge of his conduct. A Child, surely, conceives itself as accountable to its parents, and is elevated or cast down by the thought of their merited approbation or disapprobation, long before it forms any idea of its

but the amplification was omitted in ed. 6, which has itself an extensive addition in this part of the book. The 12th and last paragraph of the amendment, which was of course in ed. 1, is to be found in the 6th (Glasgow edn., III.4.2).

Accountableness to the Deity, or of the rules by which that Divine being will judge of its conduct.

The Great Judge of the World, has, for the wisest reasons, thought proper to interpose, between the weak eye of human reason and the throne of his eternal justice, a degree of obscurity and darkness which, tho it does not entirely cover that great tribunal from the view of mankind, yet renders the impression of it faint and feeble in comparison of what might be expected from the grandeur and importance of so mighty an object. If those infinite rewards and punishments, which the almighty has prepared for those who obey or transgress his will, were perceived as distinctly as we foresee the frivolous and temporary retaliations which we may expect from one another, the weakness of human nature, astonished at the immensity of objects so little fitted to its comprehension, could no longer attend to the little affairs of this world; and it is absolutely impossible that the business of society could have been carried on, if, in this respect, there had been a fuller revelation of the intentions of providence than that which has already been made. That men, however, might never be without a rule to direct their conduct by, nor without a judge whose authority should enforce its observation, the author of nature has made man the immediate judge of mankind, and has, in this respect, as in many others, created him after his own image, and appointed him his vicegerent upon earth to Superintend the behaviour of his brethren. They are taught by Nature to acknowledge that power and jurisdiction which has thus been confered upon him, and to tremble or exult according as they imagine that they have either merited his Censure or deserved his Applause.

But whatever may be the authority of this inferior tribunal, which is continually before their eyes, if at any time it should decide contrary to these rules and principles which nature has established for regulating its Judgements, men appeal from this unjust decision, and call upon a Superior tribunal established in their own minds, to redress the unjustice of this weak or partial judgement.

There are certain principles established by nature for governing our judgements concerning the conduct of those we live with. As long as we decide according to those principles, and neither applaud nor condemn any thing which nature has not rendered the proper object of Applause or condemnation, nor any further than she has rendered them such, the person, concerning whom we form these Judgements must himself necessarily approve of them. When he puts himself into our situation, he cannot avoid entering into those views of his own conduct which, he feels, must naturally occur to us, and he is obliged to Consider it himself in the very same light in which we represent it. Our sentiments, therefore, must necessarily produce their full effect upon him, and he cannot faill to conceive all the triumph of self approbation from what appears to him such merited applause, as well as all the horrors of Shame from what, he is sensible, is such deserved condemnation. But it is otherwise if we have either applauded or condemned him, contrary to those principles and rules which nature has established for the direction of our judgements concerning every thing of this kind. If we have either applauded or Condemned him for what, when he puts himself in our Situation, does not appear to him to be the object either of applause or Condemnation; as, in this case, he cannot enter into our Sentiments, if he has any constancy or firmness, he is little affected by them, and can neither be elevated by the favourable nor mortified by the unfavourable decision. The applause of the whole world will avail but little if our own conscience condemns us; and the disapprobation of all mankind is not capable of oppressing us when we are absolved by the tribunal within our own breast, and when our own mind tells us that mankind are in the wrong.

But tho this tribunal within the breast be thus the supreme arbiter of all our actions, tho' it can reverse the decisions of all mankind with regard to our character and Conduct, tho it can mortify us amidst the Applauses and Support us under the Censure of the world, yet if we enquire into the origin of its institution, its jurisdiction, we shall find, is in a great measure derived from the authority of that very tribunal, whose decisions it so often and so justly reverses. When we first come into the world, being desireous to please those we live with, we are accustomed to Consider what behaviour is likely to be agreeable to every person we converse with, to our parents, to our masters, to our companions. We address ourselves to individuals, and for some time fondly pursue the impossible and absurd project of rendering ourselves universally agreable, and of gaining the good will and approbation of every body. We soon Learn, however, from experience, that this universal approbation is altogether unattainable. As soon as we come to have more important interests to manage, we find, that by pleasing one man we almost certainly disoblige another, and that by humouring an individual, we may often irritate a whole people. The fairest and most equitable conduct must frequently obstruct the interests or thwart the inclinations of particular persons, who will seldome have candour eneough to enter into the propriety of our motives, or to see that our conduct, how disagreable soever to them, is perfectly suitable to our situation. We soon learn, therefore, to sett up in our own minds a judge between ourselves and those we live with. We Conceive ourselves as acting in the presence of a person quite candid and equitable, of one who has no particular relation, either to ourselves, or to those whose interests are affected by our conduct; who is neither father, nor Brother, nor friend, either to them, or to us; but is meerly a man in general, an impartial Spectator who considers our conduct with the same indifference with which we regard that of other people. If when we place ourselves in the Situation of such a person, our own actions appear to us under an agreable aspect, if we feel that such a Spectator cannot avoid entering into all the motives which influenced us, whatever may be the judgements of the world, we cannot help being pleased with our own behaviour, and regarding ourselves, in spite of the Censure of our companions, as the just and proper objects of approbation. On the contrary, if the man within condemns us, the loudest acclamations of mankind appear but as the noise of ignorance and folly, and whenever we assume the Character of this impartial judge, we cannot avoid viewing our own actions with his distaste and dissatisfaction. The weak, the vain and the frivolous, indeed, may be mortified by the most groundless Censure or elated by the most absurd applause. Such persons are not accustomed to consult the judge within concerning the oppinion which they ought to form of their own conduct. This inmate of the breast, this abstract man, the representative of mankind and Substitute of the Deity, whom nature has appointed the Supreme arbiter of all their actions is seldome appealed to by them. They are contented with the decision of the inferior tribunal. The approbation of their companions, of the particular persons whom they have lived and conversed with, has generally been the ultimate object of all their wishes. If they Succeed in this their Joy is compleat; and if they faill they are entirely disappointed. They never think of appealing to the Superior court. They have Seldome enquired after its decisions and are altogether unacquainted with the rules and forms of its procedure. When the world injures them, therefore, they are incapable of doing themselves Justice and are in consequence necessarily the Slaves of the world. But it is otherwise with the man who has, upon all occasions, been accustomed to have recourse to the judge within and to consider, not what the world approves or disapproves of, but what appears to this impartial Spectator the natural and proper object of approbation and disapprobation. The judgement of this supreme arbiter of his conduct is the applause which he has been accustomed principally to court, is the Censure which he has been accustomed principally to fear. Compared with this final decision, the sentiments of all mankind, tho' not altogether indifferent, appear to be but of small moment; and he is incapable of being either much elivated by their favourable, or greatly depressed by their most disadvantageous Judgement.

It is only by consulting this judge within that we can see whatever relates to ourselves in its proper shape and dimensions, or that we can make any proper comparison between our own interests and those of other men.

As to the eye of the body objects appear great or small, not so much according to their real dimensions, as according to the nearness or distance of their situation; so do they likewise to, what may be called, the natural eye of the mind: and we remedy the defects of both these organs pretty much in the same manner. In my present situation an immense landscape of Lawns and woods and distant mountains, seems to do no more than cover the little window which I write by, and to be out of all proportion less than the chamber in which I am sitting. I can form a just comparison between those great objects and the little objects around me, in no other way, than by transporting myself, at least in fancy, to a different station, from whence I can survey both at nearly equal distances, and thereby form some judgement of their real proportions. Habit and experience have taught me to do this so easily and so readily, that I am scarce sensible that I do it; and a man must be, in some measure, acquainted with the philosophy of vision, before he can be thoroughly convinced, how little those distant objects would appear to the eye, if the imagination, from a knowledge of their real magnitudes, did not swell and dilate them.

In the same manner to the selfish and original passions of human nature, the loss or gain of a very small interest of our own, appears to be of vastly more importance, excites a much more passionate joy or sorrow, a much more ardent desire or aversion, than the greatest concern of another with whom we have no particular connection. His interests as long as they are surveyed from this station, can never be put into the ballance with our own, can never restrain us from doing whatever may tend to promote our own, how ruinous soever to him. Before we can make any proper comparison of those opposite interests we must change our position. We must view them, neither from our own place, nor yet from his, neither with our own eyes nor yet with his, but from the place and with the eyes of a third person, who has no particular connection with either and who judges with impartiality between us. This is the only station from which both can be seen at equal distances, or from which any proper comparison can be made between them. Here too habit and experience have taught us to assume this station so easily and so readily that we are scarce sensible that we assume it; and it requires, in this case too, some degree of reflection and even of philosophy to convince us, how little interest we should take in the greatest concerns of our neighbour, how little we should be affected by whatever relates to him, if the sense of propriety and justice did not correct the other wise natural inequality of our sentiments. It is from this station only that we can see the propriety of generosity and the deformity of injustice; the propriety of resigning the greatest interests of our own for the yet more important interests of others, and the deformity of doing the smallest injury to another in order to obtain the greatest benefite to ourselves. The real littleness of ourselves and of whatever relates to ourselves can be seen from this Station only; and it is here only that we can learn the great lesson of Stoical magnanimity and firmness, to be no more affected by what befalls ourselves than by what befalls our neighbour, or, what comes to the same thing, than our neighbour is capable of being affected by what befalls us. 'When our neighbour, says Epictetus, loses his wife or his son, there is nobody who is not sensible that this is a human calamity, a natural event altogether according to the ordinary course of things. But, when the same thing happens to ourselves, then we cry out, as if we had suffered the most dreadful misfortune. We ought, however, to remember how we were affected when this accident happened to another, and such as we were in his case such ought we to be in our own.'

It is not upon all occasions, however, that we are capable of judging with this perfect impartiality between ourselves and others. Even the judge within is often in danger of being corrupted by the violence and injustice of our selfish passions, and is often induced to make a report very different from what the real circumstances of the case are capable of authorizing.

There are two different occasions upon which we examine our conduct, and endeavour to view it in the light in which the impartial spectator would view it. First, when we are about to act; and secondly &c. continue as in page 261.

41. *To* [ARCHIBALD CAMPBELL][1]

MS., SRO Buccleuch Collection GD224/377/9/1 p. 3; unpubl.

Glasgow, 24 Oct. 1759

Sir,

I am much obliged to you for the trouble you have taken in remembering so small an affair. I send you the account discharged.[2] I made Mr Foulis

[1] Writer to the Signet: agent of the Buccleuch family.

[2] Account for £17-9-2 rendered by Robert and Andrew Foulis for books supplied for the Duke of Buccleuch. Smith settled the account on 29 Aug., the books reached the Duke on 17 Dec., and Charles Townshend instructed John Craigie of Kilgraston on 22 Dec. to pay the amount to Smith. The account bears a receipt to Craigie by Alexander Kincaid & Co., booksellers, on Smith's orders. See Letter 39 addressed to Charles Townshend, dated 17 Sept. 1759, and Letter 44 addressed to Archibald Campbell, dated 9 Jan. 1760. The account lists the following books and prices:

Homeri Ilias 2 Vol. large folio	2 1	
——Odyssea 2 Vol. large folio	2 1	
Callimachus Gr. cum figuris folio	10	
Caesaris Opera folio	14	
Sophocles Gr. 4to	10	6
Aeschylus Gr. 4to	9	6
Plinij Epistolae & Panegyricus 4to	10	6
Theocritus Gr. 4to	6	6
Minucius Felix 4to	4	6
Homeri Ilias 2 Vol. Gr. 4to	12	
Caesaris Opera 4to	12	
Boetius de Consolatione Philosophiae	5	
Tyrtaeus Gr. Lat. 4to	3	
Demetrius Phalereus de Elocutione	4	
Terentij Comoediae, 8vo	3	9

Footnote 2 continued overleaf

copy it out of his books a second time as Mr Townshend may possibly have lost the copy I sent him. I am with great regard

Your most obedient humble Servant

Adam Smith

42. *To* LORD SHELBURNE

MS., Bowood Libr., Marquess of Lansdowne; Scott 250–1 (in part).

Glasgow, 29 Oct. 1759

My Lord

Your Lordship will receive by the same post which brings you this letter two other packets, of which the one contains Mr. Fitzmaurices receipts

Homeri Ilias Gr. Lat. 3 Vol. 8vo	8	9
Sophocles Gr. Lat. 2 Vol. 8vo	8	6
Aeschylus Gr. Lat. 2 Vol. 8vo	7	6
Theocritus Gr. Lat. 8vo	3	3
Minucius Felix 8vo	2	3
Aristophanis Nubes Gr. Lat. 8vo	2	3
Boetius de Consolatione, &c. 8vo	2	6
Antoninus Gr. Lat. 8vo 2 Vol.	5	
Plutarchus de Poetis audiendis Gr. Lat. 8vo	2	9
Euripidis Orestes Gr. Lat. 8vo	2	9
Aristoteles de Mundo Gr. Lat. 8vo	2	
Epictetus & Cebes Gr. Lat. 8vo large print	3	3
Anacreon Gr. large print, 8vo	2	
Theophrasti Characteres Gr. Lat. large print 8vo	2	3
Horatius, editio ultima 8vo	3	9
Virgilius, editio ult. 8vo	5	3
Sallustius 8vo	3	3
Lucretius 8vo	3	3
Paterculus 8vo	2	9
Tibullus & Propertius 8vo	3	
Poetae Latini minores 8vo	2	6
Iuvenalis & Persius 8vo	2	3
Pomponius Mela de situ Orbis 8vo	2	9
Phaedrus & P. Syrus 8vo	2	3
Thucydides de Peste Gr. Lat. 8vo	2	3
Plinij Epist. & Panegyr. 2 Vol. 12mo	5	
Tacitus 4 Vol. 12mo	10	
Hippocratis Aphorismi Gr. Lat. 12mo	1	8
Epictetus & Cebes Gr. Lat. 12mo	2	6
Pindari Opera 3 Vol. Gr. small size	5	
Ciceronis Opera 20 Vol. fine	2 9	6

The list is instructive in representing the range of authors thought suitable for educating the young Duke, and for reflecting the stock of the Foulis brothers, both as booksellers and printers. Noticeable among their books on the list are the *De elocutione* of Demetrius Phalereus, which was the first Greek text published in Glasgow (1743), and the one submitted by the Robert Foulis when applying to be University Printer at Glasgow; the magnificent Homer folios of 1756–8, with the typefount specially designed by Alexander Wilson, and meticulously proof-read; and the ingenious miniature Pindar (1754–8), measuring only 3 ins. by 1·9 ins.

for the money he has received at different times from me since he came here, the other, the different accounts of the way in which part of this money has been expended. I have marked every receipt with a letter of the Alphabet. Your Lordship will find the same letter upon the back of the Account or accounts which correspond to it.

Your Lordship will observe several receipts that have no accounts corresponding to them. It is always mentioned in the body of the receipt what the money was given for, but there is not always any discharged account from a third person vouching that it was actually so expended. This is the case with regard to all those articles which concern the payment of any of his masters, none of whom ever give any discharge; with regard to those for the fees of a Physician and Surgeon; with regard to those for pocket money; with regard to those for some books which were bought for ready money and which are named in the body of the receipt, for a set of Silver buckles, for a case of mathematical instruments and for some other smaller articles of a few shillings value. The two principal articles of which there is no account are that for a journey to Edinburgh: and that for another to the Duke of Argylls at Inverara.[1] I am answerable for the first of these, as it was upon my account that he went to Edinburgh, I not chusing to leave him behind me. I expected to have brought him back with me for fourty shillings; But when I came there I was often obliged either to sup or dine at places where it was improper to carry him. When this happened to be the case, that I might be sure what company he was in in a very dissolute town, I ordered a small entertainment at our lodgings and invited two or three young lawiers to keep him company in my absence. Inverara is two days journey from Glasgow and we happened to be misinformed with regard to Dukes motions and came there two days before him during which time we stayed at a very expensive Inn. At both these places I laid out the money and Mr. Fitzmaurice kept the account and when we came home we divided the expence between us.

The fees of the four Masters whose classes he attended last winter your Lordship may justly think extravagant. But it is the fee which is expected from all noblemens sons. Not above the half would be expected from any Gentlemans son.

Your Lordship will observe the first Article for Pocket to be four Pounds. He asked it and as it was the beginning of my government I gave it. It was spent in less than a month, not upon any vitious pleasure, but upon prints and baubles of no great utility and a considerable portion of it upon nuts, apples and oranges. After that I capitulated with him for a guinea a month and he has kept to this pretty nearly. You will observe two guineas for

[1] Perhaps this was the occasion when Smith heard the piper of the Argyleshire Militia repeating 'all those poems which Mr. Macpherson has translated and many more of equal beauty'; see Hume to ? Sir David Dalrymple, 16 Aug. 1760, HL i. 329.

Pocket charged in one or two articles. This, however, you will observe is the always the allowance not only of the month in which it is charged but of the preceding month for which my own indolence had made me defer taking any receipt.

Your Lordship expresses in a letter I received from you sometime ago, a very laudible anxiety that your son should be held to Oeconomy not that he might hoard, but that he might be able to give. I did not at that time take any notice of that part of your Lordships letter. I can now venture to assure your Lordship that, tho' you may think this account a bad specimen of his management, he is punctual, regular and orderly beyond almost anybody of his age and condition I have ever known, that he is careful of every thing upon which he sets any value, of his books, of his cloaths, and will I am perswaded be so of his money, whenever he comes to have any money to manage that is worth caring for. His regularity is tempered by a great desire of distinguishing himself by doing actions of eclat that will draw upon him the Attention of the world. He is even animated by this passion to a degree that is a little hazardous and is capable of venturing to expose his talents, which are naturally excellent, before they are perfectly matured. If he lives to be a man, he will, I imagine be firm, steady and resolute in an uncommon degree, and by the time he comes to the meridian of Life, will be a man of severe and even of rigid morals. I am your Lordships

Most Obliged and
Most Obedient
humble Servant
Adam Smith

43. *To* LORD SHELBURNE

MS., Bowood Libr., Marquess of Lansdowne; Scott 251–2

Glasgow, 3 Dec. 1759

My Lord

I received by this Post the honour of your Lordships Letter of the 17th November, with the two draughts enclosed. Your Lordship has remitted the money in the manner that is most advantageous to me. As the ballance of Exchange is almost always against Glasgow and in favour of London, all London bills commonly sell above Par, and I this day received $\frac{1}{2}$ per cent advanced price for the two draughts you sent me. I should abuse your Lordships Generosity very grossly if I took advantage of what you are so good as to put into my Power or did not declare that I think the sum you have remitted me full compensation for all the trouble I have been at with Mr Fitzmaurice. That trouble, indeed, is very Little. I have never known anybody more easily governed, or who more readily adopted any advice when the propriety of it is fairly explained to him. Since he came here, he has been, perhaps, the most regular student in the whole University. I shall give your Lordship but one instance of it. We have a meeting of the whole University every Saturday morning for discipline; the whole business of this meeting is to enquire into the delinquencies of the former week and to punish them with some small fine. A very strict attendance upon this meeting is not insisted on and the most regular commonly think they do enough if they attend once in three times. Mr Fitzmaurice never missed this meeting till Saturday last when he happened to oversleep himself and as I did not go out myself that day, I did not think it worth while to set him up. This absence was so remarkable that I had messages that forenoon, from, I believe, half the University to enquire if he was well. I cannot give your Lordship a stronger instance how much he takes it a point of honour to observe the most frivolous parts of his duty as a student with exact regularity. He gives very good application and has a very great ambition to distinguish himself as a man of Learning. He seems to have a particular turn for and delight in Mechanics[1] and Mathematics which make the principal part of his business this year continuing, however, all his last year's studies except Logic. What he is most defective in is Grammar, especially english Grammar, in which he is apt some times to blunder to a degree that I am some times at a loss to account for. This, however, I expect will soon be mended.

Your Lordship will receive along with this letter two covers containing four sheets of Anecdotes relating to the King of Prussia.[2] My Lord Fitzmaurice received them from a friend of his in Germany. He sent them to one Mr Boyle at London, I suppose my Lord Orrerys Son,[3] in order to be sent to me whom he desired to transmit them to your Lordship that *when you had read them, you might burn them, for he was not at liberty to give a copy*; These were his Lordships words. I received them about three weeks ago and have read them over and over with great pleasure. They will, I dare to say, give your Lordship the same satisfaction. Mr Boyle desired me to return them to him. I chose, however, to obey My Lord Fitzmaurice, The channel, besides, by which Mr Boyle proposed they should be returned did not appear to me to be perfectly secure, and he did not favour me with his direction. I would, however beg of [your] Lordship not to burn them, till I can clear up this with Mr Boyle, that if My Lord Fitzmaurice intended

---

[1] Of the period when Thomas Fitzmaurice was a bleacher of linen, a contemporary wrote: 'The buildings which he has erected, and the machines and apparatus which he has placed in them are really astonishing' (20 July 1785: HP i. 430).

[2] Frederick the Great.

[3] Edmund Boyle (1742–89), 3rd son of John Boyle (1707–62), 5th Earl of Cork and 5th Earl of Orrery, friend of Swift, Pope, and Johnson. Edmund became the 7th Earl of Orrery.

them to be seen by any fourth person his intention may yet be fulfilled. I ever am

Your Lordships
Most Obliged and most Obedient humble Servant
Adam Smith

44. *To* [ARCHIBALD CAMPBELL]

MS., SRO Buccleuch Collection GD224/377/9/4; unpubl.

Glasgow, 9 Jan. 1760

Sir,

I am very much obliged to you for taking the trouble to remember such a trifle and being so much at pains about it. If you will be so good as to pay the money to Mr Kincaid the Bookseller, he will account for it to me.[1] The sum, if you remember, is seventeen pounds, nine Shillings. His receipt I suppose may stand for a discharge: but if any more formal discharge is requisite I shall send it. Remember me to Mrs Campbell and family. I heartily wish you and them a good new year and many of them, and ever am with great esteem and regard

Most sincerely yours
Adam Smith

45. *To* LORD SHELBURNE

MS., Bowood Libr., Marquess of Lansdowne; unpubl.

Glasgow, 10 Mar. 1760

My Lord

I think it my Duty to inform your Lordship that Mr. Fitzmaurice has been for some days past ill of a slight fever, from which, however, he never appeared to be in the least danger and from which I hope he is now in a fair way of recovery.[1]

He was seized with it on Wednesday last. I missed him that forenoon from the Class, which I had never done before and upon my return to my own house, I found him lying upon his bed and complaining of a headache. I immediately sent for a Physician who ordered him to be blooded. He was

---

[1] See Letter 41 addressed to Archibald Campbell, dated 24 Oct. 1759.

[1] Smith's solicitude here parallels that for his later pupils, the Duke of Buccleuch and the Hon. Hew Campbell Scott; see Letters 94 and 95 addressed to Charles Townshend, dated 26 and 27 Aug. 1766, and Letters 97 and 98 addressed to Lady Frances Scott, dated 15 and 19 Oct. of the same year.

a good deal relieved by the bleeding, but became very feverish that evening. He continued so all next day but the day following found himself greatly relieved in consequence of a sweat and a sound Sleep. I should have written to your Lordship that evening, that is by fridays post, for I could have written no sooner, but he appeared to be so much better and Dr. Black assured me so positively that all danger was now over, and that he would probably be quite well next day, that I resolved to wait one other post before I wrote anything that could possibly alarm your Lordship. The Doctors prediction was in part fulfilled. He was very chearful and easy during all Saturday, the fourth day, till about six in the Evening. At that time he began again to complain of his headache and appeared a little feverish. Both the fever and headache, however, were much slighter than they had been the first two days. He became very drowsy and slept with very little interruption all that night and all next day. On Sunday, the fifth day, at six in the Evening, he awaked, found himself quite relieved; complained of nothing but hunger; eat a good deal of bread and drunk tea. He has been very easy ever since and seems at present quite free of all fever. The Doctor, however, expects that he may have some slight attack either this night or tomorrow, which is the seventh day. He thinks himself, however, morally certain that it will both be very trifling and that it will be the last of this ailment. Your Lordship, perhaps, may think that as I ventured to delay writing to you by last post, I ought not to have written by this: and I shall readily acknowledge that my behaviour in this respect is not very consistent. But when Mr. Fitzmaurice had a slight relapse on Saturday evening I felt so much uneasiness for not having written to your Lordship the day before that I resolved never to expose myself to the like; your Lordship may depend upon his being treated with the utmost care and attention. I have the greatest trust in the two Medical Gentlemen who waited upon him, Dr. Black and Mr. Hamilton. They are both with him at least five times a day. They never have suspected the least danger from this ailment which they now think is over, and it is contrary to both their opinions that I give your Lordship the trouble of this alarm. Your Lordship may depend upon hearing from me by every post till Mr. Fitzmaurice is able to write himself. I ever [am]

My Lord
Your Lordships
Most Obedient and obliged
Servant
Adam Smith

46. *To* LORD SHELBURNE

MS., Bowood Libr., Marquess of Lansdowne; unpubl.

Glasgow, 12 Mar. 1760

My Lord

It gives me as much pleasure to write to your Lordship today as it gave me pain to write to you by last post. The Doctors Predictions have upon this occasion been literally and exactly fulfilled. Mr. Fitzmaurice had the night before last a very slight attack of his fever which he was relieved from by a gentle sweat; and last night he had a bleeding at the nose which Dr. Black regards as a perfect crisis. He has ever since been entirely free from all feverish ailments or symptoms. He slept very sound all last night without any disturbance, and has been very easy and hearty all this day. He has been out of bed a great part of it, and has been amusing himself by reading the new Tragedy. His two Physicians Drunk tea with him and neither of them apprehend him in any danger of a relapse. There has appeared too that sediment in his urine which is regarded by them as the most certain symptom of recovery in all feverish complaints. I write this after seven o'clock at night. He has just now gone to bed and, tho weary and exhausted, seems perfectly well in every other respect. It gives me great pleasure to be able to relieve your Lordship so soon from the Alarm of which my last letter may have given you. I shall write to your Lordship whatever happens by next post. By the Post thereafter he will probably be able to write himself. I ever am with the greatest respect, My Lord

Your Lordships

Most Obliged and obedient

Servant

Adam Smith

47. *From* WILLIAM WILSON *to* THE MAGISTRATES OF THE BURGH OF LANARK

MS., GUA 2750; unpubl.

Glasgow, 15 Mar. 1760

Gentlemen

Mr. Andrew Stuart[1] desired me to send you a Copy of a Letter He has

---

[1] Andrew Stuart (1725–1801), W.S.; law agent to the Hamilton family; tutor to the children of the 6th Duke of Hamilton; resolved the Hamilton arguments in the Douglas Cause (see Letter 116 addressed to Lord Hailes, dated 5 Mar. 1769); fought a duel with Thurlow, counsel for Archibald Douglas: 'eased his mind' about the decision in the Douglas Cause in *Letters to Lord Mansfield* (1773); M.P. 1774–1801; appointed to the Board of Trade, 1779; member of the Select Society and close friend of Hume, George Dempster, Johnstone (Pulteney), and Wedderburn; wrote a *Genealogical History of the Stewarts*, (1798).

from Mr. Smith one of the Professors of the College of Glasgow in which you See the difficulty anent the Presentation[2] to Mr. Watson[3] to remove which He desires Mr. Watson may return to Him the Presentation and He will obtain a new one for Him whereby He will enter to the Logick Class next october and be received by the Colledge agreeable to the Statutes[4] and Get a year more than He had before him

Gentlemen, Your most obedient Servt

Wm Wilson

Edinburgh, 15 March, 1760

Copy Letter by Professor Smith *to* Mr. Stuart [?13 March 1760]

Dear Sir

I give you the trouble of this Letter to acquaint you of the Distress which a very Small oversight of Duke Hamiltons Tutors is likely to bring upon two very worthy young Men. They have presented one Mr. Watson [and] in order to be entitled to this Bursary He must enter the Moral Philosophy class But by the Statutes of Last Visitation no Scotch Man can pass the Logick Class unless He has Studied Logic at Some other College. Besides in two years Mr. Watson must take a degree in order to be entitled to the Divinity Bursary But by the same Statutes no Scotch Man can take a degree who has not gone thro' a compleat course of Philosophy. We dare not dispense with these Statutes which are the very Supports of the College. Mr. Watson's presentation therefore so far as I can judge of the Opinion of my Collegues cannot be received.

Mr. Bruce[5] I understand has the promise of the Vacancy which will occur next year in the Logic Class He is at present in the Moral Philosophy Class and it will be a great hardship upon Him to goe back as it will retard the course of his education.

The best way to make all easy is to give Mr. Bruce Mr. Watsons Presentation and to reserve for Mr. Watson that which is intended for Mr. Bruce. This will be equally for the benefite of both the Young Gentlemen and I am assured is agreeable to both their inclinations.

Signed / Adam Smith

   [2] Anne, Duchess of Hamilton, founded six bursaries in philosophy and divinity in 1694.

   [3] ? John Watson, Glasgow M.A. 1763.

   [4] In 1758 an Act of Parliament was obtained altering the terms of the Hamilton bursaries so that three students would be provided for, apiece, in logic and metaphysics, ethics, and natural philosophy; and three other students, apiece, for one, two, and three years of theology (*Deeds Instituting Scholarships . . . In the College . . . of Glasgow*, 1850, 102–19).

   [5] ? Archibald Bruce (d. 1799), Glasgow M.A. 1762; Minister of Fintry and then Shotts.

48. *To* LORD SHELBURNE

MS., Bowood Libr., Marquess of Lansdowne; unpubl.

Glasgow, 17 Mar. 1760

My Lord

I expected that Mr. Fitzmaurice would have been able to have acquainted your Lordship by this Post of the entire reestablishment of his health. An accident, however, has prevented this from taking place as soon as I expected. I never saw any body appear to recover faster than he did on Friday and Saturday last. On Saturday, particularly, he was surprisingly well and went to bed about 8 o'clock, in appearance, in as good health as it is possible for anybody to have, who had so lately recovered of a fever. On Sunday morning he was seized with a purging which continued all that day, raised his pulse and seemed to threaten a return of his fever. The Doctor assured me that this would in all proba[bility] prove a final crisis, that his former bleeding at the nose had not been so plentiful as he could have wished and that he had always suspected that something of this kind might happen: And I remember, indeed, that after the bleeding of his nose had stopped the Dr. told him that it would probably bleed again that night, which, however, did not happen and is the only prediction of his in this disease that has not in some degree been fulfilled. Mr. Fitzmaurice continued being very feverish all Sunday: about 8 o'clock at night he fell fast asleep and slept very sound, without once waking, till this morning (Monday) at 10 o'clock. He appeared then to be perfectly refreshed and free from all symptoms of fever. The inclination to stool, too, was much abated and seems now to be entirely gone. I write this at 8 o'clock at night. Tho' much exhausted by the Disorder of yesterday, he is quite cool and easy and free from every symptom of fever. This slight fit, I hope, tho it has retarded, will ensure his future recovery. I am

Your Lordships
most Obedient humble Servant
Adam Smith

49. *To* LORD SHELBURNE

MS., Bowood Libr., Marquess of Lansdowne; unpubl.

Glasgow, 19 Mar. 1760

My Lord

Mr. Fitzmaurice has been quite free from all feverish symptoms since Monday last, and begins now to recover his strength very fast: he has been out of bed all day and has written to my Lady Shelburne. He would have written to your Lordship at the same time, but as he took physic this

Morning he is a good deal exhausted and desired that I would make his excuse. This is the only drug he has been desired to take since the commencement of his illness. He was only once blooded and the rest of his cure has been wrought by a dark, quiet room and great plenty of lemonade made of warm barley water. I am with the highest respect My Lord

Your Lordships

Most Obedient and most

humble Servant

Adam Smith

9: o'clock at night

50. *To* WILLIAM STRAHAN[1]

MS., Goldsmith Libr., University of London, A.L. 709; Bonar, facing xxviii (facsim.); Rae 149–50.

Glasgow, 4 Apr. 1760

Dear Strahan

I sent up to Mr Millar four or five Posts ago the same additions which I had formerly sent to you, with a good many corrections and improvements which occurred to me since.[2] If there are any typographical errors remaining in the last edition which had escaped me, I hope you will correct them. In other respects I could wish it was printed pretty exactly according to the copy which I delivered to you. A man, says the Spanish proverb, had better be a Cuckold and know nothing of the matter, than not be Cuckold and believe himself to be one. And in the same manner, say I, An Author had sometimes better be in the wrong and believe himself in the right; than be in the right and believe or even suspect himself in the wrong. To desire you to read my book over and mark all the corrections you would wish me to make upon a sheet of paper and send it to me, would, I fear, be giving you too much trouble. If, however, you could induce yourself to take this trouble, you would oblige me greatly: I know how much I shall be benefitted and I shall at the same time preserve the pretious right of private

---

[1] William Strahan (1715–85) of Little New St., London, printer, publisher, and politician; son of a Writer to the Signet; educ. Edinburgh High School; apprenticed as printer in Edinburgh, then moved to London; entrusted with printing Johnson's dictionary, 1754; by 1760, he was laying up £1,000 a year after maintaining his family and paying his charges; the authors he published, together with Andrew Millar and later Thomas Cadell, included Hume, Robertson, Gibbon, Johnson, Blackstone, Blair, Beattie, Mackenzie, Macpherson, and Hawkesworth, as well as Smith; M.P., 1774–94. He sent valuable reports of parliamentary debates to Ralph Allen (Fielding's 'Allworthy'), Hume, and David Hall in Philadelphia.

[2] See Letter 40 addressed to Gilbert Elliot, dated 10 Oct. 1759, and its enclosure, for some of the improvements to TMS; also, see Letter 54 addressed to William Strahan, dated 30 Dec. 1760, for a list of errata. The intro. to Glasgow TMS presents details of alterations in ed. 2.

judgement for the sake of which our forefathers kicked out the Pope and the Pretender. I believe you to be much more infallible than the Pope, but as I am a Protestant my conscience makes me scruple to submit to any unscriptural authority.

A propos to the Pope and the Pretender, have you read Hooks memoirs?[3] I have been ill these ten days, otherwise I should have written to you sooner, but I sat up the day before yesterday in my bed and read them thro' with infinite satisfaction, tho they are by no means well written. The substance of what is in them I knew before tho not in such detail. I am afraid they are published at an unlucky time, and may throw a damp upon our militia. Nothing, however, appears to me more excusable than the disaffection of Scotland at that time. The Union was a measure from which infinite Good has been derived to this country.[4] The Prospect of that good, however, must then have appeared very remote and very uncertain. The immediate effect of it was to hurt the interest of every single order of men in the country. The dignity of the nobility was undone by it. The greater part of the Gentry who had been accustomed to represent their own country in its own Parliament were cut out for ever from all hopes of representing it in a British Parliament. Even the merchants seemed to suffer at first. The trade to the Plantations was, indeed, opened to them. But that was a trade which they knew nothing about: the trade they were acquainted with, that to France, Holland and the Baltic, was laid under new embarrassments which almost totally annihilated the two first and most important branches of it. The Clergy too, who were then far from insignificant, were alarmed about the Church. No wonder if at that time all orders of men conspired in cursing a measure so hurtful to their immediate interest. The views of their Posterity are now very different; but those views could be seen by but few of our forefathers, by those few in but a confused and imperfect manner.

It will give me the greatest satisfaction to hear from you. I pray you write to me soon. Remember me to the Franklins.[5] I hope I shall have the Grace to write to the youngest by next post to thank him in the name both of the College and of myself for his very agreable present.[6] Remember me

---

[3] Nathaniel Hooke, *The Secret History of Colonel Hooke's Negotiations in Scotland, in Favour of the Pretender; in 1707* (London, 1760). GUL copy has Smith's bookplate and a pencilled note from this letter.

[4] See WN I.xi.m.13 and I.xi.b.8 for discussions of the economic effects of the Union, e.g. the fall in the price of wool and the rise in that of cattle; also, V.iii.89 for analysis of political effects.

[5] Benjamin Franklin (1706–90), American printer, man of letters, scientist, and statesman; intimate friend of Strahan; had visited Glasgow in the autumn of 1759 with his son William (1731–1813), who was the last royal Governor of New Jersey. The elder Franklin was interested in economics and wrote on that subject. Together with Smith, he was a believer in the value of high wages as a spur to productivity, not then a common view (see J. A. Schumpeter, *History of Economic Analysis*, New York, 1954).

[6] Not traced.

likewise to Mr Griffiths.[7] I am greatly obliged to him for the very handsom Character he gave of my book in his review. I ever am Dear Strahan

Most faithfully, Sincerely yours

Adam Smith

51. *To* LORD SHELBURNE

MS., Bowood Libr., Marquess of Lansdowne; Scott 253–4 (in part).

Glasgow, 15 July 1760

My Lord

I send your Lordship enclosed in the same packet with this letter Mr. Fitzmaurices receipts for the money he has got from me since the beginning of November last. The Sum, you will see, is upwards of ninety Pounds. I did not propose to trouble your Lordship upon this subject till November next. But I happened unluckily to catch cold in March last and I suffered this illness, thro' carelessness, to hang about me till within these three weeks. I then thought I had got entirely the better of it. But upon going into Edinburgh about ten days ago, having lain in a damp bed in a house in that neighbourhood, it returned upon me with so much violence that two days ago, My friend Dr. Cullen took me aside on the street of Edinburgh, and told me that he thought it his duty to inform me plainly that if I had any hope of surviving next winter I must ride at least five hundred miles before the beginning of September. I came home yesterday to settle my affairs which, so well as I can judge, will take me up near a fortnight. If I was in health, it would not take up two days, but at present I can give so little continued application that I have already been obliged to interrupt this letter twice in order to let the profuse sweat, which the labour of writing three lines had thrown me into, go off. I am besides obliged to employ a great deal of time in Riding. I propose going the length of York and returning by the West of England as soon as my affairs will allow me. If, indeed, I run down as fast for these ten days to come as I have done for these ten days past, I think I shall save myself the trouble and My Mother, who is my heir, the expence of following my freinds prescription.

As the expence of this proposed journey comes upon me a little unexpectedly I find myself obliged to begg that your Lordship would order payment immediately of the money I have advanced. Besides the money contained in the enclosed account Mr. Fitzmaurice owes three different accounts, two to different Booksellers and one to a Clothier. It will be three

---

[7] Ralph Griffiths (1720–1803), founder (1749), owner, and publisher (with Strahan) of the *Monthly Review*. The notice of TMS appeared anonymously in Vol. xxi (July, 1759), 1–18, but it is marked 'R' in Griffiths's own run of the periodical, now in the Bodleian, indicating that TMS was reviewed by William Rose. See Benjamin C. Nangle, *The Monthly Review, First Series, 1749–1789, Indexes of Contributors and Articles* (Oxford, 1934), 199.

or four days before I can get in these different accounts. By what he tells me they will amount to between thirty and fourty Pounds Sterling. I fancy nearer the latter than the former. I must likewise beg of your Lordship to remit the last of these sums upon trust and I shall immediately take care that the Accounts themselves be transmitted to you. I would chuse to leave him behind me free in the world and as my intended journey will run away with all my ready Cash I cannot do it otherwise.

It would be throwing away Mr. Fitzmaurices time to make him accompany me on this expedition. He has had amusement and Dissipation enough during the ten days he staid with me in Edinburgh. A longer relaxation is altogether unnecessary to one of his hardy and strong constitution. He is at present and has been ever since the rising of the College extremely well employed. He stays at home all the forenoon which Time he employs in reading the best English Authors. Immediately after dinner he read with me L'Esprit des Loix for an hour or more till I caught my Last cold. That lecture is now, indeed, probably at an end for this Summer. The Evening he spends in exercises, in Dancing or in learning the exercise of an Officer and a Soldier. He learns them with no other view than to form his body, for I do not discover in him the least inclination towards the army. He has less disposition towards those parts of Science which are in some respects the objects of taste; than towards the mathematical and mechanical learning. In these he makes extraordinary progress but seems to have less time for what is called polite literature and his mind is in some respects like his body, rather strong and firm and masculine than very graceful or very elegant. No man can have a stronger or a more steady resolution to act what, he thinks, the right part, and if you can once satisfy him that any thing is fit to be done you may perfectly depend upon his doing it. To this excellent disposition he joins a certain hardness of character, if I may call it so, which hinders him from suiting himself, so readily as is agreeable, to the different situations and companies in which he has occasion to act. The great outlines of essential duty which are always the same, you may depend upon his never transgressing, but those little properties which are continually varying and for which no certain rule can be given he often mistakes. He has upon this account little address and cannot easily adjust himself to the different characters of those whom he desires to gain. He had learned at Eton a sort of flippant smartness which, not having been natural to him at first, has now left him almost entirely. In a few months more it will probably fall off altogether. The real bottom of his character is very grave and very serious, and by the time he is five and twenty, whatever faults he has will be the faults of the grave and serious character, with all its faults the best of Characters. I heard some time in April last that his companions accused him of narrowness. I told him of it immediately, and he soon explained to me what had given occasion to the accusation. I have ever since been more liberal to him and soon after gave him first six and then four Pounds to spend during the time of the Assizes. This has raised a good deal the article for pocket. As I am thoroughly convinced that there is now no chance of his ever being a spendthrift, I do not think that it could have any good effect to pinch him at present and it might have a very bad one. Take him altogether he is one of the best young men I have known, and since he came here has done more good than I ever knew anybody do in the same time. I have not the least fear that any thing will go wrong in my absence. I do not propose being away above a month. He will be in my house and have the conversation and assistance of several of my colleagues whenever he pleases to call for it. Independent of this my confidence in his own steadyness is now perfect and entire, and my illness will only be the loss of a lecture to him. Remember me in the most respectful manner to Lady Shelburne. I began this letter in the forenoon and finish it at night. It has been the labour of almost a day, you may judge how often I have been obliged to interrupt it. I am with the greatest respect

Your Lordships

most Obliged and obedient

Servant

Adam Smith

Mr. Fitzmaurice has gone out and has forgot to leave the Accounts with the vouchers of his receipts. Your Lordship will receive them in another packet by next post. His receipts come by this post in a packet by themselves. Your Lordship will observe that the date of his receipt for the jaunt to Edinburgh is yesterday, the day we came home and settled accounts. He had received the money as he had occasion for it and kept the rest of it. The same was the case of several of his other receipts, their dates are often posterior to the real time in which the money was received.

[Endorsed: 'July 15. 1760. Mr. Smith of Glasgow giving account of his ill state of health and desiring a remittance of Money on acct. of my Son Thomas. I have accordingly remitted to him two Drafts on Gosling & Co. for £100 each this 23 July 1760.']

52. *To* LORD SHELBURNE

MS., Bowood Libr., Marquess of Lansdowne; unpubl.

Glasgow, 11 Nov. 1760

My Lord

Mr Fitzmaurice being at present indisposed with sore eyes I write this letter to make his apology to your Lordship and to Lady Shelburne for his not having written so regularly of late as usual. He got cold at Inveraray, the effect of which was to make the scurvy on his face strike in and fall upon his eyes. They were, he tells me, ill there, and have been so ever since his return. These three days he has been confined to a dark room. Had he taken proper care of them immediately upon his return, they probably would have given him less trouble. But his manliness hinders him from being so careful of his person, or as attentive to the first beginning of Disorder as I would wish him. The inflammation is in the ball of one of his eyes. By the application of Leeches it is this day a good deal reduced and he is free from all pain. I have no doubt, as he has at last agreed to sit at home for all the remaining part of this week and read none, that by the beginning of next week they will be well. Till they are so and he is able to write himself I shall write either to your Lordship or to Lady Shelburne every post to inform you how they are. I reckon this accident a little unlucky as he must probably use them very sparingly on account of the weakness which may remain when the inflammation is entirely gone; He had resumed his studies with great spirit immediately on his return and did not appear to have been at all dissipated by his journey. While I make his apology I am sensible that I have much more reason to make my own for having, without any such excuse, so long neglected to thank your Lordship for the many obligations your Lordship and Lady Shelburne laid me under while at Wycombe.[1] I shall, however, trust entirely to your goodness in this respect for forgiveness, and without any take the liberty to subscribe myself your Lordships

> most Obliged and
> most Obedient Servant
> Adam Smith

[Endorsed: 'Nov.11.1760 Mr Smith with account of my Son Thomas his Complaint in his Eyes I sent this letter to the Bishop of Killala by post Nov. 20 1760. Answer'd Nov. 25. 1760'.]

53. *To* LORD SHELBURNE

MS., Bowood Libr., Marquess of Lansdowne; unpubl.

Glasgow, 11 Nov. 1760

My Lord

It was not in my Power to write to your Lordship by either of the two Last Posts. The hour that I had set aside for that purpose was broke in upon by business that would not allow a moments delay. Mr Fitzmaurices eyes are much better. He has been abroad, yesterday to take the air in a

---

[1] Smith had presumably visited Lord Shelburne's home on the jaunt anticipated in Letter 51, but nothing is recorded about this occasion.

Post Chaise, today to attend his Classes. He is still, however, obliged to wear a piece of Black Silk over them and cannot yet venture to use them. He will probably be able to write to Lady Shelburne tomorrow or next day. I am your Lordships

Most obliged and

most humble Servant

Adam Smith

[Endorsed: 'Nov. 18. 1760 Mr Smith giving Account of the abatement of the Soreness in my Son Thomas his Eyes. Answer'd Nov. 25. 1760.']

54. *To* WILLIAM STRAHAN

Address: To Mr William Strahan, Printer in London
MS., Boston Public Libr., Mellen Chamberlain Autograph Collection Ch.H.12.13; Scott 254–5 (in part).

Glasgow, 30 Dec. 1760

My Dear Strahan

The opposite leaf will set before your eyes the manifold sins and iniquities you have been guilty of in printing my book. The first six, at least the first, third and fourth and sixth are what you call sins against the holy Ghost which cannot upon any account be pardoned. The Remainder are capable of remission in case of repentance, humiliation and contrition. I should have sent you them sooner.[1]

Remember me to Rose. Tell him I have not forgot what I promised him but have been excessively hurried. My Delay, I hope, will occasion him no inconvenienancy: if it does I shall be excessively concerned and shall order some papers I left in England to be given to him.[2] They are not what I would wish them, but I had rather lose a little reputation with the public as let him suffer by my negligence. It will give me infinite pleasure to hear both from him and from you.

I hear much good of our King;[3] I ever am my Dear friend

Yours

Adam Smith

Remember me to Mrs Strahan and likewise to Dr Franklin and Son.

---

[1] See the errata which follow the letter. The first six were corrected in ed. 3, 1767; of the twenty-five errors of the second group, fifteen were corrected piecemeal up to ed. 6, 1790; and the remainder were never corrected. The details are noted within square brackets on the errata list.

[2] Possibly 'Considerations concerning the First Formation of Languages', published in *The Philological Miscellany*, i (1761) 440–79, and reprinted in TMS ed. 3, 1767.

[3] On 31 Oct. 1760, a week after his accession, George III (1738–1820) issued a royal proclamation: 'For the encouragement of piety and virtue, and for preventing and punishing of vice, profaneness, and immorality.' He also declared that he 'gloried in the name of Briton'.

The following Errata must be corrected as totally disfiguring the sense

Page	Line		
17	22.	approbation. Read. disapprobation	
188	12.	justness. Read justest.	
ditto.	15.	utility - - - - inutility	
201.	30.	pleased - - - - displeased	
204.	10.	relations - - - retaliations	
375.	10.	public or private - public to private	

Errata of less consequence

Page	Line		
13	23.	occasion. Read - occasioned.	[never corrected]
47	27 [l. 26].	interests. - - - - - interest.	[corrected ed. 4]
52	31 [l. 30].	the - - - - - - - - their.	[n.c.]
53	19	turn - - - - - - - his turn	[n.c.]
56	29	force - - - - - - forces	[ed. 4]
129	24	in every respect - - - and in every respect.	[ed. 6]
131	21	himself - - - - - - - myself	[ed. 3]
150	33	Tis - - - - - - - - - Its	[ed. 3]
161	6	last to all - - - - - last of all, to	['lastly', ed. 6]
180	29	will - - - - - - - - - would	[ed. 6]
183	28 [l. 26]	the - - - - - - - - - this	[ed. 4]
185	2	consequence - - - - - consequences	[n.c.]
187	17	men - - - - - - - - - man	[n.c.]
190	3	efforts. - - - - - - - effort.	[n.c.]
211	18	to this - - - - - - - - - to do this.	[ed. 3]
219	27	this even - - - - - - - even this	[ed. 3]
220.	20	call - - - - - - - - - - calls	[ed. 3]
252	30	loss of acquisition - - loss or acquisition.	[ed. 6]
289	21	his - - - - - - - - - this	[n.c.]
296	20 [l. 17]	measure or verse - - - - measure of verse	[n.c.]
306	26	these - - - - - - - - - the	[n.c.]
315	29 [l. 28]	the - - - - - - - - - - this	[ed. 3]
330	37 [l. 27]	subject - - - - - - - - subjects	[ed. 6]
349	30 [l. 29]	expose - - - - - - - - exposed	[ed. 3]
408	30	to what - - - - - - - Or to what.	[n.c.]

55. *From* LORD CARDROSS[1]

MS., GUL Gen. 1035/140; unpubl.

St. Andrews, 6 June 1761

Dear Sir,

The post will bring this and a Letter[2] from my Father at the same Time, Begging your Interest and Assistance in an Affair which deeply concerns us both. It will be needless for me to recapitulate the nature of this affair or the Circumstances which render the Success of our Sollicitation, much to be wished for and of great Importance to our Family.

The Multiplyed Civilities and Kindnesse's I have receiv'd at Your Hands, have Emboldened me to Second my Father's Letter to you, assuring you of my Gratitude for these Marks of your Goodness and Friendship to me.

I won't follow the common System of Letters of Sollicitation in setting forth the merits of the Object for whom we Sollicit; If my Brother[3] is honour'd by your University to be their Exhibitioner,[4] He will come and remain at Glasgow to study with You and I flatter myself will give more Substantial proofs of his merit and Capacity than I would do were I to write a Quire of Paper upon the Head; Indeed these Encomiums are always fulsome, Ill timed, and Disagreeable.

As I have heard you say you compleated your Studys at Oxford, It will be needless for me to Display the many Unavoidable Expenses to which a Student of any Denomination is Liable but particularly a Lad of Rank and a Lively Spirit; These Motives Induced Lord Buchan to ask the first vacancy of the High Exhibitions that you are not Enter'd into Engagements for; as the Nature of an Entailed Estate does not Admitt of large Allowances to his Children; the Proffitts of the Exhibition would remove a part of the Expense which the Education of a Churchman Incurrs, and the Objections which were laid to my Brothers following The Strong Inclinations He has for the Church. I have taken the Liberty to Inclose a Letter to Mr Fitzmaurice,[5] I beg you will Remember me to Mrs Smith, and

---

[1] The cover is endorsed with a note stating that the letter is from the 'son of the Earl of Buchan', i.e. David Stewart Erskine (1742–1829) later 11th Earl of Buchan, who left somewhat unreliable reminiscences of his time as a student at Glasgow under Smith (GUL Buchan MSS.). He founded the Society of Antiquaries of Scotland, and wrote literary biographies and essays.

[2] Letter not traced; the fa. was the 10th Earl of Buchan.

[3] Henry Erskine (1746–1817) lawyer, politician, poet, and wit: when he was presented to Johnson by Boswell in 1773, he dropped a shilling into Boswell's hand, whispering that 'it was for the sight of his *bear*' (BLJ v.39, n.4). He was educated at St Andrews, Edinburgh, and Glasgow; advocate 1768; Lord Advocate 1783, 1806; Dean of Faculty 1785–95; condemned the Sedition and Treason Bills of 1795 as unconstitutional—his equally brilliant bro. Thomas (1750–1823) fought against them in the English courts; M.P. 1806–7; Commissioner to inquire into the administration of justice in Scotland 1808.

[4] Snell Exhibition.   [5] Hon. Thomas Fitzmaurice.

Miss Douglass. I have heard nothing of Poor Dr Lindsay[6] which makes me hope His Distemper has abated.

I Know your Usual Indulgence will Induce you to forgive my troubling you with this Letter So I finish this without any other Apology than Assuring You That I am

Dear Sir

with Sincere Regard

your Obliged

and Humble Servant

[signature cut out]

P.S. Pray Remember me Kindly to Mr Fitzmaurice. Something has c[ome] in the which prevents my writing this Post.

56. *From* ROBERT CULLEN[1]

Address: To Mr Adam Smith, Professor of Moral Philosophy, College at Glasgow
MS., GUL Gen. 1035/141; Scott 255.

Edinburgh, 24 June 1761

Dear Sir

My Papa intended to have writ you this night himself but he is this day in particular so excessively hurried that he has not a moments time to sit down. He has therefore desired me to write for him. We are excessively sorry to hear that you have had the misfortune to lose Mr Buchanan. My Papa desires me to inform you that if you would desire a Successor to him, a young man of very good parts of a Literary turn one who has applied with Success to the Oriental Languages and one who would be contented with that Place alone you may find such a one in Dr Cumings[2] Son Peter.[3] I am Sir

Your most humble Servant

Robert Cullen

---

[6] Hercules Lindesay, Professor of Civil Law (d. 1761).

[1] Robert Cullen (?1740–1810), s. of Dr. William Cullen; educ. Glasgow ('the best student I ever had', according to Smith) and Edinburgh; lived with Lord Kames; advocate, 1764; Lord of Session (Lord Cullen) 1796; Lord Commissioner of Justiciary 1799.

[2] Patrick Cumin or Cuming (1695–1776), D.D., Minister of the Old Kirk, Edinburgh, and Professor of Church History there, 1737–62, then of Divinity; one time leader of the moderate party in the Church of Scotland; much consulted by the 3rd Duke of Argyll about patronage in Scotland; called 'Dr Turnstile' by the *literati* for his feeble behaviour in the affair of Home's *Douglas*.

[3] Patrick Cumin (1741–1820), 3rd s. of Dr. Patrick Cumin. Hume also wrote to Smith on his behalf (Letter 57, dated 29 June 1761), and Cumin was elected Professor of Oriental Languages on 26 Oct. 1761. In addition to his own subject, he taught French and Italian. Though he had retired from active teaching in 1814, his death marked the end of fifty-nine years' tenure of his Chair, which remains a record at Glasgow.

57. *From* DAVID HUME

Address: To Mr Professor Smith at Glasgow
MS., RSE ii. 31; HL i. 345–6.

Ninewells, 29 June 1761

Dear Smith.

As your Professorship of Hebrew is vacant, I have been applyd to in behalf of young Mr Cummin,[1] and you are the Person with whom I am supposed to have some Interest. But as I imagine you will not put this Election on the Footing of Interest, I shall say nothing on that head; but shall speak much more to the Purpose, by informing you, that I have known Mr Cummin for some time, and have esteemed him a young Man of exceeding good Capacity, and of a Turn towards Literature. He tells me, that he has made the Oriental Tongues and particularly the Hebrew a Part of his Study and has made some Proficiency in them: But of this Fact, craving his Pardon, I must be allowd to entertain some Doubt: For if Hebrew Roots, as Cowley says, thrive best in barren Soil,[2] he has a small Chance of producing any great Crop of them. But as you commonly regard the Professorship of Hebrew as a Step towards other Professorships, in which a good Capacity can better display itself; you will permit me to give it as my Opinion, that you will find it difficult to pitch on a young Man, who is more likely to be a Credit to your College, by his Knowlege and Industry.

I am so far on my Road to London, where I hope to see you this Season. I shall lodge in Miss Elliots Lisle Street Leicester Fields; and I beg it of you to let me hear from you the Moment of your Arrival.[3] I am Dear Smith

Yours sincerely
David Hume

58. *From* DR. WILLIAM LEECHMAN

Address: To Mr Adam Smith, Professor of Moral Philosophy in the University of Glasgow
MS., GUA University MSS. vol. 30. 62–5; Scott 200.

Glasgow July 15th 1761

Sir,

I acquaint you and the other Professors by this that unless the Rector himself[1] is to be present in the Meeting to preside there can be no meeting

[1] Patrick Cumin: see Letter 56 from Robert Cullen, dated 24 June 1761, n. 3.
[2] Hume is recalling the couplet by Samuel Butler:

> For Hebrew roots although th'are found
> To flourish most in barren ground

Hudibras Pt. i, canto i, 59–60.

[3] Smith visited London some time between 27 Aug. and 15 Oct. 1761.

[1] Lord Erroll.

today as I have already resigned the Office of Vice-Rector.[2] I likewise by this inform you that His Majesty has been graciously pleased by his Royal letter dated at St James's the 6th of July to nominate me to be principal which I have also intimated to the Lord Rector and as soon as it can be done shall qualifye before the Presbytery and desire the Rector to call a meeting for my admission. Please to communicate this to all the Gentlemen my colleagues.

I am Sir your most obedient humble Servt
Sic Subscribitur Will. Leechman

59. *From* LORD ERROLL[1]

MS., GUA University MSS. vol. 30. 95 (copy); James Coutts, *A History of the University of Glasgow* (Glasgow, 1909), 243.

London, 27 Oct. 1761

Dear Sir

I am this moment come from Lord Bute, and he desires me to inform the University that the King's orders are that you immediately vacate Mr Rouets place de novo,[2] and that every thing may be done in a legal way,[3] as

---

[2] Adam Smith as Vice-Rector had called a University Meeting for 15 July 1761 to admit John Millar as Professor of Law and to elect a Professor of Oriental Languages. By this letter Leechman sought to exert his influence, but Smith's colleagues considered they had been legally summoned to meet. Entreaties to attend the meeting were carried by Smith to Leechman but he refused, so the Meeting proceeded without him. Its acts were confirmed at another University Meeting attended by the Rector on 26 Aug. 1761. See Scott 200–2. This affair led to a controversy about the respective powers of the Rector and Principal: Scott 91–6, 202–19.

[1] James Hay (1726–78), 15th Earl of Erroll and High Constable of Scotland; Lord Rector of Glasgow University, 1760–1.

[2] In Sept. 1759, William Rouet deserted his Chair of Church History to act as travelling tutor to Lord Hope, eldest son of the Earl of Hopetoun. The University Meeting of 2 Feb. 1760 declared the Chair vacant but Rouet was not cited beforehand. The minutes of this Meeting and other documents were sent to Erroll for presentation to the Government and this is his reply. He alludes also to a loyal address on the King's marriage.

[3] Erroll's letter was read at the Meeting of 11 Nov. 1761, which resolved 'to send Mr Smith and Mr Millar [John Millar, Professor of Civil Law] to Edinburgh to consult two Advocates Viz Mr James Ferguson of Pitfour and Mr James Burnet of [Monboddo] upon the legality of the Sentence of the University meeting of the 2d of February 1760 by which Sentence the Professorship of Ecclesiastical History in this University was declared vacant, particularly upon the following Queries [:] Query 1st Does the want of the formality of a Summons invalidate the Sentence of the University in the particular circumstances of the affair of Mr Rouet? Query 2d Is the Action of deserting his office after leave of absence has been refused relevant to infer the censure that is passed [upon] the conduct of Mr Rouet in the body of the Sentence?' Smith and Millar gave in the advice of the advocates on 26 Nov. to the effect that want of a citation was a material defect in the proceedings. The decision of 2 Feb. 1760 was reversed and Rouet was cited to appear at Glasgow on 19 Jan. 1762. He did not appear but sent a letter of resignation from Utrecht dated 22 Dec. 1761, holding out for his salary. He finally got a favourable decision about his salary in 1767.

soon as that is done His Majesty will appoint a Successor.[4] There is a Necessity of complying with this else it may be of the worst consequences to the University, I could do no more, I said all that was possible but to no effect. One thing Lord Bute told me is that he is engaged to no body, but that the man who is recommended as the fittest for filling the place properly will be his man. I beg to hear from you soon on this Subject, and I likewise hope our address will be Sent up immediately. With my compliments to all my friends I ever am

most Sincerely Yours

Sic Subs.   Erroll

60. *To* JOSHUA SHARPE[1]

MS., Houghton Libr., Harvard, Eng. 870 (57) 124; unpubl.

Glasgow, 2 Nov. 1761

Dear Sir

I am desired by the University to beg of you to consult Mr Wedderburn about the propriety of pushing a separate agreement with the Lessee in the way that I talked of to you, and to take his advice about every part of the future management of that affair. I shall write to Oxford to press the Agreement with Baliol College. I ever am

Dear Sir

Your most humble

Servant

Adam Smith

61. *From* ADAM FERGUSON

Address: To Mr Adam Smith, Professor of Philosophy in The College of Glasgow.
MS., GUL Gen. 1035/142; Scott 255–6.

Edinburgh, 5 Nov. 1761

Dear Sir

Two or three days before I got your letter I happened to be applyed to by Mr Alexander Merchant here,[1] to recommend a young man if I knew

---

[4] William Wight (1730–82), a relation and intimate friend of Dr. Alexander Carlyle, formerly a Presbyterian minister in Dublin, was elected Rouet's successor; in 1778, he became Professor of Divinity at Glasgow.

[1] London solicitor with a Chancery practice; he dealt with Glasgow University business, in particular, the long-standing dispute with Balliol College about the Snell Exhibitions: see Scott 156, 161–3.

[1] Perhaps William or Robert Alexander, the 'sons' represented in William Alexander and Sons, bankers and merchants in Edinburgh who held for many years the Scottish

any fit to be tutor to his Son. I immediately carryed your letter to him and he is perfectly Satisfyed with the recommendation and I am well Satisfyed that as far as relates to Mr Alexander himself and his family your friend[2] will have every reason to applaud his good fortune in meeting with him. He has very right Ideas with respect to his Children and very noble ones with respect to the person whom he trusts with the charge of them. He told me when he first mentioned this Subject that it would be a pleasure to him to meet with such a Young Man as he coud forward through life and that he woud not scruple to risk of his fortune in doing it if his Subject was promising. The only difficulty with Mr Alexander with respect to your Friend is that his view to Physic may carry him away from him sooner than he woud wish. And it may be a difficulty with your friend that the two boys of whom the charge is proposed to him are so young the one being eight and the other six but they are equally advanced being to begin the Latin together. He proposes that they shall attend the Public School while they have the advantage of a Tutor at home. He leaves the terms to you or me and will be inclined to increase them as the boys advance especially if that will induce a person to his mind to continue with him the full time. Remember me affectionately to J. Black and all friends with you. Youll please let me know your friends resolution when he had determined himself. I am Dear Sir

Your most affectionate
humble Servant
Adam Ferguson

62. *From* DAVID LYLE[1]

Address: To Mr Professor Smith in the University of Glasgow
MS., GUL Gen. 1035/143; unpubl.

London, 12 Nov. 1761

[He has missed seeing Smith in London and wishes to have a place at the Board of Works. When he gets one, he will present his 'new mathematical instruments' to the King. He asks Smith to write a covering letter to the 2nd Earl of Shelburne to accompany a gift of 'Volume Compasses'. He comments on the elder Pitts' resignation as Prime Minister, Oct. 1761, as that of 'too great and too violent a man to be a servant to a young King of our sovereign's disposition'.]

contract from the French Farmers General of Tobacco. Robert Alexander was a candidate in the notorious Anstruther Burghs parliamentary election of 1776 (HP i. 499).

[2] Not identified.

[1] ? David Lyle, Glasgow M.A. 1755; possibly the man described in DNB as a stenographer and author of *The Art of Shorthand Improved* (1762).

63. *From* THOMAS WALLACE[1]

Address: Mr Smith, Professor of Moral Philosophy, Glasgow
MS., GUL Gen. 1035/144; unpubl.

Dunlop, 4 Jan. 1762

Sir,

Please receive Mr Maupertuis works and at the Same time my most
hearty thanks for having put me on a peice of reading that has given me So
much pleasure—but however well he writes you must allow me to Say
that the System he concludes his Venus physique with is every whit as un-
philosophical as any of those he runs down and that in any other hand it
must have made a very poor figure.[2]

Pray did you observe how much he weakens his own Arguments for his
new principle from which he deduces the Laws of motion Staticks and
mechanicks Viz that the quantity of Action employ'd by nature is always
a minimum. One cannot help being Struck by the notion of that universal
Saving but when he applys the principle to Staticks One is Surpriz'd to
find it either a maximum or a minimum.

Again I must thank you for the pleasure you have given me. I wish I
could make you a proper return but I most Sincerely am

Sir

Your most humble Servant

Thomas Wallace

If you have any commands for our Side of the country I shall be glad to
receive them.[3] We Sett [? out] first fair day. My compliments to Mrs
Smith.

64. *From* HON. THOMAS FITZMAURICE

MS., GUL Gen. 1035/145; unpubl.

St. Mary Hall, Oxford, Friday 26 Feb. 1762

My Dear Smith

I have this instant receiv'd your Letter of the 19th Inst.[1] nor do I delay
to give you any satisfaction that lies in my power. The Letter which you

---

[1] ? Sir Thomas Wallace tutored by Patrick Clason; see Letter 131 from David Hume,
dated 27 June 1772.

[2] GUL has *Œuvres de Mr De Maupertius. Nouvelle edition, corrigée et argumentée*, 4 t.
(Lyons, 1756). The 2nd vol. contains *Venus Physique*, see 243–51, Lettre XI: 'Sur ce qui
s'est passé à l'occasion du principe de la moindre quantité d'action'.

[3] Dunlop in Ayrshire is famous for cheese-making.

[1] Not traced.

wrote to my Brother I saw and think that had it been for an Affair of £10,000 instead of £200 it could not have been more accurately drawn up, so anxious were you to clear yourself of what you imagin'd my Lady Shelburne[2] thought was in you unfair dealing, which you were just as clear of before you took that trouble as anything could possibly make you, even in *her Eyes*. I give you my Word that the Account itself was found and I made that appear to my Mother to be perfectly exact and right which she once, Indeed I can assure you 'twas but for a very short time, by my giddiness thought was somewhat otherwise. The reason that I did not write to you sooner concerning this matter, was, because my Brother said he would write himself, which, tho' he has not done I am not very much surpris'd upon account of his Politics which have of late been rather intricate, which by this time I dare say you must have heard of.[3] During this last vacation of Dr Blackstones[4] I spent five weeks in London. The two first I spent with My Lady Shelburne in Hanover Square, the 3 last with my Brother in a New House which he has taken in Hill Street late belonging to Lord Weymouth[5] a very good one.

My Brother told me that he had had a letter from you to me inclos'd to him but that he had put it up with some other papers and could not get at it which was in shorter words that he had lost it, so that for the future as your Letters will always be very agreable to me and as they come but Seldom, I should be glad if, whether you have a Frank or no, you would send them to me directly to Oxford and the oft'ner they come, I need not assure you that they will be the more acceptable.

My Mother has desir'd me to ask you concerning the Epitaph which I told her you promis'd to take into Consideration but that you were not certain whether you could do it or no. I inclose to you a Letter from the Bishop of Killala[6] to me concerning Godfrey[7] which I shall tell him I leave entirely to you as being the most proper person in the World to get information from, should be glad if you would take the trouble to answer. I hope Mr Godfrey is going on well pray my Compliments to him. Your young People are in general rather brighter than they were in my time I'm told at present.

[2] Writer's mother, widow of 1st Earl of Shelburne.

[3] The 2nd Earl of Shelburne at this time was acting as a link between Henry Fox and Lord Bute who became First Lord of the Treasury on 29 May. The issue dividing the cabinet was that of making peace with France.

[4] Fitzmaurice was attending the Oxford law lectures of William Blackstone; see Letter No. 27, n. 5.

[5] Thomas Thynne (1734–96), 3rd Viscount and 1st Marquis of Bath (created 1789), 'a man of dissipated and extravagant tastes' (*The Complete Peerage*, ed. Hon. Vicary Gibbs); made Lord Lieutenant of Ireland, 1764, but never set foot there though he drew the attached salary and allowances.

[6] Nicholas Synge (d. 1771), 2nd s. of the Archbishop of Tuam; advanced to see of Killaloe, 1746.

[7] ? Luke Godfrey, M.A. 1763, D.D. 1795; later Rector of Middleton, County Cork.

I attend Chapple very regularly and Dr. Blackstone more so whose Lectures during the next Summer I hope to make myself more Master of than I am at present.

I am oblig'd to you for delivering My Message to Prof. Wilson[8] but have not as yet receiv'd the Thermometers.

Drs King and Smith and Riall[9] are all well. They desire their Compliments to you.

The Expence of this place is prodigious. Tradesmen certainly make at least cent. per cent. of their Money here. I have often heard you say that Coals were very expensive here, it is very extraordinary that they have they have cost me since I came upwards of £12.

There is as much good Company here just now as have been for this many years.—Lord Pembrokes[10] Affair with Miss Hunter makes a prodigious noise just now and indeed very Justly 'tis the oddest thing I ever heard of; They have [taken] his Regiment and his Bed-Chambership from him. They say he can never return to England again. The story is, if You should not have heard it, that he has run away with Miss. Hunter a young Lady of equal Beauty and Fashion. They say they are gone to Bremen in Germany. He did it with premeditation too. You know he is remarkable for having a very Handsome Wife a Daughter of the Duke of Marlborough, whom he never us'd well.

Pray have you seen Dr Louths English Grammar[11] which is just come out? It is talk'd of much. Some of the *ingenious men* with whom this University overflows, are picking faults and finding Errors in it at present. Pray what do you think of it? I am going to read Harris's Hermes[12] now, having read this Grammar. I heard lately an objection to an Expression in your Book, which I think has some foundation. It is in the Beginning of the 1st Section upon Custom: the Expression is a *Haunch* Button, which is not, I imagine exactly English.[13]

I saw your Friend Michael Ramsay[14] in London as also young Alexander

---

[8] Alexander Wilson.

[9] Friends of Adam Smith from his time at Oxford: on John Smith, see Letter 15, n. 4, also Scott 39; James King, D.D. 1740; ? relative of Samuel Riall, matriculated at Glasgow in 1756, entered St Mary's Hall, Oxford, 1761.

[10] Henry Herbert (1734–94), Earl of Pembroke; after his affair with Catherine (Kitty) Hunter, dau. of a Lord of Admiralty, he had 'amorous connexions' with several ladies of less note (*The Complete Peerage*).

[11] Robert Lowth or Louth (1710–87), D.D. 1753; Bishop of London 1777; Professor of Poetry at Oxford 1741–50; published lectures on Hebrew poetry (1753), *A Short Introduction to English Grammar* (1762), and a new translation of Isaiah (1778).

[12] James Harris (1709–80), M.P. 1761–80; Lord of Treasury 1763–5; published *Hermes: or a Philosophical Inquiry concerning Universal Grammar* (1751).

[13] TMS ed. 1, 1759, p. 292 (V.1): 'we find a meanness or awkwardness in the absence even of a haunch button.' The word was kept up to and including ed. 6, 1790, and seems to be good enough English (see OED).

[14] Michael Ramsay of Mungale, inclined at first to take orders in the Church of England but accepted posts as travelling tutor to families of Earls of Home and Eglintoun; later

the Merchant[15] just come from France, both of whom wer going to Scotland with one of Whom I intended to have sent a parcel containing Dr Blacks [? scale] of Faranheits Thermometer and a Book of Robin Foulis's both of which were pack'd up without my knowledge. Pray make my Compliments to both these Gentlemen as likewise to all my other good Friends of the College. Pray how does Mrs Smith and Miss. Douglas do do not forget me, by any means to them and Believe me to be

With very great Sincerity your very Affectionate
Thomas Fitzmaurice

P.S. I need not tell you that I shall be glad to hear from you as soon as may be Convenient, tho' to you I think I may say rather sooner than that. Do not forget [me] to Doctor Simson my old Friend. Dr Johnston is, I hear, at last dead.[16]

65. *To* WILLIAM JOHNSTONE

Address: To William Johnstone Esqr, Advocate, Edinburgh
MS., Pierpont Morgan Libr., New York; unpubl.

Glasgow, Tuesday 9 Mar. 1762

Dear Johnstoune

This Letter will be delivered to you by Mr Trail[1] who has been sent in from the College to consult your sage headpiece with regard to a point of Law along with Lockart.[2] He has also directions to take a private advice from you with regard to a point which is not to be communicated to any other Person whatever. You will find him an excessive clever fellow, I therefor recommend him to you as an acquaintance as well as a client. Remember me respectfully to Mrs Johnstoune[3] and believe me most faithfully yours

Adam Smith

Chamberlain to the Duke of Roxburgh; early intimate friend of David Hume and Lord Kames.

[15] ? John Alexander, 3rd son of William Alexander (d. 1761); see Letter 61 from Ferguson, dated 5 Nov. 1761.

[16] Dr John Johnstoun, died 26 Jan. 1762, Professor of Medicine at Glasgow; showed an aversion to teaching and was suspended in 1718: he allowed Dr William Cullen to teach *c.* 1746.

[1] Robert Trail (d. 1775), Professor of Divinity at Glasgow.

[2] Alexander Lockhart (1701–82); advocate 1772; Dean of Faculty 1764; Lord of Session, as Lord Covington, 1775; for many years he was the leader of the Scottish Bar, noted for his torrent of eloquence as a pleader.

[3] William Johnstone md. 10 Nov. 1760 Frances (d. 1782), dau. and heiress of Daniel Pulteney (1st cousin of William Pulteney, Earl of Bath).

66. *To* SIR GILBERT ELLIOT, LORD MINTO[1]

Address: To the Honourable The Lord Minto, Edinburgh
MS., GUL Gen. 1465/5; unpubl.

Glasgow, 9 Apr. 1762

My Lord

I received some time ago a letter from Mr James Clarke[2] in which he informed me that your Lordship had a long time before that sent him a letter of recommendation to your Son Mr Elliot, that, however, as he had no opportunity of going to London he had sent the Letter by a friend, imagining, I suppose, that it was necessary to deliver it immediately. Your Lordship will very easily excuse this impropriety in a very honest Tar who is not much acquainted with the way of the world. He is now of full standing to press for a Lieutenant and proposes to come to London soon in order to be examined for that purpose. By every account that I can hear he is perfectly well qualified and is, in every respect, a brave, honest and expert Seaman. He is extremely desirous that your Lordship should send him another letter to the same Purpose as the former and wrote to me to apply to you for that Purpose, which is the occasion of your getting this trouble. If your Lordship will be so good as to enclose that letter to me I shall send it to him by the first Post. He is doing well in every sense of the word and has even made a little money which he has disposed of in favour of his Sister. All the family, indeed, behave very well and I hope will do credit to their friends. I am My Lord, with very great respect,

your Lordships most obliged
and most Obedient
Servant
Adam Smith

67. *To* JOSHUA SHARPE

Address: To Mr Joshua Sharpe, Lincolns Inn, London
MS., GUA MS/B/15625; unpubl.

Glasgow College, 15 June 1762

Sir

We have had of Late several remonstrances from the Exhibitioners on Snells foundation at Balliol College complaining that they yet enjoy but a very small part of the Advantages which they expect to derive from the

[1] Sir Gilbert Elliot (1693–1766); advocate 1715; M.P. 1722–6; Lord of Session 1726; Lord Commissioner of Justiciary 1733; Lord Justice-Clerk, 1763–6; father of Smith's friend Gilbert Elliot, then a Lord of Admiralty.
[2] Not identified.

late degree in Chancery[1] and that those which they do enjoy are by no means the most essential. What they mean, no doubt, is that they have yet received no part of the augmentation of the pecuniary appointment which was decreed to them, which, I suppose, is occasioned by the delays which may have occurred in settling the conjunct Agreement. I wrote to Dr King of St. Mary Hall[2] to apply to Balliol College to give orders to Mr Cater[3] to give his consent to the Agreement, and received soon after enclosed in a letter from Dr. King an unsigned paper which in his letter he said was delivered to him by Mr Watkins of B.C.[4] in which it was said that Balliol College was very well disposed towards the Agreement and that they would soon write to Mr Cater in such terms as was desired. In your letter to Mr Simson of the 8th of March last you say 'that Balliol College has become very tractable of Late and we are going on quite amicably before the Master to settle the division of the lands the scheme of which I have laid before Mr Wedderburn as you desir'd and I hope it will be at last brought to a speedy conclusion'. My application to Dr King, therefor, I hope, has not been altogether ineffectual. We would beg to know at present what it is that hinders the final conclusion of this Agreement, in order that we may be able to give some satisfaction to the very natural and reasonable impatience of the young Gentlemen upon that foundation. In a letter of yours to Mr Simson of an earlier date than the foregoing, I think it was in the October preceeding, you seemed to think that if proper application was made to Balliol College, the conjunct agreement might be concluded in the ensuing term. I can very easily, however, imagine the difficulties which might occu[r] in the conduct of so very complex a transaction.

I write you this letter in the Presence and by the appointment of the University meeting, who likewise desire me to acquaint you that as our late worthy Collegue Dr Simson has resigned his office[5] on account of his age, Dr Joseph Black Professor of Medicine is now Clerk to the University. The University meeting desires, theref[ore] that for the future you would correspond either with him or with me as you think proper. Remember me to Mr Wedderburn and tell him I have been long looking for a letter from him and believe me to be Sir

Your very humble Servant
Adam Smith

[1] The important provisions of the decree of 23 Mar. 1759 were as follows: no restraint as to conformity or ordination was to be placed on the Snell Exhibitioners; £70 per annum was to be given to the five ablest Exhibitioners and £65 to the others; vacancies were to be intimated to the College of Glasgow, and failing nomination within six months a vacancy was to be filled by Glasgow (W. Innes Addison, *The Snell Exhibitions*, Glasgow, 1901, 21).

[2] William King (1685-1763), D.C.L. 1715; Principal of St. Mary Hall from 1719.

[3] ? John Cater (b. 1704) of Farendon, Berks., M.A. Oxford 1727.

[4] ? Robert Watkins of Kentchurch, Hereford., M.A. Oxford 1728; ? associated with Balliol College.   [5] As Clerk of Senate.

68. *From* LORD ERROLL

Address: To Mr Smith, Professor of Moral Philosophy, In the University of Glasgow, by Edinburgh
MS., GUL Gen. 1035/146; unpubl.

Slains Castle, 8 July 1762

Sir

I am Extremely Sorry to hear of the Death of poor Mr Buchanan. I Really think He will be a considerable Loss to the University as He was so rising a young man. If His Place is not already fill'd up I wou'd beg Leave to Recommend to the University, Mr James Crombie.[1] I have heard a very good Character of him, and as to his Capacity you must Certainly know something of that as He has been at Glasgow with Mr Duffe.[2] As to the other Affair about Mr Ruats place, the Memorial came at a time when my mind was so much taken up In attending Poor Lady Erroll, and as the fatal Event to me, soon follow'd,[3] It was not In my power to do In It what I cou'd have wished, but I go to London In September, and then I hope I shall be able to put a favourable End to it.[4] I am with great Esteem Dear Sir

Your most Obedient Servant

Erroll

69. *To* GEORGE BAIRD[1]

Address: To Mr George Baird at Scotstoun, to the care of Mr George Oswald
MS., University of Illinois Libr., Rae 159–60.

Glasgow, 7 Feb. 1763

Dear Sir

I have read over the contents of your friends work with very great pleasure, and heartily wish it was in my power to give or to procure him all the encouragement which his ingenuity and industry deserve. I think myself greatly obliged to him for the very obliging notice he has been pleased to take of me, and should be glad to contribute any thing in my power towards compleating his design. I approve greatly of his plan for a Rational Grammar and am convinced that a work of this kind executed with his abilities and industry, may prove not only the best System of

[1] James Crombie (1730–90), educ. St. Andrews, Edinburgh, and Glasgow, 1760–4; though then nominally Minister of Llanboyd, Presbytery of Elgin; became Minister of Presbyterian, later Unitarian, congregation, Belfast 1769–70; founded the Belfast Academy and was its first Principal 1786–90

[2] Not identified

[3] Rebecca, Countess of Erroll, dau. of Alexander Lockhart, died on 2 May 1761, presumably the 'fatal event'.

[4] See Letter 59 from Erroll, dated 27 Oct 1761.

[1] Owned property at Bo'ness, Linlithgowshire; fa. of Principal George Baird of Edinburgh University (1761–1840).

Grammar, but the best System of Logic in any Language, as well as the best History of the natural progress of the Human mind in forming the most important abstractions upon which all reasoning depends. From the short abstract which Mr Ward[2] has been so good as to send me, it is impossible for me to form any very decisive judgement concerning the propriety of every part of his method, particularly of some of his divisions. If I was to treat the same subject I should endeavour to begin with the consideration of Verbs; these being, in my apprehension, the original parts of speech, first invented to express in one word a compleat event; I should then have endeavoured to shew how the Subject was divided first from the Attribute; and afterwards, how the object was distinguished from both, and in this Manner I should have tried to investigate the origin and use of all the different parts of speech and of all their different modifications, considered as necessary to express all the different qualifications and relations of any single event.[3] Mr Ward, however, may have excellent reasons for following his own method, and perhaps if I was engaged in the same task I should find it necessary to follow the same; things frequently appearing in a very different light when taken in a general view, which is the only view that I can pretend to have taken of them, and when considered in detail.

Mr Ward, when he mentions the definitions which different Authors have given of Nouns Substantive takes no notice of that of the Abbé Girard the Author of a Book called *Les vrais principes de la Langue Françoise* which made me think it might be possible that he had not seen it.[4] It is the book which first set me a thinking upon these subjects and I have received more instruction from it than from any other I have yet seen upon them. If Mr Ward has not seen it, I have it at his Service. The Grammatical Articles too in the French Encyclopedie have given me a good deal of entertainment. Very probably Mr Ward has seen both these works and as he may have considered the subject more than I have done, may think less of them.

Remember me to Mrs Baird and Mr Oswald[5] and believe me to be with great truth

Dear Sir
Sincerely yours
Adam Smith

[2] William Ward of Broughton, Master of the Grammar School at Beverley, Yorks., wrote *An Essay on Grammar, as it may be applied to the English language. In two treatises. The one speculative . . . The other practical* (London, 1765).

[3] For Smith's views on language, see his criticism of Johnson's *Dictionary* in the *Edinburgh Review* of 1755, and 'Considerations concerning the First Formation of Languages', *The Philological Miscellany*, i (1761), 440–79, also printed in TMS ed. 3, 1767.

[4] Abbé Gabriel Girard, *Les Vrais Principes de la langue françoise, ou la parole réduite en methode conformément aux lois d'usage*, 2 t. (Paris, 1747); see Bonar 75.

[5] George Oswald (1753–1819) of Scotstoun and Auchincruive, tobacco merchant in Glasgow.

70. *To* DAVID HUME

Address: To David Hume Esqr, James's Court, Edinburgh
MS., RSE vii. 31; Rae 161.

Glasgow, 22 Feb. 1763

My dear Hume

This Letter will be presented to you by Mr Henry Herbert,[1] a young Gentleman who is very well acquainted with your works, and upon that account extremely desirous of being introduced to the Author. As I am convinced that you will find him extremely agreable I shall make no apology for introducing him. He proposes to stay a few weeks in Edinburgh while the Company are in town and would be glad to have the liberty of calling upon you sometime when it suits your conveniency to receive him. If you indulge him in this, Both he and I will think ourselves infinitely obliged to you.

You have been long promising us a visit at Glasgow and I have made Mr Herbert promise to endeavour to bring you along with him. Tho you have resisted all my Sollicitations, I hope you will not resist this. I hope, I need not tell you that it will give me the greatest pleasure to see you. I ever am
My Dear Friend, Most affectionately
and Sincerely yours,
Adam Smith

71. *From* DAVID HUME

Address: To Mr Professor Smith at Glasgow
MS., RSE ii. 32; HL i. 381.

Edinburgh, 28 Mar. 1763

Dear Smith

I was obligd to you both for your kind Letter and for the Opportunity which you afforded me of making Acquaintance with Mr Herbert, who appears to me a very promising young man.[1] I set up a Chaise in May next, which will give me the Liberty of travelling about; and you may be sure a Journey to Glasgow will be one of the first I shall undertake. I intend to require with great Strictness an Account how you have been employing

[1] Henry Herbert (1741–1811) of Christian Malford, Wilts. and Highclere, Hants., cr. Baron Porchester 1780, Earl of Carnarvon 1793; educ. Eton, Oxford, and Glasgow *c.* 1762; M.P. 1768–80; Privy Councillor 1806; Master of the Horse 1806–7. Horace Walpole described him as 'a young man of great fortune and good principles'. He was a frequent speaker in the House of Commons, never attached himself to any party, and judged issues on their merits.

[1] See Letter 70 addressed to Hume, dated 22 Feb. 1763.

your Leizure; and I desire you to be ready for that purpose. Wo be to you, if the Ballance be against you. Your Friends here will also expect, that I should bring you with me. It seems to me very long since I saw you. I am Dear Smith

Yours most sincerely
David Hume

72. *From* DAVID HUME

MS., RSE ii. 33; HL i. 390–1.

Edinburgh, 21 July 1763

Dear Smith

To-day is the grand Question decided by our Judges, whether they will admit of any farther Proof with regard to the Douglas Affair, or whether they will rest contented with the Proofs already produc'd.[1] Their Partiality is palpable and astonishing; yet few people think, that they will dare to refuse enquiring into Facts so remarkable and so strongly attested. They are at present sitting, but I hope to tell you the Issue in a Postscript.[2] Our friend, Johnstone,[3] has wrote the most-super-excellentest Paper in the World, which he has promis'd to send to you this Evening in Franks. Please to deliver the enclosed to Colonel Barré.[4] I am Dear Smith

Yours most sincerely
David Hume

[1] The Douglas Cause, which 'shook the sacred security of *birth-right* in Scotland to its foundations' according to Boswell (BLJ v. 28), concerned the opposition of two claimants to the estates of Archibald, 1st and last Duke of Douglas (d. 1761). The claimants were (1) Archibald James Edward Steuart (1748–1827), acknowledged as son by the Duke's sister, Lady Jane Douglas (d. 1753), who claimed he was the surviving child of twin boys born to her in Paris when she was fifty-one; and (2) James George, 7th Duke of Hamilton (1755–69). The first claimant was served heir to the Douglas estates but actions were brought by the Hamilton trustees alleging that he was not Lady Jane Douglas's son by Col. John Steuart, but the child of a poor French worker secured to inherit the Duke of Douglas's property. In 1763 the Court of Session decided to hear further evidence, and inquiries were later set afoot in France to obtain evidence. In October 1765, Smith was sworn as a Commissioner at Toulouse for this purpose (Scott 259–60). The Court of Session heard the cause from 7 to 14 July 1767, and after seven judges had voted for each side, the Lord President (Robert Dundas of Arniston) gave his casting vote in favour of the Hamiltons. The House of Lords, however, reversed this decision on appeal in 1769 (see Letter 116 addressed to Lord Hailes, dated 5 Mar. 1769). Hume like most of the Scottish *literati* supported the Hamiltons, possibly through friendship with William Mure of Caldwell and Andrew Stuart of Torrance, WS, who were Hamilton trustees.

[2] The issue decided was that of hearing further evidence.

[3] William Johnstone (later Pulteney). His 'Paper' has not [been traced. He was an advocate for the Hamilton side and had been to France with Andrew Stuart in this connection.

[4] Isaac Barré (1726–1802), soldier and politician, M.P. for Chipping Wycombe, noted for his fiery speeches. He was a political adherent of Lord Shelburne, whose fall from office in 1763 he shared.

73. *From* DAVID HUME

Address: To Mr Professor Smith at Glasgow
MS., RSE ii. 33; HL i. 391–2.

Edinburgh, 9 Aug. 1763

My dear Friend

I have got an Invitation, accompany'd with great Prospects and Expectations, from Lord Hartford,[1] if I woud accompany him, tho' at first without any Character, in his Embassy to Paris. I hesitated much on the Acceptance of this Offer, tho' in Appearance very inviting; and I thought it ridiculous, at my Years, to be entering on a new Scene, and to put myself in the Lists as a Candidate of Fortune. But I reflected, that I had in a manner abjur'd all literary Occupations, that I resolvd to give up my future Life entirely to Amusements, that there coud not be a better Pastime than such a Journey, especially with a Man of Lord Hertford's Character, and that it wou'd be easy to prevent my Acceptance from having the least Appearance of Dependance: For these Reasons, and by the Advice of every Friend, whom I consulted, I at last agreed to accompany his Lordship, and I set out to morrow for London. I am a little hurry'd in my Preparations: But I coud not depart without bidding you Adieu, my good Friend, and without acquainting you with the Reasons of so sudden a Movement. I have not great Expectations of revisiting this Country soon; but I hope it will not be impossible but we may meet abroad, which will be a great Satisfaction to me. I am dear Smith

Yours most sincerely
David Hume

74. *From* HENRY HERBERT

MS., GUL Gen. 1035/147; unpubl. (see Scott 68 n. 2)

Aberdeen, 11 Sept. 1763

My Dear Sir

I ought to have wrote before this to have acquainted you with my Direction, I am affraid my negligence may have lost me some Letters, the last I received was at Alloa, I hope none have been sent since that; pray keep those which shall arrive after this till my return; I have seen Dr Reed.[1]

---

[1] Francis Seymour Conway (1718–94), 2nd Baron Conway; cr. Earl of Hertford 1750, and Marquis 1793; Ambassador to France 1763–5; Lord Lieutenant of Ireland 1765–6; Master of the Horse 1766; Lord Chamberlain 1766–82. He was Sir Robert Walpole's nephew and Horace Walpole's cousin.

[1] Thomas Reid (1710–96), Professor of Philosophy, King's College, Aberdeen; appointed Smith's successor at Glasgow, 1764; chief proponent of the Scottish Common Sense philosophy whose tenets seem to have been developed first by his teacher at Aberdeen, George Turnbull, and his friend Lord Kames; published his Glasgow lectures as *Essays on the Intellectual Powers of Man* (1785), and *Essays on the Active Powers of Man* (1788).

He is a very sensible man. His Book is in the press and we may expect it out this Winter;[2] Campbell[3] David Humes Antagonist is an agreable man; I met Lord Marshall[4] at Lord Panmures[5] and was much taken with him. He imagines Rousseau may come over to Scotland but at present is too ill to travel; Lord Panmures Seat is the finest I have seen since my arrival in Scotland; I leave this Place to morrow. Lord Kames is already gone to Lord Des[k]fords[6] at Bamf, I go first to Mr Ferguson of Pitfours[7] where I stay a Day or two and from thence to Lord Des[k]fords,

I met Coll Gordon[8] at the Ball here; my Compliments to all your Family and beleive me

My Dear Sir
Your Affectionate Friend
Hen. Herbert

75. *From* DAVID HUME

MS., RSE ii. 35; HL i. 394–7.

Lisle Street, Leicester Fields, 13 Sept. 1763

My dear Smith

The Settlement, which I had made in Scotland, was so much to my Mind, I had indeed struck Root so heartily, that it was with the outmost

---

[2] *An Inquiry into the Human Mind, on the Principles of Common Sense*, published in 1764, made Reid's reputation, for a time, as a philosopher who answered Hume's scepticism.

[3] George Campbell (1719–96), Principal of Marischal College, Aberdeen, from 1759; D.D. 1764; Professor of Divinity at Aberdeen 1771; his *Dissertation on Miracles* (1762), attempted to answer Hume's 'Essay on Miracles' (in *Enquiry concerning Human Understanding*); his *Philosophy on Rhetoric* (1776), was read by Hume on his death-bed.

[4] George Keith (? 1692–1778), 10th Earl Marischal of Scotland; took part in Jacobite rising of 1715 and the abortive one of 1719; attainted, fled to the Continent, and entered the service of Frederick the Great, 1745; attainder removed, 1759; befriended Rousseau when Governor of Neuchâtel, then Prussian territory.

[5] William Maule (1700–82), 1st Earl of Panmure of Forth, soldier and politician; commanded Royal Scots Fusiliers and Scots Greys; General 1770; M.P. 1735–82; his seat near Carnoustie, Angus, was built *c.* 1671, according to the plans of James Milne (d. 1667), King's Master Mason in Scotland.

[6] James Ogilvy (? 1714–70) agriculturalist; known as Lord Deskford until 1764, when he became 6th Earl of Findlater and 3rd Earl of Seafield (his grandfather holding that title was the last Lord Chancellor of Scotland); friend of Lord Kames, with whom he served on the Boards for the Improvement of Fisheries and Manufactures in Scotland and for the Forfeited Estates.

[7] James Ferguson (1700–77) of Pitfour; advocate 1722; Dean of Faculty 1760–4; Lord of Session, taking Pitfour as his title, 1764, also Lord Commissioner of Justiciary. When the Earl Marischal decided that he could not live in Scotland and sold part of his estates in 1764, Ferguson was a purchaser, thus acquiring a major political interest in Banffshire and Aberdeenshire. Ramsay of Ochtertyre (i.150) said Ferguson was 'one of the greatest and most popular lawyers of that period'.

[8] Lord Adam Gordon (? 1726–1801) soldier and politician; s. of the 2nd Duke of Gordon; Col. 66th Foot 1762–6; C.-in-C. Scotland 1782; General 1796; M.P. 1754–88.

Reluctance I could think of transplanting myself; and I began to approach towards that Age, in which these Experiments become no longer practicable with Safety. I own, that, on my arrival in London, I found every Circumstance more inviting than I had reason to expect; particularly the Characters of Lord and Lady Hertford,[1] who are allowd to be the two Persons the most unexceptionable among all the English Nobility. Even that Circumstance of Lord Hertford's Character, his great Piety, ought to make my Connexions with him more agreeable, both because it is not attended with any thing sour and rigid, and because I draw the more Honour from his Choice, while he overlookd so many seeming Objections which lay against me on that head. My Fortune also receives a great Addition during Life from the Connexion; besides many Openings to Ambition, were I so simple as to be exposed to Temptation from that Passion. But notwithstanding all these Considerations; shall I tell you the Truth? I repine at my Loss of Ease and Leizure and Retirement and Independance, and it is not without a Sigh I look backwards nor without Reluctance that I cast my Eye forwards. Is this Sentiment an Instinct which admonishes me of the Situation most proper and suitable to me? Or is it a momentary Disgust, the Effect of low Spirits, which Company and Amusement and a better State of Health will soon dissipate and remove? I must wait with Patience, till I see the Decision of this Question.

I find, that one View of Lord Hertford in engaging me to go along with him, is that he thinks I may be useful to Lord Beauchamp[2] in his Studies. That young Nobleman is generally spoke of as very amiable and very promising: But I remember, tho' faintly, to have heard from you something to the contrary, which you had from that severe Critic, Mr Herbert.[3] I shoud be obligd to you for informing me of it. I have not yet seen My Lord Beauchamp, who is at this time in Paris. We shall not leave London these three Weeks.

You have, no doubt, heard of the strange Jumble among our Ministers, and of the Negotiation open'd with Mr Pit. Never Story was told with such contrary Circumstances as that of his secret Conference with the King, and of the Terms demanded by that popular Leader. The general Outlines of the whole Story seem to be these. Lord Bute disgusted with the Ministers, who had almost universally conspir'd to neglect him, and suspecting their bottom to be too narrow, had, before Lord Egremont's[4] Death, opend a Negotiation with Mr Pit, by means of Lord Shelburn, who employ'd

---

[1] In 1741 Lord Hertford md. Isabella (1726–82), 4th dau. of the 2nd Duke of Grafton.

[2] Francis Seymour Conway, afterwards Ingram-Seymour (1743–1822), Lord Beauchamp, eldest s. of Lord Hertford, whom he succeeded as the 2nd Marquis 1794.

[3] Henry Herbert: see Letter 70 addressed to Hume, dated 22 Feb. 1763.

[4] Sir Charles Wyndham (1710–63), 4th Bt., succeeded as 2nd Earl of Egremont 1750; Secretary of State, Southern Dept., 1763.

From David Hume, 13 Sept. 1763

Colcraft, the Agent.[5] Mr Pit says, that he always declard it highly improper that he should be brought to the King, before all Terms were settled on such a Footing as to render it impossible for them to separate without agreeing. He accordingly thought they were settled: His first Conference with the King confirm'd him in that Opinion, and he wrote to the Duke of Devonshire[6] to come to Town in order to place himself at the head of the Treasury: The Duke of Newcastle[7] said at his Table, on Sunday was a Fortnight, that the Ministry was settled: But when Mr Pit came to the King that Afternoon, he found him entirely chang'd, and every thing was retracted, that had been agreed on. This is his Story: The other Party says, that he rose in his Terms and wanted to impose the most exorbitant Conditions on his Sovereign. I suppose, that the first Conference pass'd chiefly in generals, and that Mr Pit would then be extremely humble and submissive and polite and dutiful in his Expressions: But when he came to particulars, they did not seem to correspond to these Appearances. At least, this is the best Account I can devise of the Matter, consistent with the Honour of both Parties.

You woud see the present Ministry by the Papers. It is pretended, that they are enragd against Lord Bute for negotiating without their Knowledge or Consent; and that the other Party are no less displeasd with him for not finishing the Treaty with them. That Nobleman declard his Resolution of going abroad a week or two ago: Now, he is determind to pass the Winter in London. Our Countymen are visibly hurt in this Justle of Parties; which I believe to be far from the Intentions of Lord Bute.

Lord Shelburne resignd because he found himself obnoxious on account of his Share in the Negotiation. I see you are much displeasd with that Nobleman but he always speaks of you with regard. I hear that your Pupil, Mr Fitzmaurice, makes a very good figure at Paris.

It is generally thought, that Mr Pit has gaind Credit and Force by this Negotiation. It turns the Eyes of the Public towards him: It shows that the King can overlook personal Resentment against him and Lord Temple.[8] It gains him the Confidence of his own Party, who see that he was negotiating for the whole of them: And puts People in mind of the French Rhyme Ville qui parle et femme qui ecoute &c.

You wou'd hear, that the Case of the Douglas is now made clear even in

[5] John Calcraft (1726–72), political and army agent; a protégé of Henry Fox, but deserted to Pitt 1763; M.P. for Calne 1766–8, and Rochester 1768–72. On 15 Aug. 1763, he tried during an interview of three hours to reconcile Pitt and the Duke of Bedford.

[6] William Cavendish (1720–64), 4th Duke of Devonshire; Master of the Horse 1751–5; Ld. Lt. of Ireland 1755–7; Prime Minister and First Lord of the Treasury 1756–7; Lord Chamberlain 1757–62.

[7] Thomas Pelham-Holles (1693–1768), 1st Duke of Newcastle; Prime Minister and First Lord of the Treasury 1745–6, and 1757–62.

[8] Richard (1711–79), 2nd Earl Temple; bro. of George Grenville and bro.-in-law of Pitt; Lord Privy Seal 1757–61.

the Eyes the most blinded and most prejudicd; which I am glad of, on account of our Friends.[9] I am Dear Smith

Yours most sincerely

David Hume

76. *From* CHARLES TOWNSHEND

MS., GUL Gen. 1464/8; Rae 164–5.

Adderbury, 25 Oct. 1763

Dear Sir

The time now drawing near when the Duke of Buccleugh intends to go abroad, I take the liberty of renewing the subject to you: that if you should still have the same disposition to travel with him I may have the satisfaction of informing Lady Dalkeith[1] and His Grace of it, and of congratulating them upon an event which I know that they, as well as myself, have so much at heart. The Duke is now at Eton: He will remain there until Christmass. He will then spend some short time in London, that he may be presented at Court, and not pass instantaneously from school to a foreign country; but it were to be wished He should not be long in Town, exposed to the habits and companions of London, before his mind has been more formed and better guarded by education and experience.

I do not enter at this moment upon the subject of establishment, because if you have no objection to the situation, I know we cannot differ about the terms. On the contrary, you will find me more sollicitous than yourself to make the connection with Buccleugh as satisfactory and advantageous to you as I am persuaded it will be essentially beneficial to him.

The Duke of Buccleugh has lately made great progress both in his knowledge of ancient languages and in his general taste for composition.[2] With these improvements his amusement from reading and his love of instruction have naturally increased. He has sufficient talents: a very manly temper, and an integrity of heart and reverence for truth, which in a person of his rank and fortune are the firmest foundation of weight in life and uniform greatness. If it should be agreeable to you to finish his education, and mould these excellent materials into a settled character, I make no doubt but he will return to his family and country the very man our fondest hopes have fancied him.

---

[9] e.g. William Mure and Andrew Stuart.

[1] Caroline Campbell, dau. of John 2nd Duke of Argyll and 1st Duke of Greenwich; widow of Lord Dalkeith M.P., mother of Henry 3rd Duke of Buccleuch; md. Charles Townshend 18 Sept. 1755.

[2] Townshend took a keen interest in the Duke's education: see I. Ross, 'Educating an Eighteenth-Century Duke', *The Scottish Tradition: Essays in honour of Ronald Gordon Cant* (Edinburgh, 1974), 178–97.

I go to Town next Friday, and should be obliged to you for your answer to this letter.—I am, with sincere affection and esteem, dear sir, your most faithful and most obedient humble servant,

C. Townshend.

Lady Dalkeith presents her compliments to you.

77. *From* DAVID HUME

MS., RSE ii. 36; HL i. 407–10.

Fontainebleau, 28 Oct. 1763

My dear Smith

I have been three days at Paris and two at Fontainbleau; and have every where met with the most extraordinary Honours which the most exorbitant Vanity cou'd wish or desire. The Compliments of Dukes and Marischals of France and foreign Ambassadors go for nothing with me at present: I retain a Relish for no kind of Flattery but that which comes from the Ladies. All the Courtiers, who stood around when I was introduc'd to Me de Pompadour,[1] assurd me that she was never heard [?] to say so much to any Man; and her Brother, [words obliterated] But I forget already, that I am to scorn all the Civilities. [ ] However, even Me Pompadour's Civilities were, if possible, exceeded by those of the Dutchess de Choiseul,[2] the Wife of the Favourite and prime Minister, and one of the Lady of the most distinguish'd Merit in France. Not contented with the very obliging things she said to me on my first Introduction, she sent to call me from the other End of the Room, in order to repeat them and to enter into a short Conversation with me: And not contented with that, she sent the Danish Ambassador after me to assure me, that what she said was not from Politeness, but that she seriously desir'd to be in Friendship and Correspondence with me. There is not a Courtier in France, who wou'd not have been transported with Joy, to have had the half of these obliging things said to him, by either of these great Ladies; but what may appear more extraordinary, both of them, as far as I could conjecture, have read with some Care all my Writings that have been translated into French, that is, almost all my Writings. The King said nothing particular to me, when I was introduced to him; and (can you imagine it) I was becoming so silly

---

[1] Jeanne-Antoinette Poisson, marquise de Pompadour (1721-64) mistress of Louis XV.

[2] Louise-Honorine Crozat du Châtel (1736–1801) md. in 1750 Étienne François de Choiseul-Stainville (1719–85), duc de Choiseul, Minister for War. In 1766 he became Minister for Foreign Affairs, but was disgraced and exiled four years later as a result of the intrigues of Mme du Barri. Mme de Choiseul (referred to as 'grand'maman' in Mme du Deffand's letters) was perhaps the most charming of the ladies at the French Court, and was greatly admired by British visitors such as Horace Walpole and Hume. She returned Hume's affection.

as to be a little mortify'd by it, till they told me, that he never says any thing to any body, the first time he sees them. The Dauphin[3] as I am told from all hands, declares himself on every Occasion very strongly in my favour; and many people assure me, that I have reason to be proud of his Judgement, even were he an Individual. I have scarce seen any of the Geniuses of Paris, who, I think, have in general great Merit, as Men of Letters. But every body is forward to tell me the high Panegyrics I receive from [them;] and you may believe that [words obliterated] Approbation which has procur'd me all these Civilities from the Courtiers.

I know you are ready to ask me, my dear Friend, if all this does not make me very happy: No, I feel little or no Difference. As this is the first Letter I write to my Friends at home, I have amus'd myself (and hope I have amus'd you) by giving you a very abridg'd Account of these Transactions: But can I ever forget, that it is the very same Species, that wou'd scarce show me common Civilities a very few Years ago at Edinburgh, who now receive me with such Applauses at Paris? I assure you I reap more internal Satisfaction from the very amiable Manners and Character of the Family in which I live (I mean Lord and Lady Hertford and Lord Beauchamp) than from all these external Vanities; and it is that domestic Enjoyment which must be considerd as the agreeable Circumstance in my Situation. During the two last days in particular, that I have been at Fontainebleau, I have sufferd (the Expression is not improper) as much Flattery as almost any man has ever done in the same time: But there are few days in my Life, when I have been in good Health, that I would not rather pass over again. Mr Neville,[4] our Minister, an honest worthy English Gentleman, who carry'd me about, was astonishd at the Civilities I met with; and has assurd me, that, on his Return, he will not fail to inform the King of England and the English Ministry of all these particulars. But enough of all these Follies. You see I trust to your Friendship, that you will forgive me; and to your Discretion, that you will keep my Secret.

I had almost forgot in these Effusions, shall I say of my Misanthropy or my Vanity, to mention the Subject which first put my Pen in my hand. The Baron d'Holbac,[5] whom I saw at Paris, told me, that there was one

---

[3] Louis (1729–65), s. of Louis XV, and fa. of Louis XVI, Louis XVII, and Charles X. Unlike his father, he was thoughtful and pious.

[4] Richard Neville Aldworth Neville (1717–93), M.P. for Reading 1747, Under-Secretary of State, Southern Dept. 1748–51; 4 Sept. 1762, apptd. Secretary to the Duke of Bedford's embassy to France. On 15 Feb. 1763 he brought to London the definitive Peace of Paris, and then returned to France to act as British Minister Plenipotentiary till Lord Hertford's arrival.

[5] Paul-Henri Thiry, Baron d'Holbach (1723–89), born in the Palatinate but lived from his childhood in Paris, where he was the friend of Diderot, d'Alembert, Helvétius, and Condorcet. His best-known work is the *Système de la nature* (1770), which expresses cogently his naturalistic and materialistic views. From 1759 until 1788, his Paris house at No. 8, rue des Moulins, was the chief rendezvous of men of letters and distinguished

under his Eye that was translating your Theory of moral Sentiments;[6] and desird me to inform you of it: Mr Fitzmaurice, your old Friend, interests himself strongly in this Undertaking: Both of them wish to know, if you propose to make any Alterations on the Work, and desire you to inform me of your Intentions in that particular. Please direct to me under Cover to the Earl of Hertford at Northumberland House, London. Letters so directed will be sent to us at Paris. I desire my Compliments to all Friends.

I am My Dear Smith Yours sincerely

David Hume

78. *To* DAVID HUME

Fraser, *Scotts of Buccleuch*, ii. 403; Rae 168–9.

Glasgow, 12 Dec. 1763

My Dear Hume,

The day before I received your last letter[1] I had the honour of a letter from Charles Townshend,[2] renewing in the most obliging manner his former proposal that I should travel with the Duke of Buccleugh, and informing me that his Grace was to leave Eton at Christmas, and would go abroad very soon after that. I accepted the proposal, but at the same time expressed to Mr Townshend the difficulties I should have in leaving the University before the beginning of April, and begged to know if my attendance upon his Grace would be necessary before that time. I have yet received no answer to that letter,[3] which, I suppose, is owing to this, that his Grace is not yet come from Eton, and that nothing is yet settled with regard to the time of his going abroad. I delayed answering your letter till I should be able to inform you at what time I should have the pleasure of seeing you. . . . I ever am, my dearest friend, most faithfully yours,

Adam Smith

79. *From* JOSEPH BLACK

MS., GUL Gen. 1035/148; Scott 256–7.

Glasgow, 23 Jan. 1764

Dear Sir

Inclosed I send you a letter from Ireland and the one to my Brother which you may deliver when you please. Mrs Smith and Miss Douglass

---

visitors for dinners on Sundays and Thursdays: 'Une grosse chère, mais bonne, d'excellent vin, d'excellent café, beaucoup de disputes, jamais de querelles' (Morellet, *Mémoires*, 1821).

[6] M.A. Eidous published a French translation of TMS in 1764, in two vols.

[1] Letter 77, dated 28 Oct. 1763. [2] Letter 76, dated 25 Oct. 1763.
[3] Not traced.

are perfectly well and you made your Mother very happy with the letter which came last night. She was particularly overjoyed at the hint that your stay abroad was not to be so long as you expected. She begs you will write as often as you can. I received your line from Edinburgh about Balfour[1] and as to the affair of the House.[2] Mrs Smith will certainly be allowed to stay in it untill martinmass and it is even probable she may keep it untill the whitsunday after. T. Young[3] performs admirably well and is much respected by the Students—

Farewell and beleive me
Yours Joseph Black

80. *From* JOHN MILLAR[1]

Address: To Dr Adam Smith, to the care of Andrew Miller, Bookseller, opposite St Catharine Street in the Strand, London
MS., GUL Gen. 1035/149; Scott 257.

Glasgow, 2 Feb. 1764

Dr Sir

I write this to you, with the concurrence of Dr Black to acquaint you of the State of our affairs since you left us. Dr Reid at Aberdeen has been strongly recommended by Lord Kames.[2] He is also recommended to Dr Traill[3] by Lord Deskford. There is great reason to believe that interest

---

[1] John Balfour, Edinburgh Bailie and bookseller, partner of Gavin Hamilton. On 16 June 1776, Smith asked Hume to direct his letters to him in Edinburgh c/o Balfour; see Letter 161.

[2] Smith had a tied house in Professors' Court of the Old College which he would be expected to vacate on demitting his Chair. Black indicates that the University was prepared to let Smith's mother retain the house for another session of three terms: Martinmas (Oct.–Dec.), Candlemas (Jan.–Mar.), and Whitsunday (Apr.–June).

[3] Thomas Young, 3rd son of Thomas Young of Burntisland, Fife; M.A. Glasgow 1763; Smith's substitute as teacher of the Moral Philosophy class and unsuccessful candidate for the Chair.

---

[1] John Millar (1735–1801), jurist and historian; educ. at Glasgow under Smith; tutor to Lord Kames's son George, late 1750s; advocate 1760; Professor of Civil Law, Glasgow, from 1761, lecturing on civil law, jurisprudence, and both Scots and English law; prominent member of the University Literary Soc.; upheld radical political views, opposing the slave trade and sympathizing with the French Revolution; his distinguished pupils included David Hume the Younger, Lord Melbourne, Thomas Muir, and Smith's nephew and heir, David Douglas (Lord Reston); published *The Origin of the Distinction of Ranks* (1771), and *Historical View of the English Government* (1787), offering a materialist analysis of history. While in general following Smith's lead as a social scientist, Millar was critical of Smith's conclusions expressed in WN, in particular that concerning 'unbounded freedom of trade'. Millar held that when public interest warranted it, there should be 'a regulation of trade' (*Letters of Eminent Persons addressed to David Hume*, ed. J. Hill Burton, Edinburgh, 1849, ii. 479).

[2] Thomas Reid was elected Smith's successor on 22 May 1764. Kames and Reid developed a lifelong friendship, in part based on sharing the Common Sense philosophy.

[3] Robert Traill (d. 1775), Professor of Oriental Languages, then Divinity, from 1761.

will be used from all these different quarters with Mr. Mckenzie.[4] Possibly too the Duke of Queensberry[5] and Lord Hopeton[6] will be engaged in his behalf, the consequence of which in the present state of things is altogether uncertain.

Black and I still think that Young is by far the best man who has appeared; for Morehead[7] refuses to accept. We earnestly beg that if you can do any thing in counterworking these extraneous operations you will exert yourself. I cannot but say that we join also in wishing that if you know any place where your opinion of Young would be of Service, you would take an opportunity of giving it. I can assure you he needs that assistance. There is now a strong circumstance in his favour which we could not know formerly. He has taught the class hitherto with great and universal applause, and by all accounts discovers an ease and fluency in Speaking which, I own, I scarce expected. No body knows of my writing this but Black. Yours sincerely

John Millar

Your mother is in good health.

81. *To* THOMAS MILLER[1]

Address: To the Right Honourable Thomas Miller Esqr. His Majesty's Advocate for Scotland
MS., GUA University MSS. vol. 31. 13; Rae 172; Scott 220–1.

Paris, 14 Feb. 1764

My Lord
I take this first opportunity, after my arrival in this Place, which was not till yesterday to resign my Office into the hands of Your Lordship, of the Dean of Faculty,[2] of the Principal of the College[3] and of all my other most

[4] John Mackenzie (d. 1778) of Delvin, agent of the Duke of Argyll; WS 1737; Clerk to Signet 1766, Deputy-Keeper 1770–8; Principal Clerk of Session 1776.
[5] Charles Douglas (1698–1778) 3rd Duke of Queensberry and 2nd Duke of Dover; Privy Councillor; Vice-Admiral of Scotland; Keeper of the Great Seal of Scotland 1760; Lord Justice-General 1763–78.
[6] John, 2nd Earl of Hopetoun (1704–81), one of the Lords of Police 1744–60, said to have spent all of his salary on charity; his first wife was a sister of Lord Deskford.
[7] George Muirhead (d. 1773), Professor of Oriental Languages 1753, of Humanity 1754–d.

[1] Thomas Miller (1717–89) of Glenlee, Kirkcudbright, and Barskimming, Ayr; lawyer, politician, and judge; educ. Glasgow and Edinburgh; advocate 1742; Town Clerk, Glasgow 1748–66; Solicitor of Excise 1755–9; Solicitor-General 1759–60; Lord Advocate 1760–6; M.P. 1761–6; Lord Rector, Glasgow University 1762–4; Lord Justice-Clerk 1766 (as Lord Barskimming 1766–80, then Glenlee); Lord President of the Court of Session 1787–d.
[2] James Clow.   [3] William Leechman.

respectable and worthy collegues. Into Your and their hands therefor I do hereby resign my Office of Professor of Moral Philosophy in the University of Glasgow and in the College thereof, with all the emoluments Privileges and advantages which belong to it. I reserve however my Right to the Salary for the current half year which commenced at the 10th of October for one part of my salary and at Martinmass last for another; and I desire that this Salary may be paid to the Gentleman who does that part of my Duty which I was obliged to leave undone, in the manner agreed on between my very worthy Collegues and me before we parted. I never was more anxious for the Good of the College than at this moment and I sincerely wish that whoever is my Successor[4] may not only do Credit to the Office by his Abilities but be a comfort to the very excellent Men with whom he is likely to spend his life, by the Probity of his heart and the Goodness of his Temper.

I have the Honour to be my Lord, your Lordship's
most obedient and most faithfull Servant
Adam Smith

82. *To* DAVID HUME

Address: A Monsieur, Monsieur Hume, chez L'Ambassadeur de L'Angleterre a Paris [readdressed to 'Compiegne']
MS., RSE vii. 32; Rae 178–9.

Toulouse, 5 July 1764

My Dearest Friend

The Duke of Buccleugh proposes soon to set out for Bordeaux where he intends to stay a fortnight or more. I should be much obliged to you if you could send us recommendations to the Duke of Richelieu,[1] the Marquis de Lorges[2] and Intendant of the Province.[3] Mr Townshend assured me that the Duke de Choiseul[4] was to recommend us to all the people of fashion here and everywhere else in France. We have heard nothing, however, of these recommendations and have had our way to make as well as we could by the help of the Abbé[5] who is a Stranger here almost as much as we. The

---

[4] Dr. Thomas Reid.

[1] Louis-François Armand Duplessis (1696–1788), duc de Richelieu; soldier, diplomat, administrator, and libertine, his old age being as amorous as his youth; Governor of Guienne from 1758, but alienated the people of Bordeaux by his hauteur and arbitrary acts; detested the *philosophes*, though Voltaire spoke of him as his hero.
[2] Louis de Durfort Duras (b. 1714), cr. duc de Lorges, 1759, soldier and administrator; served in Guienne under Richelieu and commanded in his absence.
[3] Not identified.
[4] Étienne-François, duc de Choiseul (1719–85), Prime Minister of France till Dec. 1770.
[5] Abbé Seignelay Colbert (1736–?) eldest son of Cuthbert of Castlehill, Inverness; cousin of Hume; went to France 1750, and entered Gallican Church; made Vicar-General

Progress, indeed, we have made is not very great. The Duke is acquainted with no french man whatever. I cannot cultivate the acquaintance of the few with whom I am acquainted, as I cannot bring them to our house and am not always at liberty to go to theirs. The Life which I led at Glasgow was a pleasurable, dissipated life in comparison of that which I lead here at Present. I have begun to write a book in order to pass away the time.[6] You may believe I have very little to do. If Sir James[7] would come and spend a month with us in his travels it would not only be a great Satisfaction to me but he might by his influence and example be of great service to the Duke. Mention these matters, however, to nobody but to him. Remember me in the most respectful manner to Lord Beauchamp[8] and to Dr Trail[9] and believe me my Dear Friend

Ever yours,
Adam Smith

83. *To* DAVID HUME

MS., RSE vii. 33; Rae 181–2.

Toulouse, 21 Oct. 1764

My Dear Hume

I take this opportunity of Mr Cooks[1] going to Paris to return to you, and thro' you, to the Ambassador,[2] my very sincere and hearty thanks for the very honourable manner in which he was so good as to mention me to the Duke of Richelieu in the letter of recommendation which you sent us. There was indeed one small mistake in it. He called me Robinson instead of Smith. I took upon me to correct this mistake myself before the Duke delivered the letter. We were all treated by the Marechal with the utmost Politeness and attention, particularly the Duke whom he distinguished in a very proper manner. The intendant[3] was not at Bordeaux, but we shall soon have an opportunity of delivering his letter as we propose to return that Place in order to meet my Lords Brother.[4]

---

of diocese of Toulouse 1764; Bishop of Rodez 1781; had agricultural and industrial interests; attended the meeting of the States General, 1789, and proposed union of the clergy and the third estate; resisted the civil constitution of the clergy; ended his days as secretary to Louis XVIII.

[6] First mention of writing of WN.

[7] Sir James Macdonald (1741–66), 8th Bt. of Sleat, Isle of Skye; educ. at Eton; in Paris, autumn and winter of 1764, where his intellect and personality charmed everyone; an early death while in Rome on the Grand Tour ended a most promising career.

[8] Eldest son of Lord Hertford, the British Ambassador in France.

[9] James Trail (d. 1783), Chaplain to the Ambassador, later Bishop of Down and Connor, when Lord Hertford became Lord Lieutenant of Ireland.

[1] Servant to the Duke of Buccleuch; see letter 92.   [2] Lord Hertford.
[3] Not identified.
[4] Hon. Hew Campbell Scott (1747–66), younger bro. of the Duke of Buccleuch.

Mr Cook goes to Caen to wait upon Mr Scot, and to attend him from that place to Toulouse. He will pass by Paris, and I must beg the favour of you that as soon as you understand he is in town you will be so good as to call upon him and carry him to the Ambassadours as well as to any other Place where he would chuse to go. I must beg the same favour of Sir James.[5] Mr Cook will let you know when he comes to town. I have great reason to entertain a most favorable opinion of Mr Scot, [and] I flatter myself, his company will be both useful and agreable to his Brother. Our expedition to Bordeaux, and another we have made since to Bagneres,[6] has made a great change upon the Duke. He begins now to familiarize himself to French company and I flatter myself I shall spend the rest of the Time we are to live together, not only in Peace and contentment but in gayety and amusement.

When Mr Scot joins us we propose to go to see the meeting of the States of Languedoc, at Montpelier. Could you procure us recommendations to the Comte d'Eu[7] to the Archbishop of Narbonne[8] and to the Intendant?[9] These expeditions, I find, are of the greatest service to My Lord. I ever am my Dear friend most Faithfully yours

Adam Smith

84. *To* DAVID HUME

Address: To David Hume Esqr, Paris
MS., RSE vii. 34; Rae 183.

Toulouse, 4 Nov. 1764

My dear friend,

This letter will be delivered to you by Mr Urquhart,[1] the only man I ever knew that had a better temper than yourself. You will find him most perfectly amiable. I recommend him in the most earnest manner to your advice and protection. He is not a man of letters and is just a plain, sensible, agreeable man of no pretentions of any kind, but whom you will love every-day better and better. I ever am

My Dear Friend, Most faithfully yours
Adam Smith

[5] Sir James Macdonald of Sleat.
[6] Bagnères-de-Bigorre, watering place in the Pyrénées, visited by Montaigne and Mme de Maintenon.
[7] Son of the duc de Maine (d. 1736), prince souverain de Dombes et de Trévoux, Feb. 1762.
[8] Charles-Antoine de la Roche-Aymon (1692–1777), Archbishop of Narbonne 1752; Grand-Aumônier de France 1760; Archbishop of Rheims 1762; Cardinal 1771; a moderate in Church disputes, presided over the assemblies of the clergy and directed them according to the interests of the court.   [9] Not traced.

[1] ? William Urquhart, 2nd of Craigston, who sold the estate of Cromarty bought by his fa. Captain John Urquhart (d. 1756).

85. *From* JOHN GLASSFORD[1]

Address: To Dr Smith
MS., GUL Gen. 1035/150; Scott 258-9.

Glasgow, 5 Nov. 1764

Dear Sir

I have at different Times had the Pleasure of hearing of your wellfare Since you left Glasgow, altho not favoured with any Letter from yourself. I hope that your Time passes agreeably and that you are bringing forward at your Leisure Hours the usefull work that was so well advanced here.[2] It would be a Pity to want it longer than you find necessary to finish it to your own liking, as it may then very safely make its appearance.

This I send under cover to Mr George Kippen[3] of this Place who I expect will be at London about the Time this gets there as he sett out from Glasgow on the 29th of last Month with an Intention to go from London to France in order to pass the Winter in one of the Southern provinces of that Kingdom for the Benefit of his Health which for upwards of a year has been very indifferent But which Doctor Black thinks will be greatly benefited by the exercise that he gets in this journey thither and which the Mildness of the Winter Season in the South of France will permit his taking in these Months that you know are too unfavourable here for Valetudinary people to go much abroad. Mrs Kippen goes along with Mr Kippen as does Mr Clawson[4] whom you probably have known at the university here and who will make an agreeable Companion to Him.

You no doubt are Accquainted with Mr Kippens Character and use-fullness in Society which makes it unnecessary for me to say much in Recommendation of Him to your Civilities if he fixes at Tholouse or its neighbourhood. I know that he can depend on your best advice and friendship in directing him to a proper House to lodge in That they may have as many of the conveniences as are to be afforded to Strangers in their Situation.

You no doubt know that your friend Mr William Smith[5] came to the Incle factory[6] Warehouse as was proposed before you left Glasgow where

---

[1] John Glassford (1715-83), tobacco merchant and shipowner, one of the richest men in Glasgow; Bailie 1751; purchased Dougalston, Dumbarton; is remembered in his native city by a street named after him.

[2] WN: an indication that Smith's Glasgow friends knew of this work on economics during his professorial years. The scene for discussion of this was probably Provost Andrew Cochrane's Political Economy Club (Rae 90-1).

[3] George Kippen, junior, merchant, admitted burgess of Glasgow, 1737; he was still alive in 1781.

[4] Patrick Clason (d. 1811), Glasgow M.A. 1758, tutor to the Earl of Dunmore; school-master of Logie.

[5] Probably a distant cousin of Adam Smith.

[6] Made broad tapes; founded in 1732 by Alexander Harvey, who brought at great risk two looms and a worker from Haarlem to start the industry in Glasgow.

he gives application and seems in general very qualified for Business of that sort. His younger Brother[7] is gone upon a Voyage in one of my Ships from hence to Havre de grace and from thence to Maryland and back to this place with an Intention to keep at Sea if this trying voyage pleases Him.

I referr you to some of your other Correspondents for any News that are going here. Indeed I do not remember any worth noticing to you and my now writing you except that the Members for Scotland seem now resolved to carry the Bill for abolishing the optional Clause in Bank and Bankers notes[8] this ensuing Session which you know was drop'd in the Last. I am with great regard

Dear Sir, Your most obedient and Humble Servant

John Glassford

86. *To* DAVID HUME

Address: A Monsieur, Monsieur Hume, chez L'Ambassadeur de L'Angleterre a Paris
MS., GUL Gen. 1035/129; Scott 262–3.

[?Toulouse, Aug. 1765]

My Dear Friend

Nothing has alarmed us so much among all the late extraordinary changes, as Lord Hertford quitting Paris and Lord George Lenox[1] being appointed secretary to the English Embassy. Let me beg to know immediately if you leave Paris likewise, and if any proper provision has been made for you. We propose being at Paris by the beginning of November and it will be the greatest disappointment to the Duke of Buccleugh not to find you there. He has read almost all your works several times over, and was it not for the more wholesome doctrine which I take care to instill into him, I am afraid he might be in danger of adopting some of your wicked Principles. You will find him very much improved.

I should be glad to know the causes of this astonishing change. It appears at present quite a riddle to me unless the Queen[2] is supposed to take a

---

[7] ?An Adam Smith who left Glasgow University in 1764 without taking a degree.

[8] Dealt with payment of bank notes in cash or notes of other banks; the 'optional clause' was not abolished until much later; see Hamilton 300, 305, 311–12, 315. Glassford was a partner in the Glasgow Arms Bank, founded in 1750, and a founder of the Thistle Bank in 1761.

[1] Lord George Henry Lennox (1737–1805) of West Stoke, Sussex; soldier, politician, and diplomat; Secretary to the British Embassy 1765–6, replacing Hume, as his brother, the Duke of Richmond, replaced Lord Hertford; M.P. 1761–90.

[2] George III married Princess Charlotte Sophia, 2nd dau. of the late Duke of Mecklenburg-Strelitz on 8 Sept. 1761.

little more upon her than usual. I beg to hear from you as soon as Possible.

> I ever am, My Dearest Friend,
> Yours entirely
> Adam Smith

87. *From* DAVID HUME

MS., RSE ii. 37; NHL 130–2.

Paris, 5 [Sept.]¹ 1765

Dear Smith

I have been whirled about lately in a strange Manner; but besides that none of the Revolutions have ever threatened me much, or been able to give me a Moment's Anxiety, all has ended very happily and to my wish. In June last,² I got my Patent for Secretary to the Embassy, which plac'd me in as agreeable a situation as possible, and one likely to last, with 1200 a year. A few Weeks after, Lord Hertford got a Letter from which he learnd, that he must go over Lord Lieutenant to Ireland; he told me, that he was averse to this Employment for many good Reasons, and wou'd not accept of it unless gratifyd in some Demands, particularly in appointing me Secretary for that kingdom, in conjunct Commission with his son, Lord Beauchamp. This is an Office of great Dignity, as the Secretary is in a manner Prime Minister of that kingdom, it has 2000 a year Sallary, and always entitles the Person afterwards to some considerable Employment, whatever may be the Fate of the Lord Lieutenant. Notwithstanding these Advantages, I was very averse to the office, as it obligd me to enter on a new Scene at my Years, and a Scene for which, I appre[he]nded I was not well qualifyd. I said so to Lord Hertford; but he still persisted in his Resolution. A few Weeks after, when he went over to London, he found the Rage against the Scots so high, that he was oblig'd to depart from his Resolution: Perhaps, the zeal against Deists enter'd for a Share. On the whole, he appointed his Son, sole Secretary; but he told me that he had obtaind the King's Promise to provide me in Something that shou'd not be precarious. Ten days after, he wrote me that he had procured me a Pension of 400 a Year for Life. Nothing coud be more to my Mind: I have now Opulence and Liberty: The last formerly renderd me content: Both together must do so, so far as the Encrease of Years will permit.

I stay here till the Arrival of the Duke of Richmond, which will be sometime in October,³ after which I must soon return to England: I shall set out thence in a Visit to Ireland. I decline all farther Engagements. Lord

---

¹ Hume mistakenly wrote 'Nov.' for Sept.; see the third para. of the letter.
² The commission under the Great Seal is dated 3 July 1765.
³ Richmond reached Paris on 11 Nov., and was presented to Louis XV on 17 Nov.

Hertford wrote me, that the Office of Usher to the House of Commons in Ireland commonly yielded 900 during a Session: He coud get one to serve for 300 and destind the rest for me, if I pleas'd: But I have refusd this Emolument, because I woud not run into the Ways of the World and catch at Profit from all hands. I am sure you approve of my Philosophy.

As a new Vexation to temper my good Fortune, I am much in Perplexity about fixing the Place of my future Abode for Life. Paris is the most agreeable Town in Europe, and suits me best; but it is a foreign Country. London is the Capital of my own Country; but it never pleasd me much. Letters are there held in no honour: Scotsmen are hated: Superstition and Ignorance gain Ground daily. Edinburgh has many Objections and many Allurements. My present Mind, this Forenoon the fifth of September is to return to France. I am much pressd here to accept of Offers, which woud contribute to my agreeable Living, but might encroach on my Independence, by making me enter into Engagements with Princes and great Lords and Ladies. Pray give me your Judgement.[4]

I regreat much I shall not see you. I have been looking for you every day these three Months. Your Satisfaction in your Pupil gives me equal Satisfaction.

You must direct to me under the Title of *Chargé des Affaires d'Angleterre à la Cour de France*, without anything farther.

I cannot by the Post enter into a Detail of our late strange Revolutions: But it is suspected, that the Accession of Mr Pit will be necessary to give Stability to the present Ministry.

The Duke of Richmond coud not appoint me Secretary. He coud appoint none but his Brother, without affronting Sir Charles Bunbury, his Brother in law, who had been rejected by Lord Hertford.

Yours most sincerely

David Hume

88. *To* DAVID HUME

MS., GUL Gen. 1035/130 (portions cut out); Scott 263–4.

[? Toulouse, Sept. 1765][1]

My Dear friend

It gives me the Greatest pleasure to find that you are so well contented with your present situation. I think however you are wrong in thinking

---

[4] See Letter 88 addressed to Hume, dated ? Sept. 1765, and Letter 99 addressed to Andrew Millar, dated in the autumn of 1766.

[1] The letter is undated, but seems to be a reply to Letter 87 from Hume, dated 5 Sept. Smith was travelling in the south of France later in Sept. See Letter 99 addressed to Andrew Millar, dated ? autumn 1766, for another comment on Hume's notion about settling in Paris.

of settling at Paris. A man is always displaced in a forreign Country, and notwithstanding the boasted humanity and politeness of this Nation, they appear to me to be, in general, more meanly interested, and that the cordiality of their friendship is much less to be depended on than that of our own countrymen. They live in such large societies and their affections are dissipated among so great a variety of objects, that they can bestow but a very small share of them upon any individual. Do not imagine that the great Princes and Ladies who want you to live with them make this proposal from real and sincere affection to you. They mean nothing but to gratify their own vanity by having an illustrious man in their house, and you would soon feel the want of that cordial and trusty affection which you enjoyed in the family of Lord and Lady Hertford, to whom I must beg to be remembered in the most dutiful and respectful manner. Your objections to London appear to me to be without foundation. The hatred of Scotch men can subsist, even at present, among nobody but the stupidest of the People, and is such a piece of nonsense that it must fall even among them in a twelvemonth. The Clamour against you on account of Deism is stronger, no doubt, at London where you are a Native and consequently may be a candidate for everything, than at Paris where as a forreigner, you possibly can be a candidate for nothing. Your Presence dissipated in six months time much stronger prejudices in Edinburgh, and when you appear at Court, in open day light, as you must do upon your return, and not live obscurely at Miss Elliots[2] with six or seven scotchmen as before, the same irresistible good temper will in a very few weeks dissipate much weaker prejudices at London and [   ][3] to hold their tongues. In short I have a very great interest in your settling at London, where, after many firm resolutions to return to Scotland, I think it is most likely I shall settle myself.[4] Let us make short excursions together sometimes to see our friends in France and sometimes to see our friends in Scotland, but let London be the place of our ordinary residence. Before you set out from Paris I would beg of you to leave me some letters to honest men and women. You may leave them either with Foley or with Thellason and Neckar,[5] to be delivered on my arrival at paris. The Duke desires to be remembered[   ][3]

[2] Miss Ann Elliot of Middlemiln, a poor relation of the Minto family; with her sister Peggy, she kept a boarding-establishment, much frequented by Scotsmen, in Lisle Street, Leicester Fields. While in London, Hume lodged there, *c.* 1758–*c.* 1768.

[3] Portions cut out.

[4] Smith visited London, 1766–7, 1773–6, 1777 (Jan.–*c.* Nov.), 1782, 1786 (Apr.–May), and 1787 (Mar.–Aug.), but made his home in Kirkcaldy and Edinburgh.

[5] Paris bankers.

89. *From* MARIE LOUISE DENIS[1]

MS., GUL Bi 15–d.8; Scott 260–1; Voltaire, *Corr.* (1960), lix. 255–6.

Ferney, 10–11 Dec. 1765

Samedy 7ᵉ du mois, vers les onze heures du matin, les gardes chasses de Madame Denis, Dame de ferney, vinrent avertir que des gens du Village de Saconnex chassaient au nombre de cinq dans les allées du bois de ferney qui est fermé de trois portes, et qui fait partie des jardins du château de ferney.

Joseph Fillon, charpentier, demeurant à Saconnez, a déposé aujourd'hui 10 Decembré devant le procureur fiscal, que c'était Monsieur Dillon[2] qui était venu le prendre à Saconney, avec un soldat de la garnison de genêve pour le mener chasser avec lui à ferney. Que lui, Joseph Fillon, lui avait réprésenté que celà n'était pas permis; que Monsieur Dillon lui répondit que Madame Denis lui avait donné la permission et qu'il lui répondait de tout.

Quatre personnes ont déposés que Monsieur Dillon a dit en leur présence, qu'il mettrait le feu au château.

Trois personnes ont déposé que Monsieur Dillon était venu à midy dans le village de fernex hier 9ᵉ du présent mois avec quatre personnes armées de fusils et de pistolets, qu'ils sont entrés chez le garde, qu'ils l'ont cherché chez lui et dans les maisons voisines et que Monsieur Dillon a dit en jurant qu'il l'aurait mort ou vif. Madame Denis fait juges de ces procédés tous les gentils hommes anglais qui sont à genêve.

Monsieur Dillon se plaint qu'on a tué un de ses chiens de chasse; mais ce ne sont pas les gardes qui l'ont tué puisqu'il fut tué pendant que les gardes faisaient leur raport juridique, et qu'il le fut par les gens du village de ferney, qui croyaient que ce chien appartenait à un braconier nommé Simon, du village D'Ornex, et qu'ils ne pouvaient pas savoir que ce chien avait été vendu quatre jours auparavant à Monsieur Dillon qu'ils ne connaissaient pas et qu'ils n'avaient jamais vû.

Il résulte de tous ces faits déposés dans le procez, que Monsieur Dillon doit réparer L'insulte faite à Madame Denis et payer les frais du procez qui tombe sur les habitants de Sacconey.

NB: Le garde chasse chez lequel Monsieur Dillon alla avec main forte à ferney, aiant voulu se dérober à sa poursuitte, s'est cassé les reins, et est en danger de la vie.

Madame Denis comptait envoier ce mémoire hier à Monsieur Schmidt; elle avait dicté quatre mots pour être mis au bas du mémoire; on les a par inadvertance écrit sur une Lettre séparée. Madame Denis répète qu'elle

---

[1] Marie Louise Denis, niece, housekeeper, and (latterly) mistress of Voltaire.

[2] Charles Dillon (1745–1813), afterwards 12th Viscount Dillon; visited Geneva 1764, as pupil of John Turberville Needham, F.R.S., who was on bad terms with Voltaire. Dillon's behaviour may have resulted from this.

s'en raporte à la morale de Monsieur Schmidt, et au jugement de toute la noblesse anglaise qui est à genêve; elle lui présente ses obéïssances ainsi que Monsieur De Voltaire.[3]

a Ferney 11 Décembre 1765.

90. *From* DAVID HUME

Address: A Monsieur Monsieur Adam Smith Chez Monsieur Foley, Banquier a Paris

MS., RSE ii. 38; HL ii. 5–6.

[London, ? end of Jan. 1766]

Dear Smith

I can write as seldom and as Short as you—I am sorry I did not see you before I left Paris. I am also sorry I shall not see you there soon. I shall not be able to fix Rousseau to his Mind for some Weeks yet: He is a little variable and fanciful, tho' very agreeable.[1] Lord Hertford is to be over some time in April. I must then wait for him; and afterwards must be dispos'd of, for some time, by his Commands. I recommended my Servant St Jean to you: If he be with you or the Duke, I am sure you will like him and keep him on; and you need say nothing of this to him. But if you did not engage him, please send to him and tell him, that as I cannot promise on my Return to Paris soon, I do not wish he woud deprive himself of any other good Service that offers. He lives at Collet's, a Hirer of Coaches in the Rue des vieux Augustins, a few Doors from the Hotel du Parc roiale where you intended to lodge. He is known either by the Name of St Jean or Jean Garneaux—Some push me to continue my History. Millar offers me any Price: All the Marlborough Papers are offerd me.[2] And I believe no body woud venture to refuse me: But cui bono? Why shoud I forgo Idleness and Sauntering and Society; and expose myself again to the Clamours of a stupid, factious Public? I am not yet tir'd of doing nothing; and am become too wise either to mind Censure or Applause. By and bye I shall be too old to undergo so much Labour: Adieu

David Hume.

---

[3] Samuel Rogers said Smith had been in Voltaire's company 'five or six times', P. W. Clayden, *The Early Life of Samuel Rogers* (London, 1887), 95–110; Sir Gavin de Beer ed., 'Voltaire's British Visitors', *Voltaire Studies* iii–iv (1957), 71–4.

[1] Rather a different report comes from William Rouet, writing to William Mure from London on 25 Jan. 1766: 'David Hume, and J. J. Rousseau, are in Buckingham Street, next door to J. Stuart's [John Stewart's, the wine merchant], where many go from civility to see him; and our friend David is made the shower of the Lion. He is confoundedly weary of his pupil, as he calls him; he is full of oddities and even absurdities . . .' (*Caldwell Papers*, II. ii. 63).

[2] Very likely the papers which David Mallet had by him for more than twenty years without producing the history of the great Duke of Marlborough which he had undertaken to write.

91. *From* 'LE GR[AND] VIC[AIRE] ECCOSSOIS'[1]

MS., Buccleuch Collection (acc. to Scott); Scott 109–10.

[?Toulouse,] 18 Feb. 1766

Et toi, Adam Smith, Philosophe de Glascow, héros et idole des high-broad[2] Ladys, que fais-tu, mon cher ami? Comment gouvernes-tu La Duchesse d'Anville[3] et Mad. de Bouflers,[4] ou ton coeur est-il toujours épris des charmes de Mad. Nicol[5] et des appas tant apparens que cachés de cetter autre dame de fife[6] que vous aimiéz tant? Ne puis-je recevoir de vos nouvelles, milord?[7] Si vous ne vouléz pas écrire vous-même, parce que vous êtes paresseux ou parce que vous griffonéz comme un chat ou, ce qui est pire, comme un duc, si Adam Smith ne veut pas m'écrire par les mêmes raisons, si l'honorable M. Scot[8] garde aussi le silence, dites au moins à quelcun de votre maison de me mander quelque chose de votre part; je suis chargé de savoir si vois devéz rester à Paris cet hyver ou si vous alléz courir le monde, j'ai promis de m'en informer. Si les ecrivains vous manquent, vous avèz mon ami et Cousin, Duncan le Piper,[9] qui me mandera en Erse tout ce que vous voudréz me faire savoir, et m'enverra un morceau digne de fingal, d'oscian ou de Mac Ullin.[10]

Le Gr[and] Vic[aire] Eccossois, fait en congregation

[1] The writer was a Scotsman, resident in France, who assumed here the character of a churchman on the suggestion of his companion, a Capuchin monk, during a journey from Paris to Toulouse (Scott 109).

[2] ?Anticipation of 'high-brow'.

[3] Marie-Louise-Nicole Elizabeth, duchesse d'Anville (1716–94), grand-daughter of the La Rochefoucauld of the *Maxims* and faithful friend of Turgot. With her son, the young duc de La Rochefoucauld, she met Smith at Geneva, late in 1765.

[4] Marie-Charlotte-Hippolyte de Campet de Saujeon (1725–1800), md. Edouard, marquis de Boufflers-Rouverel, Feb. 1746, then became the mistress of the prince de Conti and acted as his hostess at salons held in the Temple and at his country house, L'Isle Adam. One of the foremost anglophiles in France, she opened a correspondence with Hume in 1761 and may have used her influence to have him brought to Paris in 1763. During his two years there, she became his close friend, and for his sake welcomed Smith to her salon early in 1766. She contemplated translating TMS (Rae 198–9).

[5] ?English lady with whom Smith is supposed to have fallen in love while on a jaunt to Abbeville from Paris (Rae 213).

[6] Dugald Stewart recorded that he met a Fife lady past eighty to whom Smith was attached for several years early in life (Rae, ibid.; Scott 65).

[7] The writer addresses the Duke of Buccleuch at this point.

[8] Hon. Hew Campbell Scott.

[9] Possibly the 'piper of the Argyleshire Militia' whom David Hume mentioned to Lord Hailes as having 'repeated to [Smith] all those poems which Mr Macpherson has translated, and many more of equal beauty' (HL i. 329).

[10] James Macpherson's publications: *Fingal* (1762), *Temora* (1763), and *The Works of Ossian* (1765), with its introductory critical dissertation by Dr. Hugh Blair, pleased all of Europe and set society talking about Gaelic heroes and epic poetry.

92. *To* DAVID HUME

Address: To David Hume Esqr at Miss Elliots, Lisle Street, Leicester fields, London
MS., GUL Gen. 1035/131; Scott 264–5.

Hotel du Parc Royale, Paris, 13 Mar. 1766

Dear Hume

I am much obliged to you for recommending your Servant[1] to me. He is without exception the best I ever had in my life and I have always been very well serv'd. The main Purpose of this letter is to recommend the bearer to your Protection. He has served the Duke of Buccleugh with the most acknowledged fidelity ever since he came abroad, and has been driven out of his service by the jealousy and ill humour of Cook the Dukes Maitre d'Hotel. I will answer both for his honesty and his good nature which is such that I should have thought it impossible for any human creature to dislike him. He is very young and is upon that account thoughtless and sometimes negligent. His great perfection is as a travelling Servant. If it falls in your way easily, and without giving yourself any trouble, to recommend him to a proper place in England, you may perfectly depend upon his possessing all the above mentioned qualities in a very high degree. His name is David Challende he is a Suisse.

You are much wanted in Paris. Everybody I see enquires after the time of your return. Do not, however, for gods sake, think of settling in this country but let both of us spend the remainder of our days on the same side of the Water. Come, however, to Paris in the mean time[2] and we shall settle the plan of our future life together. I ever am

My dear friend, yours

A: Smith

93. *To* DAVID HUME

Address: To David Hume Esqr at Miss Elliots, Lisle Street, Leicester fields, London
MS., RSE vii. 35; Rae 208; HL ii. 409.

Paris, 6 July 1766

My dear friend

I am thoroughly convinced that Rousseau is as great a Rascal as you, and as every man here believes him to be; yet let me beg of you not to think of publishing anything to the world upon the very great impertinence

[1] Hume had recommended a servant known as 'St Jean or Jean Garneaux' to Smith in Jan. 1766; see Letter 90 from Hume, dated ? Jan. 1766.
[2] Hume never did return to Paris.

which he has been guilty of to you.[1] By refusing the Pension which you had the goodness to sollicit for him with his own consent, he may have thrown, by the baseness of his Proceeding some little ridicule upon you in the eyes of the Court and the ministry. Stand this ridicule, expose his brutal letter, but without giving it out of your own hand so that it may never be printed, and if you can, laugh at yourself, and I shall pawn my life that before three weeks are at an end, this little affair, which at present gives you so much uneasiness, shall be understood to do you as much honor as any thing that has ever happened to you. By endeavouring to unmask before the Public this hypocritical Pedant, you run the risk, of disturbing the tranquillity of your whole life. By letting him alone he cannot give you a fortnights uneasiness. To write against him, is, you may depend upon it, the very thing he wishes you to do. He is in danger of falling into obscurity in England and he hopes to make himself considerable by provoking an illustrious adversary. He will have a great party. The church, the Whigs, the Jacobites, the whole wise English nation, who will love to mortify a Scotchman, and to applaud a man that has refused a Pension from the King. It is not unlikely too that they may pay him very well for having refused it, and that even he may have had in view this compensation. Your whole friends here wish you not to write, the Baron,[2] D'Alembert,[3] Madame Riccaboni,[4] Mademoiselle Riancourt,[5] Mr Turgot[6] etc. etc. Mr Turgot, a friend everyway worthy of you, desired me to recommend this advice to you in a Particular manner, as his most earnest entreaty and opinion. He and I are both afraid that you are surrounded with evil counsellours, and that the Advice of your English literati, who are themselves accustomed to publish all their little gossiping stories in Newspapers, may have too much influence upon you. Remember me to Mr Walpole and believe me to be with the most sincere affection ever yours

Adam Smith

[1] Hume secured a pension from George III for Rousseau and a haven for him in Derbyshire, but Rousseau refused the first and fled from the second, prompted by his paranoia. Smarting from absurd accusations brought against him by Rousseau and fearing the publication of private letters containing them, Hume wrote a *Concise and Genuine Account of the Dispute between Mr Hume and Mr Rousseau* which was translated by J.-B.-A. Suard and published by d'Alembert in Paris as *Exposé succinct de la contestation . . . entre M. Hume et M. Rousseau* (1776).

[2] Paul-Henri Thiry, Baron d'Holbach (1723–89).

[3] Jean le Rond d'Alembert (1717–83), the *philosophe* closest to Hume; associated with Diderot until 1759 in preparing the *Encyclopédie*, which Smith arranged to have bought for GUL and reviewed in the *Edinburgh Review* (1755).

[4] Marie-Jeanne Laboras de Mézières, Mme Riccoboni, (1714–92), novelist; wife of an actor and, for a time, actress; Hume sought to interest Strahan in publishing a translation of one of her novels, HL i. 426–7. She was an effusive admirer of Smith.

[5] Not identified but presumably one of the circle of *philosophes*.

[6] Anne-Robert-Jacques Turgot (1727–81), baron de l'Aulne, statesman and economist; intendant of Limoges 1761–74; Minister of Marine 1774; Contrôleur Général des Finances 1774–6.

Make my apology to Millar[7] for not having yet answered his last very kind letter. I am preparing the Answer to it which he will certainly receive by next post. Remember me to Mrs Millar Do you ever see Mr Townshend.

94. *To* CHARLES TOWNSHEND

Sir William Fraser, *Scotts of Buccleuch*, Edinburgh, 1878, ii. 405; Rae 222–4.

Compiègne, Wednesday, 5 o'clock afternoon, 26 Aug. 1766

Dear Sir,

It is, you may believe, with the greatest concern that I find myself obliged to give you an account of a slight fever from which the Duke of Buccleugh is not yet entirely recovered, tho' it is this day very much abated. He came here to see the camp and to hunt with the King and the Court. On Thursday last he returned from hunting about seven at night very hungry, and eat heartily of a cold supper, with a vast quantity of sallad, and drank some cold punch after it. This supper, it seems, disagreed with him. He had no appetite next day, but appeared well and hearty as usual. He found himself uneasy in the field, and returned home before the rest of the company. He dined with my Lord George Lennox, and, as he tells me eat heartily. He found himself very much fatigued after dinner, and threw himself upon his servant's bed. He slept there about an hour, awaked about eight at night in a good deal of disorder. He vomited, but not enough to relieve him. I found his pulse extremely quick; he went to bed immediately and drank some vinegar whey, quite confident that a night's rest and a sweat, his usual remedy, would relieve him. He slept little that night but sweat profusely. The moment I saw him next day (Sunday) I was sure he had a fever, and begged of him to send for a physician. He refused a long time, but at last, upon seeing me uneasy, consented. I sent for Quenay,[1] first ordinary physician to the King. He sent

---

[7] Andrew Millar the publisher: no letter of about this date from him has been traced.

[1] François Quesnay (1694–1774), physician and economist: see his article on 'Fermiers' for the *Encyclopédie* and *Tableau oeconomique* (1758); to come were the pieces in *Ephémérides du citoyen* (1767), published as *Physiocratie*, 2 vols. (1767). He gave a copy of the latter work to Smith (Bonar 153), and Smith would have returned the compliment by dedicating WN to Quesnay had he lived until 1776. Dugald Stewart had this story from Smith himself: see his 'Account of the Life and Writings of Adam Smith', *Works of Smith* (1811–12), v. 470. Smith praised Quesnay in WN (IV.ix.27): 'the very ingenious and profound author of this [physiocratic] system', but thought of it as entirely speculative: 'that system which represents the produce of land as the sole source of the revenue and wealth of every country has, so far as I know, never been adopted by any nation, and it at present exists only in the speculations of a few men of great learning and ingenuity in France' (IV.ix.2: viz, the physiocrats: Quesnay, Mirabeau, and Mercier de la Rivière). Hume took a more vehement line. In 1769 he expressed surprise that Turgot would 'herd' with the physiocrats, and incited the Abbé Morellet to attack them in his *Dictionnaire du commerce*: 'I hope that in your work you will thunder them, and crush them, and pound them, and reduce them to dust

me word he was ill. I then sent for Senac;² he was ill likewise. I went to Quenay myself to beg that, notwithstanding his illness, which was not dangerous, he would come to see the Duke. He told me he was an old infirm man, whose attendance could not be depended on, and advised me, as his friend, to depend upon De la Saone,³ first physician to the Queen. I went to De la Saone, who was gone out and was not expected home till late that night. I returned to Quenay, who followed me immediately to the Duke. It was by this time seven at night. The Duke was in the same profuse sweat which he had been in all day and all the preceding night. In this situation Quenay declared that it was improper to do anything till the sweat should be over. He only ordered him some cooling ptisane⁴ drink. Quenay's illness made it impossible for him to return next day (Monday) and De la Saone has waited on the Duke ever since, to my entire satisfaction. On Monday he found the Duke's fever so moderate that he judged it unnecessary to bleed him. . . . To-day, Wednesday, upon finding some little extraordinary heat upon the Duke's skin in the morning, he proposed ordering a small quantity of blood to be taken from him at two o'clock. But upon returning at that hour he found him so very cool and easy, that he judged it unnecessary. When a French physician judges bleeding unnecessary, you may be sure that the fever is not very violent. The Duke has never had the smallest headach, nor any pain in any part of his body: he has good spirits: his head and his eyes are both clear: he has no extraordinary redness in his face: his tongue is not more foul than in a common cold. There is some little quickness in his pulse: but it is soft, full, and regular. In short, there is no one bad symptom about him: only he has a fever and keeps his bed. . . . De la Saone imagines the whole illness owing to the indigestion of Thursday night, some part of the undigested matter having got into his blood, the violent commotion which this had occasioned had burst, he supposes, some small vessel in his veins. . . . Depend upon hearing from me by every post till his perfect recovery: if any threatening symptom should appear, I shall immediately despatch an express to you; so keep your mind as easy as possible.⁵ There is not the least probability that any such symptom ever will appear. I never stir from his room from eight in the morning till ten at night, and watch for the smallest change that happens to him. I should sit by him all night too, if the ridiculous, impertinent jealousy of Cook,⁶ who thinks my assiduity an encroachment upon his duty, had not been so

and ashes! They are, indeed, the set of men the most chimerical and most arrogant that now exist, since the annihilation of the Sorbonne' (HL ii. 205). See also, WN IV.ix.38.

² Jean-Baptiste Senac (1693–1770), premier physician to Louis XV from 1752.
³ Not traced.   ⁴ A slightly medicinal concoction, originally barley-water.
⁵ Smith's solicitude (witness the next letter also) on this occasion, and for the Duke's brother on 15 Oct. (Letter 97 addressed to Lady Frances Scott), resembles that for his former pupil the Hon. Thomas Fitzmaurice; see the letters of 1759–60 to Lord Shelburne.
⁶ The Duke's servant.

much alarmed as to give some disturbance even to his master in his present illness.

The King has enquired almost every day at his levée of my Lord George and of Mr. De la Saone, concerning the Duke's illness. The Duke and Dutchess of Fitzjames,[7] the Chevalier de Clermont,[8] the Comte de Guerchy,[9] etc. etc., together with the whole English nation here and at Paris, have expressed the greatest anxiety for his recovery. Remember me in the most respectful manner to Lady Dalkeith, and believe me to be with the greatest regard, Dear Sir, Your most obliged and most humble servant,

Adam Smith.

95. *To* [CHARLES TOWNSHEND]

MS., GUL Gen. 1464/7; unpubl.

Compiègne, Thursday 6 o'clock afternoon, 27 Aug. 1766

Dear Sir

I resume the history of the Dukes illness from the moment in which I left it of yesterday.[1] I had scarce sealed up my Letter when de la Saone came into the Room. He found that the fever was somewhat increased since the time that he had seen him before which was at two o'clock afternoon. Its paroxysme is always from about seven in the evening till about twelve or one in the morning. He thought that a gentle bleeding would diminish this paroxysme which had entirely broke his rest the night before. He ordered accordingly three moderate tea cupfuls of blood to be taken from him, which was accordingly done at eight at night. The Duke accordingly spent that night more agreably than he had done any since the commencement of his illness. De la Saone found him this morning, still feverish, but more cool than he had ever seen him before. His urine, however, had returned last night to its old, bad colour but not quite so dark. De la Saone desird that I would give him leave to consult with Senac upon this singular symptom. He brought Senac accordingly at one o'clock this afternoon to see the Duke. Senac examined very carefully into all his symptoms, into the whole history of the disease from the beginning, even into his way of living and into the Accidents which had happened to his health for these twelvemonths past. He then went into a long consultation with la Saone upon this accident and upon the whole disease. I was present at this consultation and I can assure it had no resemblance to what we commonly suppose the consultations of Physicians to be. They were both

---

[7] The duc de Fitzjames was commandant of Languedoc.   [8] Not traced.
[9] Claude-Louis-François de Régnier (1715–67), comte de Guerchy, French Ambassador to England, 1763–7; exceedingly popular in London.

[1] See Letter 94 addressed to Townshend, dated 26 Aug.

of opinion that the fever was independent of this symptom and caused by an indigestion; and that it was the effect either of some strain, or of the fever itself; probably of the fever itself; as it increases with every increase of the fever and diminishes upon every relaxation; that it was blood which discoloured the Urine; they were in some doubt, however, whether this blood had come from some small vessel in the reins or in the Bladder. Its being so perfectly mixed and blended with the urine was the only symptom which disposed them to believe that it might come from the reins; But as the Duke even upon pinching his reins feels no pain or uneasiness in any part of them; they were disposed to believe that it rather came from the inside of the Bladder; in which case they both agreed that it was not likely to be of any consequence. The extreme good success of last nights bleeding inclines them to take a little more blood from the Duke, provided the fever increases as usual towards seven or eight at night. Senac is more formal than la Saone who is one of the most engaging men I ever saw; In his reasonings and Judgements, however, Senac is one of the clearest, distinctest and most rational Physicians I ever saw. La Saone is not less so.

Since I wrote the above la Saone has been to see the Duke. He finds him so easy that he imagines it will be unnecessary to bleed him to night. He is to return, however, at eight o'clock in order to decide that point along with Senac. I ever am Your most Obliged and most humble Servant

Adam Smith

The King and Queen both enquired very particularly about the Duke this morning, first from his Physicians, and afterwards, from the Sardinian Ambassadour and from the Duke of Richmond who expresses the most anxious concern about him. Senac is now quite well.

96. *From* DAVID HUME

Address: A Monsieur Monsieur Smith Gentilhomme Anglois Hotel du Parc roiale, Fauxbourg St Germain a Paris[1]
MS., RSE ii. 39; HL ii. 82–3.

[Lisle Street, Leicester Fields, Aug. 1766][2]

Dear Smith

There is a Bookseller at Paris, one Dessain,[3] who has some Character, but has play'd me a very ugly Trick. I bought of him two Volumes of

---

[1] 'Paris' is struck through and 'a Compiegne' added twice, in another hand.

[2] As the Postscript indicates, Hume was staying at the London boarding house kept by the sisters Ann and Peggy Elliot. The date of the letter is suggested by the references to the quarrel with Rousseau.

[3] Jean Dessaint (d. 1776), commenced bookseller in 1720; associated with Charles Saillant (1716–86): their firm is mentioned *passim* in Rousseau's *Correspondence*, ed. R. A. Leigh (Geneva, 1964–).

Buffon's Natural History and paid him thirty Livres[4] for them; but as M. Buffon made me a Present of them afterwards, Dessain took them back. I gave him a pretty large Commission of Books to be sent to me to the Care of David Wilson,[5] and I left among the rest, these two Volumes of Buffon, together with Mrs Macaulay's History[6] and some other Books. He has sent over several Parcels to Mr Wilson, but will neither send over my Books, nor answer my Letters nor take any Notice of me. He lives on the Quay des Augustins, not far from you: I wish you woud speak to him and threaten him a little. Tell him I shall prosecute him either myself on my Return to Paris or by Order, if he do not send over my Books and Money. I wonder he acts so foolishly: For my Commission woud be more profitable to him, than so small a Pittance as this sum.

You may see in M. Dalembert's hands the whole Narrative of my Affair with Rousseau along with the whole Train of Correspondence. Pray is it not a nice Problem, whether he be not an arrant Villain or an arrant Madman or both: The last is my Opinion; but the Villain seems to me to predominate most in his Character. I shall not publish them unless forc'd, which you will own to be a very great Degree of Self denial. My Conduct, in this Affair, woud do me a great deal of Honour; and his woud blast him for ever; and blast his Writings at the same time: For as these have been exalted much above their Merit, when his personal Character falls, they woud of Course fall below their Merit. I am however apprehensive that in the End I shall be oblig'd to publish. About two or three days ago, there was an Article in the St. James's Chronicle copyd from the Brussels Gazette, which pointed at this Dispute. This may probably put Rousseau in a Rage; he will publish something, which may oblige me for my own Honour to give the Narrative to the Public. There will be no Reason to dread a long Train of disagreeable Controversy: One Publication begins and ends it on my Side. Pray, tell me your Judgement of my Work, if it deserves the Name: Tell D'alembert I make him absolute Master to retrench or alter what he thinks proper, in order to suit it to the Latitude of Paris.

Were you and I together Dear Smith we shoud shed Tears at present for the Death of poor Sir James Macdonald. We coud not possibly have sufferd a greater Loss than in that valuable young Man.

I am
Yours most sincerely
David Hume

[4] In WN (I.iv. 10), Smith stated that the English pound was reduced to a third of its original value, and the French pound to one sixty-sixth, by his time. This would suggest that the livre was worth about one shilling.   [5] Bookseller in the Strand, London (d. 1777).
[6] Catherine Sawbridge (1731–91), md. (1) Dr. George Macaulay, and (2) William Graham. The first volume of her *History of England* was published in 1763, and Dr. Macaulay sent a copy to Hume in Paris. The last of the eight volumes appeared in 1783.

P.S.

In a little time, I go down to pass a few Weeks with my Friends in Scotland but direct still to me at Miss Elliots: My Letters will follow me. I wish I had a strong unanswerable Motive to determine me whether I shall live henceforth in London or in Paris. My Inclination and indeed my Resolutions lead me to the latter place; but my Reason points out the former. I for [   ]⁷ :ar, that I woud have a great Facility to continue my History [   ]. Clamour of Faction on both Sides seems to have subsided: But c[   ] me a good Reason, why I should put myself to that Trouble? [   ] Compliments to Baron D Holbach.

97. *To* LADY FRANCES SCOTT¹

MS., SRO GD1/479/14; unpubl.

Paris, Wednesday 11 o'clock at night, 15 Oct. 1766

I resume the very melancholy History of Mr Scott's illness from where I left it off in my last letter.²

On Monday morning Dr Gem³ observed some degree of fever in Mr Scott's pulse which he had thought entirely free of it for some days before. Mr Quenay observed the same thing. His vomitings, however, and Purgings continued with great violence all day, notwithstanding a dose of ipp[eca]cuana which they had given him in the morning. His fever seemed to go off almost entirely in the evening, and they gave him, what they had given for two days before, a very gentle opiat to quiet his stomach and to give him a little rest in the night time. Yesterday morning Dr Gem imagined he felt more quickness in his pulse than he had ever done before; this, however, soon subsided and his pulse returned to a degree of frequency that was not much beyond its natural state. He was all day much freer from vomitings than he had been for some days before, and his purgings seemed to be no greater than what might be expected from fifteen grains of Rhubarb which they had given him the night before and that morning: from one to about three o'clock afternoon I thought I observed some alterations in his

---

⁷ MS. torn.

¹ Younger sister of Duke of Buccleuch, b. (posthumous) 26 July 1750; md. Archibald, Lord Douglas, 13 May 1783; d. 31 Mar. 1817. This letter and the following one reveal that her brother, the Hon. Hew Campbell Scott, died of illness and was not 'assassinated on the streets of Paris' as was claimed in *The New Statistical Account of Scotland* (Edinburgh, 1845), i. 490, by Dr. Peter Steele, 'lately rector of Dalkeith Grammar School'.

² Not traced.

³ Dr. Richard Gem (? 1716–1800), educ. at Cambridge, settled in Paris; physician to the British Embassy there, 1762; he was steeped in French philosophy and in 1765–6 was often to be found dining at the Baron d'Holbach's house in the Rue Royale, in the company of Diderot and Helvétius; later in life Franklin and Jefferson were his intimate friends, and he supervised the education of the statesman William Huskisson.

speech, and an extraordinary hurry and confusion in his Ideas. This disagreeable symptom, however, soon went off, so as to have me uncertain whether I had not fancy'd it from my own apprehensions; His pulse continuing all the while, tho' a little feverish, extremely gentle and moderate. In the evening he appeared easier than he had been for some days before: They gave him no opiat that night and he Passed it very easily notwithstanding. This morning he ordered himself to be taken out of bed at eight o'clock and sit up to Eleven. He was entirely free from sickness and vomiting; his pulse had very little quickness; and his purging was no greater than what was to be expected from the fifteen grains of Rhubarb he had taken this morning and the night before. The Physicians were both much pleased with his situation and imagined that all the violence of his disorder was over. Quenay said that he had been at a loss before but he now knew what to do. I thought I might venture to go to my Bankers to get some money which, tho I had much occasion for it, I had put off doing for eight days before in order not to leave him. Dr Gem undertook to sit by him till I should return. I stayed out about an hour happy to imagine that all my anxiety was likely to be at an end. Upon my return I found him quite delirious, and that too with no very violent fever. I immediately sent for Quenai who ordered him instantly to be blooded. The delirium diminished upon bleeding: he fell into a sleep and into a sweat; his pulse rose; and in about two hours after he bled very copiously at the nose. Tho' he speaks distinctly sometimes, the delirium is not yet, however, entirely gone of. All his other symptoms, however, are abated: His stomach is quite easy; he has no complaint in his bowls; he complains of no pain anywhere, not even of a headach. This terrible symptom only remains. I have already wrote twice to the Duke to return; in a way, however, that will not alarm him. I have sent an express to him this afternoon besides. Tho' I have entire confidence in the skill of the Physicians that have hitherto attended him, notwithstanding they have been mistaken in their predictions, I have thought proper to call in Tronchin,[4] who will attend him for the future along with them. He is my particular and intimate friend, Quênai is one of the worthiest men in France and one of the best Physicians that is to be met with in any country. He was not only the Physician but the friend and confident of Madame Pompadour a women who was no contemptible Judge of merit. Gem is a man of the most perfect probity and friendship. Since the beginning of Mr Scotts illness he has seldom been less than twelve hours a day by his bedside and has all along acted the part of a Nurse as well as of a Physician. Tho' the event has not hitherto

---

4 Théodore Tronchin (1709–81), Genevan physician and contributor to the *Encyclopédie*: his early education was supervised by Bolingbroke and continued under Hermann Boerhaave at Leyden. He was principal physician to the house of Orleans and attended Voltaire. In 1761 he sent his son to Glasgow to be educated by Smith. His friendship with Smith would be strengthened by latter's residence in Geneva, Oct.–Dec. 1766.

answered their expectations I am convinced, they have both acted a very prudent and proper part. They both have still good hopes. Your humanity will excuse the confusion of this letter. The very sound of Mr Scotts voice, when I hear it from the next room, makes me almost as delirious as he is. I dare not desire you to say anything from me to Lady Dalkeith at present: I pray God to preserve and to prepare her for whatever may be the event of this terrible disorder. I ever am

etc. etc.
Adam Smith

Mr Scott has had a very good night. He has raved at intervals, but in general had been very quiet and distinct and has slept for a good deal. Dr Gem finds his Pulse not very quick and rather weak than strong. Thursday 7 o'clock in the morning.

98. *To* [LADY FRANCES SCOTT]

MS., SRO GD1/479/14; unpubl.

Paris, 19 Oct. 1766

It is my misfortune to be under the necessity of acquainting you of the most terrible calamity that has befallen us. Mr Scott dyed this Evening at seven o'clock.[1] I had gone to the Duke of Richmonds in order to acquaint the Duke of Buccleugh that all hope was over and that his Brother could not outlive tomorrow morning: I returned in less than half an hour to do the last duty to my best friend. He had expired about five minutes before I could get back and I had not the satisfaction of closing his eyes with my own hands. I have no force to continue this letter; The Duke, tho' in very great affliction, is otherwise in perfect health. I ever am etc. etc.

Adam Smith

99. *To* ANDREW MILLAR

MS., RSE vi. 34; HL i. 521, n. 1 (extract passed on to Hume by Millar)

Paris, Oct. 1766

Though I am very happy here, I long passionately to rejoin my old friends, and if I had once got fairly to your side of the water, I think I should never cross it again. Recommend the same sober way of thinking to Hume. He is light-headed, tell him, when he talks of coming to spend the remainder of his days here, or in France.[1]

[1] See previous letter; on 'fevers' in late eighteenth-century France, see J.-P. Peter in *Annales: E.S.C.* (July–Aug. 1967) 711–51.

[1] See Letter 87 from Hume, dated 5 Sept. 1765, and Smith's reply, ? Sept. 1765, Letter 88, for another discussion of Hume's wish to settle in Paris.

100. *To* WILLIAM STRAHAN

Rae 234; Bonar 147–8 (excerpt).

[London, winter 1766–67]
Friday

My Dear Strahan

I go to the country for a few days this afternoon, so that it will be unnecessary to send me any more sheets till I return. The *Dissertation upon the Origin of Languages* is to be printed at the end of the *Theory*.[1] There are some literal errors in the printed copy of it which I should have been glad to have corrected, but have not the opportunity, as I have no copy by me. They are of no great consequenc. In the titles, both of the *Theory* and *Dissertation*, call me simply Adam Smith without any addition either before or behind.[2]

I ever am, etc.,
Adam Smith.

101. *To* LORD SHELBURNE

Address: To Lord Shelburne
MS., Bowood Libr., Marquess of Lansdowne; Rae 235–6.

[London,] Thursday 12 Feb. 1767

My Lord

I send you enclosed Quiros's memorial presented to Philip the second after his return from his voyage, translated from the Spanish in which it is published in Purches.[1] The Voyage itself is long, obscure, and difficult to

[1] Ed. 3, 1767: the *Dissertation* was first published in *The Philological Miscellany*, i (1761) 440–79.
[2] TMS eds. 1 (1759) and 2 (1761) described the author on the title-page as 'Professor of Moral Philosophy in the University of Glasgow'. Ed. 3 placed 'LL.D.' after his name, as do eds. 4 (1774) and 5 (1781). Ed. 6 (1790) described him as 'Adam Smith, LL.D. Fellow of the Royal Societies of London and Edinburgh; One of the Commissioners of his Majesty's Customs in Scotland; and formerly Professor of Moral Philosophy in the University of Glasgow'.

[1] Pedro Fernández de Quirós (d. 1615), Portuguese visionary and sailor; pilot on the expedition of Mendaña to the Solomons, 1595–6; led search for the unknown continent in the South Seas and discovered the New Hebrides, 1605–7, which he called La Austrialia del Espíritu Santo in honour of Philip III of Spain, scion of the house of Austria. He addressed over seventy memorials to Philip on his return, the 8th (Xa he dicho) was printed in *Purchas His Pilgrimes* (London, 1624–6), the great collection of voyages published in 5 vols. by the Revd. Samuel Purchas (1577–1628). One narrative of the 1605–6 expedition (Archivo del Museo Naval, Madrid, MS. 951) was edited about 1758, probably by Don Bernardo de Iriarte. A transcription of the Simancas original of the report by Luis Vaz de Torres was sent to Dalrymple (see below) by Juan Bautista Muñoz, translated into English and printed by Rear-Admiral James Burney, who had accompanied Captain

be understood except by those who are particularly acquainted with the geography and navigation of those countries; and upon looking over a great number of Dalrymples papers[2] I imagined this was what you would like best to see. He is besides just finishing a Geographical account of all the discoveries that have yet been made in the South seas from the west coast of America to Tasmans discoveries.[3] If your Lordship will give him leave he would be glad to read this to you himself and shew you on his map the geographical ascertainment of the situation of each island. I have seen it; it is extremely short; not much longer than this memorial of Quiros. Whether this may be convenient for your Lordship I know not. Whether this continent exists or not may perhaps be uncertain; but supposing it does exist, I am very certain you never will find a man fitter for discovering it, or more determined to hazard everything in order to discover it.[4] The terms that he would ask are first, the Absolute command of the Ship with the naming of all the officers in order that he may have people who both have confidence in him and in whom he has confidence: and secondly that, in case he should lose his ship by the common course of accidents before he gets into the South Sea, that the Government will undertake to give him another. These are all the terms he would insist upon. The ship properest for such an expedition, he says, would be an old fifty gun ship without her Guns. He does not, however, insist upon this, as, a sine quâ non, but will go in any ship from an hundred to a thousand tons. He wishes to have but one ship with a good many boats. Most expeditions of this kind, he says, have miscarried from one ships being obliged to wait for the other, or losing time in looking out for the other.

Within these two days I have looked over every thing I can find relating to the Roman Colonys.[5] I have not found any thing of much consequence.

Cook in his Voyages, in *A Chronological History of Discoveries in the Pacific* (1806); see *La Austrialia del Espiritu Santo* ed. Celsus Kelly, 2 vols. (Cambridge, 1966); also Colin Jack-Hinton, *The Search for the Islands of Solomon, 1567–1838* (Oxford, 1969).

[2] Alexander Dalrymple (1737–1808), younger bro. of Lord Hailes, hydrographer; served in the East India Co., charted the northern part of the Bay of Bengal; in the Admiralty's service, 1795, and died broken-hearted on his dismissal, 1808. He published *An Historical Collection of the Several Voyages and Discoveries in the South Pacific Ocean* (1769) and *An Account of the Discoveries Made in the South Pacific Ocean, Previous to 1764* (1767).

[3] Abel Janszoon Tasman (? 1603–59), great Dutch navigator; his trading and exploratory voyages for the Dutch East India Co., 1632–53, yielded knowledge of the Pacific, Philippines, Formosa, and Japan; in 1642–3 he discovered Tasmania and New Zealand and circumnavigated Australia; his voyage of 1644 clarified the relationship between New Guinea, Tasmania, and the known parts of Australia.

[4] As Secretary of State, Shelburne had an interest in the debate over the command of the expedition to chart the transit of Venus. Lord Hawke appointed Cook who sailed in the *Endeavour*, 1768–71, to carry out the astronomical work and explore the coasts of New Zealand and eastern Australia. Cook's expedition of 1772–5 in the *Resolution* disproved the contention of Dalrymple and others about the existence of a great southern continent.

[5] Roman colonies were usually governed by a commission of three elected by the people; Smith discussed Roman colonies in WN, IV.vii.a.3.

They were governed upon the model of the Republic: had two consuls called *duumviri*; a Senate called decuriones or collegium decurionum and other magistrats similar to those of the Republic: The colonists lost their right of voting or of being elected to any magistry in the Roman comitia. In this respect they were inferior to many municipia. They retained, however, all the other privileges of Roman citizens. They seem to have been very independent. Of thirty colonies of whom the Romans demanded troops in the second carthagenian war twelve refused to obey. They frequently rebelled and joined the enemies of the Republic. Being in some measure little independent republics they naturally followed the interests which their peculiar Situation pointed out to them. I have the honour to be with the highest regard My Lord

Your Lordships

most obedient humble

Servant

Adam Smith

102. *To* THOMAS CADELL[1]

Address: To Mr Thomas Caddel
MS., Bodleian Montagu d. 10, fol. 58ᵛ; *Economic Journal* viii (1898), 402–3.

Lower Grosvenor Street, London, 25 Mar. [1767][2]

Dear Sir

After thanking you very sincerely for the trouble you have already taken about my affairs, I must still beg of you to take a little more; which is that you would not only send all the four boxes as soon as possible to Edinburgh directed to the care of Mr Kincaid, but that you would ensure them to the value of two hundred Pounds; and that likewise you would send me as soon as possible the Account of the whole expence including that of the two last books you was so good as to procure for me; viz, Anderson[3] and Postlethwait.[4]

Dear Sir, Yours sincerely

Adam Smith

[1] Thomas Cadell (1742–1802), publisher; apprenticed to Andrew Millar as printer, 1758; partner 1765; took over the business 1767; London Alderman 1798; Sheriff 1801–2.

[2] Smith gave the date as March 1766, but he was then in Paris.

[3] Adam Anderson (1692–1765), author of *Historical and Chronological Deduction of the Origin of Commerce* (new ed. 1764), much drawn upon in WN; Smith had a copy in his library (1781 list).

[4] Malachi Postlethwayt (1717–67), author of *The Universal Dictionary of Trade and Commerce* (3rd ed. 2 vols., 1766), an expanded English version of the *Dictionnaire universel de commerce* (1st ed. 3 vols., 1723–30), written mostly by Jacques Savary des Brulons (1657–1716). Both the *Dictionary* and James Postlethwayt's *History of the Public Revenues from the Revolution to the Present Time* (1759) were in Smith's library.

103. *To* DAVID HUME

Address: To David Hume Esqr, Under Secretary for the Northern department, a Mr Secretary Conways house, London
MS., RSE vii. 36 (sheet torn); Rae 241–2 (in part).

Kirkaldy, 7 June 1767

My Dearest friend

The Principal design of this Letter is to Recommend to your particular Attention the Count de Sarsfield,[1] the best and the most agreable friend I had in france. Introduce him, if you find it proper, to all the friends of your absent friend, to Oswald and to Elliot in Particular. I cannot express to you how anxious I am that his stay in London should be rendered agreeable to him. You know him and must know what a plain, worthy honourable man he is. I have enclosed a letter for him which you may either send to him or rather, if the weighty affairs of state will permit it, deliver it to him yourself. The letter to Dr Morton[2] you may send by the Penny Post.

My Business here is Study in which I have been very deeply engaged for about a Month past. My Amusements are long, solitary walks by the Sea side. You may judge how I spend my time. I feel myself, however, extremely happy, comfortable and contented. I never was, perhaps, more so in all my life.

You will give me great comfort by writing to me now and then, and by letting me know what is passing among my friends at London. Remember me to them all particularly to Mr Adams's family[3] and to Mrs. Montague.[4]

What has become of Rousseau? Has he gone abroad, because he cannot continue to get himself sufficiently persecuted in Great Britain?[5]

What is the meaning of the Bargain that your Ministry have made with the India Company?[6] They have not, I see prolonged their Charter, which is a good circumstance. What are you going to do, or rather [ ]

[1] Count de Sarsfield, of Irish extraction; for a time it was thought he would succeed M. de Guerchy as Ambassador to Britain in 1767, but he did not. Hume knew him well; see Letter 104 from Hume, dated 13 June 1767.

[2] Charles Morton (1716–99), M.D. Leyden, 1748; practised in London; F.R.S. 1751, Secretary to the Royal Society 1760–74; Under-Librarian of the British Museum 1756, Secretary to the Trustees and Principal Librarian 1776, succeeding Dr. Maty. His chief work was an edition of Whitelock's *Embassy to Sweden* (1772).

[3] ? that of the architects, Robert Adam (1728–92) and James Adam (1732–94), boyhood friends of Smith in Kirkaldy. In 1763 they returned to London after studies in Rome and on the Grand Tour which completed an education begun through apprenticeship under their father William.

[4] Mrs. Elizabeth Robinson Montagu (1720–1800), bluestocking and enthusiastic admirer of Ossian; visited Scotland in 1766; from 1750, her London house was much frequented by intellectuals; contributed to Lyttleton's *Dialogues of the Dead* (1760) and attacked Voltaire in *An Essay on the Writings and Genius of Shakespear* (1769).

[5] Rousseau was back in France by this time.

[6] Both the Government and the Opposition sought to make friends in East India House: reform was in the air but not so seriously as to affect the fortunes being made,

104. *From* DAVID HUME

MS., RSE ii. 40; HL ii. 142–3.

London, 13 June 1767

Dear Smith

The Count de Sarsfield[1] is a good Acquaintance of mine from the time I saw him at Paris; and as he is really a Man of Merit, I have great Pleasure whenever I meet him here: My Occupations keep me from cultivating his Friendship as much as I should incline. I did not introduce him to Elliot, because I knew that this Gentleman's Reserve and Indolence wou'd make him neglect the Acquaintance, and I did not introduce him to Oswald, because I fear that he and I are broke for ever: At least, he does not seem inclined to take any Steps towards an Accommodation with me. I am to tell you the strangest Story you ever heard of. I was dining with him above two Months ago, where among other Company was the Bishop of Raphoe.[2] After dinner, we were disposed to me merry; I said to the Company that I had been very ill us'd by Lord Hertford: For that I always expected to be made a Bishop by him during his Lieutenancy, but he had given away two Sees from me, to my great Vexation and Disappointment. The Right Reverend, without any farther Provocation, burst out into the most furious, and indecent, and orthodox Rage, that ever was seen: Told me that I was most impertinent; that if he did not wear a Gown I durst not, no, I durst not have us'd him so; that none but a Coward woud treat a Clergy-man in that manner; that henceforth he must either abstain from his Brother's House or I must; and that this was not the first time he had heard this stupid Joke from my Mouth. With the utmost Tranquillity and Temper, I askd his Pardon; assurd him upon my honour that I did not mean him the least Offence; if I had imagind he coud possibly have been displeas'd I never shoud have mentiond the Subject; but the Joke was not in the least against him, but entirely against myself, as if I were capable of such an Expectation as that of being a Bishop; my Regard for himself and still more for his Brother, with whom I had long been more particularly connected, wou'd certainly restrain me from either Joke or Earnest, which coud be offensive to him: And that if I had ever touchd on the same Topick before, I had entirely forgot it; and it must have been above a twelvemonth

---

e.g. by Robert Clive. Chatham's ministry extracted £400,000 a year, and simultaneously limited the dividend to 10 per cent. If the dividend fell below 6 per cent, the Company was not obliged to pay the subsidy. See L. S. Sutherland, *The East India Company in Eighteenth Century Politics* (London, 1952).

[1] See Letter 103 addressed to David Hume, dated 7 June 1767.
[2] John Oswald (d. 1780), younger bro. of James Oswald of Dunnikier; a school friend of Adam Smith; Bishop of Clonfert and Kilmacduagh 1762; of Dromore 1763; and of Raphoe 1763. See Letter 109 addressed to Hume, dated 13 Sept. 1767.

ago. He was no wise appeas'd, ravd on in the same Style for a long time: At last, I got the Discourse diverted and took my Leave seemingly with great Indifference and even good humour. I was no wise surprizd nor concernd about his Lordship; because I had on other Occasions observ'd the same orthodox Zeal swell within him, and it was often difficult for him to converse with Temper when I was in the Company: But what really surprizd and vexd me, was, that his Brother kept Silence all the time; I met him in the Passage when I went away, and he made me no Apology; he has never since calld on me; and tho he sees, that I never come near his House, tho formerly I us'd to be three or four time a week with him, he never takes the least Notice of it: I own this gives me Vexation, because I have a sincere Value and Affection for him: It is only some Satisfaction to me to find, that I am so palpably in the right, as not to leave the least Room for Doubt or Ambiguity. Dr Pitcairne,[3] who was in the Company, says, that he never saw such a Scene in his Life time. If I were sure Dear Smith that you and I shoud not one day quarrel in some such manner, I shoud tell you, that I am Yours very affectionately and sincerely

D. H.

105. *From* [GEORGE LOUIS LE SAGE][1]

MS., GUL Gen. 1035/239; unpubl.

A londres le 23 Juin 1767

J'ay recue, Monsieur, la lettre que vous m'avez fait l'honneur de m'ecrire le 7[2] et qui m'a fait le plaisir qui accompagnera toujours tout ce qui me donnera une marque de la continuation de l'amitié dont vous m'avez flatté. J'espere me dedommager Du malheur que j'ay eu de ne pas vous trouver icy en allant vous troubler dans votre Solitude Et faire quelques promenades avec vous Sur le bord de la Mer. Un le plus Seduisant de mes projets Made d'Enville me reproche de ne L'avoir pas Encore Executé. Mais je Suis retenu icy par une affaire ou La folie des hommes me donne beaucoup de tourment et d'impatience. Je vous diray ce que c'est, quand nous nous verrons. Mais dans quelque tems que ce Soit Je vous prie de ne dire a personne que Je n'aie En une icy, il m'est important qu'on ne le Sache jamais. Je ne vous parlerois pas Sans l'incertitude qu'elle met dans ma marche et la necessité ou je me trouve par cette raison de vous demander

---

[3] William Pitcairne (1711–91), also from Fife; M.D. Oxford, 1749; began practice in London, 1750; President of the Royal College of Physicians 1775–85.

[1] The signature is torn off but the references in the letter point to George Louis Le Sage (1724–1803), philosopher, physician, mathematician, and Professor of Physics at Geneva, where Smith met him in the house of Mme d'Anville when she was being attended by Dr. Tronchin. See Rae 191–2.

[2] Not traced.

ce que vous serez cet Eté. Si vous Restez constamment a Kircaldy, J'y irai quand je pourray: Si vous avez quelque projet d'en Sortir, dites m'en le tems, Je tacheray de faire un effort pour aller vous voir Auparavant ou apres. Je Servis desesperé d'etre venu dans cette ile Sans avoir cette Satisfaction.

La mort de Made la dauphine a fait tort a notre ami Tronchin.[3] Je crois que Sa plus grande faute en de n'avoir pas menagé les medecins qui Sont en fureur contre luy. Il faut a jouter qu'il a dit dans le commencement que la maladie de made La dauphine ne venoit pas de la poitrine mais du foie. C'est une fantasie qu'il a que de ne pas croire aux maux de poitrine et qui me Surprend toujours. J'en ai vu un example dans la maladie d'une fille de made d'Enville. Il est vray que pour made la dauphine S'il ne dit pas des le premier moment que le foe avois gaté les poumoux, ce fut au bout de bien peu de jours. Mais cela S'est oublié on n'à retenue de Sa phrase que la partie la plus remarquable. En ce qu'elle contredisoit l'opinion commune qui S'est [trouvée] la vraie. Il donna avant l'ouverture du cadavre un papier cacheté dans le quel il avoit mis Sa facon de penser. Le roy a qui on le lut le lendemain dit que cetoit se qu'il luy avoit toujours dit. Elle Se rapportoit a l'ouverture du cadavre ou on trouva le foie tres sain avec petite cicatrice pres qui paroissoit ancienne. Je ne Scai s'il ne convenoit pas de S'etre trompé dans les premiers jours on a dit qu'il avoit eté plus longtems dans l'erreur et on donnoit pour pruve les remedes chauds qu'il a donnés constamment. Quelques gens puissans ont pris parti contre luy. Ainsy a tout prendre quoyque Ses partisans n'aient pas perdre de terrein, quoy qu'on voie evidemment que tout cecy n'en qu'une question de mots puisque made la dauphine etoit Sans Esperance lorsqu'on l'a apellée. Quoyque Mr Le duc d'Orleans ait tente bon Et que made adelaide L'ait demandé une fois avec beaucoup dempressement, Il vaudroit mieux que cela ne fut jamais arrivé. Je luy ai envoyé le livre de dimsdale Sur L'inoculation[4] pour qu'il connoisse cette methode de qu'il la preuve peu a peu car il faut S'y rendre. Mais Il faut convenir que c'est une chose delicate pour luy.

Vous avez oublié une chose dans la comparaison que vous avez faite des hommes des differentes nations. C'est la liberté de parler les femmes l'ont plus que nous en france. Cest ce qui fait un de leurs avantages vous avez été temoin de l'effet qu'elles ont fais dans l'affaire du pauvre Latey.

Je viens de lire un livre dun de vos Compatriotes Mr Deferguson.[5] Il m'a fait grand plaisir mais j'ay ete fache d'y trouver Son Eloge des Lace-demoniens.[6] Je ne puis reconnoitre pour une nation une institution bisarre qui ne formoit des hommes que par les memes principes qui en forment chez les moines, qui avoit besoin d'esclaves pour Se Soutenir Et un mot

---

[3] Dr. Théodore Tronchin.
[4] Thomas, Baron Dimsdale, M.D. (1712–1800) published his book *The Present Method of Inoculating for the Small-Pox* in 1767.
[5] Adam Ferguson, *An Essay on the History of Civil Society* (1767).
[6] Ibid. Pt. III. vi, 'Of Civil Liberty'.

dont on auroit ete fors malheureux d'Etre voisin. J'aurois voulu qu'un aussi grand philosophe en nous citant ces Examples puis qu'il n'en trouvoit psa de meilleur pour montrer jusqu'on on pouvoit porter. L'amour de la patrie, nous eut averti qu'il croit imparfait: 1° parce que l'institutions En elle meme n'est pas bonne. Elle privoit les hommes de l'employ De la plus grande partie de leurs talens. 2° parce que pour Se former et Etre durable Elle avoit besoin d'un concours de circonstances qu'il n'est pas vraisemblable qu'on voit jamais reunie. Je trouve aussi qu'il n'a pas assez rendre justice a nos peres. Il est vray qu'il convient que les grecs doivent une grande partie de leur lustre a leurs historiens. Mais il luy eut eté facile de faire voir que nos peres ont beaucoup a Se plaindre des leurs. Je trouve encore qu'il ne rend pas assez de justice a la noblesse de leur caractere qui a Si remarquablement affoibli les horreurs de la Guerre Chez nous. Les grecs la faisoient avec toutes les passions de l'homme qui Se livre a luy meme. La Generosité de nos peres ne vient pas seulement comme le dit M ferguson de l'autorité des femmes sur eux ni de leurs livres de chevalerie.[7] Ils faisoient taire leurs femmes quand Il s'agissoit de Guerre. Vous n'avez qu'a lire la vie de bertrand du Guesclin.[8] Il ne faut pour expliquer cette difference d'Eux aux grecs que dire que Ceux icy agissoient toujours en Societé ils n'etoient rien quen Societé. Un chevalier Seul Se croyoit quelque chose et en consequence tout ce qui pouvoit l'honorer etait precieux. Quelques generaux Le sont appliqué a la tete de Leurs armés les memes principes ils avoient tout. Vos [? capitaines] anglois [? Savent] tres bien Se conduire avec finesse pendant que le brave roy jean ne Savoit aller que tout droit devant luy. Nous ne voyons pas que leur reputation ait eté attaquée dans [? cet avis là]. En un mot a force d'Etudier les peuples qui habitoient des villes Mr ferguson me paroit avoir un peu oublié les habitants des Campagnes. Je ne croiray jamais qu'un gouvernement d'ou celuy d'angleterre en derivé ne merite pas beaucoup d'attention Et n'ont pas droit a quelques eloges.

Envoilá bien long monsieur mais vous connoissez de plaisir que jay a m'entretenir avec vous. On dit rousseau a St Denis on dit qu'il est fort feté. J'ay peine a croire que le parlement l'y laisse longtems. Je ne Scai rien directement de paris. Ce Sont des gens de ce pais icy qui me l'ont dit Adieu Monsieur je finirai sans ceremonie [   ][9]

---

[7] Ibid. Pt. IV. iv, 'Manners of Polished and Commercial Nations'.
[8] Bertrand Du Guesclin (d. 1380) Constable of France under Charles V; freed France from the English.
[9] Signature torn off.

106. *To* JOHN CRAIGIE[1]

Fraser, *Scotts of Buccleuch*, facsim. facing i. 491.

Kirkcaldy, 26 June 1767

Kirkaldy 26 June 1767 Then received of Mr John Craigie of Kilgarston, in name and upon Account of the Duke of Buccleugh, the sum of one hundred and fifty Pounds Sterling due on the twenty fourth of this present month of June one thousand seven hundred and sixty seven years, being one half years payment of the Annuity of three hundred pounds a year settled upon me by his Grace;[2] of which half years payment and all pre-ceedings I hereby discharge the Said Duke of Buccleugh and all others con-cerned; at Kirkaldy this twenty sixth day of June one thousand seven hundred and sixty seven years. Witness my hand

Adam Smith

107. *From* DAVID HUME

MS., RSE ii. 41; HL ii. 150.

London, 14 July 1767

Dear Smith

I send you the enclosd with a large Packet for Count Sarsfield. This is the last ministerial Act, which I shall probably perform; and with this Exertion I finish my Functions. I shall not leave this Country presently: Perhaps I may go over to France. Our Ressignation[1] is a very extraordinary Incident; and will probably occasion a total Change of Ministry. Are you busy? Yours

David Hume

You must keep Count Sarsfield's Papers till a proper Method of return-ing them be pointed out to you. Have you read Lord Lyttleton?[2] Do you not admire his Whiggery and his Piety; Qualities so useful both for this World and the next?

---

[1] Agent of the Duke of Buccleuch.

[2] As travelling tutor to Buccleuch, Smith had received £300 p.a. and this was converted to an annuity for life on completion of the Tour.

[1] That of Hume and General Henry Seymour Conway (1721–95) in the Department of Northern Affairs, Secretary of State's office. Presumably these were not accepted; Hume remained an Under-Secretary of State until Jan. 1768. The resignations hinged on the illness of Chatham, his recovery being despaired of in July 1767. Grafton was the real leader at this time.

[2] The long-delayed *History of Henry the Second*, the 1st 3 vols. of which had just appeared.

108. *To* [WILLIAM STRAHAN]

MS., University of Illinois Libr.; Scott 265.

Kirkcaldy, 30 Aug. 1767

Dear Sir

I send you enclosed a bill for twelve Pounds eleven Shillings. When it is paid, and it is due more than a fortnight ago, I will begg the favour of you to deliver [two pounds?] eleven Shillings to Dr Morton Secretary to the Royal Society which he has been so good as to lay out for me.[1] To the best of my Remembrance I owe you about or near ten Pounds, the shilling or two that is either under or over we shall adjust at meeting. I must beg the favour of you to present my most respectful complements to Dr Morton and to tell him how much I think myself [obliged] to him for his many civilities. There is no need of taking any receipt from him. Remember me likewise to Mr and Mrs Millar and to all other friends. I ever am

Dear Sir

Most Sincerely yours

Adam Smith

109. *To* DAVID HUME

Address: To David Hume Esqr, Under Secretary for the Northern Department, London
MS., RSE vii. 37; Rae 243 (in part).

Dalkieth house,[1] 13 Sept. 1767

My Dear friend

I cannot easily express to you the indignation with which your last letter[2] filled me. The Bishop is a brute and a beast and unmerited preferment has rendered him, it seems, still more so.[3] I am very much ashamed that the very great affection which I owe to his Brother[4] had ever imposed upon me so much as to give me a good opinion of him. He was at Kirkaldy since I received your letter and I was obliged to see him, but I did not behave to him as I otherwise would have done. He thought proper to leave Edinburgh the day or the day before his brother arrived in it, without waiting

---

[1] Smith was elected a Fellow of the Royal Society on 21 May 1767, but was not admitted until 27 May 1773.

[1] Dalkeith House or Palace, Midlothian, one of the residences of the Buccleuch family; rebuilt for Duchess Anne 1700 by James Smith, and said to be an imitation of Het Loo in the Netherlands.
[2] Letter 104, dated 13 June 1767.
[3] See Letter 104 for Hume's account of Bishop John Oswald's 'rage'.
[4] James Oswald of Dunnikier.

to see that Brother to whom he owes everything, who was then, and is still
in the most terrible distress, and who used to have no other foible so great
as his esteem and regard to this haughty Blockhead. I excuse our old friend
for not having taken more notice of this affair on account of the present
state of his health upon which I shall explain myself to you more fully at
meeting.[5]

Be so good as to convey the enclosed letter to the Count de Sarsfield;
I have been much in the wrong for having delayed so long to write both to
him and you.

There is a very amiable, modest, brave worthy young Gentleman who
lives in the same house with you. His name is David Skeene.[6] He and I are
Sisters sons; but my regard for him is much more founded upon his
personal qualities than upon the relation in which he stands to me. He
acted lately in a very gallant manner in America of which he never
acquainted me himself and of which I came to the knowledge only within
these few days. If you can be of any service to him you could not possibly
do a more obliging thing to me.

The Duke and Duchess of Buccleugh have been here now for almost a
fortnight.[7] They begin to open their house on Monday next and I flatter
myself will both be very agreable to the People of this country. I am not
sure that I have ever seen a more agreeable woman than the Dutchess. I am
sorry that you are not here because I am sure you would be perfectly in
love with her. I shall probably be here some weeks; I would wish, however,
that both you and the Count de Sarsfield would direct for me as usual at
Kirkaldy. I should be glad to know the true history of Rousseau before and
since he left England.[8] You may perfectly depend upon my never quoting
you to any living soul upon that Subject. I ever am Dear Sir, Most faithfully yours

Adam Smith

[5] James Oswald was in failing health.

[6] Afterwards of Pitlour; appointed Inspector of Roads in Scotland 1787.

[7] The Duke md. Lady Betsy only dau. of the Duke of Montagu on 3 May 1767. The
newly-married couple came to Dalkeith at the beginning of September and were to celebrate the Duke's birthday on the 13th, but the news of Charles Townshend's death
caused the celebrations to be put off. Smith stayed with the Buccleuchs two months at
this time, though he was not a man 'to promote jollity at a birthday party', according to
Carlyle 511–12.

[8] See Letters 111 and 112 from Hume, dated 8 and 17 Oct. 1767.

110. *From* DAVID HUME

MS., RSE ii. 42; HL ii. 163.

[London, ? end of Sept. 1767]

Dear Smith,

I thank you for your friendly Resentment against the Right Reverend,[1] I easily forgive our Friend for not making me any Apology. Tis with great Concern I observe, that he has not Spirits enough for such an Effort, and perhaps is fetterd by some kind of Dependance on his Brute of a Brother. I have receivd two Letters from him in our usual friendly Style and have answered him in the same. Yours

D. H.

111. *From* DAVID HUME

MS., RSE ii. 43; NHL 176–9.

London, 8 Oct. 1767

Dear Smith

I shall give you an Account[1] of the late heteroclite Exploits of Rousseau, as far as I can recollect them: There is no Need of any Secrecy: They are most of them pretty public, and are well known to every body that had Curiosity to observe the Actions of that strange, undefineable Existence, whom one would be apt to imagine an imaginary Being, tho' surely not an *Ens rationis.*

I believe you know, that in Spring last, Rousseau apply'd to General Conway to have his Pension. The General answered to Mr Davenport[2] who carry'd the Application, that I was expected to Town in a few days; and without my Consent and Approbation he woud take no Steps in that Affair. You may believe I readily gave my Consent: I also sollicited the Affair thro' the Treasury; and the whole being finish'd, I wrote to Mr Davenport and desir'd him to inform his Guest that he needed only appoint any Person to receive Payment. Mr Davenport answered me that it was out of his Power to execute my Commission: For that his wild Philosopher, as he called him, had elop'd of a sudden, leaving a great Part of his Baggage behind him, some Money in Davenports hands, and a Letter on the Table, as odd, he says, as the one he wrote to me, and implying that Mr Davenport was engag'd with me in a treacherous Conspiracy against him. He was not

---

[1] See Letter 109 addressed to Hume, dated 13 Sept. 1767. 'Our friend' is James Oswald who was a sick man by this time. He resigned from Parliament in 1768 and retired from public life.

[1] This account should be compared with several others in HL and NHL; see, also NHL, Appendix A.

[2] Richard Davenport offered Rousseau the use of a house at Wootton, Staffordshire.

heard of for a fortnight; till the Chancellor receiv'd a Letter from him, dated at Spalding in Lincolnshire; in which he said, that he had been seduc'd into this Country by a Promise of Hospitality, that he had met with the worst Usage, that he was in Danger of his Life from the Plots of his Enemies, and that he apply'd to the Chancellor, as the first civil Magistrate of the Kingdom, desiring him to appoint a Guard at his own (Rousseau's) Expence, who might safely conduct him out of the Kingdom. The Chancellor made his Secretary reply to him that he was mistaken in the Nature of the Country, for that the first Post-boy he coud apply to was as safe a Guide as the Chancellor coud appoint. At the very same time, that Rousseau wrote this Letter to the Chancellor, he wrote to Davenport, that he had elop'd from him, actuated by a very natural Desire, that of recovering his Liberty, but finding he must still be in Captivity, he preferd that at Wootton; For his Captivity at Spalding was intolerable beyond all human Patience; and he was at present the most wretched being on the Face of the Globe: He wou'd therefore return to Wootton, if he were assur'd that Davenport wou'd receive him. Here I must tell you, that the Parson of Spalding[3] was about two Months ago in London, and told Mr Fitzherbert[4] from whom I had it, that he had passed several Hours every day with Rousseau while he was in that Place; that he was chearful, good-humoured, easy, and enjoyd himself perfectly well, without the least Fear or Complaint of any kind. However, this may be, our Hero, without waiting for any Answer either from the Chancellor or Mr Daveport, decamps on a sudden from Spalding, and takes the Road directly to Dover; whence he writes a Letter to General Conway seven Pages long, and full of the wildest Extravagance in the World, He says, that he had endur'd a Captivity in England which it was impossible any longer to submit to. It was strange, that the greatest in the Nation, and the whole Nation itself, should have been seducd by one private Man, to serve his Vengeance against another private Man: He found in every Face that he was here the Object of general Derision and Aversion, and he was therefore infinitely desirous to remove from this Country. He therefore begs the General to restore him to his Liberty and allow him to leave England: He warns him of the danger there may be of cutting his Throat in private; as he is un-happily a Man too well known, not to have Enquiries made after him, shou'd he disappear of a Sudden: He promised, on Condition of his being permitted to depart the Kingdom, to speak no ill of the King or Country or ministers, or even of Mr. Hume; As indeed, says he, I have perhaps no Reason; my Jealousy of him having probably arisen from my own suspicious Temper, sour'd by Misfortunes. He says, that he

---

[3] The Revd. Samuel Dinham, Rector of Spalding.
[4] William Fitzherbert (d. 1772), M.P. for Derby, had arranged in March 1766 for a servant to accompany Rousseau from Derby to Ashburn.

was wrote a Volume of Memoirs, chiefly regarding the Treatment he was met with in England; he has left it in safe hands and will order it to be burnd, in case he be permitted to go beyond Seas, and nothing shall remain to the Dishonour of the King and his Ministers.

This Letter is very well wrote, so far as regards the Style and Composition; and the Author is so vain of it, that he has given about Copies as of a rare Production. It is indeed, as General Conway says, the Composition of a whimsical Man; not of a Madman. But what is more remarkable, the very same Post he wrote to Davenport, that having arrivd within Sight of the Sea, and finding he was really at Liberty to go or stay, as he pleas'd, he had intended voluntarily to return to him; but seeing in a News Paper an account of his Departure from Wootton and concluding his Offences were too great to be forgiven, he was resolvd to depart for France. Accordingly, without any farther Preparation and without waiting General Conway's Answer, he took his Passage on a Packet Boat, and went off that very Evening. Thus you see, he is a Composition of Whim, Affectation, Wickedness, Vanity, and Inquietude, with a very small, if any Ingredient of Madness. He is always complaining of his Health; yet I have scarce ever seen a more robust little Man of his Years; He was tird in England, where he was neither persecuted nor caress'd, and where, he was sensible, he had expos'd himself: He resolvd therefore to leave it; and having no Pretence, he is oblig'd to contrive all those Absurdities, which, he himself, extravagant as he is, gives no Credit to. At least, this is the only Key I can devise to his Character. The ruling Qualities abovementioned, together with Ingratitude, Ferocity, and Lying, I need not mention, Eloquence and Invention, form the whole of the Composition.

When he arrivd at Paris, all my Friends, who were likewise all his, agreed totally to neglect him: The Public too disgusted with his multiplyd and indeed criminal Extravagancies, showd no manner of concern about him. Never was such a Fall from the time I took him up, about a Year and a half before. I am told by D'Alembert[5] and Horace Walpole, that, sensible of this great Alteration, he endeavourd to regain his Credit by acknowledging to every body his Fault with regard to me: But all in vain. He has retird to a Village in the Mountains of Auvergne as M. Durand[6] tells me; where no body enquires after him. He will probably endeavour to recover his Fame by new Publications; and I expect with some Curiosity the Reading of his Memoirs, which will I suppose suffice to justify me in every body's Eyes, and in my own, for the Publication of his Letters and my Narrative of the Case. You will see by the Papers, that a new Letter of his to M.D, which I imagine to be Davenport, is publishd. This Letter was probably wrote

---

[5] D'Alembert wrote to Hume on 13 July 1767 (RSE iii. 15); see *Letters of Eminent Persons to David Hume*, ed. J. H. Burton (1849), 210–11.
[6] 'Ministre et résident' at the French Embassy in London.

immediatly on his Arrival at Paris; or perhaps is an Effect of his usual Inconsistence: I do not much concern myself which: Thus he has had the Satisfaction, during a time, of being much talkd of, for his late Transactions; the thing in the World he most desires: But it has been at the Expence of being consign'd to perpetual Neglect and Oblivion. My compliments to Mr Oswald; and also to Mrs Smith. I am Dear Smith Yours sincerely

David Hume

P.S. Will you be in Town next Winter.

112. *From* DAVID HUME

MS., RSE ii. 44; HL ii. 168–9.

London, 17 Oct. 1767.

Dear Smith.

I sit down to correct a Mistake or two, in the former Account which I gave you of Rousseau. I saw Davenport a few days ago, who tells me, that the Letter, inserted in all the News Papers, was never addressd to him: He even doubts its being genuine; both because he knows it to be opposite to all his Sentiments with regard to me, to whom he desires earnestly to be reconcild, and because it is too absurd and extravagant, and seems to be contriv'd rather as a Banter upon him. Davenport added, that Rousseau was retir'd to some Place in France, and had chang'd his Name and his Dress; but wrote to him, that he was the most miserable of all Beings; that it was impossible for him to stay where he was; and that he wou'd return to his old Hermitage, if Davenport wou'd accept of him. Indeed, he has some Reason to be mortify'd with his Reception in France: For Horace Walpole, who has very lately returnd thence, tells me, that, tho' Rousseau is settled at Cliché,[1] within a League of Paris, no body enquired after him, no body visits him, no body talks of him, every one has agreed to neglect and disregard him: A more sudden Revolution of Fortune than almost ever happend to any man, at least to any man of Letters.

I ask'd Mr Davenport about those Memoirs, which Rousseau said he was writing, and whether he had ever seen them: He said Yes, he had: It was projected to be a Work in twelve Volumes; but he has as yet gone no farther than the first Volume, which he had entirely compos'd at Wootton. It was charmingly wrote, and concluded with a very particular and interesting Account of his first Love, the Object of which was a Person,

[1] Rousseau was not in the Paris suburb of Clichy, but had been given asylum by the prince of Conti at Trie-Château (Oise). He remained there until 1768 and finished writing the *Confessions*, which do not go beyond the year 1765 and so do not deal with the quarrel with Hume.

whose first Love it also was. Davenport, who is no bad Judge, says, that these Memoirs will be the most taking of all his Works; and indeed, you may easily imagine what such a Pen wou'd make of such a Subject as that I mentiond. Mean-while, it appears clearly, what I told you before, that he is no more mad at present, than he has been during the whole Course of his Life, and that he is capable of the same Efforts of Genius. I think I may wait in Security his Account of the Transactions between us: But however, this Incident, which I forsaw, is some Justification of me for publishing his Letters, and may apologize for a Step, which you, and even myself, have been inclind sometimes to blame and always to regreat.

Tell Mr Oswald, that I saw yesterday young Fitz-patrick,[2] Lord Ossory's Brother, who is just returnd from Caen, and who gave me very good Accounts of Jemmy[3] in every Respect.

113. *To* LORD SHELBURNE

MS., University of Michigan Libr.; *Quarterly Journal of Economics* lxxiii (1958), 157–65.

Kirkcaldy, 27 Jan. 1768

My Lord

I should have written to your Lordship a long time ago, to thank you for the very great kindness which you was so good as to shew me when I was last at London: but I flattered myself that your Lordship knew me too well to need to be assured of my sense of it by letter: and the little transactions of this Country afford nothing that can furnish any amusement to your Lordship. I now write to your Lordship to thank you for your kindness to another man, I mean my very worthy and excellent friend the Count de Sarsfield. He writes me that you have been excessively good to him: and I have the vanity, which perhaps you will laugh at, to impute some part of the kindness which you have shewn to him, to the regard with which you have been so good as to honour me. There is nothing that your Lordship could Possibly have done that would have bound me more effectually to you. I have no doubt but you have found him the same plain, worthy, sensible man which I described him to be.

Since I came to this country I have employed myself pretty much in the manner that I proposed. I have not, however, made all the Progress that I expected; I have resolved, therefor, to prolong my stay here till November next, perhaps, till after the Christmass holidays next winter.

---

[2] Hon. Richard Fitzpatrick (1747–1813), soldier who saw service in America; Secretary-at-War 1783.

[3] James Townsend Oswald (1748–1814), s. of James Oswald of Dunnikier. He was Hugh Blair's pupil in Edinburgh, and he took his father's place in the House of Commons in 1768.

When your Lordship sees Colonel Clerk[1] I beg that you would tell him that I have followed his advice exactly with regard to a change which he proposed I should make in the original contract I made with the Duke of Buccleugh.[2] I am very much obliged to him for his counsell and I feel the good effects of it every day. He will explain this to your Lordship by word of mouth much better than I could by a long letter written in so very bad a hand.

I beg to be remembered in the most respectful manner to Lady Shelburne[3] and that your Lordship would believe me to be with the highest respect and esteem My Lord   Your Lordships most obliged

and devoted Servant
Adam Smith

114. *To* ARCHIBALD CAMPBELL[1]

Address: To Mr. Archibald Campbell, Writer to the Signet, James's Court, Edinburgh
Fraser, *Scotts of Buccleuch*, ii. 406; Rae 246 (reference).

25 Dec. 1768
Kirkcaldy

Dear Sir,—I have sent by this day's post the discharge you wish for Mr. John Ross;[2] he is the gentleman I mentioned to you before. He will deliver it to you to-morrow, and you may either pay the money to him, or give him an order upon the bank for it. I am very much obliged to you for your friendly remembrance of me.

I received lately a letter from Sir James Johnstoune.[3] He has explained to you what is Mr. Scott of Davington's claim, as heir of Rennaldburn, upon the Duke of Buccleuch.[4] If it would not be too much trouble to you I should be much obliged to you if you could let me know in two lines wherein it consists.

I ever [am], dear Sir,
Your most affectionate humble servant,
Adam Smith

[1] Robert Clerk; see Letter 40, n. 5.
[2] Clerk's advice is unknown; for details of the contract see Letter 106 addressed to John Craigie, dated 26 June 1767.
[3] Shelburne married Lady Sophia Cartaret in 1765. When she died in 1771, her husband fell into a depression and went abroad for a time to recruit his spirits.

[1] Law-agent to the Duke of Buccleuch; see Letters 41 and 44.
[2] Ross was presumably Smith's law-agent in Edinburgh.
[3] Of Westerhall, fa. of Smith's friend William Johnstone (Pulteney).
[4] Possibly some affair of feudal property: the Duke was the chief of the Scott family.

115. *To* LORD HAILES[1]

Address: To the Honble The Lord Hales, Edinburgh
MS., University of Tokyo Libr.; *Sotheby's Catalogue* 21 May 1968, 65 (extract).

Kirkcaldy, 15 Jan. 1769

My Lord

I am extremely obliged to your Lordship for the very polite Message you was [so] good as to send me last by Mr John Balfour. The Use of your Lordships collection of Papers concerning the Prices of Corn and other Provisions in Antient times will lay me under a very great obligation.[2] I have no papers upon this subject except an account of the fiars[3] of Mid-Lothian from the [year] 1626 and this was copied too from a Printed Paper produced in a process before the Court of Session some years ago. I expect soon to get some others, particularly an account from the Victualling office.[4] I have, however, a good number of printed Books such as Fleetwood,[5] Du Pré de St Maur,[6] Police des Grains,[7] Messance sur la Population et sur les prise des grains,[8] Essays on the Corn Trade,[9] &c; All of which, except Messance, your Lordship has probably seen: His accounts go no farther back than 1670. I look upon him, however, to be the most judicious author of them all. I have made a good number of remarks both upon the accounts given in these books, and upon some things relating to the same subject which I have found in the History of the Exchequer,[10] in the English Acts of Parliament,[11] and in the Ordonnances of the french Kings.[11]

---

[1] Sir David Dalrymple (1726–92), Bt., of Hailes; lawyer, antiquary, and man of letters; educ. Eton, Edinburgh, and Utrecht; advocate 1748; Lord of Session (as Lord Hailes) 1766; Lord Commissioner of Justiciary 1776.

[2] See the accompaniment to Hailes's letter to Smith of 6 Mar. 1769, No. 114.

[3] Smith defined 'fiars' as 'annual valuations made upon oath, according to the actual state of the markets, of all the different sorts of grain in every different county of Scotland' (WN I.viii. 34and I.xi. e. 17).

[4] Port office for victualling ships of the Royal Navy.

[5] William Fleetwood, Bishop of Ely, *Chronicum Preciosum* (London, 1707). This and the following books were in Smith's library (see Bonar's catalogue) and are referred to in WN.

[6] N.-F. Dupré de St. Maur, *Essai sur les monnoies, ou réflexions sur la rapport entre l'argent et les denrées* (Paris, 1746); *Recherches sur la valeur des monnoies et sur les prix des grains avant et après le concile de Francfort en 794* (Paris, 1762).

[7] C. J. Herbert, *Essai sur la police générale des grains, sur leur prix et sur les effets de l'agriculture* (Berlin, 1757).

[8] *Recherches sur la population des généralités d'Auvergne, de Lyon, de Rouen, et de quelques provinces et villes du royaume, avec des reflexions sur la valeur du bled tant en France qu'en Angleterre, depuis 1674 jusqu'en 1764*, par M. Messance, receveur des tailles de l'élection de Saint-Etienne (Paris, 1766).

[9] Charles Smith, *Three Tracts on the Corn Trade and Corn Laws*, 2nd ed. (London, 1766).

[10] Thomas Madox, *History and Antiquities of the Exchequer of the Kings of England. From the Norman Conquest to Edward II* (London, 1711); referred to in WN III.iii.3.

[11] It is not known which editions of these Smith consulted.

My own Papers [12] are in very great disorder and I wait for some further informations which I expect from different quarters before I attempt to give them the last Arrangement. As soon as they are fit to be seen I shall be very happy to communicate them to your Lordship, if you will give me leave either to send them to you or to read them to you.

I am very much ashamed of having delayed so long to answer a very Polite letter[13] I had the honour to receive from your Lordship some time ago. I proposed to read over the Scotch Acts[14] and to compare them both with our own historians and with the laws of some other nations that I have had occasions to look into, in order to answer it as much to your satisfaction as I could. I have not yet had time to do this; for tho' in my present situation I have properly speaking nothing to do, my own schemes of Study leave me very little leisure, which go forward too like the web of penelope, so that I scarce see any Probability of their ending. Your Lordships remarks upon the Scotch Acts seem to be very much of the same nature with those of Judge Barrington[15] upon the English Statutes which have been so universally approved of. A work of this kind cannot fail to [be] both extremely useful and very amusing to all those that are curious in the History of their own country. I should be very happy to contribute anything in my Power to the improvement of it. I am afraid however I shall be able to contribute but very little; and it will be some time before I can contribute even that little.[16] I have the honour to be with highest respect and esteem

My Lord your Lordships Most Obedient Servant
Adam Smith

If your Lordship wishes to see any of the Books I have on the Prices of Provisions they are all at your service, as are likewise any Papers upon the same subject which I may hereafter be able to collect.

---

[12] ? Of parts of WN.

[13] Not traced.

[14] Smith had a copy of *The Actis and Constitutionis of the Realme of Scotland, 1424–1564* (Edinburgh, 1566), commonly known as 'the Black Acts'. This copy is now in the Mitchell Library, Glasgow.

[15] Hon. Daines Barrington, Recorder of Bristol and Justice of Chester, *Observations on the Statutes chiefly from Magna Carta to the twenty-first of James the First, chap. XXVII* (London, 1766). This book is not listed in Bonar's catalogue of Smith's library. Barrington had two excellent ideas: he used the statue book to illustrate English history, and he adopted a comparative approach when explaining the meaning of the earlier statutes (Holdsworth, *History of English Law*, London, 1966 reprint, xii. 401).

[16] Though Hailes circulated in printed form a specimen of his observations on the Scots Acts, he did not get the help he expected, and his scheme came to nothing (Woodhouselee, *Kames*, 1807, i. 290).

116. *To* LORD HAILES

Address: To the Honble The Lord Hales, Edinburgh
MS., University of Tokyo Libr., Brougham ii. 219; Rae 247–8.

Kirkcaldy, 5 Mar. 1769

My Lord,

I should now be extremely obliged to your Lordship if you would send me the Papers you mentioned upon the prices of Provisions in former times.[1] In order that the conveyance may be perfectly secure, if your Lordship will give me leave, I shall send my own servant sometime this week to receive them at your Lordships house at Edinburgh.[2] I have not been able to get the Papers in the cause of Lord Galloway and Lord Morton.[3] If your Lordship is Possessed of them it would likewise be a great obligation if you could send them. I shall return both as soon as Possible. If your Lordship will give me leave, I shall transcribe the Mss Papers; this, however depends entirely upon your Lordship.

Since the last time I had the honour of writing to your Lordship,[4] I have read over with more care than before, the Acts of James 1st and compared them with your Lordships remarks. From these last I have received both much pleasure and much instruction. Your Lordships remarks will, I plainly see, be of much more use to me, that I am afraid mine will be to you. I have read law entirely with a view to form some general notion of the great outlines of the plan according to which justice has [been] administered in different ages and nations: and I have entered very little into the detail of Particulars,[5] of which, I see, your Lordship is very much master. Your Lordships particular facts will be of great use to correct my general views; but the latter, I fear, will always be too vague and superficial to be of much use to your Lordship.

I have nothing to add to what your Lordship has observed upon the Acts of James 1st. The[y] are penned, in general in a much ruder and more inaccurate manner than either the English Statutes or French ordinances of the Same Period; and Scotland seems to have been, even during this vigorous reign as our historians represent it, in greater disorder than either France or England had been from the time of the Danish and

---

[1] See 'Prices of Corn' etc. printed after Letter 117 from Hailes, dated 6 Mar. 1769.

[2] New Street, Canongate.

[3] Alexander Stewart (*c.* 1694–1773), succeeded to the earldom of Galloway, 1746; James Douglas (1702–68), 14th Earl of Morton; see Sir David Dalrymple, *Remarks for Alexander Earl of Galloway and others, Pursuers, upon the Information for James Earl of Morton, Defender, etc.* (Edinburgh, 1759).

[4] See Letter 115 addressed to Hailes, dated 15 Jan. 1769.

[5] Smith's final course of Lectures in Edinburgh in the years 1748–51 concerned law. John Callander of Craigforth reported '[Smith] taught Civil Law to students of Jurisprudence' (EUL, La. ii. 451–2). Smith gave lectures along the lines described in the letter in Glasgow during his professorial years; see LJ.

Norwegian incursions. The 5. 24. 56. and 85, Statutes, seem all to attempt a remedy to one and the same abuse.[6] Travelling, from the disorders of the Country, must have been extremely dangerous, and consequently very rare. Few People, therefor, could propose to live by entertaining travellers; and consequently there would be few or no inns. Travellers would be obliged to have recourse to the hospitality of private families: in the same manner as in all other barbarous Countries: And being in this situation real objects of Compassion, private families would think themselves obliged to receive them, even though this Hospitality was extremely oppressive. Strangers, says Homer, are sacred Persons, and under the protection of jupiter;[7] but no wise man would ever chuse to send for a Stranger unless he was either a Bard or a Soothsayer. The danger, too, of travelling either alone or with few attendants, made all men of any consequence carry along with them a numerous suite of retainers which rendered this Hospitality still more oppressive. Hence the orders to build Hostellaries in 24 and 85. And as many people had chosen to follow the old fashion and to live rather at the expense of other people than at their own, hence the Complaint of the Keepers of the Hostellaries, and the order thereupon in Act 56.

I cannot conclude this letter, though already too long, without expressing to your Lordship my concern and still more, my indignation at what has lately passed both at London and at Edinburgh.[8] I have often thought that the supreme court of the United Kingdom very much resembled a jury. The Law Lords generally take upon them, to sum up the Evidence, and to explain the Law to the other peers; who generally follow their opinion implicitly. Of the two Law Lords, who upon this occasion, instructed them, the one has always run after the Applause of the Mob:[9] the other, by far the most intelligent, has always shewn the greatest dread of popular

---

[6] Statute 5: Na man suld travell with maa men, nor he may susteine. 24: Of Hostillaries in Burrowes and throuch-fares. 56: All men suld Ludge with Hostillares. 85: Anent Hostillares (see *The Laws and Acts of Parliament Made by King James the First and his Royal Successors*, 1682, i). Smith deals with the cause and effect of hospitality in feudal times in WN, III.iv.5.

[7] See *Odyssey* vi, 207–8: Nausicaa addressing her handmaidens in the presence of Odysseus: '. . . for all strangers and beggars / Are in the care of Zeus'; also *Od.* ix 271, and *Il.* xiii 625.

[8] On the Douglas Cause, see letters No. 72, n. 1. Hailes before his elevation to the Bench had been an advocate on the Hamilton side. The Scottish *literati* were Hamiltonians almost to a man, while the Douglasians (who included Boswell) were the popular party. When the Court of Session decided in favour of the Duke of Hamilton, the Douglas party appealed to the House of Lords, and on 27 Feb. 1769 in that chamber the decision of Scotland's supreme civil court was reversed. This was followed by popular rejoicing in Edinburgh; see Hailes's letter of 6 Mar., No. 117, n. 4.

[9] Charles Pratt (1713–94), Earl Camden; called to the Bar 1738; Attorney-Gen. 1757; Chief Justice of the Common Please 1761; Lord Chancellor 1766–70; President of the Council 1784–94; a great common law and equity judge, whose speech to the House of Lords was decisive in overturning the Court of Session decision.

odium; which, however, [he][10] has not been able to avoid.[11] His inclinations [also] have always been suspected to favour one of the [par]ties. He
has upon this occasion, I suspect, followed rather his fears and his inclinations, than his judgment. I could say a great deal more upon this subject
to your Lordship, but I am afraid I have already said too much. I would
rather, for my own part, have the solid reputation of your most respectable
President,[12] though exposed to the insults of a brutal mob, than all the vain
and flimsy applause that has ever yet been bestowed upon either or both
the other two. I have the honour to be,

with the highest esteem and regard,

My Lord,

Your Lordships most obedient

and obliged Servant

Adam Smith

117. *From* LORD HAILES

Address: To Adam Smith Esqr. at Kirkaldy, To the Care of the Postmaster of
Kirkaldy
MS., Newhailes MSS. (1805 copy) No. 432, NLS microfilm; unpubl.

Edinburgh, 6 Mar. 1769

Dear Sir

Instead of giving you the trouble of sending a Servant for the papers[1]
I transmit them to you by the post; they are at your Service absolutely,
I have gone little farther than you see, in writing out; the principal
materials were in the Records, and I knew I could have them when I
pleased; if you have occasion for the materials, on Record, I can assist you.
I have looked out for the papers in the Orkney cause[2] and I miss many of

---

[10] MS. damaged.

[11] Concerning William Murray, Earl Mansfield, see Letter 33, n. 5. He was unpopular
with the mob for mitigating the rigours of the laws decreed against Roman Catholics, also
with some constitutionalists for introducing into common law principles derived from
equity. His house with its remarkable library was burned during the Gordon Riots of 1780.

[12] Robert Dundas of Armiston the Younger: see Letter 19, n. 2. He was a vigorous
occupant of the President's chair who cleared off the arrears of causes on the Court of
Session rolls: 'the business of the country was thus carried on with a degree of regularity
and dispatch hitherto without a parallel in the annals of that Court' (Brunton and Haig,
Senators of the College of Justice, 1836, 525).

[1] Printed at the end of this letter.

[2] Not identified. Orkney had a distinctive legal system, based on that of Norway, in
force until the formal introduction of Scots law in the seventeenth century. Information
about that system (Udal law) was presented in James Mackenzie, Writer, *The General
Grievances and Oppression of the Isles Orkney and Shetland* (1750). This book was prompted
by the 'Pundlar process' about weights and measures, a 'pundlar' being the Orkney and
Shetland word for a steelyard or Danish balance with movable fulcrum.

them, but I can easily get a compleat set for you. There is a Book lately published as to the prices of Corn &c in England since the Conquest,[3] but I have not seen it, and indeed I have no time to think of any thing at present but the duty of my profession, if matters go on in the present course the Business of a judge will be very easy, he need not consult the law, nor his Conscience, he will find an infallible Rule in the Enemys of Glass windows, has any man an antipathy of Glass windows then he is in the right.

Seriously this is an unhappy Crisis, *incidimus in ea tempora*, that a Judge must study Causes under the protection of skrewed Bayonets; this was my case for two nights; and I assure you, that next to Window-breakers they were the most disagreeable attendants that I ever met with. Judges must not only be free, but they must feel themselves free and the whole nation must have the Conviction of their being free—hitherto I imagined that I was answerable for my Conduct to the laws of my Country and to my God, and that I was subject to no other Tribunal—*now* there is a sovereign Tribunal at every Bonfire.

When the Mob first attacked the President's house, he went to his Door, and walked before it for a quarter of an hour, till assistance came. I heard this Anecdote from an Eye-witness and I mention it to you as a Confirmation of the opinion which you entertain of his Steadiness.[4]

An odd accident happened to me in the Outer-House, between nine and ten—while I was sitting and hearing a Cause,[5] at once, the whole house broke loose, I asked what was the matter, the answer was 'they are putting the President out of his Chair'. My judicial Ideas made me forget that the President could have any Chair but that in the Court. I went to Lord Pitfour[6] who was at another Bar and said 'My Lord, they are pulling the President out of his Chair, we must go and share the same fate with him' —he followed me into the Inner-house where there was not a Soul; this

---

[3] Not traced.

[4] The popular exuberance took place on the nights of 2 and 3 March following the arrival of Ilay Campbell in Edinburgh with the news that the House of Lords had reversed the decision of the Court of Session in the Douglas Cause. As the stones shattered the windows of the Lord President on 2 March, Boswell is said to have remarked that 'other honest fellows were giving *their* casting votes in their turn' (F. A. Pottle, *James Boswell: The Earlier Years*, New York, 1966, 299). The Lord Justice-Clerk appealed to the Commander-in-Chief for Scotland on 3 March, and a detachment of dragoons was sent to maintain order in the city.

[5] The Court of Session transacted its business in two divisions: the Outer and Inner House. Since 1642 it had met in the Parliament House, to the south of the High Kirk of St. Giles. The Parliament Hall was the court-room of Outer House, and there each week in his turn a Lord Ordinary sat as a judge of first instance, occupying the sovereign's throne. Appeals were made to the Inner House, where the 'haill fifteen' with the Lord President in the chair, or a quorum of at least nine of them, reviewed the judgements of the Ordinaries.

[6] James Ferguson of Pitfour, also hearing causes as a Lord Ordinary on this occasion, was connected on his wife's side with the Douglas family, which was thought to influence his verdict as a judge in the Douglas Cause (Ramsay of Ochtertyre, i. 155, n. 1).

still confirmed me in my Error, I imagined that the Court was dispersed—
my next thought was to call a Macer, that I might go out in form—and
then I found that the Insult had not been committed in Court—the Insult
may be palliated, but I have no doubt the Mob went the length of crying
'pull him down', and *entre nous*, they certainly cryed out at his Back-
windows the night before, 'Porteus him'.[7]

At present all is quiet, but while we are ruled by an unthinking and
unthinkable Multitude, we hold our Security by a precarious tenure.
Mean time

I am Dear Sir with great Esteem
Your most obedient
and obliged humble Servant
Dav: Dalrymple.

Prices of Corn, Cattle &c in Scotland from the
earliest accounts to the death of James V.[8]

1243   Charter by David Bishop of Murray bears this Clause 'Animad-
       vertentes Rebendam Centum Solidorum predictae nostrae Ecclesiae
       tenuem esse et exilem.' Ch. Morav. fol. 48.[9] This example does
       not determine anything with precision. It may, however, be pre-
       sumed that the assertion of the Bishop is not far wide of truth
       or probability.
            See Wilkin's *Concilia* Vol. 1. p. 609. Anno 1249.
1253   Ten Merks of Silver, six acres of arable land and one acre of
       Meadow ground, provided to the Vicar of Worgo in Galloway.
       Confirmed by Gilbert Episcopus Candidae Casae. Ch. Dryburgh
       fol. 23.
            Before 1253 when Bishop Gilbert died.
1268   A Pension of ten Merks Sterling to the Vicar of Kilrethny. Of
       ten Merks to the Vicar of Salton. Ten pounds to the Vicar of

---

[7] At the hanging of a smuggler on 14 April 1736, John Porteous, Captain of the City
Guard of Edinburgh, ordered his men to fire on the crowd and discharged a weapon himself. He was tried and sentenced to death, then reprieved by Queen Caroline. On 7
September, the day before Porteous was originally sentenced to hang, a disciplined crowd
took the law into its own hands and hanged him in the Grass Market. See Walter Scott's
Heart of Midlothian and William Roughead's *The Trial of Captain Porteous* (Edinburgh,
1909).

[8] Reproduced here is the 1805 copy of the MS. sent to Smith. Ampersands have been
expanded, but other contractions and the copyist's peculiarities left.

[9] Hailes's sources are the cartularies (registers of accounts) of the bishoprics of Moray
and Aberdeen, and of the monasteries of Dryburgh, Arbroath (Aberbrothock), Kelso,
Scone, Cambuskenneth, and Dunfermline. For details of these cartularies, see G. R. C.
Davis, *Medieval Cartularies of Great Britain* (London, 1958). Hailes also refers to the
Books of Sederunt of the Court of Session.

Childenkirk, who is also to do duty at the Chappel of Lawder. Twelve merks to the vicar of Golyn. Kilrethny is Kilrenny in Fife. Childenkirk, otherwise Childinchle now called Ginglekirk in Merse. Golyn, Gulane in East Lothian.

1285   The Chaplain of Fivin has a grant from the Monastery of Aberbrothock of '100 Solidi per Annum'. Ch. Abbr. Vol. 1. fol. 14.

1304   The monastery of Abberbrothock enters into a Contract with the Bishop of Brechin, whereby it is provided 'quod non licebit Domini Brechin Episcopo alicujus Vicarii portionem ultra decem libros Sterlingorum augmentare'. Ch. Abbr. Vol. 1. fol. 21.

Before 1316   'Dominus Abbas capiet de qualibet domo villae de Bolden ante Natalem, unam Gallinam pro obolo'. Rent Roll of Kelso, subjoined to Ch. Kelso.

This Rent-roll mentions Abbot Richard, and consequently cannot be older than about 1295 when Richard became Abbot. It does not mention the Church of Newthorn, and consequently cannot be later than 1316, when the monastery acquired that Church Ant. Natalem Noel. Christmas Day.

1316   The Vicar of Naithanthern was to have a 'portio Centum solidorum' Ch. Kelso f. 120. Naithenthern, now Newthorn in Merse.

1317   A payment of four Oxen by the Earl of Lenox was converted into a payment of two Merks of Silver. So that, at that time, the price of an Ox was six Shillings and eightpence. Ch. Abbr. Vol. 2. fol. 12. This deed is so anxiously conceived that it would seem the conversion was near the real value.

1328   'Assedatio terrarum de Dunnethyn David de Manuel et si dictus David amerciatus fuerit in curiâ Domini Abbatis pro propriâ querelâ debit pro amerciamento quociens acciderit quinque solidos vel unam vaccam'. Ch. Abbr. Vol. 2, fol. 12. So that it would seem the price of a Cow was five Shillings. The lease is granted by Abbot Bernard who was elected Bishop of Sodor in 1328.

1329   The Abbot and Convent of Abberbrothock acknowledged themselves to be debtors to John Scot in the Sum of Six pounds thirteen Shillings and four pence 'pro uno palfrido ab illo'. Ch. Abbr. V. 2. f. 17.

In simple times the prices of riding Horses would not greatly vary.

1342   The Vicar of Tarras is provided by the Monastery of Aberbrothock in Twenty four merks. Ch. Aber. Vol. 2. fol. 42.

1344   William Plommer of Tweedale to have iii d. 'for ilk stane fynyne that he fynys of lede and a stane of ilke hundyr that he fynys till his travel, and that day that he wyrks he sal haf a penny till his nayn saykis'. Ch. Abbr. Vol. 2. fol. 25.

1355 A pension of ten merks payable to the vicar of Carington in Mid-Lothian. Ch. Scone Vol. 1, fol. 40.

1370 Salary of the Dempster of the Territory of Abberbrothock twenty shillings Sterling 'de exitibus curiarum'. Ch. Abbr. Vol. 2. f. 53.

1380 The monastery of Aberbrothock having been burnt and the monks dispersed, there was provided twelve Marks 'cuilibet per an. pro victu et vestitu'. Ch. Abbr. Vol. 2. f. 24.

Between 1362 and 1397 Grant by the Bishop of Murray to 'Andreas filius Roberti' of a piece of Ground at Elgyn, 'reddendo annuatim sex Solidos et octo denarios vel unam petram bonae cerae'. Ch. Morav. fol. 110.

Alexander Bishop of Murray makes this grant. He was Bishop from 1362 to 1397.

1395 A pension of forty five Marks of the usual money of Scotland payable to the Vicar of St Giles's Edinburgh for his Maintenance. Ch. Scone Vol. XX 1. fol. 40.

1422 In a Contract between the Abbacy of Dunfermeline and the abbacy of Cambuskenneth, it was agreed that four Marks should be paid for a Chalder of Meal i.e. 3sh. 4d. pr Boll. Ch. Cambuskenneth fol. 68.

1462 Salary of the Mair and Coroner of Aberbrothock 40sh. 12 Bolls Bear and 12 Bolls [oat]meal. Ch. Abbr. Vol. 2. fol. 60.

1466 In a poynding for Rent at Aberdeen, the following pieces of house-hold furniture were thus valued.

Unae sistae, a Countyr	4 Merks
Unam screnium, a schrevyn	50 Shillings
Unam longum Sedile, viz. a landsadile[10]	40 do.

Usualis monetae Scotiae pro summa septem librarum et decem solidorum. Ch. Abbr. Vol. 2. fol. 65. There is certainly some mistake here; for the sum total agrees not with the particulars and the prices are beyond measure exorbitant.

1474 Contract with Steven Lyel Carpenter to work for the Abbacy all the days of his Life—to have twenty Marks per annum payable quarterly 'pro mercede suâ ac pro suis esculentis et poculentis'.

'Alterius si prefatus Stephanus oneratus fuerit per dictos Abbatem et Conventionem ad[11] extra pro reparatione Ecclesiarum suarum operari, dicti Abbas et conventus persolvent dicto Stephano omni die operabile pro expensis suis quatuor denarios'.

'Et praefatus Stephanus inchoabit opus omni die operabili hora quinta ante meridiem et finiet hora septima post meridiem tam in

---

[10] Error for 'langsadile', i.e. a long settle or bench, usually with arms and a high back.
[11] ? ab.

aestate quam hyeme et si sic continuaverit omni die operabili dictus Stephanus habebit ad gentaculum suam et suam servium[12] si quem habuerit unam parvam panem aulae et unam pinetam cervisiae conventualis et tantum recipiet post meridiem pro refectione sua et servi sui si quem habeat'. Ch. Abbr. Vol. 2.

1483 Lease of the Mill of Craquhy 'cum 40 denariis monetae Scotiae pro dimidiâ parte porci.' So that the price of a hog appears to have been six shillings and eight pence. Ch. Abbr. Vol. 2. fol. 48.

1484 Lease of the Wardmill by the monastery of Aberbrothock. The Lesee taken bound to deliver 'unum porcum bene pastum vel dimidiam marcam' 6sh. 8d. vid. the lease of Craquhy 1483. Lesee also taken bound to provide a servant for working at the mill of the monastery 'quantum spectat ad officium Molendinarii pro viginti sex Solidis et octo denarii annuatim' £1. 6. 8 or two marks. Ch. Abbr. Vol. 2. fol. 113.

1484 In payment for Debt Lease of the tythes of Balmarmuir by the Monastery of Aberbrothock wherein Bear and Meal are thus estimated 'ad valorem quatuor librarum pro celdra'—four pounds per Chalder or five Shillings per Boll. Ch. Abbr. Vol. 2. fol. 109.

1486 Lease of the tythes of Balgello. '20 lib. ad rationem, 4. celdrarum et 6 Bollarum ordei et farina' i.e. 5sh. 8d. and about 1/17 of a penny pr Boll. Ch. Abbr. Vol. 2. fol. 120.

1486 Archibald Lame hired to be Schoolmaster His Salary ten marks 'una cum cotidiana portione sicut conventus quotidie recipet'.[13] Ch. Abbr. Vol. 2 fol. 131.

1488 Salary to be paid to the Coroner of the Regality of Aberbrothock 24 Bolls Bear and Meal, and 40 Shillings of Silver. Ch. Abbr. Vol. 2 fol. 127.

1489 The yearly expences of the Monastery of Abberbrothock called 'ordinatio David (Leighton) Abbatis'.

	£		
Wedders 800 at 3/- each	120		
Marts i.e. Beeves salt and fresh 900 Price of ilk piece 15/-	675		
Keling lard i.e. salted ling 1500 at £3 pr 100	45		
Fish in winter 500, in Lent 1000	320	6	8
Dry Haddocks and Speldings 1200 at 16s pr 100	8		
Saffron 4 lib at £1. 15. pr lb	7		
Pepper 16 lb at 6sh 8d pr lb	5	6	8
Ginger 2 lb at 10/- pr lb	1		
Canel (Cinnamon) 2 lb at 16/- per lb	1	12	
Cloves 2 lb at 13/4 pr lb.	1	6	8

---

[12] ? suum servum.   [13] ? recipit or recipiet.

Granis (Incense) 1 lb at 13/4 . . . .   13 4
Mace 1 lb . . . .   16 .
Almonds 100 lb at 20d pr lb 8 6 4
3 Dozn rise (probably 36 lb rice) at 8/-⎫
pr Dozn or 8d per lb . . . . . ⎭   . . .   1 4 .
Vinegar X 8 Gallons at 8d pr pint . . . . .   1 12 .
Honey six Gallons at 8d pr pint . . . . . .   1 12 .
Swyne and Bars (Barrow hogs) 2 Dozn⎫
at 8/4 each . . . . ⎭   . . .   10 . .
Habit silver to the Cellerar 6 13 4
Servants fees in the Kitchen . . . .   3 10 .
    Ch. Abbr. Vol. 2. fol. 126.

There are several curious particulars to be learnt from this
Account. The extravagant price of Spiceries in the 15th Century.
Vinegar and Honey bear the same price, which shows that the
people on the Continent kept to themselves the secret of making
Vinegar and thereby enhanced the price. The Article of Fish must
mean 1500 Dozn otherwise the price would be exorbitant. The
Article Swyne and Bars 2 Dozn must mean two Dozn of each. We
have seen in 1483 and 1484 that a hog went at the rate of 6/8 a
Barrow hog must have been at 1/8 in order to make up the total of
8/4 each.

1507   The Abbot and Convent of Dunfermlyne entered into an Indenture
with 'Simon Karnor Wright and his parentys'. Karnor became bound
to work for the Convent during Life. His wages were settled at
20 Merks of usual money of Scotland; one Chalder meal and three
Bolls Malt pr annum, payable quarterly. The wages of the Apprentice were settled at five merks and one Chalder meal. Their Utensils
were to be kept in repair and maintained by the Convent. Ch. Dunfermline fol. 120.

1525   In a question between the monastery of Cambuskenneth and
[?word illegible] Lords of Council estimated meal and Barley three
Chalders each on an Average at 13/4 pr Boll on the parish of Lenye,
shire of Dumbarton. Ch. Cambuskenneth fol. 91.

1525   In a Decreet of the Lords of Council a Hen valued at 4d. Ch.
Cambuskenneth fol. 91.

1527   Fourteen Marks and two acres of Ground provided as a Salary to
the Chaplain of Arringask. Ch. Cambuskenneth fol. 112.

1528   Decreet for abstracted tythes by the Lords of Council estimating
Oats with fodder at 6/8 pr Boll. This was in the high Grounds of
Stirlingshire. Ch. Cambuskenneth fol. 112.

1530   The Salary settled on the Door-keeper of the Abbacy of Dunfermline was £4 and one Chalder meal. Ch. Dunfermline fol. 120.

1540   Decreet of Non-entry in the lands of Haydail where the price of Grain are thus settled

Wheat pr Boll	£1 15	.
Bear pr Do	13	4
Meal pr Do	13	4

     Books of Sederunt 14th March 1540.

1540   In a Charter granted by the Bishop of Murray 3 Marts are converted at £1 4. each. Six Bolls Oats at 4/- each. Ch. Morav. fol. 171.

1540   In a Charter granted by the Bishop of Murray six Bolls of dry Multure are converted at 6Sh 8d pr Boll. Ch. Morav. fol. 177.

1544 and 1554   In deeds made by the Bishop of Murray the following conversions occur:

	1544			*1554*		
Mart	£1	4	.	£2 13	4	
Mutton (killed sheep) . .		4	.	8	.	
Kid		1	2	.	.	
Capon			6		12	
Poultrie			3	.	.	
Goose (auca)		.	8	1	4	
Boll of Oats		4	.	6	8	fodder
Dry Multure pr Boll . .		6	8	6	8	
Mers Fish 16 at 22/- . .		1	4	.	.	
Barrel of Salmon . . .	2	10	.	.	.	

     Ch. Morav. fol. 194 et seq.

1545   A Lamb is converted at 1Sh. 2d. Ch. Morav, fol. 197, but in 1554 at 2Sh. The Conversions 1554 are contained in a Lease for two lives granted by Patrick Hepburn Bishop of Murray to Thomas and David Hepburn. It is not easy at first Sight to account for the great difference between the Conversions 1544 and 1554. and this the more especially, as the higher Conversions are in a Lease to persons of the Bishops own name and who, probably were his near Relations.

1561   In a feu-Charter granted by the Bishop of Murray, Bear dry Multure is converted at 6Sh. 8d. per Boll. Ch. Morav. fol. 122.

1561   In a feu-Charter granted by the Bishop of Murray there occurs the following Clause 'Reservato tamen nobis et successoribus nostris Moravien[sis] Episcopis piscibus captabilibus vulgariter the *tak fish* prout usus est levori et percipi de lie Scotsold seys ex pretiis sequentibus respective vizt viginti lie *Haddokis* sive *Quhittingis* et aliorum piscium minorum pro denario pro uno lie *Keling* duos denarios pro uno lie *Scait* duos denarios pro uno lie *ling* duos denarios pro uno lie *turbet* quatuor denarios pro uno lie *Selch* quatuor Solidos'. Ch. Morav. fol. 122.

118. *To* LORD HAILES

Address: To the Honble The Lord Hales, Edinburgh
MS., University of Tokyo Libr.; Brougham ii. 219; Rae 249; *Sotheby's Catalogue*
21 May 1968, 65 (all ptd. texts, in part).

Kirkcaldy, 12 Mar. 1769

My Lord

I received the favour of your Lordships Letter in due course of Post and have read over the Papers you enclosed along with it; with great pleasure and attention.[1] I am greatly obliged to your Lordship for them: they will be of a very great use to me.

I shall only observe to your Lordship that all the estimated prices of grain among our ancestors seem to have been extremely Loose and inaccurate: and that the same nominal sum was frequently considered as the Average price both of grain and of other things during a course of years in which considerable alterations had been made upon the intrinsick value of the Coin.[2] Thus both in 1523. and in 1540. the Boll[3] of barley and meal is estimated at 13S and 4D, tho in the first of these two periods there were only seven money pounds coined out of the pound weight of Silver; and tho' in the second there were nine pounds, twelve Shillings coined out of it.[4] This estimation is made, however, by the Lords of council and Session[5] from whom the greatest accuracy might have been expected. It is not conceivable that during the course of the sixteenth century, so long after the discovery of the Spanish west Indies, grain should have sunk near one third in its average Price, or in the real quantity of silver that was given for it.[6] The market price of Grain was in those times extremely fluctuating, much more so than at present, and people seem to have been so much at a Loss how to fix an average, that they were happy to catch at any average that had been fixed in some former period without always attending to the difference of circumstances. In the conversion Prices that are agreed upon in Leases, the option whether to pay or take the rent in kind or in money, is sometimes in the Tennant, and sometimes in the Landlord. When it is in

---

[1] See Letter 117 from Hailes, dated 6 Mar. 1769.

[2] Cf. WN I.v. and I.xi. e. 28 on real and nominal price and corn as a 'more accurate measure of value than any other commodity or set of commodities'.

[3] 'The Scotch boll, equal to about half the English quarter' (WN I.xi.e.22).

[4] Smith's information about Scots money came from James Anderson, *Selectus diplomatum et numismatum Scotiae thesaurus* (1739) and Thomas Ruddiman's intro. to this book. It was in Smith's library.

[5] In their judicial capacity, judges of the Court of Session are addressed as Lords of Council and Session, recalling their origin in the Curia Regis; see *Acts of the Parliaments of Scotland*, ed. T. Thomson and C. Innes, Record Edition, 12 vols. (1814–75), ii. 226. c. 16, by which the Chancellor was directed to preside over such 'lordis of consale or ellis the lordis of sessioun' who were to administer justice at three fixed terms. These Lords specialized in law, leaving others free for other functions of government.

[6] WN I.xi.e.

the Landlord, and when the Landlord generally resides upon his estate and chuses, for the conveniency of his family, to receive the rent in kind, it is very indifferent to him how low the conversion price is.[7] In this neighbourhood the price of a good fowl, a hen, has been for many years from ten pence, to a Shilling and fifteen pence. Several years ago a friend of mine converted all the Poultry upon his estate at a Shilling. Five pence, however, is a common conversion price in a lease, the option being in the Landlord. Leases of this kind have been let within [?these] two or three years. I should be glad to know, if your Lordship remembers it, for I should be very sorry to give you the trouble to consult the record, whether in the leases of the Abbays and Bishopriks which you have looked into,[8] the option was in the Landlord or in Tennant. If it was in the former, as a Monastery is always, and in old times a Bishop was generally resident, we need not wonder either at the irregularity, or at the lowness of some of the conversion prices. I have the honour to be with the greatest respect and regard

My Lord

Your Lordships

most obedient and obliged

Servant

Adam Smith

If the rejoicings, which I read of in the public papers, in different places on account of the Douglass Cause, had no more foundation than those which were said to have been in this place, there has been very little joy upon the occasion. There was here no sort of rejoicing of any kind; unless four schoolboys having set up three candles upon the trone,[9] by way of an illumination, is to be considered as such.

119. *To* LORD HAILES

Address: To the Right Honble The Lord Hales, Edinburgh
MS., University of Tokyo Libr.; *Sotheby's Catalogue* 21 May 1698, illus. facing p. 65 (in part); unpubl.

Kirkcaldy, Tuesday 16 May [1769]

My Lord

I have read over with very great pleasure your Lordships discourse on

---

[7] 'In antient times almost all rents were paid in kind; in a certain quantity of corn, cattle, poultry, etc. It sometimes happened, however, that the landlord would stipulate, that he should be at liberty to demand of the tenant, either the annual payment in kind, or a certain sum of money instead of it. The price at which the payment in kind was in this manner exchanged for a certain sum of money, is in Scotland called the conversion price' (WN I.xi.e.17).

[8] See the memorandum on 'Prices' accompanying Hailes's letter of 6 Mar., above. Hailes had consulted charters and rent rolls of abbeys and bishopries.

[9] Usually 'tron': public weighing apparatus in a burgh; the post for the scales could be used as a place for public exposure and punishment of criminals.

the Laws of Malcolm.[1] I am entirely of your Lordships opinion that they are not the Laws of any King Malcolm; but the composition of some private man, who meant to describe the great outlines of the Laws and customs of his Country, which he supposed, or had been told by tradition, were first introduced by some antient and famous king of the name of Malcolm; either Malcolm McKenneth or Malcolm Canmore;[2] the former just as probably as the latter. It does not, I think, appear that the Author himself ever meant that they should pass for the original Statutes of that King. The Whole book is a narrative or History of the Regulations which he supposed had been made in times that were antient in comparision of his own. The Style is every where, not Statutory, but Historical. He intitled them the *Laws of Malcolm*, because he supposed that they had originally been instituted by some King of that name in the manner in which he tells; which tho' very absurd, is not more so than the account given in many antient Books of the origin of other laws and customs. The supposition of their being the Statutes of any King is a blunder, and a very gross one, of later writers for which the Author is not answerable. Your Lordship, has, I think, proved very clearly that this author must have lived in the Norman times and was probably posterior to Richard 2d.[3] The Discrepancies which your Lordship has taken notice of in the prices of several different things, are very look [?like those] which occur in the antient Coutumes of many different provinces of france. Mr Du Pré de St Maur has tortured his brain to reconcile them and make them all consistent.[4] The real cause of those discrepancies seems to have been that either the Authors of those compilements, or perhaps the courts in the particulare Province had in some cases simply followed some antient valuation, and in others had accomodated that antient valuation to the changes that had afterwards been made in the Standard of the coin; and this pretty much as accidental circumstances had directed.

I am greatly obliged to your Lordship for your attention in sending me the Orkney Process.[5] I had before got together all the Papers except two; which two will be of the greatest use to me. I have taken a copy, as your Lordship allowed me, of your Manuscript upon the antient Prices of Corn etc.[6] I shall therefor return the two Manuscripts along with all the Orkney Papers that I had not before collected; by next weeks carrier I shall come to

---

[1] *An Examination of Some of the Arguments for the High Antiquity of Regiam Majestatem; and an Inquiry into the Authenticity of Leges Malcolmi* (Edinburgh, 1769).

[2] Malcolm II, reigned 1005–34; Malcolm III, 1058–93.

[3] Modern scholars ascribe the *Regiam Maiestatem* to the fourteenth century, after 1318, and acknowledge its borrowings from Anglo-Norman, as well as Roman and canon law sources; see A. A. M. Duncan, '*Regiam Maiestatem*; a reconsideration', *Juridical Review* (1961), 199–217; and Peter Stein, 'The source of the Romano-Canonical Part of *Regiam Maiestatem*', *Scottish Historical Review* xlviii (1969), 107–23.

[4] See Letter 115, dated 15 Jan., n. 6.　　　　[5] See Letter 117, dated 6 Mar., n. 2.

[6] See the memorandum printed with Letter 117.

Edinburgh in the end of Summer Session[7] when I shall beg your Lordships assistance to get access to the Chartularies[8] from which you have copied the Prices of corn &c. I ever am

with the greatest Respect
My Lord
your Lordships
most obliged humble Servant
Adam Smith

120. *To* [LORD HAILES]

MS., University of Illinois Libr.; Scott 265–7.

Kirkcaldy, 23 May 1769

My Lord

I return your Lordship your two Manuscripts, having taken a copy of that upon prices,[1] as your Lordship permitted me to do it.

I have not the Latin copy of Laws of Malcolm by me; but Skeene[2] appears to have understood one passage differently from your Lordship. It is Chap: 3. S5. Item, for ilk man not found the time of the Attachment the Crowner sall remain at his house quhere he dwells be the space of ane day ane nicht; and sall have his reasonable sustentation for himself and twa of his servants and for twa other men brought with him to be witness; and for his Clerk twa Shillinges and sall take na mair. According to this Passage, as here translated and pointed; the reasonable sustentation is for the five persons, and the twa Shillings is the fee of the Clerk. If the twa Shillings are to be understood to be the value of the reasonable sustentation, it is for six persons and is 4.d apiece. 4d. is the day wages of a Master mason of free stone as appointed by the statute of Labourers, of the 25 of Edward 3.[3] This therefor would not in those days have appeared an Unreasonable sustentation for a Crowner and five Attendants.

[7] The Court of Session sat from 12 June to 12 August in the summer.

[8] Of Aberdeen, Arbroath, Cambuskenneth, Dunfermline, Dryburgh, Kelso, Moray, and Scone—possibly in the Advocates' Library. Hailes was not thought to be able to read charter-hand (Cosmo Innes, *Lectures on Scotch Legal Antiquities*, 1872, i, n. 1), but Smith could call on the help of his friend, John Davidson, Clerk to the Signet.

[1] See the memorandum printed with Letter 117 from Hailes, dated 6 Mar. 1769.

[2] *Regiam Majestatem. The Auld Lawes and Constitutions of Scotland. Faithfullie collected furth of the Register, and other auld authentick Bukes, from the Dayes of King Malcolme the Second untill the Time of King James the First . . . translated out Latine in Scottish Language . . . Be Sir John Skene of Curriehill, Clerk of our Soveraigne Lordis Register, Counsell, and Rollis* (Edinburgh, 1609). Skene began his work in 1574, when he was commissioned by the Regent Morton to 'visit the Bukis of the Law'. His editorial work is much criticized. Smith has a copy of the 2nd Latin edn. (1613) of Skene's book (Bonar 168).

[3] The Statute of Labourers of 1350 attempted to fix wages at the level reached *c.* 1340–5: see WN I.xi.e.2.

I last week happened to see the Case of Lady Sutherland, your Lordships ward.[4] There is at present depending before the Parliament of Paris a process of the same kind between the Marechal of Clermont Tonnerre and the Countess of Lannion, for the Honours and estate of Clermont in Dauphine. The Lady is much connected with some of my friends,[5] who have sent me all her Papers. There is a good deal of affinity between her case and that of the countess of Sutherland. Both turn upon the Antiquity of female honours and female fiefs. If your Lordship thinks they can be of any use I shall send them by the Carrier next week. I have the honour to be with great regard

My Lord
Your Lordships obliged and
Most humble Servant
Adam Smith

121. *From* DAVID HUME

MS., RSE ii. 45; HL ii. 206–7.

James's Court, Edinburgh, 20 Aug. 1769

Dear Smith

I am glad to have come within sight of you, and to have a View of Kirkaldy from my Windows: But as I wish also to be within speaking terms of you, I wish we coud concert measures for that purpose. I am mortally sick at Sea, and regard with horror, and a kind of hydrophobia the great Gulph that lies between us. I am also tir'd of travelling, as much as you ought naturally to be, of staying at home: I therefore propose to you to come hither, and pass some days with me in this Solitude. I want to know what you have been doing, and propose to exact a rigorous Account of the method, in which you have employed yourself during your Retreat. I am positive you are in the wrong in many of your Speculations, especially where you have the Misfortune to differ from me. All these are Reasons for our meeting, and I wish you woud make me some reasonable Proposal for the Purpose. There is no Habitation on the Island of Inch-keith; otherwise I shoud challenge you to meet me on that Spot, and neither [of] us ever to leave the Place, till we were fully agreed on all points of Controversy. I expect General Conway here tomorrow, whom I shall attend to

---

⁴ As guardian of Elizabeth Gordon (1765–1839), Hailes drew up her claim to be Countess of Sutherland. His written appeal is still regarded as an important source of peerage law. Smith had copies of the printed pleadings (Bonar 181, Mizuta 57).

⁵ Perhaps among his Toulouse acquaintances or the d'Anville–La Rochefoucauld circle; the chevalier de Clermont was one of those concerned about the illness of the Duke of Buccleuch in 1766 (Letter 94 addressed to Charles Townshend, dated 26 Aug.).

Roseneath,[1] and I shall remain there a few days. On my Return, I expect to find a Letter from you, containing a bold Acceptance of this Defiance. I am Dear Smith Yours sincerely

David Hume

122. *From* JAMES BOSWELL[1]

Address: To Adam Smith Esqr at Kirkaldie
MS., Yale University Libr. L1161 (copy in hand of John Johnston of Grange); unpubl. (to appear in Yale *Boswell Correspondence*).

Edinburgh, 28 Aug. 1769[2]

Dear Sir

As I know your benevolence; I readily take the liberty to Solicite you in behalf of the Widow of Mr. Francis Scot of Johnston, who was a very worthy man, and a Descendant of the Family of Buccleugh.

The Good old woman has a Small possession under the Duke, Called Knollyholm in the parish of Cannobie, where She is anxious to end her days, She is under Some fears of its being taken from her, I would therefore beg that you may take the trouble to mention this Case to the Duke and prevent an inhuman thing from being done; I am always with much regard

Dear Sir,
Your obliged humble Servt.
(Signed) James Boswell

123. *From* DAVID HUME

Address: To Adam Smith Esqr at Kirkaldy
MS., RSE ii. 46; HL ii. 214–15.

Edinburgh, 6 Feb. 1770

What is the Meaning of this, Dear Smith, which we hear, that you are not to be here above a day or two, in your Passage to London? How can

---

[1] On the Gareloch, Firth of Clyde, owned by the Duke of Argyll. General Conway's wife, Lady Ailesbury, was the daughter of John, 4th Duke of Argyll.

[1] James Boswell (1740–95) lawyer, journalist, and biographer; educ. Edinburgh, Glasgow, Leyden, and on the Grand Tour 1764–6. Smith was his teacher at Glasgow and praised him, according to Boswell, for his 'happy facility of manners'. He passed advocate in 1766, but his first love was writing: *Account of Corsica* (1768); *Journal of a Tour to the Hebrides* (1785), giving an account of his 1773 tour with Johnson; and *The Life of Johnson* (1791). The discovery and publication in recent years of the journals found at Malahide Castle and Fettercairn have brought him renewed fame.

[2] Boswell wrote letters from the evening of 27 Aug. until 5 a.m. the next morning, then set out for London at 8 o'clock.

you so much as entertain a thought of publishing a Book,[1] full of Reason, Sense, and Learning, to these wicked, abandon'd Madmen?

I suppose you have not yet got over your Astonishment at this most astonishing Resignation.[2] For my part, I knew not at first whether to throw the Blame on the Duke or the King; but I now find it is entirely and compleatly the Dukes own; and I think him dishonourd for ever. Here is the Passage of a Letter, which I receivd yesterday from a very good hand. 'The most wonderful political Event that ever happened in this Country happend yesterday. The Duke of Grafton, who, it seems, has bad Nerves, thought proper to resign on Tuesday the 30th of Jany at 12 of the clock forenoon. The King, who showd a Firmness, which few people thought he possess'd and a rage that no body expected from him, absolutely refus'd to treat with the Opposition, and calld upon Lord North to stand forth, assuring him, that he would never yield.[3] Lord North accordingly took the Duke of Grafton's place, and yesterday met the house of Commons as Minister. The great danger was the Effect of the Pannic, and he checkt the Pannic by his Declaration, that he woud never resign, and whilst his breathe was in his body that he would support the King's faithful Servants, and the Dignity of Parliament against faction and Conspiracy: They renewd the same captious and popular Question about the Middlesex Election; and after a long and warm debate, they divided and Lord North carryd the Question by forty Votes. This is reckond the most spirited Conduct that any man has held since the Revolution, and he is extolld to the Skies. The Opposition, who were parcelling out the Kingdom, are in despair; as there is no doubt that the new Minister will gather force every hour, as he has upon this critical occasion shown that strength of Mind, which is the precise thing hitherto wanting to give permanence to administration. Without doors there is nothing but peace and quietness; not a mouse stirring among the Mob; and I think the times will mend.'

So far my Friend, whose Prophesy I hope will be fulfilld; tho' for my part I am rather inclind to give myself up to despair: Nothing but a Rebellion and Bloodshed will open the Eyes of that deluded People, tho' were they alone concernd I think it is no matter what becomes of them. Be sure to bring over the Northumberland Household Book[4] and Priestley's Grammar.[5] Yours Dear Smith

David Hume

---

[1] WN.

[2] The Duke of Grafton (1735–1811) resigned as First Lord of the Treasury in Jan. 1770, when his colleagues, prompted by Chatham, fell away from him.

[3] George III concerted matters with Lord North before Grafton resigned (Geo. III, *Corr.* ii. 126 f.).

[4] *The Regulations and Establishment of the Household of Henry Algernon, the fifth Earl of Northumberland, at his castles of Wresill and Lekinfield in Yorkshire, begun anno domini MDXII,* ed. Thomas Percy (London, 1770); referred to in WN at I.xi.e.9, where Smith deals with fluctuations in the prices of wheat. He seems to be misled, however, by a mistake

[*continuation of footnote 4 and footnote 5 overleaf*

124. *From* DAVID HUME

Address: To Adam Smith Esqr at Kirkaldy
MS., RSE ii. 50; HL ii. 217.

[Edinburgh, Feb. 1770][1]

'This Night Opposition produc'd a Motion to overwhelm Administration as they said; that no Officer, employ'd in collecting his Majesty's Revenue should be allowed to vote in the Election of a Member of Parliament: Administration carry'd the Question 263 to 188, so administration has gaind 35 since the last Division. At the same Moment the House of Lords divided 81 against 41. We look upon Opposition to be over.'[2]

Pray when do you come over to us? Do not buy any Claret to me

D H

125. *To* JOHN DAVIDSON

Address: To Mr John Davidson, Writer to the Signet, Castle Hill, Edinburgh, with a watch
MS., EUL La. ii. 191; Scott 267.

Kirkcaldy, 11 Mar. 1771

Dear Sir,

Your friend Cowan[1] has not done justice to my Watch. Since I came to this side of the Water she runs down as fasr as I wind her up: the latch, I suspect, is either much damaged or lost altogether. I suppose he had given her to some of his apprentices. I must now beg that he will take the trouble to look at her with some care himself. I ever am

My Dear Sir, Most faithfully and
affectionately yours
Adam Smith

in the text of the *Household Book*: see WN, 6th edn. ed. Cannan (1950), i. 200, n. 1. Hume was later engaged in controversy with Percy over a note to the *History of England* referring to the *Household Book*: see NHL, pp. xvii–xix, 197–9.

[5] Joseph Priestley, *Rudiments of English Grammar* (London, 1769).

[1] The provenance is suggested by the phrase 'over to us', i.e. across the Firth of Forth to Edinburgh, in the last para. of the letter. The date is indicated by the reference in the first para. to the motion seeking to disenfranchise the revenue officers.

[2] In this para. Hume is quoting from a letter from someone in London. The motion was one proposed on 12 Feb. 1770 by William Dowdeswell, leader of the Rockingham group in the House of Commons. It was intended to reduce the influence of the Government, and it foreshadowed Crewe's Act of 1782. Its defeat marked the growing power in the Commons of Lord North.

[1] Watchmaker in Edinburgh.

126. *From* COUNT DE SARSFIELD

MS., GUL Gen. 1035/239; unpubl.

Paris, 7 Juin 1771

Je ne doute point Monsieur que vous ne pensiez que jay oublié Lengagement que Jay pris avec vous de vous envoyer le memoire[2] Cy joint. Peut etre l'avez vous oublié vous meme. Mais, quant a moi, Je vous assure que Je ne lay pas perdu de vue, parce que cela ne marrivera jamais, Quand Il Sagira dune Chose qui vous regarde et qui peut Contribuer a me rappeller dans votre souvenir.

Depuis mon retour en france, Jay passé beaucoup de tems en province. Ce Sejour m'a Eloigné des occasions De Vous faire passer cecy.

Je retourne incessament a Rennes en Bretagne. Partout ou je Serai soyez Sur que vous avez un serviteur et un ami

Sarsfield

Si vous voyez mr hume Je vous prie de Lui dire mille Choses pour moy. Lhistoire de Charles quint a icy un tres grand Succes.[3] Quand verrons nous quelque chose de vous?

127. *To* JOHN SPOTTISWOODE[1]

MS., Pierpont Morgan Libr., New York; unpubl.

Kirkcaldy, 26 July 1771

Dear Sir,

I have written to the D[uke][2] a letter which I hope will prevent the effect of any other application whatever. If Simson[3] dies let me know by the first Post. I have forgot the name of the Kirk where our friend is minister. I ever am most faithfully yours

Adam Smith

---

[1] See Letter 103, n. 1.

[2] Not traced.

[3] William Robertson's *History of Charles V* (1769) was translated into French (1771) by J.-B.-A. Suard (1733–1817).

[1] Nephew to William Strahan.   [2] Of Buccleuch.

[3] Presumably a minister whose church might be secured for 'our friend'.

128. *To* JOHN DAVIDSON

Address: To Mr John Davidson, Writer to the Signet, Castle Hill, Edinburgh
MS., EUL La. ii.191; Scott 267.

Kirkcaldy, Thursday [autumn 1771][1]

My Dear Sir

I should be glad to see the Duke of Buccleugh before he leaves this country. I should, therefore, be very much obliged to you if you would let me know when he returns to Dalkieth and how long he proposes to stay there.

If you see Andrew Stuart you may tell him that I am longing very much to see him; as he promised me a call.

I intended about a week ago to make a long visit to my friends on your side of the water.[2] I had got wind in my stomach which I suspected a little dissipation might be necessary to dispel. By taking three or four very laborious walks I have entirely rid of it: so that I shall not [leave][3] my retreat for above a day these six months [to come].[3]

I ever am

My Dear Sir, Most faithfully and affectionately yours.

Adam Smith

129. *From* DAVID HUME

Address: To Adam Smith Esqr at Kirkaldy
MS., RSE ii. 47; HL ii. 256.

Edinburgh, 28 Jan. 1772

Dear Smith

I shoud certainly, before this time, have challenged the Performance of your Promise, of being with me about Christmas, had it not been for the Misfortunes of my Family. Last Month, my Sister fell dangerously ill of a Fever; and though the Fever be now gone, she is still so weak and low, and recovers so slowly, that I was afraid it woud be but a melancholy House to invite you to. However, I expect, that time will re-instate her in her former Health, in which case, I shall look for your Company. I shall not take any Excuse from your own State of Health, which I suppose only a Subterfuges invented by Indolence and Love of Solitude. Indeed, my Dear Smith, if you continue to hearken to Complaints of this Nature, you will cut Yourself out entirely from human Society, to the great Loss of both Parties.

---

[1] The letter is undated, and the reasonable conjecture is Scott's.
[2] River Forth.
[3] The breaking of the seal removed some words.

The Lady's Direction is Me la Comtesse de B. Douairiere au Temple.¹
She has a Daughter in law, which makes it requisite to distinguish her

Yours sincerely
David Hume

P.S.

I have not yet read Orlando inamorato;² but intend soon to do it. I am now in a course of reading the Italian Historians, and am confirmd in my former Opinion that that Language has not produced one Author who knew how to write elegant correct Prose, though it contains several excellent Poets. You say nothing to me of your own work.

130. *To* MME DE BOUFFLERS

Recherches sur la nature et les causes de la richesse des nations, trad. . . . par le citoyen Blavet (Paris, 1800), xxiv (extract).

[? Edinburgh, Kirkcaldy, Feb. 1772]¹

C'était une grande mortification pour moi de voir la manière dont mon livre (Théorie des Sentimens Moraux)² avait été traduit dans la langue d'une nation où je n'ambitionne sûrement pas d'être estimé plus que je ne le mérite. Votre bonté généreuse m'a délivré de cette peine, et m'a rendu le plus grand service qu'on puisse rendre à un homme de lettres.³ Je me promets un grand plaisir à lire une traduction faite, parce que vous l'avez desiré. Si ce n'est pas être trop curieux, je serais bien aise de savoir le nom de la personne qui m'a fait l'honneur de me traduire.

131. *From* DAVID HUME

Address: To Adam Smith Esqr Kirkaldy
MS., RSE ii. 48; HL ii. 262–4.

St Andrews Square, 27 June 1772

Done ere you bade: I receivd a Letter from Clason¹ himself, and

---

¹ Comtesse de Boufflers: see Letter 91, n. 4.
² By Matteo Boiardo (c.1430–94).

¹ See Letter 129 from Hume, dated 28 Jan. 1772. Smith presumably wrote this letter soon thereafter.
² The earliest French trans. of TMS was by Marc-Antoine Eidous (in 2 vols. Paris, 1764). Smith had a copy of this.
³ The Abbé Blavet published his trans. in 1774 (2 vols. Paris). In a note to this letter he mentions that Mme de Boufflers compared it with the original from beginning to end. Smith's library contained a presentation copy of the Blavet trans. (Bonar 171.)

¹ Patrick Clason; see Letter 85, n. 4: his letter to Hume has not been found, but see Letter 144 from Clason, dated 25 Feb. 1775.

immediately wrote to Lord Chesterfield.[2] Baron Mure told me of the good
Behaviour of Mr Clason, in attending Sir Thomas Wallace, of which I
also informd his Lordship. I hope the young Man will meet with Success.

We are here in a very melancholy Situation: Continual Bankruptcies,
universal Loss of Credit, and endless Suspicions.[3] There are but two standing Houses in this Place, Mansfield's[4] and the Couttses: For I comprehend
not Cummin,[5] whose dealings were always very narrow. Mansfield has
pay'd away 40.000 pounds in a few days; but it is apprehended, that neither
he nor any of them can hold out till the End of next Week, if no Alteration
happen.[6] The Case is little better in London. It is thought, that Sir George
Colebroke[7] must soon stop; and even the Bank of England is not entirely
free from Suspicion. Those of Newcastle, Norwich and Bristol are said
to be stopp'd: The Thistle Bank[8] has been reported to be in the same Condition: The Carron Company[9] is reeling, which is one of the greatest
Calamities of the whole; as they gave Employment to near 10.000 People.
Do these Events any-wise affect your Theory? Or will it occasion the
Revisal of any Chapters?

Of all the Sufferers I am the most concern'd for the Adams, particularly
John. But their Undertakings were so vast that nothing coud support them:[10]

---

[2] Chesterfield was supervising the education of his godson, Philip Stanhope, who succeeded him as 5th Earl in 1773. Probably Clason was seeking a post as tutor. In the end
Adam Ferguson became Chesterfield's tutor and travelled with him on the Continent for
two years: see Letter 139, n. 2.

[3] At the end of the 1760s there was considerable economic development in Scotland
coupled with problems over shortage of capital and banking facilities. To increase the
supply of finance, a new bank was established, Douglas, Heron & Co., better known as
the Ayr Bank, with landowners prominent among the shareholders, which commenced
business on 6 Nov. 1769. Principally to support land improvement schemes, it adopted
policies that proved ruinous: 'This bank was more liberal than any other had ever been,
both in granting cash accounts, and in discounting bills of exchange' (WN II.ii.73). As the
bank got going, there was an economic crisis in Scotland caused through investments
outrunning savings, a fall in prices of such commodities as linen, and a 'spirit of over-
trading'. The years 1772–4 saw a movement towards a depression. In June 1772 the failure
of a London banking house that had extensive dealings with the Ayr Bank resulted in a
financial panic in Edinburgh, and a run on the Ayr Bank for specie forced it to suspend
payments on the 25th of that month. See Letter 132 addressed to Sir William Pulteney,
dated 3 Sept. 1772, and Letter 133 from Hume, dated Oct. 1772; also Hamilton 317–25.

[4] Edinburgh banking house, founded in 1738, known as Mansfield, Ramsay & Co.

[5] William Cuming & Sons, private bank founded in Edinburgh between 1750 and 1760.

[6] Only four private banks in Edinburgh survived the crisis: Mansfields' and Cumings'
among them.

[7] Head of a London bank, and in 1769 chairman of the Directors of the East India
Company.

[8] A Glasgow bank founded in 1761, which lasted until 1836 then merged with the
Glasgow Union Bank.

[9] Founded in 1760 by Dr. Roebuck and by this time the largest industrial operation in
Scotland. For some years it had suffered from a shortage of capital, and during the crisis
of 1772 several partners faced bankruptcy, but the Company survived.

[10] The Adam brothers, Robert, James, and William, were heavily involved in the
Adelphi, an imaginative scheme to embank the Thames at Durham House and combine

They must dismiss 3000 Workmen, who, comprehending the Materials, must have expended above 100.000 a Year. They have great Funds; but if these must be dispos'd of, in a hurry and to disadvantage, I am afraid the Remainder will amount to little or nothing. People's [Compa]ssion, I see, was exhausted for John in his last Calamity,[11] and every body asks why he incurr'd any more hazards. But his Friendship for his Brothers is an Apology; tho' I believe he has a projecting Turn of his own. To me, the Scheme of the Adelphi always appeared so imprudent, that my wonder is, how they cou'd have gone on so long.

If Sir George Colebroke stop, it will probably disconcert all the Plans of our Friends, as it will diminish their Patron's Influence; which is a new Misfortune.

On the whole, I believe, that the Check given to our exorbitant and ill grounded Credit will prove of Advantage in the long run, as it will reduce people to more solid and less sanguine Projects, and at the same time introduce Frugality among the Merchants and Manufacturers:[12] What say you? Here is Food for your Speculation.

Shall we see you again this Summer?

132. *To* WILLIAM PULTENEY[1]

Address: To William Pulteney Esqr, Member of Parliament, Bath House, London
MS., Pierpont Morgan Libr., New York; Rae 253–4 (misdated 5 Sept.).

Kirkcaldy, 3 Sept. 1772

My Dearest Pulteney

I received your most friendly letter in due course, and I have delayed a great deal too long to answer it. Tho I have had no concern myself in the Public calamities, some of the friends for whom I interest myself the most have been deeply concerned in them; and my attention has been a good deal occupied about the most proper method of extricating them.[2] In the Book[3] which I am now preparing for the Press I have treated fully and

warehouse facilities with low-cost housing. The scheme failed financially, and the Adams escaped bankruptcy by resorting to the device of a lottery: see John Summerson, *Georgian London* (revised edn. 1962), 138–40.

[11] The failure of John Adam and Thomas Fairholme in 1764.

[12] These sentiments of Hume's are echoed in WN II.ii.72, and the lesson of the Ayr Bank's history was recorded in *The Precipitation and Fall of Messrs. Douglas, Heron and Company, late Bankers in Air with the Causes of their Distress and Ruin investigated and considered by a Committee of Inquiry appointed by the Proprietors* (Edinburgh, 1778).

[1] Formerly William Johnstone: see Letter 11 addressed to James Oswald, dated 19 Jan. 1752.

[2] Difficulties of Scottish businessmen and banks, in particular the Ayr Bank of which the Duke of Buccleuch was one of the largest shareholders. See Letters 131 and 133 from Hume, dated 27 June and Oct. 1772.   [3] WN.

distinctly of every part of the subject which you have recommended to me; and I intended to have sent you some extracts from it; but upon looking them over, I find that they are too much interwoven with other parts of the work to be easily separated from it. I have the same opinion of Sir James Stewarts Book that you have. Without once mentioning it, I flatter myself, that every false principle in it, will meet with a clear and distinct confutation in mine.[4]

I think myself very much honoured and obliged to you for having mentioned me to the east India Directors as a person who could be of any use to them. You have acted in your old way of doing your friends a good office behind their backs, pretty much as other people do them a bad one. There is no labour of any kind which you can impose upon me which I will not readily undertake. By what Mr Stewart and Mr Ferguson hinted to me concerning your notion of the proper remedy for the disorders of the coin in Bengal, I believe our opinions upon that subject are perfectly the same.[5]

My book would have been ready for the Press by the beginning of this winter; but the interruptions occasioned partly by bad health arising from want of amusement and from thinking too much upon one thing; and partly by the avocations above mentioned will oblige me to retard its publication for a few months longer. I ever am

My Dearest Pulteney
Most faithfully and affectionately
your obliged Servant
Adam Smith

133. *From* DAVID HUME

MS., RSE ii. 49; HL ii. 265–6.

[Oct. 1772]

My dear Sir

Yours came to hand, while I was in the Country[1] where I should have

---

[4] Sir James Steuart (later Steuart-Denham), *Inquiry into the Principles of Political Œconomy* (1767): the 'false principles' may be those concerning government intervention in economic affairs. Smith is said to have observed that he understood Steuart's system better from his talk than from his books (Rae 61).

[5] See Letter 133, n. 6. Pulteney had suggested Adam Ferguson and Andrew Stuart as well as Smith as members of a commission to study the affairs of the East India Company, which in 1772 had fallen into confusion. Sir James Steuart was asked to examine the grave currency problems of the Company, because he had written a book on the German coinage and had friends in the British Government. His report was published as *Principles of Money Applied to the State of the Coin in Bengal* (1772); see S. R. Sen, *Economics of Sir James Steuart* (1957), ch. 10; and Stuart, *Principles*, ed. A. S. Skinner (Edinburgh, 1966), i. xlix and n.

[1] Hume visited Ninewells and Minto in the autumn of 1772, then hurried back to Edinburgh hearing that the French Ambassador, the duc de Guines (1735–1806), was expected there.

been still, had it not been for a Letter of the French Ambassador, who expected to see me here in Town: He is lookd for to morrow Evening. As soon as I came to Town, I ask'd the Question you proposd; and was told by Sir William Forbes,[2] that tho' they did not commonly take the Air Notes,[3] yet he woud upon your Account: You may therefore send them over by the first Opportunity. I think that Bank more discredited by the last Step than by all their former Operations. They pretend to open at Air, in order to have a Pretence for striking off any farther Interest but as soon as great Sums are demanded, they pretend, that they are only to change small Notes for the Circulation of the Country; and so refuse Payment: This is in effect shutting up again: They do not seem to have forseen, that it was the Interest of the two Banks here and of all the Bankers to make a Run upon them; for which they ought to have been prepar'd. As far as I can learn, the Duke of Queensberry[4] alone signs the Bonds of Annuity in his own Name; but it is imagind that the Duke of Buccleugh, Mr Douglas[5] etc., have enterd into an Agreement to bear their Share: Otherwise it were Madness in him; and indeed not very wise in him and them in any case. I had last post a Letter from Andrew Stuart: I do not like the present Situation of that Supervisorship. Six to go from Europe, three to join them in the Indies: Corruption will get in among them; and probably Absurdity and Folly. And at best nine Persons can never do any Business. He tells me, that Ferguson is sure of going out Secretary.[6] I wish it may be so. It will be a great Vexation and Disappointment to him to return to his Office with which he was before somewhat disgusted.

Yours

D H

[2] Sir William Forbes (1739–1806), Edinburgh banker; apprenticed to Messrs. Coutts, 1753; partner, 1761; formed Messrs. Forbes, Hunter & Herries, 1763, which became Forbes, Hunter & Co. 1773, wrote a *Life of James Beattie* (1806).

[3] See Letter 131 from Hume, dated 27 June 1772. The directors reopened their head office in Ayr on 28 September 1772, seeking to exchange notes for specie, but they were finally forced to give up business in August 1773.

[4] Charles, 3rd Duke of Queensberry, owned extensive property in the Lowlands and was a distinguished agricultural improver. Already Chairman of the Forth and Clyde Canal Company, he was elected Chairman of the Ayr Bank in 1769. After the crash of June 1772, the directors proceeded to raise money in London by means of terminable annuities at an extremely high rate.

[5] Archibald Douglas of the Douglas Cause: he and Queensberry and the other partners of the Ayr Bank were liable to the full extent of their wealth. Ultimately the creditors were paid in full at a cost of £663,397, and it is said that £750,000 worth of landed property had to be sold.

[6] In Feb. 1772 Hume heard that Andrew Stuart was to be appointed as one of the supervisors to inquire into the affairs of the East India Company. Adam Ferguson's name was mentioned for the post of secretary to the commission, but neither he nor Stuart was appointed; see Letter 132 addressed to Sir William Pulteney, dated 3 Sept. 1772.

134. *From* DAVID HUME

Address: To Adam Smith Esqr at Kirkaldy
MS., RSE ii. 51; HL ii. 266–7.

St. Andrews Square, 23 Nov. 1772

Dear Smith

I shou'd agree to your Reasoning,[1] if I coud trust your Resolution. Come hither for some weeks about Christmas; dissipate yourself a little; return to Kirkaldy; finish your Work before Autumn; go to London; print it; return and settle in this Town, which suits your studious, independant turn even better than London: Execute this plan faithfully; and I forgive you.

I was apply'd to, a few days ago, by poor Roby Arbuthnot,[2] in favour of his Son, now 13 years of Age, and a promising boy, as I am told, whom he intends to send to Glasgow, in a view of procuring him an Exhibition at Oxford. You know the State of that Family; and have probably heard that both the Parents of the boy are unfortunate People of Merit. I own, that, trusting to your Humanity, I promisd them your Interest and Advice in that Scheme: I hope you are not pre-engaged for any other Person: Otherwise I cannot doubt of your Concurrence.

Ferguson has return'd, fat and fair; and in good humour, notwithstanding his Disappointment,[3] which I am glad of. He comes over next week, to a house in this neighbourhood. Pray, come over this winter, and join us.

I am My Dear Smith Ever yours
David Hume

135. *From* DAVID HUME

Address: To Adam Smith Esqr at Kirkaldy
MS., RSE ii. 52; HL ii. 276–7.

St. Andrews Square, 24 Feb. 1773

Dear Smith

There are two late Publications here which I advise you to commission. The first is Andrew Stuarts Letters to Lord Mansfield which they say have met with vast Success in London; Andrew has easd his own Mind, and no bad Effects are to follow: Lord Mansfield is determind absolutely to neglect them.[1] The other is Lord Monboddo's Treatise on the Origin

---

[1] Possibly referring to a letter from Smith that has not been traced.

[2] ? Robert Arbuthnot of Kirkbraehead (1708–73), who had three sons, or perhaps a member of the private banking firm of Arbuthnot and Guthrie, which failed in June 1772.

[3] Perhaps at failure to secure a post as Secretary to the Committee of Inquiry on East Indian Affairs: see Letter 133, n. 6.

[1] In *Letters to the Right Honourable Lord Mansfield*, privately printed in Jan. 1773, Andrew Stuart attacked Mansfield in an ironic vein for his partiality in the Douglas Cause: see Letter 72, n. 1.

and Progress of Language,[2] which is only part of a larger work. It contains all the Absurdity and malignity which I expected; but is writ with more Ingenuity and in a better Stile than I look'd for.

Surge et inhumanæ senium depone Camenæ.[3] Yours

D. H.

P.S.

I shoud save you Expence, by sending you over both these works, if I knew how.

136. *From* DAVID HUME

Address: To Adam Smith Esqr Kirkaldy
MS., RSE ii. 53; HL ii. 280–1.

St. Andrews Square, 10 Apr. 1773.

To day News arriv'd in town that the Air Bank had shut up; and as many people think for ever.[1] I hear that the Duke of Bucleugh is on the Road: The Country will be in prodigious distress for Money this term. Sir G. Colebroke's Bankruptcy is thought to be the immediate Cause of this Event.

Have you seen Macpherson's Homer?[2] It is hard to tell whether the Attempt or the Execution be worse. I hear he is employd by the Booksellers to continue my History: But in my Opinion, of all men of Parts, he has the most anti-historical Head in the Universe.

Have you seen Sir John Dalrymple?[3] It is strange what a Rage is against him, on account of the most commendable Action in his Life.[4] His

---

[2] The first volume of Monboddo's book *Of the Origin and Progress of Language* was advertised in the *Edinburgh Advertiser* on 23 Feb. 1773, and in the London press on 29 March. Monboddo's stories of cat-tailed men and the essential humanity of the orang-outang diverted the reading public, but his central thesis was an original one: 'The matter of my Book . . . may be reduced to three heads—first, that Language is not natural to Man—second, that it is possible (for I say no more) that it may have been invented—and, lastly—upon that Supposition—to show how it was invented.' See E. L. Cloyd, *James Burnett, Lord Monboddo* (1972), ch. IV. The sixth and last volume of the *Origin* was published in 1792.

[3] Horace, *Epistles* i. 18, l. 47: 'Rise up and abandon the peevishness of the unsociable muse.' Doubtless another exhortation to Smith to visit Hume in Edinburgh.

[1] See Letter 131 from Hume, dated 27 June 1772.

[2] James Macpherson's translation of the *Iliad* into Ossianic prose appeared early in 1773; his *History of Great Britain, from the Restoration to the accession of the House of Hanover* was published by Strahan and Cadell in 1775.

[3] Sir James Dalrymple of Cranstoun (1726–1810), 4th Bt.; educ. Edinburgh and Cambridge; advocate 1748; Baron of the Scottish Exchequer, 1776–1807; friend of Smith. His chief works are *General History of Feudal Property in Great Britain* (1759); and *Memoirs of Great Britain and Ireland* (1st vol. 1771; 2nd 1773). He discovered a way of making soap from herrings.

[4] His *Memoirs of Great Britain* enraged the Whigs.

Collection is curious but introduces no new Light into the civil, whatever it may, into the biographical and anecdotical History of the times.

Have you seen Alonzo?[5] Very slovenly Versification, some pathetic, but too much resembling Douglas.

I expect to see you soon. Have you been busy, and whether in pulling down or building up?

D. H.

137. *To* DAVID HUME

Address: To David Hume Esqr, of St Andrews Square, Edinburgh
MS., RSE vii. 38; Rae 262–3.

Edinburgh, 16 Apr. 1773

My Dear Friend

As I have left the care of all my literary papers to you,[1] I must tell you that except those which I carry along with me[2] there are none worth the publishing, but a fragment of a great work which contains a history of the Astronomical Systems that were successively in fashion down to the time of Des Cartes.[3] Whether that might not be published as a fragment of an intended juvenile work, I leave entirely to your judgement; tho I begin to suspect myself that there is more refinement[4] than solidity in some parts of it. This little work you will find in a thin folio paper book in my writing desk in my bedroom. All the other loose papers which you will find either in that desk or within the glass folding doors of a bureau which stands in My bed room together with about eighteen thin paper folio books which you will likewise find within the same glass folding doors I desire may be destroyed without any examination.[5] Unless I die very suddenly I shall take care that the Papers I carry with me shall be carefully sent to you. I ever am

My Dear Friend, Most faithfully yours
Adam Smith

[5] Another of John Home's tragedies, produced at Drury Lane this year.

[1] The precarious state of his health led Smith to make Hume his literary executor, but Hume died first (1776) leaving Smith in charge of the publication of *Dialogues Concerning Natural Religion*, a duty which Smith evaded and left to Hume's nephew, David Hume the Younger. See Letters 156 and 157 from Hume, dated 3 May 1776.

[2] MS. of WN.

[3] Posthumously published as 'The Principles which lead and direct Philosophical Enquiries; illustrated by the History of Astronomy' in *Essays on Philosophical Subjects*, ed. by Smith's literary executors Joseph Black and James Hutton (Edinburgh, 1795). For a commentary on the 'Principles' as guidelines to Smith's view of scientific method, see A. S. Skinner, 'Adam Smith: Philosophy and Science', *Scottish Journal of Political Economy* xix. 3 (1972), 307–19.

[4] Repetition omitted of five previous words.

[5] Black and Hutton followed similar instructions in 1790 and committed sixteen vols. of MSS. to the flames (Rae 434).

138. *From* ADAM FERGUSON

Small 614 n.

Edinburgh, 2 Sept. 1773

My Dear Sir,

I am told that Dr Beaty,[1] or his party, give out that he has not only refuted but killed D. Hume. I should be very glad of the first, but sorry for the other; and I have the pleasure to inform you that he is in perfect good health; if he had been otherwise I should have certainly mentioned it in some of my letters. He had a cough, and lost flesh, soon after you went from home,[2] which we did not know what to think of, but it turned out a mere cold, and it went off without leaving any ill effects; he has still some less flesh than usual, which nobody regrets, but in point of health and spirits I never saw him better. You seemed to doubt whether I should not write to Lord Stanhope.[3] I had inclination enough, but was not so decided as to send my letter to himself without putting it in your power to withhold it if proper, and therefore I stayed for a frank; what is disagreeable is, laying him under the obligation to make a ceremonious answer, and, if he be gone, subjecting him to Continental postage, so you will judge. I have not seen J. Ferguson,[4] but he must acquiesce.

I am, dear Sir,
most affectionately yours,
Adam Ferguson

139. *From* ADAM FERGUSON

Small 614.

Edinburgh, 23 Jan. 1774

My Dear Friend

It has given me great pleasure that you have avoided doing anything that might tend to urge Lord Stanhope farther than he has already gone

[1] James Beattie (1735–1823), poet and Professor of Moral Philosophy, Marischal College, Aberdeen (from 1760); abused Hume in *An Essay on the Nature and Immutability of Truth; in opposition to Sophistry and Scepticism* (1st edn. 1770). In 1773 Beattie was much taken up in London by the Johnson circle and given a pension by George III. In an 'Advertisment' to the first posthumous edition of his *Essays and Treatises* (1777), Hume gave 'a compleat Answer to Dr Reid and to that bigotted silly Fellow, Beattie' (HL ii. 301) by disowning the 'juvenile' *Treatise of Human Nature* and asking that his later works be regarded 'as containing his philosophical sentiments and principles'.

[2] Smith went to London in May 1773 and remained there until April 1776, about a month after publication of WN.

[3] Philip, 2nd Earl Stanhope (1717–86), mathematician; friend of Smith since his stay in Geneva; had consulted Smith about the education of his ward, Philip Stanhope, 5th Earl of Chesterfield (1755–1815). Adam Ferguson was recommended as tutor.

[4] ? Relative of Adam Ferguson who was to travel with him to London in 1774: see Letter 141.

in the proposal respecting Lord Chesterfield.[1] If I had known the part he took in that business, I should certainly at first have either frankly accepted of the offer made me, or declined it in a way that could not imply an intention to raise the terms. This is certainly the only alternative that is now left me. I have revolved the subject all night and this morning, and the possibility of my becoming a burden on Lord Stanhope's family weighs much, but the odds on Lord Chesterfield's life is so great as very much to reduce that consideration. My place here, a few years ago, was worth about £300 a-year, but this and the preceding year it has fallen considerably short; and while the present alarm of the scarcity of money, and the expense of education at Edinburgh, continues, it may not rise again to its former value. To this I must add, that in case of debility or old age, I shall probably be reduced to my salary, which is no more than £100 a-year. For these reasons I think that I can fully justify myself to my family in accepting of £200 a-year certain, with the privilege of choosing my place and my occupations; and if my Lord Chesterfield's guardians should be of opinion that he ought, when he comes of age, not only to relieve my Lord Stanhope of his engagement, but likewise, in case I shall have acquitted myself faithfully and properly, to make some such addition to my annuity as I mentioned, I shall then likewise think that I can justify my conduct to the world, who rate men commonly as they do horses, by the price that is put upon them.[2] But of this I would not have the least hint to my Lord Chesterfield at present. I have so far proceeded without consulting anybody, and have formed an opinion subject to correction. I mean to read your letters, and this I am writing to one or two of my friends. If they approve, it shall go to you; and if you agree with me, be so good as intimate my resolution to the guardians of my Lord Chesterfield; or, if you have any objections of moment, delay it till I shall have heard from you. My own present feeling is, that I should be to blame if I omitted putting myself and family under the protection of persons so worthy and so respectable, when I have an opportunity of doing it without any real hazard to my interest. But I shall not enter on this subject, my heart, indeed, being too full, especially with respect to Lord Stanhope. I am etc.

Adam Ferguson

[1] See previous Letter.

[2] Ferguson gave up teaching Moral Philosophy and acted as travelling tutor to Chesterfield at a salary of £400. He was promised a pension of £200 for life. The Edinburgh Town Council dismissed him from his professorship in 1774, then reinstated him two years later as a result of legal action.

140. *From* DAVID HUME

MS., RSE ii. 54; HL ii. 285–6.

St. Andrews Square, 13 Feb. 1774

Dear Smith

You are in the wrong for never informing me of your Intentions and Resolutions, if you have fix'd any. I am now oblig'd to write to you on a Subject, without knowing whether the Proposal, or rather Hint, which I am to give you, be an Absurdity or not. The Settlement to be made on Ferguson is a very narrow Compensation for his Class, if he must lose it: He wishes to keep it, and to serve by a Deputy in his Absence. But besides that this Scheme will appear invidious and is really scarce admissible, those in the Town Council, who aim at filling the Vacancy with a Friend, will strenuously object to it; and he himself cannot think of one who will make a proper Substitute. I fancy, that the chief Difficulty wou'd be remov'd, if you cou'd offer to supply his Class, either as his Substitute or his Successor, with a Purpose of resigning upon his return. This notion is entirely my own, and shall never be known to Ferguson, if it appear to you improper. I shall only say, that he deserves this friendly Treatment, by his friendly Conduct, of a similar kind, towards poor Russel's Family.[1]

Pray, what strange Accounts are these we hear of Franklyn's Conduct?[2] I am very slow in believing that he has been guilty in the extreme Degree that is pretended; tho' I always knew him to be a very factious man, and Faction, next to Fanaticism, is, of all passions, the most destructive of Morality. How is it suppos'd, he got Possession of these Letters? I hear that Wedderburn's Treatment of him before the Council, was most cruel, without being in the least blameable. What a Pity![3]

---

[1] James Russel (d. 1773), Edinburgh surgeon and Professor of Natural Philosophy from 1764 until his death. Ferguson had become Professor of Moral Philosophy in 1764 as a result of a deal involving Russel (HL i. 438, n. 2). For Ferguson's account of his negotiations with the Stanhope family, see Letters 138 and 139.

[2] On 29 Jan. 1774 Franklin was examined before the Privy Council in the Cockpit, government buildings opposite Whitehall, for transmitting to Boston letters from Governor Hutchinson advocating the use of force against Massachusetts. The examination was pressed in a scurrilous manner by the Solicitor-General, Alexander Wedderburn. It has been claimed that thereafter war with the American colonies became inevitable:

> Sarcastic Sawney, swol'n with spite and prate
> On silent Franklin poured his venal hate.
> The calm philosopher, without reply,
> Withdrew and gave his country liberty.

(Quoted in Fay 125.)

[3] The letter has no signature, and is perhaps unfinished. The folded sheet containing the letter has neither address nor postmark.

141. *From* ADAM FERGUSON

Address: To Mr Adam Smith at the British Coffeehouse, Charing Cross, London
MS., Priv. coll. James R. Abbey, 31 Meadowside Rd., Edinburgh; unpubl.

Edinburgh, 11 Mar. 1774

My Dear Sir

I don't know whether you may not allude[1] to a letter that I have not received, but it is likely that none have miscarried. And I thought my last[2] decisive as to my resolutions and intended Motions. I have laboured hard to finish at the College and have put an end to one Species of Philosophy today and shall to another tomorrow. I have fixed to set out for London with J. Ferguson on Tuesday the Fifteenth of this Month, but as my Companion is indulgent to himself and Lazy may not be in London before Sunday or Monday thereafter. I write this merely because you say you are uneasy at not hearing from me. Am perfectly Satisfied with the whole manner and State of the Transactions and defer particularly till we meet. I have been dining with D. Hume who says you have never yet made any attempt to cure him of his Pet altho it be a great and a growing distemper.[3]
I am

My Dear Sir
Your most affectionately
humble Servant
Adam Ferguson

142. *From* ADAM FERGUSON

Small 618.

Geneva, 1 June, 1774

My Dear Smith,

You see I have taken full benefit of the time you allowed me to form my opinion of this situation,[1] and have the pleasure to inform you it is in most material circumstances very agreeable. I was received with great politeness, and continue to be treated with sufficient marks of regard. I have found not only vivacity and parts as I was made to expect, but likewise good dispositions and attachments, servants all of an old standing, and become friends without any improper influence or disorder that I have yet observed. I was made to expect great jealousy of control, and set out with a resolution to employ no other than what a sense of my great regard might give me. It is

---

[1] Presumably in a letter from Smith that has not been traced.
[2] ? Letter 139 from Ferguson, dated 23 Jan. 1774.
[3] Hume wrote to Smith about Ferguson's affairs on 13 Feb. (No. 140).

[1] See Letters 138 and 139 from Ferguson, dated 2 Sept. 1773 and 1 June 1774.

likely that a person of a different character was expected, and the disappointment, I believe, has had a good effect. My journey hither furnished no adventures worth relating. My Lord Stanhope's being at Paris gave me access, for the few days I stayed, to some very respectable and agreeable company, in which I was questioned concerning you, particularly by the Duchess D'Enville who complained of your French,[2] as she did of mine, but said that before you left Paris she had the happiness to learn your language. I likewise met with your friend, Count Sarsfield, to whom I had great obligations, and if you write I beg that you will thank him, etc. etc.

Adam Ferguson

143. *To* WILLIAM CULLEN

Thomson i. 473–81; Rae 273–80.

London, 20 Sept. 1774

My Dear Doctor,

I have been very much in the wrong both to you and to the Duke of Buccleugh,[1] to whom I certainly promised to write you in a post or two, for having delayed so long to fulfil my promise. The truth is, some occurrences which interested me a good deal, and which happened here immediately after the Duke's departure, made me forget altogether a business which I do acknowledge interested me very little.

In the present state of the Scotch Universities, I do most sincerely look upon them as, in spite of all their faults, without exception the best seminaries of learning that are to be found any where in Europe. They are perhaps, upon the whole, as unexceptionable as any public institutions of that kind, which all contain in their very nature the seeds and causes of negligency and corruption, have ever been, or are ever likely to be. That, however, they are still capable of amendment, and even of considerable amendment, I know very well, and a Visitation is, I believe, the only proper means of procuring them this amendment. Before any wise man, however, would apply for the appointment of so arbitrary a tribunal, in order to improve what is already, upon the whole, very *well*, he ought

---

[2] The Abbé Morellet, translator of WN, also said Smith's French was very bad (*Mémoires*, i. 127).

[1] When the Duke was elected an honorary Fellow of the College of Physicians of Edinburgh, 1774, he offered to have the question of examination for medical degrees opened in Parliament. The College drafted a memorial urging that medical degrees, rather than honorary ones, should be granted by the Scottish Universities only after personal examination of candidates and presentation of a certificate of pursuance of medical studies for at least two years. Failing immediate Government action, a Royal Commission of inquiry was advocated. The memorial was sent to Smith for his consideration.

certainly to know with some degree of certainty, first, who are likely to be appointed visitors, and secondly, what plan of reformation those visitors are likely to follow. But, in the present multiplicity of pretenders to some share in the prudential management of Scotch affairs, these are two points which I apprehend neither you nor I, nor the Solicitor-General,[2] nor the Duke of Buccleugh, can possibly know any thing about. In the present state of our affairs, therefore, to apply for a Visition in order to remedy an abuse, which is not perhaps of great consequence to the public, would appear to me to be extremely unwise. Hereafter, perhaps an opportunity may present itself for making such an application with more safety.

With regard to an admonition or threatening, or any other method of interfering in the affairs of a body corporate, which is not perfectly and strictly regular and legal, these are expedients which I am convinced neither his Majesty nor any of his present Ministers would choose to employ either now or at any time hereafter, in order to obtain an object even of much greater consequence than this reformation of Scotch degrees.

You propose, I observe, that no person should be admitted to examination for his degrees unless he brought a certificate of his having studied at least two years in some University. Would not such a regulation be oppressive upon all private teachers, such as the Hunters,[3] Hewson,[4] Fordyce,[5] etc.? The scholars of such teachers surely merit whatever honour or advantage a degree can confer, much more than the greater part of those who have spent many years in some Universities, where the different branches of medical knowledge are either not taught at all, or are taught so superficially that they had as well not be taught at all. When a man has learnt his lesson very well, it surely can be of little importance where or from whom he has learnt it.

The monopoly of medical education which this regulation would establish in favour of Universities would, I apprehend, be hurtful to the lasting prosperity of such bodies-coporate. Monopolists very seldom make good work, and a lecture which a certain number of students must attend, whether they profit by it or no, is certainly not very likely to be a good one. I have thought a great deal upon this subject, and have inquired very carefully into the constitution and history of several of the principal Universities of Europe:[6] I have satisfied myself that the present state of degradation and contempt into which the greater part of those societies

[2] Alexander Wedderburn.

[3] When in London, Smith along with Gibbon attended lectures on anatomy by Dr. William Hunter (1718–83), brother of Dr. John Hunter (1728–93), who lectured on surgery. Glasgow University was bequeathed the specimens and books of Dr. William Hunter now in the Hunterian Museum.

[4] William Hewson (1739–74), surgeon and anatomist, partner of Dr. William Hunter.

[5] Sir William Fordyce (1724–92), physician, practised in London from 1750 on.

[6] See WN I.x.c. 34 and v.i.f.

have fallen in almost every part of Europe, arises principally, first, from the large salaries which in some universities are given to professors, and which render them altogether independent of their diligence and success in their professions; and secondly, from the great number of students who, in order to get degrees or to be admitted to exercise certain professions, or who, for the sake of bursaries, exhibitions, scholarships, fellowships, etc., are obliged to resort to certain societies of this kind, whether the instructions which they are likely to receive there are or are not worth the receiving. All those different causes of negligence and corruption, no doubt take place in some degree in all our Scotch Universities. In the best of them, however, these cases take place in a much less degree than in the greater part of other considerable societies of the same kind; and I look upon this circumstance as the real cause of their present excellence. In the medical College of Edinburgh in particular, the salaries of the Professors are insignificant. There are few or no bursaries or exhibitions, and their monopoly of degrees is broken in upon by all other Universities, foreign and domestic. I require no other explication of its present acknowledged superiority over every other society of the same kind in Europe.

To sign a certificate in favour of any man whom we know little or nothing about, is most certainly a practice which cannot be strictly vindicated. It is a practice, however, which, from mere good nature, and without interest of any kind, the most scrupulous men in the world are sometimes guilty of. I certainly do not mean to defend it. Bating the unhandsomeness of the practice, however, I would ask in what manner does the public suffer by it? The title of Doctor, such as it is, you will say, gives some credit and authority to the man upon whom it is bestowed; it extends his practice, and consequently his field for doing mischief; it is not improbable too that it may increase his presumption, and consequently his disposition to do mischief. That a degree injudiciously conferred may sometimes have some little effect of this kind, it would surely be absurd to deny; but that this effect should be very considerable, I cannot bring myself to believe. That Doctors are sometimes fools as well as other people, is not, in the present times, one of those profound secrets which is known only to the learned. The title is not so very imposing, and it very seldom happens that a man trusts his health to another merely because that other is a doctor. The person so trusted has almost always either some knowledge or some craft which would procure him nearly the same trust, though he was not decorated with any such title. In fact the persons who apply for degrees in the irregular manner complained of, are, the greater part of them, surgeons or apothecaries, who are in the custom of advising and prescribing, that is, of practising as physicians; but who, being only surgeons and apothecaries, are not fee-ed as physicians. It is not so much to extend their practice as to increase their fees, that they are desirious of being made Doctors.

Degrees conferred, even undeservedly, upon such persons can surely do very little harm to the public. When the University of St Andrew's very rashly and imprudently, conferred a degree upon one Green, who happened to be a stage-doctor, they no doubt brought much ridicule and discredit upon themselves; but in what respect did they hurt the public? Green still continued to be what he was before, a stage-doctor, and probably never poisoned a single man more than he would have done though the honours of graduation had never been conferred upon him. Stage-doctors, I must observe, do not much excite the indignation of the faculty; more reputable quacks do. The former are too contemptible to be considered as rivals: They only poison the poor people; and the copper pence which are thrown up to them in handkerchiefs, could never find their way to the pocket of a regular physician. It is otherwise with the latter: They some-times intercept a part of what perhaps would have been better bestowed in another place. Do not all the old women in the country practice physic without exciting murmur or complaint? And if here and there a graduated doctor should be as ignorant as an old women, where can be the great harm? The beardless old woman, indeed, takes no fees; the bearded one does, and it is this circumstance I strongly suspect, which exasperates his bretheren so much against him.

There never was, and I will venture to say there never will be, a Univer-sity from which a degree could give any tolerable security, that the person upon whom it had been conferred, was fit to practise physic. The strictest Universities confer degrees only upon students of a certain standing. Their real motive for requiring this standing is, that the student may spend more money among them, and that they may make more profit by him. When he has attained this standing, therefore, though he still undergoes what they call an examination, it scarce ever happens that he is refused his degree. Your examination at Edinburgh, I have all reason to believe, is as serious, and perhaps more so than that of any other University in Europe. But when a student has resided a few years among you, has behaved dutifully to all his Professors, and has attended regularly all their lectures, when he comes to his examination, I suspect you are disposed to be as good-natured as other people. Several of your graduates, upon applying for license to the College of Physicians here, have had it recommended to them to continue their studies. From a particular knowledge of some of the cases, I am satisfied that the decision of the College in refusing them their license, was perfectly just; that is, was perfectly agreeable to the principles which ought to regulate all such decisions, and that the candidates were really very ignorant of their profession.

A degree can pretend to give security for nothing but the science of the graduate; and even for that it can give but a very slender security. For his good sense and discretion, qualities not discoverable by an academical examination, it can give no security at all. But without these, the presumption which commonly attends science must render it, in the practice of physic, ten times more dangerous than the grossest ignorance when accompanied, as it sometimes is, with some degree of modesty and diffidence.

If a degree, in short, always has been, and, in spite of all the regulations which can be made, always must be, a mere piece of quackery, it is certainly for the advantage of the public that it should be understood to be so. It is in a particular manner for the advantage of the Universities that, for the resort of students, they should be obliged to depend, not upon their privileges, but upon their merit, upon their abilities to teach and their diligence in teaching; and that they should not have it in their power to use any of those quackish arts which have disgraced and degraded the half of them.

A degree which can be conferred only upon students of a certain standing, is a statute of apprenticeship which is likely to contribute to the advancement of science, just as other statutes of apprenticeship have contributed to that of arts and manufactures. Those statutes of apprenticeship, assisted by other corporation laws, have banished arts and manufactures from the greater part of towns-corporate. Such degrees, assisted by some other regulations of a similar tendency, have banished almost all useful and solid education from the greater part of Universities. Bad work and high price have been the effects of the monopoly introduced by the former. Quackery, imposture, and exorbitant fees, have been the consequences of that established by the latter. The industry of manufacturing villages has remedied in part the inconveniences which the monopolies established by towns-corporate had occasioned. The private interest of some poor Professors of Physic in some poor Universities, inconveniently situated for the resort of students, has in part remedied the inconveniences which would certainly have resulted from that sort of monopoly which the great and rich Universities had attempted to establish. The great and rich Universities seldom graduated any body but their own students, and not even then till after a long and tedious standing; five and seven years for a Master of Arts; eleven and sixteen for a Doctor of Law, Physic, or Divinity. The poor Universities, on account of the inconveniency of their situation, not being able to get many students, endeavoured to turn the penny in the only way in which they could turn it, and sold their Degrees to whoever would buy them, generally without requiring any residence or standing, and frequently without subjecting the candidate even to a decent examination. The less trouble they gave the more money they got, and I certainly do not pretend to vindicate so dirty a practice. All universities being ecclesiastical establishments, under the immediate protection of the Pope, a degree from one of them gave, all over Christendom, very nearly the same privileges which a degree from any other could have given; and the respect which is to this day paid to foreign degrees, even in Protestant countries, must be considered as a remnant of Popery. The facility of obtaining degrees, particularly in physic, from those poor Universities, had two effects, both extremely advantageous to the public, but extremely disagreeable to graduates of other Universities, whose degrees had cost them much time and expense. *First*, It multiplied very much the number of doctors, and thereby no doubt sunk their fees, or at least hindered them from rising so very high as they otherwise would have done. Had the Universities of Oxford and Cambridge been able to maintain themselves in the exclusive privilege of graduating all the doctors who could practise in England, the price of feeling a pulse might by this time have risen from two and three guineas, the price which it has now happily arrived at, to double or triple that sum; and English physicians might, and probably would, have been at the same time the most ignorant and quackish in the world. *Secondly*, It reduced a good deal the rank and dignity of a doctor. But if the physician was a man of sense and science, it would not surely prevent his being respected and employed as a man of sense and science. If he was neither the one nor the other, indeed, his doctorship would no doubt avail him the less. But ought it in this case to avail him at all? Had the hopeful project of the rich and great Universities succeeded, there would have been no occasion for sense or science. To have been a doctor would alone have been sufficient to give any man rank, dignity, and fortune enough. That in every profession the fortune of every individual should depend as much as possible upon his merit, and as little as possible upon his privilege, is certainly for the interest of the public. It is even for the interest of every particular profession, which can never so effectually support the general merit and real honour of the greater part of those who exercise it, as by resting on such liberal principles. Those principles are even most effectual for procuring them all the employment which the country can afford. The great success of quacks in England has been altogether owing to the real quackery of the regular physicians. Our regular physicians in Scotland have little quackery, and no quack accordingly has ever made his fortune among us.

After all, this trade in degrees I acknowledge to be a most disgraceful trade to those who exercise it; and I am extremely sorry that it should be exercised by such respectable bodies as any of our Scotch Universities. But as it serves as a corrective to what would otherwise soon grow up to be an intolerable nuisance, the exclusive and corporation spirit of all thriving professions and of all great Universities, I deny that it is hurtful to the public.

What the physicians of Edinburgh at present feel as a hardship is, perhaps, the real cause of their acknowledged superiority over the greater part of other physicians. The Royal College of Physicians there, you say, are obliged by their charter to grant a license, without examination, to all the graduates of Scotch Universities. You are all obliged, I suppose, in consequence of this, to consult sometimes with very unworthy brethren. You are all made to feel that you must rest no part of your dignity upon your degree, a distinction which you share with the men in the world, perhaps, whom you despise the most, but that you must found the whole of it upon your merit. Not being able to derive much consequence from the character of Doctor, you are obliged, perhaps, to attend more to your characters as men, as gentlemen, and as men of letters. The unworthiness of some of your brethren may, perhaps, in this manner be in part the cause of the very eminent and superior worth of many of the rest. The very abuse which you complain of may in this manner, perhaps, be the real source of your present excellence. You are at present well, wonderfully well, and when you are so, be assured there is always some danger in attempting to be better.

Adieu, my dear Doctor; after having delayed so long to write to you, I am afraid I shall *get my lug in my lufe*,⁷ as we say, for what I have written. But I ever am, most affectionately yours,

Adam Smith.

144. *From* PATRICK CLASON

Address: Adam Smith Esqr, Care of Mr Cadell, Bookseller in the Strand, London
MS., RSE viii. 14; unpubl.

Geneva, 25 Feb. 1775

Sir

Mr Bonnet, the natural historian, has given me a commission which I cannot execute without your assistance. He wished to send his *Reche[r]ches* and *Palingenesie*¹ to Mr Hume, but was at a loss in what manner he should send them. I desired him to write to Mr Hume [   ]² his answer.

Vous le dirai-je Monsr? plus j'y reflechis, et moins je me sens porté s'ecrire à votre illustre compatriote. Je paroitrois trop rechercher son suffrage; je lui laisserois même supçonner que je fais assez de cas de mes petits ecrits pour esperer qu'ils feroient sur lui quelqu' impression; enfin, ce que seroit pis encore, j'aurois l'air de tenter une conversion, et je n'ais jamais eu la manie des conversions. Je sçais bien que son coeur honnête et vertueux se plairoit à applaudir mes faibles efforts, et a la moderation que

---

⁷ 'Lug' is Scots for ear, and 'lufe' means hand or palm. The saying is equivalent to 'getting one's ear warmed', or 'ears boxed', and then rubbing the affected part.

¹ The works of Charles Bonnet (1720–93) mentioned are *Recherches sur l'usage des feuilles dans les plantes* (1754) and *Palingénésie philosophique* (1769–70). For the result of Bonnet's request, see Letter 146 addressed to Hume, dated 9 May 1775.

² Writing has faded here.

j'ai porté dans des Recherches qui n'ont malheureusement excités que trop souvent la Bile des Ecrivains. Si vous presumés que ces ouvrages puissent interesser, tant soit peu, l'illustre philosophe, je vous prie de les lui envoyer, en l'assurant du cas singulier que l'Auteur fait de son merite, de ses talens et de ses lumieres. Mais, vous n'oublieres pas, surtout de lui dire bien que l'Auteur n'a pas songé le moins du monde à rompre une Lance avec le plus fameux Athlete de notre Siecle.

Ne vous oublies pas, je vous prie, auprés du Sage de Glascow vous voyés asses qui je parle de Mr Smith, dont nous nous ouviendrons toujours avec grand plaisir.

This gentleman and his Lady have been remarkably civil to me since I came to Geneva; and I was introduced to them as your acquaintance. He is, you know, of one of the first families here and a very estimable man. His religious ideas are probably different from Mr Hume's—mais qu'est que ça fait. I beg you to send those two books, which Mr Cadell will deliver to you free of carriage, accompanied with a letter to Mr Hume; and I wish much that he may take in good part the good intentions of Mr Bonnet. I should be glad if you or Mr Hume would write him. This would gratify him extremely.

I remain here till Lord Lumley[3] join me: I know nothing of our future expeditions nor of the time fixed for our travels.

I expected before this time to have seen you ag[ain] [   ]⁴ Tronchin and Le Sage beg to be remembered to you.

With great respect and Esteem I [have the] honour to be

Sir
Your most obedient humble Servant
Pat Clason

145. *From* EDMUND BURKE

MS., sold at Sotheby's, 8 Feb. 1955; *Burke Corr.* iii. 152–3.

Westminster, 1 May 1775

Dear Sir

You will be so good as to excuse an application upon a Business which I have very much at heart. The renewal of Mr Champions[1] Patent for his China Manufacture is opposed by Mr Wedgewood,[2] who does not so

---

³ Clason's pupil, Hon. Richard Lumley (1757–1832), 2nd s. of the 4th Earl of Scarborough; later M.P. for Lincoln 1784–90, and well known as possessor of one of the most valuable racing studs in the kingdom.   ⁴ Writing has faded here.

¹ Richard Champion (1743–91), Bristol ceramist and friend of Burke.

² Josiah Wedgwood (1730–95), master potter; founded the pre-eminent firm in the English Midland potteries district; developed such wares as Egyptian marbled, queen's, and jasper.

much as pretend to have ever had a Manufacture of that kind and consequently can feel no injury except in his imaginations of unmeasurable
gain. He pretends indeed that he is actuated, (and so he told me,) by nothing but a desire of the publick good. I confess a declaration of the lowest
species of any honest self Interest, would have much greater weight with
me, from the mouth of a Tradesman. He goes this day into Staffordshire
to stir up the Potters there to petition against us. This he does now, at the
close of the Session; though our petition has stood unopposed in the house
from the 2nd of February.[3] I should be very much obligd to you if you
could apply to the Duke of Buccleugh that he may keep his mind open to
the merits of this Cause, in Case we can get it through the house of Commons. His Grace should be furnished with the exact state of the Case, and
the merits of the Manufacture and the manufacturers. If you can serve in
this matter I shall take it as a real kindness and am with the greatest regard
and Esteem,

Dear Sir
your very faithful
and obedient humble Servant
Edm Burke

146. *To* DAVID HUME

MS., Muzeum Czartoryskich, Cracow, Poland; ed. Tadeusz Kozanecki, 'Dawida
Hume'a Nieznane Listy W Zbiorach Muzeum Czartoryskich (Polska)', *Archiwum
Historii Filozofii I Myśli Społecznej*, ix (1963), 150.

No. 24 Suffolk Street, Charing Cross, London,[1]
9 May 1775

My Dear Friend

I should be ashamed to write to you, if I had not long ago conquered
all modesty of that sort. Taking it for granted, therefore, that you hate
apologies as much as I do, I meant both making them and receiving them,
I shall not pretend to make any for my having so long neglected to write
to you. I hope I need not tell you that my long silence did not arise from
any want of the most affectionate and most grateful remembrance of you.

Mr Bonnet, the Gentleman mentioned in the enclosed letter from Mr
Clawson,[2] is one of the worthiest, and best hearted men in Geneva or

---

[3] The date should be 22 Feb., when Burke first presented Champion's petition (see
Burke Corr. iii. 138). The Bill to extend the patent was read on 1 May, committed on the
5th, and given its second reading on the 17th. Most of the controversy about it took place
during the committee stage. Burke's notes for a speech supporting Champion's patent,
and defending him against the charge of monopoly, are in the National Library of Ireland.

[1] The cover to Letter 147 gives Smith's address as No. 27 Suffolk Street.
[2] See Letter 144 from Patrick Clason, dated 25 Feb. 1775.

indeed in the world; notwithstanding he is one of the most religious. I delayed sending you this letter, till I should have an opportunity of sending you the Books which your Neighbour Mr Ross will bring you.[3]

Your friends here have been all much diverted with Priestly's answer to Beatie.[4] We were in great hopes that Beatie would have replyed and we are assured he has a reply ready written; but your old friend Hurd,[5] whom my Lord Mansfield, has with great judgement, made a Bishop, wrote to Beatie, I am assured, and advised him against answering; telling him that so excellent a work as the immutability of truth required no defence. We by this means have lost a most incomparable controversy. Priestly was perfectly prepared to carry it on thro' at least twenty rejoinders. I have some hopes still of getting somebody to provoke Beatie to draw his Pen again. I shall send my own book to the Press in the end of this month or the beginning of the next.[6]

There is a young man at Edinburgh, Mr Hugh Dalrymple,[7] for whom, on account of his Father, I at first conceived a most august aversion. Upon conversing with him, I found him one of the most amiable men I have ever known. His Father is not the only one of his family connections in which he has been unfortunate. But, in my opinion, he is upon that very account more entitled to the Protection of all good men. If he falls in your way I most earnestly recommend him to your countenance and good advice. I ought to have done this, I am ashamed to say, how many months ago. I ever am

My Dear Friend
Most faithfully yours
Adam Smith

147. *From* JOHN ROEBUCK[1]

Address: Adam Smith Esqr, Suffolk Street No 27, Charing Cross, London
MS., GUL Gen. 1035/152; Scott 268–9.

Bo'ness, 1 Nov. 1775

Dear Sir

I have so long delayed writing that I blush to take the Pen. Yet I know

---

[3] David Ross (1727–1805); advocate 1751; Lord of Session (Lord Ankerville) 1776. He lived at No. 3 St. Andrew's Square, near Hume's house on the south-west corner.

[4] Joseph Priestley, *An Examination of Reid's Inquiry, Beattie's Essay, and Oswald's Appeal to Common Sense* (1774). Concerning Beattie, see Letter 138 from Adam Ferguson, dated 2 Sept. 1773.

[5] Richard Hurd (1720–1808); Bishop of Lichfield 1774; one of the 'Warburton School' responsible for attacks on Hume's *Natural History of Religion* (1757).

[6] WN, published 9 Mar. 1776.   [7] Not identified.

[1] John Roebuck (1718–94), inventor and projector; studied Chemistry and Medicine at Edinburgh and Leyden (M.D. 1742); developed techniques for smelting precious

you will believe me when I say if my writing would have been of real service to you no consideration should have made me omit it. Since I left London I have not enjoyed good Health but have been dul and inactive and yet not so ill as to be confined to the House or take Medicines. I have trusted to indolence and temperance to restore me to health and have therefore attended only to absolutely necessary Business.

On my return home I found Mr Miller[2] rather more tractable than I expected. My concerns[3] however suffered a good deal by my absence not for want of either knowledge or industry in my Son John who truly executed his part to admiration but for want of sufficient Authority which necessitated him to yield to the Controul of my Trustees when I might have resisted. Sometimes I think Mr Miller disposed to [be]have candidly according to his knowledge at other times I find it difficult to refrain from contrary sentiments. I am daily however becoming more independent. These reflections to ourselves I should weary you with the subject if I was placed in your easy Chair.

Business and want of good Health has so confined me to Kinneil[4] that I have nothing but News Paper Politicks to furnish me with a little Zest which has roused me to write the inclosed Paper[5] I will not say in answer for I did not chuse to be personal but on the occasion of the publication of Mr Burks Letter to Mr [   ] of Bristol.[6] I sent it last Post to a Friend to put it in some of the Papers (of course without mentioning my name). But perhaps it may not see the light.

I have inclosed you a Coppy of a Letter from Capt. Lowrie with the Characters of some of the Boston Politicians.[7] Though the Pictures are not well painted yet I am inclined to think they are not much unlike the Originals.

I this day received the Kings Speech which delights me much as I perceive the Ministry are now creating a proper spirit.

I sometime ago received a Coppie of Letters to T.R.[8] by which I perceive both you and Mr W[9] have been attentive to my Interest. In hopes it

---

metals and producing sulphuric acid; formed the Carron Iron Company, 1760; Fellow of the Royal Societies of London and Edinburgh; friend and partner of James Watt. He went bankrupt in 1773, and Matthew Boulton bought his share in the partnership with Watt.

[2] Patrick Miller (1731–1815), Edinburgh banker and shareholder in Carron Co.; director of the Bank of Scotland (from 1767), then Deputy Governor; later associated, as projector, with the development of steam navigation.

[3] Roebuck lost heavily through ill success at this period with salt-works and coalmines at Bo'ness, Linlithgowshire. Latterly he was employed there as manager by his creditors.

[4] 16th–17th-century mansion S.W. of Bo'ness; the park was the scene of experiments with Watt's condensing steam engine.

[5] Not traced.

[6] Blank in text: ? Richard Champion—see Letter 145 from Burke, dated 1 May 1775.

[7] Walter S. Laurie, 'Camp on Charles Town heights 23 June 1775', GUL MS. Gen. 1035(y): the 'Boston Politicians' include Samuel Adams and Josiah Quincy.

[8] Not traced.   [9] ? Alexander Wedderburn.

will take place I have been instructing Ben.[10] in some branches of Chymistry so as to enable him to carry on Business with advantage soon after his arrival.

I hoped by this time to have seen your Name in the Papers. The meeting of Parliament is a proper time for the Publication of such a work as yours.[11] It might also have been of general use in influencing the Opinion of many in this American contest.

Mrs Roebuck sends her kind Compliments to you. I am Dear Sir ever your Affectionate Friend and Humble Servant

John Roebuck

[　　] letter and a Plan of the Pr[　　]ers shall be sent to TR under [　　] next Post.[12]

148. *To* [HENRY DUNDAS][1]

MS., SRO GD51/1/198/10/2; unpubl.

[London,] 13 Dec. 1775

My Dear Lord

I had yesterday a very long conversation with the Sollicitor General[2] and Andrew Stuart concerning the Politicks of fifeshire.[3] I told them exactly what I had done in favour of my Cousin;[4] and they told me as

---

[10] Another son of Roebuck.　　　　[11] WN.　　　　[12] The postscript is torn.

[1] Addressee identified by SRO as Henry Dundas (1742–1811), lawyer and statesman; son of Robert Dundas of Arniston the Elder, and half-brother of the Younger, both Lord Presidents of the Court of Session; advocate 1763; Solicitor-Gen. of Scotland 1766; M.P. 1774–1802; appointed Lord Advocate 1775, giving him control of political patronage in Scotland which he retained for most of his life. He was the friend and colleague of Pitt, holding high office in his administrations with particular responsibility for waging war against revolutionary France. In 1802 he was created Viscount Melville; after serving as First Lord of the Admiralty 1804–5, he was impeached in 1806 for malversion, found guilty of negligence, but acquitted and restored to the roll of the Privy Council 1807.

[2] Alexander Murray (1736–95) of Murrayfield, Edinburgh, and Henderland, Peebles; educ. Edinburgh University; advocate 1758; Sheriff Depute, Peebles 1761–75; one of the Commissaries of Edinburgh 1765; succeeded Henry Dundas as Solicitor-Gen. 1775–83; M.P. for Peebles 1780–3; Commissioner for Fisheries and Manufactures 1777; raised to the Bench as Lord Henderland 1783, and made a Lord Commissioner of Justiciary; Clerk of the Pipe in Exchequer 1786–d. His influential connections included the Marquess of Tweeddale and Lord Mansfield, and he was a loyal colleague to Henry Dundas. Boswell admired him for his 'ornate eloquence'.

[3] The sitting M.P., Col. John Scott of Balcomie, died in 1775. Henry Dundas, guardian of Scott's children, took control of the Balcomie interest which was much sought after. The previous member, James Wemyss, gave his interest to James Townsend Oswald.

[4] Robert Skene (1719–87) of Hallyards, entered the Army 1743; Adjutant Gen. 1763; Inspector of Roads in the Highlands 1767–80; Col. 1772; Maj. Gen. 1777. He stood for Fife in 1776, supported by John, 5th Duke of Argyll, but gave his interest to James Townsend Oswald who was elected. When the latter resigned in 1779, Skene was returned as M.P., then unseated in Feb. 1780 because he held the office of Inspector of Roads. He was

exactly what they had done in favour of their respective friends. The Sollicitor General, I understand, has recommended to you, in the first place, his friend Sir John Hackit; and supposing that he should decline standing, Mr Stuarts nephew, Mr Henderson.[5] If Sir John Hackit is a candidate, there is an end of the Business. Collonel Skeene will not oppose his nearest relation and his best friend. If Sir John should decline, which it is here believed he will do, I have some reason to believe that My Lord Mansfield will not chuse that the remains of General Scott's interest should go to a Nephew of Andrew Stuart.[6] If my information should happen to be Just, I am thoroughly convinced that Skeene is as good a man as any you could pitch upon. He has been one of the best Sons, Brothers and Unkles that I have ever known; and, I am thoroughly convinced, will be an equally faithful supporter of whoever supports him. I have desired him to wait upon your Brother and you as soon as he gets to Scotland. I will pawn my head that he makes no dishonourable use of any confidence you chuse to put in him. I ever am

My Dear Lord
most faithfully yours
Adam Smith

149. *From* DAVID HUME

Address: To Adam Smith Esqr at the British Coffee-house, Charing cross London
MS., RSE ii. 55; HL ii. 308.

Edinburgh, 8 Feb. 1776

Dear Smith

I am as lazy a Correspondent as you; yet my Anxiety about you makes me write.

By all Accounts, your Book has been printed long ago; yet it has never yet been so much as advertised.[1] What is the Reason? If you wait till the Fate of America be decided, you may wait long.

By all accounts, you intend to settle with us this Spring: Yet we hear no more of it: What is the Reason? Your Chamber in my House is always unoccupied: I am always at home: I expect you to land here.

returned again in the General Election of 1780. Skene supported North's administration, was listed among Shelburne's friends, and was regarded latterly as an opponent of Pitt. He was an authority on Road Bills.

5 John Henderson (1752–1817) of Fordell, succeeded his fa. as 5th Bt. 1781; educ. St Andrews and Oxford; M.P. 1780–1807 for, successively, Fife, Dysart, Seaford, and Stirling.

6 In the House of Lords Mansfield attacked Stuart's Douglas Cause proofs as gross perjury, and Stuart retaliated with the ironic *Letters to Lord Mansfield* (1773).

1 WN, published 9 March 1776; advertised in *London Chronicle* of 5–7 Mar.

I have been, am, and shall be probably in an indifferent State of Health. I weighed myself t'other day, and find I have fallen five compleat Stones. If you delay much longer, I shall probably disappear altogether.

The Duke of Bucleugh tells me, that you are very zealous in American Affairs.[2] My Notion is, that the Matter is not so important as is commonly imagind. If I be mistaken, I shall probably correct my Error, when I see you or read you. Our Navigation and general Commerce may suffer more than our Manufactures. Shoud London fall as much in its Size, as I have done, it will be the better. It is nothing but a Hulk of bad and unclean Humours. Yours

David Hume

150. *From* DAVID HUME

Address: To Adam Smith Esqr
MS., RSE ii. 56; HL ii. 311–12.

Edinburgh, 1 Apr. 1776

Euge![1] Belle! Dear Mr Smith: I am much pleas'd with your Performance, and the Perusal of it has taken me from a State of great Anxiety. It was a Work of so much Expectation, by yourself, by your Friends, and by the Public, that I trembled for its Appearance; but am now much relieved. Not but that the Reading of it necessarily requires so much Attention, and the Public is disposed to give so little, that I shall still doubt for some time of its being at first very popular:[2] But it has Depth and Solidity and Acuteness, and is so much illustrated by curious Facts, that it must at last take the public Attention. It is probably much improved by your last Abode in London. If you were here at my Fireside, I shoud dispute some of your Principles. I cannot think, that the Rent of Farms makes any part of the Price of the Produce, but that the Price is determined altogether by the Quantity and the Demand.[3] It appears to me impossible, that the King of France can take a Seigniorage of 8 per cent upon the Coinage. No body would bring Bullion to the mint:[4] It woud be all sent to Holland or

---

[2] Presumably Smith was impressing on influential friends such as Wedderburn and Strahan, the views brought out in WN IV.vii.c. and at the conclusion of his book. See Letter 158 addressed to Strahan, dated 3 June 1776; 159 from Wedderburn, dated 6 June; and 160 from Strahan, dated 10 June; also, Appendix B.

[1] Greek for 'Well done!'

[2] The *Gentleman's Magazine* ignored WN, and it received only a two-page review in the 1776 *Annual Register*, though this is thought to have been written by Burke.

[3] At WN I.vi.8, Smith states that the rent of land constitutes a third part of the price of most kinds of goods, but notes later that rent enters into the composition of the price of commodities in a different way from wages and profit' (I. xi. a. 8). Hume's criticism foreshadows that of Ricardo: *The Principles of Political Economy and Taxation*, ch. xxiv.

[4] In WN IV.vi.20, 'of Treaties of Commerce', Smith stated on the authority of Bazinghen's *Traité des monnoies* (1764), that the coinage in France increases the value of a mark of standard gold bullion, by the difference between 671 livres 10 deniers, and 720 livres; or

England, where it might be coined and sent back to France for less than two per cent. Accordingly Neckre⁵ says, that the French King takes only two per cent of Seigniorage. But these and a hundred other Points are fit only to be discussed in Conversation; which, till you tell me the contrary, I shall still flatter myself with soon. I hope it will be soon: For I am in a very bad State of Health and cannot afford a long Delay.

I fancy you are acquainted with Mr Gibbon: I like his Performance extremely and have ventured to tell him, that, had I not been personally acquainted with him, I shoud never have expected such an excellent Work from the Pen of an Englishman.⁶ It is lamentable to consider how much that Nation has declined in Literature during our time. I hope he did not take amiss the national Reflection.

All your Friends here are in great Grief at present for the Death of Baron Mure,⁷ which is an irreparable Loss to our Society. He was among the oldest and best Friends I had in the World.

I wrote you about six Weeks ago,⁸ which I hope you received: You may certainly at present have the Subject of a Letter to me; and you have no longer any very pressing Occupation. But our Friendship does not depend on these Ceremonials.

D H

151. From HUGH BLAIR¹

MS., NLS 1005 fols. 21–22ᵛ; Fay 39–40 (in part).

Edinburgh, 3 Apr. [1776]

My Dear Sir

I Cannot forbear writing to Congratulate you upon your Book. I have

---

by 48 livres 19 sous and 2 deniers. This works out at a seignorage of slightly over 7% (not 8% as Hume claimed). But Hume's criticism was just, for Garnier in his translation of WN (v. 234) points out that the mint price referred to by Bazinghen remained in force a very short time. When it failed to bring bullion to the mint, higher prices were offered, and at the time of the publication of WN, the seignorage amounted to approximately 3%.

⁵ The reference is to Jacques Necker's *Essai sur la législation et le commerce des grains* (1775), which Smith cites, e.g. at WN V.ii.k.78. See Letter 159, n. 5.

⁶ The first volume of *The Decline and Fall of the Roman Empire* was published by Strahan on 20 February. Hume congratulated Gibbon on 18 March (HL ii. 309–11), in a letter which the author said 'overpaid the labour of ten years'. Gibbon's book sold better than WN (Rae 286).

⁷ Baron Mure died at Caldwell on 25 March 1776, of gout in the stomach.

⁸ Letter 149, dated 8 Feb. 1776.

¹ Hugh Blair (1718–1800), leader among the moderates of the Edinburgh ministers, successively incumbent of the Canongate Kirk, Lady Yester's, and the High Kirk of St. Giles (after 1758); famous as a preacher and literary critic; appointed Regius Professor of Rhetoric and Belles-Lettres at Edinburgh, 1762; remembered for his preface (anon.) to Macpherson's *Fragments of Ancient Poetry* (1760), *Critical Dissertation on the Poems of*

just finished it; and though from what you read to me some years ago, and from the great Attention which I knew you had bestowed on the Subject, I expected much, yet I Confess you have exceeded my expectations. One writer after another on these Subjects did nothing but puzzle me. I despaired of ever arriving at clear Ideas. You have given me full and Compleat Satisfaction and my Faith is fixed. I do think the Age is highly indebted to you, and I wish they may be duly Sensible of the Obligation. You have done great Service to the World by overturning all that interested Sophistry of Merchants, with which they had Confounded the whole Subject of Commerce. Your work ought to be, and I am perswaded will in some degree become, the Commercial Code of Nations. I did not read one Chapter of it without Acquiring much Light and instruction. I am Convinced that since Montesquieu's *Esprit des Loix*, Europe has not received any Publication which tends so much to Enlarge and Rectify the ideas of mankind.

Your Arrangement is excellent. One chapter paves the way for another; and your System gradually erects itself. Nothing was ever better suited than your Style is to the Subject; clear and distinct to the last degree, full without being too much so, and as tercly as the Subject could admit. Dry as some of the Subjects are, It carried me along. I read the whole with avidity; and have pleasure in thinking that I shall within some short time give it a Second and more deliberate perusal.

But have I no faults to find? There are some pages about the middle of the Second Volume where you enter into a description about the measures we ought at present to take with respect to America, giving them a representation etc.[2] which I wish had been omitted, because it is too much like a publication for the present moment. In Subsequent editions when publick Measures come to be Settled, these pages will fall to be omitted or Altered. But in the mean time they will go into the Translation of your work (unless, which perhaps might deserve your Consideration, you write to prevent it) into French, and may remain in Europe unaltered. By your two Chapters on Universities and the Church,[3] you have raised up very formidable adversaries who will do all they can to decry you. There is so much good Sense and Truth in your doctrine about Universities, and it is so fit that your doctrine should be preached to the World, that I own I would have regretted the Want of that Chapter. But in your System about the Church I cannot wholly agree with you. Independency was at no time

Ossian (1763), *Lectures on Rhetoric and Belles-Lettres* (1783), and *Sermons* (1778–1801). Blair followed Smith and Robert Watson in lecturing on rhetoric at Edinburgh. He was shown by Smith 'part of a manuscript treatise on rhetoric', presumably a version of the later LRBL, and he incorporated ideas from it in his own lectures. Also, he is reported as making use of Smith's ideas on jurisprudence in his sermons, but Smith did not complain, remarking: 'He is very welcome. There is enough left' (Rae 33, quoting indirectly Henry Mackenzie).

   [2] WN IV.vii.c. 75–9.   [3] WN V.i.f. and g.

a popular or practicable System. The little Sects you Speak of, would for many reasons, have Combined together into greater bodies, and done much Mischief to Society. You are, I think, too favourable by much to Presbytery. It Connects the Teachers too closely with the People; and gives too much aid to that Austere System you Speak of,[4] which is never favourable to the great improvements of mankind.

But the chief Improvement I wish for in the next Edition is that you take some method to point out in what parts of the Book we may find out any thing we wish to look for. You travel thro' a great Variety of Subjects. One has frequently occasion to reflect and look back. The Contents of your chapters are so short as to afford little direction. An Index (which however will be Necessary) does not fully Supply the want.[5] My Idea is this; That at the beginning or end of the work you should give us a Syllabus of the whole; expressed in short independent Propositions, like the Syllabus's we are in use to give of our College Lectures; with references under each, to the pages in which these propositions are handled and proved. The Benefit of this would not only be that it would lead us to any part of the work we wanted to Consult, but (which would be a much higher advantage) it would Exhibit a Scientifical View of the whole System; it would impress your Principles on our Memory; it would show us how they hang upon one another, and give mutual Support and Con[s]istency to the Fabrick; it would gather together the Scatter'd Ideas which many of your Readers will form, and give them something like real improvement. I do not know whether I have made you clearly understand my Idea. But I am Convinced that something of this kind would be a great and material improvement of your work. Ten or fifteen Additional pages would comprize it all; and they would be the most Valuable pages of the whole. Pray think of this. I want exceedingly to have it done. It would give both more eclat and more usefulness to your System.

This has been a fortunate Season. Gibbon has given us an Elegant and Masterly Book. But what the Deuce had he to do with Attacking Religion?[6] It will both Clog his Work, and it is in itself Unhistorical, and out of place. I heartily wish him to go on; but for Gods sake let him for the future keep off that ground as much as possible.

Your Friends here are well; except (how miserable it is that we must make that exception!) poor D. Hume.[7] He is declining Sadly. I dread,

[4] According to Smith the 'austere system' of morality was favoured by the 'common people' and the 'liberal' or 'loose' one by the people of fashion: see WN V.i.g.10, also 34 and 37.

[5] An index was added to the 3rd edn. of WN in 1784; see Letter 242 addressed to Thomas Cadell, dated 18 Nov. of that year.

[6] Chs. 15 and 16 of *The Decline and Fall of the Roman Empire*.

[7] 'In spring 1775', Hume wrote, 'I was struck with a Disorder in my Bowels, which at first gave me no Alarm, but has since, as I apprehend it, become mortal and incurable' (*My Own Life*, 18 Apr. 1776).

I dread—and I shudder at the prospect. We have suffered so much by the loss of Friends in our Circle here of late,[8] that such a blow as that would be utterly overwhelming. We have often flattered our Selves with the prospect of your Settling amongst us in a Station that would be both Creditable and Usefull. But I own that I have less prospect of that than I had. I Cannot believe but that they will place you at some of the great Boards in England. They are Idiots if they do not: Tho perhaps you might pass your days as Comfortably at some of our Boards here.[9] Wherever you are, God bless you. The D[uke] of B[uccleuch] your friend goes up, I hear it said, next week. I ever am, with great respect and Esteem

My Dear Sir
Your Affectionate and Faithful
Hugh Blair

152. *From* JOSEPH BLACK

Address: To Mr Adam Smith
MS., RSE viii. 6; unpubl.

[Edinburgh, Apr. 1776][1]

Dear Sir

Tho I sit down to write to you upon another account I cannot help expressing the pleasure and Satisfaction I frequently meet with in hearing the Opinions of good Judges concerning your Book. I most heartily rejoice in the prospect of the additional Credit and reputation which you cannot miss to gain by it and which must encrease as long as you live for I have no doubt that the Views you have given of many parts of your Subject will be found by experience to be as just as they are new and interesting and although it be admired immediately by discerning and impartial Judges[,] It will require some time before others who are not so quick sighted and whose minds are warped by Prejudice or Interest can understand and relish such a comprehensive System composed with such just and liberal Sentiments. But I write at present cheifly to acquaint you with the State of your Freind David Humes' Health which is so bad that I am quite melancholy upon it and as I hear that you intend a Visit to this country, soon, I wish if possible to hasten your coming that he may have the Comfort of your Company so much the sooner. He has been declining several years and this in a Slow and gradual manner untill about a twelve month agoe Since which the progress of his Disorder has been more

---

[8] Baron Mure and Lord Alemoor.
[9] Smith was made a Commissioner of Customs for Scotland in January 1778.

[1] The letter must have been written after WN reached Scotland and before Hume left for England on 21 April.

rapid.[2] One of his Distresses has been a Sensation of excessive Heat cheifly in the nighttime and which was only external for it occasioned no internal distress or anxiety or thirst. It has been greatly alleviated by the use of the tepid Bath which he still finds very comfortable. But there is another Disorder in his Constitution which is undermining him I am afraid in an irresistable manner. This is a Diarrhea with Colicy Pains attended with and I beleive proceeding from an internal Haemorrage. He has been all his life Subject to fits of Diarrhea which returned at pretty regular intervals [,] he has also been long subject to haemorrhoidal Discharges—but the Diarhhea has become gradually more frequent and now returns every 3 or 4 days—and when it comes he passes a large quantity of blood which from its appearance and from the Seat of his Colicy pains must proceed from some of the higher parts of the intestines—he is greatly weakened and looks very ill after every discharge but recovers next day in some measure and enjoys upon the whole a Surprising degree of ease and good Spirits and takes a moderate quantity of food with appetite and relish. His mother he says had precisely the same constitution with himself and dyed of this very disorder, which has made him give up any hopes of his getting the better of it. I have given you this particular account of his Situation that you may Communicate it to Sir John Pringle[3] with my respectfull Compliments. I know that they have a great freindship for one another and Sir John must be anxious to hear a particular account of his freind. If he has any remarks to make or hints to give I shall be glad to receive them.

Do not however say much on this Subject to any one else, as he does not like to have it spoke of and has even been shy and slow in acquainting me fully with this State of his health.

Forgive this Scrawl which I have not time to transcribe and beleive me ever

My Dear Sir
Most faithfully and affectionately
Yours
Joseph Black

[2] Cancer of the bowel cannot be ruled out, but Hume probably died of chronic ulcerative colitis, following an acute bacillary dysentery (Mossner, *Life of Hume*, 596).

[3] Sir John Pringle (1707–82), physician, friend of Smith and Hume; studied at Leyden; joint Professor of Pneumatics and Moral Philosophy at Edinburgh 1734–44; resigned professorship to become Physician-General to British forces in Flanders 1744; settled in London, 1748; physician to George III, 1774; President of the Royal Soc. 1772; reformed military medicine and sanitation: *Observations on Diseases of the Army* (1752).

153. *From* WILLIAM ROBERTSON

Lady Dorothea Charnwood, *An Autograph Collection* (London, 1930), 121–2.

North Murchiston, 8 Apr. 1776

My Dear Sir

Though I am little disposed to write letters, and nobody, I know, is less apt to expect them than you, I cannot rise from finishing my first reading of the *Inquiry*, full of the new ideas and knowledge which it has communicated to me, without expressing somewhat of the cordial satisfaction which one naturally feels upon contemplating any uncommon and meritorious exertion of a friend. As I knew how much time and attention you had bestowed upon this work, I had raised my expectations of it very high, but it has gone far beyond what I expected. You have formed into a regular and consistent system one of the most intricate and important parts of political science, and if the English be capable of extending their ideas beyond the narrow and illiberal arrangements introduced by the mercantile supporters of Revolution principles, and countenanced by Locke and some of their favourite writers, I should think your Book will occasion a total change in several important articles both in police[1] and finance. All your friends here have but one opinion concerning your work. Perhaps, however, when we have the pleasure of seeing you, we may venture to discuss some articles of your Creed, and to dispute others, but in the spirit of meekness, non ita certandi cupidi, quam propter amorem. None of your friends, however, will profit more by your labours and discoveries than I.[2] Many of your observations concerning the Colonies are of capital importance to me. I shall often follow you as my Guide and instructor. I am happy to find my own ideas concerning the absurdity of the limitations upon the Colony trade established much better than I could have done myself. I have now finished all my work, but what relates to the British Colonies, and in the present uncertain state into which they are thrown, I go on writing with hesitation.[3]

[1] At the opening of his Lectures on Jurisprudence, Smith said: 'The four great objects of law are justice, police, revenue, and arms.' Later came a definition: 'Police is the second general division of jurisprudence. The name is French, and is originally derived from the Greek πολιτεία, which properly signified the policy of civil government, but now it only means the regulation of the inferior parts of government, *viz.*: cleanliness, security, and cheapness or plenty' (LJ(B), 5, 203; ed. Cannan, 3, 154).

[2] Evidence exists about Robertson making use of Smith's ideas at an earlier stage in his career. John Callander of Craigforth who heard Smith's lectures on jurisprudence *c.* 1750–1 averred that 'Dr Robertson had borrowed the first volume of his History of Charles V. from them as every student could testify'. The reference is to the first vol. of the *History: A View of the Progress of Society in Europe from the Subversion of the Roman Empire to the Beginning of the Sixteenth Century.* According to Callander, Smith said Robertson 'was able to form a good outline but he wanted industry to fill up the plan' (EUL MSS. La. ii. 451–2, quoted in Scott 55–6).

[3] In the first eight books of his *History of America* (1777), Robertson gave 'an account

As your Book must necessarily become a Political or Commercial Code to all Europe, which must be often consulted both by men of Practice and Speculation, I should wish that in the 2d Edition you would give a copious index,[4] and likewise what the Book-sellers call *Side-notes*, pointing out the progress of the subject in every paragraph. This will greatly facilitate the consulting or referring to it. I hope now that your Book is off your hand, that we may have the pleasure of seeing you in Scotland. Our society here has suffered cruel loppings. Mr Hume declines so fast, that I am under the greatest sollicitude about him. If he does not recruit with the return of good weather, I shall become very apprehensive about his fate. I need not say to you what a loss we shall all suffer. Believe me My Dear Sir ever to be

Your affectionate and faithfull

friend
William Robertson

154. *From* ADAM FERGUSON

Small 621; Rae 138 (in part).

Edinburgh, 18 Apr. 1776.

My Dear Sir,

I have been for some time so busy reading you, and recommending and quoting you, to my students, that I have not had leisure to trouble you with letters. I suppose, however, that of all the opinions on which you have any curiosity, mine is among the least doubtful. You may believe, that on further acquaintance with your work my esteem is not a little increased. You are surely to reign alone on these subjects, to form the opinions, and I hope to govern at least the coming generations. I see no addition your work can receive except such little matters as may occur to yourself in subsequent editions. You are not to expect the run of a novel, nor even of a true history; but you may venture to assure your booksellers of a steady and continual sale, as long as people wish for information on these subjects.[1] You have provoked, it is true, the church, the universities, and the merchants, against all of whom I am willing to take your part; but

---

of the discovery of the New World, and of the progress of the Spanish arms and Colonies there'. The last two books dealt with the history of Virginia to 1688 and of New England to 1652. In the preface he promised he would return to the British colonies when the 'civil war with Great Britain terminated', but he did not do so.

4 See Letter 151 from Hugh Blair, dated 3 April 1776, n. 5.

1 Hume thought WN required 'too much thought to be as popular as Mr Gibbon's [History]' (HL, ii. 314), and Strahan concurred: 'What you say of Mr Gibbon's and Dr Smith's book is exactly just. The former is the more popular work; but the sale of the latter, though nor near so rapid, has been more than I could have expected from a work that requires much thought and reflection (qualities that do not much abound among modern readers) to peruse to any purpose' (12 Apr. 1776, RSE Hume MSS.) Ed. 1 of WN was exhausted in six months.

you have likewise provoked the militia, and there I must be against you.[2] The gentlemen and peasants of this country do not need the authority of philosophers to make them supine and negligent of every resource they might have in themselves, in the case of certain extremities, of which the pressure, God knows, may be at no great distance. But of this more at Philippi. You have heard from Black of our worthy friend D. Hume. If anything in such a case could be agreeable, the easy and pleasant state of his mind and spirits would be really so. I believe he will be prevailed on at least to get in motion, and to try the effect of Bath, or anything else Sir John Pringle may recommend.[3] I have said more on this subject to Mr Gibbon who, if you be found at London, will communicate to you. If not, I hope we shall soon meet here. And am, etc.

Adam Ferguson

155. *From* ADAM FERGUSON

Small 623, n. (extract).

[Edinburgh, Apr. 1776][1]

. . . David, I am afraid, loses ground. He is cheerful, and in good spirits as usual; but I confess that my hopes from the effects of the turn of the season towards spring have very much abated . . .

156. *From* DAVID HUME

Address: To Adam Smith Esqr at Kirkcaldy
MS., ii. 57; HL ii. 316–17.

London 3d of May 1776

My dear Friend

I send you enclosed an ostensible Letter,[1] conformably to your Desire. I think, however, your Scruples groundless.[2] Was Mallet any wise hurt by

---

[2] In general, Smith argued a militia would be inferior to a professional standing army, since modern war made demands ill-trained soldiers could not meet, but with a prophetic eye on America he noted a militia long in the field could become the equal of a standing army: WN V.i.a. 23 and 27. Ferguson, was a leader in the campaign to get a Scottish militia: *The Proceedings in the Case of Margaret, called Peg, only Sister of John Bull* (1761). In 1775, he enthused to Alexander Carlyle about seeing the Swiss militia under arm.

[3] This month of April, Sir John Pringle persuaded Hume to come to London for a medical examination and then to try the waters at Bath and Buxton. Hume left Edinburgh on 21 April, meeting Smith and John Home the dramatist two days later at Morpeth. Smith continued on to Kirkcaldy to see his ailing mother, while his companion returned to London with Hume.

[1] Undated, but presumably written before Hume left Edinburgh for London on 21 Apr.

[1] Letter 157 also dated 3 May 1776.
[2] Subsequent letters show that Smith would not take the responsibility of publishing the *Dialogues concerning Natural Religion*.

his Publication of Lord Bolingbroke? He received an Office afterwards from the present King and Lord Bute, the most prudish Man in the World; and he always justify'd himself by his sacred Regard to the Will of a dead Friend. At the same time, I own, that your Scruples have a specious Appearance. But my Opinion is, that, if, upon my Death, you determine never to publish these papers, you shoud leave them, seal'd up with my Brother and Family, with some Inscription, that you reserve to Yourself the Power of reclaiming them, whenever you think proper. If I live a few Years longer, I shall publish them myself. I consider an Observation of Rochefoucault, that a Wind, though it extinguishes a Candle, blows up a fire.

You may be surpriz'd to hear me talk of living Years, considering the State you saw me in, and the Sentiments which both I and all my Friends at Edinburgh entertaind on that Subject. But though I cannot come up entirely to the sanguine Notions of our Friend, John,[3] I find myself very much recovered on the Road, and I hope Bath Waters, and farther Journeys may effect my Cure.

By the little Company I have seen, I find the Town very full of your Book, which meets with general Approbation. Many People think particular Points disputable; but this you certainly expected: I am glad, that I am one of the Number; as these points will be the Subject of future Conversation between us.

I set out for Bath, I believe on Monday, by Sir John Pringle's Directions who says that he sees nothing to be apprehended in my Case. If you write to me, hem! hem! I say, if you write to me, send your Letters under Cover to Mr Strahan, who will have my Direction.

I regret much, in leaving Edinburgh, that I shall lose much of your Company, which I shoud have enjoy'd this Summer. I am Dear Smith

Yours sincerely and affectionately

David Hume

157. *From* DAVID HUME

Address: Dr Adam Smith
MS., RSE ii. 58; HL ii. 317–18.

London, 3 May 1776

My dear Sir

After reflecting more maturely on that Article of my Will by which I left you the Disposal of all my Papers,[1] with a Request that you shou'd

---

[3] John Home the dramatist.

[1] The article reads: 'To my friend Dr Adam Smith, late Professor of Moral Philosophy in Glasgow, I leave all my manuscripts without exception, desiring him to publish my

publish my *Dialogues concerning natural Religion,* I have become sensible, that, both on account of the Nature of the Work, and of your Situation, it may be improper to hurry on that Publication. I therefore take the present Opportunity of qualifying that friendly Request: I am content, to leave it entirely to your Discretion at what time you will publish that Piece, or whether you will publish it at all. You will find among my Papers a very inoffensive Piece, called *My Own Life,* which I composed a few days before I left Edinburgh, when I thought, as did all my Friends, that my Life was despaired of. There can be no Objection, that this small piece shoud be sent to Messrs. Strahan and Cadell and the Proprietors of my other Works to be prefixed to any future Edition of them. I am Dear Sir

Your most affectionate Friend and Servant
David Hume

158. *To* [WILLIAM STRAHAN]

MS., Huntington Libr., San Marino, California; unpubl.

Kirkcaldy, 3 June 1776

Dear Sir

I have very little to say to you besides what I have said to Mr Cadell in the enclosed to which I refer.[1] In business I consider him and you as the same person.

From this obscure and remote part of the country there is nothing to write you about except, the worst of all subjects, ones self. And even upon that subject I have nothing to say except that I am in perfect health and that I found my mother as much so as it is possible for anybody to be who is past eighty.

The American Campaign has begun awkwardly.[2] I hope, I cannot say that I expect, it will end better. England, tho' in the present times it breeds men of great professional abilities in all different ways, great Lawyers, great watch makers and Clockmakers, etc. etc., seems to breed

Dialogues concerning Natural Religion, which are comprehended in this present bequest; but to publish no other papers which he suspects not to have been written within these five years, but to destroy them all at his leisure. And I even leave him full power over all my papers, except the Dialogues above mentioned; and though I can trust to that intimate and sincere friendship, which has ever subsisted between us, for his faithful execution of this part of my will, yet, as a small recompense of his pains in correcting and publishing this work, I leave him two hundred pounds, to be paid immediately after the publication of it.' (Will dated 4 Jan. 1776, *Register of Testaments,* H.M. Register House, Edinburgh.)

[1] The enclosures to Cadell have not been traced but presumably were a bill and a communication about the sale of WN. See Letter 160 from Strahan, dated 10 June.

[2] At the beginning of 1776, General Howe was forced to evacuate Boston and retire to Halifax, Nova Scotia.

neither Statesmen nor Generals. A letter from you, with your opinion upon the State of the times, will be a great comfort.[3] I ever am

My Dear Sir, Most faithfully & affectionately yours

Adam Smith

159. *From* ALEXANDER WEDDERBURN

MS., GUL Gen. 1035/153; Scott 269–71.

[? London,] 6 June 1776

My Dear Smith,

Your Reflections a month ago upon the bad advices from America are all confuted by the favourable accounts lately received, which prove that our preparations have been seasonable, our Plans wise and the execution of them in all the departments of government active and vigorous. The next westerly wind may possibly reestablish your doctrines,[1] but in the mean time because Quebeck is not taken and General Lee is, and because five American frigates were not able to beat an old twenty Gun Ship, we are wonderfully well pleased with ourselves;[2] I have neither desponded very much nor been at all elated by any accounts from America, But I have a strong persuasion that in spite of all our wretched Conduct, the mere force of government clumsily and unsteadily applied will beat down the more unsteady and unmanageable Force of a democratical Rebellion. Fortune must be very adverse to us indeed, if distraction, folly, Envy and Faction should not fight for, as well as against us. So much for Politicks, of which at this time of the year I always have a perfect distaste, but I never felt it so strong as at present. Were the Session to open at this moment I know no man with whom I am fit to act except our friend Herbert.[3] Would It in

[3] Strahan's views on politics and his reports of parliamentary debates were highly regarded. Hume wrote in 1770: 'Nothing could be more agreeable than your political Intelligence. I have always said, without Flattery, that you may give Instructions to Statesmen' (HL ii. 224). Originally well-disposed through friendship with Franklin to favour the American colonists, he came to take the British Government's side with increasing partiality after becoming an M.P. in 1774. By 1775 he could write to Hume: 'I am entirely for coercive methods with these obstinate madmen. Why should we suffer the Empire to be so dismembered without the utmost exertions on our part? . . . Not that I wish to enslave the colonists . . . but I am for keeping them subordinate to the British legislature' (HP ii. 490–1).

[1] See Letter 158 addressed to William Strahan, dated 3 June 1776, and the MS. in Wedderburn's hand, 'Smith's Thoughts on the State of the Contest with America, February 1778', which is presented in Appendix B; also WN V.i.a. 27.

[2] Admiral Charles Douglas landed supplies at Quebec on 6 Mar. and the American investment was raised on 6 May. Gen. Charles Lee was not captured until 13 Dec. 1776.

[3] Henry Herbert: see Letter 70, n.1. Wedderburn urged conciliation with the Americans and drafted proposals to this end in 1776 and 1778. He became disenchanted with North's conduct of the war and intrigued against him.

your opinion be justifiable in Any Man, and if so would It be fit for me to take up the System of pursuing my own Ideas without the least Attention to the Sentiments or Situations of other People. I am at present disposed to think that this is the best line a Man can follow, provided he acts so as to shew that It is System and not Caprice which directs him.

I saw some of your French friends, Suard[4] was my Old acquaintance, a very reasonable Man, well informed and free from prejudices; Necker's conversation shews that he is very rich and accustomed to be heard with complaisance.[5] I did not take him to be very profound even in the Subjects he has had the greatest opportunity of knowing. He seems to think that a Book of rates is a good method of augmenting the industry of a Country, a Great quantity of Coin the certain proof of Wealth, and that a nation is the poorer for all the manufacturers bought of foreigners. He will not be a Convert to your System, for he is in possession of three or four terms that are of too much use in all his arguments to be easily dropped and that you do not much employ. Corn is with him La Matiere premiere, Coin, Le Tresor Publique, and by a dextrous application of the various literal and figurative senses of these phrases, he is very successful in every argument. I was unlucky in not meeting Made. Necker,[6] but I could not prevail on Mrs Wedderburn[7] to make a Party for her, and had only the Men.

I remember you mentioned two Books to me that would be of service to Sir James Erskine,[8] and I have forgot the titles of them. If they occurr to you, I should be very glad to have them, as I must in a few weeks find some employment for his Curiosity.

I saw a very chearfull Letter from D. Hume, who I am happy to hear from other accounts is not likely to leave you any Commissions[9] for a considerable time—

I ever am, My Dear Smith
Yours most sincerely
Al: Wedderburn

---

[4] J.-.B.-A. Suard (1733–1817) co-editor of *La Gazette littéraire*, translator of Robertson's *History of Charles V*.

[5] Jacques Necker (1732–1804) financier and statesman, Louis XVI's finance minister 1776–81, 1788–9; opposed the Physiocrats, as in his *Essai sur la legislation et le commerce des grains* (1775), which took issue with Turgot's advocacy of a free trade in grains. Smith accepted an estimate of the French population from the *Essai*, but is said to have had no high opinion of Necker, calling him a 'mere man of detail' (Rae 206). See Letter 150, n. 5.

[6] Born Suzanne Curchod (1739–94); Gibbon 'sighed as a lover' for her, but 'obeyed as a son' when his father disapproved of their engagement. As Mme Necker, she conducted a famous salon in Paris and wrote on literary and moral topics. She was the mother of Mme de Staël.

[7] Betty Anne (d. 1781) dau. and heiress of John Dawson of Morley, Yorks.

[8] Sir James Erskine (1762–1837) s. of Wedderburn's sister; at Eton 1772–7. His uncle supervised his education, secured him a seat in Parliament in 1782, though he was under age, and made him his heir. See letter 163, n. 5.

[9] Smith was Hume's literary executor.

160. *From* WILLIAM STRAHAN

Address: Dr Adam Smith, Kirkaldy, N.B.
MS., RSE viii. 48 (marked 'copy'); J. A. Cochrane, *Dr Johnson's Printer: The Life of William Strachan* (London, 1964), 138, 202 (in part).

London, 10 June 1776

Dear Sir

I am favoured with yours.[1] You rightly consider writing to Mr Cadell or to me as the same, when you write about Business. Your Bill shall be duly honoured, and Mr Cadell will write you particularly about the Sale of your Book in a few Days.

I am very glad to hear you are in perfect Health, and that your worthy Parent is as well as can be expected. I beg you will remember me to her with great Respect. Pray do you think she will be able to accompany you to London about the End of the Summer?

Sir John Pringle had a Letter from Mr Hume a few Days ago, and I had one today, by which I am sorry to find all the good Symptoms that attended his first Tryal of the Bath Water are now vanished. His Distemper has returned with its usual Violence; So he intends to leave that Place, and try Buxton. I expect him in Town every Hour in his way thither. You cannot think how much Concern I feel for his present Situation, tho' he himself writes with Magnanimity and Resignation. Some Particulars he has communicated,[2] and some Directions he has given about his Works, in case of his Death, which shall be duly attended to and religiously observed. You already know all, for I need not say more of this to you till I see you. My Instructions are to keep an entire Silence upon the Subject to every body else.

Along with this melancholy Account of our most valuable Friend, I have the Satisfaction to acquaint you, from the best Authority, that General Carlton[3] having received some Succours about the 9th of May by two of our Men of War (I forget their Names) made a Sally from Quebec with a thousand Men, before whom the Besiegers, thrice their Number, fled with the utmost Precipitation without making the least Resistance, leaving behind them their whole Artillery, Stores, and every thing, even their very Dinners upon their Tables. The General had sent Parties in Pursuit of them; but I have heard no farther Particulars. This important News came

---

[1] Letter 158 addressed to William Strahan, dated 3 June 1776.

[2] About the *Dialogues concerning Natural Religion*, see Letter 166 addressed to David Hume, dated 22 Aug. 1776, and Letter 172 addressed to Strahan, dated 5 Sept. 1776, together with Letter 173 from Strahan, dated 16 Sept.

[3] Guy Carleton (1724–1806), 1st Baron Dorchester, soldier and administrator; Governor of Quebec 1775–7; successfully defended Quebec against the Americans, Dec. 1775–May 1776; C.-in-C. America, 1782–3.

by a Capt Hamilton, and I had this Account of [it] from Sir Hugh Palliser[4] and Mr Stephens's[5] own mouths at the Admiralty this Morning. It will doubtless be in tomorrow's Gazette; but I write tonight to give you a Chance of having [it] a Day sooner than your Neighbour will probably have. As General Burgoyne[6] is doubtless got there, our Force in that Province is now very respectable. Indeed the Preservation of it was of the utmost Consequence, as had it been lost, our affairs in America would have been nearly desperate. Two hundred men were on their way to reinforce the Provincials before Quebec; so that it is matter of great Surprise what could induce them to act so cowardly a Part. You would see by the last Gazette, at the same time, what Havock our Navy was making among their Shipping, no less than 70 and upwards of their Ships having already fallen into our Hands. If we proceed at this Rate we shall soon make them weary of opposing themselves to the Strength of Old England, which I hope will still prove triumphant over all her Enemies, Domestic as well as Foreign. This is no awkward beginning of the Campaign; nor is little to be expected from the Operations of our Fleet during the Summer, as they are but just now *got into their Gears*, as Sir H. Palliser expressed it a few Days ago.

Whenever I can convey to you any Intelligence which you are not likely to receive from any other Quarter, or can give it you sooner than you can have it by the usual Channels of Conveyance, I shall be sure to write you, that I may contri[bute] my Mite towards making your Retirement as agreeable to you as possible.

I am
Dear Sir
Your most affectionate and
faithful humble Servt
Will: Strahan

General Carlton has great Merit as a Soldier, and will, I hope, prove an Exception to the general Maxim with regard to the Characters of the Age.

---

[4] Sir Hugh Palliser (1723–96), 1st Bt.; entered Royal Navy 1735; Rear-Admiral 1775; Lord of Admiralty 1775; Admiral 1787; acted insubordinately under Keppel 1778, court-martialled and acquitted; Governor of Greenwich Hospital 1782.

[5] Sir Philip Stephens (1725–1809), 1st Bt.; Secretary of the Admiralty 1763–95; M.P. (Sandwich) 1768–1806; F.R.S. 1771; Bt. 1795.

[6] John Burgoyne (1722–92), dramatist and soldier; Second-in-Command, Canada 1776; C.-in-C. Canada 1777, but capitulated to Americans at Saratoga in Oct.; C.-in-C. Ireland 1782; his plays include *The Heiress* (1786).

161. *To* DAVID HUME

Address: To David Hume Esqr
MS., GUL Gen. 1035/132; Scott 271–2.

Kirkcaldy, 16 June 1776

My Dear Friend

I am very sorry to Learn by Mr Strahan that the Bath Waters have not agreed with you for some time, so well as they appeared to do at first. You have found one Medicine which has agreed with you; travelling and change of air. I would continue, if I was you, during the continuance of the fine Season the constant application of that medicine without troubling myself with any other, and would spend the summer in Sauntering thro all the different corners of England without halting above two or three nights in any one place. If before the month of October you do not find yourself thoroughly re'established, you may then think of changing this cold climate for a better, and of visiting the venerable remains of antient and modern arts that are to be seen about Rome and the Kingdom of Naples. A mineral water is as much a drug as any that comes out of the Apothecaries Shop. It produces the same violent effects upon the Body. It occasions a real disease, tho' a transitory one, over and above that which nature occasions. If the new disease is not so hostile to the old one as to contribute to expell it, it necessarily weakens the Power which nature might otherwise have to expell it. Change of air and moderate exercise occasion no new disease: they only moderate the hurtful effects of any lingering disease which may be lurking in the constitution; and thereby preserve the body in as good order as it is capable of being during the continuance of that morbid state. They do not weaken, but invigorate, the power of Nature to expel the disease. I reckon it probable that the Bath Waters had never agreed with you, but that the good effects of your journey not being spent when you began to use them, you continued for some time to recover, not by means of them, but in spite of them. Is it probable that the Buxton waters will do you more good? The Prescription supposed most likely to do good is always given first. If it fails, which it does nine times in ten, the second is surely likely to fail ninety nine time in a hundred. The journey to Buxton, however, may be of great service to you; but I would be sparing in the use of the water.

I am greatly obliged to you for your letter[1] and for the unlimited confidence which you repose in me. If I should have the misfortune to survive you, you may depend upon my taking every possible measure which may

---

[1] See Letters 156 and 157 from David Hume, both dated 3 May 1776, with directions about *Dialogues concerning Natural Religion* and *My Own Life*.

prevent anything from being lost which you wish should be preserved. I ever am my Dearest friend

Most faithfully and affectionately yours
Adam Smith

I go to Edinburgh the day after tomorrow and it will be some weeks before I return to this town. I will therefore beg of you to direct to me to the care of Mr John Balfour, Bookseller.

162. *To* [WILLIAM STRAHAN]

MS., Yale University Libr.; unpubl.

Edinburgh, 6 July 1776

Dear Sir

Mr Hume arrived here on Wednesday last, by no means in the state in which I could have wished to have seen him. His spirits, however, continue perfectly good; and his complexion, I think, is clearer than when I saw him at Morpeth; But his strength, I am afraid, is a good deal wasted so that he cannot now bear the jolting of a Post chaise upon our rough roads. He desired me to write to him under your cover when he was in England. I accordingly did so; but he has never received my letter.[1] I wish you would still send it to him; because, I think, he takes my supposed neglect unkindly.

Who is this Arnold, the new sub-preceptor to the princes? I do not remember to have heard of him. And what was the cause of so unexpected a revolution in that very important department of the Kings Household?[2] The cause of Lord Bruces resignation I know.[3]

I have drawn upon Cadell; but I have yet had no letter from him. I ever am

My Dear Sir
Most faithfully and sincerely
Yours
Adam Smith

Direct for me to the care of Mr John Balfour Bookseller. There is good

---

[1] Presumably Letter 161 addressed to Hume, dated 16 June 1776.

[2] The Earl of Holderness, governor to the children of George III, had a lengthy quarrel with Cyril Jackson, the sub-preceptor. The latter was dismissed and the former resigned. The new sub-preceptor was the Revd. William Arnold (d. 1802).

[3] Thomas Bruce Bruce-Brudenell (later Brudenell-Bruce: 1729–1814; 2nd Baron Bruce, 1747; cr. Earl of Ailesbury 10 June 1776) and Bishop Hurd kissed the King's hands on 31 May 1776 as governors of the royal children. Two days later Lord Bruce resigned: 'This day I saw the Bishop of Litchfield who brought me the melancholy news that some difficulties from Lady Bruce has so agitated her husband that he was come to acquaint me from him that he could not think of being governor to my children' (George III to North, 2 June 1776: *Geo. III Corr.* iii. 370). Bruce was succeeded by his brother, the Duke of Montagu. See Walpole, *Corr.* xxiv. 217–18.

sense, and learning, and philosophy in Campbells Book:[4] But it is so un-fashioned that I am afraid you will not be a great gainer by it. Remember me to Mrs and Miss Strahan and all the rest of the family.

163. *To* ALEXANDER WEDDERBURN

Address: To Alexander Wedderburne, Esquire, M.P., Lincolns Inn Fields, London
MS., GUL Gen. 4131; unpubl.

Kirkcaldy, 14 Aug. 1776

My Dear Sir

It gives me very great concern to learn by Mr Cunningham that Mrs Wedderburnes state of Health obliges you to pass some months at Spaw. I would hope, however, that necessity is only the pretence, and that amuse-ment is the real purpose of your journey, which will at any rate remove you from a scene of Business and anxiety to one of Pleasure and dissipation.

I have nothing to tell you that will be very agreable. Poor David Hume is dying very fast, but with great chearfulness and good humour and with more real resignation to the necessary course of things, than any Whining Christian ever dyed with pretended resignation to the will of God.[1] On thursday last he showed me a letter from his old friend Collonel Edmond-stone[2] bidding him an eternal adieu. I alledged that as his spirits were so very good there was still some chance that his disease might take a favour-able turn. He answered, 'Smith, your hopes are groundless; an habitual diarrhaea, which has now continued for several years, is a dangerous disease to a man of any age. At my age it is a mortal one. When I rise in the morning I find myself weaker than when I went to bed at night, and when I go to bed at night weaker than when I rose in the morning, so that in a few days I trust the business will be over.' I said, that at any rate he had the comfort of thinking that he left all his friends in prosperity particularly his brothers family whose circumstances would be greatly improved by his means. He replied, their circumstances were good independent of me and gave me some account of them: but, continued he, I so far agree with you, that when I was lately reading the dialogues of Lucian[3] in which he

[4] George Campbell's *Philosophy of Rhetoric*, published by Strahan in 1776.

[1] Smith had been staying with Hume in Edinburgh.

[2] James Edmonstoune of Newton; entered the Army in 1739 and rose to be Lt. Col. (1762) before resigning in 1770; an old friend of Hume, whose companion he had been on the L'Orient expedition of 1746. The letter read, in part: 'My Heart is very full. I could not see you this Morning; I thought it was better for us both. You can't die, you must live in the Memory of all your friends and Acquaintances and your Works will render you immortal. I could never conceive that it was possible for any one to dislike you or hate you, he must be more than savage who could be an Enemy to a Man of the best Head and Heart and of the most amiable Manners' (RSE v. 7).

[3] Lucian was Hume's favourite author, according to Morellet, who sent him a transla-tion of one of the dialogues in 1766 (HL ii. 157, n. 1).

represents one Ghost as pleading for a short delay till he should marry a young daughter, another till he should finish a house he had begun, a third till he had provided a portion for two or three young Children, I began to think of what Excuse I could alledge to Charon in order to procure a short delay, and as I have now done everything that I ever intended to do, I acknowledge that for some time no tolerable one occurred to me; at last I thought I might say, Good Charon, I have been endeavouring to open the eyes of people; have a little patience only till I have the pleasure of seeing the churches shut up, and the Clergy sent about their business; but Charon would reply, O you loitering rogue; that wont happen these two hundred years; do you fancy I will give you a lease for so long a time? Get into the boat this instant.[4] Since we must lose our friend the most agreable thing that can happen is that he dyes [as] a man of sense ought to do. I left Edinburgh for a few days till he should recall me. He is so weak, that even my company fatigues him, especially as his spirits are so good that he cannot help talking incessantly when anybody is with him. When alone he diverts himself with with correcting his own works, and with all [the] ordinary amusements.

I do not very well remember what were the books I recommended to Sir James Erskine. The [?*Cours*] *des Etudes du duc de Parme* was probably [among] them.[5] I cannot guess at the other.

Is McDonald of your Party?[6] His health, I hear, is not good. I should be much obliged to you for an account of it. After Hume there is scarce anybody I would more sincerely regret. I ever am

My Dear Sir, Yours entirely

Adam Smith

164. *From* JOSEPH BLACK

Address: Mr Adam Smith, Kirkaldy
MS., RSE viii. 7; unpubl.

Edinburgh, 14 Aug. 1776

Dear Sir

I have the pleasure to return for answer to your Enquiry about Mr Hume that he had been remarkably Easy and chearfull, these three last days. He

---

⁴ This account of Hume's last days was elaborated on by Smith in Letter 178 addressed to Strahan, dated 9 Nov. 1776, which was subsequently published by Strahan. One striking difference, however, is that for the purposes of publication, Smith toned down the reference to religion and, in particular, he omitted the remark about 'any whining Christian'.

⁵ See Letter 159 from Alexander Wedderburn, dated 6 June 1776. Condillac's *Cours d'étude pour l'instruction du Prince de Parme* is listed in the 1781 catalogue of Smith's books (Mizuta 14).

⁶ ? Archibald Macdonald (1747–1826), a rising lawyer who entered Parliament in 1777 as a supporter of North.

had before been much shocked with the appearance of his Nephew[1] and was fatigued with the Stir and Noise which his living in the House occasioned. His disorder at the same time changed a little for the worse and was attended with an obstruction of the Bile, a sickness and feeling of a dull Pain and load at his Stomach and sometimes Vomiting of very bad stuff— but all these appearances are now gone, and he is very much at his Ease. This will encrease your Hopes and it is so pleasant to Hope that I would rather join you, then desire you to give them up. Present my Compliments to Mrs Smith and Miss Douglas and beleive me

Yours affectionately

Joseph Black

165. *From* DAVID HUME

Address: To Adam Smith Esqr at Kirkaldy
MS., RSE ii. 59; H: ii. 334.

Edinburgh 15 of Augt 1776

My dear Smith

I have orderd a new Copy of my Dialogues to be made besides that which will be sent to Mr Strahan, and to be kept by my Nephew.[1] If you will permit me, I shall order a third Copy to be made, and consignd to you. It will bind you to nothing, but will serve as a Security. On revising them (which I have not done these 15 Years) I find that nothing can be more cautiously and more artfully written. You had certainly forgotten them. Will you permit me to leave you the Property of the Copy, in case they shoud not be published in five Years after my Decease? Be so good as to write me an answer soon.[2] My State of Health does not permit me to wait Months for it.

Yours affectionately

David Hume

[1] Joseph Home (1752–1872), eldest son of David's bro. John. David Hume bought him a Cornetcy (14 Dec. 1770) and then a Lieutenancy (28 Mar. 1776) in the second regiment of the Dragoon Guards. He came to stay with his uncle on 4 Aug. and had left by 13 Aug. (HL ii. 330, 332). Joseph had a reputation for being 'dissipated and idle' (HL ii. 207).

[1] Appreciating that Smith was not keen to publish the *Dialogues concerning Natural Religion*, Hume thought of publishing the book himself but realized that he was too ill. On 7 Aug. he added a codicil to his will, leaving his MSS. to Strahan and desiring him to bring out the *Dialogues* within two years, also two suppressed essays, 'Of Suicide' and 'Of the Immortality of the Soul'. A further codicil was appended, 'I also ordain, that if my Dialogues from whatever Cause, be not publishd within two Years and a half after my Death, as also the Account of my Life, the Property shall return to my Nephew, David, whose Duty, in publishing them as the last Request of his Uncle, must be approved of by all the World' (RSE ix. 24).

[2] Smith replied in Letter 166, dated 22 Aug. Hume's letter had been delayed in transit through coming via carrier rather than by the post.

166. *To* DAVID HUME

Address: To David Hume Esq, St Andrews Square, Edinburgh
MS., RSE vii.39; Rae 300–1.

Kirkcaldy, 22 Aug. 1776.

My Dearest friend

I have this moment received your Letter of the 15 inst. You had, in order to save me the sum of one penny Sterling, sent it by the carrier instead of the Post; and (if you have not mistaken the date,) it has lain at his quarters these eight days and was, I presume, very likely to lie there for ever.

I shall be very happy to receive a copy of your dialogues; and, if I should happen to die before they are published, I shall take care that my copy shall be as carefully preserved as if I was to live a hundred years. With regard to leaving me the property in case they are not published within five years after your decease, you may do as you think proper. I think, however, you should not menace Strahan with the loss of anything in case he does not publish your work within a certain time. There is no probability of his delaying it, and if anything could make him delay it, it would be a clause of this kind, which would give him an honourable pretence for doing so. It would then be said that I had published, for the sake of an Emolument, not from respect to the memory of my friend, what even a printer for the sake of the same emolument had not published. That Strahan is sufficiently zealous you will see by the enclosed letter,[1] which I will beg the favour of you to return to me, but by the Post and not by the carrier.

If you will give me leave I will add a few lines to your account of your own life;[2] giving some account, in my own name, of your behaviour in this illness, if, contrary to my own hopes, it should prove your last. Some conversations we had lately together, particularly that concerning your want of an excuse to make to Charon, the excuse you at last thought of, and the very bad reception which Charon was likely to give it, would, I imagine, make no disagreeable part of the history. You have in a declining state of health, under an exhausting disease, for more than two years together, now looked at the approach, or what you at least believed to be the approach of Death with a steady chearfulness such as very few men have been able to maintain for a few hours, tho' otherwise in the most perfect Health.

I shall likewise, if you will give me leave, correct the Sheets of the new edition of your works, and shall take care that it shall be published exactly according to your last corrections. As I shall be at London this winter it will cost me very little trouble.

---

[1] Presumably Letter 160 from Strahan, dated 10 June 1776.
[2] Smith chose to print Letter 178 addressed to Strahan, dated 9 Nov. 1776.

All this, I have written upon the supposition that the event of your disease should prove different from what I still hope it may do. For your spirits are so good, the Spirit of Life is still so very strong in you, and the progress of your disorder is as slow and gradual that I still hope it may take a turn. Even the cool and steady Dr Black, by a letter I received from him last week,[3] seems not to be averse to the same hopes.

I hope I need not repeat to you that I am ready to wait on you whenever you wish to see me. Whenever you do so, I hope you will not scruple to call on me. I beg to be remembered in the kindest and most respectful manner to your Brother, Your Sister, Your Nephew[4] and all other friends

I ever am

My Dearest friend, Most affectionately yours

Adam Smith

167. *From* JOSEPH BLACK

Address: To Mr Adam Smith, Kirkaldy
MS., RSE viii. 8; unpubl.

Edinburgh, 22 Aug. 1776

Dear Sir

I said lately to Mr Hume that I should write to you now and then an account of his health to save him the trouble of doing it. Since my last he has past his time pretty well but is much weaker—he sits up, goes down Stairs once a day and amuses himself with reading,[1] but hardly sees any Body. He finds that the conversation of even his most intimate freinds fatigues and oppresses him for the most part. And it is happy that he does not need it for he is quite free from Anxiety impatience or low Spirits and passes his time very well with the assistance of amuseing Books. He says he wrote to you lately[2] and expects an answer.

I am Dear Sir

Yours affectionately

Joseph Black

[3] Letter 164 from Black, dated 14 Aug. 1776.
[4] John Home of Ninewells (1709–85); Katherine Home (? 1710–90); and either Joseph or David Hume the Younger (1757–1838), sons of Home of Ninewells (see HL ii. 333–4).

[1] During the journey to England in April, Hume read 'chiefly in the classics' (Mossner 594), and early in August he was reading Lucian's *Dialogues of the Dead* (see Letter 163 addressed to Alexander Wedderburn, dated 14 Aug. 1776).
[2] Letter 165 from Hume, dated 15 Aug. 1776.

168. *From* DAVID HUME

Address: Adam Smith Esqr Kirkaldy
MS., RSE ii. 60; HL ii. 335–6.

Edinburgh, 23 Aug. 1776

My Dearest Friend

I am obliged to make use of my Nephews hand in writing to you as I do not rise to day.

There is No Man in whom I have a greater Confidence than Mr Strahan, yet have I left the property of that Manuscript[1] to my Nephew David in case by any accident it should not be published within three years after my decease. The only accident I could forsee, was one to Mr Strahans Life, and without this clause My Nephew would have had no right to publish it. Be so good as to inform Mr Strahan of this Circumstance.

You are too good in thinking any trifles that concern me are so much worth your attention, but I give you entire liberty to make what Additions you please to the account of my Life.[2]

I go very fast to decline, and last night had a small fever, which I hoped might put a quicker period to this tedious Illness, but unluckily it has in a great measure gone of. I cannot submit to your coming over here on my account as it is possible for me to see you so small a Part of the day but Dr Black can better inform you concerning the degree of strength which may from time to time remain with Me.[3]

Adieu My dearest Friend

David Hume

P.S. It was a strange blunder to send your Letter by the Carrier.

169. *From* JOSEPH BLACK

Address: Mr Adam Smith, Kirkaldy
MS., RSE viii. 9; William Smellie, *Characteristical Lives of . . . Gregory, Kames, Hume, and Smith* (Edinburgh, 1800), 172 (in part); HL ii. 449.

Edinburgh, Monday 26 Aug. 1776

Dear Sir

Yesterday about 4 o'clock afternoon Mr Hume expired. The immediate approach of his Death became evident in the night between Thursday

---

[1] *Dialogues concerning Natural Religion*: see Letter 167 n. 1.

[2] In 1777, Smith arranged that with Hume's autobiography, *My Own Life*, there was printed Letter 178 addressed to Strahan, dated 9 Nov. 1776. This letter includes extracts from Letters 166, 168, and 169. See Letter 163, n. 2.

[3] See the opening sentence of Letter 169 from Joseph Black, dated 26 Aug.

and Friday when the looseness became very excessive and was attended
with vomiting now and then. This continued the greater part of the time
that remained and soon weakened him so much that he could no longer
rise out of his bed. He continued to the last perfectly sensible and free from
much pain or feelings of distress. He never dropped the smallest expression
of impatience but when he had occasion to speak to the people about him
always did it with affection and tenderness. I thought it improper to
write to bring you over, especially as I heard that he had dictated a letter
to you on Thursday or wednesday desiring you not to come. When he
became very weak it cost him an effort to speak and he died in such a happy
composure of mind that nothing could have made it better.

Yours affectionately

J. Black

170. *To* JOHN HOME OF NINEWELLS[1]

Address: John Home Esqr, of Ninewells, St Davids Street, Edinburgh
MS., RSE viii. 38; Rae 302–3.

Dalkieth House 31. August. 1776

Dear Sir

As the Duke[2] proposes to stay here till thursday next, I may not have
an opportunity of seeing you before your return to Ninewells. I, therefore,
take this opportunity of discharging you and all others concerned of the
Legacy which you was so good as to think might, upon a certain event,
became due to me by your Brothers will; but which, I think, could upon
no event become so; viz the legacy of two hundred pounds Sterling. I
hereby therefore discharge it for ever; and least this discharge should be
lost I shall be careful to mention it in a note at the bottom of my will.
I shall be glad to hear that you have received this Letter; and hope you will
believe me to be, both on your Brothers account and your own, with great
truth, most affectionately yours—

Adam Smith

P.S. I do not hereby mean to discharge the other Legacy, viz that of a copy
of his works.

[1] As David's elder brother, John had inherited the family estate of Ninewells, Chirn-
side, Berwickshire.
[2] Of Buccleuch.

171. *From* JOHN HOME OF NINEWELLS

Address: To Adam Smith Esq, att Dalkeith house
MS., RSE viii. 17; Rae 303.

Edinburgh, 2 Sept. 1776

Dear Sir

I was favoured with yours of Saturday,[1] and I asure you, that on peruse-ing the destinations; I was more of opinion, than when I saw you, that the pecuniary part of it, was not was not altered by the codocill: and that it was intended for you at all events, that my brother knowing your liberal way of thinking, laid on you something as an equivalent, not imagineing you would refuse, a small gratuity from the funds it was to come from, as a testimony of his freindship. And tho I must highly esteem the motives and manner: I cannot agree to accept of your renounciation, but leave you full master, to dispose of it which way is most agreeable to you.

The Copys of the Dialogues are finished and of the life, and will be sent to Mr Strahan to morrow;[2] and I will mention to him your intention of adding to the last, something to finish so valuable a life, and will leave you at liberty, to look into the correction of the first, as it either answers your leisure, or ideas with regard to the composition, or what effects you think it may have with regard to your self. The two copys intended for you, will be left with my sister, when you please to require them; and the copy of the new edition of his works,[3] you shall be sure to receive; tho you have no better title to that part, than the other. Tho much you have to the freind-ship and esteem of Dear Sir of him who is most sincerely

Yours
John Home

172. *To* WILLIAM STRAHAN

Address: To William Strahan Esqr, M.P., New Street, Shoe Lane, London
MS., NYPL Miscell. MSS.; Rae 305–6 (noting that there is an unsigned draft of this letter in RSE viii. 41, omitting the last para.)

Dalkeith House, 5 Sept. 1776

My Dear Strahan

By a codicil[1] to the will of our late most valuable friend, Mr Hume, the

---

[1] Letter 170, dated 31 Aug.

[2] Strahan replied by promising to fulfill Hume's intentions 'most exactly' (Cochrane, *Dr Johnson's Printer*, 167), but his resolution was affected by Smith's Letters 172, dated 5 Sept.

[3] *Essays and Treatises on Several Subjects* (1777): which Hume wished to be regarded as 'containing his philosophical sentiments and principles', and from which he excluded *A Treatise of Human Nature* (Advertisement-preface).

[1] Added 7 Aug. 1776.

care of his manuscripts is left to you. Both from his will and from his conversation, I understand that there are only two which he meant should be published. An account of his life and, Dialogues concerning natural religion. The latter tho' finely written I could have wished had remained in Manuscript to be communicated only to a few people. When you read the work you will see my reasons without my giving you the trouble of reading them in a letter. But he has ordered it otherwise. In case of their not being published within three years after his decease he has left the property of them to his Nephew.[2] Upon my objecting to this clause as unnecessary, and improper, he wrote to me in the following terms: 'There is no man in whom I have a greater confidence that Mr Strahan; yet have I left the property of that Manuscript to my Nephew David in case, by any accident, it should not be published within three years after my decease. The only accident I could forsee was one to Mr Strahans life; and without this clause my Nephew would have no right to publish it. Be so good as to inform Mr Strahan of this circumstance.' Thus far his letter which was dated on 23rd of August.[3] He dyed on the 25th at 4 o'clock afternoon. I once had persuaded him to leave it entirely to my discretion either to publish them at what time I thought proper or not to publish them at all. Had he continued of this mind the manuscript should have been most carefully preserved and upon my decease restored to his family; but it never should have been published in my lifetime. When you have read it you will, perhaps, think it not unreasonable to consult some prudent friend about what you ought to do.

I propose to add to his life a very well authenticated account of his behaviour during his last Illness.[4] I must, however, beg that his life and those dialogues may not be published together; as I am resolved, for many reasons, to have no concern in the publication of those dialogues. His life, I think, ought to be prefixed to the next edition of his former works[5] upon which he has made many very proper corrections, chiefly in what concerns the language. If this Edition is published while I am in London I shall revise the sheets and Authenticate its being according to his last corrections. I promised him that I would do so.

If my mothers health will permit me to leave her, I shall be in London by the beginning of November. I shall write to Mr Home[6] to take my Lodgings as soon as I return to Fife which will be on Monday or tuesday

[2] David Hume (1757–1839), 2nd s. of John Home of Ninewells; advocate 1779; Professor of Scots Law, Edinburgh, 1786; Baron of Exchequer 1822; succeeded to Ninewells 1832, on death of Joseph, his elder brother.

[3] See Letter 168.

[4] See Letter 178 addressed to Strahan, dated 9 Nov. 1776.

[5] 1777 edition of *Essays and Treatises; My Own Life* was first printed in the January 1777 issue of the *Scots Magazine*. See W. B. Todd, 'First Printing of Hume's *Life*', *Library*, 5th Series, vi (1951), 123–5.

[6] John Home the poet.

next. The Duke of Buccleugh leaves this on Sunday. Direct for me at Kirkaldy, Fifeshire, where I shall remain all the rest of the Season. I ever am
My Dear Strahan
Most faithfully
Yours
Adam Smith

Let me hear from you soon

173. *From* WILLIAM STRAHAN

Address: Adam Smith Esqr., Kirkaldy, Fifeshire, N.B.
MS., RSE viii. 149; *Letters of David Hume to William Strahan*, ed. G. Birkbeck Hill (Oxford, 1888), 349 n. 2 (in part).

Southampton, 16 Sept. 1776
Dear Sir

I received yours[1] in the Neighbourhood of this Place where I was upon a Visit to a Friend, and for a little fresh Air and Relaxation. I am now come to Southampton, where I shall not stay many Days before I return home, but that will somewhat depend upon the Weather. I had a Letter from the Brother of our late excellent Friend, a few days before I received yours, and my Son[2] writes me that the MSS. are also come to hand, but the Parcel will not be opened till my Return. All therefore that I can say just now, is, that I shall do nothing precipitately, and without the Advice of my Friends, to whose Opinion, and particularly to yours, I shall pay great Regard. I will likewise give the *Dialogues* a very attentive Perusal, before I consult any body, that I may at once see how far their Judgments coincide with my own. I own I did not expect to hear they were so very exceptionable, as in one of his late Letters to me he tells me *there is nothing in them worse than what I have already published*, or Words to that Effect. But at any Rate, they shall certainly be published distinct from the *Life*, which I think we may throw out this Winter, and afterwards prefix to the Edition of his History now printing. I have not the least doubt that your Addition[3] to it will be highly proper, and if it is ready, I beg you would transmit it to me without Delay; for I long very much to see it. Every Particular respecting that great and good Man I would wish to know and to remember. You see by his leaving the *Dialogues* ultimately to his Nephew[4] in case of any Accident to me his extreme Solicitude that they should not be suppressed, so that if it is at all judged proper to let them see

[1] Letter 172, dated 5 Sept.
[2] Andrew Strahan (1750–1831), who inherited the family printing business and, like his father, became an M.P.
[3] *The Life of David Hume, Esq; Written by Himself* was published in London, together with a preface by Strahan and Smith's letter to Strahan of 9 Nov. 1776 (No. 178), on 11 Mar. 1777 and went through three eds.
[4] David Hume the Younger.

the Light, I should wish to execute his Intentions. But, of this, as I said before, I shall not hastily determine. I shall write you again from London as soon as I have read them.

I hope your Mother's Health will not prevent you from returning hither at the time you propose. You know I once mentioned to you how happy I thought it would make you both if you could bring her along with you to spend the Remainder of her Days in this Place, but perhaps it will not be easy to remove her so far at this time of her Life. I pray you offer her the respectful Compliments of my Family, who do not forget her genteel and hospitable Reception at Kircaldy some Years ago.

I hope you will excuse this hasty Scrawl; but as you desired to hear from me soon, I would not delay writing tho from a Place of Dissipation, and without having much to say. As for our late worthy and most valuable Friend, I shall only say, that all who knew him have sustained a Loss by his Death which is altogether irreparable, and which they must all feel, and chiefly those who knew him best. I will add no more.

Believe me, with the sincerest Respect and Esteem

Dear Sir
Your affectionate and faithful
Will: Strahan

174. *From* THOMAS POWNALL[1]

A Letter from Governor Pownall to Adam Smith, L.L.D., F.R.S., Being an Examination of Several Points of Doctrine Laid Down in His Enquiry into the Nature and Causes of the Wealth of Nations, London, [25 Sept.] 1776[2]

[A text of the *Letter* corrected from the BM copy is presented in Appendix A.]

[1] Thomas Pownall (1722–1805), clerk at the Board of Trade 1743–54; Secretary to Gov. of New York 1753; Lt. Gov. New Jersey 1755; Gov. Massachusetts Bay 1757–9; Gov. South Carolina 1760 (did not take up his post); published *The Administration of Colonies* (1764). As an M.P. 1767–80, he advocated conciliation with America and spoke against Government policy. He was a noted controversialist and when one of his publications appeared in red ink, a contemporary supposed 'that the Governor was determined that one of his books at least should be red' (*Journal and Corr. of William, Lord Auckland* (London, 1861), ii. 237). See Letter 208 addressed to Andreas Holt, dated 26 Oct. 1780, for Smith's views on his attempt to answer Pownall's criticisms of WN.

[2] Pownall recognizes in WN 'moral newtonianism' bearing upon political economy. As a man of experience, he challenges some of the views of Smith the theorist. The most interesting criticisms concern price, patterns of trade, restraints on importations, and the monopoly of the colony trade.

175. *To* [JOHN HOME OF NINEWELLS]

MS., RSE viii. 40 (39: draft); Rae 304.

Kirkcaldy, 7 Oct. 1776

Dear Sir

I send you, under the same cover with this letter, what I propose should be added to the account which your never to be forgotten[1] brother has left of his own life. When you have read it, I beg you will return it to me and at the same time let me know if you would wish to have anything either added to it or taken from it. I think there is a propriety in addressing it as a letter to Mr Strahan to whom he has left the care of his works.[2] If you approve of it, I shall send it to him, as soon as I receive it from you.

I have added at the bottom of my will the note discharging the legacy of two hundred pounds which your Brother was so kind as to leave me. Upon the most mature deliberation I am fully Satisfied that in justice it is not due to me. Tho it should be due to me, therefore, in strict law, I cannot with honour accept of it. You will easily believe that my refusal does not proceed from any want of the highest respect for the memory of your deceased Brother. I have the Honour to be, with the highest respect and esteem

Dear Sir, Most Sincerely and Affectionately yours

Adam Smith

176. *From* JOHN HOME OF NINEWELLS

MS., RSE viii. 18; unpubl.

Ninewells, 14 Oct. 1776

Dear Sir

I was favoured with yours of the 7th instant;[1] along with the addition you proposed should be printed of our worthy freind, and my deceast brothers account of himself: in consequence of your request to him, and his aprobabation of it. I reckon myself much obliged to you, for having communicated it to me, and of haveing asked my oppinion of it, of which I should be very unworthy, if I did not give you an ingenous one; such as it is: and it is this, that I much approve of your thought in addressing it in a letter to Mr Strahan; as well as of the whole performance, only you will forgive me, for observeing that as it is to be aded, to what is wrote in so short and

---

[1] The phrase was later applied by Smith to his teacher Frances Hutcheson; see Letter 274 addressed to Dr. Archibald Davidson, dated 16 Nov. 1787, in which Smith accepted the rectorship of Glasgow University.

[2] See Letter 173, n. 3, and Letter 178, addressed to Strahan, dated 9 Nov. 1776.

[1] Letter 175.

simple a manner would have wished, that the detail had been less minutely entered into, particularly of the journey, which being of a private concern, and haveing drawn to no consequences, does not interest the publick. But on the other hand, when I consider, that any alterations, might require the new modeling of the whole: as well as with what diffidence, I must give my oppinion when deviating from you I beleive it had best be published as it is. I imagine however that in page 2d line 2d the words submitted to or some such words to prevent the obscurity of the sense, is wanted and near the bottom of the same page, instead of 'as my worst enemies [   ]² I was told he said, 'as my enemies,—If I have any, could wish'³ which if it was [true was] better: but if I am wrong informed, I stand corrected. Colonel Edmiston wrote his letter⁴ from Lithgow, which I saw, and is in toun.

Since I came here I had a letter from Mr Strahan,⁵ informing me of his haveing received the account of his life and the Dialogues on Natural Religion; which last he makes no difficulty of publishing, as he had promised, and will print the first [w]ith the edition of his works, at present in the press, along with what you are to send him.

I wrote you directed to Dalkeith house, immediately on the receit, and in answer to yours from thence, which if it came to hand, would show you, that In [my] oppinion, [that] the legacy was due you, both in Law and equity, and tho by a[n] uncommo[n] [g]enerous way of thinking you refuse it, that it was still [   ]² or at any time after to accept of it, which I again repeat in case my letter has not come to hand.

I shall leave this in less then 3 weeks for toun, and if you write me after please direct it there, and where at all times, it would be a great favour to see you, and to cultivate a connexion, that is so much regarded, and so justly esteemed by

Dear Sir

your much obliged and sincere

humble Servant

John Home

Tho it cannot enter properly into the publication, I thought it proper, to transcribe a copy of a letter dated the 13th of August⁶ as a strong mark of the [courage?] and Spirits our friend [possessed].⁷ [There follows a transcription of the letter of 13 Aug. printed at HL, ii. 332.]

---

² Lacuna in MS.

³ This wording is found in Letter 178 addressed to Strahan, dated 9 Nov. 1776.

⁴ Col. James Edmonstoune wrote a letter of 'eternal adieu' to Hume on 7 Aug. 1776 (RSE v. 7). Smith quotes from this in Letter 178.   ⁵ Dated 9 Sept., RSE viii. 43.

⁶ David Hume wrote to his brother John on 13 Aug. 1776: 'Dr Black tells me plainly, like a man of Sense, that I shall dye soon, which is no disagreeable news to me' (HL ii. 332).

⁷ The writing is difficult to make out here.

177A. *To* WILLIAM STRAHAN

Earlier draft, 1st para. scored through: *Letters of David Hume to William Strahan,* ed. G. Birkbeck Hill (Oxford, 1888), 354.

[Oct. 1776]

You are certainly right in publishing the new Edition of Mr Hume's works before you publish the dialogues. They might prevent the sale of this Edition; and it is not impossible that they may hereafter [affect] the sale of another. I am still uneasy about the clamour which I foresee they will excite, and could . . .

I am much obliged to you for so readily agreeing to print the Life together with my addition separate from the Dialogues.[1] I even flatter myself that this arrangement will contribute not only to my quiet, but to your interest. The clamour against the Dialogues, if published first, might for some time hurt the sale of the new edition of his works;[2] and when the clamour has a little subsided the dialogues may hereafter occasion a quicker sale of another edition.

177B. *To* [WILLIAM STRAHAN]

MS., RSE viii. 42 (unsigned draft letter); Rae 306–7.

[Kirkcaldy, Oct. 1776]

Dear Sir

When I received your last letter[1] I had not begun the small addition which I proposed to make to the life of our late friend. It is now more than three weeks since I finished it and sent one copy to his Brother and another to Dr Black. That which I sent to his Brother is returned with remarks,[2] all of which I approve of and shall adopt. Dr Black waits for John Home, the Poet, who is expected every day in Edinburgh whose remarks he proposes to send along with those of all our common friends. The work consists only of two sheets in the form of a letter to you; but without one word of flattery or compliment. It will not cost my servant a forenoon to transcribe it, so that you will receive it by the first post after it is returned to me.

I am much obliged to you for so readily agreeing to [print] the life, together with my addition separate from the Dialogues. I even flatter myself that this arrangement will contribute, not only to my quiet, but to

---

[1] See Letter 173 from Strahan, dated 16 Sept. 1776.
[2] The *Dialogues* caused no uproar, but Letter 178 addressed to Strahan, dated 9 Nov. 1776, was violently attacked. See Letter 208 addressed to Andreas Holt, dated 26 Oct. 1780.

[1] Letter 173 from Strahan, dated 16 Sept. 1776.
[2] See Letter 176 from John Home of Ninewells, dated 14 Oct. 1776.

your interest. The clamour against the dialogues, if published first, might hurt for some time the sale of the new edition of his works and when the Clamour has a little subsided, the dialogues might hereafter occasion a quicker sale of another edition.

I do not propose being with you till the Christmas holidays; in the meantime I should be glad to know how things stand between us; what copies of my last book[3] are either sold or unsold and when the balance of our bargain is likely to be due to me. I beg my most respectful and affectionate complements to Mr Cadell; I should have written to him but you know the pain it gives me to write with my own hand and I look upon writing to him and you as the same thing. I have been since I came to Scotland, most exceedingly idle. It is partly in order to bring up in some measure my leeway that I propose to stay here two months longer than I had intended. If my presence however was at all necessary in London I could easily set out immediately.[4]

I beg the favour of you to send the enclosed to Mr Home.[5] The purpose of it is to bespeak my Lodgings.

178. *To* WILLIAM STRAHAN

'Letter from Adam Smith, LL.D. to William Strahan, Esq.',[1] *The Life of David Hume, Esq.: Written by Himself* (London, 1777), 37–62.

Kirkaldy, Fifeshire, 9 Nov. 1776

Dear Sir,

It is with a real, though a very melancholy pleasure, that I sit down to give you some account of the behaviour of our late excellent friend, Mr. Hume, during his last illness.

Though, in his own judgement, his disease was mortal and incurable, yet he allowed himself to be prevailed upon, by the entreaty of his friends, to try what might be the effects of a long journey. A few days before he set out, he wrote that account of his own life, which, together with his other papers, he has left to your care. My account, therefore, shall begin where his ends.

He set out for London towards the end of April, and at Morpeth met with Mr. John Home and myself, who had both come down from London on purpose to see him, expecting to have found him at Edinburgh. Mr. Home returned with him, and attended him during the whole of his stay

---

[3] WN.
[4] Smith went to London in Jan. 1777 and remained until Oct. of that year.
[5] The poet.

[1] This is the ostensible letter that Smith showed to Hume's brother and to intimate friends; see Letters 175 and 177A, B.

in England, with that care and attention which might be expected from a temper so perfectly friendly and affectionate. As I had written to my mother that she might expect me in Scotland, I was under the necessity of continuing my journey. His disease seemed to yield to exercise and change of air, and when he arrived in London, he was apparently in much better health than when he left Edinburgh. He was advised to go to Bath to drink the waters, which appeared for some time to have so good an effect upon him, that even he himself began to entertain, what he was not apt to do, a better opinion of his own health. His symptoms, however, soon returned with their usual violence, and from that moment he gave up all thoughts of recovery, but submitted with the utmost cheerfulness, and the most perfect complacency and resignation. Upon his return to Edinburgh, though he found himself much weaker, yet his cheerfulness never abated, and he continued to divert himself, as usual, with correcting his own works for a new edition, with reading books of amusement, with the conversation of his friends; and, sometimes in the evening, with a party at his favourite game of whist. His cheerfulness was so great, and his conversation and amusements run so much in their usual strain, that, notwithstanding all bad symptoms, many people could not believe he was dying. 'I shall tell your friend, Colonel Edmondstone,' said Doctor Dundas to him one day, 'that I left you much better, and in a fair way of recovery.' 'Doctor', said he, 'as I believe you would not chuse to tell any thing but the truth, you had better tell him, that I am dying as fast as my enemies, if I have any, could wish, and as easily and cheerfully as my best friends could desire.' Colonel Edmondstone soon afterwards came to see him, and take leave of him; and on his way home, he could not forbear writing him a letter bidding him once more an eternal adieu, and applying to him, as to a dying man, the beautiful French verses in which the Abbé Chaulieu, in expectation of his own death, laments his approaching separation from his friend, the Marquis de la Fare. Mr. Hume's magnanimity and firmness were such, that his most affectionate friends knew, that they hazarded nothing in talking or writing to him as to a dying man, and that so far from being hurt by this frankness, he was rather pleased and flattered by it. I happened to come into his room while he was reading this letter, which he had just received, and which he immediately showed me. I told him, that though I was sensible how very much he was weakened, and that appearances were in many respects very bad, yet his cheerfulness was still so great, the spirit of life seemed still to be so very strong in him, that I could not help entertaining some faint hopes. He answered, 'Your hopes are groundless. An habitual diarrhoea of more than a year's standing, would be a very bad disease at any age: at my age it is a mortal one. When I lie down in the evening, I feel myself weaker than when I rose in the morning; and when I rise in the morning, weaker than when I lay down in the evening. I am sensible, besides, that some of my vital parts are affected, so that I must soon die.' 'Well,' said I, 'if it must be so, you have at least the satisfaction of leaving all your friends, your brother's family in particular, in great prosperity.' He said that he felt that satisfaction so sensibly, that when he was reading a few days before, Lucian's Dialogues of the Dead, among all the excuses which are alleged to Charon for not entering readily into his boat, he could not find one that fitted him; he had no house to finish, he had no daughter to provide for, he had no enemies upon whom he wished to revenge himself. 'I could not well imagine,' said he, 'what excuse I could make to Charon in order to obtain a little delay. I have done every thing of consequence which I ever meant to do, and I could at no time expect to leave my relations and friends in a better situation than that in which I am now likely to leave them; I, therefore, have all reason to die contented.' He then diverted himself with inventing several jocular excuses, which he supposed he might make to Charon, and with imagining the very surly answers which it might suit the character of Charon to return to them. 'Upon further consideration,' said he, 'I thought I might say to him, Good Charon, I have been correcting my works for a new edition. Allow me a little time, that I may see how the Public receives the alterations.' But Charon would answer, 'When you have seen the effect of these, you will be for making other alterations. There will be no end of such excuses; so, honest friend, please step into the boat.' But I might still urge, 'Have a little patience, good Charon, I have been endeavouring to open the eyes of the Public. If I live a few years longer, I may have the satisfaction of seeing the downfal of some of the prevailing systems of superstition.' But Charon would then lose all temper and decency. 'You loitering rogue, that will not happen these many hundred years. Do you fancy I will grant you a lease for so long a term? Get into the boat this instant, you lazy loitering rogue.'

But, though Mr. Hume always talked of his approaching dissolution with great cheerfulness, he never affected to make any parade of his magnanimity. He never mentioned the subject but when the conversation naturally led to it, and never dwelt longer upon it than the course of the conversation happened to require: it was a subject indeed which occurred pretty frequently, in consequence of the inquiries which his friends, who came to see him, naturally made concerning the state of his health. The conversation which I mentioned above, and which passed on Thursday the 8th of August, was the last, except one, that I ever had with him. He had now become so very weak, that the company of his most intimate friends fatigued him; for his cheerfulness was still so great, his complaisance and social disposition were still so entire, that when any friend was with him, he could not help talking more, and with greater exertion, than suited the weakness of his body. At his own desire, therefore, I agreed to leave

Edinburgh, where I was staying partly upon his account, and returned to my mother's house here, at Kirkaldy, upon condition that he would send for me whenever he wished to see me; the physician who saw him most frequently, Doctor Black, undertaking, in the mean time, to write me occasionally an account of the state of his health.

On the 22d of August, the Doctor wrote me the following letter:

'Since my last, Mr. Hume has passed his time pretty easily, but is much weaker. He sits up, goes down stairs once a day, and amuses himself with reading, but seldom sees any body. He finds that even the conversation of his most intimate friends fatigues and oppresses him; and it is happy that he does not need it, for he is quite free from anxiety, impatience, or low spirits, and passes his time very well with the assistance of amusing books.'

I received the day after a letter from Mr. Hume himself, of which the following is an extract

Edinburgh, 23d August, 1776.

'My Dearest Friend,

I am obliged to make use of my nephew's hand in writing to you, as I do not rise today . . . I go very fast to decline, and last night had a small fever, which I hoped might put a quicker period to this tedious illness, but unluckily it has, in a great measure, gone off. I cannot submit to your coming over here on my account, as it is possible for me to see you so small a part of the day, but Doctor Black can better inform you concerning the degree of strength which may from time to time remain with me. Adieu, &c.'

Three days after I received the following letter from Doctor Black.

Edinburgh, Monday, 26th August, 1776.

'Dear Sir,

Yesterday about four o'clock afternoon, Mr. Hume expired. The near approach of his death became evident in the night between Thursday and Friday, when his disease became excessive, and soon weakened him so much, that he could no longer rise out of his bed. He continued to the last perfectly sensible, and free from much pain or feelings of distress. He never dropped the smallest expression of impatience; but when he had occasion to speak to the people about him, always did it with affection and tenderness. I thought it improper to write to bring you over, especially as I heard that he had dictated a letter to you desiring you not to come. When he became very weak, it cost him an effort to speak, and he died in such a happy composure of mind, that nothing could exceeed it.'

Thus died out most excellent, and never to be forgotten friend; concerning whose philosophical opinions men will, no doubt, judge variously, every one approving or condemning them, according as they happen to coincide or disagree with his own; but concerning whose character and conduct there can scarce be a difference of opinion. His temper, indeed, seemed to be more happily balanced, if I may be allowed such an expression, than that perhaps of any other man I have ever known. Even in the lowest state of his fortune, his great and necessary frugality never hindered him from exercising, upon proper occasions, acts both of charity and generosity. It was a frugality founded, not upon avarice, but upon the love of independency. The extreme gentleness of his nature never weakened either the firmness of his mind, or the steadiness of his resolutions. His constant pleasantry was the genuine effusion of good-nature and good-humour, tempered with delicacy and modesty, and without even the slightest tincture of malignity, so frequently the disagreeable source of what is called wit in other men. It never was the meaning of his raillery to mortify; and therefore, far from offending, it seldom failed to please and delight, even those who were the objects of it. To his friends, who were frequently the objects of it, there was not perhaps any one of all his great and amiable qualities, which contributed more to endear his conversation. And that gaiety of temper, so agreeable in society, but which is so often accompanied with frivolous and superficial qualities, was in him certainly attended with the most severe application, the most extensive learning, the greatest depth of thought, and a capacity in every respect the most comprehensive. Upon the whole, I have always considered him, both in his lifetime and since his death, as approaching as nearly to the idea of a perfectly wise and virtuous man, as perhaps the nature of human frailty will permit.

> I ever am, dear Sir,
> Most affectionately your's,
> Adam Smith.

179. *To* WILLIAM STRAHAN

Rae 308.

Kirkcaldy, 13 Nov. 1776

Dear Sir

The enclosed is the small addition which I propose to make to the account which our late invaluable friend left of his own life.[1]

I have received £300 of the copy money of the first edition of my book. But as I got a good number of copies to make presents of from Mr Cadell, I do not exactly know what balance may be due to me. I should therefore be glad he would send me the account. I shall write to him upon this subject.

[1] Letter 178, ostensibly addressed to Strahan on 9 Nov. 1776.

With regard to the next edition,[2] my present opinion is that it should be printed in four vol. octavo; and I would propose that it should be printed at your expense, and that we should divide the profits. Let me know if this is agreeable to you.

My mother begs to be remembered to Mrs Strahan and Miss Strahan,[3] and thinks herself much obliged both to you and them for being so good as to remember her.

I ever am, dear sir,
most affectionately yours,
Adam Smith

I shall certainly be in town before the end of the Christmas holidays. I do not apprehend it can be necessary for me to come sooner. I have therefore written to Mr Home to bespeak my lodgings from Christmas.

180. *From* WILLIAM STRAHAN

Address: Adam Smith Esqr., Kirkaldy, Fife Shire, N.B.
MS., RSE viii. 50; Rae 309–10.

London, 26 Nov. 1776

Dear Sir

I received yours of the 13th inclosing the Addition to Mr Hume's Life, which I like exceedingly.[1] But as the whole put together is very short and will not make a Volume even of the *smallest Size*, I have been advised by some very good Judges to annex some of his Letters to me on political Subjects. What think you of this? I will do nothing without your Advice and Approbation;[2] nor would I, for the World publish any Letter of his, but such as, in your Opinion, would do him Honour. Mr Gibbon thinks such as I have shewn him would have that Tendency. Now, if you approve of this in any Manner, you may perhaps add greatly to the Collection from your own Cabinet and those of Mr John Home, Dr Robertson, and others of your mutual Friends, which you may pick up before you return hither. But if you wholly disapprove of this Scheme, say nothing of it, here let it drop, for without your Concurrence I will not publish *a single Word* of his. I should be glad, however, of your Sentiments as soon as you can, and let me know, at the same time, as nearly as may be, what Day you propose to

---

[2] WN ed. 2 appeared in 2 vols. early in 1778: see Letter 180 from Strahan, dated 26 Nov. 1776.
[3] Margaret Penelope Strahan (b. 1751) md. John Spottiswoode of Spottiswoode on 10 June 1779. She was known as Peggy.

[1] See Letters 178 and 179.
[2] See Letter 181 addressed to Strahan, dated 2 Dec. 1776. Predictably Smith was against publishing private correspondence.

be in London; for I must again repeat to you, that without your Approbation I will do nothing.

Your Proposal to print the next Edition of your Work in 4 vols Octavo, at *our* Expence, and to divide the Profits,[3] is a very fair one, and therefore very agreeable to Mr Cadell and me. Inclosed is the List of Books delivered to you of the 1st Edit.

My Wife and Daughter join kindest Compliments to your amiable Parent, who I hope is still able to enjoy your Company, which must be her greatest Comfort. I am ever

Dear Sir

Your faithful and affectionate

humble Servant

Will: Strahan

181. *To* WILLIAM STRAHAN

Letters of David Hume to William Strahan, ed. G. Birkbeck Hill (Oxford, 1888), 351–2; Rae 310.

Kirkcaldy, 2 Dec. 1776

Dear Sir

It always gives me great uneasiness whenever I am obliged to give an opinion contrary to the inclination of my friend.[1] I am sensible that many of Mr Humes letters would do him great honour and that you would publish none but such as would. But what in this case ought principally to be considered is the will of the Dead. Mr Humes constant injunction was to burn all his Papers, except the Dialogues and the account of his own life. This injunction was even inserted in the body of his will. I know he always disliked the thought of his letters ever being published. He had been in long and intimate correspondence with a relation of his own who dyed a few years ago. When that Gentlemans health began to decline he was extremely anxious to get back his letters, least the heir should think of publishing them. They were accordingly returned and burnt as soon as returned. If a collection of Mr Humes letters, besides, was to receive the public approbation, as yours certainly would, the Curls[2] of the times would immediately set about rummaging the cabinets of all those who had ever received a scrap of paper from him. Many things would be published not fit to see the light to the great mortification of all those who wish well to his

---

[3] Refers to WN ed. 2. See Letter 179, n. 2.

[1] This is an answer to the previous Letter 180.

[2] Edmund Curll (1675–1747), the contemporary of Swift and Pope whose name was a byword as that of an unscrupulous bookseller; he specialized in publishing poetical miscellanies, ramshackle biographies ('one of the new terrors of death', according to Arbuthnot), and pornographic pamphlets.

memory. Nothing has contributed so much to sink the value of Swifts works as the undistinguished publication of his letters;[3] and be assured that your publication, however select, would soon be followed by an undistinguished one. I should, therefore, be sorry to see any beginning given to the publication of his letters. His life will not make a volume; but it will make a small pamphlet. I shall certainly be in London by the tenth of January at furthest. I have a little business at Edinburgh which may detain me a few days about Christmass, otherwise I should be with you by the new year. I have a great deal more to say to you; but the post is just going. I shall write to Mr. Cadell by next post.

I ever am Dear Sir
Most affectionately yours
Adam Smith

182. *To* GOVERNOR POWNALL

Gentleman's Magazine, lxv (1795), 635; Rae 319.

Suffolk Street, London, 19 Jan. 1777

Sir,

I received, the day before I left Edinburgh, the very great honour of your letter.[1] Though I arrived here on Sunday last, I have been, almost from the day of my arrival, confined by a cold, which I caught upon the road; otherwise I should, before this time, have done myself the honour of waiting on you in person, and of thanking you for the very great politeness with which you have treated me. There is not, I give you my word, in your whole letter, a single syllable, relating to myself, which I could wish to have altered; and the publication of your remarks does me much more honour than the communication of them by a private letter could have done.

I hope in a few days to have the honour of waiting on you, and of discussing in person with you both the points in which we agree and those in which we differ. Whether you will think me, what I mean to be, a fair disputant, I know not; I can venture to promise, you will not find me an irascible one. In the mean time, I have the honour to be, with the highest respect and esteem, etc. etc.

Adam Smith

[3] Without authorization, Curll published *Dean Swift's Literary Correspondence, For Twenty-Four Years* in 1741; and Swift's official publisher, Faulkner, put out in the same year *Letters To and From Dr J. Swift, D.S.P.D. From the Year 1714, to 1738.* In LRBL, Smith commented on Shaftesbury's letters adversely and represented them as 'not near so animated as those of Swift and Pope' (Wed. 15 Dec.).

[1] Letter 174, dated 25 Sept. 1776. See Appendix A; also Letter 208, for Smith's subsequent views on his attempts to answer Pownall's criticisms of WN.

183. *From* ADAM FERGUSON

Address: To Adam Smith Esqr at Mr Home's in Suffolk Street, London
MS., GUL Gen. 1035/154; Scott 273.

My Dear Smith,   Edinburgh, 12 Apr 1777

I heard from Mr Chalmers[1] of your being again intangled in my disagreeable affairs[2] and have since received your own letter[3] inclosing one from My Lord Stanhope to you. I have been greatly at a loss on this occasion for want of my usual Counsellor Mr Davidson. After mature consideration it appears to my friends here as well as to myself that a requisition to produce the original of Earl Stanhopes letter to me dated at Paris Aprile 6th 1774 may be a matter of Course in Bussiness But that it may proceed likewise from some degree of suspicion that my Copie of this Letter particularly that transcribed in my own hand writeing and sent to the Earl of Chesterfield in January last is not exact. That if the original letter were by any Accident lost the suspicion might produce Insinuations of which I shoud in that case have no direct refutation. And that in this View of the matter I ought not to expose this letter to any Avoidable Accident whatever. If My Lord Chesterfield declare his Intention in case my Copy is verified by the original, to fullfill the condition which will Relieve My Lord Stanhope of his Obligation, I will if he give me leave without loss of time go to London and wait upon his Lordship with the original Letter. In the meantime I send by this post Copys of this and two other letters from My Lord Stanhope to me Collated and Attested by a Notary Public and By The Lord Provost of Edinburgh In hopes that this may be sufficient. These Copys go in a Packet to Mr Chalmers who will communicate them to you and otherwise employ them for any purpose they can Serve. I return you with this Lord Stanhopes letter to yourself and send to His Lordship the Copy he desires in my own hand writeing very sorry any difficulty shoud hinder me from sending the Originall.

I am My Dear Smith
Your most affectionate
and most humble servant
Adam Ferguson

[1] George Chalmers (1742–1825), antiquary; educ. Aberdeen and Edinburgh; emigrated to America in 1763 and became a successful lawyer in Baltimore; settled in London 1775; wrote pamphlets on the American colonies 1777–82; appointed Clerk to the Board of Trade 1786. He wrote lives of Defoe (1786), Sir John Davies (1786), Tom Paine (1793), and a number of Scottish figures, among them Thomas Ruddiman (1794). The last work contains copious information about Scotland in the first half of the eighteenth century. His chief work is said to be *Caledonia: an Account of . . . North Britain* (1807–24).

[2] Connected with the financial arrangements for Ferguson's tour of the Continent with the Earl of Chesterfield 1773–5, and his withdrawal from teaching Moral Philosophy at Edinburgh at this time.

[3] Not traced. Smith met Stanhope at Geneva in 1765, and subsequently recommended Ferguson as a tutor for Chesterfield.

184. *To* WILLIAM STRAHAN

Address: William Strahan Esqr M.P., New Street, Shoe Lane, London
MS., Liverpool Central Librs.; unpubl.

Kirkcaldy, 27 Oct. 1777

Dear Sir

By the death of Mr Menzies,[1] one of the Commissioners at the board of customs here, I am now a candidate for a seat at that Board. The purpose of this letter is to beg the favour of you to endeavour to get me from the board of treasury the first and best intelligence you can either of my final success or disappointment, or of the probability or improbability of either. You know that I am not apt to be over-sanguine in my expectations; and my mind has not upon the present occasion, lost its usual temper.

I sent this day was se'n'night a very important cancel to Mr Andrew.[2] It saves a very great apparent inconsistency between some of the new corrections and a part of the old text as it stood before. I had not observed it till it was shewn to me by a friend. I shall be anxious to know that he has received it and executed it with his usual attention. It is certainly reasonable that I should be at the expence at least of this cancel. Remember me to Mrs and Miss Strahan and to all the rest of your family; Remember me likewise to Mr and Mrs Cadell; and believe me to be ever yours

Adam Smith

185. *From* ALEXANDER WEDDERBURN

MS., GUL Gen. 1035/155; Scott 274–5.

London, 30 Oct. 1777

My Dear Smith

I have long intended to answer your Letter[1] which I received very regularly, but in a Situation where I could not gain the least Intelligence about Mr Nelthorp.[2] That Part of your Letter is now as much out of date as the Account of your mercy to the highwayman, in which I suspect there was a little mixture of Prudence; Nor I am convinced that the ardour of

---

[1] Archibald Menzies (d. 1777), appointed in 1770 one of the five 'Commissioners for Managing and Causing to be Levied and Collected His Majesty's Customs, and Subsidies and other Duties in that part of Great Britain called Scotland, and also the Duties of Excise upon all Salt and Rock Salt Imported or to be Imported into that part of Great Britain called Scotland', as they were styled in official documents.

[2] Andrew Strahan; the 'cancel' concerned changes in WN ed. 2 (1778)—see Letter 208 addressed to Andreas Holt, dated 26 Oct. 1780.

[1] Not traced: presumably dealt with Smith's candidacy for the post of Commissioner of Customs.

[2] William Nelthorp, appointed Commissioner of Customs, 1774.

your Mans Courage[3] would have misdirected his Pistol, and if he had shot I shou'd have been in more pain for your danger than the Highwayman's. I believe I may venture to assure you that neither of the two Gentlemen you recommend so warmly will succeed Mr Menzies. I am sorry that I did not know how much you interested yourself in their favour before I received the D[uchess] of B[uccleuch]'s note, which I immediately conveyed to Lord North[4] and I am assured It has had its full effect. I have often heard that Ladys interfering in Business never fail to spoil it. This Dutchess, meaning no doubt very well runs counter to your recommendation very unluckily, disappoints you of the pleasure of seeing either a very able or a very jolly Commissioner of the Customs, and deprives one of these Gentlemen of the more substantial pleasure of enjoying a very good Office.

If you do not come up to London directly and for some months at least keep Mr Nelthorp in countenance, I shall as little forgive the Duchess for her meddling in this Business, as you ought to do.

There is a Packet arrived from Howe[5] which has been two months upon Its passage. People seem pleased with the accounts but I do not know what they are having only been a few hours in town.

> I ever am, My Dr Smith
> Yours most sincerely
> Al Wedderburn

186. *From* SIR GREY COOPER[1]

MS., GUL Gen. 1035/156; Scott 275.

> Parliament Street, [Westminster,]
> 7 Nov. 1777.

Dear Sir!

I assure you with great sincerity and truth that I am much flattered and pleased with your letter which was delivered to me last week by our friend Mr Sollicitor General,[2] and who at the same time was so good as to show me one he has received from you on the same subject. There is a character

---

[3] Possibly Robert Reid, servant who left Smith's employment before 1784, and wrote to him from New Brunswick, on 11 Sept. 1785; see Letter 246.

[4] Frederick, Lord North (1732–92), M.P.; Chancellor of the Exchequer 1767–82; First Lord of the Treasury 1770–82, and as such Prime Minister during the crisis of the American War of Independence. He succeeded his father as 2nd Earl of Guilford in 1790.

[5] Either Admiral Richard Lord Howe or General Sir William Howe, brothers who commanded by sea and land in America.

[1] Sir Grey Cooper (? 1726–1801), successful lawyer and M.P. (1765–84; 1786–90); Secretary to the Treasury 1765–82; Lord of Treasury 1783; noted for his accurate knowledge of financial matters. In the Treasury, he took charge of the revenue side, though John Robinson, the Joint Secretary (1770–82), thought his conduct of affairs was 'slovenly' (HP ii. 251). He was allied politically with Henry Dundas and Alexander Wedderburn.

[2] Alexander Wedderburn.

of sentiment in these letters so very different from the applications and sollicitations which I have been long accustomed to receive, that the Singularity and novelty of it gave me uncommon pleasure. When you sollicited the appointment of your friends Son to the Collectorship of Grenville Harbour, I remember well the zeal, the assiduity, and the warmth of heart with which you recommended him, and I reflect with satisfaction that it was in my power to give success to that application; you now sollicit a place at the Board of Customs at Edinburgh for another Person, but in this case, instead of a warm and eager application, I find nothing But Phlegm, Composure and Indifference; It is however fortunate that the person whom you so faintly support, does not want yours or any other great mans recommendation; and tho you seem to have no very high opinion of him, His merit is so well known to Lord North and to all the world, That (Alas what a Bathos!) He will very soon, if I am not much mistaken be appointed a Commissioner of the Customs in Scotland.

I am Dear Sir

with real esteem and regard

Your faithfull

Humble Servant

Grey Cooper

187. *From* EDWARD GIBBON

MS., Honeyman Coll., Lehigh University Libr., Bethlehem, Penn.; *Review of English Studies*, N.S. x (1950), 401–2; *Letters of Gibbon*, ed. J. E. Norton (1956), ii. 166 (in part).

Almacks [Club, London,] 26 Nov. 1777

Dear Sir

Among the strange reports, which are every day circulated in this wide town, I heard one to-day so very extraordinary, that I know not how to give credit to it. I was informed that a place of Commissioner of the Customs in Scotland had been given to a Philosopher who for his own glory and for the benefit of mankind had enlightened the world by the most profound and systematic treatise on the great objects of trade and revenue which had ever been published in any age or in any Country. But as I was told at the same time that this Philosopher was my particular friend, I found myself very forcible inclined to believe, what I most sincerely wished and desired.

After a very pleasant summer passed in Paris where I often heard your name, and saw several of your friends particularly the Dutchess Danville, and the Countess de Bouflers, I returned to England about the beginning of this Month. If I was guilty of any intemperance I have been punished by a very severe fit of the Gout, from which I am now recovering to mix again in the more tumultuous but perhaps less pleasing Society of London. If your new dignity should [not] allow you to make us a regular visit every spring or summer I am afraid I shall be selfish enough to murmur at your promotion. In case you should be at Edinburgh, I must trouble you with my Compliments to Dr Robertson: in a post or two I hope to satisfy him by what a strange concurrence of accidents I have appeared so very careless. Beauclerc,[1] who is playing at Whisk, desires me to assure you that he is warmly interested in whatever may be agreable or avantageous to you.

I am Dear Sir with the highest regard

most sincerely yours

E. Gibbon.

188. *To* [WILLIAM STRAHAN]

MS., Goldsmith Libr., University of London, A.L. 110; Rae 321–2.

Edinburgh, 20 Dec. 1777

Dear Sir

The last letter[1] I had the pleasure of receiving from you congratulated me upon by being appointed one of the commissioners of customs in Scotland. You told me at the same time that you had dined that day with Sir Grey Cooper, and that you had both been so good as to speak very favourably of me. I have received from London several other congratulations of the same kind. But I have not yet received, nor has the Office here received any official information that any such appointment had been made. It is possible that the Commission is not made out on account of the fees. If this is the case, you may either draw upon me for the Amount which I understand to be about £160; or you may write to me and I shall by return of Post remit you the money to London. Whatever be the cause of the delay I beg you will endeavour to find it out and let me know as soon as possible, that I may at least be at the end of my hope. Remember me most affectionately to all your family and believe me to be

Most faithfully yours

Adam Smith

Neither you nor Mr Cadell have wrote me anything concerning the new Edition of My Book[2] It is Published? Does it sell well? does it sell ill? does it sell at all? I left directions with Mr Cadell to send copies of it to

[1] Topham Beauclerk (1739–80), fellow member, together with Gibbon and Smith, of Dr. Johnson's Club. He owned a library of 30,000 volumes, especially rich in English literature and history, also travels and science.

[1] Not traced.

[2] Ed. 2 WN appeared early in 1778 with numerous though minor changes for the sake of style, factual accuracy, and additional information, along with some theoretical adjustments.

several of my friends. If John Hunter[3] was not among the Number, put him in ex dono authoris; and desire Cadell to send me the Account of the whole that I may pay it. I should write to him; but it would only be plaguing him. If you draw upon me make your bill payable at five days sight. I return to Kirkaldy on Christmas day.

189. *From* GEORGE HORNE[1]

[The Revd. George Horne], *A Letter to Adam Smith, LL.D. on the Life, Death, and Philosophy of his Friend David Hume Esq. By One of the People Called Christians* (Oxford, 1777).

[This *Letter* is an attack on Smith for praising Hume. Its tone and nature are sufficiently indicated by a quotation from the first page: 'You have been lately employed in embalming a philosopher; his *body*, I believe I must say; for concerning the other part of him, neither you nor he seem to have entertained an idea sleeping or waking. Else, it surely might have claimed a little of your care and attention; and one would think, the belief of the soul's existence and immortality could do no harm, if it did no good, in a *Theory of Moral Sentiments*. But every gentleman understands his own business best.' This kind of thing was the 'abuse' of which Smith complained in Letter 208 Addressed to Andreas Holt. dated 26 Oct. 1780.]

190. *To* WILLIAM STRAHAN

MS., University of Illinois Libr.; Rae 322–3.

Kirkcaldy, 14 Jan. 1778

Dear Sir

I should have sent you the enclosed bill the day after I received your letter accompanyed with a note from Mr Spottiswood,[1] had not Mr Charteris, the Sollicitor to the Customs here, told me that the fees were not paid at London, but at Edinburgh; where Mr Shadrach Moyes acted as receiver and agent for the officers of the treasury at London. I have drawn the bill for the £120. in order to pay, first what you have advanced for me; secondly, the exchange between Edinburgh and London; and lastly, the account which I shall owe to Mr Cadell after he has delivered

---

[3] The famous surgeon and anatomist whose collections were acquired by the College of Surgeons, London.

[1] George Horne (1730–92), Fellow of Magdalen College, Oxford, then President 1768–90; Royal Chaplain 1771–81; Dean of Canterbury 1781; Bishop of Norwich 1790–2; orthodox Anglican, though he allowed John Wesley to preach in his diocese.

[1] John Spottiswoode, nephew of Strahan. The letter and note have not been traced.

the presents I desired him to make of the second edition of my book.[2] To these I beg he will add two copies handsomely bound and guilt, one to Lord North, the other to Sir Gray Cooper. I received Sir Grays letter[3] and shall write to him as soon as the new commission arrives, in order not to trouble him with answering two Letter[s]. I believe that I have been very highly obliged to him in this business. I shall not say anything to you of the obligations I owe you for the concern you have shewn and the diligence you have exerted on my account. Remember me to Mr Spottiswood. I shall write to him as soon as the affair is over. Would it be proper to send him any present or fee? I am much obliged to him and should be glad to express my sense of it in every way in my power.

I would not make any alteration in my title page on account of my new office.

Remember me to Mrs and Miss Strahan, likewise to the Humes[4] and the Hunters. How does the Painter[5] go on? I hope, he thrives. I ever am

My Dear Sir
most faithfully and
affectionately yours
Adam Smith

191. *To* JOHN SPOTTISWOODE

Address: Mr Spottiswood
MS., Pierpont Morgan Libr., New York; Scott 275–6.

Kirkcaldy, 21 Jan. 1778

Dear Sir

I do not know how to express my thankfulness to you for voluntarily undertaking to transact my business at the treasury. A man of honour who undertakes to execute a trust for another very often thinks that he cannot save his money too much. This may be for the honour of the trustee but it is not always for that of the truster. You rate the fees at 90 or 100 pounds. Everbody else tells me they amount to 150 or 160 pounds. May I beg that I may have no dispute with the Clerks of the treasury and that everything may be paid as liberally as it usually is by other people. I am with the highest sense of your kindness, Dear Sir

Your most obliged
and most obedient
Servant
Adam Smith

[2] WN ed. 2, 1778.   [3] Letter 186, dated 7 Nov. 1777.
[4] ? John Home the poet and his wife.
[5] ? Allan Ramsay (1713–84), settled in England *c.* 1756 and became portrait-painter to George III, 1767.

192. *To* [ANDREW] STRAHAN[1]

MS., University of Illinois Libr.; Rae 323–4.

Edinburgh, 5 Feb. 1778

My Dear Strahan

I received the commission in due Course and have only to thank you for your great attention to my interest in every respect; but above all for your generosity in so readily forgiving the sally of bad humour, which in consequence of General Skeenes,[2] who meant too very well, most unreasonably broke out upon you. I can only say in my own vindication, that I am not very subject to such sallies; and that upon the very few occasions in which I have happened to fall into them, I have soon recovered from them. I am told that no commission ever came so soon to Edinburgh; many having been delayed three weeks or a month after appearing in the Gazette. This extraordinary dispatch I can impute to nothing but your friendly diligence and that of Mr Spottiswood; to whom I beg to be remembered in the most respectfull manner.

You have made a small mistake in stating our account; you credit me with £150 only, instead of £170; the first bill being for £120 the second for £50.[3] Cadell, however, still remains unpaid.[4] As soon as I understand he has delivered the books, or before it, if he will send me the account of them, I shall send him the money. I ever am Dear Sir

Most faithfully yours
Adam Smith

193. *To* WILLIAM STRAHAN

Address: William Strahan Esqr, M.P., New Street, Shoe Lane, London
MS., Goldsmith Libr., University of London, A.L. 111; Scott 276.

Edinburgh, 5 Feb. 1778

Dear Sir

I received the Commission on Monday the 2d inst; four days after my name had appeared in the Gazette; I am assured that there is scarce an example of any such commissions coming to Edinburgh in less than four weeks after that publication. I do not know in what manner to thank you

---

[1] Presumably Andrew; the son; even the absent-minded Smith could hardly have written two letters on the same day covering the same ground to William Strahan (see Letter 193 addressed to William Strahan, dated 4 Feb. 1778).

[2] Smith's cousin, Robert Skene; his part in the affair of the commission is unknown; and Smith's 'sally' is a mystery also.

[3] Calculations on the back of the letter suggest that the commission fees came to '£147. 18s'. Possibly Smith sent two bills (£120 and £50) to pay the fees; see Letter 191 addressd to William Spottiswoode, dated 21 Jan. 1778.

[4] For printing WN ed. 2; see Letter 184 addressed to William Strahan, dated 27 Oct. 1777.

for your friendly diligence in procuring me this ready dispatch, which at this moment happened to be of very great consequence to me.¹ I am much afraid it may never be in my power to make you a proper return; I can only assure you that I shall always retain the most lively sense of your very great kindness; I ever am

Dear Sir, Your much obliged, and most
obedient humble Servant
Adam Smith

194. *From* LE DUC DE LA ROCHEFOUCAULD¹

Smith's Works, ed. Dugald Stewart, v. 467–8; Rae 339–40.

Paris, 3 Mars 1778

Le desir de se rappeller à votre souvenir, Monsieur, quand on a eu l'honneur de vous connoître, doit vous paroitre fort naturel; permettez que nous saisissions pour cela, ma Mère² et moi, l'occasion d'une édition nouvelle des *Maximes de la Rochefoucauld*,³ dont nous prenons la liberté de vous offrir un exemplaire. Vous voyez que nous n'avons point de rancune, puisque le mal que vous avez dit de lui dans la *Théorie des Sentimens Moraux*,⁴ ne nous empêche point de vous envoyer ce même ouvrage. Il s'en est même fallu de peu que je ne fisse encore plus, car j'avois eu peut-être la temerité d'entreprendre une traduction de votre *Théorie*; mais comme je venois de terminer la première partie, j'ai vu paroitre la traduction de M. l'Abbé Blavet,⁵ et j'ai été forcé de renoncer au plaisir que j'aurois eu de fair passer dans ma langue un des meilleurs ouvrages de la vôtre.

Il auroit bien fallu pour lors entreprendre une justification de mon grandpère.⁶ Peut-être n'auroit-il pas été difficile, premièrement de l' excuser, en disant, qu'il avoit toujours vu les hommes à la Cour, et dans la guerre civile, *deux théatres sur lesquels ils sont certainement plus mauvais*

---

¹ Possibly Smith's benefactions to friends embarrassed by the difficulties with America had left him short of funds.

¹ Louis-Alexandre, Duc de La Rochefoucauld (1743–92), active in cultural affairs and, later, radical politics; he took part in the French revolution and was killed in the September massacres of 1792. See Letter 199 from La Rochefoucauld, dated 6 Aug. 1779; and Letter 248 addressed to La Rochefoucauld, dated 1 Nov. 1785.

² Duchesse d'Anville.   ³ Paris, 1778.

⁴ The reference to the famous La Rochefoucauld came in TMS, VII.ii.4.6, eds. 1–5, and was dropped in ed. 6. Smith still called the chapter 'Of licentious Systems', even though he dealt only with Mandeville. The grandson was justified in objecting to Smith's treatment of the author of the *Maxims* in the early editions. While the style of La Rochefoucauld had been aptly characterized as possessing 'elegance and delicate precision' as against the 'lively and humourous, tho' coarse and rustic eloquence' of Mandeville, their philosophical positions were not distinguished.   ⁵ 1774.

⁶ François VI Duc de La Rochefoucauld (1613–80), author of the *Maxims*.

qu' ailleurs; et ensuite de justifier par la conduite personelle de l'auteur, les principes qui sont certainement trop généralisés dans son ouvrage. Il a pris la partie pour le tout; et parceque les gens qu'il avoit eu le plus sous les yeux étoient animés par *l'amour propre*, il en a fait le mobile général de tous les hommes. Au reste, quoique son ouvrage merite à certains égards d'être combattu, il est cependant estimable même pour le fond, et beaucoup pour la forme.

Permettex-moi de vous demander, si nous aurons bientôt une édition complette des oeuvres de votre illustre ami M. Hume? Nous l'avons sincèrement regretté.

Recevez, je vous supplie, l'expression sincère de tous les sentimens d'estime et d'attachement avec lesquels j'ai l'honneur d'être Monsieur, votre très humble et très obeissant serviteur,

Le Duc de La Rochefoucauld

195. *To* LORD KAMES

Address: The Right Honble, The Lord Kaimes
MS., SRO GD24/1/586; Rae 341.

Edinburgh, 16 Nov. 1778

My Dear Lord

I am much obliged to your Lordship for the kind communication of the objections you propose to make in your new Edition[1] to my System. Nothing can be more perfectly friendly and polite than the terms in which you express yourself with regard to me; and I should be extremely peevish and ill-tempered if I could make the slightest opposition to their publication. I am no doubt extremely sorry to find myself of a different opinion both from so able a judge of the subject and from so old and so good a friend.[2] But differences of this kind are unavoidable;[3] and besides, *partium contentionibus respublica crescit*. I should have been waiting on your Lordship before this time; but the remains of a cold have for these four or five days past made it inconvenient to go out in the evening. Remember me to Mrs Drummond[4] and believe me to be

Your most obliged and most humble Servant.

Adam Smith

[1] *Essays on the Principles of Morality and Natural Religion*, (ed. 3, 1779).

[2] Kames had sponsored Smith's Edinburgh lectures on rhetoric and jurisprudence, 1748–51.

[3] Kames resisted Smith's moral doctrine concerning sympathy on three grounds: putting oneself in the place of a sufferer leads to self-satisfaction and diminution of pity; those with the liveliest imaginations are not the most moral of men; moral sentiments towards our own actions are not explained by sympathy.

[4] Agatha, dau. of James Drummond of Blair Drummond; md. Kames (Henry Home) 1741; unexpectedly became heiress to Blair Drummond 1766, and assumed the name Home Drummond; d. 1795.

196. *To* JOHN SINCLAIR OF ULBSTER[1]

MS., Thurso East Mains, Caithness, Viscount Thurso of Ulbster; *Sinclair Corr.* (1831), i. 388; Rae 343-4; Rosalind Mitchison, *Agricultural Sir John* (London, 1962), facsim. facing p. 5 (in part).

Edinburgh, 24 Nov. 1778

Mr Smith presents his most respectful complements to Mr Sinclair of Ulbster.

The memoires sur les finances[2] are engaged for four months to come to Mr John Davidson. When he has done with them Mr Smith would be very happy to accomodate Mr Sinclair; but acknowledges he is a little uneasy about the safety of the conveyance and the Greatness of the Distance; he has frequent occasion to consult the book himself both in the course of his private studies and in the business of his present employment; and is, therefore, not very willing to let it go out of Edinburgh. The Book[3] was never properly published, but there were a few more copies printed than was necessary for the Commission, for whose use it was compiled.[4]

One of these I obtained by the particular favour of Mr Turgot, the late Controller-General of the Finances. I have heard but of three copies in Great Britain: one belongs to a noble lord, who obtained it by connivance, as he told me,[5] one is in the Secretary of State's office, and the third belongs

---

[1] John Sinclair (1754–1835) of Ulbster and Thurso Castle, Caithness; agriculturalist, politician, and economic geographer; educ. at the Universities of Edinburgh, Glasgow, and Oxford; advocate 1775; called to the English Bar 1783; M.P. 1780–1811; cr. Baronet, 1786; president of the Board of Agriculture, 1793–8, 1806–14; member of the Scottish Board of Trustees for Manufacturers, from 1808; Cashier of Excise in Scotland, 1811 until he died; Privy Councillor, 1810. His most famous work was the compilation of the *Statistical Account of Scotland* (1790–7), the first complete picture of a nation, parish by parish.

[2] *Mémoires concernant les impositions et droits en Europe*, 4 t. (Paris, 1768–9), by J. L. Moreau de Beaumont (1715–85). Smith's WN note (V.ii.a.4) reads: 'This work was compiled by order of the court for the use of a commission employed for some years past in considering the proper means for reforming the finances of France. The account of the French taxes, which takes up three volumes in quarto, may be regarded as perfectly authentic. That of those of other European nations was compiled from such information as the French ministers at the different courts could procure. It is much shorter, and probably not quite so exact as that of the French taxes.' Smith actually quoted more from the later volumes; see WN V.ii. for references to European taxes, in Hamburgh, Holland, Switzerland, Prussia, and Venice (Bonar 18–21).

[3] End of facsimile text; remainder of the letter is taken from Rae.

[4] Rae states that 100 copies of the *Mémoires* were printed in 1768, and argues 'it may be reasonably inferred, from Smith's account of the extreme difficulty of getting a copy, that he only obtained his in 1774, on the advent of Turgot to power. If that be so, much in the chapters on taxation in the *Wealth of Nations* must have been written in London after that date' (343–4).

[5] 'Probably Lord Rosslyn, for Bentham, in writing to advise Lord Shelburne to procure a copy of this book, mentions that he knew Lord Rosslyn had a copy, which he had obtained from Mr Anstruther, M.P., who happened to be in Paris when it was printed, and contrived to get a copy somehow there' (Rae 344).

to a private gentleman. How these two were obtained I know not, but suspect it was in the same manner. If any accident should happen to my book, the loss is perfectly irreparable. When Mr Sinclair comes to Edinburgh I shall be very happy to communicate to him not only that book, but everything else I have upon the subject, both printed and manuscript, and am, with the highest respect for his character his most obedient humble servant,

Adam Smith

197. *From* [JOHN MACPHERSON][1]

MS., GUL Gen. 1035/157, end missing; Scott 276–8.

Kensington Gore, 28 Nov. 1778

My dear Sir.

I meant to have written you long since, and wished to have communicated some public news, that might have at least amused you as much as a common Advertiser. But tho' I have been much at the first Source of Intelligence, and tho' I know almost all that can be known yet have I little to tell you. You perhaps Remember the Speech which I spouted for the Premier[2] at your Table at 2 in the morning of the Day I left Edinburgh. It was so well relished, that you would have found from it all the Features of what was afterwards spoken in the House. It was a lucky Coincidence with times and Sentiments.

I had a most ample Discussion with Lord North at Bushy Park on my Return from Scotland. I will get him to do something Essential for the Nabob.[3] We went over all India America Scotland and England. I pledged your Authority about importing part of the Dead Treasure of Calcutta.[4] He felt the Authority with Respect, but hesitated about a measure so novel. He thought the Treasury of Bengal was a kind of Bank. Finding the

---

[1] The letter has no signature, but the hand was identified by Sir Lewis Namier as that of John Macpherson (c. 1745–1821), Bt. 1786; M.P. 1779–82, 1796–1802. Macpherson was deeply involved in Indian affairs for much of his career, first as servant of the Nawab of Arcot, then as agent in England for the Nawab and Warren Hastings (1777–81), and latterly as member of the Bengal Council. He became Acting Governor of Bengal when Hastings resigned, and his successor in 1786 described Macpherson's administration as 'a system of the dirtiest jobbing'. On his return to England in 1787, Macpherson made the acquaintance of the Prince of Wales, whose friendship he enjoyed, and joined the Opposition.

[2] Lord North.   [3] Warren Hastings.

[4] In WN I.xi.h. 2, Smith states that the quantities of silver carried annually to India have reduced the value of that metal in relation to gold and instances depreciation in Calcutta. Perhaps he had suggested to Macpherson that part of Calcutta's treasury holdings could be imported to Britain during the distresses of the American war without loss of fiscal advantage to Bengal. Smith's strictures on the East India Company and references to the Calcutta treasury are found in WN I.viii. 26, IV.vii.c. 101–8, and V.i.e. 26.

necessity of remaining in office he is become more manly and his Speech the first Day of the Session was in a firmer tone than usual. He was inquisitive about your Duke and the Advocate.[5] To my astonishment he had all the little History of Edinburgh and in rather a wrong light. It seems you have awaked some new Ideas about improving the Revenue. For he said the absurdity of enforcing the prevention of Contraband Trade in America was evinced from the Difficulties of it in the faithful Kingdom of Scotland, as appeared by late Representations.

Your Letter to the Attorney General[6] he spoke of to me with warmth, and I hope to turn it to our mutual Good. I have since dined twice with him, and he is to taste my Magnums at Kensington Gore soon. Of all the Speakers and *Men* who distinguished themselves on the 26th he shone most and with most Efficacy. I sat near Mr Andrew Stuart and Robinson[7] while he was speaking; and we all felt his commanding Superiority. All the gloss Reasoning and prismatic figures in Burkes long Speech, as well as the more solid Vehemence of Foxes harangue he broke down as you would a Pile of glasses with the Sweep of your arm. He covered the Minister by desiring to lay open his Conduct, and he drew the House to the original Motion amidst the firmest conviction of his own Position. Lord North felt the Telamonian Shield as well as the Edge which at once protected him and galled his opponents. This is no Exaggeration, and I believe North for the first time feels Regard where before he had only Respect. I have aided the impression by even an accident. [   ][8]

198. *To* [Unidentified Nobleman]

Lady Charnwood, *An Autograph Collection*, 120.

Canongate, Edinburgh, Jan. 1779

My Lord,

I am extremely sorry that all the copies of my Book that I ever was possessed of have been long ago given away, a single one excepted of each of the two editions[1] which I am obliged to keep for my own use in order to mark the corrections or additions which I may hereafter have occasion

---

[5] The Duke of Buccleuch and Henry Dundas.   [6] Alexander Wedderburn.

[7] John Robinson (1727–1802) M.P. 1764–1802; Jt. Secretary to Treasury 1770–82; Surveyor Gen. of Woods and Forests 1786–d. His Treasury work brought him responsibility for the political management of East India Co. affairs, also for a time Irish commercial legislative, and political management. During North's Administration he was the Government teller and whip and acted as a liaison with the King's circle. Subsequently, he supplied political intelligence to Shelburne and Pitt, since he considered that his first loyalty was to the King and the government of the King's choice (HP iii. 364–6).

[8] The end of the letter is missing.

[1] WN ed. 1, 1776; ed. 2, 1778.

to make. I should otherwise have been very happy to have presented one
to your Lordship. I have the honour to be, with great respect,

My Lord, Your Lordship's Most obedient

and most humble Servant,

Adam Smith

199. *From* LE DUC DE LA ROCHEFOUCAULD

MS., GUL Gen. 1035/158; Scott 278–9.

Verteuil,[1] 6 Aout 1779

C'est ici, Monsieur, au fond d'une Province où sont situées no sterres,
et où le voisinage de ma garnison m'a permis de venir passer quelque tems
avec ma mere, que me sont parvenus votre lettre du 15. Mai,[2] et l'ouvrage
posthume de votre digne ami que vous avez eu la bonté de m'envoier.[3]
Il est tel que son esprit aussi délicat que profond, et sa manière de penser
fort connue devoient le faire présumer en voiant son titre; je l'ai lû
avec un véritable plaisir; on ne peut pas mieux plaider le *Scepticisme*; mais
comme il le dit lui même, s'il y a de veritable *Sceptiques*, ils sont en bien
petit nombre, et cette doctrine ne convient qu'à bien peu de gens: je vous
avoue que je ne le suis point sur l'existence d'un Etre premier, et je crois
qu'il seroit très avantageux que tout le monde crût a son existence dépouil-
lée des accompagnemens dangereux que la superstition y a joints dans
presque tous les pais; mais je ne voudrois pas que l'on regardât son
existence comme si peu liée avec qui se passe ici bas. Mais je m'appercois
que, insensiblement, j'entre en matière sur un sujet bien au dessus de mes
forces, et qui appartiendroit â l'Auteur de la *Théory of Moral Sentiments*.

Je reçois avec bien du plaisir l'annonce de la nouvelle Edition que vous
préparez de cet excellent ouvrage;[4] je pousserai l'indiscretion jusqu'à vous
en demander un Exemplaire quand il paroîtra: et si les changemens que
vous y aurez faits, exigeoient une nouvelle Edition françoise, et que M.
l'Abbé Blavet ne la donnât pas, j'aurois peut être la témérité de reprendre
mon entreprise,[5] mais il faudroit que j'y fusse autorisé par votre aveu, et
par l'assurance que vous voudriez bien revoir la traduction avant qu'elle
vît le jour.

Je suis ici dans un lieu qu'a beaucoup habité mon grandpere Auteur
des Maximes, et je vous dois en son nom des remercimens de la justice que
vous voulez lui rendre, et qu'il mérite: la reputation de son esprit est bien

---

[1] Near Angoulême; the fifteenth-century château was the principal domain of the
author of the *Maxims*.

[2] Not traced.

[3] David Hume, *Dialogues concerning Natural Religion* (1779).

[4] TMS ed. 5 was published in 1781.

[5] See Letter 194 from La Rochefoucauld, dated 3 Mar. 1778.

établie, et celle de son coeur a été injustement attaquée, car il étoit honnête homme, et croioit à la vertu qu'il pratiquoit. Il a fait comme beaucoup d'Auteurs, il a trop generalisé les conséquences d'un principe vrai; et Diderot[6] me disoit un jour au sujet de son livre, que le moien de lui éviter les reproches qu'il a quelque fois encourus, c'étoit de l'intituler, *Réflexions Morales, a l'usage des Cours.*

J'ai recu en même tems que le vôtre, un autre Exemplaire de l'ouvrage de M. hume par un de ses neveux que j'ai connu il y a quelques années a Metz, et qui étoit alors Militaire;[7] je voudrois bien lui en témoigner ma reconnoissance, mais j'ignore son adresse; si vous pouvez me mander où et par quel moien je pourrois lui faire parvenir une lettre, je vous en Serai infiniment obligé.

Ma mere me charge de vous faire ses complimens; recevez, je vous supplie, l'expression sincere de tous les sentimens d'estime et d'attachement avec lesquels j'ai l'honneur d'être, Monsieur, Votre très humble et très obeissant Serviteur.

Le Duc de la Rochefoucauld

200. *From* HENRY DUNDAS

MS., among papers of William Eden, Lord Auckland (copy of letter sent to Smith); *English Historical Review* i (1886), 308–11; Rae 352–3.

Melville, 30 Oct. 1779

Dear Sir,

I received the enclosed last night from Mr Eden.[1] The questions he puts would require a volume to answer them in place of a Letter.[2] Think of it however and let me have your ideas upon it.[3] For my own part I confess

---

[6] Denis Diderot (1713–84), chief editor of the *Encyclopédie* and best known of the *philosophes.*

[7] Joseph Home was at Metz, 1775–6 (HL ii. 296).

[1] William Eden (1744–1814), M.P. 1774–93; md. a dau. of Gilbert Elliot of Minto; politically allied with Alexander Wedderburn; Lord of Trade 1776–82; Commissioner for Conciliation with America 1778–9; Secretary to the Lord Lieutenant of Ireland 1780–2; envoy to France on special commercial mission 1785–8; Ambassador to Spain 1788–9, and to the United Provinces 1789–93; President of the Board of Trade 1806–7; cr. Baron Auckland 1789. In France Eden negotiated a commercial treaty named after himself, whose provisions were based on the argument advanced in WN IV.iii.c.12 ('Additions', 3rd edn. 1784) that France would provide a better market than the American colonies. The chief beneficiaries, as Smith had predicted, proved to be British industry and the French vineyards.

[2] On 12 Oct. the Irish Parliament had unanimously approved free trade for Ireland. Eden solicited Dundas's opinion on this issue.

[3] See Letter 201 addressed to Dundas, dated 1 Nov., the same day that a politely ambiguous royal message was made known on the Irish question. Smith sent a similar copy to Lord Carlisle on 8 Nov.; see Letter 202.

myself little alarmed about what others seem so much alarmed. I doubt much if a free trade to Ireland is so very much to be dreaded. There is trade enough in the world for the Industry both of Britain and Ireland, and if two or three places either in south or north Britain should suffer some damage, which by the bye will be very gradual, from the loss of their monopoly, that is a very small consideration in the general scale and policy of the Country. The only thing to be guarded against is the people in Ireland being able to undersell us in foreign mercates from the want of Taxes and the Cheapness of labour. But a wise Statesman will be able to regulate that by proper distribution of taxes upon the materials and Commodities of the respective Countrys. I believe an union would be the best if it can be accomplished, if not the Irish Parliament must be managed by the proper distribution of the Loaves and fishes, so that the Legislatures of the two Countrys may act in union together. In short, it has long appeared to me that the bearing down of Ireland, was in truth bearing down a substantial part of the Naval and Military strength of our own Country. Indeed it has often shocked me in the House of Commons for these two years past, when anything was hinted in favour of Ireland by its friends, of even giving them only the benefit of making the most of what their soil or climate afforded them, to hear it received as a sufficient answer, that a town in England or Scotland would be hurt by such an Indulgence. This kind of reasoning will no longer do. But I find in place of asking yours I am giving you my opinion, so adieu.

Yours sincerely,
Henry Dundas

201. *To* [HENRY DUNDAS]

MS., SRO GD51/1/355; BM Add. MSS. 34416 (copy: shorter version); Rae 353–5.

Edinburgh, 1 Nov. 1779

My Dear Lord

I am very happy to find that your Lordships opinion concerning the consequences of granting a free trade to Ireland[1] coincides so perfectly with my own.

I cannot believe that the manufactures of G.B. can, for a century to come, suffer much from the rivalship of those of Ireland, even tho' the Irish should be indulged in a free trade. Ireland has neither the Skill, nor the Stock which could enable her to rival England; and tho' both may be acquired in time, to acquire them compleatly will require the operation of little less than a century. Ireland has neither coal nor Wood. The former

---

[1] See Letter 200 from Dundas, dated 30 Oct., and Letter 202 addressed to Lord Carlisle, dated 8 Nov. 1779, also WN I.xi.m. 9 and V.iii.72.

seems to have been denied to her by nature; and tho her soil and climate are perfectly suited for raising the latter; yet to raise it to the same degree as in England will require more than a century. I perfectly agree with your Lordship too, that to crush the Industry of so great and so fine a province of the empire, in order to favour the monopoly of some particular towns in Scotland or England, is equally unjust and impolitic. The general opulence and improvement of Ireland might certainly, under proper management, afford much greater resources to Government, than can ever be drawn from a few mercantile or manufacturing towns.

Till the Irish Parliament sends over the Heads of their proposed Bill it may, perhaps, be uncertain what they understand by a free trade.

They may, perhaps, understand by it no more than the power of exporting their own produce to the forreign country where they can find the best Market. Nothing can be more just and reasonable than this demand; nor can anything be more unjust and unreasonable than some of the restraints which their industry in this respect at present labours under. They are prohibited under the heaviest penalties to export Glass to any country. Wool they can export only to G.B. Woollen goods they can export only from certain ports in their own country and to certain Ports in Great Britain.

They may mean to demand the power of importing such goods as they have occasion for, from any country where they can find them cheapest, subject to no other duties and restraints than such as may be imposed by their own parliament. This freedom, tho in my opinion perfectly reasonable, will interfere a little with some of our paltry monopolies. Glass, Hops, forreign Sugars, several sorts of East India goods can at present be imported only from Great Britain.

They may mean to demand a free trade to our american and African Plantations, free from the restraints which the 18th of the Present King imposed upon it, or at least from some of those restraints; such as, the prohibition of Exporting thither their own Woollen and Cotton Manufactures, Glass, Hats, Hops, gunpowder etc.[2] This freedom, tho it would interfere with some of our monopolies, I am convinced, would do no harm to Great Britain. It would be reasonable indeed that whatever goods were exported from Ireland to those plantations should be subject to the like duties as those of the same kind exported from England; in the terms of the 18th of the present King.

They may mean to demand a free trade to Great Britain, their manufactures and produce when imported into this country being subjected to no other duties than the like manufactures and produce of our own. Nothing, in my opinion, would be more highly advantageous to both countries than this mutual freedom of trade. It would help to break down that

[2] 18 Geo. III (1778) c.55.

absurd monopoly which we have most absurdly established against ourselves in favour of almost all the different classes of our own manufacturers.

Whatever the Irish mean to demand in this way, in the present situation of our affairs, I should think it madness not to grant it. Whatever they may demand our manufacturers, unless the leading and principal men among them are properly dealt with beforehand, will probably oppose it. That they may be so dealt with, I know from experience, and that it may be done at little expense and with no great trouble. I could even point out some persons, who, I think, are fit and likely to deal with them successfully for this purpose. I shall not say more upon this till I see you; which I shall do the first moment I can get out of this town.

I am much honoured by Mr Edens remembrance of me. I beg you will present my most respectful complements to him and that you will believe me to be

My Dear Lord, Most faithfully yours

Adam Smith

202. *To* [LORD CARLISLE][1]

MS., Kress Libr., Harvard University; Rae 350–2.

Edinburgh, 8 Nov. 1779

My Lord

My friend Mr Fergusson[2] showed me, a few days ago, a letter in which your Lordship was so good as to say that you wished to know my opinion concerning the consequence of granting to the Irish that *free trade* which they at present demand so importunately.[3] I shall not attempt to express how much I feel myself flattered by your Lordships very honourable remembrance of me; but shall, without further preface, endeavour to explain that opinion, such as it may be, as distinctly as I can.

Till we see the heads of the bill which the Irish propose to send over, it is impossible to know precisely what they mean by a free trade.

It is possible they may mean by it no more than the freedom of exporting all goods, whether of their own produce or imported from abroad, to all Countries (Great Britain and the british settlements excepted) subject to no other duties or restraints than such as their own Parliament may impose. At present they can export Glass, tho' of their own manufacture, to no country whatever. Raw Silk, a forreign commodity, is under the same restraint. Wool they can export only to Great Britain.—Woollen Manufactures they can export only from certain Ports in Ireland to certain Ports

---

[1] Frederick Howard, 5th Earl of Carlisle (1748–1825), statesman, dramatist, and poet; President of the Board of Trade 1779; Viceroy of Ireland 1780–2; member of American Conciliation Commission of 1778–9, together with Eden and Governor Johnstone.

[2] Adam Ferguson served as Secretary to the American Conciliation Commission.

[3] See Letter 200 from Dundas, dated 30 Oct., and Letter 201 addressed to Dundas, dated 1 Nov.

in Great Britain. A very slender interest of our own Manufacturers is the foundation of all these unjust and oppressive restraints. The watchful jealousy of those Gentlemen is alarmed least the Irish, who have never been able to supply compleatly even their own market with Glass or Woollen manufactures, should be able to rival them in forreign Markets.

The Irish may mean by *a free trade* to demand besides, the freedom of importing from wherever they can buy them cheapest, all such forreign goods as they have occasion for. At present they can import Glass, Sugars of forreign plantations, except those of Spain and Portugal, and certain sorts of East India Goods from no Country but Great Britain. Tho' Ireland was relieved from these and from all other restraints of the same kind, the Interest of Great Britain could surely suffer very little. The Irish probably mean to demand no more than this most just and reasonable freedom of exportation and importation; in restraining which we seem to me rather to have gratified the impertinence than to have promoted any solid interest of our Merchants and Manufacturers.

The Irish may, however, mean to demand, besides, the same freedom of exportation and importation to and from the British settlements in Africa and America which is enjoyed by the Inhabitants of Great Britain. As Ireland has contributed little either to the establishment or defence of those Settlements, this demand would be less reasonable than the other two. But as I never believed that the monopoly of our Plantation trade was really advantageous to Great Britain; so I cannot believe that the admission of Ireland to a share in that Monopoly, or the extension of this monopoly to all the British Islands, would be really disadvantageous.

Over and above all this the Irish may mean to demand the freedom of importing their own produce and manufactures into Great Britain; subject to no other duties than such as are equivalent to the duties imposed upon the like goods of British produce or Manufacture. Tho' even this demand, the most unreasonable of all, should be granted, I cannot believe a that the interest of Britain would be hurt by it. On the contrary, the Competition of Irish goods in the British market might contribute to break down in Part that monopoly which we have most absurdly granted to the greater part of our own workmen against our selves. It would, however, be a long time, before, this competition could be very considerable. In the present state of Ireland, centuries must pass away before the greater part of its manufactures could vie with those of England. Ireland has little Coal; the Coallieries about Lough Neagh being of little consequence to the greater part of the Country. It is ill provided with Wood; two articles essentially necessary to the progress of Great Manufactures. It wants order, police, and a regular administration of justice both to protect and to restrain the inferior ranks of people, articles more essential to the progress of Industry than both coal and wood put together, and which

Ireland must continue to want as long as it continues to be divided between two hostile nations, the oppressors and the oppressed, the protestants and the Papists.[4]

Should the Industry of Ireland, in consequence of freedom and Good Government, ever equal that of England, so much the better would it be, not only for the whole British empire, but for the particular province of England. As the wealth and industry of Lancashire does not obstruct, but promote that of Yorkshire; so the wealth and industry of Ireland, would not abstruct, but promote that of England.

It makes me very happy to find, that in the midst of the Public misfortunes, a person of Your Lordships rank and elevation of mind doth not despair of the Commonwealth; but is willing to accept of an active share in Administration. That your Lordship may be the happy means of restoring vigour and decision to our councils and in consequence of them, success to our arms is the sincere wish of My Lord

Your Lordships
Most obliged and
Most obedient Servant
Adam Smith

203. *To* [WILLIAM EDEN]

MS., Lincoln Savings and Loan Association, Los Angeles 17; unpubl.

Edinburgh, 3 Jan. 1780

Dear Sir

It gives me very great pleasure to hear of the success of your Letters to Lord Carlyle.[1] I acknowledge I was not a little anxious about the success of a pamphlet which abused no party and no person and which represented the state of public affairs as less desperate than it is commonly believed to be. The Nation, I hope, is coming both into better humour and better spirits than I believed it to be. Besides the Editions you mention your letters have gone thro' an edition even in this narrow country.[2] I do not know how to thank you for the very honourable mention you have made of me.

It does not occur to me that much can be added to what you have already said. The difficulty of either inventing new taxes or increasing the old, is,

---

[4] See WN V.iii.89 for Smith's arguments about the advantages to Ireland of union with Great Britain, for promoting the deliverance of the 'people of all ranks' from an 'oppressive aristocracy . . . founded in the most odious of all distinctions, those of religious and political prejudices'.

[1] *Four Letters to the Earl of Carlisle* (London, 1779), in which Eden defended the Government's American policy.

[2] At least three London editions of Eden's *Letters* had appeared in 1779. As yet no Scottish edition has been traced.

I apprehend, the principal cause of our embarrassment. Besides a strict attention to Oeconomy, there appears to me to be three very obvious methods by which the public revenue can be increased without laying any new burthen upon the people.[3]

The first is a repeal of all bounties upon exportation. These in Scotland and England together amount to about £300,000 a year; exclusive of the Bounty upon Corn which in some years has amounted to a sum equal to all the other bounties. It will probably amount to a very considerable sum this year. When we cannot find taxes to carry on a defensive war; our Merchants ought not to complain if we refuse to tax ourselves any longer in order to support a few feeble and languishing branches of their commerce.

The second is a repeal of all prohibitions of importation, whether absolute or circumstantial, and the substitution of moderate and reasonable duties in the room of them. A prohibition can answer no purpose but that of monopoly. No revenue can arise from it, but in consequence of its violation and of the forfeiture of the prohibited goods. Instead of encouraging, it commonly prevents the improvement and extension of the branch of industry it is meant to promote. Dutch cured Herrings cannot be imported upon forfeiture of Ship and cargo. They are, however, vastly superior to British cured you can scarce imagine the difference. The price of a barrel of british cured Herrings is about a guinea and that of the Dutch, I imagine, is nearly the same. Instead of the prohibition, lay a tax of half a guinea a barrel upon dutch Herrings. Dutch Herrings will, in this case, sell in great Britain at S. 33 or Sh 34 Shillings, a circumstance which will confine them altogether to the tables of the better sort of people. The British curers will immediately endeavour to get this high price, and by superior care and cleanliness to raise their goods to an equality with the Dutch, and this emulation will, probably, in five or six years time raise the manufacture to a degree of improvement, which at present I despair of its attaining to in fifty or Sixty years. Our fisheries may then rival the Dutch in forreign Markets, where at present they cannot come into competition with them, and the manufacture may not only be much improved, but greatly extended. Prohibitions do not prevent the importation of the prohibited goods. They are bought everywhere, in the fair way of trade, by people who are not in the least aware that they are buying them. About a week after I was made a Commissioner of the Customs,[4] upon looking over the list of prohibited goods, (which is hung up in every Customhouse and which is well worth your considering) and upon examining my own wearing apparel, I found, to my great astonishment, that I had scarce a stock,

---

[3] The strength of the views expressed in this letter about bounties and prohibitions is reflected in the additions Smith made to WN ed. 3 (1784) concerning the absurdity of restrictions on trade with France, the herring fishing bounty, and the corn bounty; see the note to Letter 222 addressed to Cadell, dated 7 Dec. 1782; also WN IV.v.a. 29–31.

[4] Smith was appointed a Commissioner of Customs for Scotland in Jan. 1778.

a cravat, a pair of ruffles, or a pocket handkerchief which was not prohibited to be worn or used in Great Britain. I wished to set an example and burnt them all. I will not advise you to examine either your own or Mrs. Edens apparel or household furniture, least you be brought into a scrape of the same kind. The sole effect of a prohibition is to hinder the revenue from profiting by the importation. All those high duties, which make it scarce possible to trade fairly in the goods upon which they are imposed, are equally hurtful to the revenue and equally favourable to smuggling, as absolute prohibitions. It is difficult to say what such a repeal of all prohibitions and of such exorbitant duties as are scarce ever fairly paid, might produce. I imagine it would produce a still greater sum than the repeal of all bounties; provided a reasonable tax was always substituted in the room both of the exorbitant tax and of the prohibition.[5]

The third is a repeal of the prohibition of exporting wool and a substitution of a pretty high duty in the room of it. The Price of wool is now lower than in the time of Edward III; because now it is confined to the market of Great Britain; whereas then the market of the world was open to it. The low price of wool tends to debase the [qua]lity[6] of the commodity, and may thus hurt the woollen manufacture in one way, as much as it may benefit it in another. By this prohibition, besides, the interest of the [grower] is evidently sacrificed to the interest of the manufacturer. A real tax is laid upon the one for the benefit of the other. In old times a duty upon the exportation of wool was the most important branch of the Custom.

I heartily congratulate you upon the unexpected good temper of Ireland. I trust in God that Administrators will be wise and steady enough not to disappoint the people in any one thing they have given them reason to expect. Give them as much more as you will, but never throw out a single hint that you wish to give them anything less. Remember me to all friends and believe me to be, with great esteem and regard,

Dear Sir, Most entirely yours
Adam Smith

204. *To* HENRY MACKENZIE[1]

Address: Mr Mackinzie *MS.*, Columbia University Libr., unpubl.

Edinburgh, Tuesday 23 May 1780

Dear Sir

I have read with great attention twice over the two draughts of the

---

[5] See Appendix D, comment on No. 11.   [6] Torn MS.

[1] Henry Mackenzie (1745–1831) novelist and essayist; Attorney for the Crown in Scotland; edited *The Mirror* 1779–80, and *The Lounger* 1785–7.

mirror.² The first appears to me by much the best. The objection of its being too humble does not strike me as well founded. It is at least ten times more interesting than the second, where there seems to be too much general talk which, tho it relates to the mirror, is not directly applied to it till the end of the paper, and, in the reading, appears on that account much flatter and colder. The observations are, in other respects, perfectly just and proper in both. I have taken the liberty to make a few marginal remarks upon the language of both; they are of no great consequence whether adopted or rejected. I ever am

Dear Sir
Most faithfully yours
Adam Smith

205. *To* JOHN DAVIDSON

Address: Mr Davidson, Castle Hill
MS., EUL, La. ii. 191; unpubl.

Custom-house, Edinburgh, 5 July 1780

Dear Sir
   I send you the Duke of Buccleughs discharge which you may send back if payment is not perfectly convenient.¹ I ever am

Dear Sir, most faithfully yours
Adam Smith

206. *To* [THOMAS CADELL]

MS., Yale University Libr., unpubl.

Canongate, Edinburgh, 25 Oct. [1780]¹

Dear Sir
   May I beg the favour of you, immediately after receiving this letter to send three copies of the second edition of My book concerning the Wealth of nations to Mr Peter Anker, Consul General of Denmark;² writing upon the blank leaf of one of them to Mr Anker from the Authour; of another,

   ² Most likely Mackenzie submitted to Smith drafts of the farewell retrospect of the editor of *The Mirror* (iii, No. 110, Sat. 27 May 1780), in which he comments on the intentions and performance of the small circle of contributors to the periodical.

   ¹ Presumably refers to the payment of Smith's pension from the Duke.

   ¹ The year '1760' at the end of the letter is an error, for it obviously belongs with the Letters 208 and 209, dated 26 Oct. 1780 and addressed to Holt and Anker.
   ² Karsten and Peter Anker (1744–1832), sons of a Norwegian timber merchant, travelled to Britain in 1760, and were in Glasgow in 1762 when they met Adam Smith. They were in his company again in Toulouse in 1764 when he was writing WN.

To Mr Holt[3] from the Authour, and of the third to Mr Dreby[4] from the Authour. Mr Dreby has lately translated me into Danish[5] These copies must be handsomely bound and Guilded. I am afraid I am not only your best, but almost your only customer for this second Edition. Let me know, however, how this matter goes on.

So long ago as the year 1767, sometime in the month of march, a few days before I left London, I bought of you a copy of Andersons History of Commerce.[6] You happened not to have it in your own shop but you procured it for me from some of your Neighbours. In this copy I lately discovered an Imperfection of which John Balfour wrote to you sometime ago. If you could get this imperfection supplied, you would oblige me greatly. I ever am Dear Sir

Most faithfully and
affectionately yours
Adam Smith

207. *To* [WILLIAM STRAHAN]

MS., Boston Public Libr., Virginia and Richard Ehrlich Autograph Coll.; Rae 357–8.

Canongate, Edinburgh, 26 Oct. 1780

Dear Sir:

I think it is predestined that I shall never write a letter to you; except to ask some favour of you, or to put you to some trouble. This letter is not to depart from the style of all the rest. I am a subscriber for Watts copying machine.[1] The price is six Guineas for the machine and five Shillings for the packing box; I should be glad too [if] he would send me a ream of the copying Paper, together with all the other specimens of Ink etc. which

---

[3] Andreas Holt (1729–84), tutor to the Ankers, then Danish civil servant, head of the Norwegian Secretariat of the Economic and Trade Department, and finally a State Councillor.

[4] Frants Dræbye (1740–1814), tutor to the sons of a Norwegian merchant, James Collett, visited England with them 1773–6; trans. WN into Danish when he was head of the Norwegian Secretariat of the Economic and Trade Department in succession to Holt. The Ankers and Holt probably persuaded him to do the translating.

[5] *Undersøgelser om National-Volstands Natur og Aarsag af Doctor Adam Smith . . .* Af det Engelske oversat og med nogle anmærkninger oplyst af F. Dræbye (Copenhagen, 1779–80). To the second volume was added Gov. Pownall's letter of 1776.

[6] See Letter 102 addressed to Cadell, dated 25 Mar. 1767.

[1] One of the remarkable inventions of James Watt (1736–1819), a device as universally employed as his more familiar mechanical productions. Patented 14 Feb. 1780, the duplicator employed a specially prepared ink impressed on a damp sheet of paper to produce a facsimile. Smith had known Watt since 1757, when the latter was appointed mathematical instrument-maker to Glasgow University. It was in his workshop there that Watt repaired the Newcomen steam engine in 1764, leading to his own discoveries in that field of technology.

commonly accompany the Machine. For payment of this to Mr Wood-
mason, the seller, whose printed letter I have enclosed, you will herewith
receive a bill of eight Guineas payable at sight. If after paying for all this
there should be any remnant, there is a taylour in Craven Street, one
Heddington, an acquaintance of James McPherson to whom I owe some
shillings, I believe under ten, certainly under twenty, pay him what I owe.
He is a very honest man and will ask no more than is due. Before I left
London I had sent several times for his account, but he always put it off.

I had almost forgot I was the Author of the enquiry concerning the
Wealth of Nations; but some time ago I received a letter from a friend in
Denmark telling me that it had been translated into Danish by one Mr
Dreby, Secretary to a new erected board of trade and Oeconomy in that
Kingdom.[2] My correspondent, Mr Holt, who is an assessor of that Board,
desires in the name of Mr Dreby, to know what alterations I propose to
make in a second Edition. The shortest answer to this is to send them the
second Edition. I propose, therefore, by this Post to desire Mr Cadell to
send three copies of the second edition, handsomely bound and gilt, to
Mr Anker, Consul General of Denmark, who is an old acquaintance, one
for himself, and the other two to be by him transmitted to Mr Holt, and
Mr Dreby. At our final settlement I shall debit myself with these three
Books. I suspect I am now almost your only customer for my own book.
Let me know however how matters go on in this respect.

After begging your pardon a thousand times for having so long neglected
to write to you, I shall conclude with assuring you that notwithstanding
this neglect, I have the highest respect, and esteem for you and for your
whole family and that I am

Most Sincerely
and affectionately
ever yours
Adam Smith

208. *To* [ANDREAS HOLT, Commissioner of the Danish Board of
Trade and Economy]

MS., GUL Gen. 1035/133 (copy letter, unsigned); Scott 281–4.

[Edinburgh, 26 Oct. 1780]

Dear Sir

I am ashamed of having delayed so long to answer your very obliging
letter;[1] but I am occupied four days in every Week at the Custom House;

---

[2] See Letter 206 to Cadell, dated 25 Oct. 1780; also Letter 208 to Holt and Letter
209 to Anker, both dated 26 Oct. 1780.

[1] Not traced.

during which it is impossible to sit down seriously to any other business: during the other three days too, I am liable to be frequently interrupted by the extraordinary duties of my office, as well as by my own private affairs, and the common duties of society.

It gives me the greatest pleasure to hear that Mr Dreby has done me the distinguished honour of translating my Book into the Danish language.[2] I beg you will present to him my most sincere thanks and most respectful Compliments. I am much concerned that I cannot have the pleasure of reading it in his translation, as I am so unfortunate as not to understand the Danish language.

I Published more than two years ago a second edition of the inquiry concerning the Wealth of Nations, in which though I have made no material alteration, I have made a good number of corrections, none of which, however, affect even in the slightest degree, the general principles, or Plan of the System. I have by this Post directed Mr Cadell, to deliver two copies of this second edition, to your friend and pupil Mr Anker, of whom I have taken the liberty to ask the favour, of transmitting them by the first convenient opportunity to you. I hope you will be so good as to accept of one of them for yourself and present the other in my name to Mr Dreby.

I do not pretend that this second edition though a good deal more correct that the first, is entirely exempted from all errors. I have myself discovered several inaccurasies. The most considerable is in Vol. 2. page 482 where I say 'In England for example, when by the land-tax, every other sort of revenue was supposed to be assessed at four shillings in the pound, it was very popular to lay a real tax of five shillings in the pound upon the salaries of offices which exceeded a hundred pounds a year, those of the Judges and a few others less obnoxious to envy excepted.'[3] The tax upon such salaries amounts, not to five shillings only, but to five and six pence in the pound; and the salaries of Judges are not exempted from it. The only salaries exempted are the pensions of the younger branches of the Royal family, and the pay of the Officers of the army and Navy. This blunder which so far as I know is the grossest in the whole Book, and which arose from trusting too much to memory, does not in the least affect the reasoning, or conclusion which it was brought to support.

I have not thought it proper to make any direct answer to any of my adversaries. In the second edition I flattered myself that I had obviated all the objections of Governor Pownal.[4] I find however, he is by no means satisfied, and as Authors are not much disposed to alter the opinions they have once published, I am not much surprized at it.

---

[2] See Letter 206, n. 5. [3] WN V.ii.i.7 (conclusion).

[4] See Letter 174 from Pownall, dated 15 Sept. 1776 (Appendix A), and Smith's reply, Letter 182, dated 19 Jan. 1777.

The anonymous author of a pamphlet concerning national defense, who I have been told is a Gentleman of the name of Douglas, has Written against Me. When he Wrote his book, he had not read mine to the end. He fancies that because I insist that a Militia is in all cases inferior to a well regulated and well disciplined standing Army, that I disapprove of Militias altogether. With regard to that subject, he and I happened to be precisly of the same opinion. This Gentleman, if I am rightly informed of his name, is a man of parts and one of my acquaintance, so that I was a little surprized at his attack upon Me, and still more at the mode of it.[5]

A very diligent, laborious, honest Man of the name of Anderson, has published a large quarto volume concerning improvements; in this volume he has done me the honour to employ a very long chapter in answering my objections to the bounty upon the exportation of Corn.[6] In volume second page 101 of the first edition, I happened to say that the nature of things had stamped a real value upon Corn which no human institution can alter. The expression was certainly too strong, and had escaped me in the heat of Writing. I ought to have said that the nature of things had stamped upon corn a real value which could not be altered merely by altering its Money price. This was all that the argument required, and all that I really meant. Mr Anderson takes advantage of this hasty expression, and triumphs very much by showing that in several other parts of my Work I had acknowledged that whatever lowered the real price of manu-factur'd produce, rais'd the price of rude produce, and consequently of corn. In the second edition I have corrected this careless expression, which I apprehend takes away the foundation of the whole argument of Mr Anderson.[7]

It is not worth while to take notice even to you of the innumerable squibs thrown out upon me in the newspapers. I have however, upon the whole been much less abused than I had reason to expect; so that in this respect I think myself rather lucky than otherwise. A single, and as, I thought a very harmless Sheet of paper, which I happened to Write concerning the death of our late friend Mr Hume,[8] brought upon me ten times more abuse than the very violent attack I had made upon the whole commercial system of Great Britain. So much for what relates to my Book.

[5] *A Letter from a Gentleman in Edinburgh to his Grace the Duke of Buccleugh on National Defence, with some Remarks on Dr Smith's Chapter on that Subject in his Book, entitled 'An Enquiry into the Nature and Causes of the Wealth of Nations'* (London, 1778). The initials 'M.T.' appear at the end of the preface; see WN V.i.a. 23, 27.

[6] James Anderson, *Observations on the Means of Exciting a Spirit of National Industry* (London, 1777); WN IV.v. 4–25, also V.ii.k. 13.

[7] See WN IV.v.a.23. Ed. 2 reads 'The nature of things has stamped upon corn a real value which cannot be altered by merely altering its money price'. Pownall in his *Letter* notices a similarity between Smith's arguments about the corn bounty and those of Necker in *Sur la législation et le commerce des grains* (1775); see Appendix A, pp. 361–6.

[8] Letter 178 dated 9 Nov. 1776, addressed to William Strahan.

I was much intertained with the account which you was so good as [to] send me of your travels into Iceland,[9] and of the different situation you have been in since I had the pleasure of seeing you in France,[10] and was Very happy to find in the end that you had obtained so comfortable and honourable an establishment at Copenhagen. The revolution in the administration of your Government, which you mention, I always believed to have been conducted with great prudence and moderation, and to have been indispensibly necessary for the preservation of the State.[11] It gives me great pleasure to hear the agreeable accounts which you give me of the young Prince and of the very proper manner in which he is educated. Since I had the pleasure of seeing you, my own life has been extremely uniform.[12] Upon my return to Britain I retired to a small Town in Scotland the place of my nativity, where I continued to live for six years in great tranquillity, and almost in complete retirement. During this time I amused myself principally with writing my Enquiry concerning the Wealth of Nations, in studying Botany (in which however I made no great progress) as well as some other sciences to which I had never given much attention before. In the Spring of 1773 a proposal, which many of my friends thought very advantageous was made to me to go abroad a second time.[13] The discussion of this proposal obliged me to go to London, where the Duke of Buccleugh was so good as to disuade [me] from accepting it. For four years after this London was my principal residence, where I finished and published my Book. I had returned to my old retirement at Kirkaldy and was employing myself in writing another Work concerning the imitative arts,[14] when by the interest of the Duke of Buccleugh, I was appointed to my present Office; which though it requires a good deal of attendance is both easy and honourable, and for my Way of living sufficiently beneficial. Upon my appointment I proposed to surrender the annuity which had been settled upon me by the Tutors of the Duke of Buccleugh, before I went abroad with him, and which had been renewed by his Grace after he became of age, as a thing for which I had no farther occasion. But his Grace sent me word by his Cashier, to whom I had offered to deliver up his bond, that though I had considered what was fit for my own honour, I had not consider'd what was fit for his; and that he never would suffer it to be suspected that he had procured an office for his friend, in order

---

[9] Holt was overlandskommissær there. [10] They met at Toulouse in 1764.

[11] A coup d'état in 1772 resulted in the exile of Queen Caroline Mathilde; the execution of her lover, Struensee, a German physician who had become Prime Minister after dominating King Christian VII from 1768; and the restoration of Danish leadership.

[12] This para. presents a brief autobiography of the years 1766–80. The account of how Smith became a Commissioner of Customs is to be compared with his letters of Dec. 1777–Feb. 1778.

[13] As travelling tutor to the Duke of Hamilton.

[14] EPS, 'Of the Nature of that Imitation which takes place in what are called the Imitative Arts'.

to relieve himself from the burden of such an annuity. My present situation is therefore fully as affluent as I could wish it to be. The only thing I regret in it is the interruptions to my literary pursuits, which the duties of my office necessarily occasion. Several Works which I had projected are likely to go on much more slowly than they otherwise would have done. Wishing you every sort of happiness and prosperity, I have the honour to be with the highest respect and esteem

Dear Sir your most affectionate
humble Servant

209. *To* [PETER ANKER, Consul General of Denmark in Great Britain]

MS., GUL Gen. 1035/133 (copy letter, unsigned); Scott 280–1.

[Edinburgh, 26 Oct. 1780]

Dear Sir,

It gave me very great pleasure to find that I had not been altogether forgotten, either by you, or by your valuable friend Mr Holt. I can plead no other excuse for having delayed so very long to answer your very obliging letter,[1] except the great number of occupations in which I am necessarily involved by the duties of my Office and by my own private affairs. I did not chuse to answer your letter till I had answer'd Mr Holts.[2] which required more time than I have commonly to spare. I have at last taken the liberty to inclose to you my answer to his letter which I must beg the favour of you to transmitte to him.

I have likewise taken the liberty to desire Mr Cadell to deliver to you, three copies of the second edition of my Book; I hope you will be so good as [to] accept of one of them as a memorandum of old friendship and transmitte the other two to Mr Holt, the one as a memorandum of the same kind to him, the other as a present to Mr Dreby who has done me the honour to translate my Book into your language.

It gives me great pleasure to hear from you that the arm'd Neutrality of the northern powers, does not mean to be hostile to Great Britain.[3] Notwithstanding, however, the very high respect which I have for your authority, I must acknowledge that I dread a great deal from it, and hope very little. But whatever alterations may happen in the dispositions of our

[1] Not traced; possibly these letters gave news of Dræbye's trans. of WN; see Letter 206 addressed to Cadell, dated 25 Oct. 1780.

[2] Letter 208, dated 26 Oct. 1780.

[3] On 9 July 1780, Denmark and Russia signed a treaty declaring 'armed neutrality' in the face of the British Navy's enforcement of a policy of searching neutral vessels for arms and supplies for France and the former American colonies. The treaty was joined by Sweden and Prussia but proved of little value. The principles were reasserted, however, in 1797, in another treaty between Denmark, Norway, and Sweden, and this led to the battle of Copenhagen, 1801.

respective Nations towards one another, I trust no alterations will ever happen in those of our private friendship. I have the honour to be with the highest respect and esteem

Dear Sir, Your Most affectionate
humble Servant

P.S. I am not sure if my address to Mr Holt at Copenhagen is sufficiently distinct. After sealing the letter you will be so good as to supply what is defective.

Copies Letters to Messrs Holt and Anker[4] October 26 1780[4]

210. *From* THE DUKE OF BUCCLEUCH

Address: Adam Smith Esqr. Custom House, Edinburgh
MS., GUL Gen. 1035/159; unpubl.

Bath, 26 Nov. 1780

My Dear Sir

I am now within two Stages of Bath, expecting that the Waters are to strengthen my stomach which is already better than when I left Scotland. The Advocate[1] will explain to you what is to be done about the vacant place at your Board, he will inform you that Nelthrope[2] has some chance of being removed but in what way I do not know. I think Gala[3] might be provided for in a better way, and more suited to his abilities. When I say 'better' I do not mean, more honorable or lucrative than what you proposed. London is quite dull and quiet at present, but you may expect violent Storms after Xmas, if the opposing Parties can unite and agree, at present I believe they cannot. All my family are well.

I am yours Sincerely
Buccleugh

211. *From* SAMUEL CHARTERS

MS., GUL Gen. 1035/160; unpubl.

Calcutta, 30 Nov. 1780

[A letter from Samuel Charters, addressed Calcutta, in which he gives Smith an account of neglect and injuries he has received in the service of the East India Company. No doubt he hoped Smith would intercede for him with Alexander Wedderburn.]

---

[4] Date added in a later hand.

[1] Henry Dundas.
[2] William Nelthorp, up to this time one of the Commissioners of Customs. His name does not appear on later board documents, e.g. that of 19 Dec. 1780, SRO GD 24/1/591, to Lord Kames, so it is likely that he was removed.
[3] Not traced.

212. *To* THOMAS CADELL

New York Evening Post 30 Apr. 1887; Rae 361.

[Edinburgh, 1780]

Dear Sir

Mrs Ross of Crighton,[1] now living in Welbeck Street is my particular friend, and the wife of Lieutenant-Collonel Patrick Ross, in the service of the East India Company, my very near relation. When she left this [? place] she seemed to intimate that she wished to have a copy of my last book from the author. May I therefore beg the favour of you to send her a copy of both my books, viz. of the Theory of Moral Sentiments and of the Enquiry concerning the 'Wealth of Nations', handsomely bound and gilt, placing the same to my account, and writing upon the blank-leaf of each, *From the Author*. Be so good as to remember me to Mrs Cadell, Mr Strahan and family, and all other friends, and believe me, ever yours,

Adam Smith

213. *From* THE MARQUIS DE BOMBELLES[1]

Address; To Adam Smith Esq; Kircaldy near Edinburgh
MS., GUL Gen. 1035/161; unpubl.

Rue pot de fer, [? Paris,] le 18 Juin 1781

My dear friend

Il y a bien longtems que nous n'avons Entendu parler l'un de l'autre. C'est depuis l'arrivee du Mr Gibbon icy, il y a 4 ans. Vous paroissez rarement dans les newspapers parce que vos ouvrages ne Sont pas de Ceux qui naissent tous les ans. Moy on ne m'y voit Jamais. C'est Made la duchesse de Chabot, la fille de made la duchesse d'Enville qui m'engage a vous attaquer de Conversation aujourdhuy. Elle aprend l'anglois comme font toutes nos dames que vous trouverez, quand vous viendrez icy, qui le lisent passablement. Elle vous demande Si Il est vray que vous ayez donne une Edition complette de toutes vos oeuvres. Je n'entends pas trop ce que ce peut Etre. Je ne connois de vous que The theory of moral Sentiments et the Wealth of Nations. Et C'est bien assez voila pourquoy Il faut que Je m'adresse a vous pour le Savoir. Je n'ay pas eu de peine a me decider a Saisir cette occasion de me rappeler dans votre souvenir et de vous demander de vos nouvelles.[2]

---

[1] Mrs. Ross (d. 1803) was the wife of Smith's cousin, Patrick Ross.

[1] Marc Marie Bombelles (1744–1821), diplomat; emigré, fought with the royalists; took orders and became Bishop of Amiens after the restoration of the Bourbons.

[2] Smith arranged to have copies of WN ed. 3 (1784) sent to Bombelles and the La Rochefoucauld family; see Letter 241 addressed to Cadell, dated 16 Nov. 1784.

Donnez m'en Je vous prie un peu en detail.

Un homme de mes amis a la Haie a Ecrit quelques oeuvrages de meta-physique dans lesquels Il etablit lexistence dun Sens moral qui ressemble bien a votre Simpathee.³ Si vous etez curieux de les Connoitre, Je pourrai vous en faire passer un Exemplaire que Jay a ma disposition.

Comment reussissent les deux derniers volumes du Mr Gibbon⁴ Je vois des gens qui Craignent qu'il ne les ait pas autant travaillés que le premier, qu'il ne laisse Echapper un peu trop d'empressement de parler de la Religion Et un peu plus de Galanterie ou d'Occupation des femmes quil ne Convient a la Gravité de l'Histoire Et surtout d'une histoire aussi belle aussi profonde et aussi Savante que la Sienne.

Adieu my dear friend Reconnoitrez vous la main dun homme qui vous est bien sincerement attaché.

Ne trouvez vous pas que nous avons fait un pas vers la civilisation lorsque dans une guerre comme celle cy,⁵ nous avons la liberté de corres-pondre ensemble Et qui plus Est, celle daller Les uns chez les autres. Il y a icy beaucoup d'Anglois. Ils y viennent tant quils voulent.

214. *To* JAMES HUNTER BLAIR¹

Address: James Hunter Blair Esqr, George's Street, Edinburgh
MS., SRO Blairquhan Muniments; unpubl.

Custom-house Edinburgh, 29 Oct. 1781

Dear Sir,

I am extremely sorry that it is [not] in my power to wait upon [you] at dinner today. I had all yesterday a very disagreable pain in my stomach, and in addition I have got this day a pain in my side. I am afraid an Election dinner² is not the proper remedy for these complaints. I most sincerely congratulate you and ever am

Dear Sir
Most faithfully
Yours
Adam Smith

---

³ Not traced.
⁴ Vols. ii and iii were published 1 May 1781. The offensive chapters about religion were 15 and 16 which concluded vol. i (published 17 Feb. 1776). Gibbon was at work on vol. iv from 1 Mar. 1782 to June 1784.
⁵ War broke out between Britain and France, together with her ally Spain, in 1778.

¹ James Hunter Blair (1741–87) of Dunsky, Wigtown; banker, partner of Sir William Forbes (see the latter's *Memoirs of a Banking-House*, 1803); M.P. for Edinburgh 1781–4; Ld. Provost of Edinburgh 1784–6; noted for his extensive knowledge of the trade and manufactures of Scotland.
² Blair was elected M.P. the day the letter was written.

215. *From* HENRY MACKENZIE

Address: Adam Smith Esqr., No. 27. Suffolk Street, Charing Cross, London
MS., GUL Gen. 1035/162; Scott 284-5.

Edinburgh, 7 June 1782

Dear Sir

The inclosed Letter[1] will serve as my Apology, and explain the Reason, for my troubling you once more with a Letter. It happens whimsically enough, that it should be on a similar Subject with my last.[1] This second Application I could not well avoid, without giving some Offence to a Man[2] whose Genius, as well as the Warmth and Goodness of his Heart, I respect, and who being of the 'Genus irritabile vatum'[3] is I am afraid, somewhat easily offended.

He left his *Runnamede* two Days with me; I gave it such a Perusal as the Leisure of those two Days would allow, sufficient to judge of it's general Effect on my Feelings, but by no means equal to the forming any critical opinion upon it. I offerd however to the Author, when he called again for his Tragedy, some Observations I had made on the leading Incidents of the Piece, some of which I thought faulty; on the other hand I gave the Commendation I thought they merited to certain Passages, and added in general that if it were now to be brought on the Stage, the Spirit of Liberty it breath'd might catch an Audience, and that some of the Declamation of it, which, critically speaking, I might find fault with, was such as I had seen procure loud Applause in an English Theatre. These were the Observations which produced the inclosed Letter from Mr Logan, which I take the Liberty of sending to you, to save a long Narrative which would be awkward to me, and possibly not very intelligible to you. My Opinion of it (which Mr Logan does me the honor of supposing might have some Influence with you) is nearly as above, allowing for that Delicacy which the 'sturdiest Moralist'[4] must temper his Truth with, in speaking to an Author of his Works.

[1] Not traced.

[2] John Logan (1748–88), poet, pamphleteer, and historical writer. He was educated for the ministry of the Church of Scotland and during his college days was a friend of a young poet, Michael Bruce (1746–67). Logan edited and published Bruce's poems in 1770, and eleven years later published his own poems, but was accused by Bruce's relatives of having issued as his own work poems by Bruce. The accusation was directed chiefly at an ode, 'To the Cuckoo', which excited contemporary interest. From 1779 to 1781, Logan gave lectures on history at Edinburgh, and he published an analysis of these: *Elements of the Philosophy of History* (1783). A tragedy, *Runnamede*, containing advanced political views, was produced at Edinburgh in 1783. His metrical paraphrases found much acceptance in Scotland (and still do), but he was driven from his charge at Leith as a result of scandalous allegations about his publishing ventures, and thereafter he went to London. Undoubtedly able, Logan could not resist finessing about his publishing ventures: see Letter 273 addressed to Smith, dated 20 Aug. 1787.

[3] Horace, *Epistles*, ii. 2, l. 102.

[4] An echo from Johnson's gibe at the Scottish reception of the Ossian fabrications of

I hope your former Indisposition has been long quite removed, and that you have escaped the Influenza, which has raged in London and now begins to rage here. About 240 of the S. [Southern] Fencibles are down with it.[5] Our weather, however, is now milder, and I hope may blunt it's Effects with us.

> I am Dear Sir,
> With the greatest Regard,
> Your most obedient Servant
> Henry Mackenzie

216. *To* EDMUND BURKE

Address: The Honble Edmund Burke Esqr., Pay Office[1]
MS., Sheffield City Librs.; *Burke Corr.* v.3.

London, Monday 1 July 1782

My dear friend

I cannot avoid writing you a few lines to tell you how deeply I feel your affliction.[2] I hope and trust that you will exert your usual firmness and that your friends and you will immediately plight unalterable faith to one another, and with unanimous consent chuse a leader whose virtues may command the same confidence with that which you all had in the worthy man whom it has pleased God to take from you.[3] When I first heard of the misfortune my first movement was to run to your house; but I restrained myself for fear of disturbing your sorrow. I am ever yours

> Adam Smith

James Macpherson: 'A Scotchman must be a very sturdy moralist, who does not love *Scotland* better than the truth' (*A Journey to the Western Islands*, 1775).

[5] In London on 29 May, Gibbon described the 'present influenza' as a 'plague' (*Letters*, ii. 296), and under 2 June the *Gentleman's Magazine* noted its ravages among sailors at naval stations (LII, 1782, p. 306).

[1] As Paymaster General, Burke had an office in Whitehall which he vacated on 17 July after resigning (*Burke Corr.* v. 18–19, 21).

[2] The Prime Minister, 2nd Marquis of Rockingham, died at noon on 1 July. He was head of the Administration that succeeded North's, in March 1782, with a view to concluding peace with the Americans.

[3] Smith no doubt hoped Burke would rally Rockingham's followers, e.g. Charles James Fox and Lord John Cavendish, to the side of Shelburne, then Secretary of State for Home Affairs. Shelburne did become Prime Minister, but Burke saw this as 'a sore, a very sore tryal' (*Burke Corr.* v. 20). Such was the suspicion of Shelburne that Burke, Fox, and Cavendish all resigned office.

217. *To* EDMUND BURKE

MS., Sheffield City Librs.; *Burke Corr.* v. 9–10.

London, 6 July 1782

My Dear Sir

I cannot go into the Post Chaise[1] without writing these few lines to you to tell you how much I approve and admire every part of your conduct, tho' I feel, perhaps, more than you do, for some of the effects of it.[2] *Tout est perdu horsmis l'honneur*, was the saying of Francis the first after the battle of Pavia,[3] and when honour is not only perfectly and compleatly saved, but acquired and augmented, all other losses are insignificant.

Remember me in the most respectful and affectionate manner to Mrs Burke and to your Brother.[4] I beg likewise to be remembered to My Lord John Cavendish[5] and to Mr Frederick Montagu.[6] I called yesterday at the Door of the former to return him my most sincere thanks for his politeness and attention. It must afflict every good citizen that any circumstance should occur which could make men of their probity, prudence and moderation judge it proper in these times to withdraw from the service of their country. Farewell, my Dear Friend; I hope we shall soon meet again even in this world in times of more joy and prosperity. I ever am

Most sincerely yours
Adam Smith

218. *To* ABBÉ BLAVET

[L'Abbé Blavet] *Recherches sur la nature et les causes de la richesses des nations*, xxv–xxvii (extract, Blavet's translation); Luigi Einaudi, *Saggi bibliografici e storici intorno alle dottrine economiche* (Rome, 1953), 80.

Edinburgh, 23 July 1782

Monsieur, mon respectable ami, Mr. Lumsden,[1] m'a fait l'honneur de me remettre votre lettre avec votre excellente traduction de mon ouvrage[2]

---

[1] To return to Scotland.   [2] See Smith's letter of 1 July, above (216).

[3] After the battle of Pavia (1525), Francis I is said to have written to his mother, 'nothing remains to me but honour and life.'

[4] Richard Burke (1733–94), a businessman.

[5] Lord John Cavendish (1732–96), uncle of the Duke of Devonshire; M.P. for York; had been Chancellor of the Exchequer under Rockingham.

[6] Frederick Montagu (1733–1800), M.P. for Higham Ferrers; resigned as a Lord of the Treasury July 1782, and opposed Shelburne's ministry.

[1] ?Andrew Lumsden (1720–1801), private secretary to Prince Charles Edward 1745; in exile in France and Rome till 1773; pardoned, 1778.

[2] Blavet's translation of WN was first sent in weekly instalments to the *Journal de l'agriculture, du commerce, des arts et des finances* (Jan. 1779–Dec. 1780). It was then printed as a book, both at Yverdon and Paris, in 1781. The Abbé Morellet, who had an unpublished translation on his hands, said 'poor Smith was traduced [by Blavet] rather than translated'. See David Murray, *French Translations of the Wealth of Nations* (Glasgow, 1905), 4–5.

dans le dernier séjour que j'ai fait à Londres, où j'ai été si occupé de différentes affaires, que je n'ai pas eu le tems ni le loisir de vous remercier de la grande faveur, ainsi que de l'honneur que vous m'avez fait. Je suis charmé de cette traduction et vous m'avez rendu le plus grand service qu'on puisse rendre à un auteur, en faisant connaître mon livre à la nation de l'Europe dont je considère le plus le gout et le jugement. J'étais fort content de votre traduction de mon premier ouvrage; mais je le suis encore plus de la manière dont vous avez rendu ce dernier. Je puis vous dire, sans flatterie, que par-tout où j'ai jeté les yeus dessus, (car comme il n'y a que peu de jours que je suis parti de Londres, je n'ai pas encore eu le tems de la lire en entier) je l'ai trouvée, à tous égards, parfaitement égale à l'original.

Quelques jours après avoir quitté Londres, j'ai reçu une lettre d'un gentilhomme qui est à Bordeaux. Il s'appelle le comte de Nort,[3] et il est colonel d'infanterie au service de France. Il me mande qu'il a traduit mon livre en français et qu'il se propose de venir à Ecosse pour soumettre sa traduction a mon jugement avant de la publier. Je lui écrirai par le prochain courier que je suis si satisfait de la votre, et que je vous ai personnellement tant d'obligation, que je ne puis encourager ni en favoriser aucune autre.

219. *To* CHARLES McKINNON OF McKINNON[1]

Address: Charles McKinnon Esqr, of McKinnon, Kilmorie, Skye
MS., BM Add. MSS. 5035; Rae 380–1.

Custom-house, Edinburgh, 21 Aug. 1782
Dear Sir
I received your favour of the thirteenth of this month and am under some concern to be obliged to tell you that I am not only not yet out of the press, but that I have not yet gone into it; and would most earnestly once more recommend it to your consideration whether upon this occasion we should go into it at all. It was but within these few days that I could obtain a meeting with Mr McKinzie who was occupied with the Exchequer Business.[2] I found he had seen your Papers before and was of the same opinion with me, that in their present condition they would not do you the honour we wish you to derive from whatever work you publish. We read them over together with great care and attention, and we both continued of our first opinion. I hope you will pardon me, if I take the liberty to tell you that I cannot discover in them those original ideas which you seem to

---

[3] Not traced.

[1] Charles Mackinnon of Mackinnon, Chief of Clan, had composed a treatise on fortification which he wished to have published. To this end he sent £5 to Smith to cover expenses, but Smith wanted him to abandon the whole idea of publication.

[2] Henry Mackenzie, the novelist.

suppose that they contain. I am not very certain whether I understand what you hint obscurely in your former letter; but it seems to me as if you had some fear that some person might anticipate you and claim the merit of your discoveries by publishing them as his own. From the Characters of the Gentlemen to whom your Papers have been communicated, I should hope there is no danger of this. But to prevent the Possibility of the Public being imposed upon in this manner, your Papers now lie sealed up in my writing Desk, superscribed with directions to my Executors[3] to return them unopened to you or your heirs as their proper owners. In case of my Death and that of McKinzie the production of these papers under my seal and superscribed by my hand will be sufficient to refute any plagiarism of this kind. While we live our evidence will secure to you the reputation of whatever discoveries may be contained in them. I return you the five Pound note in hopes that you will not insist upon this publication at least for some time; at any rate I shall always be happy to advance a larger sum upon your account, tho I own, I could wish it was for some other purpose. I have not shown your Papers to Smellie.[4] It will give me great pleasure to hear from you and to be informed that you forgive the freedom I have used in offering you, I am afraid, a disagreable advice. I can assure you that nothing but the respect which, I think, I owe to the character of a person whom I know to be a man of worth, delicacy and honour could have extorted it from me. I ever am

Dear Sir, most faithfully yours
Adam Smith

If you should not chuse that your papers should remain in my custody, I shall either send them to you, or deliver to whom you please.

220. *To* [Unknown Correspondent]

Caxton Head Catalogue: excerpt quoted, Scott 103.

Sept. 1782

[To a recommendation made to Adam Smith, when Commissioner of Customs of a person for the post of boatman, he replied that he refused to support him, for] he was a shortsighted land-lubber.[1]

---

[3] Drs. John Black and James Hutton.
[4] William Smellie (1740–95), printer, naturalist, and antiquary; edited and contributed to ed. 1 of *Encyclopoedia Britannica*, 1771; wrote a brief life of Smith.

[1] The applicant was John Greig, and the tide surveyor at Newburgh reported he was unfitted for the post; see Appendix D under correspondence of Aug.–Oct. 1782.

221. *To* JOHN SINCLAIR OF ULBSTER

Sinclair Corr., i. 389–90; Rae 382–3.

Custom-House, Edinburgh, 14 Oct. 1782

My Dear Sir,

I have read your pamphlet several times over, with great pleasure, and am very much pleased with the style and composition.[1] As to what effect it might produce, if translated, upon the Powers concerned in the armed neutrality,[2] I am a little doubtful. It is too plainly partial to England. It proposes that the force of the armed neutrality should be employed in recovering to England the islands she has lost; and the compensation which it is proposed that England should give for this service, is the islands which they may conquer for themselves, with the assistance of England, indeed, from France and Spain. There seems to me, besides, to be some inconsistency in the argument. If it be just to emancipate the Continent of America from the dominion of every European power, how can it be just to subject the islands to such dominion? And if the monopoly of the trade of the Continent be contrary to the rights of mankind, how can that of the islands be agreeable to those rights? The real futility of all distant dominions, of which the defence is necessarily most expensive, and which contribute nothing, either by revenue or military force, to the general defence of the empire, and very little even to their own particular defence, is, I think, the subject upon which the public prejudices of Europe require most to be set right.[3] In order to defend the barren rock of Gibraltar, (to the possession of which we owe the union of France and Spain, contrary to the natural interests and inveterate prejudices of both countries, the important enmity of Spain, and the futile and expensive friendship of Portugal,) we have now left our own coasts defenceless, and sent out a great fleet, to which any considerable disaster may prove fatal to our domestic security; and which, in order to effectuate its purpose, must probably engage a fleet of superior force.[4] Sore eyes have made me delay writing to you so long. I ever am, my Dear Sir, your most faithful and affectionate humble servant,

Adam Smith

[1] *Thoughts on the Naval Strength of the British Empire*, Pt. II (London, 1782); published anonymously.

[2] Denmark, Russia, Sweden, and Prussia: see Letter 209 addressed to Peter Anker, dated 26 Oct. 1780.

[3] Cf. WN IV.vii.c.64.n.52. When Sinclair lamented to Smith the misfortunes of the American war, exclaiming: 'If we go on at this rate, the nation *must be ruined*,' Smith replied: 'Be assured, my young friend, that there is a great deal of *ruin* in a nation' (*Sinclair Corr.*, i. 390–1).

[4] The siege of Gibraltar lasted from 1780 to 1782 and severely strained British naval resources during the American war.

222. *To* THOMAS CADELL

Address: Mr Thomas Cadell, Bookseller, over against Catharine Street, Strand, London
MS., Hyde Collection, Four Oaks Farm, RFD 3, Somerville, New Jersey: Mrs. Donald F. Hyde; Rae 362.

Edinburgh, 7 Dec. 1782

Dear Sir

I have many apologies to make to you for my Idleness since I came to Scotland. The truth is, I bought at London a good many, partly new books, and partly either new editions of old books, or editions that were new to me; and the amusement I found in reading and diverting myself with them debauched me from my proper business; the preparing a new edition of the Wealth of nations. I am now, however, heartily engaged at my proper work and I hope in two or three months to send you up the second Edition corrected in many places, with three or four very considerable additions; chiefly to the second volume; among the rest is a short, but I flatter myself, a compleat History of all the trading companies in G. Britain. These Additions, I mean not only to be inserted at their proper places into the new edition, but to be printed separately and to be sold for a shilling, or half a Crown, to the purchasers of the old Edition.[1] The price must depend upon the bulk of the Additions when they are all written out. It would give me great satisfaction if you would let me know by the return of the Post if this delay will not be inconvenient. Remember me to Strahan. He will be so good as to excuse my not writing to him as I have nothing to

---

[1] Considerable differences exist between WN ed. 2 (1778) and ed. 3 (1784), The Advertisement to ed. 3 refers to 'additions . . . to the chapter on Drawbacks, and to that upon Bounties; likewise a new chapter entitled, The Conclusion of the Mercantile System; and a new article to the chapter upon the expences. In all these additions, *the present state of things* means always the state in which they were during the year 1783 and the beginning of the present year 1784.' The references to the additions are:

	6th Cannan ed. 1950	Glasgow WN
'Conclusion of the Mercantile System'	ii. 159–81	IV.viii
'of the Public Works . . .'	ii. 253–82	V.i.d–e
'absurdity of restrictions on trade with France'	i. 496–7; 521–2	IV.iii.a.1, IV.iii.c.12–13
on various drawbacks	ii. 3–7	IV.iv.3–11
herring fishing bounty	ii. 24–8	IV.v.a.28–37.
appendix on the same	ii. 487–9	Appendix
portion of discussion of effects of the corn bounty	ii. 13–14	IV.v.a.8–9

These passages and others were published on 20 Nov. 1784 as 'Additions and Corrections to the First and Second Editions of Dr Adam Smith's Inquiry into the Nature and Causes of the Wealth of Nations'. See Letter 223 from Cadell, dated 12 Dec. 1782, and Letter 227 addressed to William Strahan, dated 22 May 1783, also Letter 231 addressed to William Strahan, dated 6 Oct. 1783, and Glasgow WN 62–3.

say to him but what I have now said to you; and he knows my aversion to writing. I ever am

> Dear Sir
> Most faithfully yours
> Adam Smith

223. *From* THOMAS CADELL

MS., GUL Gen. 1035/164; Scott 286.

London, 12 Dec. 1782

Dear Sir

I was favoured with yours of the 7th[1] and communicated its contents to our Friend Strahan who desires his best Compliments. I am happy to hear you are preparing for a new Edition of the Wealth of Nations—the delay will I am afraid prevent our publishing this new Edition this Winter —We will however set about it as soon as we receive the Copy, and if we cannot get [it] in time to publish before the Town is empty we will postpone it to the meeting of Parliament in the ensuing Winter. I heartily approve of selling the Additions separate, but as they will be very valuable we must, if possible, prevent them being sold but to those who purchased the Book. I have nothing further to add but that I remain with great respect and regard, Dear Sir,

> Your obliged and
> affectionate Humble Servant
> Tho: Cadell

Will you be so obliging to let your Servant deliver the Inclosed to Dr Stedman.[2]

224. *To* JOHN DAVIDSON

Address: John Davidson Esqr, Castle Hill
MS., Columbia University Libr.; Scott 288.

Edinburgh, Tuesday, 25 Feb. 1783

Dear Sir

William Donald Landwaiter[1] doing duty at Greenock, but standing on the establishment at Port Glasgow is dead. Gabriel Millar will be presented

---

[1] Letter 222 addressed to Cadell, dated 7 Dec. 1782.
[2] Possibly Dr. John Stedman, physician and translator; author of *Physiological Essays* (1769); *Laelius and Hortensia; or, Thoughts on the Nature and Objects of Taste and Genius* (1782); *Moral Fables* (1784).

[1] Customs officer whose duty it was to superintend the landing of goods and to examine them.

by this nights post, But our presentation will be of little weight unless he is supported by better interest. I ever am etc

Adam Smith

225. *To* LADY FRANCES SCOTT

MS., SRO GD1/479/14; unpubl.

Edinburgh, 17 Mar. 1783

Mr Smith presents his most respectful compliments to Lady Frances Scot: is extremely obliged to her Ladyship for her attention in sending him his paper upon Italian and English Verse,[1] and will certainly not forget his promise to send her a more perfect copy as soon as he has compleated his plan: It will, however, be some time before he can set about it, as he is at present very much engaged in another business;[2] which it is not in his power to delay.

226. *To* EDMUND BURKE

MS., Sheffield City Librs.; *Burke Corr.* v. 86–7.

Custom-house, [Edinburgh,] 15 Apr. 1783

My Dear Friend

Nothing ever gave me more pleasure than to see your name in the last Gazette,[1] I never should have changed my opinion concerning the propriety of your conduct last summer,[2] whatever might have been the event of it; and, I dare to say, you would still less have changed your own. It gives me, however, great satisfaction to see, that what was so agreeable to the highest principles of honour may in the end prove not inconsistent with interest. Be so good as to remember me in the most respectful and most affectionate manner to Mrs Burke and to your Brother; and believe me to be, with the highest respect and esteem.

Dear Sir,
ever yours
Adam Smith

---

[1] 'Of the Affinity between certain English and Italian Verses'; MS. GUL Gen. 1035/226 (facsim. Scott 371–3); publ. posthumously in EPS (1795).
[2] Smith was at work on the additions to WN ed. 3; see Letter 227 addressed to William Strahan, dated 22 May 1783.

[1] Burke's appointment as Paymaster General was announced in the *London Gazette* 5–8 Apr.
[2] See Letter 216 addressed to Burke, dated 1 July 1782.

227. *To* WILLIAM STRAHAN

MS., Pennsylvania Historical Society; Scott 286–7.

Custom-house, Edinburgh, 22 May 1783

My Dear Strahan

I have for these several months been labouring[1] as hard as the continual interruption which my employment necessarily occasions, will allow me. I now only wait for some accounts which my friend Sir Grey Cooper was so good as to promise me from the treasury,[2] in order to compleat all the Additions which I propose to make to my third edition. This Edition will probably see me out and I should therefor chuse to leave it behind me as perfect as I can make it. The Principal additions are to the second Volume. Some new arguments against the corn bounty; against the Herring buss bounty; a new concluding Chapter upon the mercantile System; A short History and, I presume, a full exposition of the Absurdity and hurtfulness of almost all our chartered trading companies; I expect to be able to finish it in about a month after I receive the treasury accounts which are now preparing. I must correct the press myself and you must, therefor, frank me the sheets as they are printed. I would even rather than not correct it myself come up to London in the beginning of next winter and attend the Press myself. Remember me to Cadel, to Rose[3] and to Griffiths.[3] I long to have more dinners at the Packhorse. If you have any literary news, I should be glad to hear it. I should likewise be glad to know your judgement concerning the present state of our affairs. I ever am

My Dear friend
most affectionately
yours.
Adam Smith

228. *To* [SIR GREY COOPER]

MS., NLS 3278, fol. 56; Fay 38.

Custom-house, Edinburgh, 2 June 1783

My Dear Sir

I most sincerely congratulate you upon the new taxes,[1] which are in every respect as happily devised as any thing I ever saw. I acknowledge,

---

[1] On additions to WN ed. see Letter 222 addressed to Cadell, dated 7 Nov. 1782.
[2] Sir Grey Cooper had access to the bounty accounts as Secretary to the Treasury.
[3] William Rose and Ralph Griffiths: associates in publishing the *Monthly Review*.

[1] Lord John Cavendish, Chancellor of the Exchequer and Cooper's superior in the Treasury, introduced in the budget of 1782–3 a receipts tax which proved unpopular.

I had not the most distant idea that the stamp duties could have afforded such resources as My Lord John Cavendish had shewn that they can. I was extremely anxious about what might be the effect of opening this part of the budget; and tho' I had turned over in my mind the subject of our national resources with as much attention as I could, I must own that none occurred to me that would be so little burdensome to the People as these that have been fallen upon.

I forgot, I believe, in my last long and tiresome letter[2] to tell you how much I think myself obliged to you for ordering the accounts[3] I took the liberty to apply for. I ever am

Dear Sir
Your most obliged
and most affectionate
humble Servant
Adam Smith

I am very greatly obliged to you for your attention to my friend Mr Reid.[4]

229. *To* [EDWARD GIBBON]

MS., BM Add. MSS. 34,886, fol. 138; unpubl.

Custom-house, Edinburgh, 19 June 1783

Dear Sir

The principal purpose of this letter is to recommend to your notice a particular friend of Mine, Mr. Dalziel,[1] professor of Greek in this University, a Gentleman who has probably been sufficiently recommended to your attention already by Dr Robertson. He wished, however, that I should write to you likewise, and I promised to do so, but either from indolence or forgetfulness delayed it till this moment. You will find him, not only a very accurate and acute Grammarian, but in other respects a man of the greatest prudence and discretion, and as sensible and Judicious a man of Learning as any you have been acquainted with.

I would fain hope to have the pleasure of seeing you in London in the

---

[2] Not traced.
[3] Concerning bounties; see Letter 227 addressed to Strahan, dated 22 May 1783, n. 2.
[4] Smith's servant Robert Reid; see Letter 246 from Reid, dated 11 Sept. 1785.

[1] Andrew Dalziel (1742–1806), classical scholar; Professor of Greek at Edinburgh 1779–1805; corresponded with Heine; historian of his University; intimate friend of Smith whose accurate knowledge of Greek grammar and authors aroused his admiration (Rae 23).

course of next winter. Remember me to Sir Joshua[2] and believe me to be with the sincerest esteem and affection

Dear Sir, Most faithfully yours
Adam Smith

230. *From* EDMUND BURKE

MS., Lowell Autograph Coll., Houghton Libr., Harvard; *Burke Corr.* v. 98–9.

Horseguards, [London,] 20 June 1783

My dear Sir,

I received your very kind Letter of congratulations, on my return to Office.[1] I received your Condolence at my Departure from it.[2] In what state I am to be met with by your Sympathising Sentiments when you receive this, I know not. That such a friend, and such a man as you are, should take any concern in my fortunes is a Circumstance very flattering to me. I want some consolation I assure you—not with relation to such paltry affairs as mine, which I hope I do not rate a great deal above their Value; but on account of finding, that the Labours of many years are likely to produce few or none of the advantages, with regard to objects (for which I readily forget myself) which ought to be, and are far nearer to your heart and to mine. We had a shake of a Court Earthquake a day or two ago[3]— All is settled again; and in great apparent Tranquility on the old Foundations. But we walk the Streets of Naples.[4] Your ingenious and publick Spirited fellow Citizen—Mr. Miller[5] will give you this. Mrs Burke and a family much obliged to you entreat you to continue your old partiality to us all. I have the honour to be with the most sincere regard and Esteem

My dear Sir
Your most faithful
and affectionate humble Servant
Edm Burke

[2] Sir Joshua Reynolds (1723–92), painter; founded the Literary Club to give Dr. Johnson unlimited opportunities of talking 1764; President of the Royal Academy 1768; his *Discourses* (annual addresses) to the Academy are a valuable guide to his changing ideas as an artist.

[1] Letter 226 addressed to Burke, dated 15 Apr. 1783.
[2] Letter 217 addressed to Burke, dated 6 July 1782.
[3] The King had quarrelled with the Duke of Portland, First Lord of the Treasury, over the best way to relieve the financial embarrassments of the Prince of Wales (*Geo. III, Corr.* vi. 400–10). A compromise was arranged on 25 June (*Parliamentary History* ed. T. C. Hansard, London, 1814, xxiii. 1030–41).
[4] The recent eruptions of Vesuvius had attracted much attention (*Annual Register* for 1780, publ. Jan. 1782, 72–96).
[5] Not identified.

231. To [WILLIAM STRAHAN]

Extracts in Goodspeed (18 Beacon Street, Boston), *Catalogue* No. 526, item 315; letter sold 22 Oct. 1963, Parke-Bernet Galleries: *American Book-Prices Current* (1964), 870.

Custom-house, Edinburgh, 6 Oct. 1783

The alterations and additions which I propose to make to my new Edition of the Wealth of Nations are now either finished compleatly [or soon will be] . . . I still . . . wait for the Accounts which our good friend Sir Grey Cooper was so kind as to promise me[1] soon after the late political revolution.[2] . . . It is possible some fees may be due to the Clerks who copied the Accounts. . . .

I intended to have asked a four months leave of absence . . . in order to have attended the reprinting of my Book. But a Welch Nephew of mine tells me that unless I advance him two hundred pounds he must sell his commission in the army. This robs me of the money with which I intended to defray the expence of my expedition.[3] . . .

I wrote to Mr Cadell . . . recommending to his attention (for I never pretend to recommend to anything else) a theory and History of Music by the revd. Mr Robertson Minister of Dalmeny.[4] I read the theory (not the History) and was much instructed. [Smith also recommends publication of the sermons of the Revd. Mr. Samuel Charteris[5]]. . . .

It would give me the greatest pleasure to believe that the present Administration rests on a solid Basis.[6] It comprehends the worthiest and ablest men in the nation, the heads of the two great Aristocracies, whose disunion had weakened the . . . Government so much as at last to occasion the dismemberment of the empire. Their coalition, instead of being unpopular, was most devoutly to be wished for. . . . I trust that the usual folly and impertinence of next winters opposition will more effectually reconcile the King to his new ministers, than . . . any address of theirs has yet been able to do. . . .

---

[1] See Letter 227, n. 2; also, Letters 222, 223, 228, and 232.

[2] The fall of Shelburne in Feb. 1783.

[3] The nephew has not been traced, but the details of the story agree with what is known about Smith's charitable activities as reported to Dugald Stewart by 'a near relation of [Smith's] and one of his most confidential friends, Miss Ross, daughter of the late Patrick Ross, Esq., of Innernethy' (Rae 437).

[4] Thomas Robertson (d. 1799), Minister of Dalmeny 1775–99; published a *History of Music* (1784) and a *History of Mary Queen of Scots* (1793); see Letter 237 addressed to William Strahan, dated 10 June 1784.

[5] Not traced.

[6] The Fox–North coalition came to power in April 1783 and survived until December of the same year, when Pitt took over as First Lord of the Treasury with the backing of the King.

232. *To* [WILLIAM STRAHAN]

MS., Kress Libr., Harvard University; unpubl.

Canongate, Edinburgh, 20 Nov. 1783

My Dear Sir

I have been looking every post day for the arrival of the Accounts which our friend Sir Grey Cooper has been so good as to promise me;[1] and which, in a letter I received from him a few weeks ago he was so good as to say he would deliver to you. May I beg the favour of you to call upon him a second time for the same purpose. I have written to him myself by this days post.

I have a thousand thanks to return to you for your proffered kindness which I shall certainly accept of if there is any necessary occasion. But as my own funds will before the sixth day of January produce what will be sufficient for my purpose, I intend to set out on that day. If I am disappointed I shall certainly apply to you, and I can assure you with great truth, that there is no man living from whom I would more willingly receive a favour of this kind. I have, however, a mortal aversion to all anticipations.

If my old friend, Mr Home,[2] will receive me I shall be happy to take up my quarters with him, in whatever part of the town he may happen to be settled. But if that should be inconvenient I will beg the favour either of you or of him, to look out for a good lodging to me on a first floor somewhere in Suffolk Street, the price not to exceed two guineas a week. I beg to be remembered in the most respectful and affectionate manner to the whole family of the Homes and that you will believe me to with very great regard, My Dear Sir

> Your most obliged
> and most affectionate
> humble Servant
> Adam Smith

Cadel, to whom I beg to be remembered, is anxious, on account of something which fell the other day from Mr Rose[3] that we should set about the new edition immediately. I do not apprehend that a delay of six weeks can be of any consequence. If you think otherwise, however, be so good as to let me know and I shall endeavour to accomodate. I consider writing to you and writing to him as the same thing. I intend that this should be my last visit to London.

[1] Bounty accounts needed for additions to WN ed. 3; see Letter 227 addressed to Strahan, dated 22 May 1783, and Letter 228 addressed to Sir Grey Cooper, dated 2 June 1783.
[2] John Home the dramatist.　　　　[3] William Rose.

233. *To* WILLIAM EDEN[1]

Journal and Corr. of William, Lord Auckland (London, 1861), i. 64–6; Rae 385–6

Edinburgh, 15 Dec. 1783

Dear Sir,

If the Americans really mean to subject the goods of all different nations to the same duties, and to grant them the same indulgences, they set an example of good sense which all other nations ought to imitate. At any rate, it is certainly just that their goods, their naval stores for example, should be subjected to the same duties to which we subject those of Russia, Sweden and Denmark, and that we should treat them as they mean to treat us, and all other nations.

What degree of commercial connection we should allow between the remaining colonies, whether in North America or the West Indies, and the United States, may to some people appear a more difficult question. My own opinion is that it should be allowed to go on as before, and whatever inconveniences may result from this freedom may be remedied as they occur. The lumber and provisions of the United States are more necessary to our West India Islands, than the rum and sugar of the latter are to the former. Any interruption or restraint of commerce would hurt our loyal much more than our revolted subjects. Canada and Nova Scotia cannot justly be refused at least the same freedom of commerce which we grant to the United States.

I suspect the Americans do not mean what they say. I have seen a Revenue Act of South Carolina by which two shillings are laid upon every hundredweight of brown sugar imported from the British plantations, and only eighteen-pence upon that imported from any foreign colony. Upon every pound of refined sugar from the former one penny, from the latter one halfpenny. Upon every gallon of French wine, two-pence; of Spanish wine, three-pence; of Portuguese wine, four-pence.

I have little anxiety about what becomes of the American commerce. By an equality of treatment to all nations, we might soon open a commerce with the neighbouring nations of Europe infinitely more advantageous than that of so distant a country as America.[2] This is an immense subject, upon which, when I wrote to you last,[3] I intended to have sent you a letter of many sheets, but as I expect to see you in a few weeks, I shall not trouble you with so tedious a dissertation. I shall only say at present that every

---

[1] See his *Letters to . . . Carlisle* (1779), for a defence of the Government's policy on America, also Letter 203 addressed to William Eden dated 3 Jan. 1780.

[2] Shelburne and others had a vision of an Atlantic trading community as an answer to the economic problems arising from the loss of the American colonies.

[3] Not traced.

extraordinary either encouragement or discouragement that is given to the trade of any country more than to that of another, may, I think, be demonstrated to be in every case a complete piece of dupery, by which the interest of the State and the nation is constantly sacrificed to that of some particular class of traders. I heartily congratulate you upon the triumphant manner in which the East India Bill has been carried through the Lower House.[4] I have no doubt of its passing through the Upper House in the same manner. The decisive judgment and resolution with which Mr Fox has introduced and supported that Bill does him the highest honour.

I ever am, with the greatest respect and esteem, dear Sir, your most affectionate and most obedient humble servant,

Adam Smith

234. *From* GEORGE DEMPSTER[1]

MS., GUL Gen. 1035/165; Scott 287-8.

London, 18 Dec. 1783

Dear Sir

Will you forgive my troubling you with the inclosed.[2] It is the Effusion of a very gratefull Heart, and the writer a good man and deserving officer.

I dare say you have heard of a smuggling Committee lately appointed.[3] I promised to Mr Eden our Chairman that I would drop you a hint of the intention of the Committee to desire the favour of your attendance in Town after the Holidays. Strange Events have since happend which render doubtfull the existence of the House itself and of course of all its Committees even to the beginning of the Holidays.[4] So far as I can judge there is as great a probability of your seeing some of the Committee in Scotland as of the Committee seeing you in London. Should however the present

---

[4] Fox's India Bill, drafted by Burke, was passed by the House of Commons in Nov. 1783. It sought to establish a measure of public control over the East India Co., but the Commissioners to be appointed were placemen and they were to be based in London. The King intervened and the Bill was defeated by the Lords. Fox went into Opposition and Pitt headed the Administration.

[1] George Dempster (1732–1818) of Dunnichen, Forfar; M.P. for Perth Burghs 1761–8, 1769–70; educ. St Andrews, Edinburgh, and Brussels; advocate 1755; Director, East India Co. 1769, 1772–3; member of the Select Soc.; a dedicated improver, especially with respect to the Scottish fisheries, responsible for the practice of sending salmon on ice to London; championed reform of Scottish franchise.

[2] Not traced.

[3] A 'Committee on Smuggling and other Illicit Practices used in Defrauding the Revenue', met Dec. 1783–Mar. 1784. The ensuing Report does not appear to contain or mention a contribution from Smith. For his views on preventing smuggling, see WN V.ii.k.27, 35–6. See also Letter 235, WN V.ii.k.64, and Appendix D, No. 11.

[4] The controversy over Fox's India Bill and the fall of the North–Fox administration; a general election was held in 1784.

surmises of a dissolution prove groundless, the Committee will be much indebted to you for your Ideas of the most effectual means to prevent smuggling, which by all the Information we have received has come to an alarming height, threatening the destruction of the Revenue, the fair trader, the Health and morals of the People.

I am with most sincere respect

Dear Sir

Your most Obedient

and most humble Servant

George Dempster

235. *To* [?WILLIAM EDEN][1]

MS., GUL Gen. 1035/134 (draft, unsigned); Scott 288-90.

[Edinburgh, 1783?]

My Dear Sir

After making you wait a fortnight, in expectation of an account from the excise which I have not yet received, I at last sit down to answer your very obliging letter, not one bit better informed than I was an hour after I received it. As soon as I get more information you shall have it.[2]

By the 1st George 3. Cap: 1 Sect: 8, all the duties and revenues which were payable to the late king during his life in Scotland were reserved to his present majesty; over and above the £800,000 per an granted to him from the aggregate fund.

By the 10th Anne Cap: 26. Sect: 108, all the duties of customs and excise at that time payable in Scotland were made liable to the expense of keeping up the three courts of Session, Justiciary and Exchequer.

In consequence of the first of these clauses, not only the rents of the Crown lands, and the feudal Casualties arising in Scotland but the produce of all fines and forfeitures and consequently of all Seizures, the new Subsidy, the Hereditary and temporary excise, as well as several other branches of revenue are, by our Barons of Exchequer, considered as making part of the private estate of the king; to be disposed of in what manner he pleases, and consequently applicable to pensions and Gratuities.

In consequence of the second of these clauses combined with the first, when if those private funds should be so far exhausted by pensions and Gratuities as not to be sufficient for the maintenance of the 3 courts, the

---

[1] This letter was meant for someone in the Treasury, possibly William Eden. See Letter 234 from George Dempster, dated 18 Dec. 1783.

[2] A manuscript in the Bannerman Coll., GUL, may be the information in question: 'Calculation of Loss to the Revenue in North Britain from the Abuse of Small Stills'. 1,000 stills were believed to exist, causing a loss of £182,000 to the Excise collectors.

same Judges consider all the different branches of customs and excise payable to Scotland in the 10th of Queen Anne as liable to make up the deficiency.

The pensions upon the civil list of Scotland at the death of the late king did not, I have been assured, much exceed four thousand pounds a year. They at present amount to upwards of eighteen thousand pounds a year. I should have enclosed a list of them, had I not known that it was sent up quarterly to the treasury.

The amount of the civil establishment in Scotland during the last year has been as follows.

Michaelmass quarter 1782	£15,550.	1	
Christmas 1782 . . .	16,798	12	1
Ladyday 1783	16,615	15	5½
Midsummer 1783 . . .	17,915.	2.	1½
	66,879:	10:	8

Whatever part of the funds which are considered as the private property of the king is not exhausted by pensions is applied to the payment of the three courts, and the other necessary charges of the civil establishment of Scotland. So far as those private funds are not sufficient for this purpose, the deficiency is supplied by having recourse to the subsidiary funds applicable to the same purpose by the above clause in the 10th of Queen Anne. The remainder of those subsidiary funds is remitted by the order of the boards of Customs and Excise to the Receivers general of those respective Revenues in England.

The enclosed Account will sufficiently explain to you the nature of the funds under the management of our board which are applicable to the civil list, and the manner in which they are applied. In a post or two I shall probably be able to send you a similar account of those under the management of the Excise.

236. *To* JOHN DAVIDSON

MS., EUL (now missing); Rae 392.

Friday 7 May [1784]

My Lord Stonefield[1] is an old attached and faithful friend of A. Stuart. The papers relative to the County of Lanark may safely be communicated to him. He is perfectly convinced of the propriety of what you and I agreed

---

[1] John Campbell of Stonefield (d. 1801); advocate 1748; Session Court Judge, 1762; Lord Commissioner of Justiciary, 1787 (resigned 1792); brother-in-law of Lord Bute.

upon, that the subject[2] ought to be talked of as little as possible, and never but among his most intimate and cordial friends.

A. Smith

237. *To* [WILLIAM STRAHAN]

MS., Pennsylvania Historical Society; Scott 290.

Custom-house, Edinburgh, 10 June 1784

My Dear Sir

I return you the Proof[1] which, indeed, requires little correction, except in the pointing, and not much in that. I received the fair sheets by the Coach, and sent Robertson of Dalmenie[2] his parcel. I [am] much pleased with the Paper and letter, and am obliged to you for sending the fair sheets rather by the cheap conveyance of the Coach than by the expensive one of the Post. I should be glad, however, to receive the proofs of the Manuscript part by the Post as the speedier conveyance; and if it gives you much trouble to procure franks I shall willingly pay the postage. I should immediately have acknowledged the receipt of the fair sheets; but I had just then come from performing the last duty to my poor old Mother;[3] and tho' the death of a person in the ninetieth year of her age was no doubt an event most agreable to the course of nature; and, therefore, to be foreseen and prepared for; yet I must say to you, what I have said to other people, that the final separation from a person who certainly loved me more than any other person ever did or ever will love me; and whom I certainly loved and respected more than I ever shall either love or respect any other person, I cannot help feeling, even at this hour, as a very heavy stroke upon me. Even in this state of mind, however, it gives me very great concern to hear that there is any failure in your health and spirits.[4] The good weather, I hope, will soon reestablish both in their ordinary vigour. My friends grow very thin in the world, and I do not find that my new ones are likely to supply their place. I shall be very anxious to hear from you as soon as your

---

[2] At the General Election of 1784, Stuart withdrew his candidature over some difference with the Duke of Hamilton. The day before withdrawing he sent the whole correspondence with the Duke concerning this matter to John Davidson, for the perusal of his Edinburgh friends: 'There is particularly one friend, Mr. Adam Smith, whom I wish to be fully informed of everything'.

[1] WN ed. 3; see Letter 222 to Cadell, date 7 Dec. 1782, and Nos. 227 and 232 to Strahan, dated 22 May and 20 Nov. 1783, also No. 223 from Cadell, dated 12 Dec. 1782.

[2] See Letter 231, n. 4.

[3] Smith's mother, Margaret Douglas, died on 23 May 1784.

[4] Strahan did not stand at the general election of 1784 and died on 9 July 1785.

conveniency will permit. Remember me to Mr and Mrs Spottiswood[5] and to all other friends and believe me to be

My Dear friend
most faithfully and affectionately
ever yours
Adam Smith

238. *To* DR. MAXWELL GARTHSHORE[1]

Address: Dr Garthshore
MS., Kress Libr., Harvard University; Homer Vanderblue, *Adam Smith and the Wealth of Nations* (Boston, 1936), 6.

[Edinburgh,] 18 June 1784

My Dear Doctor

Our friend Mr Peter Maine[2] has been advised to offer himself a candidate for the office of Overseer of the Kings works, which, he tells me, is vacant by the Death of Mr Thomas Tyers,[2] who was bred a joiner, and who dyed last night. You and I both know what an ingenious Mechanick Maine is, and if this office could be procured for him, I have no doubt of his being better qualified for it than any joiner in Great Britain. I should write at more length, but am much indisposed. I ever am, My Dear Doctor

Most faithfully
Yours
Adam Smith

239. *To* [THOMAS CADELL]

MS., NYPL Berg Collection; unpubl.

Custom-house, Edinburgh, 19 June 1784

Dear Sir

I received your very obliging letter in due course, and the Edition of my book now goes on in a manner that is most agreable to me; for which I consider myself as much beholden to you.[1]

I understand that the Abbé Morellet has translated my Book into french and has published it in Holland in four or six octavo Volumes with large

---

5 John Spottiswoode and his wife Peggy, dau. of William Strahan.

1 Maxwell Garthshore (1732–1812), physician; M.D. Edinburgh 1764; F.R.S.; published works on obstetrics.
2 Not traced.

1 Not traced but presumably dealing with WN ed. 3; see Letter 237, n. 1.

notes.[2] I should be much obliged to you if you could procure me a copy of this translation and send it to me by the first convenient opportunity.

As a Member of the Royal Society I am entitled to the annual transactions. I have been negligent in making good this right. I became in a member in 1767. I have the transactions for 1766 which were sent me by Dr Morton soon after my election: but I want those for 1767 and 1768, that is, I want the 57th and 58th Volumes. I have the 59th, 60th, 61st, 62nd, 63rd, and the first part of the 64th volume; but I want the second part of the 64th volume and all that has been published since. May I beg the favour of you to endeavour to procure me these imperfections, and if I am out of time in making this demand for any part of them, as I suspect I am, may I beg the favour of you to buy them for me;[3] and when you let me know the price I shall remit you the money by return of Post.

When I was last in London I bought at your Shop Maty's Edition of Chesterfields miscellaneous works. The third volume wants the last page; viz; page 401. It is, indeed, an imperfection of very small consequence; it being only the french original of the conclusion of a letter from Voltaire, of which the English translation is on the opposite page. If you could, however, make up to me this small imperfection, I should be much obliged to you.

You see how dangerous it is to do one favour to a troublesome man. It brings many other requests upon you. Let me advise you, therefore, to be cautious in time coming and this counsel I look upon as well worth at least part of the trouble.

It gives me great concern to learn from Strahan that his health and spirits are not what they used to be. Remember me most affectionately to him and likewise to Rose and Griffiths;[4] and believe me to be

Dear Sir
most faithfully
and affectionately
ever yours
Adam Smith

---

[2] Morellet did translate WN but did not publish his work (*Mémoires*, 1823, 243). A French trans. of WN had appeared in Holland: *Recherches sur la nature et les causes de la richesse des nations* . . . traduit de l'Anglois de M. Adam Smith, par M***. [4 t.] (The Hague, 1778–9).

[3] There is a note on the letter, ?in Cadell's hand, to the effect that Smith was intitled to the *Transactions of the Royal Soc.* for 1780, 1781, 1782, 1783, but had forfeited the rest because members had to demand the vols. every four years. Among its holdings of Smith's books, New College, Edinburgh University, has from the 56th to the 76th vol. of the *Transactions*, covering the years 1766–86 (Mizuta 46).

[4] William Rose and Ralph Griffiths.

240. *To* [THOMAS CADELL]

MS., University of Illinois Libr.; Scott 291.

Custom-house, Edinburgh, 10 Aug. 1784

Dear Sir

I received last week all the Volumes of the Philosophical transactions which I wanted except the Volumes 70. 71. and the first part of 72. I received the second part of 72 and both parts of Volume 73.[1] I am much obliged to you for the trouble you have been at; those still wanting, I suppose, will come when the Society meets.

I wrote to Strahan desiring a few presents to be made in my name before the Publication;[2] viz, to Lady Louisa MacDonald,[3] to Lords Stanhope,[4] Mahon,[5] Loughborough[6] and Sheffield;[7] to these let me add a Sixth to Sir Grey Cooper. The copy to Lady Louisa to be finely bound and and Gilt; the rest in boards. I should likewise be glad you would send me six copies in boards (by the first Leith Ship) to be distributed to some of my friends here.

I received the leaf that was wanting in Chesterfields miscellanies:[8] But you say nothing to me about the french translation by the Abbé Morellet which I am very anxious to see. I have another french translation by the Abbé Blavet.[9] Remember me to all friends and believe me to be

My Dear Sir
Most faithfully
yours
Adam Smith

[1] See Letter 239 addressed to Cadell, dated 19 June 1784.

[2] Of WN ed. 3, published on 20 Nov. 1784.

[3] Lady Louise Gower, dau. of Granville 2nd Earl Gower, md. Sir Archibald MacDonald of Armadale Castle, Skye, 26 Dec. 1777.

[4] Philip 2nd Earl Stanhope.

[5] Charles Stanhope (1753–1816), styled Viscount Mahon until 1786 when he succeeded his fa. and became the 3rd Earl Stanhope. He was noted for his radical politics, scientific work, and inventions. Smith met him and his fa. during his visit to Geneva, Oct.–Dec. 1765.

[6] Alexander Wedderburn, cr. Baron Loughborough 1780.

[7] John Baker Holroyd (1735–1821), Gibbon's 'best friend' and executor; owned estates in Yorkshire, Scotland, and Ireland; M.P. for Coventry 1780–4, and Bristol 1790–1802; F.R.S. 1783; particularly interested in agriculture, trade, and finance. He acquired Sheffield Place, Sussex, in 1769; became Baron Sheffield of Dunamore 1780 (Irish peerage), Baron Sheffield of Sheffield, Yorks. 1802, and Viscount Pevensey and 1st Earl of Sheffield 1816. Gibbon was buried in the Sheffield burial-place, in Fletching parish church, near Sheffield Place, now known as Sheffield Park.

[8] See Letter 239.

[9] Published in 1781; see Letter 218, n. 2 and Bonar 174.

241. *To* [THOMAS CADELL]

MS., Kress Libr., Harvard University; Scott 292.

Custom-house, Edinburgh, 16 Nov. 1784

Dear Sir

For these several weeks past I have been looking for a letter from you by every Post, in answer to the last I wrote you.[1] I see that you have executed my commissions, as I have received the thanks of some of the persons to whom I had begged the favour of you to send copies. To those which in my former letter I desired you to deliver as presents from the Authour I must beg the favour of you to add four more: one to Lord Shelburne; and three to the Marquis de Bombelles; one to the Marquis himself; one to the Duke of Rochefoucault; and one to the Dutchess Chabot, the Sister of the Duke of Rochefoucault and the Daughter of the Dutchess D'Anville.[2] My Lord Shelburne will be so good as to deliver the three copies to the Marquis de Bombelles, who will be so good as to deliver at Paris the two copies for the Duke of Rochefoucault and the Dutchess Chabot. Remember me most respectfully and affectionately to Strahan and believe me to be

Dear Sir

ever yours

Adam Smith

242. *To* [THOMAS CADELL]

MS., Bodleian, Montagu d.10, fol. 60; *Economic Journal* viii (1898), 403.

Custom-house, Edinburgh, 18 Nov. 1784

Dear Sir

I received this moment your favour of the 12 instt. I am much obliged to you for your attention in procuring me the Volumes of the Philosophical transactions which I wanted;[1] But you say nothing to me of the Abbé Morellet's translation of my Book, which I am extremely desirous of seeing.[2] I am sorry to give you so much trouble, but I beg you would endeavour to procure me a copy of it for Love or Money. The Abbé himselfe, I understand, is now or was lately in London with Lord Shelburne.[3]

Yesterday Mr Spottiswood delivered me a Packet from Strahan containing some part of the index of my Book. A note on the outside of it

[1] Letter 240 addressed to Cadell, dated 10 Aug. 1784.

[2] See Letter 213 from the Marquis de Bombelles, dated 18 June 1781, asking for news of Smith's publications.

[1] Cadell's letter has not been traced; for Smith's request about the *Transactions*, see Letter 239, dated 19 June 1784, n. 2.   [2] See Letter 239, n. 2.

[3] Morellet was in London with Shelburne in Oct. 1784. They had resumed their association at Spa after the fall of Shelburne's Administration in 1783.

requested to know if I wished the index to be printed in Quarto and to be delivered, with the other Additions, to the Purchasers of the former Editions. I am afraid it is now too late, as all the numerals in the index must be altered in order to accomodate them to either of the two former editions of which the Pages do not in many places correspond.[4] I am afraid therefor, this must be omitted. I shall agree, however, to whatever you and he think proper. I ever am

Dear Sir, Most affectionately, Yours
Adam Smith

243. *To* DR. JAMES MENTEATH[1]

Address: The Revd Dr James Menteath, Barrowby, near Grantham
MS., GUL Gen. 1464/1; Scott 292–3.

Custom-house, Edinburgh, 22 Feb. 1785

My Dear James

I received your very kind and friendly letter in due course; and have no hesitation to recommend the University of Edinburgh in preference to any other. It is at present better provided in Professors than any other Society of the kind that I ever knew; and it is likely soon to be still better provided than at present.[2] While my own residence, besides, is here, which it is now very likely to be for life, I would fain flatter myself I may be of some use in rendering both your stay here agreable and your sons useful. I approve entirely of your attending your son[3] to the place of his education yourself as his principal Governour and Preceptor. I consider it as the most sacred as well as the most important duty of a father. But I disapprove altogether of your proposal to resign your Living. It may happen that Scotland may not turn out to be so agreeable a place of residence either to you or to your family as you at present hope; and it will certainly be more prudent to take a trial of us for a year or two at least, before you take the final and irrevocable resolution of giving up altogether your connection with your present Neighbourhood and abode. You have hitherto been so

---

[4] The index was made an integral part of the book. Either the person who compiled it had an intimate knowledge of Scottish banking, or Smith corrected the index himself (according to Edwin Cannan, WN 1950, i. xvi).

[1] A friend of Smith from his Oxford days, he was Rector of Barrowby in Lincolnshire until he inherited Closeburn, Dumfriesshire. He assumed the additional surname of Stuart by sign-manual in 1770. Smith sometimes spelled the name Monteath, and the family is now known as Stuart-Menteth.

[2] Adam Ferguson gave up the Chair of Moral Philosophy in 1785 and was succeeded by Dugald Stewart. Other distinguished teachers at Edinburgh University were the Principal, William Robertson; Joseph Black, Chemistry; William Cullen, Physic; John Robinson, Natural Philosophy; John Bruce, Logic; and A. F. Tytler, Universal History.

[3] Charles Granville Stuart Menteith, created a Baronet in 1838.

religiously exact in the performance of all your pastoral duties, that you are well entitled to demand a vacation for at least three or four winters in order to attend upon the education of your son. I give you this caution, much against my own interest and inclination, and merely for Conscience sake. You are now, except one or two old Cousins,[4] the oldest friend I have now remaining in the world, and it gives me the most unspeakable satisfaction to think that I have some chance of ending my days in your Society and neighbourhood. I ever am

My Dearest friend, your most
affectionate and most faithful
humble Servant
Adam Smith

244. *To* [THOMAS CADELL][1]

MS., Mrs. John Mildmay-White, c/o her Trustees, Messrs Baring Bros. & Co., 8 Bishopsgate, London, EC2N 4AE; *Important Autograph Letters*, Christie's Sale Cat., London, 2 Apr. 1975, No. 167 (extract).

Custom-house, Edinburgh, 21 Apr. 1785

Dear Sir

Your letter of the 25th of March was extremely agreeable to me, as you may well imagine, and I am very much obliged to you for it. I shall be very glad to hear that a new edition is called for and we shall have no difference about the terms of Publication. If a new edition of the theory is wanted I have a few alterations to make of no great consequence which I shall send to you. Let me hear from you soon.

I was misinformed with regard to the Abbé Morellet having translated my book.

My Philosophical transactions are now compleat. I am much obliged to you for the trouble you have had about it. I ever am

My Dear Sir
your most affectionate
humble Servant
Adam Smith

[4] General Robert Skene; Col. Robert Douglas of Strathenry; Miss Janet Douglas, Smith's housekeeper; and Col. Patrick Ross of Innernethy and his wife. See Letter 281 addressed to James Menteath, dated 16 Sept. 1788, for an account of the last illness of Miss Douglas.

[1] This letter is presumably to Thomas Cadell, Smith's London publisher; see the forerunner, Letter 239, dated 19 June 1784, in which mention is made of Morellet's translation of WN and Smith's request for the *Transactions* of the Royal Society. The editions referred to are the 4th of WN, published in 1786, and the 6th of TMS, which was available by May 1790. This latter came to incorporate extensive additions and substantial revisions; see Letters 276 and 287, addressed to Cadell, dated 15 Mar. 1788 and 31 Mar. 1789.

245. *From* HENRY HERBERT, LORD PORCHESTER

MS., GUL Gen. 1035/166; Scott 293–4.

Highclere, 24 Aug. 1785

My Dear Smith

Least you should be surprized with the sudden appearance of a little Man in black presenting a Letter to you desiring your acquaintance I must apprize you that on the receipt of the enclosed Letter[1] I have just sent to Doctor Ogle[2] Dean of Winchester a Letter of introduction to you; he is a very worthy respectable Man as little of a high priest as a priest can possibly be, and a great deal more of a Republican than will ever lead the Dean to a Bishoprick, a very Zealous man in every thing he undertakes and will at any time sacrifice his interest to his Principles which are all strongly tinged with a Republican cast; I shall really be much obliged to you for any civility you can without inconvenience to yourself show him; he is Brother to Admiral Sir Chaloner Ogle,[3] married the Daughter of the Late Bishop of Winchester from whom he got great preferment in the Church and would have long ago been higher but for his uncourtly disposition; never having been able to resist an opportunity of showing his Enthusiasm in any Cause coloured with Publick Liberty:—I hope you continue in perfect Health and happiness, and not idly bent to keep the result of your Studies to yourself; Lady Porchester desires to be remembered to you, and with me wishes you would persuade yourself to come up and spend on[e] of your vacations here with us, for I think you have arranged your attendance on your official Duties so as to have several months in the year to spare; in the strange arrangement of this world one lives daily with People one cares little about and does not see above once an age those one Esteems most; pray remember me kindly to all your Family not forgetting my good friend Miss Douglas,

I remain My Dear Smith
with the greatest esteem and regard
Most faithfully and Affectionately yours
Porchester

[1] Not traced.

[2] Newton Ogle (b. 1726) md. Susanna dau. of Dr. John Thomas, Bishop of Winchester. Ogle became Dean of Winchester in 1769, but never achieved the mitre.

[3] Sir Chaloner Ogle (? 1681–1750) Admiral from 1744, having entered the Navy in 1697; he was with Vernon in the attack on Carthagena 1742, and succeeded him in command. A gap of forty-five years between brothers, though possible, seems unlikely, and Porchester may be wrong about the relationship.

246. *From* ROBERT REID[1]

Address: Adam Smith Esqr
MS., GUL Gen. 1035/167; unpubl.

Miramichi, 11 Sept. 1785

With due respect I would humbly beg leave to trouble you with a few lines informing of my present situation and give you some account of my peregrinations last winter. Know, then, Sir, that I am settled upon the Banks of a very pleasant and navigable River called Miramichi in the Province of New Brunswic and County of Northumberland, of which Governor Carleton has been pleased to appoint me Coroner. I have got an estate of some hundreds of Acres of Land of which the soil is but indifferent. Every tree that I cut down, however, serves two purposes; first, it affords firewood; and, secondly, it clears so much Land which with a little culture will produce tollerable good grain, Potatoes, and Cabbages etc. The woods abound with game of different sorts, particularly with what the Savages call Moose; an animal about the size of a Bullock and its flesh eats equally well. The Mapple tree in spring affords a juice which in my opinion makes sugar of a much more wholesome quality than that imported from the west Indies. We have also several herbs, particularly what is called Maidenhair, which serve as an excellent Substitute for Tea. The river is amply stored with various sorts of fish, particularly Salmon. I am now therefore become both a farmer and a fisherman, and by exerting my Industry can live comfortably. Our Co-partnery have two vessels one of which goes to the foreign Market with the produce of our Industry in fish and returns with such British goods as suits the market here. In short, Sir, I have at present the prospect of becoming what I call Rich.

I shall now, according to promise, give you some account of my peregrinations last winter. One of my Partners and self went to Quebec where we purchased a Schooner and being detained at that place too long could not reach this place before the frost set it. We were therefore under the necessity of putting into a place called Pabo in the Bay de Chaleur where the vessel wintered; and I undertook the arduous task of traversing about five hundred miles thro' the wild woods of America in order to transact some necessary business at Halifax. I accordingly set out about the middle of December thro' an almost un-inhabited Country and entirely covered with Snow. I was, however, equipt with a pair of good snowshoes, a very happy invention which in winter greatly facilitates the Business of this Country and without the use of which scarce any out-door business can be carried on. I had not travelled many miles when I fell in with three Savages one of whom I soon understood bore the rank of Captain, who seeing my blue Cloaths immediately announced me *Brother*. I entered chearfully into

[1] Former servant to Smith.

conversation with them, and as I was going the same road they proposed to conduct me to their Wigwams which were only a few leagues distance. We travelled on till evening approached and my companions then proposed to encamp for the night; but think what were my ideas to lye down to sleep in a wild lonesome wood, surrounded by savages, in so very cold a climate, in the depth of winter and during a very heavy fall of Snow! There was, however, no alternative. My companions went to work with their Tomahawks and cut down some trees for firewood, and with the larger branches made our wigwam, while the smaller ones were alloted for our Beds. Fire serves two purposes; first, it prevents any attack from wild Beasts who never approach it; and, secondly, by turning our feet towards it prevents their being frost-bit; an accident very common in cold climates. We lay down and my companions slept very comfortably after regaling themselves with a bumper or two of my Rum. The only inconveniency I felt was the necessity of rising frequently to shake my Blanket clear of the Snow which continued to fall incessantly thro' the night. Morning approach'd and we resumed our journey after treating my friends with another bumper which had such an effect on my *Brother* that for one single bottle he proposed I should have *his* squaw (or wife) for my Bed-fellow upon our arrival at his Wigwam. I was introduced as a brother Captain; but the appearance of the Lady was not a motive sufficient to excite me to part, either with my Rum, or accept of the honour of such a Bed-fellow. I remained among them a few days which gave me an opportunity of observing their manners. But a particular and proper description of their Wigwams, their furniture, their Customs and manners of Life would far exceed the bounds of a Letter. I have since that time navigated rivers some hundreds of miles with other Savages in their Canoes made of the bark of the birch tree. If I could find a favourable opportunity I would send home one of these Canoes as a present for Lord Dalkeith.[2]

I called upon Sir Charles Douglass[3] when at Halifax and met with a most friendly reception both from Lady Douglass and from him which I shall ever remember with gratitude. Her Ladyship sets a great value upon the skin of a black fox which I hope soon to procure from some of my friends, the Savages. It was at Breakfast with Sir Charles that I first heard my late worthy Mistress Smith had paid the debt of Nature. The powers of language fail to express my feelings when I heard the melancholy news. Permit me to say that I sympathise with you on the loss of so virtuous and so loving a mother.—Please to offer my most respectful Compliments to Miss Douglass. I am now entirely at a loss in what manner to apologise for my conduct in presuming to trouble you with so very long an epistle,

[2] Heir of the Duke of Buccleuch.

[3] Sir Charles Douglas, 1st Bt. (d. 1789), Rear-admiral; Captain of the Fleet at the battle of Dominica, 1782; C.-in-C. Halifax station, 1783–6; distant relative of Smith.

especially when I consider how trifling the greater part of the subject is. My fears already suggest that your not honouring me with an answer will confirm my suspicion.—Our Correspondent Mr William Annand[4] in Bow Lane, London will forward any letters address'd for me. I am, Sir with the greatest respect

Your much obliged
and most Obedient Humble Servant
Robt Reid

247. *To* ANDREW STRAHAN

Address: To Mr Andrew Strahan, New Street, Shoe Lane, London
MS., Kress Libr., Harvard University; Rae 396–7.

Edinburgh, 29 Sept. 1785

Dear Sir

Mr. Logan, a Clergyman of uncommon learning, taste and ingenuity; but who cannot easily submit to the puritanical spirit of this country, quits his charge and proposes to settle in London; where he will probably exercise what may be called the trade of a man of Letters.[1] He has published a few poems, of which several have great merit and which are probably not unknown to you. He has likewise published a tragedy, which, I cannot say I admire in the least.[2] He has another in manuscript, founded and almost translated from a french drama, which is much better. But the best of all his works which I have seen, are some lectures upon Universal History,[3] which were read here some years ago, but which, notwithstanding they were approved and even admired by some of the best and most impartial judges, were run down by the prevalence of a hostile literary faction, to the leaders of which he had imprudently given some personal offence. Give me leave to recommend him most earnestly to your countenance and protection. If he was employed in a review he would be an excellent hand for giving an account of all Books of taste, of history, and of moral and abstract Philosophy. I ever am,

My Dear Sir
Most faithfully
and Affectionately yours
Adam Smith

[4] Not traced.

[1] See Letter 215 from Henry Mackenzie, dated 7 June 1782.

[2] There exists a letter from Logan to Mackenzie with another version of Smith's opinion of *Runnamede*: 'tho' [Smith] expressed his approbation of it as a poem in terms that I would not chuse to repeat, he seemed to doubt of its being adapted to the English Stage' (Scott 285–6).

[3] *Elements of the Philosophy of History* (1781), based on lectures given at Edinburgh, 1779–81.

248. *To* LE DUC DE LA ROCHEFOUCAULD

Economic Journal vi (1896), 165–6; I.C. Lundberg, *Turgot's Unknown Translator: The Réflexions and Adam Smith* (The Hague, 1964), 44–5.

Edinburgh, 1 Nov. 1785

My Lord Duke,

I should certainly have been very happy to have communicated to your Grace any letters which the ever-to-be-regretted Mr Turgot had done me the honour to write to me; and by that means, to have the distinguished honour of being recorded as one of his correspondents.[1] But tho' I had the happiness of his acquaintance, and, I flattered myself, even of his friendship and esteem, I never had that of his correspondence. He was so good as to send me a copy of the *Proces Verbal* of what passed at the bed of justice upon the registration of his six edicts which did so much honour to their Author, and, had they been executed without alteration, would have proved so beneficial to his country.[2] But the Present (which I preserve as I most valuable monument of a person whom I remember with so much veneration) was not accompanied with any Letter.

I expect all the bad consequences from the chambers of Commerce and manufactures establishing in different parts of this Country, which your Grace seems to foresee.[3] In a Country where Clamour always intimidates and faction often oppresses the Government, the regulations of Commerce are commonly dictated by those who are most interested to deceive and impose upon the Public.

I have not forgot what I promised to your Grace in an edition of the 'Theory of Moral Sentiments,' which I hope to execute before the end of the ensuing winter.[4] I have likewise two other great works upon the anvil;

[1] No letter asking about Turgot's correspondence with Smith has survived; for other topics of common interest, see La Rochefoucauld's letters of 3 Mar. 1778 and 6 Aug. 1779 (Nos. 194 and 199).

[2] Smith's copy of *Procès verbal de ce qui s'est passé au Lit de Justice tenu par le Roi à Versailles, le mardi douze mars 1776* (Paris, 1776) is bound with Gabriel Sénac de Meilhan, *Considérations sur les richesses et le luxe* (Amsterdam, 1787) in EUL (Bonar 102, 157–8).

[3] The first meeting of the Glasgow Chamber of Commerce was held on 1 Jan. 1783. It was interested chiefly in raising the standard of goods for sale, urging the Government to ease the burden of taxation, reducing tariffs on a reciprocal basis, and eliminating illicit trading and smuggling. Correspondence was carried on with London merchants and the Chambers of Commerce of Bristol and Liverpool. On 14 Mar. 1785 a decision was taken in London to form 'The General Chamber of Manufacturers of Great Britain'. In Feb. 1786 there was established 'The Chamber of Commerce and Manufactures in the City of Edinburgh'. Predictably, from Smith's point of view, the Chambers of Commerce were opposed to free trade with Ireland, but they were more favourably disposed to the Eden Treaty of 1786 which aimed at opening up trade with France (Hamilton 272–8).

[4] During the years left to him, Smith laboured at revising TMS; see Letters 244, 276, and 287 addressed to Cadell, dated 21 Apr. 1785, 15 Mar. 1788, and 31 Mar. 1789. The corrected and expanded ed. 6 was available by May 1790; see Letters 294 and 295 also to Cadell, dated 16 and 25 May 1790.

the one is a sort of Philosophical History of all the different branches of Literature, of Philosophy, Poetry and Eloquence; the other is a sort of theory and History of Law and Government.[5] The materials of both are in a great measure collected, and some Part of both is put into tollerable good order. But the indolence of old age, tho' I struggle violently against it, I feel coming fast upon me, and whether I shall ever be able to finish either is extremely uncertain.

May I beg to be remembered in the most respectful manner to the Dutchess D'Anville and to the Dutchess Chabot and that your Grace will do me the honour to believe me to be, with the highest regard,

My Lord Duke,

Your Grace's most obliged, most obedient

and most faithful humble servant

Adam Smith

249. *To* GEORGE CHALMERS[1]

Address: George Chalmers Esqr, Berkely Square No. 31, London
MS., NLS 582 No. 680; HMC Laing MSS. (1925), ii. 522; Scott 294–5.

Custom-house, Edinburgh, 10 Nov. 1785

Sir

I received the honour of your very polite and obliging letter of the 3 Nov, and shall be very happy to give you every information in my power towards perfecting so very useful and comfortable a work as your estimate. The two accounts you wish for are official accounts which have been annually transmitted to the treasury in consequence of an annual order for that purpose. It is contrary to the practise of this Board to communicate accounts of this nature to any private person without a particular order or permission from a secretary of the treasury. The slightest card from Mr Rose[2] either to me, if he will do me that honour, or to any other member of our Board will

---

[5] For the history of the 'great works' that Smith had 'upon the anvil' see EPS, LJ (A and B), and LRBL. His executors Joseph Black and James Hutton made a selection for EPS (1795).

[1] See Letter 183 n. 1. The letter of 3 Nov. 1784 to Smith has not been traced, but it probably contained queries relating to *An Estimate of the comparative Strength of Great Britain*, which Chalmers republished frequently: 1782, 1786, 1794, 1802, 1804, 1812. See Letters 250, 251, and 252 addressed to Chalmers, dated 3 and 22 Dec. 1785 and 3 Jan. 1786.

[2] George Rose (1744–1818) government clerk, then keeper of various records; Secretary of the Board of Taxes 1777–82; Secretary to the Treasury 1782–1801; Clerk of the Parliaments 1788–d.: 'indefatigable, methodical, and yet rapid, equal to but not above the business of the Treasury', according to Nathaniel Wraxall (*Memoirs*, iii. 457, quoted in HP iii. 376).

procure you that and any other information in our power to give without a moments delay.

The accounts of the tunnage of British shipping entered and cleared out from the ports of Scotland does not comprehend the Coast trade. The account of that trade may easily be had from the year 1779. It cannot easily be had from the year 1759.

The late reverend Mr Webster,[3] of all the men I have ever known, the most skilful in Political Arithmetic,[4] had made out what seemed a very accurate account of the Population of Scotland as it stood in the year 1755. He had collected the lists of births, burials and marriages in all the different Parishes in Scotland. In many of the parishes he had got the people counted accurately. In others, he had got the lists of what are called examinable persons, that is, of people who are fit to be examined before the Kirk session in the Scotch Catechism. Children of seven and eight years of age are considered as examinable persons. In several parishes he had got the ages of all the different inhabitants ascertained. He had computed the numbers in the Parishes where he had got only the lists of the Births, Burials and Marriages, by those in the Parishes which were in nearly similar circumstances and had been accurately counted. This account filled a pretty large Volume in folio. About ten years ago I had the use of this account for many months. By it the whole number of souls in Scotland amounted to little more than 1,250,000. The same Gentleman a few months before his death told me that he had stated the numbers too low; and that, upon better information, he believed they might amount to 1,500,000, according to the best of my recollection. I acknowledge, however, I cannot be very positive about the precise number mentioned in this verbal information. If he has left any papers behind him upon this subject which I can either get access to, or get any distinct account of, I shall immediately inform you. You know that I have little faith in Political Arithmetic and this story does not contribute to mend my opinion of it.[5]

[3] Dr. Alexander Webster (1707–84), Minister of the Tolbooth Kirk, Edinburgh; leader of the 'High-flyers' of the Church of Scotland; author of an 'Account of the Number of People in Scotland in the year 1755' (ed. Sir James Gray Kyd, Scottish History Society, Edinburgh, 1952). The 'Account' was compiled for a pension scheme to assist the widows and children of ministers. Webster got statistical returns because of a prestige in Church affairs that was unimpaired by convivial habits earning him the title of Dr. Bonum Magnum.

[4] Statistics of population, trade, revenue, expenditure, etc. of a state. The OED notes as the first known use of the term, the title of Sir William Petty's 'Essay in Political Arithmetick, concerning the Growth of the City of London' (1682). See also, the preface to his *Political Arithmetic* (1691) for what is believed to be the earliest advocacy of quantitative empirical methods in the study of social and political phenomena.

[5] Smith expressed the same reservation in WN IV.v.6.30, 'Digression on the Corn Trade': 'I have no great faith in political arithmetick.' A similar scepticism is the basis of Hume's dissertation, 'Of the Populousness of Ancient Nations'. Smith, however, had second thoughts about the implications of Webster's revised figure; see Letter 252, last para

I am very much flattered by your good opinion of my book. There is no man living whose approbation I set more value upon. I have the honour to be, with the highest respect and esteem

Sir

Your most obedient

and most faithful

humble Servant

Adam Smith

250. *To* GEORGE CHALMERS

MS., NLS Add. MSS., 2.1.15, fol. 60; Scott 296.

[Edinburgh], Friday 3 Dec. 1785

Mr Smiths most respectful compliments to Mr Chalmers. He sends him the tunnage account corrected in the way he wished. The other accounts which he wanted will be forwarded with all possible dispatch on Monday or tuesday next at furthest[1]

251. *To* [GEORGE CHALMERS]

MS., Kress Libr., Harvard University; Rae 400.

Custom-house, Edinburgh, 22 Dec. 1785

Sir

I have been so long in answering your very obliging letter of the 8th instt, that I am afraid you will imagine I have been forgetting or neglecting it. I hoped to send one of the accounts by the post after I received your letter; but some difficulties have occurred which I was [not] aware of and you may yet be obliged to wait a few days for it. In the mean time I send you a note extracted from Mr Websters book by his Clerk, who was of great use to him in composing it and who has made several corrections upon it since[1]

My letters as a Commissioner of the Customs are paid at the Custom house and my correspondents receive them duty free. I should, otherwise, have taken the liberty to inclose them, as you direct, under Mr Roses[2] Cover It may, perhaps, give that Gentleman pleasure to be informed that the net

---

[1] See Letter 249, addressed to George Chalmers, dated 10 Nov. 1785.

[1] See Letters 249 and 250 addressed to Chalmers, dated 10 Nov. and 3 Dec. 1785, also 252 dated 3 Jan. 1786.
[2] George Rose.

revenue arising from the customs in Scotland is at least four times greater that it was seven or eight years ago. It has been increasing rapidly these four or five years past; and the revenue of this year has overleaped by at least one half the revenue of the greatest former year. I flatter myself it is likely to increase still further. The development of the causes of this augmentation would require a longer discussion than this letter will admit of.

Prices speculations cannot fail to sink into the neglect that they always deserved. I have always considered him as a factious citizen, a most superficial Philosopher and by no means an able calculator.[3] I have the honour to be, with great respect and esteem,

Sir
Your most faithfull
humble Servant
Adam Smith

I shall certainly think myself very much honoured by any notice you may think proper to take of me in your book.[4]

252. *To* [GEORGE CHALMERS]

MS., EUL La. ii. 191, Rae 400–1.

Edinburgh, 3 Jan. 1786

Sir

The accounts of the Imports and Exports of Scotland, which you wanted, are sent by this days Post to Mr Rose.[1]

Since I wrote to you last I have conversed with Sir Henry Moncrieff,[2] Dr. Websters successor as Collector of the fund for the Maintenance of Clergymens Widows, and with his Clerk, who was likewise Clerk to Dr Webster, and who was of great use to the Doctor in the composition of the very book which I mentioned to you in a former letter. They are both of opinion that the conversation I had with Dr Webster a few months before

[3] Dr. Richard Price (1723–91), Nonconformist minister and writer on morals, politics, and economics; supporter of the American and French revolutions; his *Review of the Principal Questions in Morals* (1758), *National Debt* (2nd ed., 1772), *Civil Liberty* (6th ed., 1776; 1778 ed.), *Reversionary Payments* (4th ed., 1783), and *American Revolution* (2nd ed., 1785) were in Smith's library (Bonar 150–1, Mizuta 48).

[4] Chalmers wrote of Smith's views on foreign trade: 'This subject has been amply discussed and finely illustrated by Dr Adam Smith, who merits the praise of having formerly strengthened our morals and lately enlightened our intellects' (*Estimate of the Comparative Strength of Britain, 1785* (1786), 76; see also 17, 158, 164, 191).

[1] See Letters 249, 250, and 251 addressed to Chalmers, dated 10 Nov., 3 Dec., and 22 Dec. 1785.

[2] Sir Henry Moncrieff, 8th Bt. (1750–1827), Minister of St. Cuthbert's, Edinburgh, from 1775; Moderator of the General Assembly of the Church of Scotland, 1785.

his Death, must have been the effect of a momentary and sudden thought, and not of any serious or deliberate consideration or enquiry. It was, indeed, at a very jolly table, and in the midst of much mirth and jollity, of which the worthy Doctor, among many other useful and amiable qualities, was a very great lover and promoter. They told me that in the year 1779; a copy of the Doctors book was made out by his Clerk for the use of my Lord North. That in the end of that Book the Doctor had subjoined a note to the following purpose; that tho' between 1755 and 1779, the numbers in the great trading and manufacturing towns and Villages were considerably increased, yet the Highlands and islands were much depopulated, and even the Low Country, by the enlargement of farms, in some degree; so that the whole numbers, he imagined, might be nearly the same at both periods. Both these gentlemen believe that this was the last deliberate Judgement which Dr Webster ever formed upon this subject. The lists mentioned in the note are the lists of what are called examinable persons; that is of persons upwards of seven or eight years of age, who are supposed fit to be publicly examined upon religious and moral subjects. Most of our country Clergy keep examination rolls of this kind.

My Lord North will, I dare to say, be happy to accomodate you with the use of this book. It is a great curiosity, tho the conversation I mentioned to you, had a little shaken my faith in it, I am glad now to suppose, without much reason.[3] I have the honour to be with the highest regard Sir

your most obedient
humble Servant
Adam Smith

253. *To* JOHN SINCLAIR OF ULBSTER

MS., Thurso East Mains, Caithness: Viscount Thurso of Ulbster; Mitchison, *Agricultural Sir John* (London, 1962), 36 n. 2 (reference).

30 Jan. 1786

[This letter cannot be traced now, but is said by Mitchison to contain a 'criticism of Sinclair's first serious book, *A History of the Public Revenue of the British Empire* (1784)'. Part of this letter may be the item listed below as Letter 299.]

[3] See Letter 249.

254. *To* FRASER TYTLER[1]

Address: Mr Fraser Tytler, George Square
MS., NLS Acc. 3639, fol. 19; RSE *Transactions* viii (1818), 538,

[Edinburgh,] 4 Feb. 1786

Dear Sir

I have read over your Paper[2] with the greatest pleasure. The composition is, what it ought to be, simple, elegant and perfectly perspicuous, and will be a very great ornament to our memoirs. Some of my Chymical friends, however, are of opinion that the degree of Vitrification, which takes place in the specimens of those forts, is too great to be the effect of any accidental fire such as you suppose, and could be produced only by a great accumulation of wood heaped upon the wall after it was built. This is a subject of which I am totally ignorant. You had convinced me who fancied that this imperfect vitrification was more likely to be the effect of accident than of knowledge. The friends I mean are Dr Black and Dr Hutton,[3] who, in every other respect, entertain the same high opinion of your composition that [I][4] do. You had better c[onsult] with them, or they may convince you; and even tho neither of these two events should happen, the offense, I apprehend, will not be great either to them or to you. I have the honour to be, with the greatest respect and esteem, Dear Sir

Your most humble Servant
Adam Smith

255. *From* BUCCLEUCH SHARP

MS., GUL Gen. 1035/168; unpubl.

5 Feb. 1786

[Sharp has done badly as a printer in London under Andrew Strahan and wants Smith to arrange his return to Scotland, where he might be of service as a copyist. See Letter 256.]

[1] Alexander Fraser Tytler (1747–1813), lawyer and historian; educ. Edinburgh; advocate 1770; protégé of Lord Kames, whose *Dictionary of Decisions* he continued (1778, 1797); Professor of Universal History at Edinburgh 1780—published his lectures, *Elements of General History* (1801); Judge-Advocate for North Britain 1790; Court of Session Judge, as Lord Woodhouselee 1802, and Lord Commissioner of Justiciary 1811; notable works: *Essay on the Principles of Translation* (1791) and *Memoirs of . . . Henry Home of Kames* (1807, 1814).

[2] Read to RSE in 1789: *Transactions* viii (1818) 537; Smith was one of the presidents of the RSE literary class. Tytler was one of the secretaries of RSE by 1788 (Rae 377).

[3] Dr. Joseph Black, Smith's co-executor with Dr. James Hutton (1726–97), geologist, educ. Edinburgh, Paris, and Leyden (M.D. 1749). Hutton's *Theory of the Earth* (1795) established uniformitarianism in geology, and the modern theory of the formation of the earth's crust.

[4] MS. damaged.

256. *To* ANDREW STRAHAN

MS., University of Illinois Libr., Scott 296.

Edinburgh, 13 Feb. 1786

Dear Sir

I must beg the favour of you to endeavour to employ Sharp[1] for three or four weeks to come in the best way you can, till we have time to look about us. I see he does not spell well, which alone must make him a bad compositor. I have wrote him an encouraging letter, as his letter to me expressed great dejection of spirits. I have, however, (as you will see by the inclosed, which I beg you will read) taken notice of this defect. If in the meantime you could recommend him as clerk to any Warehouse keeper, an employment for which you think him qualified, I should be much obliged to you.

I beg you will employ one of your best compositors in printing the new edition of my book.[2] I must, likewise beg that a compleat copy be sent to me before it is published, that I may revise and correct it. You may depend upon my not detaining you above a week. I should likewise be glad to know when I may draw for the money; I wish to conclude the transaction, least Mr Cadell should take another fit of the ague and make another request which may not be so well received as the former. I ever am

Dear Sir
Most faithfully
yours
Adam Smith

257. *To* [THOMAS CADELL]

Sotheby's Catalogue 478 (27 Oct. 1959), 96 (extract).

14 Mar. 1786

. . . I should be glad to know in what degree of demand the theory of Moral Sentiments still continues to be. The eight and twenty years property are now near expired. But I hope to be able to secure you in the property for at least fourteen years more . . .[1]

[1] See Letter 256 from Buccleuch Sharp, dated 5 Feb.

[2] WN ed. 4 published 6 Nov. 1786; there are a few, trifling alterations of the ed. 3 text made (or permitted) by the author. Other changes appear to be misreadings or corrections of the printers.

[1] By the Copyright Act of 1709, fourteen years of exclusive rights were secured upon publication of a book, after which the author, if alive, had another fourteen years of copyright. Since much of his investment was in the copyright of books, William Strahan supported a movement for perpetual copyright in 1774, but the House of Lords rejected the Bill. Johnson and Hume were opposed to perpetual copyright (Cochrane, *Life of Strahan*, London, 1964, 132–5). Smith objected to monopolies as hindering competition, but put the case for the temporary monopoly granted to inventors of new machines and authors of new books in LJ (A) 2, 31–3 and WN V.i.e.30.

258. *To* [SIR JOHN SINCLAIR OF ULBSTER]

MS., State Historical Museum, Moscow; Scott 297.

Edinburgh, 11 Apr. 1786

Dear Sir

I took the liberty to write you some weeks ago a pretty long letter[1] which I should be glad to hear you had received; and that you have, from the bottom of your heart, forgiven the very great freedom which I have used with you.

In that letter I said that I had no particular remark to make upon what you had said concerning sugar. Upon further recollection, however, I suspect you are wrong with regard to the prices of Muscovado Sugar. I never have bought any of that sugar for family use, so that I have no personal experience of the price. I remember, I think, having told you that during the late war I used to pay fourteen and fifteen pence for the same sugar which I now buy for eight pence and nine pence. I wish you would make some further enquiry concerning the prices of Muscovado Sugar. It certainly could never be so low as a penny a pound. When I lived at Glasgow a hoghead of Muscovado Sugar was valued at importation from thirty to thirty six Shillings the hundred weight of 112 lib. The pound could not be sold, at this rate, under four or five pence. I am told that it sells at present for six pence. The sugar which I principally make use of is what good Housewives call breakfast Sugar and which I buy at the price above mentioned eight pence or nine pence a pound.[2]

I heartily congratulate you upon your late acquisition of Title;[3] and hope I may still live to see you arrive at still higher honours.

I ever am
My Dear Sir
Most faithfully and affectionately Yours
Adam Smith

[1] Letter 253, dated 30 Jan. 1786.

[2] According to Walter Scott, Smith had an inordinate love for lump sugar: 'We shall never forget one particular evening, when [Smith] put an elderly maiden lady, who presided at the tea-table, to some confusion, by neglecting utterly her invitations to be seated, and walking round and round the circle, stopping ever and anon to steal a lump from the sugar-basin, which the venerable spinster was at length constrained to place on her own knee, as the only method of securing it from his most uneconomical depredations. His appearance, mumping the eternal sugar, was something indescribable': Scott, rev. of *The Works of John Home* (1824) in *Quarterly Rev.* xxxvi (1827), 200.

[3] Sinclair was created a baronet on 14 Feb. 1786.

259. *To* ABBÉ MORELLET

Address: A Monsieur, Monsieur L'Abbé Morellet, Paris
MS., University of Illinois Libr.; Scott 298–9.

Edinburgh, 1 May 1786

Dear Sir

After so long an Interruption of our correspondence, I should have been afraid to put you in mind of an old acquaintance, if I had not understood from our most valuable friend, the Marquis of Landsdown,[1] that you still did me the honour to remember me with some degree of kindness. It is in consequence of this that I now venture to introduce to your acquaintance my particular friend, Mr John Bruce, Professor of Logic in the University of Edinburgh.[2] He accompanies on his travels Mr Dundas, a young gentleman of great modesty and property of manners and of great application to his studies and to all his other duties, the son of the Gentleman who may be considered as our present Minister for Scotland. Give me leave to recommend them both to your advice and protection during whatever stay they may think proper to make in your Capital.

Give me leave to condole with you on the many heavy losses which the Society,[3] in which I had so often the Pleasure of seeing you about twenty years ago, have sustained by the death of so many of its greatest ornaments, of Helvetius, of Mr Turgot, of Mademoiselle D'Espinasse, of Mr D'Alembert, of Mr Diderot. I have not heard of Baron D'Holbach these two or three years past. I hope he is happy and in good health. Be so good as to assure him of my most affectionate and respectfull remembrance, and that I never shall forget the very great kindness he did me the honour to shew me during my residence at Paris.[4] Excuse this very great freedom, and believe me to be, with the highest respect and esteem, Dear Sir

your most obliged
and most obedient Servant
Adam Smith

---

[1] The 2nd Earl of Shelburne was created Marquess of Lansdowne, 6 Dec. 1784.

[2] John Bruce (1744–1826), Professor of Logic at Edinburgh, 1774–86; resigned to become travelling tutor to Robert Saunders Dundas (1771–1851), later 2nd Viscount Melville, son of Henry Dundas.

[3] The *philosophes* and ladies of the *salons* known to Smith as a result of his visits to Paris, 1764–6.

[4] D'Holbach no doubt invited Smith to dinners in his house on the rue Royale, Butte St Roche, to meet the leading intellectuals of Paris.

260. *From* SIR CHARLES DOUGLAS

MS., GUL Gen. 1035/169; unpubl.

Gosport, 2 May 1786

[A letter to Smith from a distant relative who discusses his sister's legal difficulties and a plan to enter a son in the Royal Naval Academy, Portsmouth.]

261. *To* THOMAS CADELL

Address: Mr Cadell
MS., Pierpont Morgan Libr., New York; Scott 299.

Edinburgh, 7 May 1786

Dear Sir

This Letter will be delivered to you by my very intimate and particular friend Mr John Bruce. He has a work upon moral Philosophy¹ which; tho' he and I differ a little, as David Hume and I used to do; I expect will do him very great honour. It is as free of Metaphysics as is possible for any work upon that subject to be. Its fault, in my opinion, is that it is too free of them. But what is a fault to me, may very probably, be a recommendation to the Public. It is extremely well written; with simplicity and perspicuity everywhere, and in proper places with the warmth which becomes the subject. I most earnestly recommend it to your attention. I ever am Dear Sir

Most faithfully yours
Adam Smith

262. *To* JOHN BRUCE

Address: John Bruce Esq, chez Mons. de la Serriere, Rue des Fossez St Jacques, à Paris
MS., SRO Hamilton Bruce 104/71; Scott 299–30.

Edinburgh, 3 Oct. 1786

My Dear John

After begging your pardon for having so long delayed writing to you, at last I send you the letter I promised you to Professor Meiner.¹ My mortal aversion to letters of compliment and ceremony has been the

---

¹ *Elements of the Science of Ethics on the Principles of Natural Philosophy* (London, 1786).

¹ ? J.W. Meiner (1723–89), Rector of Langen-Salz, Thuringia, a polyglot linguist; or ? Christoph Meiners (1747–1810), Göttingen professor, prolific writer on the philosophy and history of religion.

principal cause of the delay. Remember me most affectionately to your Pupil[2] and believe, with the greatest love and regard

My Dear John Most faithfully and
sincerely yours
Adam Smith

263. *From* EDMUND BURKE

MS., J. M. and Marie-Louise Osborn Coll., Yale University Libr.; *Burke Corr.* v. 296–8.

Beconsfield, 7 Dec. 1786

My dear friend,

During the whole of the last Winter I flatterd myself that I might have the pleasure of seeing you in London; though I could not hope, that I should have much enjoyment of your Company from the troublesome Nature of the Business in which I was necessarily engaged. I have no Doubt, that in so important and so clear a Case, that on the whole I have met your approbation; and that you do not altogether think, that I wanted the patience and Temper proper to carry me reputably through an undertaking begun under such difficulties on all sides as that was, and conducted under so litigious and vexatious, as well as powerful opposition. This Session will finally dispose of the affair[1]—and then having no engagements on my hands—I may take other matters as they arise with more or less application to them as I think proper, or as my health and strength may admit. I think it right however to caution any friend of mine in judging of me at a distance to look to my papers of charge as the sole things authentick, and to pay no regard to the Speeches in the Newspaper, which so far as regards me, I am persuaded are often misrepresented wilfully; but almost always are misrepresented from the total ignorance of the Speech makers in the matters treated of.

In the Course of Last Winter, Lord Cornwallis was appointed to India with powers totally unlimited.[2] I have reason to believe, that in order to justifye these powers, changes (whether reformations I know not) to which such powers are commensurate will be made. He has gone out with a full spirit of that kind—a very zealous Courtier—no friend of mine—

[2] Robert Saunders Dundas; see Letter 259, addressed to the Abbé Morellet, dated 1 May 1786, n. 2.

[1] The session ended with Warren Hastings being impeached by the Commons at the Bar of the House of Lords, but the trial did not end until April 1795.

[2] Charles Cornwallis (1738–1805), 2nd Earl and later 1st Marquis, was given the power of acting without the consent of his Council on certain occasions (26 Geo. III, c. 16, sec. 7) and of combining the offices of Commander-in-Chief and Governor General (sec. 6) of India.

etc etc. With those dispositions I trust you will not accuse me of being unreasonably timid, when I apprehend it to be possible, that there may be a selection of proper Objects in those changes; and that any friend of mine is not likely to be the better secured for my Wishes in his favour. I do not know Lord Cornwallis in the least—and Mr Ross I have seen only at your House.[3] You know, and you partake in, my regards for my old and valuable friend Will Burke.[4] Thro' what things he has gone, and what his Merits are I need not say. But surely he ought to be sufferd in his Banishment to try to make up some little matter honourably, (he would not make any thing otherwise,) for the little remainder of his Life.[5] Little he can make; and no long time he can live. He has no Enemies but such as are so, and some are so very bitterly, on account of my Conduct. On his own Account he had made nothing but friends; and is, I am well informed, the best beloved man that ever went out to India, both by the Civil, and the Military Lines. I gave him the place of Deputy Paymaster whilst I was in Office. Attempts have been made to remove him. Hitherto they have failed; and for this Service, the old friendship to him of Governor Johnstone,[6] as well as some resort to generosity on the part of Mr Dundas, are to be acknowledged by Mr Burke.

Now my dear friend, may I beg the favour of you to write to Col Ross yourself;[7] and if you can interest any other friends it will be the more obliging, to entreat his friendship and protection to Mr Burke. This you will not do coldly; but with your usual goodnature, and I entreat it may be (*your own* Letter at least) so speedy as to go by the next Ships. I make no apology for desiring an act of kindness at your hands. I am ever with my Wifes and my Sons most cordial regards

My dear Sir
Your most faithful
and affectionate humble Servant
Edm Burke

I do not wish you to particularise any Service to Mr Burke but a general, and, (as you will make it,) strong recommendation. You need not make mention of any attempts against him; this is for yourself, with them it might do harm.

---

[3] Colonel Alexander Ross (1742–1827) was Cornwallis's secretary. Windham records in his *Diary*, ed. Mrs. H. Baring (London, 1866), 63–4, that he and Burke met Ross at Adam Smith's in Edinburgh on 13 September 1785.

[4] William Burke (1729–98), M.P. 1766–74, Deputy-Paymaster of the Forces in India, 1782–93. Edmund recognized him as a cousin.

[5] Cornwallis kept a tight grip on affairs in India, and William Burke was not allowed to make a profit from the money paid to the troops.

[6] George Johnstone (1730–87), M.P. for Ilchester, was usually called 'Governor Johnstone', having been Governor of West Florida from 1763 to 1767. He had a long and stormy career in East India Company politics.

[7] Smith complied; see Letter 264 addressed to Col. Alexander Ross, dated 13 Dec. 1786.

264. *To* LT. COL. ALEXANDER ROSS

MS., Treasure Room, Widener Libr., Harvard University; Scott 300–1.

Edinburgh, 13 Dec. 1786

My Dear Sir

When I had the honour to wait upon you immediately before you left Scotland, I told you that there was only one Man in India whom I would presume to recommend to your particular countenance and protection; viz, your namesake Lieutenant Collonel Ross cheif Engineer upon the Madras Establishment.[1] A very particular circumstance obliges me to depart from this resolution. My old and most valuable friend, Mr William Burke, was appointed deputy paymaster General to the Kings forces in India when his Cousin Edmund was paymaster General. He still continues to enjoy that office. May I most earnestly recommend him, not only to your notice and kindness, but even to your friendship. I am sure you will find him worthy of it. You never knew an honester hearted fellow; social, convivial, perfectly good natured, and quite frank and open; naturally the friend of every man that stood in need of a friend. He is a real man of Business of excellent abilities; and as he went out to India immediately after the first intimation of Lord Pigots affair arrived in England,[2] he must by this time have acquired great knowledge and experience in the Affairs of that country. You will, I imagine, find few men more capable of giving both good information and good advice.[3]

I need not tell you, how much all your friends in this country lament and regret your absence. Nothing but the acquisition of distinguished honour and Glory can ever compensate the comfortable situation you left behind you, or make amends for your separation from all the love and friendship which you enjoyed in this country. Wealth and preferment are most inadequate compensations. But as I know that nothing but your generous Attachment to your friend Lord Cornwallis could have separated you from us, I have no doubt of your acquiring the only adequate compensation for what you have lost. I had the honour of seeing Lord Cornwallis twice at the Earl of Bristols.[4] He probably will not recollect me. If

---

[1] Patrick Ross, Smith's cousin.

[2] Sir George Pigot (1719–77), M.P. 1765–77, Governor of Madras, 1755–63 and 1775–7; created Baronet 1764; suspended two members of the Madras Council and was himself suspended and imprisoned; died in prison.

[3] See Letter 263 from Edmund Burke, dated 7 Dec.

[4] ? Frederick Augustus Harvey, 4th Earl of Bristol (1730–1803), took orders and became Bishop of Derry 1768–1803; studied volcanic phenomena in Italy and Dalmatia; advocated relaxation of Catholic penal laws and abolition of tithes, also parliamentary reform; succeeded his brother, Augustus John, an Admiral, as 4th Earl 1779. Their eldest brother, George William, the 2nd Earl, a diplomat and politician, died in 1775.

he does I beg to be remembered to him in the most respectful manner. I have the honour to be, with the most perfect love and esteem,

My Dear Sir
Your most affectionate
and most faithful, humble
Servant
Adam Smith

265. *From* EDMUND BURKE

MS., Pennsylvania Historical Soc.; *Burke Corr.* v. 301–2.

Beconsfield, 20 Dec. 1786

My dearest friend,

I received a Letter from you and enclosures well justifying that name. I have sent off the Letter to Col. Ross.[1] Will Burke has already received great Civilities, and some service from both the Gentlemen you mention—particularly Sir John Macpherson.[2] But your Letters will go a great way, I have no doubt, in securing the continuance of their friendship, and possibly[3] its future exertions. I wish that in your Letter to Sir John Macpherson you would Let him know that Will Burke has made, as he has, the strongest acknowledgements of his Kindness to him—and you may mention some thing of the same sort relative to Sir Archibald Campbell;[4] for in Truth he received him with a strong memory of their old acquaintance and had been remarkably attentive to him; though, (possibly from want of opportunity) he had not the same particular obligations to him that he had to Sir John Macpherson. Many Many thanks to you and the cordial good wishes of all here. Remember me and my Son most respectfully to Mrs Douglas. I am ever My dear Sir

Your most faithful
and obedient humble Servant
Edm Burke

I send this to London which gets it some hours forward. My Richard retains a most grateful Sense and he bids me to tell you so, of your constant kindness to him whilst he was in Scotland.[5]

---

[1] See Letter 264 addressed to Lt. Col. Alexander Ross, dated 13 Dec. Smith sent it to Burke first, but the accompanying letter has not been traced.

[2] See Letter 197, n. 1. [3] MS.: possible.

[4] Sir Archibald Campbell (1739–91), of Inverneil; General and M.P.; served in America and India; Governor of Madras, 1786–9.

[5] Richard Burke (1758–94), son of the statesman; one of the youngest members of The Club, to which he was elected in 1782; visited Scotland in the summer of 1785; briefly an M.P.; Burke was inconsolable after his death.

266. *To* [BISHOP JOHN DOUGLAS][1]

MS., BM Egerton 2181; NYPL (scribe's copy); Rae 403.

Edinburgh, 6 Mar. 1787

Dear Sir

This letter will be delivered to you by Mr Robert Beatson of Vicars Grange in Fifeshire,[2] a very worthy friend of mine and my Neighbour in the Country for more than ten years together. He has lately published a very useful book called a political index, which has been very successful and which he now proposes to republish with some additions. He wishes much to have your good advice with regard to those additions, and indeed with regard to every other part of his book. And, indeed, without flattering you, I know no man so fit to give him good advice upon this subject. May I, therefor, beg leave to introduce him to your acquaintance and to recommend him most earnestly to your best advice and assistance. You will find him a very good natured, well informed, inoffensive and obliging companion.

I was excessively vexed and not a little offended when I heard that you had passed thro' this town, some time ago, without calling upon me or letting me know that you was in our Neighbourhood. My anger, however, which was very fierce, is now a good deal abated, and if you promise to behave better for the future, it is not impossible but I may forgive the past.

This year I am in my grand Climacteric; and the state of my health has been a good deal worse than usual. I am getting better and better, however, every day; and I begin to flatter myself that, with good pilotage, I shall be able to weather this dangerous promontory of Human life; after which, I hope to sail in smooth water for the remainder of my days. I ever am

My Dear Sir, Most faithfully and

Affectionately yours

Adam Smith

[1] John Douglas (1721–1807) son of a Pittenweem merchant, and friend of Smith from his time as a Snell Exhibitioner at Balliol; controverted Hume's views on miracles in the *Criterion* (1752); D.D. 1758; Canon of Windsor 1762, and St Paul's 1776; F.R.S. and F.S.A. 1778; Bishop of Carlisle 1787–91; Dean of Windsor 1788; Bishop of Salisbury 1791–1807; ed. Clarendon's *Diary and Letters* (1763), and Captain Cook's *Journals* (Second Voyage 1777).

[2] Robert Beatson (1742–1818) military engineer, served in France and West Indies; retired 1766 and devoted himself to agriculture in Fife; compiled *A Political Index to the Histories of Great Britain and Ireland, or a Complete Register of Honours and Persons in Office from the earliest Periods to the Present Time* (London, 1786), dedicating it to Adam Smith.

267. *From* HENRY DUNDAS

MS., GUL Gen. 1035/170; Scott 302.

India Board, [London,]¹ 21 Mar. 1787

Dear Smith,

I received your letter this forenoon. Ross was certainly injured, but Sir Archibald Campbell will do him justice.² I would have persevered against the Court of Directors, but I was suspicious they would have carried their bad humour so far as to dismiss him from their Service, so that by Protecting him farther I might have ruined him.

I am glad you have got Vacation. Mr Pitt,³ Mr Greenville⁴ and your humble Servant are clearly of opinion you cannot spend it so well as here.⁵ The Weather is fine, My Villa at Wimbledon a most comfortable healthy Place. You shall have a comfortable Room and as the Business is much relaxed we shall have time to discuss all your Books with you every Evening. Mr Greenville who is an uncommonly sensible man is concert in this Request.

Yours faithfully
Henry Dundas

¹ Besides being virtual minister for Scotland, Dundas had complete command of Indian affairs by this time.

² Smith no doubt hoped through Dundas to prevail on Campbell, who was Governor and C.-in-C. of Madras, to get military advancement for Patrick Ross. In the end, Ross retired with the rank of General.

³ William Pitt (1759–1806), the Younger; M.P. 1781–1806; Chancellor of the Exchequer 1782–3; First Lord of the Treasury and Chancellor of the Exchequer Dec. 1783–Mar. 1801, May 1804–d.; dominated Parliament with his calmness and assurance; began as a reformer but turned conservative in response to the stresses of a revolutionary era.

⁴ William Wyndham Grenville (1759–1834), M.P. 1782–90, sat in the Lords as Lord Grenville from 1790; Privy Councillor 1783; Paymaster-General, then Jt. Paymaster 1782–9; member of the Board of Trade 1784–9, Vice-Pres. 1786–9, member of Board of Control 1784–90, President 1790–3; Speaker of the House of Commons Jan.–June 1789; Home Sec. 1789–91; Foreign Sec. 1791–1801; First Lord of the Treasury 1806–7; *c.* 1785 was reported as having second place in Pitt's favour: 'The ties of consanguinity cemented every other motive derived from mental endowments. Nature had bestowed on him no exterior advantages. His person was heavy, and devoide of elegance or grace, his manners destitute of suavity. Even his eloquence partook of these defects. In debate he wanted Pitt's copious pomp of words, his facility and majesty of expression' (Wraxall's *Memoirs*, quoted in HP ii. 549).

⁵ Smith went to London for his last visit in March 1787 and remained there until August. He was consulted by Pitt about tax matters. In Dundas's house during this visit, Addington, Grenville, Wilberforce, and Pitt all stood until Smith was seated, because as Pitt said, they were all his scholars (Scott 302).

268. *From* JEREMY BENTHAM[1]

Letter XIII, 'To Dr Smith on Projects in Arts, &c', *Defence of Usury*, 1st edn. 1787; 2nd 1790.

Crichoff, White Russia, Mar. 1787

[Letter XIII is presented in Appendix C, the copy-text being that of the 2nd edn. (1790) as printed in *Bentham's Economic Writings*, ed. Werner Stark (London, 1952), i. 167–87.]

269. *To* JOSEPH BLACK

MS., EUL, Black MSS., Vol. iii; Scott 301.

London, 9 May 1787

My Dear Doctor

This Letter will be delivered to you by the Baron de Baert,[1] a french Gentleman of great Distinction, and of greater information. He is a great traveller and has visited a country unknown to all other travellers that ever I met with; the southern fronteer of the Russian Empire, from Kion to Astrakan and Casan. I beg you will make him acquainted with Hutton and with every other Person you think can amuse him. He is recommended to me by the Duke of Rochefoucault, the Gentleman in France to whom I owe the greatest obligations. I ever am

My Dear Doctor
Most faithfully yours
Adam Smith

270. *To* LT. COL. ALEXANDER ROSS

Address: Lieutnt Collonel Ross, Calcutta
MS., NYPL Berg Collection; unpubl.

London, 13 June 1787

My Dear Sir

When I saw you at Edinburgh, immediately before your departure for India, I told you I would trouble you with no recommendation except for

---

[1] Jeremy Bentham (1748–1832), philosopher and jurist; applied himself to a wide range of problems in ethics, jurisprudence, logic, and political economy; criticized Blackstone in *A Fragment on Government* (1776), which obtained for him the friendship of Shelburne; his *Introduction to the Principles of Morals and Legislation* (1789), in time, resulted in fundamental changes in the administration of justice. While visiting his brother in Russia, he wrote the *Defence of Usury*, advocating acceptance of a high rate of interest on loans and defending projectors as by and large a useful class. See Letter 296 from Bentham, dated 1790.

[1] Alexandre Balthazar François de Paul de Baert (*c.* 1750–1825), author of *Tableau de la Grande Bretagne et d'Irlande* (1800).

my old friend and near relation, Coll: Ross of the Madras establishment.[1] The peculiar situation of the excellent William Burke obliged me to violate this resolution; and the commands of My Lord Loughborrough, to whom you know well my very great obligations, lay me under the necessity of violating it a second time in favour of a friend of his, and of a Gentleman, for whose success, though I have not the honour to be known to him, I am myself extremely interrested. The Gentleman who will present you this Letter, Mr Royds, is the son of one of the most respectable families in Halifax.[2] His Brother is married to a young Lady of great beauty and merit, the daughter of one of the oldest and most respected friends I ever had in the world, Mr Robert White of Kirkaldy, who dyed a little more than a year ago, to the unspeakable loss of his family and friends. Give me leave, both on Lord Loughborroug[h]s account, on account of the Gentleman himself, of whom I have heard the most advantageous character, and on account of his whole family to recommend him in the most anxious and earnest manner to your best advice, countenance and Protection.

There is no news except about the unhappy confusions and disturbances in Holland, in which, I hope, we shall be wise enough to take no share.[3] The Present administration[4] seems as firmly established as it is possible for any administration to be in this country. No public or general discontent and great majorities in both Houses. Believe me to be, my Dear Sir, most faithfully

and affectionately

ever yours

Adam Smith

[1] See Letter 264 addressed to Lt. Col. Alexander Ross, dated 13 Dec. 1786, above, and Letters 263 and 265 from Burke, dated 7 and 20 Dec. 1786.

[2] A note on the cover of the letter reveals that the letter was delivered in Feb. 1788 by Royds, who had travelled to India on the *Ranger* and that a reply (which has not been traced) was sent to Britain by the *William Pitt* in Nov. 1788. Royds and his relative Robert White have not been identified.

[3] In 1787, France was supporting the republicans in the Netherlands, while the British Envoy was organizing associations to defend the constitutional rights of the Stadtholder. The new King of Prussia, Frederick William II, who was married to the Stadtholder's sister, mobilized his troops in the Rhineland. Assured of the co-operation of a Prussian army, Pitt warned France she must abandon attempts to control the Netherlands or fight. The Prussians invaded Holland, the republicans fled, the Stadtholder returned in triumph to The Hague, and the provincial Estates rescinded their suspension of him. On the eve of revolution, France could not interfere, and in April 1788 the United Provinces concluded a formal defensive alliance with Prussia and Britain.

[4] Pitt's.

271. *From* BISHOP JOHN GEDDES[1]

Address: Adam Smith Esqr., Com[missione]r [of] Customs
MS., EUL La. ii. 110 vii (copy); unpubl.

Blackfriars Wynd, Edinburgh, 8 July 1787

Dear Sir

As I am to set out tomorrow for the north, and hope that you will be returned from England with a great Stock of good Health for many years, before my Return; I leave this to be delivered to you by Mr Brydson,[2] who has lately become a particular friend of mine in consequence of the very considerable Merit, of which, if I am not very much mistaken, he is possessed. I think he has more than ordinary Talents, which it is a Pity he should not be enabled to apply to laudable purposes, as he earnestly desires to do.

He has undertaken to give an Account of the Order of the Peerage of Great Britain and Ireland; and if it should be agreeable to you, he will submit to your Perusal an introductory Discourse on the British Constitution, which, in as far as I can judge, is well done.

He has already obtained the Names of several Persons of Eminence as Subscribers to his Work, but he is particularly desirous of your's, for obvious Reasons, if you should think it proper to grant this Favour to him and me, I even entertain Hopes that after conversing with him, you may be pleased to be useful to him with others, who may be very useful to him. He labours under disadvantages; but, I think he has Pur[pose] and will have Perseverance to surmount them.

The Motives, which you will see I have for troubling you with this, will, I am confident, be a sufficient Excuse for it.

I ever am with great Esteem and Regard, Dear Sir, your much obliged and obedient humble Servant

[signed] John Geddes

---

[1] John Geddes (1735–99), Roman Catholic Bishop; educ. Scots College, Rome; Superior of Scalan 1762–7, of Semple's College in Spain 1770–9; Coadjutor of the Lowlands with the title of Bishop of Morocco 1779–97; published a life of Saint Margaret, Queen of Scotland, and a treatise against duelling.

[2] ? Thomas Brydson, author of *A Summary View of Heraldry, in reference to the usages of chivalry and the general economy of the feudal system. With an appendix respecting such distinctions of rank as have place in the British Constitution*, published by Mundell & Son, Edinburgh, 1795.

272. *To* HENRY DUNDAS

MS., NLS Melville Papers 4 fols. 53–4; Scott 303.

Buckingham Str., York Buildings, [London] N.12
Wednesday, 18 July 1787

Dear Sir

When I took the liberty to recommend to you protection, My friend and near relation, Mr Robert Douglas,[1] Lieutenant in the 58th regiment of foot, you was so good as to desire me to write you a letter to put you in mind of the Circumstances of his case. It is in consequence of this conversation that I take the liberty to trouble you at present.

He is the son of Coll: Robert Douglas of Strathendrie, the oldest friend and one of the nearest relations I have now living in the world. His two elder Brothers, Lieutnt Coll: Douglas of the Guards, and John Robert Douglas, of the corps of Engineers, are both officers of merit. His younger Brother, Charles Douglas, got a commission in Lord McLeods regiment, some years after Robert had joined his regiment at Gibraltar. But McLeods being a new raised regiment Charles's first commission was a Lieutenancy, and he had very soon after an opportunity of purchasing a company in the same regiment. He was reduced to half pay at the peace,[2] but had soon after an opportunity of exchanging into full pay with an officer who wished to retire and is now a Captain in Gibraltar; His elder Brother, Robert, an older officer, and, I believe, an officer of very great merit still remaining a lieutenant. Both Brothers served during the whole siege of Gibraltar, and were both present in the sally commanded by General Ross.[3] During the continuance of the Siege Roberts friends had several opportunities of purchasing a company for him, which they were very well disposed to embrace; but they were told, I think very properly, that he could not be removed from his regiment while in actual service. His service, therefor, has stopt his preferment, instead of promoting it. For his Character as an officer and a Gentleman, I can safely refer you to all those whom he has served either with or under; particularly to Sir George Augustus Elliot,[4] General Boyd[5] and General Ross.

[1] Robert Douglas (1760–96), died of wounds received in action at St. Vincent. See Scott Appendix IV, for a family history of this Douglas family. The youngest brother David Douglas, Lord Reston (1769–1819), became Smith's heir.

[2] Of Paris and Versailles, 1782–3, following the American war.

[3] On 27 Nov. 1781, Maj. Gen. Charles Ross (1729–97) of Invercharron led a force of about 2,000 men in a sortie from the garrison at Gibraltar and succeeded in destroying the advanced batteries of the Spaniards.

[4] Gen. George Augustus Eliott (1717–90) defended Gibraltar against D'Arzon and the Spaniards, 1779–83; cr. Baron Heathfield of Gibraltar 1787.

[5] Lt. Gen. Sir Robert Boyd (1710–94), 2nd-in-C. Gibraltar during the siege; General 1793.

I believe, I told you that one of Adairs[6] places, Chelsea Hospital, is in the Gift of the paymasters; the other, or; rather the recommendation to it in that of the Secretary at War. Chelsea Hospital is the best of the two; but both would be best of all; and nothing is too good for our friend John.[7] In the giving away of these Places, the King, I understand, sometimes interferes.

Believe me to be, with the highest sense of your kindness, Dear Sir

Your most obliged

and most faithful, humble

Servant

Adam Smith

273. *From* JOHN LOGAN

MS., GUL Gen. 1035/171; Scott 304–5.

London, 20 Aug. 1787

Dear Sir

I am happy to hear from Mr Mackenzie[1] that you have got down to Edinburgh in good health. There is an old acquaintance of mine, Dr Rutherford, a Dissenting Clergyman and Master of an Academy at Uxbridge, who is publishing 'A View of antient History' by Subscription. He is a good natured friendly man and there is something interesting in his Situation. Soon after he began the business of teaching he was called to visit one of his former pupils who was in a fever; the boy died in his arms, and at the same time the Father was arrested for the Sum of fifteen hundred pounds and would have been carried to prison if Dr Rutherford had not been Security for him, who had the whole to pay. This was probably a London trick, but embarrassed Rutherford very much. Independent of this consideration, the book will not only be a good one but the very best on the Subject.[2] May I therefor hope that you will do him the honour to be one of his Subscribers? The book is to be published in three Volumes large Octavo, but I only ask the favour of you to subscribe for the first. If you could interest the family of Buccleugh in this affair, I would look upon it as a great favour, their names would be of great Service to the keeper of an Academy.

---

[6] Robert Adair (c.1711–90), Sergeant-Surgeon to George III; Surgeon-General of the Army 1783; Surgeon of the Royal Military Hospital, Chelsea.

[7] John Hunter; he was made Surgeon-General in 1790.

[1] Henry Mackenzie the novelist.

[2] Robert Chambers states that the *View of Antient History* was written by Logan, though published over the name of Rutherford (*Dictionary of Eminent Scotsmen* iii. 492). The *View* was published in 2 vols. 1788, 1791, and reached ed. 3 in 1809. Similar letters to engage sympathy for 'Rutherford' and float the book went elsewhere, e.g., to the Revd. Alexander Carlyle (Scott 304).

The King of Prussia and our Court seem determined to support the Prince of Orange, at the same time I have no apprehension of a war.[3] The Duke of York is figuring away here at present, and is very popular, which is not wonderful when we consider the Character of the *Royal* Competitors he has to struggle with.[4]

Lord George Gordon has returned to London and what is more extraordinary has become a Jew. He lodges at the house of my Taylor, goes to the Synagogue on Saturdays and eats no meat but what is killed by the Jews. He is said to be making love to a rich Jewess but I suspect his plans are deeper, and that he intends to set up as Messiah, a trade which has never been very successful. He set up a hideous and horrid roar when he was circumcised.[5]

I set off to the country this day to remain for a fortnight which makes me Shorten my letter. Believe me to be ever,

Sir,

Your faithful humble Servant

J: Logan

274. *To* DR. ARCHIBALD DAVIDSON[1]

Address: The Reverend Dr Archibald Davidson, Principal of the College, Glasgow
MS., GUA 'Letters from Rectors, etc. 1726–87'; Rae 411–12.

Edinburgh, 16 Nov. 1787

Reverend and Dear Sir

I have this moment received the honour of your Letter of the 15th instt. I accept with Gratitude and Pleasure the very great honour which the University of Glasgow have done me in electing me for the ensuing year to be the Rector of that illustrious Body. No preferment could have given me so much real satisfaction. No man can owe greater obligations to a Society than I do to the University of Glasgow. They educated me, they

---

[3] See Letter 270, n. 3.

[4] Frederick Augustus (1763–1827) 2nd s. of George III, cr. Duke of York 1784. He made his career in the Army, and indifferent success in the Flanders campaign of 1793–5 brought him immortality in the nursery rhyme, 'The Grand Old Duke of York'. He became C.-in-C. in 1798, but lost his position in 1809 as a result of a storm in Parliament over the corrupt practices of his mistress, Mrs. Mary Anne Clarke. In 1811 he was reinstated in his command. Save for the eccentric Duke of Cambridge, all of George III's sons led irregular lives.

[5] Lord George Gordon (1751–93) 3rd s. of the 3rd Duke of Gordon, focus of the anti-Catholic riots of June 1780 in which 458 people were killed or wounded. Following his conversation to judaism, Gordon was imprisoned in 1788 for a libel on the Queen of France and died in jail five years later.

[1] Archibald Davidson (d. 1803), Minister of Inchinnan; Principal of Glasgow University 1785–d.

sent me to Oxford, soon after my return to Scotland they elected me one of their own members, and afterwards preferred me to another office, to which the abilities and Virtues of the never to be forgotten Dr Hutcheson had given a superior degree of illustration.[2] The period of thirteen years which I spent as a member of that society I remember as by far the most useful, and, therefore, as by far the happiest and most honourable period of my life; and now, after three and twenty years absence, to be remembered in so very agreable manner by my old friends and Protectors gives me a heartfelt joy which I cannot easily express to you.

I shall be happy to receive the commands of my Colleagues concerning the time when it may be convenient for them to do me the honour of admitting me to the office. Mr Millar[3] mentions Christmas. We have commonly at the board of Customs a vacation of five or six days at that time. But I am so regular an attendant that I think myself entitled to take the play for a week at any time. It will be no inconvenicy to me, therefor, to wait upon you at whatever time you please.[4] I beg to be remembered to my Colleagues in the most respectful and most affectionate manner; and that you would believe me to be, with great truth, Reverend and Dear Sir

Your and their most obliged
most obedient and most humble Servant
Adam Smith

275. *To* SIR JOSEPH BANKS[1]

Address: Sir Joseph Banks
MS., University of Illinois Libr.; Rae 413; Fay, *The World of Adam Smith* (1960), 19 n. (extract).

Edinburgh, 18 Dec. 178[7]

Sir

The great politeness and attention with which you was so good as to honour me when I was last in London, has emboldened me to use a freedom which, I am afraid, I am not intitled to, and to introduce to your acquaintance a young Gentleman of very great merit and who is very

[2] Smith's famous tribute to his former teacher, Francis Hutcheson (1694–1746), after Shaftesbury the chief founder of the Moral Sense school of philosophy. For Smith's account of Hutcheson's system, see TMS VII.iii.c.

[3] John Millar, Professor of Civil Law.

[4] In succession to Edmund Burke, Smith was Lord Rector for two years, 1787–9. He gave no inaugural address.

[1] Sir Joseph Banks (1743–1820) of Revesby Abbey, Lincs.; studied botany at Oxford; F.R.S. 1766; with Linnaeus's pupil Daniel Karl Solander, accompanied Cook on the first voyage of southern high latitude exploration in the *Endeavour*, 1768–71; intended to join Cook for the second voyage in the *Resolution*, but made impossible demands about authority and facilities and was left behind; visited Iceland with Solander 1772; President of the Royal Society 1778–d.; cr. Baronet 1781; Privy Councillor 1797; his library and collections are in the BM.

ambitious of being known to you. Mr Leslie,[2] the bearer of this letter, has been known to me for several years past. He has a very particular and happy turn for the mathematical Sciences. It is now more than two years ago that he undertook the instruction of a young Gentleman, my nearest relation, in some of the higher parts of those sciences and acquitted himself most perfectly both to my satisfaction and to that of the young Gentleman. I think myself upon this account under particular obligations to him. He proposes to pursue the same line in London and would be glad to accept of employment in some of the mathematical academies. Besides his knowledge in Mathematics, he is, I am assured, a tolerable Botanist and Chymist. Your countenance and good opinion, provided you shall find he deserves them, may be of the highest importance to him. Give me leave, upon that condition, to recommend him in the most anxious and earnest manner to your Protection. I have the honour to be, with the highest respect and regard

Sir

Your most obliged

and most obedient

humble Servant

Adam Smith

276. *To* THOMAS CADELL

MS., GUL Gen. 1035/1780; *Economic Journal* xxxiii (1923), 427–8; Scott 374–6 (facsim.)

Edinburgh, 15 Mar. 1788

Dear Sir

You have very great reason to wonder at my long silence. The weak state of my health and my atendance at the Custom house, occupied me so much after my return to Scotland, that tho' I gave as much application to study as these circumstances would permit, yet that application was neither very great, nor very steady, so that my progress was not very great. I have now taken leave of my Colleagues for four months and I am at present giving the most intense application. My subject is *the theory of moral Sentiments* to all parts of which I am making many additions and corrections.[1] The chief and the most important additions will be to the third part, that concerning *the sense of Duty* and to the last part concerning

---

[2] Sir John Leslie (1766–1832), mathematician and natural philosopher; educ. St Andrews and Edinburgh; tutor to Smith's heir David Douglas 1785–7, and then to the Wedgwoods 1790–2; Professor of Mathematics at Edinburgh 1805, and of Natural Philosophy 1819; among his scientific achievements was that of artificial freezing; Knighted 1832.

[1] TMS ed. 6; the additions were sent to the printer Dec. 1789, and the book appeared in 2 vols. before Smith's death, 17 July 1790.

the History of moral Philosophy. As I consider my tenure of this life as extremely precarious, and am very uncertain whether I shall live to finish several other works which I have projected and in which I have made some progress,[2] the best thing, I think, I can do is to leave those I have already published in the best and most perfect state behind me. I am a slow a very slow workman, who do and undo everything I write at least half a dozen of times before I can be tolerably pleased with it; and tho' I have now, I think, brought my work within compass, yet it will be the month of June before I shall be able to send it to you. I have told you already, and I need not tell you again, that I mean to make you a present of all my Additions. I must beg, therefore, that no new edition of that book may be published before that time.

I should be glad to know how the sale of my other book goes on.

I am ashamed of the trouble I have so often given you about the Philosophical transactions. The second part of 1787 is now due to me; and the first part of 1788, if it is yet published, I should be much obliged to you if you could find a clever way of sending them to me.

Remember me most affectionately to Strahan, and believe me to be

My Dear Sir
Most affectionately yours,
Adam Smith

277. *From* PIERRE-SAMUEL DUPONT DE NEMOURS[1]

MS., formerly in copy of Dupont's *Lettre à la Chambre du Commerce de Normandie* (1788), New College Libr., Edinburgh; Bonar 62–3.

Paris, 19 *juin* 1788

Monsieur

J'ai l'honneur de vous envoyer un ouvrage que je viens de publier sur le traité de commerce entre nos deux Nations.[2]

[2] See Letter 248 addressed to the Duc de La Rochefoucauld, dated 1 Nov. 1785, n. 5.

[1] Pierre-Samuel Dupont de Nemours (1739–1817), philanthropist, economist, Deputy to the National Assembly, and translator of Ariosto. He impressed the *économistes* by his *Réflexions sur l'écrit intitulé: Richesse de l'État* (1763), and publicized Quesnay's system in frequent articles for two journals he edited: *Journal de l'agriculture* (1765–6) and *Éphémérides du citoyen* (1768–72), also he published Quesnay's writings together with an analysis in *Physiocratie* (1768). His treatise *De l'origine et du progrès d'une science nouvelle* (1767) and the *Tableau raisonné des principes de l'économie politique* (1775) are among his important contributions to the literature of economics. He became the friend and confidant of Turgot and served under him in the French Government, 1774–6; later he wrote memoirs of Turgot (1782), then enlarged these for an edition of Turgot's complete works (1808–11). As a practical politician he took part in the early stages of the French Revolution, but his views clashed with those of the Jacobins, and after running a clandestine press he was imprisoned, surviving this period solely as a result of the fall of Robespierre. In 1799 he emigrated to the United States and a year later, at Jefferson's request, he

[*Continuation of footnote 1 and footnote 2 overleaf*

Je vous prie de l'agréer comme un tribut de mon respect pour le Livre excellent dont vous avez enrichi le monde.

Vous trouverez que je n'ai pas traité mon sujet assez philosophiquement; qu'il y a un grand nombre de vérités que je n'ai qu'indiquées; qu'il y a plusieurs passages dans lesquels j'ai évité de choquer de front les préjugés de mes lecteurs, et j'ai commencé par applaudir à leurs intentions et à leurs vues avant d'exposer les vues préférables qui sont à suivre.

Monsieur, je voulais persuader même avant de les convaincre des gens animés jusqu'au fanatisme, et qui croiraient faire une action louable en entraînant les deux nations à la guerre pour les replonger sous les fers des Prohibitions respectives.

J'avais à combattre une opinion unanime et universelle dans mon pays. Toute opinion publique mérite d'être traitée avec égard, surtout lors qu'il faut qu'à l'instant l'administration se détermine contre elle. C'est lorsque la nécessité de prendre un parti n'est pas pressante que l'on peut fronder l'erreur de toute la hauteur de la vérité.

J'espère donc que vous pardonnerez les défauts de mon ouvrage qui ne me sont inconnus et dont quelques-uns sont volontaires.

Il est encore plus important de bien faire que de bien dire. Si parlant comme attaché au Gouvernement on annonçait à nos négocians, a nos fabricans et à la Tourbe de nos administrateurs qu'il est inutile et dangereux de donner des encouragemens particuliers aux fabriques et à l'exportation de leurs ouvrages, non seulement on ne serait ni lu, ni écouté, mais on risquerait de décrier tellement les bons Principes qu'on en éloignerait le Gouvernement lui-même, et qu'on prolongerait de dix ans l'ignorance et ses funestes effets. En frappant les yeux d'une lumière trop vive, on leur rendrait la cécité.

Je sais que la Postérité sera éclairée. C'est à la génération présente que je voudrais être utile. Elle est dans l'enfance. Il lui faut encore des alimens proportionnés à la faiblesse.

Lorsque j'étais homme privé, j'étais plus hardi; et je le redeviendrai en quittant la très petite part que j'ai à l'administration. Un simple citoyen peut dire ce qu'il lui plaît parce que personne n'imagine que les conseils des Princes ou des nations se déterminent d'après les livres. Mais si l'administration elle-même paraît vouloir suivre uniquement les Principes

prepared a plan for national education. At this time his son, Eleuthère Irénée, set up a gunpowder mill in Delaware, thus founding the family chemical industry. The father returned to France in 1802 to assist in the negotiations for the Louisiana Purchase, and was active in bringing down Napoleon's regime in 1814, but a year later returned to America where he died.

² *Lettre à la Chambre du Commerce de Normandie sur le Mémoire qu'elle a publié relativement au Traité de Commerce avec l'Angleterre* (Rouen, 1788): an account of the negotiations that led to the signing of the Eden Treaty in 1786. It contains Dupont's *bon mot* likening commerce to Lazarus: resurrection was assured as soon as government cried out like Jesus: 'Ôtez-lui ses liens, et laissez-le aller.'

d'une nouvelle philosophie, les Préjugés s'ameutent autour d'elle manière a lui interdire tout succès.

C'est ce que j'ai vu arriver à l'excellent M. Turgot, et c'est un malheur que j'ai partagé avec lui. Il a fallu dix ans pour qu'une partie de ses plans, celui de la suppression des corvées et celui de la formation des assemblées provinciales pussent se réaliser imparfaitement, et encore au prix des orages auxquels vous voyez notre Royaume en proie.[3]

Il ne faut pas croire cependant que ces orages soient aussi nuisibles qu'ils le paraissent. Ils accoutument à réfléchir sur les intérêts et les droits des hommes; ils mûrissent l'État gouvernant et l'État gouverné.

Nous marchons avec rapidité à une bonne constitution,[4] qui contribuera ensuite à perfectionner même celle de votre Patrie; et les bons principes après été quelque tems concentrés entre les États unis d'Amérique, la France et l'Angleterre, se répandront enfin jusques sur les autres nations.

Vous avez beaucoup hâté cette utile révolution, les *Économistes* français n'y auront pas nui, et ils garderont pour vous autant de respect, Monsieur, que vous daignez leur témoigner d'estime.

J'ai l'honneur d'être avec un respectueux attachement, Monsieur, votre très humble et très obéissant serviteur.

Du Pont

278. *To* DR. ARCHIBALD DAVIDSON

Address: The Reverend, Doctor Archibald Davidson, Principal of the College, Glasgow
MS., Balliol College, Oxford, MS. 421 No. 39: unpubl.

Edinburgh, 16 July 1788

My Dear Sir

Since I received your letter I have again waited upon Baron Moncrief,

---

[3] Turgot's attempts to suppress the *corvées* and establish a tiered system of district and provincial representative bodies culminating in a *grande municipalité* were renewed during the ministry of Calonne 1783–7.

[4] To carry out his reforms, Calonne summoned an *Assemblée des notables*, which met in Feb. 1787 with Dupont serving as one of the two secretaries. There ensued the opening phase of the aristocratic revolt resulting in the fall of Calonne, and the demand by the Paris *parlement* on 26 July 1787 for the summoning of the *États généraux*. By May 1788, matters had reached the point of the Paris *parlement* drawing up a list of the fundamental laws of the monarchy in response to warnings of severe measures of repression. The *Assemblée du clergé* met in June and amid the growing financial crisis, they combined with the provincial *parlements* in calling for a meeting of the *États généraux*. The Government acceded and the meeting was fixed for 1 May 1789. It became clear that the privileged classes of the nobility and the clergy wished to retain a permanent right of veto over the *tiers état*. Dupont was sent to the *États généraux* as a Deputy for the *tiers état* of the *baillage* of Nemours, and he voted both for the establishment of two chambers and the suspensive veto. Subsequently, he presided over the National Assembly twice and often served as its Secretary.

Baron Gordon, and likewise Mr Loch the remembrancer.[1] The delay has been occasioned by a doubt whether there is any precedent of the courts reporting in favour of a lease, to be renewed four years before the expiration of the old Lease, the new lease not to commence till the expiration of the old. If the new Lease was to commence from the date of the Grant, by which four years of the old lease would in effect be given up, they seem to have no doubt. I ventured to say, that, tho' the other way would certainly be best, the College would be very well contented with the last way, if no better can be done. I meet Mr Loch tomorrow at the Exchequer; when he will either shew me his report, if it is ready, or tell me what it is to be. I shall write you again tomorrow. When I saw him today he had not examined his books so as to be able to ascertain the precedent in question. Every body seems very friendly. Mr Loch wishes to get the matter discussed on Friday, the first day of the term, for very friendly reasons. Remember me most affectionately to all my Colleagues. I am sorry for Clow;[2] tho he has dyed in the fulness of years, and I dare to say, perfectly satisfyed and contented with his share of the enjoyments of human life. I ever am

My Dear Sir, Your most faithful, humble Servant

Adam Smith

279. *From* GEORGE CUNNINGHAM

MS., Brotherton Libr., Leeds University; unpubl.

Greenock, 19 Aug. 1788

[George Cunningham, Deputy Collector of Customs at Greenock, asks Smith to favour his application to be made Collector or Comptroller when Glasgow and Greenock become separate divisions. The letter accompanies a memorial addressed to Henry Dundas as Treasurer of the Navy. Smith forwarded the memorial on 1 Sept. 1788; see Letter 280.]

280. *To* HENRY DUNDAS

Address: The Right Honble Henry Dundas, M.P., Dinero Lodge, by Crieff
MS., Brotherton Libr., Leeds University; unpubl.

Custom-house, Edinburgh, 1 Sept. 1788

Dear Sir

It gives me the greatest uneasiness to be obliged to trouble you with any sort of application. But the inclosed letter,[1] in which I perfectly know

---

[1] Officials of the Scottish Court of Exchequer; see Letter 286.
[2] James Clow (d. 1787), succeeded Smith as Professor of Logic at Glasgow.

[1] The memorial from George Cunningham; see Letter 279 from him, dated 19 Aug. 1788.

the truth of every circumstance, has moved me so very much, that I cannot avoid recommending it to your attention. I heartily beg your Pardon for this freedom and hope you will believe me to be your most obliged

and most obedient Servant

Adam Smith

281. *To* DR. JAMES MENTEATH

Address: The Revd Dr James Menteath of Closeburn, Closeburn Castle, Dumfries Shire
MS., GUL Gen. 1464/2; Scott 306.

Edinburgh, 16 Sept. 1788

My Dear James

Your Letter gave my very great pleasure as it both informed me of your good health and as it gave me the hope of seeing you here in the end October or beginning of November. Millar seldom comes into Glasgow till the beginning of November; but he will be able to receive your son[1] and you at his country house, just as conveniently as at his town house; and you and he may speculate about his farm.[2]

Poor Miss Douglas[3] has been confined to her bed now for some time. Without any hope of recovery she preserves her usual spirit and Chearfulness, directs the affairs of the family, which she expects to leave in a few days, with as much care and distinctness as ever; and tho' sorry to part with her friends, seems to die with satisfaction and contentment, happy in the life that she has spent, and very well pleased with the lot that has fallen to her, and without the slightest fear or anxiety about the change she expects so soon to undergo.

We are much obliged to you for your Game; but do not send any more. Nobody in the family can eat them and we do not at present entertain Strangers. About the end of the first week of September Miss Douglas said to me, If you do not receive Game in a day or two from your friend Monteath I shall believe that he is either not well or not in the Country. They arrived next day.

Remember me to the Ladies and the young Gentleman and believe me to be with the greatest love and regard

My Dear James ever yours,

Adam Smith

[1] See Letter 243 addressed to Menteath, dated 22 Feb. 1785.
[2] Professor John Millar's country house was Milheugh, in Blantyre. In Glasgow he occupied a University house.
[3] Janet Douglas, Smith's cousin and housekeeper.

282. *To* [?WILLIAM ROBERTSON]

MS., NYPL Miscellaneous; Scott 305.

Edinburgh, 11 Oct. 1788

Reverend and Dear Sir

This letter is to introduce and to recommend to your attention three Spanish Gentlemen.

> Collonel Francis Xavier Tyrry.
> Dr John Andrew de Temes y Prado.
> Don Francis Codon.

They are men of letters and are travelling for their instruction and improvement. Dr Temes is Rector of the University of Valladolid. They all speak french intelligibly. The Collonel even begins to make himself be understood in English. They are well informed men and their conversation will not be disagreable to you. You are, I imagine, by far the best modern linguist among us,[1] and I, therefore, have taken the liberty to give you this trouble; which I hope, you will excuse. I ever am

> Reverend and Dear Sir
> Most faithfully and affectionately
>
> > yours
> > Adam Smith

283. *To* EDWARD GIBBON

Address: Edward Gibbon, Esqr, Lausanne
MS., BM Add. 34,886, fol. 168ᵛ; Gibbon's *Miscell. Wks.* (1814), ii. 429 (misdated); Rae 414 (in part, misdated).

Edinburgh, 10 Decr. 1788

My Dear Friend

This Letter will be delivered to you by Mr Hugh Cleghorn Professor of History in the University of St Andrews.[1] He is my particular and

---

[1] Possibly the researches Robertson carried out on original European sources for his *History of Charles V* (1769) and *History of America* (1777)—which involved study of Spanish documents—also his status as a clergyman and member of the Edinburgh *literati*, qualify him for consideration as the recipient of this letter.

[1] Hugh Cleghorn (?1751–1836), Professor of Civil History, St Andrews, 1773–93. During the later years of his professorship, Cleghorn travelled a great deal on the Continent, and after 1793 he was employed on secret service by the British Government. He formed a friendship with the Count de Meuron, proprietor and Colonel of a Swiss regiment that formed the main part of the Dutch garrison of Ceylon. With Henry Dundas's support Cleghorn travelled to Ceylon with de Meuron in 1795 and secured the transference of the regiment to British service, thus setting in train the annexation of Ceylon to the British Empire. From 1798 to 1800, Cleghorn was Colonial Secretary of Ceylon, but he resigned

intimate friend, and is besides married to a very near relation of mine.[2] He accompanies upon his travels the Earl of Home,[3] the Chief of our friend Davids family, and a young man, I have every reason to believe, of very amiable and agreable manners. May I beg leave to recommend most earnestly both Pupil and Tutor to your best advice and protection.

I have ten thousand appologies to make for not having long ago returned you my best thanks for the very agreable present you made me of the three last Volumes of your History.[4] I cannot express to you the pleasure it gives me to find, that by the universal assent of every man of taste and learning, whom I either know or correspond with, it sets you at the very head of the whole literary tribe at present existing in Europe. I ever am, my Dear friend, most affectionately yours

Adam Smith

284. *To* DR. JAMES MENTEATH

Address: The Reverend, Dr James Stewart Monteith, Closeburn Castle, by Dumfries
MS., Gen. 1464/3; Scott 306–7.

Canongate, Edinburgh, 2 Feb. 1789

My Dear James

As soon as I received your letter I sent for Mr Angier,[1] who could not then give me any such distinct and satisfactory answer concerning the time in which he proposed to be at Glasgow, as was worth the communicating. I sent for him last week again, and he breakfasted with me this morning when he assured me he would be at Glasgow by the middle of next month. He said he would then be willing to charge himself with the cure of your son and upon his leaving Glasgow in the beginning of May to accompany him for some weeks to your house in the country. I have no doubt

as the result of conflicts with the Governor, Lord North. He bought the estate of Stravithie, Fife, after returning from the East; was elected Captain of the Royal and Ancient Golf Club, St Andrews 1802; and became the friend of Sir Walter Scott who wrote of him in the last diaries as an able man who had seen much and spoke well: see the Revd. William Neil, ed., *The Cleghorn Papers* (London, 1927).

[2] In 1774 Cleghorn married Rachel MackGill who came from Kemback, Fife.

[3] Alexander, 10th Earl of Home (1769–1841), succeeded his father 1786; representative peer for Scotland 1807; Ld. Lt. of Berwickshire; md. Elizabeth, 2nd dau. of the 3rd Duke of Buccleuch 1798. As the heir of the Dunglass branch, he was 'Chief' to all Homes including 'Chief' to all Homes including the Ninewells branch.

[4] Vols. iv, v, vi of the *Decline and Fall* were published on 8 May 1788. In the last volume (Ch. 61, n. 72), Gibbon paid tribute to the Scottish school of historical thinkers: 'On this interesting subject, the progress of society in Europe, a strong ray of philosophic light has broke from Scotland in our own times; and it is with private, as well as public regard, that I repeat the names of Hume, Robertson, and Adam Smith.'

[1] Language teacher who was to give speech therapy to Charles Menteath, James's son, a student at Glasgow University.

about the propriety of your accepting this proposal. He is much charmed with our friend Charles's temper and Disposition.

I am much obliged to you for your inquiries about the Bingham's:[2] they are very satisfactory and comfortable. I have had a very proper and a very affecting letter from the Young Lady. Which, however, I have not answered. She is young and I am not sure of her discretion. If Sir Charles and still more if Lady Douglas, should ever hear that I correspond with her, and disapprove of their conduct, it would put it totally out of my power ever to render her the smallest service. I expect them both here every hour when I hope to do her effectual service.

We are all longing for you at the Club[3] and if you will take up your quarters with me. Davids[4] Bed is at your service. Remember me most respectfully to Mrs Monteith and Miss Monteith and believe me to be

My Dearest James, most faithfully yours

Adam Smith

285. *From* MRS. L. M. BINGHAM

Address: Adam Smith Esqr., Panmuirs Close, Cannongate, Edinburgh.
MS., GUL Gen. 1035/172; unpubl. (Scott 307, n. 1, reference).

Gosport, 20 Feb. 1789

[Mrs. L. M. Bingham writes in French to Smith asking him to further a reconciliation with her father, Admiral Sir Charles Douglas, after her marriage to the Revd. Richard Bingham on 10 Nov. 1788. In justification of her *démarche*, she refers to the miserable life she lived with Lady Douglas when Sir Charles was away.]

286. *To* [HENRY DUNDAS]

MS., GUL Gen. 1506; *Economic History Review* iii (1931), 88–9; Scott 377–8 (facsim.)

Custom-house, Edinburgh, 25 Mar. 1789

My Dear Sir

I need not, I flatter myselfe, inform you at this time, what pleasure, the late happy, (and to my own melancholy and evil boding mind, I acknowledge, unexpected) event, has given to your friends, here and, I will venture to say, to all the real friends of the country. The firmness, propriety and prudence of every part of your young friends conduct must, as long as it

---

[2] See the note on Letter 285 from Mrs. L. M. Bingham, dated 20 Feb. 1789.
[3] ?Poker Club.   [4] David Douglas.

is remembered, place him very high in the estimation of every wise and thinking man in the Kingdom.[1]

It gives me great concern that I am obliged to put you in mind of anything that, at this time of business, can give you any trouble. But there is a very favourable report of the Scots Barons[2] lying before the Lords of the treasury for their approbation, upon the petition of the University of Glasgow for a renewal of the Grant of the Archbishopric.[3] My Colleagues at Glasgow are besides very anxious about a pension to the Widow of their late friend and assistant in their Labours, Dr Irwin.[4] My Colleagues at this board too are equally so about something of the same kind to the Daughter of the late Richard Gardiner,[5] who, before her fathers death had got some hopes of somthing of this kind, and she now certainly needs it more than ever. These are the only affairs about which I wish to trouble you; and enough, you will say, of all conscience.

The Earl of Home thinks himself very much obliged to you for your letter which I transmitted him the moment I received it. I have every reason, that good information, (for it is good information only) can give, to expect much good of this young Gentleman. I ever am, with the highest regard Dear Sir

Your most obliged and most affectionate humble
Servant
Adam Smith

287. *To* MR. THOMAS CADELL

Address: To Mr Thomas Cadell, Bookseller, Strand, London
MS., University of Illinois Libr.; Scott 309.

Custom-house, Edinburgh, 31 Mar. 1789

Dear Sir

Ever since I wrote to you last I have been labouring very hard in preparing the proposed new edition of the Theory of Moral Sentiments.[1]

---

[1] In Nov. 1788 George III had a serious illness that was regarded as insanity. A regency crisis ensued as Pitt (Dundas's 'young friend'), hoping that the King would recover, sought to limit the power of the Prince of Wales and Fox insisted on full royal power for the Prince. The King recovered his sanity in Feb. 1789, resumed his power, and thanked his ministers, with Pitt at their head, for their loyalty.

[2] Of Exchequer. See Letter 278.

[3] In 1697 or 1698, King William III granted a tack (lease) of the Archbishopric of Glasgow to fund a gift to the University of £300 a year, and this tack was renewed for about 125 years by later sovereigns.

[4] William Irvine (d. 1787); M.D., 1766; lectured at Glasgow University on Materia Medica from 1765, and on Chemistry from 1769; associated with Joseph Black in some of his experiments. In 1825, the Faculty granted an annuity of £50 to his widow.

[5] Not traced.

[1] See Letter 276 addressed to Cadell, dated 15 Mar. 1788.

I have even hurt my health and have been obliged to return, within these few days, to my usual attendance at the Custom house (from which the indulgence of my Colleagues had excused me) I may say principally for the sake of relaxation, and a much easier Business. Besides the Additions and improvements I mentioned to you; I have inserted, immediately after the fifth part, a compleat new sixth part containing a practical system of Morality, under the title of the Character of Virtue. The Book now will consist of seven Parts and will make two pretty large 8vo. Volumes. After all my labours, however, I am afraid it will be Midsummer before I can get the whole Manuscript in such proper order as to send it to you. I am very much ashamed of this delay; but the subject has grown upon me. I would fain flatter myself that your Profit from the additions will fully compensate the loss you may have suffered by the delay. Let me hear from you as soon as you conveniently can. Remember me to Strahan and Believe me

ever yours
Adam Smith

288. *From* DR. JAMES MENTEATH

Address: To Adam Smith Esq., Commissioner of the Customs, Edinburgh
MS., GUL Gen. 1035/173; Scott 308.

Closeburn Castle, 20 Apr. 1789

My dear Adam

From Your sensibility of Soul You will easily conceive the pleasure that Your most obliging Favour of the 15th gave me; and entirely relying on Professor Millars Authority and no less on good Davids for the great Service done to my Son by Mr Angier,[1] I have this Day written to Mr Erskine[2] desiring Him [to send][3] You 43 Guineas, which I must beg the favour [of] You to pay to Mr Angier on my Account, as likewise my most grateful Thanks and to tell Him that I received His Letter, which I should have answered myself but did not know where a Letter might find Him. Mr Angiers Fee for a Cure is 50 Guineas, now as I had given Him 10 Guineas for his Attendance on my Son this time twelve Months I presume that He will think the 40 Guineas now a full Payment, but if You find He expects 50 for what He has lately done I will beg the favour of You to give them, the 3 Guineas is on Account of His Expences while He was at Glasgow.

[1] No letter of Smith's to Menteath dated 15 Mar. has been traced, but Letter 284 dated 2 Feb. 1789 explains matters. 'Good David' is David Douglas, Smith's nephew: at this time a student attending Glasgow University.
[2] Not traced but presumably Menteath's man of business in Edinburgh.
[3] MS. damaged.

What You say with respect Yourself as to money Matters, is equally applicable to me; We have both much larger Incomes now than at a former period, but I am not quite certain that either of Us is more happy than we were then. Solomon sith, 'He that increaseth Knowledge increaseth Sorrow'; this may be true; but I am not quite certain of it, as I am, of this that He who increaseth Property increaseth Trouble; this I experience daily.

I am not quite determined about going to Glasgow [for] my Son, but if I go shall certainly return by Edinburgh and do [my]/self the pleasure of seeing You. My best Respects attend Your Sunday Night Friends[4] and believe me to be with great truth

My dear Adam
Your ever most obliged
and most affectionate
Jas. Stuart Menteath

289. *To* DR. JAMES MENTEATH

Address: The Revd, Dr James Stewart Menteath, Closeburn Castle, Dumfries Shire
MS., Gen. 1464/4; Scott 309.

Edinburgh 9 May 1789

My Dear James

David returned to me on Saturday the 2d instt. The first question I asked him was concerning your Son.[1] He said, Your Son was wonderfully improved by Angiers instructions; but that after Angier had left him, he (David) thought he had fallen back a little. He said your Sons industry was prodigious; and that, as their rooms were adjoining, he heard your son every day practising Angiers lessons aloud, sometimes so early as five in the morning. I was excessively vexed at this intelligence and as soon as I could see Angier complained to him of it. He said the habit might not be compleatly confirmed; but that whenever he was in the same place with Mr Menteath he was willing to attend him without fee or reward. I received the inclosed letter from him this morning in confirmation of this. Angier was perfectly satisfied with the 43 guineas. I had not lain out of the money above half a minute when James Dundas[2] repaid it. Ever yours

Adam Smith

[4] Smith's Sunday night suppers at Panmure House were an institution among Edinburgh intellectuals.

[1] See Letters 281 and 284 addressed to Menteath, dated 16 Sept. 1788 and 2 Feb. 1789, also Letter 288 from Menteath, dated 20 Apr. 1789.
[2] Not traced.

290. *To* SIR WILLIAM FORBES[1]

Address: Sir William Forbes Baronet
MS., NLS Acc. 4796 part 2, Box 10, Folder F19; unpubl.

[Edinburgh,] Friday 18 [Sept. 1789]

Dear Sir

It gives me very gr[eat][3] concern that I cannot have t[he plea]sure of waiting on you an[d Mr] Chalmers[4] today at Dinner [ac]cording to My Promise. B[?ad] pain and disorder in my st[omach] make it inconvenien[t] for me to dine out of my own house. I should be very happy to wait on Mr Chalmers if knew where he lodged. Or, if he would do me the honour to call upon me, he will find me at home always in the afternoon, and today, tomorrow and Sunday in the forenoon till two o'clock.

Yours ever
Adam Smith

291. *To* DAVID DOUGLAS

MS., University of Illinois Libr.; Scott 310.

Edinburgh, 21 Jan. 1790

My Dearest David

I have many apologies to make to you for having neglected so long to write to you. You will not, I know, impute it to any want of regard or affection but to an increased shaking in my hand which renders writing more and more inconvenient for me. Your day of tryal[1] will probably be some day in May as, it is proposed, I understand, to bring in a new act of Parliament altering the day of meeting for the court of Session from the 12th day of June to the 12th or some other day in May. You may, I believe, rest satisfied that nobody will get before you.

The illness of Mr Hamilton[2] gives me the greatest concern. His death, which God forbid, would be an irreparable loss to the College of Glasgow.

---

[1] Sir William Forbes (1739–1806), Edinburgh banker and author; entered firm of Coutts, 1754, became partner, changing the name of the firm to Coutts, Hunter & Co. 1773; friend of Boswell, for whom he read part of the MS. 'Journal of a tour to the Hebrides' in 1775 and 1777; a leader in preparing the Bankruptcy Act of 1783; consulted on financial matters by Pitt; member of Dr. Johnson's 'Club'; wrote *Memoirs of a Banking-House* (1803) and a *Life of Beattie* (1806).

[2] Forbes docketed the letter '18 Sept. 1789'.

[3] The letter is torn in a number of places, hence the conjectures about missing words.

[4] ? George Chalmers.

[1] Examination for entrance to the Faculty of Advocates.

[2] William Hamilton, Professor of Anatomy from 1781 at Glasgow University; d. 1790, when he was 32.

I saw Mr Herbert[3] at Dalkeith; but I only saw him. He was so good as to call on me at Edinburgh. But I had the ill Luck to miss him. Be so good as to deliver the inclosed letter to him; it is an invitation to spend some part of the summer with us at Edinburgh. By putting up a bed in our Drawing room we can very easily accomodate him.

I should be glad to hear how the Greek goes on. I suppose by this time you are far advanced in the Odyssey. Mrs Ross and Miss Ross[4] are both in their usual state of health: as is likewise your Brother the Colonel[5] who is here just now on his way to London. Remember me to Mr and Mrs. Millar to Mr James and to all the rest of the family.[6] I ever am my Dearest David

Most affectionately yours
Adam Smith

292. *To* ROBERT CULLEN

Address: Robert Cullen Esqr., Advocate, Argylle Square
MS., GUL Gen. 1503; unpubl.

Custom-house, Edinburgh, 9 Feb. 1790

My Dear Robert

It gives me the greatest concern that it will not be in my power to attend the funeral of my late very dear friend[1] tomorrow. A Stomach complaint has weakened me so much that I can bear no fatigue, not even that of walking from my own house to the Customhouse. I cannot tell you how much I feel both for you and all the rest of the family. I would have been to wait on you but I was afraid of being troublesome.

Ever yours, most affectionately
Adam Smith

293. *From* THE DUKE OF BUCCLEUCH

Address: Adam Smith Esqr.
MS., GUL Gen. 1035/174; Scott 311

Grovenor Square, [London], 24 Feb. 1790

My Dear Sir

I took the first opportunity in my power of speaking to Mr Dundas about Dr Cullens Daughters.[1] The enclosed letter will give you pleasure,

---

3 ? Eldest son of Henry Herbert.
4 Possibly the wife and daughter of Col. Patrick Ross.
5 Col. William Ann Douglas (1753–1803).   6 Of Professor John Millar.

1 Dr. William Cullen, d. 5 Feb. 1790.

1 Dr. William Cullen: see Letter 292, n. 1.

and I have no doubt public satisfaction. Ministers seldom gain much credit by granting of Pensions, but in this case, I am sure, Mr Pitt and Mr Dundas will be much commended. I hope this fine weather will restore you to your usual strength, I wish you could go to Dalkeith House for sometime, I am sure the Country Air and gentle exercise will be of service to you. I need not tell you how much I am interested in what ever concerns you, I should be ungrateful if I did not feel, as I do, with regard to your health and happiness. We have long lived in friendship, uninterrupted for one single moment since we first were acquainted. I hope soon to hear from you.

Yours sincerely
Buccleugh

294. *To* [THOMAS CADELL][1]

MS., NYPL Montague Coll.; unpubl.

Edinburgh, 16 May 1790

Dear Sir

I received two days ago the enclosed letter from Mr Coope of Clapham[2] to whom I have not the honour of being known. I have taken the liberty to desire him to deliver the Papers alluded to sealed up to you and that you would find some safe and easy method of conveying them to me. I hope you will excuse this freedom. I should be glad you could [send] me along with them the last volume of the Philosophical transactions. I have often given you trouble about this before.

I should be glad to hear something about the good or bad success of my new edition.[3] You may safely tell me the truth as I am grown almost perfectly indifferent both as to praise and as to abuse. Remember me most affectionately to Strahan and believe me to be

My Dear Sir
Most faithfully
Yours Adam Smith

[1] The last para. suggests Cadell was the recipient of this letter.
[2] Not identified.
[3] Most likely TMS ed. 6; see Letter 276 addressed to Cadell, dated 15 Mar. 1788, and Letter 287 dated 31 Mar. 1789.

295. *To* THOMAS CADELL

Address: Mr Thomas Cadell, Bookseller, Strand, London.[1]
MS., Kress Libr., Harvard; facsim. *Harvard Business School Alumni Bulletin*
(Nov. 1937), 18.

Edinburgh, 25 May 1790

Dear Sir

I have received this moment you[r] very obliging letter which you may
believe I read with very great satisfaction.

The twelve copies of my book[2] for which I most heartily thank you,
arrived in due course. The bookbinder informed me by, the inclosed note,
that one of the copies is imperfect, wanting the sheet [ ]. I will beg the
favour of you to send down the imperfection by the first parcel you send to
Scotland.

I expected by this time to have been setting out upon my Journey to
London. But my progress to recovery is so very slow, and so often inter-
rupted by violent relapses that the probability of my being able to execute
that Journey becomes every day more doubtful.[3] In the meantime I ever am
Most affectionately yours
Adam Smith

296. *From* JEREMY BENTHAM

MS., University College Libr., London, Bentham MSS., 169. 173–5; *Defence of
Usury* 2nd edn (1790), preface.

[1790]

[When a second edition of the *Defence of Usury* was called for, Bentham
wrote a preface in the form of a 'Letter to Dr Smith'. This 'Letter' is
presented in Appendix C. See, also, Letter 268 from Bentham, dated
March 1787.]

---

[1] After the address on the cover, the phrase 'more to pay' is written in what appears
to be Cadell's hand. The allusion is possibly to the postal charge, as the cover is franked
'post paid'.
[2] TMS, ed. 6.
[3] Smith never recovered sufficiently to travel to London. As far as is known, this is
the last letter he wrote before his death on 17 July.

297. *To* WILLIAM JOHNSTONE

Address: To William Johnstone Esqr, Advocate, at his [house] on the Castle Hill, Edinburgh
MS., Pierpont Morgan Libr., New York; unpubl.

Glasgow, Monday [Mar./Apr. 1752–63][1]

Dear Johnstoune

It gives me the greatest joy to hear that you are likely to be soon here. The sooner you come and the longer you stay the better. This week, however, is the sacrament week, so that as a friend I would advise you to keep clear of it, as I shall be almost constantly in the way of my Duty. This day se'nnight is a good travelling day and will bring you here exactly upon the conclusion of our holidays when you will find everything ten times more joyful on account of the melancholy of the foregoing week. I shall expect a fortnight of you at least. I ever am etc

A Smith

I hope I need not tell you to come directly to my house.[2]

298. *To* JOHN BRUCE

Address: Mr Professor Bruce, Pater Row
MS., SRO Hamilton Bruce 104/71; unpubl.

[Edinburgh,] Thursday 7 Sept. [1780][1]

Dear Sir

I have a good deal of private business upon my hands at present which will occupy me the greater part of to-morrow forenoon and the two following adjourment days. May I therefore beg leave to adjourn our proposed meeting till to-morrow Se'nnight when I shall be compleatly ready for you. I ever am yours entirely

Adam Smith

---

[1] This letter is undated, but the references to 'sacrament week' and 'Duty' suggest that it was written during Smith's teaching days at Glasgow University, when he would be required to perform religious exercises at Easter.
[2] Smith is thought to have occupied the 'back Divinity House', 1752–7, and then two of the houses in turn in Professors' Court, 1757–64 (Scott 420–1).

[1] The letter is undated, but 1780 is the likely year because (a) the perpetual calendar reveals that 7 Sept. fell on a Thursday in 1780 and 1786; and (b) 1786 is ruled out because Bruce was absent from Edinburgh much of that year, acting as a travelling tutor: see Letter 259 addressed to the Abbé Morellet, dated 1 May 1786, concerning Bruce's visit to Paris. The reference to 'adjour[n]ment days' suggests that the letter was written after 1778 when Smith became a Commissioner of Customs.

299. *To* SIR JOHN SINCLAIR OF ULBSTER

John Sinclair, *Life and Times of Sir John Sinclair* (1837), i. 39; Rae 344–5.

[Undated][1]

I dislike all taxes that may affect the necessary expenses of the poor. They, according to circumstances, either oppress the people immediately subject to them, or are repaid with great interest by the rich, *i.e.* by their employers in the advanced wages of their labour. Taxes on the *luxuries* of the poor, upon their beer and other spirituous liquors, for example, as long as they are so moderate as not to give much temptation to smuggling, I am so far from disapproving, that I took upon them as the best of sumptuary laws.

I could write a volume upon the folly and the bad effects of all the legal encouragements that have been given either to the linen manufacture or to the fisheries.—I have the honour to be, with most sincere regard, my dear friend, most affectionately yours,   Adam Smith

300. *From* DAVID HUME

MS., RSE ii. 61; HL ii. 338.

Edinburgh, Wednesday 3 June [Undated]

Mr Hume is very unhappy in never meeting with Mr Smith. He desires to remind him of his Engagement to dine with him tomorrow. If Mr. Smith chuses to pass this Evening with the Chief Baron [? William Mure], he will there meet with Mr. A. Stuart and Mr. Hume.

301. *From* JAMES HUTTON

Address: To Mr Adam Smith, Kirkaldy
MS., RSE 3 Gen. 1035/151; unpubl.

Edinburgh, November [undated][1]

[. . .] from this conspectus such as it is if you can form any opinion pray write me and let us know how you are doing—where do you propose to winter?—if in an enemies country it is almost time you were making good your quarters; if you are stoick enough to judge of the season of the year from the corns in Fife you will now imagine that harvest is near done—I send you this flap in the ear to inform that novem[be]r is begun and that there is now little danger of frost till after the new year; so if you have anything to do with what is without you may conduct yourself accordingly; if it is otherwise and you are made up for sleep and vision, let me know when I should waken [y]ou again. Yours Jas. Hutton

[1] Possibly this is part of Letter 253 addressed to Sinclair, dated 30 Jan. 1786. John Sinclair states in the life of his father that the original consisted of a 'holograph letter in six folio pages', and Rae adds that only the conclusion is extant.

[1] The letter was posted in Edinburgh, because the postmark is a Bishop Mark confined to the G.P.O. in that city. The mark also shows 'NO' for November. The possible years are 1767–72 and 1777 in view of Smith's periods at Kirkcaldy.

302. *From* [CHARLES TOWNSHEND]

MS., SRO Buccleuch Collection GD224/471/1; Scott, 'Adam Smith at Downing Street, 1766–7', *Economic History Review* vi (1935–6), 85–8; Fay 115–16 (excerpt).

[? end of Oct./end of Dec. 1766][1]

Dear Sir

I have the Favor of yours of the 27th of October, which is a fresh proof of your goodness to me, and an additional Specimen of your application and knowledge. Our investigation now grows more difficult and delicate, and it seems necessary to review the whole as far as we have advanced, and bring it into one state.[2] I mean to do this in this letter, and, after having opened to you my thoughts, upon the several heads, into which the subject naturally divides itself, I will venture to suggest some further matter for consideration.

In the first place, then, I think we agree in our Idea of considering the Sinking Fund as consisting of the surplusses of the Three Funds[3] seperate from other surplusses since carried to it and therefore now included in it in common Speech. You approve of the Periods which I have chosen:[4]

---

[1] This letter or 'memorial' was found among Charles Townshend's papers in the Buccleuch Collection, and it is in his hand except for some figures in that of Adam Smith. This fact and the tone of the opening sentence suggest that Smith was the person addressed, but no letter from him dated 27 Oct. 1766 has been traced. It would presumably have been sent from Paris, for Smith and the Duke of Buccleuch reached Dover on 1 Nov. (Rae 226). Scott conjectured that Townshend sought Smith's help with a research project on taxation while the latter was in France. There is some evidence to support this in the data concerning French finance also among the Townshend papers, which Smith could well have collected. This corresponds with material in a bound volume of MSS. entitled 'Etat actuel des finances' and bearing Smith's book-plate, now in the Goldsmith's Library, University of London (Scott, 'Smith at Downing Street', 83, 85; Mizuta 21–2).

[2] Townshend was engaged in writing a 'History of the Sinking Fund'. The incomplete MS. is also part of the Buccleuch Collection: SRO GD 224/47/2. The entry on the schedule of the MSS. reads: 'Mr. Townshend's History of the Funds and many calculations and other papers by Mr Smith, with other papers relating thereto. This History is very long, and copied in several parts by my brother and myself. I hope to be able to put it together. Note Mr Smith's papers were taken out' (Scott, 'Smith at Downing Street' 80). The brothers are identified in a pencilled, marginal note as 'the Messrs Barrett'. Smith was apparently asked to supply facts, theoretical points, and recent information on French finance.

[3] As a result of legislation that received royal assent on 17 July 1717, the surpluses of the 'General yearly fund', Aggregate Fund, and South Sea Fund were to be paid into a Sinking Fund, to discharge 'the principal and interest of such national Debts and Incumbrances as were incurred before the 25th day of December 1716 in such manner as shall be directed or appointed by any future Acts of Parliament and to or for none other use, intent, or purpose, whatsoever' (3 Geo. I, c. 7, s. 37, quoted in P. G. M. Dickson, *The Financial Revolution in England: A Study in the Development of Public Credit 1688–1756* (London, 1967), 86).

[4] 1688–97; 1697–1714; 1715–21 (unfinished, draws attention to Walpole's wise system of finance); 1722–9; 1730–8 (unfinished); cf. WN V.iii. 41–3 for Smith's corresponding account of the accumulation of the National Debt.

you adopt the account of the progress of the Sinking Fund by the reduction of interest and allow this to have been the only cause.[5]

In the next place our difference of Totals arises in every instance merely from your taking in the lesser figures, except in the two instances of an error of subtraction and of an oversight in the manner of transcribing the produce of the Sinking Fund in 1739 from a wrong Sum in the column. As yet I have not been able to explain the seeming inconsistency upon the comparison of the years 1729 and 1738, but I hope to reconcile the several accounts and wish you would turn your thoughts to it.

In stating the saving consequential of the reduction of the interest made by Mr Pelham in 1749 as it took place in 1758 I follow the calculation made at the time of the proposition.[6] It may be seen in the *Gentleman's Magazine* for that year, but I should be glad to know whether it took full effect, tho' I have little doubt of it.[7]

You are certainly right in stating the produce of the supply of the three funds previous to the incorporation of them into a Sinking Fund in 1717 at 239211 : 11 : 2 1/2 and I was led into my error by Mr Fane's mistake.[8]

Your table formed to illustrate my general position that the whole increase of the Sinking Fund has proceeded from reductions of interest and not from improvement of the branches is clear and decisive.

Your state of the produce of the Sinking Fund from 1717 to 1763 is I believe accurate, and the inferences from it self-evident.[9]

In addition to these preliminary materials we only want a clear state of the present sinking fund, its produce and its mortgage, and of the outstanding debts unprovided for.

[5] In WN V.iii. 27, Smith notes the first step was inducing creditors of the public to accept 5% interest, occasioning a saving of 1% on the capital of the greater part of the debts funded in perpetuity, and of one-sixth of the greater part of the annuities paid out of the General, Aggregate, and South Sea Funds. This saving left a surplus in the tax returns in these funds after annuity payments had been deducted, and by 1717 laid the foundation for the Sinking Fund. In 1727, the interest of the greater part of the public debt was reduced to 4%; in 1753 and 1757 to 3·5 and 3%; and these reductions further augmented the Sinking Fund.

[6] On 16 Nov. 1749, Henry Pelham (c.1695–1754), First Lord of the Treasury, outlined proposals to reduce the National Debt by dropping the interest on 4% debt to 3·5%; leaving it at that rate for seven years; then further dropping it to 3%. He preceded these proposals by finding means to raise 3% Government stock above par and reduce India bonds from 4 to 3% (*Gentleman's Magazine*, Nov. 1749, 1; Dickson, op. cit., 230–1; 233).

[7] By Christmas 1757, 88% of the 4% debt had been reduced to 3·5%; and seven years later to 3%. The cost of servicing the funded debt as a result was reduced by about 12% to begin with, and by nearly 25% from 1757, though war loans by this time almost negated the fall (Dickson 239).

[8] ?Henry Fane (1703–77), M.P., Chief Clerk of the Treasury 1742–57; Clerk to the Privy Council 1756–64. He was trained in Treasury business under Walpole and his uncle, John Scrope (HP ii. 413).

[9] The 'table' and 'state of the produce of the Sinking Fund' were presumably removed with other papers of Smith's; see n. 2 above.

Our foundations will then be complete, perhaps Mr D'Oyley[10] could easily get these last from Mr Bradshaw.[11] They are not secrets, not even the mysteries of office.

I will now proceed to consider our present situation in the same detail, and from thence I shall naturally be led to make some remarks upon the several applications of the Sinking Fund which you have suggested, and to add some loose and imperfect thoughts which have occurred to me.

You are sensible how much our establishments are liable to variation; of the fluctuation of the Sinking Fund and the incertainty of [?Each years] annual charges, and therefore you will of yourself consider the estimates of these, not as certain, but as presumed Expenses, to serve for the grounds of calculation and argument merely.

Our charges then last year were

for the Army	1509313 : 14 : 0
Navy	1443568 : 11 : 9
Miscellaneous Articles	295353 : 0 : 0[12]
Total	3,248,235 : 5 : 9[12]

This may presumed to be now the established plan of civil expense in time of Peace, too subject to increase upon every foreign event, and not likely to be lessened from furgality or change of system.

As to our Revenue the Sinking Fund may be fairly stated at

	1800000 £
a Land Tax of 4 shillings[13] will yield with the annual Malt [tax] a nett revenue of	2500000 £
Total	4,300,000
If you deduct from this Revenue	4,300,000 : 0 : 0
the charges	3,248,235 : 5 : 9
the Remainder will be	1051764 : 14 : 3[12]

but from this Surplus of 1,051864[14] must be deducted also the sum now taken out of the Sinking fund in payment of the interest of debts charged

---

[10] Christopher D'Oyly (*c.* 1717–95), War Office, First Clerk 1761–2, Deputy-Secretary Jan. 1763–Jan. 1772; M.P. 1774–84; confidant of Townshend.

[11] Thomas Bradshaw (1733–74), Chief Clerk at Treasury Dec. 1761–Feb. 1763; Commissioner of Taxes Feb. 1763–Aug. 1767; M.P. 1767–74.

[12] These figures are corrections in Smith's hand.

[13] On 27 Feb. 1767, the Government moved that the land tax should remain at 4*s.* in the £, but the Opposition countered by reducing the rate to 3*s.* (HP i. 527).

[14] An error of £100 corrected in the previous deduction was not caught in the subsequent figures.

for the present on this Fund viz. 140000 and the interest of 1000,000 lent last year by the Bank charged also on this Fund—30,000.[15]

The Nett Surplus of the sinking fund therefore, if computed at 1800000, after the current services have been answered and the interest already laid upon it has been discharged will be

$$1051864 : 6 : 3$$
$$170000 : 0 : 0$$
$$\overline{881,764 : 6 : 3}^{16}$$

The declared and unfunded debt is generally and fairly computed at 7000,000. This debt, once liquidated must in a short time be either provided for at 4 per cent or discharged. If it be disposed of as the former debt was at the close of the wars[17] and charged on the Sinking Fund at 4 per cent that will make another deduction of 280000 from 881764 : 6 : 3[18] and make the final free surplus of the Sinking Fund only 601764.[18] which sum, encreasing by the addition of the interest of the parts discharged, will not pay off 7,000,000 in less than about ten years.

Thus Upon this plan the most strict application of the utmost computed produce of the nett Surplus of Sinking Fund remaining after present mortgages are discharged will not bring us within sight of the Capital of our funded debt of 130000,000 til at the end of about 10 years:[19] during which time the Stocks will in that case probably remain in their present low state, and consequently no measures of any kind can be taken for the discharging any part of the capital debt. Private interests will for the same reason be kept at the present high rate, for who will lend his money upon private security at less than 4 per cent when he can have that public interest for 94£ and 3 per cent for [?] 3 [?].[20]

The evident inconvenience, oppression and danger resulting from this

[15] Eighteenth-century budgets were constructed on the basis of pledging the main items of customs and excise revenue to the interest of particular loans, also assigning the surplus from an increase of yield or reduction to interest to the discharging of debt through the Sinking Fund, as documented by Smith in WN V.iii 43–6. New taxes were commonly justified as providing interest on the capital sums that would be borrowed against them (Fay 105, n. 1).

[16] Smith corrected this figure, going back to the remainder left after deducting charges from the sum of the revenue from the Sinking Fund and the annual malt tax.

[17] Efforts were made to reduce the National Debt at the close of the War of Austrian Succession in 1748, and the close of the Seven Years War in 1763. For details, see the appropriate sections of the following vols. of *British Parliamentary Papers*: xxxiii (1857–8), Return of the National Debt of Great Britain and Ireland 1691–1857; xxxv (1868–9), Accounts of public income and expenditure of Great Britain, 1688 ff.; xlviii (1890–1), Report of the proceedings of the commissioners for reducing the National Debt 1786–1890; liii (1898), History of the earlier years of the Funded Debt from 1694 to 1786.

[18] These figures are corrected in Smith's hand.

[19] This estimate is much too low.

[20] If an investor bought 3 per cents at 94, he would obtain nearly £3. 4*s*. per cent.

dilatory plan, necessarily leads men of zeal and active minds to think of all methods of quickening and invigorating the measure.

Among the methods it has been proposed to grant annuities upon the part of the sinking fund, upon which I would make these observations. First that until the expiration of about ten years there will be no surplus of the Sinking Fund at liberty for such use. Secondly that the Terms upon which these and all Annuities must be granted would be governed by the interest of money, and therefore the present time seems to be unfavourable for such a measure, and lastly it has ever been a doubt whether the market would take off any large Sum of annuities at one time.

Others have suggested that it might be right to entrust the Treasury with the power of purchasing such parts of the debt as They judge proper from time to time. To the fairness of this proposal, I have no objection, because the sale is *voluntary*, and it is indifferent to A whether He sells to the public or to B, but great and just objection would be made to the power of purchasing and influencing stock being in one Hand. The price of the Funds turns upon the confidence in Government and Peace; the duration of Peace may be made seemingly incertain by any measure of administration and just to the degree and at the Time They please: by every such temporary variation They may lower the funds, and if They have the power of buying at the same instant, a legal stockjobbing in one sense of the word will be said to be established by act of Parliament, in which the Public indeed will be the Jew but the Minister will be the broker and the subject the Dupe. I wish this impression could be obviated, and the abuse prevented by restraints and directions, but I fear it can not.

What then remains? Are we to hesitate upon every method and propose no other—victims of irresolution and delay. No! I will suggest another Plan: which is the simple one of ameliorating the branches of your Revenue, enriching the Sinking Fund, and appropriating the frequent and future Surplus in time of peace. The Branches I would ameliorate are your Customs, by a better method of preventing illicit trade, your Excise by better changes and regulations in the Soap and tea duty: by lessening the duties on Coffee, and by varying the duties on Spirits. I would enrich the Sinking Fund by new taxes *in themselves* proper, such as the late duty on French Cambricks, a tax on Servants, and other such wise regulations for the encouragement of labour and commerce. I would also fall upon plantations in the forests, and the settlement of waste lands, which adding people and produce would of course encre[as]e interior consumption, the only true source of solid Revenue. I will add to these a *real* American Revenue.[21]

---

[21] James West, in a report to the Duke of Newcastle, described the opening of Townshend's budget on 15 Apr. 1767, as follows: 'He stated the expence of the year at £88 million and then stated the Ways and Means. Proposed the Land and Malt at £2. 7. The Sinking Fund, which with the additions he had got from the sweeping of the Treasury and the

I compute these united branches at about 400,000£ nett additional income, which added to 600000 nett present surplus would make an appropriated summ of 1,000,000 every year encreasing, the sight of which would instantly, and still more as the operation of it drew near to the Funded debt, raise the stocks, invigorate circulation, restore credit, and thereby put things into such a state as to admit of trying the reduction of interest by opening subscriptions for the same debt on lower terms, or granting Annuities, or borrowing money directly.

This is my plan; consider it, and speak without reserve upon every part of this memorial (for I cannot call it a letter) without reserve and pitty.

I have now only one article left to trouble you upon and that is the propositions of Sir J. Bernard.[22] His scheme in 1746 was formed in the hour of great distress, and his proposition in 1737 was founded, as you say, on the rate of interest and the price of Stocks at that time. When the same case exists, the same measure will be right.

Pay Office, he should make 400,000 . . . the American Revenue 110,000. . . . With regard to the funds for the payment of interest on the 1½ million proposed to be borrowed

The chip hats	£37,000
3d. per ell on Russian linens	£10,000
	£47,000

The whole received with universal satisfaction and applause.' Townshend had been interested in an American revenue as early in his parliamentary career as 1753, and was always associated with plans for remodelling the colonial administration. In 1767 the House of Commons passed resolutions inspired by Townshend that suspended the legislative functions of the New York Assembly; established Commissioners of Customs in America to superintend the trade laws; and proposed specific taxes (10 and 13 May). Among the latter was the famous imposition on tea (Financial Resolutions of 2 June), which lead in time with other incitements to the American reaction of the Boston Tea Party of 16 Dec. 1773. No evidence has been found indicating Smith suggested or approved of American duties, and Townshend's list seems to have been advised by close associates outside the Cabinet such as Samuel Touchet and John Huske (Fay 104–6; HP ii. 661; iii. 535, 540, 542, 543, 547).

[22] Sir John Barnard (c. 1685–1764), son of a Quaker wine merchant, turned Anglican, left the wine trade and made a moderate fortune as an insurer with Lloyd's; served as London alderman 1728–58, Lord Mayor 1737–8; M.P. for the City of London 1722–61. In the House of Commons and in print he argued consistently that the return on government stock truly determined private rates of interest, and that in consequence a reduction of interest in the Funded Debt was a necessary condition of cheaper capital in the economy. In 1737 he proposed that taxes should be cut proportionately after a reduction of interest to 3%, but the Government leaders convinced a majority of the Commons that taxes could not be cut until the National Debt had been reduced through the Sinking Fund. In 1746, to combat the depressed condition of the market caused by the Jacobite rising, Barnard suggested raising £3 million by lotteries, with the attached loans having different rates of interest. The aim here was to eliminate the profits of the middle men by going directly to the public for subscriptions. Loans based on Barnard's scheme were raised in 1747–8. See Sir John Barnard's two pamphlets: *Reasons for the More Speedy Lessening the National Debt and Taking Off the Most Burthensome of the Taxes* (1737), and *A Defence of several Proposals for Raising of Three Millions for the Service of the Government for the year 1746* (1746); also Dickson, op. cit., 213–14, 224–5, 478.

I recollect one thing still remaining and that is the composition of the annuities for terms and survivorship and the time of their expiration. This grows a material consideration and should be examined; I have not the means.

I will prepare a state of the branches I would regulate, and some computation of the produce of the dutys I would raise, and show them to you.

I have now done for the present. Let me hear soon from you: and when I come to Town (which will be at the end of this month) we must compare our final judgements.

Adieu! I am much obliged to you for your aid and patience with me.

303. *To* THOMAS WHARTON[1]

Address: Mr Wharton, Commissioner of Excise, Laurieston
MS., inserted in copy of vol. i of WN ed. 3 (1784), Quaritch Catalogue 937 (1974), p. 74; Faculty of Economics Libr., Nihon University, Tokyo, Japan; unpubl.

[Edinburgh], 8 Feb. 1788

My Dear Sir

Though nothing can be more tempting than the company you propose I should dine with to-morrow; yet the state of my health, the coldness of the weather, and my fear of bringing back some of my old complaints; by venturing to dine at so great a distance, oblige me to beg you would excuse me. It is a great mortification to me; but necessity must be submitted to. Remember me most respectfully to Lady Sophia and ever believe me

My Dear Sir
most affectionately
Yours
Adam Smith

304. *From* [WILLIAM CULLEN][1]

MS., GUL Cullen 2255/11; unpubl. draft.

[Glasgow,? late Jan.–Apr., 1751][2]

Dear Sir

I am sorry to find that our divisions give you so much trouble but I hope it[3] will be at an end when you come to live among us for perhaps both

---

[1] Thomas Wharton, Commissioner of Excise for Scotland, 1771–1809.

[1] The contents of this unsigned draft indicate that it is a report to Smith concerning feeling over his election as Professor of Logic at Glasgow; see Scott, pp. 66, 138–9. Cullen was Smith's informant about College affairs; see Letters 9 and 10.

[2] The professors named in the draft taught at Glasgow College. The date must lie after 16 Jan. 1751 (see note 8), but before the end of April (see note 20).

[3] 'your uneasiness' crossed out.

parties at present endeavour to take advantage of the distance you are at
to gain an influence over you. As to what you write of its being said here
that you had sent the two letters to London I had the first notice of such
a report from your letter of yesterday.[4] I have challenged the principal[5] very
freely upon this subject but he assures me in the most confident manner
that he never gave occasion to such a report. I have talked to Dr. Lindsay[6]
in the same way and have the same answers from him and I am apt to
believe they both speak sincerely and as they are the only persons I suspected for it I believe the accounts you have got are a downright falsehood
intended to do the principal a bad office with you but at the same time I
must tell you what is at the bottom and may have given occasion to this
story. When Mr Lindsay and the Principal first got notice of Mr Craigies
letter[7] about himself and six others you will remember they took it in
great dudgeon and alledged it was a false and low artifice. When you
came here to be admitted[8] Mr Lindsay was very inquisitive about that
matter and learned further that Mr Craigies stile was that he and the six
others were to be for you without regard to any great man whatever. This
upon consideration provoked Mr Lindsay very much and communicated
to the principal had the same effect upon him and upon their finding that
Mr Ruat[9] had wrote to Lord Hyndford[10] making Messrs Leechman[11] and
Craigies voting for you a compliment to Lord Hyndford and Duke of
Argyle[12] the principal thought proper to write the affair of your letter to
the Duke of Argyle and at the same time to your Cousin[13] not with a view
of getting declarations[14] from you but to get the facts confirmed from you.
I guessed that this affair when it came to your knowledge would give you
concern[15] and therefore I myself should have hesitated about it but if you
can be vindicated I am not sorry for the Duke of Argyles being acquainted
with the affair. I cannot bear with peoples doing the direct contrary to what
they profess and I can give you many reasons for my being displeased and
Mr Lindsay and the Principal thought they were at Liberty to make use of
what you had accidently dropt in mentioning with what bona fides you
had acted with Mr Craigie upon the Subject of your regard to the Duke of
Argyle.[16] I own to you that I was acquainted with the step and tho I could

---

⁴ Not traced.   ⁵ Neil Campbell.
⁶ Hercules Lindesay, Professor of Civil Law, who taught Smith's logic class when the
latter returned to Edinburgh to resume his lectures there after his admittance as a professor
at Glasgow.
⁷ Followed by 'to you' crossed out. Thomas Craigie, Professor of Moral Philosophy: his
letter has not been traced.
⁸ Smith was admitted as Professor of Logic on 16 Jan. 1751.
⁹ William Ruat or Rouet, appointed Professor of Oriental Languages on 31 Oct. 1750.
¹⁰ John Carmichael, 3rd Earl of Hyndford (1701–67); diplomat with Lanark connections.
¹¹ William Leechman, Professor of Divinity.   ¹² Archibald, 3rd Duke of Argyll.
¹³ William Smith; see Scott, p. 66.   ¹⁴ 'engagements' written above.
¹⁵ 'uneasiness' written above.
¹⁶ Followed by 'I thought the' crossed out.

not approve of it I thought it was safe enough in the Duke of Argyles own hands and if it had gone no further neither you nor Mr Craigie had heard of the matter but I find it has gone further and has been spoke of here and given occasion to [the] report you have met with. Mr Lindsay did not think you were concerned in the matter and at the same time thought he had no measures to keep with[17] other persons. I am apt to think that you may be absolutely vindicated and I can testify that your share in the matter seemed quite undesigned and accidental and I think you cannot be answerable for the use that others have made of what you innocently dropt.[18] I dare say that no member of the College ever said you had sent any of the letters to London and it has been told you with a bad intention. If you please I shall explain the matter as above to every member of the society that are any ways concerned in it but as the affair has not[19] been spoke of here of late and as it must occasion some eclairissemens which in the present state of Mr Craigies health[20] would be disagreeable I think it will be better to let the matter remain as it is till you are here yourself and can judge better how to manage it. In the mean time I have no connexion with the affair to hinder me from doing anything in it that you may desire. As to the principles solliciting declarations from you I cannot understand it for I have perceived no anxiety in him on that subject ever since you was here and as to his either solliciting at London or at Edinburgh with that view he absolutely refuses it and particularly refuses that he ever spoke or wrote to any at Edinburgh on that subject. Perhaps he has at some times been guilty of some indiscretions which indulges his enemies in charging him with more than he is guilty of. I beg that for the sake of your quiet and health you would not indulge in any anger or vexation till you are sure of your facts and which you cannot be with regard to our affairs till you are for some time on[21]

[17] Followed by 'the' crossed out.
[18] Followed by 'If you [?] please' crossed out.
[19] Followed by 'that I know of' crossed out.
[20] In April 1751 Craigie was permitted to cease teaching and go to the country for health reasons (Coutts, *History of the University of Glasgow*, p. 221).
[21] Last words of the incomplete draft at the foot of the fifth page of the MS. No letter based on this draft and received by Smith has been traced.

APPENDIX A

A Letter from Governor Pownall to Adam Smith[1]

Sir,   Richmond, 25 Sept. 1776

When I first saw the plan and superstructure of your very ingenious and very learned Treatise on the Wealth of Nations, it gave me a compleat idea of that system, which I had long wished to see the publick in possession of. A system, that might fix some first principles in the most important of sciences, the knowledge of the human community, and its operations. That might become *principia* to the knowledge of politick operations; as Mathematicks are to Mechanicks, Astronomy, and the other Sciences.

Early in my life I had begun an analysis, of *those laws of motion* (if I may so express myself) which are the source of, and give direction to, the labour of man in the individual; which form that reciprocation of wants and intercommunion of mutual supply that becomes *the creating cause of community*; which give energy, motion, and *that organized form* to the compound labour and operations of that community, *which is government*; which give source to trade and commerce, and are the forming causes of the instrument of it, *money*; of the effect of it in operation, an *influx of riches*, and of the final effect, *wealth and power*. The fate of that life called me off from study. I have however at times (never totally losing sight of it) endeavoured to resume this investigation; but fearing that the want of exercise and habit in those intellectual exertions may have rendered me unequal to the attempt, I am extremely happy to find this executed by abilities superior to what I can pretend to, and to a point beyond that which the utmost range of my shot could have attained. Not having any personal knowledge of the author, or of the port which I now understand he bears in the learned world, I read your book without prejudice.—I saw it deserved a more close and attentive application, than the season of business would allow me to give to it; I have since in the retreat of summer studied it: you have, I find, by a truly philosophic and patient analysis, endeavoured to investigate *analitically* those principles, by which nature first moves and then conducts the operations of man in the individual, and in community: And then, next, by application of these principles to fact, experience, and the institutions of men, you have endeavoured to deduce *synthetically*, by the most precise and measured steps of demonstration, those important doctrines of practice, which your very scientifick and learned book offers to the consideration of the world of business.

Viewing your book in this light, yet seeing, as my reasoning leads me to conceive, some deviations which have misled your analysis, some aberrations from

[1] *A Letter from Governor Pownall to Adam Smith, L.L.D. F.R.S., being an Examination of Several Points of Doctrine, laid down in his 'Inquiry in to the Nature and Causes of the Wealth of Nations'* (London, 1776). See Letter 174 above, also Letter 182 addressed to Governor Pownall, dated 19 Jan. 1777. This text, with the errata corrected, is reprinted from the copy in the British Library. Pownall's WN citations were from ed. 1, 1776. These have been converted to vol. and page ref. to ed. 1, and each is followed by the Glasgow Edition form. Citations and editorial notes are placed within square brackets.

the exact line of demonstration in the deductive part; and considering any errors in a work of that authority, which the learning and knowledge that abounds in yours must always give, as the most dangerous, and the more so, as they tend to mix themselves in with the reasoning and conduct of men, not of speculation, but of business—I have taken the liberty, by stating my doubts to you in this Letter, to recommend a revision of those parts which I think exceptionable.

If these doubts should appear to you to contain any matter of real objection, I should hope those parts might be corrected, or that the bad consequences of those positions, which I conceive to be dangerous, may be obviated. When I first wrote these observations, I meant to have sent them to you, by the interposition of a common friend, in a private letter; but, as I think these subjects deserve a fair, full, and publick discussion, and as there are now in the world of business many very ingenious men, who have turned their minds to these speculations, the making this publick may perhaps excite their ingenuity, and thus become the means of eliciting truth in the most important of all sciences. It may animate even your spirit of inquiry, and lead to further researches. It is not in the spirit of controversy, which I both detest and despise, but in that of fair discussion that I address this to you.

When, in your investigation of those springs, which give motion, direction, and division to labour[2]—you state '*a propensity to barter*'; as the cause of this division: when you[3] say, 'that it is that trucking business which *originally* gives occasion to the division of labour;' I think you have stopped short in your analysis before you have arrived at the first natural cause and principle of the division of labour. You do indeed[4] doubt, 'whether this propensity be one of those *original principles* in human nature, of which no farther account can be given; or whether, as seems more probable, it be the necessary consequence of the faculties of reason and speech.' Before a man can have the propensity to barter, he must have acquired somewhat, which he does not want himself, and must feel, that there is something which he does want, that another person has in his way acquired; a man has not a propensity to acquire, especially by labour, either the thing which he does not want, or more than he wants, even of necessaries; and yet nature so works in him, he is so made, that his labour, in the ordinary course of it, furnishes him in the line in which he labours, with more than he wants; but while his labour is confined in that particular line, he is deprived of the opportunity to supply himself with some other articles equally necessary to him, as that which he is in the act of acquiring. As it is with one man, so is it with the next, with every individual, and with all. Nature has so formed us, as that the labour of each must take one special direction, in preference to, and to the exclusion of some other equally necessary line of labour, by which direction of his labour, he will be but partially and imperfectly supplied. Yet while each take a different line of labour, the channels of all are abundantly supplied.

Man's wants and desires require to be supplied through many channels; his labour will more than supply him in some one or more; but through the limitation and the defined direction of his capacities he cannot actuate them all. This limitation, however, of his capacities, and the extent of his wants, necessarily creates to each man an accumulation of some articles of supply, and a defect of

2 [i. 16; I.ii.1.]				3 [i. 18; I.ii.3.]				4 [i. 16; I.ii.2.]

others, and is the original principle of his nature, which creates, by a reciprocation of wants, the necessity of an intercommunion of mutual supplies; this is the forming cause, not only of the division of labour, but the efficient cause of that community, which is the basis and origin of civil government; for, by necessarily creating an inequality of accumulation, and a consequential subordination of classes and orders of men, it puts the community under that form, and that organization of powers, which is government. It is this principle, which, operating by a reciprocation of wants in nature, as well as in man, becomes also the source to that intercommunion of supplies, which barter, trade, and general commerce, in the progress of society, give. It is not in the voluntary desires, much less in a capricious *'propensity to barter,'* that this first principle of community resides; it is not a consequence of reason and speech actuating this propensity, it is interwoven with the essence of our nature, and is there in the progress of, and as part of that nature, the creating and efficient cause of government; of government as *the true state of nature* to man, not as an artificial succedaneum to an imagined theoretic state of nature.

The pursuing of the Analysis up to this *first principle*, does not immediately, I agree with you, 'belong to the subject of your inquiries;' for the doctrine contained in the second chapter of your first book, seems only noted *en passant*, but is no where, either in the course of your Analysis, used, nor applied in the subsequent explications. But as some thirty years ago, I had made this Analysis of the ⁵*Principles of Polity*; and as I have, in the practical administration of the powers of government, found, that those powers on one hand do, as from the truest source, derive from these principles of nature, and that the liberties of mankind are most safely established on them: and as I think that great danger may arise to both, in deriving the source of community and government from passions or caprice, creating by will an artificial succedaneum to nature, I could not but in the same manner, *en passant*, make this cursory remark.

Having established and defined this first operation of man in community, that of *barter*, you proceed to consider the *natural rules* by which this is conducted; what it is which gives *value*; what it is which *measures* the relative or *comparative value*, and hence the doctrine of *price*: and by the intervention of these, the *introduction of money and coin*. As in the former doctrine, I thought you had not pursued the analysis to the real sources of nature; so here, on the contrary, I think you have stretched your doctrine beyond the garb of nature. Some of your more refined doctrines have rather subtilised ideas, as they lie in your mind, than analised those distinctions which lie in nature. On the first reading the eight first chapters of your first book, in which these matters are treated of, before I came to the use and application of your doctrines in the explication of practice and business, I began to apprehend, that some dangerous consequences in practice might be deduced from theory, instead of those sound and beneficial doctrines which derive through experience, by a true analysis of nature and her

---

⁵ [London, 1752]. A little Treatise which I wrote when I was very young, and which is very imperfect and incorrect in its manner and composition; but such in the matter and reasoning, as frequent revision and application of the principles to matters in fact, have confirmed me in the conviction of as true, although different from the common train of reasoning in those who follow Mr. Locke's phrases rather than his arguments.

principles. I thought I saw, that many mischievous impertinent meddlings might take rise from a distinction between *a natural* and *a market price*. As I had been used to hold that only to be the measure of exchangeable value, which the world generally takes and uses as such, money formed of the precious metals: I could not but apprehend, that many extensively dangerous practices might arise from your laying aside, in your Analysis of Money, the idea of its being A DEPOSIT. I saw, that that *theory of metaphysicks*, led to a destructive *practice in physicks*; to the practice of creating a *circulation of paper*, and of calling such circulation, money; and of introducing it as such. In your doctrine, that 'labour is the measure of exchangeable value of all commodities,' connected with your mode of explanation of the wages of labour, the profit of stock, the rent of land, and the effect of the progress of improvements, I thought I saw great danger, that Theory, in the pride of rectitude, might harden its heart against the real, though relative, distresses, which the labourer and the landed gentry of a country do suffer, and are oppressed by, *during the progress* of improvement, in consequence of a *continuing influx of riches*; and might therefore depreciate, or even endeavour to obstruct, all those current remedies which give comfort and relief to these distresses, and alleviate even those which cannot be remedied.

Although[6] the demand for those who live by wages must naturally increase with the increase of national wealth; and consequently the price of wages rise in proportion to the rise of every thing else; so as that the labourer will in the end partake of the general riches and happiness of the publick. Although[7] the rise in the price of all produce is in the end no calamity, but the *forerunner* of every publick advantage: Yet as those prices do *forerun*, and must, during the progress of improvement, *always forerun*; wages and rent must always continue *at an under-value* in the comparison. They will indeed rise also, but as this foreruns, they can only follow, *sed non passibus æquis*. The labourer, and he who lives on rent, therefore, must always, though improving, be unable to improve so fast as to emerge from a continued distress: if this distinction, that a flowing encrease of wealth, although it is the forerunner of every advantage to the publick in general, and *in the end* to every individual, yet is the continuing cause to the continued distress of the labourer, and of him who lives by rent, is not carefully attended to. If the state of the circumstances of distress, which continues to oppress those classes of the community, are not constantly adverted to with feeling, and with exertions of precaution and benevolence, we shall, in the triumph of our general prosperity, be the constant oppressors of those who have the best title to share in this prosperity.

Under these ideas and apprehensions I did very carefully and repeatedly, before I proceeded to the applied doctrines contained in the latter book, revise the analytic part of the former. When I came to the doctrines applied to practice, and the businesses of the world, I found that my cautions had not been unnecessary, and that my apprehensions, that some such consequences might be drawn from it, were grounded: I found also what I did not from the principles expect (nor as yet do I see how they derive from them, as any part of the chain of reasoning) that in the course of the doctrines you hold, you are led to disapprove the law giving a bounty on corn exported; and also to think, that the monopoly,

---

6 [i. 85; I.viii.21.]   7 [i. 286; I.xi.l.1 2]

which we claim in the American trade,[8] 'like all other mean and malignant expedients of the mercantile system,' without in the least increasing, doth on the contrary diminish the industry of the country, in whose favour it is established; and doth, although it may have the seducing aspect of a *relative advantage*,[9] subject the nation, its trade and commerce, to an absolute disadvantage. I hope you will not think, that I misunderstand, or mean to mis-state, your position. You allow, and very fully explain the great advantages of the colony trade, but think that the monopoly is the reason why, great as it is, we do not derive so great advantages from it to the nation and to the landed interest, and to the community in general, as we might have done, had it not been crampt and perverted by the monopoly.

In the many occasions which I have had to view this monopoly, I own, although I have seen some errors in the extension of the *measure*, further than is expedient or necessary, yet I do not see the malignancy of the principle of a monopoly; nor while I have lived amidst the daily proofs of the *relative advantage* which it gives to the mother country, by its colonies, over all other foreign nations, I have not been able to discover, nor have your arguments, although so methodically and so clearly drawn out, been able to explain to me, that absolute disadvantage which you think it subjects us to.

Although I agree entirely with you, having also previously read the same opinion in Mr. Necker's Treatise, *sur la Legislation & le Commerce des Graines*, that the bounty which our law gives to the exportation of corn, has not been the sole cause which hath rendered corn cheaper than otherwise it would have been; but, on the contrary, hath, in each direct instance, given it some small advance in the general scale of prices: Yet, considering that so far as it does this, and gives relief to the relative oppression which the landed interest must continue to feel under *a continued influx of riches*, and an advancing rise in the prices of every thing else; I think it one of the wisest measures for a country like England that could be devised.

I think with you, that many of our laws and regulations of trade are practical errors, and mischievous. I think that, while they seem to be founded on our navigation act, they mistake the spirit of it, and no less mistake the real interest of the nation: yet I cannot but hold these to be errors only, as they deviate from the true principle of the act of navigation, which is a different thing from the acts of trade.

Having prefaced thus much as to the several doctrines on which I have conceived some doubts, I will now, following the order of your work, state those doubts. When I found you discarding *metallic money*, that intervening commodity which having, by common consent, acquired a value of its own, hath been hitherto esteemed a common known measure of the value of all other things, from being any longer such common measure, and by a refinement of theory, endeavouring to establish in its place 'an abstract notion,' *that labour was the common measure of all value*; I did not only doubt the truth of the position, but, looking to the uses that might be made of the doctrine, hesitated on the principle. If labour be the only real and ultimate measure of value, money is but the instrument, like the counters on the checquer, which keeps the account; if

[8] [ii. 217; IV. vii. c. 56]   [9] [ii. 201; IV. vii.c.26]

this be all the use of money, then *circulation*, or even *an account opened with a banker* (according to a practice in Scotland, as described by you) is to all uses and ends as good as money. If it is not necessary, that the common measure should have some known permanent value in itself, so as to be a deposit of that absent value which it represents, as well as measures, so as to convey to all who possess it an absolute power of purchase, then indeed the circulating instrument, the machine that circulates, whether it be a paper or a leather one, or even an account, without any *deposit*, is equal to all the uses and end of money, is that which we may safely receive for the future. As I have been mixed in the business of a country, where the evils of this doctrine and practice have been severely felt, and where it was my duty to watch, that nothing was imposed upon the publick as money, but what was either in itself a deposit, or was established on a fund equal to a deposit, and what had *all* the uses of a permanent known measure in all cases of circulation; I could not but read this leading doctrine of your's with great caution and doubt. I must doubt, whether it be labour simply which creates and becomes the measure of value, when I find other component parts mixed in the most simple idea of value: I cannot conceive, that equal quantities of labour are absolutely of equal value, when I find the value of labour both in use and in exchange varying in all proportions, amidst the correlative values of these components parts; I cannot suppose labour to be the ultimate measure, when I find labour itself measured by something more remote.—You say very properly in the major of your syllogism, that when the division of labour has once thoroughly taken place, it is but a very small part of the necessaries and conveniences of life, with which a man's own labour can supply him. But when we come to the minor proposition of it, we must consider also the objects on which labour is employed; for it is not simply the *labour*, but the *labour mixed with these objects*, that is exchanged; it is *the composite article, the laboured article*: Some part of the exchangeable value is derived from the object itself; and in this composite value, which is the thing actually exchanged, the labour bears very different proportions of value, according to the different nature of the object on which it is employed. Labour, employed in *collecting* the *spontaneous produce* of the earth, is very different in the composite exchangeable value of the fruit collected, from that which is employed in raising and collecting the *cultured fruits* of the earth. Labour, employed on a rich, cleared, subdued and fruitful, or on a poor and unkindly soil, or on a wild uncleared waste, has a very different value in the composite object produced in the one, from what it bears in the composite value of the other. As the object then makes part of the composite value, we must consider, in the exchangeable value, the object also, as a component part. Whose then is the object? Who has acquired, and does possess, the object or objects on which the labour may be employed? Let us take up this consideration under these first scenes of man, which are usually called a state of nature, somewhat advanced in the division of labour and community. Previous to the employing of labour, there must be some acquisition of objects whereon to employ this labour; a strong and selfish man, who will not labour, sits, we will suppose, idly under a tree, loaded with the spontaneous fruits of nature; an industrious, but weaker man, wants some part of those to supply his necessity, the idler will not let him collect the fruit, unless that other collects also enough for both. Or if, still more churlish and more selfish, he will not let him who is willing, by his labour, to collect a sufficiency for *his* use, unless the labourer collects also more than sufficient for the idler's present use, sufficient for his future use also. Does the labourer here command or exchange, by his labour, any part of the labour of the idler? Certainly not. In this state *a division of the objects* on which labour must be employed, and with which it must be mixed, as well as a division of labour hath taken place; and therefore the labourer must be able, by his labour, to command in exchange a certain portion of these objects which another hath, as well as a certain part of that other's labour. It will not relieve this doubt by saying, as Mr Locke (treating of right) says, that there can be no *right of possession*, but by a man's mixing his labour with any object; because we are here not considering the matter of right, but the matter of fact: nor will it answer to say, that the acquisition itself is an act of labour, because I have here stated the case of a churlish sluggard idler, strong enough to maintain himself in idleness, by commanding not only the actual labourer, but certain *greater or lesser quantity of that labour*, according as his selfish churlish temper leads him to press upon the necessity of the weaker. Suppose the same idler, in this division of the objects of labour, to have got possession of a fishing lake, or a beaver-pond, or in a sandy desart of a spring; or of a spot of fruitful ground, amidst a barren country; or of a ford, or particular position, which commands a fine hunting-ground, so as to exclude the labourer from the objects whereon his labour must be employed, in order to form that laboured article which is to supply his wants. You see, that the means of commanding the *objects of labour, as well the labour* of another, make part of the supply whereby a man must live, whereby he may be said to be rich or poor. Even you yourself (I hope you will excuse the expression under which I quote it) say, with rather some degree of confusion in terms, 'that every thing is really *worth* to the man who has *acquired it*, and who wants to dispose of it, or exchange it for something else; the toil and trouble which it can save to himself, and which it can impose upon other people.' This expresses the conclusion which I draw from the case I have stated, and not your position, that labour is the *measure*, and that it is labour which is exchangeable for *value*: it is, on the contrary, the mixture of the labour, and the objects laboured upon, which produces the composite value. The labour must remain unproductive, unless it hath some object whereon to exert itself, and the object is of no use unless laboured upon. The exchange therefore is made by A keeping a part of his labour mixed with a part of the object, and B using a part of his objects rendered useful by the labour of A mixed with them. The consequence therefore in your syllogism cannot fairly conclude, that the value of any commodity to the person who possesses it, and who means not to use or to consume it himself, but to exchange it for other commodities, *is equal to the quantity of labour*, which it enables him to purchase or command. On the contrary, it is a composite value of the object and labour mixed, and takes part of its value from each of the component parts. It is not therefore labour (which is but one of the component parts of the exchangeable commodity) which gives the exchangeable value, but *the labour and the object mixed*, the compounded laboured article, in which the labour bears all possible proportions to the correlative value of the two component parts, according as the possessor of the object, or the exertor of the labour, or the common general course of the estimation of mankind shall settle it. Real value, if any such thing there be different from market value, is *the mixed composite laboured article*, not labour simply.

You have, Sir, made a very proper distinction of *value in use*, and *value in exchange*. That labour which varies in its productive power, according as it is differently applied, and according to the object it is employed upon, must certainly vary in its use, and equal quantities of it must be in such different circumstances of very unequal value to the labourer. *Labour in vain, lost labour—Labour which makes itself work*, (phrases which, to a proverb, express some species of labour,) *cannot be* said to be *of any use* to the labourer. He who would shave a block with razor, will labour in vain. He who sows on a rock, or on a barren sand, or in a drowned morass, will lose his labour. He who sheers his hogs, will have great cry and little wool, and only make himself work: but labour will still vary more in its *exchangeable value*; equal quantities of labour will receive very variable degrees of estimation and value. In the first operation of barter of labour (the value of the objects being, for the sake of argument, laid aside) we will suppose A to say to B, you shall have as much of the surplus of my labour on the article M, as you will exchange for the surplus of your labour on the article Δ. By this, A 'means to save as much of his toil and trouble to himself, and to impose as much upon B, as he can.' B means the same. What then is to be the real standard of measure? Not labour itself. What is to give the respective estimation in which each holds his labour? Each alternatively will be disposed to estimate his own most valuable, and to each 'the labour of the other will sometimes appear to be of greater and sometimes of smaller value[10].' This value cannot be fixed by and in the nature of the labour; it will depend upon the nature of the feelings and the activity of the persons estimating it. A and B having, by equal quantities of labour, produced equal quantities of two of the most necessary articles of supply, whose values, in the general scale of things, vary the least; each having a surplus in the article which his labour has produced, and each likewise having an equal want of what the other has produced. This *quantity* of labour, although stated as *equal*, will have very different *exchangeable values* in the hands of the one or the other, as A or B are *by nature* formed to make a good bargain in the common adjustment of the barter. He who has not an impatience in his desire on one hand, or a soon-alarmed fear on the other of losing his market; who has a certain firmness, perseverance and coldness in barter; who has a certain *natural* self-estimation, will take the lead in setting the price upon the meek and poor in spirit; upon the impatient and timid bargainer. The higher or lower value of these equal quantities of labour, will follow the one or the other spirit. The value is not equal, and is not fixed in, nor depends upon, the equal quantity of the labour, it is unequal and differs, and is fixed by, and derives from, the different *natures of the persons* bargaining. The exchangeable value of equal quantities of labour, stated equal in all circumstances, is not only not equal in this first instance, between that of A and B, but may, in other comparisons, vary both in A and in B individually.' The exchangeable value of B, although inferior in barter with A, may acquire an ascendant value, and be superior in barter with C. This difference and this variation will run through every degree

[10] [i. 39; I.v.8, also, see l.iv.13].

in the utmost extent of the markets: nay, the same person will, in different habits, relations and circumstances of life, estimate that labour (which shall be stated to be absolutely equal) as of very different value; he will, on different occasions, estimate his 'ease, liberty, and desire of happiness' differently. Equal quantities of labour, equal, I mean absolutely, and in every respect, will acquire and derive very different values both in use, and in exchange both in respect of the person by whom such is exerted, as well as in respect of the person who barters for it, from the objects with which it is mixed. Respecting the person by whom it is exerted, if a day's labour always produces a day's subsistence, the value in use is always the same; if it doth not, the value in use must vary. In respect of exchangeable value, labour will sometimes give value to things which, in themselves, had little or no value: in others, it will derive value from the things with which it is mixed; it will itself have an exchangeable value from its compounded value, that is, from the proportion of value which it bears in the composite laboured article.

What is thus varying in a relative value, must require some correlative, which, while this measures other things, in return will measure it; that which is itself measured by something more remote, cannot be the final measure or standard. It cannot[11] therefore be 'alone the ultimate and real standard by which the value of all commodities can, at all times and places, be estimated and compared: it is not their *real price*.' I must therefore conclude, in a proposition which I quote from yourself, where I wish you had let the business[12] rest; 'That there can be no accurate measure, but that exchangeable value must be settled by the higgling and bargaining of the market, according to that sort of rough equality, which, though not exact, is sufficient for the carrying on the business of life.'

You confess, that this proposition of your's. '*That labour is the measure of the value, and the real price of all commodities,*' is '*an abstract notion.*' As such I should not have taken any notice of it; but you endeavour to establish it as a leading principle, whereby I think a *practical one*, which mankind hath universally and generally acted upon, may be in dangerous speculations distinguished away. If the common forensick idea, that money which, in the common acceptation of it, hath actually been used to measure, doth in strict truth measure as 'a common intervening commodity', both labour and all other things, and their relations, is to be considered as a mere practical notion, and we are in reasoning to look to some abstract notion, as the real standard. What do we, but pervert our reasoning from distinct notions in practice, to 'abstract notions,' and subleties in theory: as I apprehend that these theories have been, and fear they may and will again be used, if admitted into the reasoning of the world, to very mischievous and destructive schemes; as I think that they remove old bounds, and erase old and solid foundations, and may be applied to the building paper castles in the air; as they lead to speculations, which swerve from the idea of *pledge and deposit in money matters*, and tend to create *an imaginary phantom of circulation*, erected on the foundation of credit and opinion of trust only, I have taken the liberty of stating my doubts upon it.

While I have thus doubted, whether labour is the ultimate measure and standard of the exchangeable value of all commodities, I should be willing with

[11] [i. 39; I.v.7.]   [12] [i. 37; I.v.4.]

you to admit, that corn will not universally answer as such a measure had not you yourself,[13] in another part of your book seemed to think, that 'the nature of things has stamped upon corn, *a real* value, which no human institution can alter; and that *corn* is that regulating commodity, by which the real value of all other commodities must *be finally measured* and determined.' Gold and silver, you say, varying as it doth in its own value, can never be an accurate measure of the value of other things. There is then, according to what I have always been used to think, and what from your Treatise I find myself confirmed in, no one commodity that will measure all others, but that all are to one another in their reciprocal value *alternate measures*; and that *gold and silver* is only the common and most general, almost the universal, measure, so found to be, and so used by the general experience and consent of mankind, as *that intervening commodity* which will most uniformly become *a common measure*, at the same that it doth (as being a deposit of value, which all mankind have agreed to receive) *give universal power of purchase.*

As I think that there is no real measure of value, so I think there is no fixed natural rate of value, or real price distinct from the market price. I think, that the doctrine which states the two definitions as an actual existing truth, and as a practical distinction formed for business, not true on one hand, but on the other a dangerous proposition.

You say,[14] 'That there is in every society or neighbourhood *an ordinary or average rate* both of wages and profit, in every different employment of labour and stock;' these average rates you call 'the *natural price*, at the time and place in which they commonly prevail.'

The actual price at which any commodity is *commonly sold*, is called its market price.

I clearly see the distinction in definition; but I do not learn how the ordinary average rates, or price paid for labour, or for the use of land or stock, or for any commodity in the neighbourhood, where it comes from the first hand, in the first act of bargain and sale, is any more natural than the price which it finds and bears in any other succeeding act of bargain and sale, at the time and place wherever it is sold. What is it, in the first instance, which settles these average rates, which you call natural, but the competition of the effectual demand, compared with the supply, and founded on some proportion whereby the price paid for labour, stock or land, will enable the seller to purchase an equivalent quantity of those necessaries and conveniences which his state of life requires? If, from this first operation of bargain and sale, the commodity, by means of carriage, and the collection, storage, and distribution of the middle man, goes to a succeeding and more complicated value with these adventitious articles of expence added to it: Is not the price which is here, also the price at which it here commonly sells, and which is in like manner precisely determined equally, that ordinary average rate and *natural price* as the former? Or rather, is not the price in the first operation of bargain and sale *equally a market price* as the latter, settled by that higgling and barter which doth and must regulate it in all times and in all cases? The refinement which, using different expressions, as in one case calling it 'the ordinary average rate,' and in the other, 'that price at which it

---

[13] [ii. 101; IV.v.a.23.]   [14] [i. 66; I.vii.1.]

is commonly sold,' is a distinction of words without scarce a difference in idea, certainly none in fact and truth. If there be any such thing as a natural price, both are natural; if not, which I rather think both are the artificial market price, such as the act of higgling and barter can settle on the reciprocation of wants and mutual supply. What else is it in *nature* which settles the ordinary average rates, which you call the natural price? This price '*naturally* increases,' as adventitious circumstances mix with the commodity brought to sale. The encreased market price encreases by the adventitious circumstances of labour in carriage, of risque, storage, and the middle-man's profit. This encrease is *naturally* regulated by the ordinary and average rates of these added circumstances in their time and place; and on these the competition, compared with the supply, doth as naturally in one case as in the other create the market price; which may be called, if you choose to call the former so, a natural price; but both are, in fact, equally in their time and place the market price. When therefore you say,[15] 'that the natural price is the *central price*, to which the prices of all commodities are perpetually gravitating'; I must own that I receive the metaphor of the proposition with great apprehensions of the uses in practice, which the doctrine may lead to. If any one, who has got a lead in business, should adopt your distinction of *natural and market price*; and, following the delusion of your metaphor, should think, that, as in nature, all market prices do perpetually gravitate to the natural *central price*, so the circuiting motion of all market prices should be made to take and keep this direction round their center; (perfectly satisfying himself, that as he ought not, so he does not, meddle with the *natural prices* of things:) he may, through a confusion and reverse of all order, so perplex the supply of the community, as totally to ruin those who are concerned in it, and intirely to obstruct it. He may render trade almost impracticable, and annihilate commerce. That the succeeding prices of the secondary operations of bargain and sale are regulated by the same rules and laws of barter as the first; and that the outset of the first will give direction of motion, as well as motion to all succeeding operations, regulated by the same laws of this motion, is certainly true; and that it will (while in the ordinary course of things) keep this motion equable by the respective average rates in their time and place; that the violence and artifices of man will ever and anon try to warp and misrate it, is certainly true; and a truth well worthy of constant attention— not with a view to interfere and intermeddle with the *market prices*, under any theory of regulating them by some supposed natural *central price*, but to obstruct and oppose all interference and meddling whatsoever; and upon this truth to maintain in the market an universal freedom, choice and liberty.

Although, as I have stated my opinion above, I think, that the general course of all prices, or that correlative value between commodities must depend upon, and derive from the reciprocal higgling of bargain and sale, and are not measured by labour: Yet so far as they depend upon, or are mixed with labour, there is some natural scale below which they cannot go; which scale takes its level from the quantity of subsistence which such labour will procure. The plain and homespun wisdom of our ancestors, therefore, did not attempt to measure the prices of things by any *abstract notion of labour being that measure*, but they measured labour itself[16] 'by the plenty or dearth of provisions,' or the subsistance, according

---

[15] [i. 70; I.vii.15.]   [16] Vide the several statutes of labourers.

to the laboured productive effects of nature from time to time. Although therefore I agree with you,[17] 'that the *common wages* of labour *depends* every where *upon the contract* made between two parties, whose interests are by no means the same;' yet in that,[18] 'a man must always live by his work, and that his wages must at least maintain him.' There is a scale of rate below which the price of labour cannot by any contract or bargain be lowered.

That the prices of wages do continually increase with the advancing prosperity of any community, and that they are the highest in those communities, who are advancing with the most rapid velocity, is a truth, a comfortable and an encouraging truth: yet as prices of wages follow but with slow and loaded steps, in proportion to the quick motions of the rise of the prices of all other things, if some care and attention is not given to aid the motion of the rise of wages, in some measure to keep it above the lowest scale, which it can subsist by; we may, in the triumph of prosperity, and in the pride of rectitude, see the poor labourer, of the lower classes, under a continued state of helpless oppression, amidst the prosperity of the community in general; but of the nature, and of the manner of regulating these, I shall have occasion to treat in another place, and on another occasion.

As value or price is not any fixed *natural* thing, but is merely the *actual* correlative proportion of exchange amongst all commodities; *so that intervening commodity which* does in fact most commonly, or on common result, and by common consent, *express this correlative proportion*, is *the common measure* of this value: It is not an abstract notion of *labour*, 'but *money*[19] (as 'Mr Hume says) which is *by agreement* the common measure.' This common measure does not barely express the proportion of value between commodities when brought together in the act of exchange, but is that something, that most common intervening commodity, which mankind hath generally and universally agreed shall not only express this act of exchange, and the relation of reciprocal value under which it is made, but which is in fact an universal equivalent deposit of value, which gives, in all places and at all times, with all persons, a power of purchase, and is in fact and truth that intervening commodity, which, as a common measure, exchanges without actually bringing the things exchanged into barter. The thing which we thus express in abstract reasoning by the word *money*, is *by use* universal, by general and common consent, *the precious metals applied as this practical common measure*, the uses which it hath, and the purposes to which it is applied amongst the acts and things of the community, gives it *a value in its exchangeable operations*. This idea of money is fixed by *old bounds* of common consent and universal practice; and as I am not willing *to remove old bounds*, fixed in a real foundation, to follow an abstract notion[20] 'on Dædalian wings through the air;' I will here next take the liberty to state the reasons which make me hesitate to follow you in those regions of theory. Although you tell me, that it is not the metallic money which is exchanged, it is the *money's worth*; that money may be the *actual* measure of this exchange, but that it is the labour which the money

---

[17] [i. 81; I.viii.11.]   [18] [i. 83; I.viii.15.]

[19] *Essay on Money*, p. 321. [Not traced in Hume. He did write 'money' is nothing but the representation of labour and commodities, and serves only as a method of rating or estimating them', *Phil. Wks.* (1875), iii. 312, 'Of Money'.]

[20] [i. 389; II.ii.86.]

represents and sells and purchases, which is the *real measure*. Yet when my ideas lead me in the very line of your analysis to conceive, that labour is not, no more than any other commodity, the ultimate measure, but is the thing measured; that when measured against subsistance, it is actually measured by that subsistance. When I consider, that although it is the money's worth which is exchanged, yet it is the money which measures and exchanges it. I cannot but think it nearest even to abstract truth, and safest in practice, to abide by *the old bounds* of that idea which mankind hath generally and universally fixed, *that money* IS THE COMMON MEASURE, to be which adequately, and in all its *uses*, it must be a DEPOSIT also.

In your account[21] of the origin and use of money, you very properly state, that 'every prudent man in every period of society (after the first establishment of the division of labour) must naturally have endeavoured to manage his affairs in such manner, as to have at all times by him, besides the peculiar produce of his own industry, a certain quantity of some one commodity or other, such as he imagined few people would be likely to refuse in exchange for the produce of their industry.' If in the doing this, all, led by any thing in the nature of any commodity itself, or by some coincidence of reasoning and consent, should agree upon any one commodity in general, which would be thus generally and universally received in exchange, *that*, in the most refined strictness of abstract reasoning, as well as in decisive fact, would become that[22] *intervening commodity* which would measure the exchangeable value, and be the real instrument of actual exchange in the market. It would not only be that *measure*, but it would become a *real* as well as *actual deposit of value*, and would convey to whomsoever possessed it, a general, universal and effective power of purchase.

When next then I inquire, what this intervening commodity is—I find,[23] that metallic money, or rather, 'silver, is that which, by the general consent of mankind, has become that deposit, which is the common measure; this is a general effect of some general cause. The experience of its degree of scarceness, compared with its common introduction amidst men, together with the facility of its being known by its visible and palpable properties, hath given this effect. Its degree of scarceness hath given it a value proportioned to the making it A DEPOSIT; and the certain quantity in which this is mixed with the possessions and transactions of men, together with the facility of its being known, had made it A COMMON MEASURE amongst those things. There are perhaps other things which might be better applied to commerce as *a common measure*, and there are perhaps other things which might better answer *as a deposit*; but there is nothing, except [the precious metals, or rather] silver, known and acknowledged by the general experience of mankind, which is *a deposit and a common measure*. Paper, leather, or parchment, may, by the sanction of government, become a common measure, to an extent beyond what silver could reach; yet all the sanction and power of government never will make it an *adequate* deposit. Diamonds, pearls, or other jewels, may, in many cases, be considered as a more apt and suitable deposit, and may be applied as such to an extant to which silver will not reach: yet their scarcity tends to thrown them into a monopoly; they cannot be subdivided nor

---

[21] [i. 28; I.iv.2.]   [22] [i.37; I.v.6.]
[23] Vide *Administration of the Colonies* [ed. 5, 1774], vol. i, ch. v.

amassed into one concrete; and the knowledge of them is more calculated for a mystery, or trade, than for the forensic uses of man in common, and they will never therefore become a common measure.

'The quantity of this deposit, and the general application of it to several different commodities, in different places and circumstances, creates a correlative proportion between it and other objects, with which it stands compared, and from this proportion forms *its own scale*; this scale derives from the effect of natural operations, and not from artificial imposition. If therefore silver was never used but by the merchant, as the general measure of his commerce and exchange, *coin* would be (as it is in such case) of no use; it would be considered as bullion only. Although bullion is thus sufficient for the measure of general commerce, yet for the daily uses of the market something more is wanted in detail; something is wanted to mark to common judgment its proportion, and to give the scale: government therefore here interposes, and by forming it into COIN gives the scale, and makes it become to forensic use AN INSTRUMENT in detail, as well as it is in bullion A MEASURE in general.'

It is here, Sir, that I think your Analysis, subtilised by too high refinement, deviates from the path in which the nature of things would have led you. Quitting the idea of money being A COMMON MEASURE, and totally leaving out all idea of its being a DEPOSIT, your Analysis leads you to conceive no other idea of it but as CIRCULATION, or, as you distinctly express it, a CIRCULATING MACHINE; and of course, according to these principles, considering it as an instrument, you state it in your account *amongst those instruments which form the fixed capital of the community.* The result of which in fair reasoning is, that as these machines cost an expence (which must be either drawn from the circulating capital of the community, or from its revenue by savings) both to erect them and to maintain them; so every saving which can be made in the erection or maintenance of such a machine, will be advantageous to the circulating capital, the source of materials and wages, and the spring of industry. In this line of deduction you come to the result in practice, and say,[23] that 'the substitution of paper, in the room of gold and silver money, replaces *a very expensive instrument* of commerce with one much less costly, and *sometimes* equally convenient; *circulation* comes to be carried on by *a new wheel*, which it costs less both to erect and to maintain than *the old one*.'

As my reasoning hath many years ago impressed it strongly on my mind, that money is a COMMON MEASURE, and must be a DEPOSIT, and *in coin an instrument* of the market; and as many years experience in a country of paper hath convinced me, that if any instrument of the exchange of commodities, other than that which, while it measures the correlative values in circulation, is founded on a DEPOSIT, equivalent at all times to the conversion of it into money, shall be introduced, it will be a source of fraud, which, leading by an unnatural influx of riches to luxury without bounds, and to enterprize without foundation, will derange all industry, and instead of substantial wealth end by bankruptcies in distress and poverty.

So far as *circulation* can carry on the exchanges of commodities in the community, so far paper bills of credit, or even accounts opened, may do in the

[24] [i. 350; II.ii.26.]

room of the metallic money; but without a deposit, which is adequate and equivalent in all times and places, and with all persons, to this conversion of it, I have no sure foundation, that I do possess, in all times and places, and with all persons, *the power of purchasing or of accumulating as I like.* Although I have all the trust and confidence in the world in the credit of this circulating machine of paper, yet it has not the universal extent in, nor the operation of all the uses of money, although therefore it may be *'sometimes equally convenient;'* it is not that intervening commodity which hath *all the uses of money,*[25] universally and adequately. Circulation, even where no paper money or credit exists, must always much exceed in its total of exchange the sum total of the money deposit, how much that is, experience in the fact can alone determine: paper may certainly, without any danger, encrease this power of circulation, if it does not exceed what the deposit will answer while it is in circulation, and is created *on such a fund, as will finally convert it into money.* So far as paper, by the extent of the uses, and the absolute security and exchangeable conversion of it into metallic money, *can be and is made a deposit,* so far it may safely measure as money, and become a convenient instrument; but in that this security is always more or less uncertain; in that it depends on the prudence and probity of the money makers, it is always liable to exception, abuse and failure. So far forth as it is defective in its fund, the creation and use of it must be always hazardous, and hath been generally ruinous; and however distant and remote the end may be, *must* be a fraud in the end. In a world of enterprize, where *trust and credit* is substituted *in the stead of fund* and prompt change, paper money loses the very essence of a deposit; unless I have *a deposit,* which gives me an absolute actual power of purchasing, in all times and places, in all events, to all intents and uses; or that which is absolutely ready and immediate change for such deposit. The bill which I have, may or may not, here or there, now and then, *sometimes* not always, maintain in me *the power of purchasing,* or of real hoarding or banking as I like. General, universal, permanent consent of all mankind, has, from *actual experience* of its uses, given to *metallic money* a permanent and absolute value: partial, local, temporary agreement, founded *in opinion of trust and credit,* can give to paper but a partial, local, temporary ideal value, which never will be a real and universal deposit; it may become to certain local temporary purposes a *circulating machine,* but money is something more: this paper is not that intervening commodity, which all mankind hath universally agreed to be *that common measure which is a deposit;* such alone is money in the strict as well as common acceptation of the word and idea.

So far as paper money can be so contrived as to have, while it is in circulation, *all the uses* of money; or is so founded, that it can in all moments and in all places be taken out of circulation by conversion into metallic money at its nominal value, so far it will be equal to money both as a measure and as a deposit. But so far as it is defective in any one use, however much it may excel in any other use, it will and must depreciate below the real value of the metallic money, which it is supposed to represent; so far as in any point of time or place the power of converting it into metallic money is remote, so for is it ideal, unsubstantial, and no deposit. Although with a fund of 20,000*l.* a banker, or the treasury

[25] [i. 351; II.ii.29.]

of a government, may circulate 100,000*l*. yet as whevever, for any reason, or by any event, it becomes necessary to take that 100,000*l*. out of circulation, the banker or the treasury can but pay 20,000*l*. or four shillings in the pound, that circulation must end in a fraud.

Where, in the circulation of capital, paper money is substituted instead of metallic money, you allow, that it will not answer in its uses to foreign trade. I, for the same reason, add, it will not *pay taxes*, so far as those taxes are to *supply expences incurred or laid out abroad*. If great variety of *reabsorbing glands* did not in Scotland take up, in the course of circulation, the amount of the taxes levied on that part of the kingdom, their paper money could not pay that amount.

Just as much gold, as paper circulation becomes a substitute for, may be spared from circulation, and will become, as you truly say, a new fund for commerce, and will go abroad in foreign trade: if it is employed in a commerce of luxury or consumption, it is in every respect hurtful to society; so far as it purchases raw and rude materials, or provisions or tools, and instruments to work with, it may be beneficial. You think that, however individuals may run into the former, bodies and societies are more likely to actuate the latter. Yet in countries where a superabundant quantity of paper money hath taken place, where the power of creating this money hath advanced faster in its creation and emissions than the labour, industry and abilities of the inhabitants would have produced it. This *artificial plenty* hath always encouraged a commerce of luxury; an over-trading; a multitude and disproportionate number of shop-keepers; extravagant expences in idle land-holders; more building than can be supported; and all kinds of ambitious and dangerous projects. '[26]The commerce and industy of a country, you must acknowledge, and do candidly confess, though they may be somewhat augmented, cannot be altogether *so secure*, when they are thus, as it were, suspended upon the *dædalian wings of paper money*, as when they travel *on the solid ground of gold and silver*. Over and above the accidents to which they are exposed from the unskilfulness (I *would here add the fraud also*) of the conductors of this paper money, they are liable to several others, from which no prudence or skill of the conductors can guard them.'—You indeed reason from the *abuse*, but all these arguments do equally derive from the *defect* of this paper money. As it creates an *influx of riches*, which does not spring from industry, which is not the effect and produce of useful labour; it creates, with aggravated circumstances, all that distress which the real useful labourer and real man of property, the land-owner, must feel, even under an influx of real riches; it gives motion and velocity to this influx, without producing any real *deposit* whereon the *riches*, which it pours in to circulation, *may be funded as* WEALTH. The land-holder lives for a while under oppression and distress; he then, raising his rents beyond what the real stock will bear, lives in a delusive abundance of luxurious expence, but is finally ruined. The successor, who purchases him out, succeeds by the same disease to the same ruin. The labourer, and all who live on fixed stipend, are under a continued series of oppression. The false wealth only of adventurers, jobbers, and cheats, become the riches of the country; that real deposit, which would be a fund of real wealth and real supply in case of distress,

[26] [i. 389; II.ii.86.]

will be chaced away. The phantom of circulation, which is substituted in its place, will, instead of coming in aid, fail, and vanish on the first alarm of distress.

'[27]An unsuccessful war, for example, in which the enemy got possession of the capital (*who does not tremble as he reads?*) and consequently of that treasure which supported the credit of paper money, would occasion *a much greater confusion* in a country where the whole circulation was carried on by paper, than in one where the greater part of it was carried on by gold and silver. The usual instrument of commerce *having lost its value*, no exchanges could be made but by barter or upon credit. All taxes having been usually paid in paper money, the prince would not have wherewithal either to pay his troops or to furnish his magazines; and the state of the country would be much more irretrievable, than if the greater part of its circulation had consisted in gold and silver. A prince, anxious to maintain his dominions in a state in which he can most easily defend them, ought, upon this account (*and I add upon all others*) to guard not only against the excessive multiplication of paper money, which ruins the very banks that issue it, but even against that multiplication of it, which enables them to fill the greater part of the circulation with it.'

I was willing to oppose, in your own words, this fair description which you give of the dangerous state of a country which abounds in *circulation of riches*, instead of a deposit, which is *wealth*, as an antidote against the delusions of this powerful temptation: and as I think the dose ought to be repeated, I will repeat it in the words of the very clear-minded and ingenious Mr. Hume.[28]

'He has entertained (*he says from similar reasons as above stated*) a great doubt concerning the benefit of banks and paper credit, which are so generally esteemed advantageous to every nation. That provisions and labour should become dear, by the encrease of trade and money, is, in many respects, an inconvenience, but an inconvenience that is unavoidable, and the effect of that publick wealth and prosperity, which is the end of all our wishes. It is compensated, however, by the advantages which we reap, from the possession of those *precious metals*, and the weight which they give the nation in all foreign wars and negotiations. But there appears no reason for the encreasing that inconvenience by *a counterfeit money*, which foreigners will not accept in any payment, and which *any great disorder in the state will reduce to* NOTHING.'

It is for these reasons, because I am not for *removing old bounds*, and that I wish to preserve the old general established opinion, that money is a *common measure*; because I am unwilling to receive that *new and delusive friend* CIRCULA- TION, instead of *the old and steady one*, MONEY, which being a DEPOSIT, will stick by us in all times, that I have taken the liberty to examine this part of your Analysis, and to wish, if you should be persuaded to revise it, that you would enquire, in the real track of nature, whether that commodity, by the intervention of which the exchanges of all commodities may in all times and cases be actuated, must not, *in truth as well as in fact*, be that common measure in the use of which all mankind have universally agreed, and must not be a deposit, which the metallic money alone is: and whether, where paper circulation is not so propor- tioned to the deposit as that, that deposit is always ready to exchange it during its circulation; is not established on such a *fund* as will *absolutely exchange it*;

[27] [i. 389; II.ii.87.] [28] Hume's third *Essay on Money* [*Phil. Wks.* iii. 311.].

whether, I say, such paper circulation is not a delusion that must finally, however remotely, lead to a fraud.

By what I have said above I do not mean to say, that paper is not useful; I think, that under such due regulations respecting the FUND, which is to exchange it, the USES to which it is to be applied, and the QUANTITY in which it may be safely issued, as will make it a common measure and a DEPOSIT, it is not only generall beneficial, but that the greatest advantages may be derived from it to the publick.

If now, Sir, by these principles, as I have stated them, as they are found in the FUND and the USES, you examine all the schemes of paper circulation from that of the bank of Amsterdam, founded on a real deposit, to that of the Scotch banks, founded on[29] trust and confidence, without any actual deposit; if you examine the paper money, and the operations of that wise and prudent institution, the loan-office of Pensylvania, examine the foundation and the succeeding operations of the bank of England, you will find, that you have a fixed canon, by which you may precisely mark what are real, what delusive; what may be beneficial, what will be ruinous in the end. Whereas, if no other idea but that of *circulation* enters into our notion of money; if it be conceived to be nothing more than *a circulating machine*, under that conception every delusive fraudulent credit, which every adventurer can establish *on a deceived and betrayed confidence*, may set in motion a circulation, that may on every ground be justified even in the moment of its bankruptcy. And even those just and wise precautions, with which you have endeavoured to guard this circulation against fraud, may tend to give an opinion of confidence to this circulation, when it shall be so guarded, which in any case it ought not to have, unless it can be so framed as to have *all the use* of money in circulation, and be so *funded* as in the end to be a real deposit.

It is impossible to pass over those parts of your learned work, wherein you treat of labour, stock, and land; of wages, profit, and rent; of the monied prices of commodities, and especially your very curious and scientifick Treatise on the Precious Metals applied as Money; it is impossible to read those parts respecting the effects of the progress of improvement in the community, of the nature, accumulation, and employment of stock, without reiterating the idea and the wish expressed in the beginning of this letter, of seeing your book considered as INSTITUTE OF THE PRINCIPIA *of those laws of motion*, by which the operations of the community are directed and regulated, and by which they should be examined. In that part, however, which explains the different effect of different employment of capital, wherein you seem rather to have engrafted some foreign shoots, than to have trained up, in the regular branchings of your Analysis, to propositions fully demonstrated, I will beg to arrest your steps for a moment, while we examine the ground whereon we tread; and the more so, as I find these propositions used in the second part of your work as data; whence you endeavour to prove, that the monopoly of the colony trade is a disadvantageous commercial institution.

After having very justly described the four different ways in which capital stock may be employed—first, in drawing from the elements of earth and water the rude, the spontaneous or cultured produce; next, in working these materials

[29] [i. 351; I.ii.28, also § 41 et seq.]

up for use; next, the general exchange or trade of these commodities, conveyed from place to place as they are wanted; and, lastly, the retail distribution of them to the consumer. After having divided by fair analysis the general trade or commerce, described under the third head, into three different operations—that is, the home trade; the foreign trade of consumption, and the carrying trade. After having shewn the just gradation of beneficial employ of capital, which these different operations produce, and how truly beneficial each in its respective *natural* gradations is,[30] 'When the course of things, without any constraint or violence, naturally introduces it;' you lay and prepare a ground of contrast, from whence in your fourth book to prove, that the establishment of a monopoly in the colony trade, by perverting this *natural order and gradation of operations* in commerce, hath rendered the commerce of such colonies less beneficial than they might otherwise in general have been; I am here marking only the order of your argument, not trying the force of it. In the order of this argument, I think I discover an essential misconception of that branch and operation of commerce, which is in nature *circuitous*, and as such beneficial; but which you conceive to be and call *a round-about commerce*, and as such of course, and in the nature of things, disadvantageous. Your argument goes to prove, that the monopoly, instead of leaving the direct trade to its full and free operation, instead of suffering the round-about trade (as you call it) to take up the *surplus only* of capital which that produces, and next the carrying trade naturally to absorb what the others disgorge, doth force capital, which might have been more beneficially employed in a direct trade, into a round-about trade; which is too commonly mistaken for the carrying trade of Great Britain.

I mean, in its place, to examine this your argument, in your application of it to the actual subject. I will here, in the mean time, with your leave, make an assay of the truth of its combination; for it appears to me, that in treating *a circuitous commerce* as *a round-about trade*, you confound two things the most distinct in their nature, and the most different in their effect of any two that could have been put together.

A CIRCUITOUS TRADE or commerce is that by which receiving, *with the due profits of return of capital*, some article of trade or some commodity, *which is better to go to market with than money*, I go to market with that commodity so received; and perhaps again with some other in like manner received; and perhaps again with a third, making by each operation my due profits, annexed to each return of my capital; and finally a greater superlucration of profit than I could have done by the same number of direct trades; and consequently either a greater revenue, or a greater accumulation of capital, that may again employ more productive labour.

A ROUND-ABOUT TRADE, on the contrary, with lost labour, with waste of expence, and unprofitable detention of capital, sends to market some commodity (as the proverb well expresses it) *by Tom-Long the carrier*.

We will suppose, that the British merchant or factor hath sold his British manufactures in Virginia, in which he vested his capital; and that he has it in speculation, whether by taking money, a bill of exchange, or some commodity, which is ready money's worth in the British market, he shall make a direct

[30] [i. 453; II.v.32.]

return of his capital, and its simple accretion of profit; or whether by taking such commodities, as by an intermediate operation in his way home, he may derive an intermediate adventitious profit from, before the same is again reinvested in British goods for the Virginian market.

In the first case, his capital may be said to return with its profit directly; in the second, although it may make a circuit, and be detained awhile in its way home, yet it is not detained, nor goes out of its way *unprofitably* to Great Britain; for by the superlucration, arising from the intermediate operation, it gives proportionably either a greater revenue, or as an encreased capital employs more productive labour.

We will suppose a second case taken up on this speculation, that he either receives corn by barter, or by purchase invests what he has received in that commodity, with which, instead of coming directly home, he calls in his way at Cadiz or Lisbon; the sale of his corn there returns him his capital with a second accretion of profit. Here again he speculates in like manner, and determines to invest this accumulated capital in wines, fruits, etc. which at the home market will again return his capital, with farther accretion of profit. Has not every movement of this circuitous trade been a different operation? Has not each operation made a distinct return of capital? Has not each return given its peculiar profit? Has any expence been wasted? Any labour lost? Has there been any detention of capital unprofitably to Great Britain, while, at its return, it affords either more revenue, or, as capital, employs more productive labour than otherwise it would.

Let us in another line suppose, that this merchant or factor receives tobacco, rice, indigo, or peltry, which he brings directly home; with these commodities at the British market he speculates, whether he shall take ready money there for them, which, vesting in British manufactures, or foreign manufactures bought with British produce, he will return directly to Virginia again with. Or whether these commodities, which represent his capital, with its accretion of profit, might not still more encrease it, if he himself sent them to that market where they are purchased for consumption. We will suppose, that his prudence directs him to the latter conduct. He fends them then to Russia or to Germany. They there return him his capital, with another accretion of profit. We will suppose, that he re-invests his capital with hemp or flax for the British, or in linnens for the American market. He is by this operation enabled to go back again to America, either with Russian or German manufactures, bought with British commodities, or selling what he bought of Russia or Germany in the British markets, with a still more increased quantity of British manufactures than what any direct trade between America and Great Britain could have purchased. Here again the same questions may be asked, and must receive the same answers.

On the contrary, wherever there is a *round-about trade*, there the commercial operations are obstructed, and the advantages greatly defalcated, if not, in many instances, entirely lost. The obliging the merchant to bring rice from the southern latitudes northward to Great Britain, which rice must go back again south to its market in the southern parts of Europe and the Streights, was a round-about trade, it was labour lost, it was a waste of expence, an unprofitable detention of capital, and the commodity was sent by *Tom Long the carrier* to market. The monopoly therefore, in that case, where it created a round-about trade, hath been relaxed. Sugars are in the same case; and a like relaxation, under peculiar regulations relating to that peculiar article, have been recommended, and might be safely and beneficially given. There are some parts of the tobacco crops, which, in the assortment, might be admitted to somewhat a similar liberty without danger, but with benefit. Nay, *that intermediate operation of the circuitous trade*, mentioned above, which obliges the Virginian tobacco to come to England before it goes to Germany, and the German linnens also to come to England before they go to America, *is a round-about trade*, a needless and very disadvantageous operation, in which some relaxation ought to be made. I can see, that the English merchant may lose a commission, but labour and expence would be saved to the community. In like manner the obliging the West India ships, which, since the interruption of the American trade, load staves, lumber and corn in England, which articles are brought from foreign parts, is obliging them to take up these things by a round-about trade; whereas, if they were permitted to ship, in British shipping only, these articles at the foreign markets directly for the West Indies, many inconveniencies, which the British part of the community experiences, might be avoided, and both labour and expence saved to the community at large. If salt fish, which is intended for the southern markets, was obliged to be brought northward first to England, and so go round about to the south, its proper market, it would create a round-about trade. If these ships loading with salt for their back carriage were obliged to come round by England, it would create a round-about trade, and in either case would waste labour, and might lose all the profit of the capital employed. The monopoly therefore does not take place in this.

The permitting, in certain cases stated, and under certain regulations specified, the Americans who go with fish directly to the Streight, Spain, or Portugal, to purchase there, if purchased of British merchants, certain articles, and to carry the same, so purchased, directly back to America, so far as it would avoid the round-about trade, persevering, and even extending at the same time the British market, has been for twelve or fourteen years successively recommended.

I think in general on this subject, that wherever the monopoly would create a round-about trade, it should not take place; and that wherever it hath occasioned any such round-about operation, if should be relaxed; always however keeping in view this object and end, namely, that so far as our colonies are to be considered as an institution, established and directed to encrease the naval force of our marine empire, and so far as that force derives in any degree from the operations of their commercial powers, so far that monopoly, which engrafts them upon our internal establishment, is indispensible, and ought never to be departed from or relaxed. The sovereign power, which hath the care of the defence and strength of the empire, ought never to permit any the most flattering idea of commercial opulence to come in competition with the solid ground of strength and defence. In this way of reasoning I find myself joined by you, who reason in the same way, and almost in the same words, when speaking of the act of navigation you say, that, 'although it be not favourable to foreign commerce, or to the growth of that general opulence which might arise from it, yet, as defence is of much more importance than opulence, it is the wisest of all the commercial regulations of England'. On the ground and deriving my reasoning from the same principle, I say, that the monopoly is of the same spirit; is not only wise, but is also necessary, and that it is not the monopoly, but the injudicious undistinguishing application of it, without that reason which alone can justify it, and in channels where it necessarily creates a round-about trade, which renders it disadvantageous, not only to the colonies, but to the general community of the empire.

As no round-about trade, unless where the obliging the colony trade to submit to such, is necessary to the system of defence, should be occasioned, but should even, where it has taken place, be relaxed, so, on the contrary,[31] I have always thought, that a circuitous operation in the colony trade, as the thing which of all others tends most to increase and extend the American markets for British manufactures, should be allowed and encouraged, provided that trade in its circuition keeps its course *in an orbit that hath Great Britain for its center.*

Having thus shewn, simply to the point of stating the case, not arguing it, that a circuitous commerce and a round-about trade are two very different and distinct things, having very different operations and very different effects: having shewn that the circuitous trade is very advantageous, while a round-about trade is always detrimental, but that the circuitous commerce of the colonies is not that hurtful round-about trade which you treat as occasioned by the monopoly, I will now proceed to examine, under their several heads, your application of the principles which you lay down in your analysis, as what directs your synthetic reasonings on the commercial institutions which have taken place in the British œconomy.

Although I perfectly agree with you, that the *restraints on the importation* of such foreign goods as can be produced cheaper at home are useless; and that the laying restraints on the importation of such as cannot be made so cheap at home, answers no good end, but may be hurtful; although I allow, that these measures, as a kind of institution of monopoly in favour of internal industry in preference, or to the exclusion of the produce of foreign industry coming to it, does not always tend to encourage the home industry, but, on the contrary, gives a false turn to it, puts it on a false ground and profit, and may have the effect of forcing an unprofitable labour: yet I am unwilling to quit the principle of encouraging the first efforts of home industry, if employed on home commodities in the home market, as I think the principle, applied only in cases where it is wanted, may be very beneficial; I had rather, in my notions of political œconomy, abide by the principle, and examine, upon each application of it, how it does or does not operate to encourage a profitable industry, skill and habit in peculiar branches of labour, which the society has to learn, and which learnt will be profitable. If a society, which once used to send abroad its rude produce to purchase manufactures made of that very rude produce so sent out, and which it knew not how to work up, had never been, by some adventitious aid, over and above what the sources of the first efforts of its industry could have given, encouraged to begin in trials of its skill; if the individual is not, while he is learning his trade, and the skill of working profitably in it, supported in part, he can never attempt to learn it; if the society does not pay for the learning, it can never have it; although it be true that at first the *apprentice* (for by that name I will express the first efforts of

[31] Vide *Administ. of the British colonies*, vol. i, ch. viii.

a manufacture) is not employed to the greatest advantage, because he might buy the articles which he is learning to make, cheaper than he can make them; although the community pays this difference; although these efforts, thus artificially forced, are at first disadvantageous and unprofitable to the community: yet by his industry being so directed to, and so supported in a line of labour, which he could not naturally have gone into, nor could have supported himself by, these first efforts, which the community pays for, do by repeated exercise produce skill, which in time will work as well, and enable the home manufacturer (if his labour is *employed on native home rude produce*) to sell as cheap, and soon cheaper, than the foreign workman and manufacturer; his labour then will become profitable to himself, and advantageous to the community of which he is a part. It was thus our woollen and hardware manufacturers were first encouraged and supported; but the very same principle, and the same reasoning upon it, hath always led me to a persuasion, that no aids of a monopoly in the home market, nor no bounties, can ever force a manufacture founded and *employed on foreign rude material*. It is an attempt, by robbing Peter to pay Paul, to establish a trade, the natural profit of which cannot support the establishment, and the loss of which must be made up to it by payments from the society at large. Against such your principle, in the full force of its arguments, stands unanswerable. Such is the linnen manufacture wrought on foreign line and flax; such is the silk in some degree; this last, however, so far differs, as that rude material may be imported full as cheap as any rival country in Europe can raise it.

You think, the restraints upon the importation of live cattle and corn an unreasonable and ungenerous monopoly, for that the grazing and farming business of Great Britain could be but little affected by a free importation of these, and not in the least hurt. As, on the contrary, I think, any change in this part of our system might be attended with the most important consequences, especially to a class of people who bear the chief burthen of all the taxes, and are the support of the state of the community. I own, I tremble for the change, and should hope this matter may be a little more thoroughly explored, in all the effects of its operation, before any such idea becomes a leading doctrine.

You have with clear and profound reasoning[32] shewn, that, in an improving state of the community, the prices of cattle and of butchers meat, and the lesser articles of the supply must start, and continue to rise until they come to such a rate, as shall make it worth the farmer's while to cultivate the land, which he rents, to the purposes of breeding and feeding such cattle, and to the raising these other articles for the market; this you properly call *the natural progress of improvement*, and these rising values *the natural course of prices*. If a free importation of cattle and of these lesser articles should be allowed, this *adventitious supply* coming from countries which have great wastes for breeding cattle, which do not pay such heavy taxes, and which are not arrived at that degree of improvement in which this country is found, such importation *must derange this scale of natural prices, and must arrest this progress of improvement in its course*. If such foreign country can breed and feed, and afford to import and bring to market cattle and these lesser articles cheaper than our grazer can, the grazing business at home must cease. Well—but say you, if under these circumstances grazing will not

[32] [i. 274ff.; I.xi.l, Second Sort of Rude Produce.]

answer, the land will be broken up for tillage. But here again, if a free importation of corn, on a like plan, derived from such reasoning on these principles, is, as you recommend, permitted, that branch of business, not capable of farther extension, and met at market by such importation, will be at a stand, and finally become retrograde; we shall be obliged to give up all our improvements, and return to our wastes and commons. In order to obviate in some measure these objections, a kind of distinction is made between the importation of lean and fat cattle. The importation of lean cattle would not, says the argument, hurt, but benefit the feeding farms. The breeding farms, however, would be ruined; and there is a link of connection, which so allies the whole progress of country business in one chain of intercommunion, that all in the end would suffer and be undone.

A second palliative used to obviate these objections, which naturally arise against this idea of giving up our system of restraints on importation of cattle,[33] is, that the importation of *salt provisions* could never come in competition with the fresh provisions of the country. To try how this would operate, let us suppose that the Victualling-Office, as the law now stands, is in the ordinary course of taking great quantities of cattle, and in the extraordinary demand which war occasions, takes off a proportionate encreased number; this of course raises the price of the grazers sales, and countervails, in some measure, with the landed interest, the burthen of the encreased taxes. But if a free importation of salt provisions is to take place as a settled system, the English grazer, while the war encreases his burthens, and raises the price of every article which he purchases, is himself met at the market by a competition brought against him from a country that does not bear this encreased burthen; and he cannot therefore find that *natural scale of price*, which the maintenance of his business and relative state in the country requires; he must be ruined, and the land soon rendered incapable of paying its rents, and of raising those very taxes.

In the same train of reasoning you think, that a free importation of corn could very little affect the interest of the farmers of Great Britain, because the quantity imported, even in times of the greatest scarcity, bears so inconsiderable a proportion to the whole stock raised. From this argument, founded in fact, you think the farmers could have nothing to fear from the freest importation; and you reproach them on the account of the system of restraint against free importation of corn, as forgetting the generosity which is natural to their station, in demanding the exclusive privilege of supplying their countrymen. If here, Sir, you had weighed well a distinction which Mons. Necker[34] has, with exquisite precision, explained, you would have spared this reproach. It is not the ratio of the quantity of corn exported or imported, and the quantity of the whole stock raised, but the ratio between the *surplus* and this quantity exported or imported, which creates the effect; it is not a ratio of $\frac{1}{571}$, but a ratio of $\frac{1}{15}$, which acts and which operates on the market; it is not the $\frac{1}{571}$ part but the $\frac{1}{15}$th part which would operate to the depression of the market and the oppression of the farmer.

Chearful under the burthen of the taxes, and spiritedly willing to pay them in support of his country, he only wishes to enable himself to do so from his industry, and the natural profits of it at his own market, without having that market loaded from an external supply, and depressed by a competition from

[33] [ii. 41; IV.ii.19.]   [34] *Sur la législation et le commerce des grains* [1775].

countries which are not in that state of improvement, and do not pay those taxes, which he must add to his price, if he is to live and pay them; he does not desire the *exclusive* supply, but a fair and equal market on the natural scale of prices, which shall give vent to his supply; this surely he may do without reproach. On the contrary, were it possible to suppose that the country gentleman could be persuaded to change the system, and give up the security which the restraint on importation gives him in his interest, he would deservedly incur the real reproach of having lost that practical sense, which the country gentlemen have always hitherto been found to have, when they come to real business.

But I think you rather misrepresent our system of restraint on importation of corn; it does not absolutely prohibit corn from being brought into the country, and does not establish *an exclusive supply* in the country land-owner; it only restrains such an importation as may either in quantity or price injure the free and fair vent of our own supply in our own market, at such prices as the general state of the improvement of the community and the scale of prices, which is the natural consequence, require.

From the consideration of our restraints on importation of corn, whose operations act as a bounty, you proceed to the consideration of the direct BOUNTY which our system gives *on the exportation of corn*, to which you make the like, but stronger objections. As you seem on this subject to have adopted the reasoning which[35] Mr. Necker uses, and to have copied it closely; and as his book, as well as your's, will carry great authority with it, I will in this place examine both your objections *ensemble*.

Contrary to the common use made of the popular argument in favour of the measure, you both say, the measure has a direct tendency *in the instant* to raise the price of corn in the interior market, and to enable the merchant to introduce it into the foreign market at a lower price. What you say is fact, and the truth rightly understood; and yet while this measure encourages a plenty, overflowing with a constant succession of surplusses, it hath a tendency, *in a series of times taken together*, to lower the price. That our measure of the bounty has not been the sole cause of lowering the price of corn, Mr. Necker gives a decisive proof in fact, which you[36] copy. That the general lowering of the price of corn is not owing to the English measure of *the bounty on exportation*, is (he says) plain, because the same general lowering of the price has taken place in France in the same period, where a direct contrary system, *a total prohibition of exportation* hath invariably prevailed till very lately. You add to his argument an assertion, 'that it raises however *not the real but nominal price only*, and is of no use to the landed interest.' There is perhaps (you say) but one set of men in the whole commonwealth to whom the bounty either was or could easily be serviceable, these are the corn-merchants; it loads (you add) the publick revenue with a very considerable expence, but does not in any respect encrease the real value of the landed man's commodity.

Mr. Necker has also said that the bounty is not necessary; for if there be a surplus, and the foreign market wants it, it will have it without the aid of the bounty. The difference only is, that if the merchant finds that he cannot export

[35] *Sur la législation et le commerce des grains.*
[36] [Vol. i. 248; l.xi.g.ll, see also V.v.a.21–2.]

it at the price of the British market, so as to carry it to the foreign market, he must wait till it falls in price in England, or rises in the foreign market, as many shillings per quarter as the bounty would give: *then* he will be equally able to export it *without* as *before with* the bounty. In a corollary of which argument you join him in saying, as he had said, that if the surplus quantity may be, by the aid of the bounty, thus exported when corn is at a high price, the surplus of a plentiful year will always so go out, as not to come in aid to relieve the scarcity of a defective one.

After having (in a manner indeed which rather has reference to the effect it might have in France) reprobrated the measure of granting a bounty on the exportation of corn, he gives an opinion, in which I own I was surprized to find you following him; that if an encouragement is necessary to agriculture, it should be given *not on the exportation, but on the production.*

I will first state what I think to be the real operations and end of the bounty on corn exported, and then consider the positions above, not by way of reply, but by comparison on fair examination, mark wherein they deviate and differ from the real state of the case.

Any country rising in that progressive state of improvement, by which England for near a century hath been rising, must have experienced *a continued influx of riches*; that continued influx must have and hath created *a continued progressive rise of prices*. If the continuation of the influx was arrested in its course, however great *the quantity of* riches which hath come in, however great the glut of money; yet, after it hath spread itself in all parts, and found its general level, *all* prices will be proportionably raised; the original proportions which they held, before the start of prices, will be restored; all therefore, however high, will be but *nominal*, and a greater or a less quantity of the precious metals will be totally indifferent; but the case is very different, while the influx is in continuance. During its operation it starts the prices of things, but of different things with very different velocity in the motion of the rise. Objects of fancy, caprice, luxurious use, and the lesser articles of food, which bore little or no price, while the necessaries must always have born a certain price, even what may be called a high price in a poor and unimproved state of the community, will, when the progression of improvement begins, start first in price, and with a velocity that will continue to *forerun* the velocity of rise in the price of necessaries. The relative proportion of the scale of prices being changed, the difference of the prices is real, and corn will be always last and lowest in the scale. Although the price of corn may and will rise, yet not rising in proportion to other things, and the rents of land and the wages of labour depending on the price of corn, the price of every other thing must not only rise before rent and wages can start in price, but must continue *so to forerun* in their rise, that the landed man and labourer must be in a continued state of oppression and distress: that they are so in fact, the invariable and universal experience of all improving countries, actuating manufactures and trades, demonstrates. In the end all must equally partake of the general prosperity; corn must rise in price; rents must rise; wages must be encreased: but during the continuance of the influx there must be a partial distress, which, although relative, is not the less but the more aggravated from being relative, others being in the actual enjoyment of a prosperity which the landed man can but look up to and hope for in the end. If the operation was short, and if the influx soon spread itself into a level, it would not be of much moment in what order the scale of prices arose. In a country where the land-workers and owners are few, in proportion to those employed in trade and commerce, as in rich commercial countries of small extent, there this effect is soon produced; there the landed interest cannot suffer much from the disproportionate velocity of the rise of prices, however accelerated, but in a trading and commercial country, *of large extent*, the spreading and level of the inflowing riches must be an operation of so long time, and the effect so far removed from the first cause, that the land-worker and owner can never receive a proportionate relief, much less the benefit of an equable scale of prices, *while that cause is in operation*. If the influx be a continued encreasing operation, the scale will always be ascending. In a country circumstanced as thus described, if the legislator is ever to intermeddle, or can ever do any good by meddling in these matters, his interference should be directed to relieve this oppressed order and class of the community. The English measure of the bounty does this, by aiding in its first effect the relative, and therefore *real price* of the produce of the land *without obstructing the natural effects* of the advancing and improving state of the community. It relieves the relative distress, which the acceleration of the inflowing of riches occasions to the land-worker; it helps to accelerate the rising of the price of his commodity, and in some measure guards them from a greater distress, which they would otherwise feel: as it is, the traders and merchants eat out the landed man: they do suffer, but much less than they would do. In a country of this sort the velocity of the influx of riches (especially if *an artificial influx* by paper money is added to the real one) may have even too much acceleration, if care is not taken at the same time to accelerate also the distribution of these riches into every channel and duct. In such a country as England, but more especially in France, if commerce be encouraged by the force of any artificial spring, if a disproportionate and[37] *more than natural* influx of riches comes in upon it, how much soever (when this influx may in the end have taken its whole effect and spread itself into a level) the land and labourer must necessarily share in the general prosperity, yet if care is not taken to give acceleration to the motion of the landed interest, in some proportion to the motion of the advance of commerce, and the influx of riches, the landed interest must remain under a continued depression of circumstances. Under this relative depression the land-worker, while he is buying every thing he wants at an advanced price, requires some adventitious force or spring to aid the velocity of the rise of the price of his commodity which he hath to sell. The wisdom of our ancestors, men of business, acting not from selfish and ungenerous motives, not from any jealousy of commerce, but from feeling and experience, gave this very encouragement, and gave it, in the very way in which it could have the truest effect; in which it could do the least harm, and the most good. They encouraged the landworker without checking the operations of commerce, or retarding the progress of improvement: and while in the direct instant they effected by the bounty a rise of price to the saleable commodity of the

[37] Either by an undue creation of paper money, or by the bringing in great quantities of money amassed by conquest or by rapine, as was the case in Rome, by the money brought from Asia; as was the case in Britain, by the money brought from Indostan.

landworker, and gave that encouragement, which was thus become necessary; yet they so gave the bounty, as that in the remote effect it would prevent the enhancing of the general price, because the bounty encouraged the raising not only a surplus, but a succession of surplusses. They converted these surplusses even of our food into an article of commerce, and encouraged, and made it the interest of the corn merchant to trade with it in every part of the world.

Thus acted the homely understanding of the country gentlemen *upon practice*; men of refined and great abilities, speculating in the closet, *decide upon theory*, that it would have answered the same ends better to have given the bounty *not on exportation, but on production.*

As the bounty on exportation goes only to the surplus exported, and as a bounty on production must have gone to the whole quantity raised, which measure do you, who made the objection, think would load the publick revenue most? But unless there was an assured constant vent by exportation of any surplus that should be raised, such a bounty as you and Mr. Necker recommend, would never encrease the quantity, or raise a surplus, (for say you, B. IV.C.V. p. 123. [IV.v.b.36]) 'unless the surplus can in all ordinary cases be exported, the grower will be careful never to grow any more than what the bare consumption of the home market requires, and that market will be very seldom over-stocked, but will be generally understocked.' To what end, say I, should the farmer work; it would be only making to himself work, to lose profit, for the more he raised, the less would be the price.

On the contrary, the bounty on the exportation, at the same time that it doth (as you and Mr. Necker justly observe) actually and directly raise the price of the commodity, it raises (I say) *not the nominal* but the *real* price, for it brings that price which was *relatively* too low, nearer to the level of the general scale of prices: At the same time that it is (as you truly say) serviceable to the corn-merchant, it enables him, without lowering the price of corn below the rate at which the farmer in the country can afford to produce it, to throw it into the general circulation of the commerce of Europe at an average rate which suits that commerce. This tends to encrease, and does encrease the quantity raised, and yet preventing on one hand a discouraging fall, or a disproportionate inhancement of price on the other, keeps that price equable; and by creating a succession of surplusses, obviates your fear, that the exportation of the surplus of the plentiful year should prevent the use of a surplus, which should relieve, and come in aid to, the defects of a scarce one; for it doth actually, by the succession of surplusses, which the high prices of the home market will always first command, provide against such scarcity, which point the regulations in the permanent corn law, of the 13th of G. III. on this head do still more effectually secure.

Let us now try how your's and Mr. Necker's objections to the English measure of granting a bounty on corn exported bear against these operations.

Let us try Mr. Necker's first objection, viz. that it is a measure unnecessary, because, says he, if there be a surplus which the foreign market wants, it will take it off, as soon as the home price falls, or the foreign prices rise, as many shillings in the quarter of corn as the amount of the bounty comes to. We shall find, that if no surplus of wheat, for instance, can go out and flow in the channels of the European market, at a higher price than 32 shillings per quarter, (the general average price of wheat in Europe) there will be no such surplus; the farmer in the present improved state of England, loaded at the same time as it is with taxes, cannot afford to raise wheat at that price: And if the British merchant did wait till the English wheat did sink to that price, he might better never export it; he would find, that the Dutch, Hambrough or Dantzic merchant had got to market before him, and had forestalled it. On the other hand considering that, at the very lowest estimation, the farmer cannot raise wheat at a lower average rate than 37 shillings per quarter, the bounty adds the five shillings, per quarter, which is just sufficient on one hand to enable the merchant to give the farmer a living price, and on the other to carry it to the foreign market at the average rates of that market; so that if the encouragement of the farmer, and of the supply be proper, and if 'the business of the corn-merchant be in reality that trade, (as you say) which, if properly protected and encouraged, would contribute the most to the raising of corn.'[38] This measure of a bounty on export is every way not only beneficial, but necessary: although you have said, in one place, that it is service-able to the corn merchant *only*, yet in this view you yourself find, that this trade of the corn merchant 'will support the trade of the farmer, in the same manner as the wholesale dealer supports that of the manufacturer.'

The next objection in which you and Mr. Necker join, is, that the doing any thing to raise the price of *corn* (as you express it, of *subsistance*, as Mr. Necker rather more logically) in the home-market, must of course raise the expence of our manufactures, and give advantage to the rival manufactures of every part of Europe against us. This objection takes rise from a total mis-stating of the case.

If corn was the first article which started in price, so that all other commodities followed it, then indeed both your positions would be true; first that so far as respects the home market, we should only raise the *nominal* price for all rising proportionably, there would be no alteration in the *ratios of the scale*: this would therefore be of no use to the farmer on one hand, but by raising *all the articles of subsistence and supply*, our manufactures must become too dear for the average rates of the general market. But the contrary is the fact. Corn is the last of all the articles of the market which starts in its price, and rises always with the slowest motion. It is only in consequence of all other commodities having arisen, that a rise in this becomes necessary, and when it does begin to rise, it follows with such unequal motion, that some encouragement becomes necessary, as a spring to aid the velocity of its rise in proportion to other things. It is not the rise of the price of corn, but the general improved state of the country, raising the rates of all things, and the burthen of taxes successively accumulated, which raises the price of our manufactures. On the contrary, encouraging the raising of corn by a good price in the direct instant, creates a plenty: a plenty, with a succession of sur-plusses, keeps down the price, taken in a general series of times; and in some measure it tends also to lower the price of manufactures, by the number of hands which plenty of subsistance, if I may so express myself, always creates.

Seeing then nothing narrow, invidious, selfish, or ungenerous in our system of restraints and bounties on our corn trade, considering it as a necessary, wife and beneficial system, interwoven into the general œconomy of our agriculture, manufactures and commerce: persuaded that a certain sober conviction of

[38] [ii. 116; IV.v. b. 18.]

experience, arising from practice, first suggested the truth, I cannot but hope, that the same wisdom which gave the bounty, will operate with the country gentlemen, to doubt every speculation of closet doctrine, and to oppose, on every occasion, every the most distant attempt to lower, or to confine within narrower limits this bounty.

You have made several observations on, some objections to, and give rather a hasty and summary judgment on the general system of our corn laws: I have made some remarks on these parts also, but I shall reserve these to another place, where I shall have occasion to examine all the regulations relative to the supply of the community with bread-corn, and to the manner in which the surplus of that supply is converted into an article of commerce.

I will now proceed to the consideration of your opinions and doctrines respecting the *monopoly of the colony trade.*

You allow,[39] 'this colony-trade to be very advantageous, though not by means, yet in spight, of the monopoly, and that the natural good effects of it more than counterbalance to Great Britain the bad effects of the monopoly; so that, monopoly and all together, that trade, even as it is carried on at present, is not only advantageous, but greatly advantageous.' Although you allow this, yet while you consider our colonies 'rather as a cause of weakness than of strength', 'as a source of expence not revenue'; while you say, that[40] 'the invidious and malignant project of excluding other nations from any share' in our colony-trade depresses the industry of all other countries, but chiefly that of the colonies, without in the least encreasing, but on the contrary diminishing, that of the country in whose favour it is established; that, in order to obtain a relative advantage, that country not only gives up an absolute one in this trade itself, but subjects itself to both an absolute and relative disadvantage in every other branch of trade wherein this monopoly does not operate. While you say this, you conclude,[41] 'that under the present system of management, Great Britain derives nothing but loss from the dominion which she assumes over her colonies.' In consequence of this doctrine, you are not only for breaking up the monopoly, but for a dismemberment of the empire,[42] by giving up the dominion over our colonies. This prompt and hasty conclusion is very unlike the author of 'the Treatise on the wealth of nations,' it savours more of the puzzled inexperience of an unpracticed surgeon, who is more ready with his amputation knife, than prepared in the skill of healing medicines. If we lose our colonies, we must submit to our fate; but the idea of parting with them on the ground of system, is much like the system which an ironical proverb recommends, '*of dying to save charges*'. When superficial importants talk, write, or vend such their idle crudities, one is not surprized; unworthy of notice they are neglected: but when a man, who, like yourself, hath joined practical knowledge to the most refined spirit of speculation, can suffer himself so to be mislead, an examination of those speculations, or at least of their consequences, as they lead to practice, is due to him and to the world: I will therefore examine your objections to the monopoly, and the reasoning whereon you found them, by the actual operations and effects of this colony-trade, acted upon by this monopoly.

[39] [ii. 214; IV.vii.c.50.]   [40] [ii. 196; IV.vii.c.18.]   [41] [ii. 224; IV.vii.c.65.]
[42] [ii. 224; IV.vii.c.66.]

But first I cannot but observe, that a round assertion, 'that our colonies have never yet furnished any military force for the defence of the mother country, and that they have been a cause rather of weakness than of strength', is such as should have followed only from a deduction of facts: and I will beg leave to suggest to you some facts that induce me, and may perhaps you also, to be of a very different opinion. That very naval force, which by their armed vessels they are now so destructively exerting against our West-India trade and transports, they did very effectively in the two late wars, especially in the last, exert to the ruin of the West Indian commerce of France and Spain, and to the almost total obstruction of all communication of those countries with their respective colonies. If you have not heard of what they did then, judge of it by what they are able to do now, against the whole undiverted power of their mother country.

The mother country, with her own immediate force, must always meet the immediate force of its enemies, wherever exerted. If therefore France sent its European forces to America, Great Britain, with her European force, must meet them in that field. If the strength of our colonies, exerted against the colonial strength of France or Spain was effective; or if it was ready to serve where it could best serve, and where most wanted; if it was not only equal to its own defence, but did act against the enemy offensively also, with effect, it did bring forth 'a military force for the defence of the mother country.' The military force of the province of Massachusett's Bay not only defended the dominions of the mother country in that province, but for many years exerted itself in defending Accadia or Nova Scotia. In the war which ended by the peace of Aix la Chapelle, the military force of that province took Louisburg and Cape Breton, an acquisition which purchased for the mother country that peace. So far as my assertion may go in proof, I will venture to assert, that had France during the last war effectuated a landing in Great Britain, and had been able to maintain themselves there until an account of it should have arrived in New England, I should have been able to have brought over, or sent from the province, Massachusett's Bay (perhaps joined by Connecticut also) 'a military force for the defence of the mother country'.

On the point of revenue, I will also beg leave to repeat, because I have now still stronger reason for it, an assertion which I made in parliament, that before we went to decided war, a revenue might have been had upon compact, on terms which would have established the constitutional sovereignty of this country, regulating at the same time the trade and naval powers of the colonies, if those terms might have gone, at the same time, to the securing the rights of those colonies as granted by the government of that mother country. As to the ways and means of coming at the *grounds of agreement*, and the nature of that revenue and compact, an explanation never will be withheld, if ever again events shall render them practical. The colonies did always raise a revenue in support of that establishment of internal government, which the mother country had set over them; I do not say that I approve the manner in which they applied it. As to their raising, while *under a state of minority*, farther taxes, *except port duties*, for the *external purposes of the empire at large*, I will give no opinion, but submit it to your judgment, who have thoroughly considered the different fructuation of surplus produce expended in revenue, or vested in circulating capital, for further improvements, which further extend the British market in America, to decide, which of the two were, in that state, most beneficial to the mother country. I reason here in the line in which you consider the subject, the line of political œconomy, not of administration of government.

Your objections to the monopoly endeavour to prove, that; in *the invidious and malignant project* (as you stile it) of excluding as much as possible all other nations from any share in the trade of our colonies, Great Britain sacrifices, in a great degree, an absolute advantage, to enjoy in a lesser degree a relative one: that if the trade had been free and open, the industry of the colonies would not only have been less cramped, but the source of all the advantages deriving to Europe, from the settlement of Europeans in America, would have been more abundant and more productive of advantage: and that, although Great Britain had sacrificed a relative advantage which she derived from the exclusive trade, she would yet have had a greater absolute advantage; as an explanatory proof you instance in the monopoly of the article of tobacco. The market opened for this article would, you think, *probably* have lowered the profits of a tobacco-plantation nearer to the level of a corn-farm; the price of the commodity would *probably* have been lowered, and an *equal quantity* of the commodities, either of England or of any other country, might have *purchased a greater quantity* of tobacco than it can at present. I will suppose with you, that by this new arrangement, and the consequential *new ratio in the scale of* prices betwixt Europe and America, that Great Britain as well as other countries would have derived a great absolute advantage: yet as these other countries would have derived the same advantage from our colonies, this fancied absolute advantage could be but merely *nominal*; for although England thus got more tobacco for a less quantity of British commodities, yet as other countries also got the same on the same terms directly from Maryland or Virginia, what Great Britain thus got would not only be less in value, but would run the risque of being a drug upon her hands. In giving up therefore the relative advantage which she enjoyed by her exclusive trade, *while she gained a nominal*, she would lose every *real* advantage. Besides, there is surely some management to be observed in the culture of an article of produce, whose consumption hath arisen from whim and caprice into an habitual, but not a necessary use: instead of encouraging an unbounded produce of this, it were best, *probably*, that it should be limited. I am sure it is an absolute advantage to Great Britain, that Virginia and Maryland should find it most to their advantage to cultivate tobacco, rice, indico, or any other exotick commodity, than that by bringing the profits of a tobacco-plantation nearer upon a level with those of a corn-farm; they should find their advantage in raising corn to the rivalling us at the European markets in our home commodity, and to the depression of our agriculture. So far therefore as this argument goes, it demonstrates to me, at least, that by quitting the relative, *a real* advantage, we should not even gain a *nominal* advantage, but should run every risque of losing every advantage, both relative and absolute, real and nominal, which is to be derived from this source restrained, and at the same time of setting up a rival culture against our own agriculture. If you see the matter in this light in which it appears to me, you will, I am sure, feel how dangerous it is to vend these novelties of speculation against the sober conviction of experience.

Your argument goes on to state, that there are *very probable reasons for believing*, that although we do sacrifice this absolute advantage (which would, *it is supposed*, probably be drawn from a free and open trade) for a narrow mean relative advantage; yet we do not possess even this relative advantage, without subjecting ourselves, at the same time, both to an absolute and to a relative disadvantage in almost every other branch of trade of which we have not the monopoly.

It strikes me as material, and I am sure, therefore, you will excuse me making, in this place, one remark even *on the manner* of your argument, and how *you stretch your reasoning nicely.* You in words advance upon the ground of *probable reasons for believing* only, you prove by probable suppositions only; yet most people who read your book, will think you mean to set up an absolute proof, and your conclusion is drawn as though you had.

You proceed to describe these absolute and relative disadvantages.

The monopoly of the colony trade, wherein the English merchant was enabled to sell dear and buy cheap, gave a rate of profit in that trade much above the level of profit in any other, and would therefore never fail of drawing capital from those other branches into this, as fast as it could employ such. This double effect of drawing capital from all other branches of trade, and of raising the rates of profit higher in our internal trades than it would otherwise have been, arose at the first establishment of the monopoly, and hath continued ever since. Having thus stated the effect, you proceed to prove them to be bad and disadvantageous.

By drawing, not through the natural effects of trade, but by the artificial operations of the monopoly, capital from other trades, and other branches of trade in Europe, which were greatly advantageous both in a commercial and in a political view, this monopoly, it is *probable* (you say) may not have occasioned *so much an addition* to the trade of Great Britain, *as a total change in its direction.*

First, as to the assertion, that capital has been drawn from certain trades and certain branches of trade in Europe, and turned by the monopoly into the colony trade, which without this would not have been so diverted; that (I answer) is a matter of fact, which must not be established by an argument, *à priori*—but on an actual deduction of facts. As I did not find the latter in your book, I looked into the only records which we have of the progressive state of our commerce, in a[43] series of returns of the imports and exports of Great Britain, as made to parliament. I cannot ascertain in our European trade that fact which your theory supposes. The tides and currents of commerce, like that of the ocean over which it passes, are constantly shifting their force and course, but this comes not up to your fact. I find no deprivation, but an encreased state of our European trade; and at the same time an immense multiplied encrease of our colony trade, and of every branch of commerce connected with it. Supposing, however, that this fact was true, that there hath been a *total change* in the direction of our trade, by drawing capital from several of the European trades, and by employing more of our general capital in the colony trade than would naturally have gone to it, had all trade been free and open: yet that supposition will never, against fact, prove, that this monopoly, thus employing more capital in, and deriving more profits from the colony-trade, hath occasioned a privation of advantage to the

---

[43] A very useful collection, published by Sir C. Whitworth, M.P. [*State of the Trade of Great Britain in its imports and exports progressively from the year 1697* (1776)].

trade of Great Britain in general—Fact contradicts that position. Well, but as Great Britain cannot have sufficient capital to actuate all, it must occasion a privation in some of the branches of its trade; for, although there may not be an absolute decrease in certain branches, there is a relative one, as they have not increased in the proportion in which they would have done. This is again argument, *à priori*, in matters of fact, wherein it cannot act as proof; however, for the sake of your argument we will even suppose it, and ask the question, what then? To which, in my way of reasoning, I should answer, that as in the division of labour no one man can actuate all the branches of it, so in the division of the commerce of the world, no nation nor no capital can carry on all the branches of it in every channel in which it flows. That country then which, while it does less in those branches of trade wherein least is to be gotten, but has the command in that which exceeds all others in profit, doth surely draw the greatest possible advantage from commerce. This part then of your argument proves to me, assisted by the reasoning which you use in other parts of your work, the very reverse of the conclusion which you here draw from it.

You say in the next place, that this monopoly has contributed to raise and keep up the rates of profit in all the different branches of the British trade higher than they would naturally have been, or, which is the same thing, to prevent them from falling so low as they would otherwise have fallen; and that this forced height of profit hath subjected the country, where it takes effect, both to an absolute and to relative disadvantage in every branch of trade, in which it has not the monopoly. I could here answer in general by your own reasoning, as you use it in the case of the profits of grazing and corn land; as when the state of the community is such, that it occasions a greater call for, and consequently a greater profit on the one than the other; that other will soon be converted into the one which is in demand, and will give the greater profits, till both come to a level: so in commerce, under whatever regulations, either those which the natural wants or the political institutions of men establish, it is carried on, will always shift about, and endeavour to flow in those channels wherein most profit is to be had. That country then which is under those fortunate and powerful circumstances, and has the wisdom so to profit of those circumstances, as to be able to maintain a monopoly of the most profitable channels; and be able to maintain, at the same time, (notwithstanding the clog of its high rates of profits) a share of other branches of trade, even where it is undersold, has surely acquired *that ascendency in trade and commerce*, which is always better understood than explained. But I will not rest within these entrenchments, I will meet your argument in your open field.

You say,[44] that in consequence of these high rates of profit, under which our commodities and manufactures must be brought to market, we must in our foreign trade 'both buy dearer and sell dearer, must both buy less and sell less;' but I deny the consequence, 'that we must profit less,'[45] because, although those high rates may confine the extent, yet raising the profit of the dealing, we enjoy as much, and produce in trade as much, as if we did more business of less profits: all is kept equal and level as to the foreign trade, and our colony trade goes on, the mean while, in a still more rapid prosperity. Your conclusion therefore,

---

[44] [ii. 201; IV.vii.c.27.]   [45] [ii. 219; IV.vii.c.59.]

'that it is in this manner that the capital of Great Britain has partly been drawn, and partly driven from the greater part of the different branches of trade, of which she has not the monopoly; from the trade of Europe in particular, and from that of the countries which lie round the Mediterranean sea,' is neither deducible from your argument, *à priori*, nor will you find it justified by fact.

Yet again that we, who think well of the monopoly, may not derive any support from thinking, that as the colony-trade is more advantageous to Great Britain than any other, so the capital being forced into that channel, is of more advantage to the country than if employed any other way. That we may not avail ourselves of this comfort, you proceed to shew it to be 'a natural effect of this monopoly; that it turns our capital from a foreign trade of consumption with a neighbouring into one with a more distant country; in many cases from a *direct trade* of consumption *into a round-about one* and in some cases from all foreign trade of consumption into a carrying one.' And as in the analytick part of your work you have shewn, that the direct trade of consumption, especially that with a neighbouring country, maintains the greatest quantity of productive labour, by the direct and frequent returns of its capital; that a round-about trade is always less advantageous, and the carrying still least so of all; you draw your conclusion, that therefore the operation of the monopoly, thus acting, turns our capital into channels where it employs less productive labour than it would naturally have done, if the trade was left to its free and natural operations. By your first position you mean, that it hath turned the capital from the European trade to the North American and West Indian trade, from whence the returns are less frequent, both on account of the greater distance, but more especially on account of the peculiar circumstances of America. An improving country, always dealing beyond their capital, must wait to pay their debts by their improvements, by which means, although the merchant may repay himself by the profit he puts upon his goods, and by other means, yet the capital of Great Britain is detained and withheld; and, thus detained, prevented from maintaining such a quantity of productive labour as otherwise it would do. In answer to this state of the argument (which I hope I have stated fairly) I say, that that part of our capital, which is some while withheld in America and does not return directly, is not withheld unprofitably to Great Britain: like that portion of the harvest which is detained for seed, it is the matrix of a succeeding and encreased production; by operating to advance still farther these improvements, and consequently the population of these countries, it is *creating and extending a new market*, whose demands for our productive labour calls forth that labour faster and to more advantage, than the same capital directly returned and vested in British goods could do; as it encreases this market in a constant progression, it calls forth more *manufacturers*; gives a spring to *agriculture*; and extends the *commerce* of Great Britain.

Well but, say you, 'secondly, the monopoly of the colony-trade has, in many cases, forced some part of the capital of Great Britain from a direct foreign trade of consumption into a round-about one.' Wherever it does so, that is an error in the system, it should be corrected and amended, so far as is consistent (as I said above) with the establishment of the unity of empire in all its orders and subordination of orders. I have in a former part of this letter, and many years ago on other occasions, pointed out some of these errors and their remedy; but

I must beg here to apply those distinctions, which, in my remarks on the analytick part of your work, I shewed to exist in nature and fact, *between a circuitous and a round-about trade*; and to observe, that where your objections are pointed against the circuitous operations of our colony-trade, they do not act with effect; for these are always advantageous, and should be even more encouraged than they are. Such a series of such circuitous operations as create and extend the market, accumulating by each operation a fresh profit, return home not only (by this accumulated capital) with the means of employing more manufacturers, but with having created[46] an encreasing demand for more and more manufactures. The encreasing market of our improving colonies, still more and more rapidly improved by the circuitous trade, must, while we have the command of that market, multiply British manufacturers; these manufacturers thus multiplied[47], 'constitute (as you state it truly) a new market for the produce of the land, and most advantageous of all markets, the home market, for corn and cattle.'

Another objection yet remains, that in many cases the colony-trade becomes, by means of the regulations of the monopoly, merely a *carrying trade*. This carrying trade, which you describe as a defect, would be so, if the carrying was the only part in which our capital was employed, and the hire of the carriage the only profit that we derive from it, but instead of that, joined as it is with the circuitous trade, it becomes, in a political as well as a commercial view, a beneficial part of the operations which employs our own shipping.

Having gone through your argument of objection, you close with some corollary observations, as deriving from it. You think, that the unnatural spring applied to the colony-trade, has destroyed the natural ballance which would otherwise have taken place amongst all the different branches of British industry, and that the direction of it is thus thrown too much into one channel. The idea then of a blood vessel, artificially swelled beyond its natural dimensions, strikes your imagination, and you are brought under an apprehension of some terrible disorder. As this disorder did not seize Great Britain in the case you supposed,[48] you then search out five unforseen and unthought-of events (to which I could add another very perfectly foreseen and thoroughly understood) which fortunately occurred to prevent it. As I am no *malade imiginair* in politicks, and have no fears of those[49] 'convulsions, apoplexy, or death,' which have been so often predicted, I know not how to go seriously, against fact into reasoning upon them. That our trade has felt, on a great and sudden shock, no such convulsions or apoplexy, but that its productive powers continue to be actuated, and its circulation to run *in some other channels*, though our American artery is obstructed, proves, that this was not our principal, much less our sole great channel of commerce; some part, perhaps great part, of our circulation passed through it into other remoter vessels,

---

[46] This is what, in *The Administration of the British colonies*, vol. i, ch. viii, I call creating and securing 'an encreasing nation of appropriated customers;' which idea, you, from that superiority that speaking *è cathedra* always inspires, treat with sovereign contempt; 'it is, you say, a project fit only for a nation of shop-keepers, governed by shop-keepers.' This idea, however, upon the closest and strictest analysis is the only one I can find precisely to define the relation which a commercial country bears to its colonies, and to express that institution of policy, in our act of navigation, which you rather too lightly and too contemptuously call (p. 222) 'a truly shop-keeper proposal'.

[47] [ii. 215; IV.vii.c.51.]   [48] [ii. 211; IV.vii.c.45.]   [49] [ii. 210; IV.vii.c.43.]

which is now perhaps full as properly with more profit to the British merchant, poured through more direct channels. In short, the whole state of our trade, as it stands in fact, and is found in effect, is to me a proof in point against your case in theory.

'[50]The effect of the monopoly (you say) has been not to encrease the *quantity*, but to alter *the quality* of the manufactures of Great Britain, suited to a market from which the returns are slow,' instead of keeping on in an old trade, 'from which the returns are frequent.'

If we consider the effect which the opening a *new market under a monopoly*, or in *a free trade*, hath on a commercial country, we shall find, if it be a market which calls for some new assortment of manufactures of a *quality different* from the ordinary and accustomed sort, in which that commercial country dealt before this new demand was opened, that *a free and open market*, into which the operations of a competition comes, *is more likely to alter the quality of the manufactures*, than where any commercial country possesses that market under a monopoly. In the former case they must watch and suit every call, every fashion, and even caprice of their free customers; in the latter case they will oblige *their appropriated customers*, to take off such goods as they please to send them, altho' the sorts do not in quality entirely suit that market; they will under this monopoly, carry this so far as to drive the country, which is subject to the monopoly, into smuggling, not only on account of the price, *but merely to get* goods of a quality which suits them. Your information in the practick, as well as theoretick knowledge of our commerce, will be able to supply proofs of this fact from many revolutions of our manufactures in different periods of our commerce. It is not therefore *the effect of a monopoly*, so much as it would be *the effect of a free and open trade, to alter the quality* of the manufactures of Great Britain. We will then next enquire, *how this monopoly operates as to the increase or not of the quantity*. In the first step we are agreed, that *this increasing market of appropriated customers* doth at this one entrance *encrease the quantity* of manufactures demanded. Let us next enquire, how 'the surplus produce of the colonies, which (you justly say[51]) is the *source of all of that encrease of enjoyments and industry*, which Europe derives from the discovery and colonization of America,' operates under a monopoly, or would operate under a free and open trade to encrease the quantity of British industry and manufactures. The articles of this produce are (it is needless to enquire how) become of accustomed demand in the markets of Europe, not only for its more pleasurable enjoyment, but in the line of industry also. So far as Great Britain hath the monopoly of these articles, she will become *a necessary trader* in these markets. She will not go to such markets with these articles only; she will make up a cargo with assortments of her manufactures also; the one will necessarily introduce the others; and if the first cannot be had without the latter it will introduce those others, where, from the disadvantages of a high scale of prices, they would not otherwise have been introduced; so that *our monopoly* of these American sources of enjoyments and industry to the Europeans, *doth not only tend to encrease* the quantity of our industry and manufactures *partially, but absolutely*. As they are interwoven with our general commerce, they do actually tend to introduce and carry on our commerce in our manufactures, even under

[50] [ii. 216; IV.vii.c.55.]   [51] [ii. 193; IV.vii.c.9.]

those disadvantages, which you have described as the effects of the monopoly; this is one ground of that *ascendancy in commerce*, which I rather referred to, than described as enjoyed by Great Britain.

As to the fact about the returns of capital, if you will compare notes between the merchant trading in British manufactures to Germany, and the merchant trading with British manufactures to America and the West Indies, you will find the returns of the latter upon the whole (if these goods go no farther than North America, or our West Indies) not slower than those from Germany. Credit has, even before the present war, been extended in Germany, and shortened towards America: inquire after this fact in Norwich, London, and the other great manufacturing places, and you will find it so.

That the productive labour of Great Britain is kept down by the monopoly; that this monopoly prevents its affording revenue so much as it might; and that rent and wages are always less abundant than otherwise they would be, is a corollary or propositions neither proved by reasoning nor established by fact. That the monopoly, raising the rates of mercantile profit, discourages the improvement of land, is still more aberrant from the line of reason, and more directly contrary to fact: the reason you give is, that the superior profits made by trade will draw capital from improvements in land. It will so in the first instance, but as this encreasing advanced interest of trade 'constitutes a new market for the produce of the land,' the rates of the price of the produce of the land will so rise, and so raise the profits made by improvements, that, although at first, as I have shewn above, it suffers a relative depression, the application of capital to it will of course and necessarily become a very advantageous employment of such: but the new and daily encreasing market of America, of which we have the monopoly, raising the rates of profit in trade, draws after it the daily ascending rates of that land, which supplies this market and the workmen in it; and is the very thing coincident with a general prosperity, that hath given such a spring to agriculture in this country.

When you say in another wreath of this corollary, that the high rates of profit necessarily keep up the high rate of interest, which *è contra* must lower the value of land. I answer, that the rate of interest does not necessarily depend on the rates of profit made by money, but on the proportion of demand for the use of it to the quantity which, and the velocity with which, the *influx* of riches, in consequence of an advancing mercantile prosperity, brings it into circulation. High profits themselves will occasion money to come in to the market which wants it; high profits, and an increasing demand, will open and give birth to a secondary source by paper circulation: so that the major of your syllogism is not founded in reason; nor is the conclusion, that the natural encrease of rent, and the rise in the value of land, is retarded by the effects of the monopoly, fact. I do here distinguish the effects of the monopoly from the effects of the trade itself: this, like all other advantageous applications of capital, where great mercantile profits are to be gotten, accelerates the rise of the profits of trade faster than those of land; but those of land are in the effect raised also by it; and although in a slower degree of velocity to that of the rise of mercantile profit, *yet not in a retarded but accelerated velocity also*.

Upon the whole, I fully and perfectly agree with you, that any regulation which gives a *confined course of direction*, and keeps in that line of direction any operation, must check and destroy part of the *vis motrix*, with which the body moving would fly off in a *direct course*. Just as the central force, which confines any body to circulate round that center in any given orbit, doth check and diminish part of the projectile force with which it would have flown off from that orbit: So the monopoly, which requires the colony-trade to observe Great Britain as its center, doth certainly check and diminish part of that *commercial activity with which it is at all points in exertion to fly off in a tangent.* Although I agree in this truth, yet being taught to think, that all separate communities, until some commercial millenium shall melt down all into one, must ever seek to give such a specifick direction to the operations of their own specifick powers, as shall maintain the separate and *relative state* of existence in which each community is placed; and knowing it to be an universal law of nature, that in any machine, part of the original *momentum* must always find itself diminished in proportion as it becomes necessary to give a *specifick direction* to its operation: So I consider the losing or lessening part of the productive activity, which the culture and commerce of the colonies might give *in a direct line, that is, to the world at large,* but not to Great Britain especially, as analogous to that law of nature; as the very essence of that combination of force, and consequential specifick direction, which confines it circulating in an orbit round Great Britain as its center; and as the precise state of that theorem, which no politician in the one case, any more than any true mechanick in the other, would deny as untrue, or condemn as wrong.

I cannot therefore but remain, and do fancy, that every sober man of business will remain in the persuasion and conviction, confirmed by experience, that while the monopoly of our colony trade gives as such to Great Britain, in its *relative state* of existence in the world, a *relative advantage* in the commercial world; Great Britain doth not lose unnecessarily any absolute advantage, nor doth subject itself to either absolute or relative disadvantage, in all other branches of commerce in which it hath not the monopoly: That it employs our capital, upon the ballance of the whole, to the greatest advantage, and conspires in the means, together with other branches of trade, of drawing forth our utmost productive industry: And that under the true system of a monopoly, Great Britain might derive from the dominion which she had in her colonies (of which dominion they were, in their due subordination, part) *force, revenue, and every commercial advantage.*

These are the matters in which I think your book has erred. I have examined them with a view to such discussion, as may occasion a review of them; because I do really think, that your book, if corrected on these points, planned and written as it is, might become an institute, containing the *principia* of those laws of motion, by which the system of the human community is framed and doth act, AN INSTITUTE *of political œconomy*, such as I could heartily wish, for the reasons given at the beginning of this letter, that some understanding Tutor in our Universities would take up, as a basis of lectures on this subject.

I should here have proceeded to the consideration of your plans of the system, which you think Great Britain should adopt in her future conduct towards America; but the present state of events suspends all political discussion on that head. If future events shall ever lay a rational, sound and true ground of colonial government, the proposing of such may then be proper, and shall not be withheld. At present *jacta est alea*, the fate of this country is now at the hazard of events, which force, and not reason, is to decide. I am afraid we are reasoning here about things which once were, and were most dear, but are no more.

I cannot conclude this letter without saying, that as I have impressed upon my mind the highest opinion of your abilities, learning, and knowledge, and think well of your fair intentions, I hope I have never deviated from the respect which is due to such. I have taken pains to comprehend fully, and have meant to state fairly, your reasoning; and to propose my own, as I ought, with diffidence. If any expression breaths the spirit of controversy, instead of what I meant, fair discussion, I disavow it; for although personally unknown to you, yet from what I learn of you by your works, I find myself in every sentiment of respect and esteem.

Sir,

Your most obedient,

And most humble Servant,

T. Pownall.

APPENDIX B

'Smiths Thoughts on the State of the Contest with America, February 1778'

EDITED BY DAVID STEVENS

In 1929 the William L. Clements Library, University of Michigan, Ann Arbor, acquired from a descendant of the heir of Alexander Wedderburn a collection of the latter's papers. Among the 158 pieces of correspondence and documents in the Rosslyn MSS. or Wedderburn Collection is an item which G. H. Guttridge identified in 1933 as a memorandum by Adam Smith on the American problem.[1]

The arguments advanced for the identification are partly biographical, and partly textual and doctrinal. The memorandum is endorsed in Wedderburn's hand: 'Smiths Thoughts on the State of the Contest with America, February 1778'. Wedderburn and Smith were friends of thirty year's standing by this date, if we accept Dugald Stewart's account that they met in 1748.[2] At the time of the memorandum, Wedderburn was North's Solicitor-General and at the centre of the discussion on American policy. Moreover, he corresponded with Smith about American matters: Letters 159 and 185. Thus he was in a position to seek Smith's advice on behalf of the Government. The need for consultation with experts at this period, following the dismaying news of Burgoyne's surrender at Saratoga in October 1777, was expressed by North in a letter of 4 December: '[The] consequences of this most fatal event may be very important and serious and will certainly require some material change of system. No time shall be lost, and no person who can give good information left unconsulted in the present moment.'[3]

Smith was well qualified as such a person. During his professor's days in Glasgow he had known merchants with direct experience of America. Subsequently, he had worked with Charles Townshend in 1766–7 when

---

[1] The MS. in question is Wedderburn Papers vol. 3, item 2; it was published by G. H. Guttridge, *American Historical Review* xxxviii (1933), 714–20 and again by Fay 110–14. Wedderburn's heir was Sir James St. Clair Erskine (2nd Earl of Rosslyn), and the heir's descendant was Captain John Erskine-Wemyss: Howard H. Peckham, *A Guide to the Manuscript Collections in the William L. Clements Library* (University of Michigan Press, Ann Arbor, 1942), 264–8.

[2] 'Account of the Life and Writings of Adam Smith', *Works of Smith*, ed. Stewart (1811), v. 410. See Letters 15 and 163 for evidence about the degree of friendship. Smith wrote articles for the *Edinburgh Review* which Wedderburn edited in 1755, and they were founder members of the Select Society, which debated in 1754 such topics as union with Ireland: John, Lord Campbell, *Lives of the Chancellors* (1868), vii. 358–61, 365–9.

[3] *Geo. III Corr.* ii. 504.

a budget was in preparation that vitally affected the relationship between the mother country and the American colonies, and at the same period he had been consulted by Lord Shelburne concerning the history of the colonies.[4] During the last stages of the composition of WN and at the time of its publication he was much preoccupied with America. Hume wrote to him on 8 February 1776: 'The Duke of Buccleugh tells me, that you are very zealous in American Affairs' (Letter 149). Also, as is seen in Governor Pownall's *Letter* (Appendix A), two parts of WN dealing with American problems and similar ones in Ireland commanded respect and added to his contemporary reputation (IV.vii, 'Of Colonies', and V.iii, 'Of publick Debts'). Further, when the North government became concerned in October 1779 with Irish demands for free trade, Smith was called upon for advice (Letters 200–3).

The negative point that the memorandum has a topical notation, I^{mo}, II^{do}, III^{tio}, and IV^{to}, which is not found elsewhere in Smith's manuscripts, does not amount to much. The memorandum is in the hand of a copyist or amanuensis, which is in line with Smith's practice with lengthy documents, e.g. the revisions sent on 10 October 1759 to Gilbert Elliot of Minto (Letter 40). The paper of the memorandum bears the Britannia watermark common on Smith manuscripts but also found on paper used in Government offices.[5]

In the memorandum, the writer describes himself as 'a solitary philosopher', which was indeed Smith's condition from 1767 until 1773 when he lived in seclusion in Kirkcaldy and worked on WN, and again from November 1777 until January 1778 while he waited for his appointment as a Commissioner of Customs in Scotland. The latter period can be postulated as that of the composition of the memorandum. As a 'solitary philosopher', however, Smith was by no means cut off from the course of public business. It has been argued that his commissionership was as much a reward for his contribution to North's budgets of 1777 and 1778 as for his service to the Buccleugh family through acting as tutor to the third Duke.[6] The memorandum, then, is not to be seen as a mere academic exercise but as advocacy in the spirit of WN, perhaps the more persuasive because couched in the language of the professional student of politics and history.

[4] See Letter 302, and Scott, 'Adam Smith at Downing Street, 1766–7', 79–89; also Letter 101. Adam Smith's attitudes to the colonies and the options open to the British Government are summarized in Donald Winch, *Classical Political Economy and Colonies* (London, 1965), 14–24.

[5] Scott 60, 321–2; R. L. Meek and A. S. Skinner, *Economic Journal* 83 (1973), 1104.

[6] Smith ascribed his appointment to the 'interest of the Duke of Buccleuch', but see Rae 320–1, for the argument that North valued Smith's advice, his evidence being the 1777 taxes on man-servants and property sold by auction, and the 1778 malt tax and duty on inhabited houses: compare WN V.ii.e.8, g,12, k.49. North's budget speech of 1777 acknowledged the support given by Smith for added impositions: Cobbett's *Parliamentary History* (1814), xix. 241–9. See also John Ehrman, *The Younger Pitt* (1969), i. 249.

This last point brings matters round to the text and the doctrines it embodies. Here, again, the reasons for detecting Smith's authorship are strong. In vocabulary, phrasing, and sentence structure the memorandum is reminiscent of parallel passages in WN. Also, the doctrines expressed are strikingly similar. Only the thesis concerning the cost to the mother country of a monopoly trade is scanted in the memorandum, possibly because the stress is on political rather than economic considerations. The other chief topics are there, discussed in the same manner: the cost of past wars, the solution of electoral and representative problems, the basis of representation upon taxation, the role and ambition of the American leaders, and the expense of a military solution.[7]

There are two curiosities of thought in the memorandum that are not unworthy of the ingenuity of Smith. One is the proposal that to secure the independent Americans as allies of Britain, Canada should be restored to the French and the Floridas to Spain. Something like this suggestion, which smacks of *Realpolitik*, had occurred to Samuel Johnson in 1775: 'one wild proposal is best answered by another. Let us restore to the French what we have taken from them. We shall see the colonists at our feet, when they have an enemy so near them' (*Taxation No Tyranny*). The other is that ostensibly the old colonial relationship of 1763 should be resumed. Secretly, however, the American and British leaders would agree to sever gradually the link between the two countries. With reason the memorandum concludes that a scheme of such finesse would probably fail in the execution.

In the opinion of the author of the memorandum, the scheme offering most advantages to the British empire was that of a constitutional union with American representation. This scheme is alleged to have scarce a single advocate except for 'a solitary philosopher' like the writer. Now, Smith himself mentions the idea of a federal union some twelve times in WN, but he was not unique in presenting this idea. Franklin had written in 1754 that union would be 'very acceptable to the colonies' with certain reservations. As late as 1775 he had a lingering sympathy for the idea, but came round thereafter to the view that nothing would serve but complete emancipation.[8] Lord Kames had suggested a 'consolidating union' in 1774, in *Sketches of the History of Man* (II.iv). Governor Pownall recommended a federal union in successive editions of *Administration of the Colonies* (1764, 1765, 1766, 1768, 1774, 1777), but on 2 December 1778, before the news of Saratoga was received, he told the House of Commons: 'Until you shall be convinced that you are no longer sovereigns over America, but that the United States are an independent sovereign people—until you are

---

[7] Parallel passages are extensively reported in the Glasgow Edition WN.

[8] Verner W. Crane, *Benjamin Franklin's Letters to the Press* (University of North Carolina Press, Chapel Hill, 1950), 72, n. 28, and Franklin, *Papers*, ed. Willcox *et al.* (Yale University Press, New Haven and London, 1972), xv. 238–9.

prepared to treat with them as such—it is of no consequence at all, what schemes or plans of conciliation this side the House or that may adopt.'[9]

Yet, if the case for constitutional union had no chance of acceptance in connection with America, something would be added by the memorandum to the quantum of opinion in Government circles concerning the appropriate way to deal with a colony inclined to rebellion. In 1800 that opinion triumphed in the parliamentary union with Ireland, when the free trade argument won the support of the Irish commercial interest, Wedderburn still in Government at that date as Lord Chancellor Loughborough, sought to prejudice George III against the expected outcome of the union in the form of Catholic emancipation. That the measure was carried forward at all was due to the exertions of another 'pupil' of Smith, the younger Pitt, who certainly had the doctrines of WN in his head, if not the 'Thoughts on the Contest with America' which usefully supplement and amplify them.[10]

There seem to be four, and but four, possible ways in which the present unhappy war with our Colonies may be conceived to end.

First, it may be conceived to end in the complete submission of America; all the different colonies, not only acknowledging, as formerly, the supremacy of the mother country; but contributing their proper proportion towards defraying the expence of the general Government and defence of the Empire.

Secondly, it may be conceived to end in the complete emancipation of America; not a single acre of land, from the enterance into Hudson's Straits to the mouth of the Mississipi, acknowledging the supremacy of Great Britain.

Thirdly, it may be conceived to end in the restoration, or something near to the restoration, of the old system; the colonies acknowledging the supremacy of the mother country, allowing the Crown to appoint the Governors, the Lieutenant-Governors, the secretaries and a few other officers in the greater part of them, and submitting to certain regulations of trade; but contributing little or nothing towards defraying the expence of the general Government and defence of the empire.[11]

Fourthly, and lastly, it may be conceived to end in the submission of a part, but of a part only, of America; Great Britain, after a long, expensive and ruinous war, being obliged to acknowledge the independency of the rest.

The probability of some of these events is, no doubt, very small; and it may not, perhaps, be worth while so say any thing about them. For the sake of order and distinctness, however, I shall say a few words concerning the advantages and disadvantages which might be expected from each.

I^{mo} The first event might be conceived to be brought about, either altogether by Conquest, or altogether by treaty, or partly by the one, and partly by the other.

If the complete submission of America was brought about altogether by Conquest, a military government would naturally be established there; and the

---

⁹ Quoted at HP iii. 318.

¹⁰ Rae 405; J. Steven Watson, *The Reign of George III: 1760–1815* (Oxford, 1960), 399–402.   ¹¹ WN IV.vii.c. 64–7; see, also Letter 221.

continuance of that submission would be supposed to depend altogether upon the continuance of the force which had originally established it. But a military government is what, of all others, the Americans hate and dread the most. While they are able to keep the field they never will submit to it; and if, in spite of their utmost resistance, it should be established, they will, for more than a century to come, be at all times ready to take arms in order to overturn it. The necessary violence of such a government would render them less able, than they otherwise would be, to contribute towards the general expence of the empire. Their dislike to it would render them less willing. Whatever could be extorted from them, and probably much more than could be extorted from them, would be spent in maintaining that military force which would be requisite to command their obedience. By our dominion over a country, which submitted so unwillingly to our authority, we could gain scarce anything but the disgrace of being supposed to oppress a people whom we have long talked of, not only as of our fellow subjects, but as of our brethren and even as of our children.

But whatever may be the impracticability of bringing about the complete submission of America in this manner; it arises altogether from the resistance of America. A plan of this kind would be agreeable to the present humour of Great Britain where, if you except a few angry speeches in Parliament, it would meet with scarce any opposition.

If the complete submission of America was brought about altogether by treaty, the most perfect equality would probably be established between the mother country and her colonies; both parts of the empire enjoying the same freedom of trade and sharing in their proper proportion both in the burden of taxation and in the benefit of representation. No expensive military force would, in this case, be necessary to maintain the allegiance of America. The principal security of every government arises always from the support of those whose dignity, authority and interest, depend upon its being supported. But the leading men of America, being either members of the general legislature of the empire, or electors of those members, would have the same interest to support the general government of the empire which the Members of the British legislature and their electors have at present to support the partciular government of Great Britain. The necessary mildness of such a government, so exactly resembling that of the mother country, would secure the continuance of the prosperity of the colonies. They would be able to contribute more largely; and, being taxed by their own representatives, they would be disposed to contribute more willingly.

That the complete submission of America, however, should be brought about by treaty only, seems not very probable at present. In their present elevation of spirits, the ulcerated minds of the Americans are not likely to consent to any union even upon terms the most advantageous to themselves. One or two campaigns, however, more successful than those we have hitherto made against them, might bring them perhaps to think more soberly upon the subject of their dispute with the mother country: And if, in this case, the Parliament and people of Great Britain appeared heartily to wish for a union of this kind, it is not, perhaps, impossible but that, partly by conquest, and partly by treaty, it might be brought about. Unfortunately, however, the plan of a constitutional union with our colonies and of an American representation seems not to be agreeable to any considerable party of men in Great Britain. The plan which, if it could be executed, would certainly tend most to the prosperity, to the splendour, and to the duration of the empire, if you except here and there a solitary philosopher like myself, seems scarce to have a single advocate.[12] A government which has failed in accomplishing, what seemed to them to be very easy, is, perhaps, with some reason, afraid to undertake what would certainly prove very difficult. After the unavoidable difficulty, however, of reconciling the discordant views both of societies and of individuals, whose interests might be affected by this union; the greatest difficulty which I have heard of, as resulting from the nature of the thing, is that of judging concerning the controverted elections which might happen in that distant country. A Worcestershire election of which the witnesses were to be brought from America, it must be acknowledged, would prove an endless business.[13] There should not, however, seem to be any great inconveniency, or such as could essentially alter the constitution of Parliament, in establishing particular courts of justice for deciding such controverted elections as might occur, either in that or in the other parts of the empire. The genius of the present election Committees of the house of Commons is in reality more different from that of the antient judicature of the whole house; than the genius of such courts of justice might be from that of those election Committees.[14]

II[do] The complete emancipation of America from all dependency upon Great Britain, would at once deliver this country from the great ordinary expence of the military establishment necessary for maintaining her authority in the colonies, and of the naval establishment necessary for defending her monopoly of their trade. It would at once deliver her likewise from the still greater extraordinary expence of defending them in time of war; whether that war was undertaken upon their account or upon our own. The two most expensive wars which Great Britain ever carried on, the Spanish war which began in 1739, and the French war which began in 1755, were undertaken, the one chiefly, the other altogether on account of the colonies. During the reign of the late king, and that of his royal father, we used to complain, that our connexion with Hanover deprived us of the advantages of our insular situation, and involved us in the quarrels of other nations, with which we should, otherwise, have had nothing to do. But we, surely, have had much more reason to complain, upon the same account, of our connexion with America. If in those days it was the general wish of the people that Hanover might some time or other be separated from the Crown of Great Britain; it ought to be much more their wish now that America should be so. If, with the complete emancipation of America, we should restore Canada to France and the two Floridas to Spain; we should render our colonies the natural enemies

---

[12] At WN IV.vii.c.60, Smith urges the advantages of the emancipation of the colonies in a similar fashion, but avers 'the most visionary enthusiast would scarce be capable of proposing such a measure, with any serious hopes at least of its ever being adopted'.

[13] Worcestershire was one of twelve counties which never went to the poll from 1754 to 1790, but in 1754 Oxfordshire had a celebrated election case involving a double return of two Whigs and two Tories: HP i. 9, 178–9.

[14] Grenville's Act of 1770 provided that each election petition should be referred to a Committee of the House of Commons chosen by lot. The measure was made a permanent one in 1774: HP i. 179.

of those two monarchies and consequently the natural allies of Great Britain. Those splendid, but unprofitable acquisitions of the late war, left our colonies no other enemies to quarrel with but their mother country. By restoring those acquisitions to their antient masters, we should certainly revive old enmities, and probably old friendships. Even without this restitution, tho' Canada, Nova Scotia, and the Floridas were all given up to our rebellious colonies, or were all conquered by them, yet the similarity of language and manners would in most cases dispose the Americans to prefer our alliance to that of any other nation. Their antient affection for the people of this country might revive, if they were once assured that we meant to claim no dominion over them; and if in the peace which we made with them, we insisted upon nothing, but the personal safety, and the restoration to their estates and possessions, of those few unfortunate individuals who have made some feeble, but ineffectual efforts to support our authority among them. By a federal union with America we should certainly incur much less expense, and might, at the same time, gain as real advantages, as any we have hitherto derived from all the nominal dominion we have ever exercised over them.

But tho' this termination of the war might be really advantageous, it would not, in the eyes of Europe appear honourable to Great Britain; and when her empire was so much curtailled, her power and dignity would be supposed to be proportionably diminished. What is of still greater importance, it could scarce fail to discredit the Government in the eyes of our own people, who would probably impute to mal-administration what might, perhaps, be no more than the unavoidable effect of the natural and necessary course of things. A government which, in times of the most profound peace, of the highest public prosperity, when the people had scarce even the pretext of a single grievance to complain of, has not always been able to make itself respected by them; would have every thing to fear from their rage and indignation at the public disgrace and calamity, for such they would suppose it to be, of thus dismembering the empire.

III[tio] The restoration, or something near to the restoration, of the old system would sufficiently preserve, both in the eyes of foreign nations and of our own people, the credit and honour of the government. Our own people seem to desire this event so ardently, that what might be the effect of mere weakness and inability, would by them be imputed to wisdom, tho' to late wisdom, and moderation. But this event would not preserve the honour of the British Government in the eyes of the Americans. After so complete a victory, as even this event would amount to; after having, not only felt their own strength, but made us feel it, they would be ten times more ungovernable than ever; factious, mutinous and discontented subjects in time of peace; at all times, upon the slightest disobligation, disposed to rebel; and, in the case of a French or Spanish war, certainly rebelling. This event, however, does not at present seem very probable. The Americans, I imagine, would be less unwilling to consent to such a union with Great Britain as Scotland made with England in 1707; than to the restoration, or to anything like the restoration, of the old systems. The leading men of America, we may believe, wish to continue to be the principal people in their own country. After a union with Great Britain, they might expect to continue to be so; in the same manner as the leading men of Scotland continued to be the principal people of their own country after the union with England.[15] But after the restoration, or any thing like the restoration, of the old system, the appointment of the principal people among them, of their Governors, Lieutenant Governors, etc., will revert to the Crown of Great Britain.

The Americans, it has been said, when they compare the mildness of their old government with the violence of that which they have established in its stead, cannot fail both to remember the one with regret and to view the other with detestation. That these will be their sentiments when the war is over and when their new government, if ever that should happen, is firmly established among them, I have no doubt. But while the war they will impute, and with appearance of reason too, the greater part of the oppressions which they suffer to the necessity of the times. Those oppressions will serve to animate them, not so much against their own leaders, as against the government of the Mother country to which they will impute the causes of that necessity. It was not till some time after the conclusion of the civil war that the people of England began to regret the loss of that regal Government which they had rashly overturned, and which was happily restored to them by such a concurrence of accidental circumstances as may not, upon any similar occasion, ever happen again.

An apparent restoration of the old system, so contrived as to lead necessarily, but insensibly to the total dismemberment of America, might, perhaps, satisfy both the people of Great Britain and the leading men of America; the former mistaking, and the latter understanding the meaning of the scheme. It might, at the same time, gradually bring about an event which, in the present distressful situation of our affairs, is, perhaps, of all those which are likely to happen, the most advantageous to the state. But the policy, the secrecy, the prudence necessary for conducting a scheme of this kind, are such as, I apprehend, a British Government, from the nature and essence of our constitution, is altogether incapable of.

IV^to The submission or conquest of a part, but of a part only, of America, seems of all the four possible terminations of this unhappy war, by far the most probable; and unfortunately it is the termination which is likely to prove most destructive to Great Britain. The defence of that part, from the attacks of the other colonies, would require a much greater military force than all the taxes which could be raised upon it could maintain. The neighbourhood of that part would keep alive the jealousy and animosity of all the other provinces, and would necessarily throw them into the alliance of the enemies of Great Britain. If all the seventeen provinces of the Netherlands had completely emancipated themselves from the dominion of Spain, their situation, as soon as their independency was acknowledged, would have rendered them the natural enemies of France and consequently the natural allies of Spain. Spain would have suffered little more than the mortification of losing the dominion of a great country, which, for some years before the revolt, had never paid the whole expence of its own government. To compensate this mortification, she would have gained the solid advantage of a powerful, and probably a faithful alliance, against the most

---

[15] Cf. WN IV.viii.c.75; but see Letter 50's account of the short-run disadvantages of the union of 1707, and WN V.iii.89 for the argument that the union freed the Scottish people from the an oppressive aristocracy.

formidable of all her enemies. Whoever considers with attention the causes of the declension of the Spanish Monarchy, will find that it was owing, more to the recovery of the ten, than to the loss of the seven united provinces. Those ten provinces, a much richer and more fertile country than any part of America; and at that time more populous than all the thirteen united colonies taken together, never paid the tenth part of the expence of the armies which Spain was obliged to maintain in them. The neighbourhood of those armies rendered the seven united provinces, for about a hundred years together; that is, till France had conquered the greater part of the ten provinces, the constant allies of France and the constant enemies of Spain.

Jeremy Bentham's 'Letters' to Adam Smith (1787, 1790)

In August 1785 Jeremy Bentham set out from England to join his younger brother Samuel, the naval architect and engineer, whose projects in Russia included helping to develop Prince Potëmkin's estate at Krichëv. Travelling via France, Italy, Smyrna, and Bucharest, Jeremy Bentham reached White Russia in February 1786 and settled himself on a farm at Zadobrast on the Sozh, near Krichëv, to live in seclusion and write. In August the brothers entertained an English M.P., Sir Richard Worsley, who reported that the British Government intended to restrict the rate of interest. Writing in December to George Wilson, a Lincoln's Inn barrister of Scottish extraction, Bentham mentioned his reaction to this report: 'Sir R.W. has a notion that Pitt means to reduce the rate of interest from five to four. Tell me what you hear about it; were it true I should like to give him a piece of my mind first. I have arguments against it *ready cut* and *dry*: the former epithet you may have some doubt about; the latter you will not dispute. You know that it is an old maxim of mine, that interest, as love and religion, and so many other pretty things, should be free.'

The topic was continued in another letter to Wilson of 9/20 February 1787: 'I am writing letters to *you* abusing Pitt for being about to reduce the rate of interest, and abusing the world for limiting the rate of interest at all.' Replying on 24 April, Wilson said that as far as he knew no proposal had been made in Parliament to reduce the rate of interest, but he encouraged Bentham to continue with his book because the subject was an important one: 'It is at all time sufficiently in people's minds to make it interesting; and perhaps new doctrines concerning it, will have more weight that they do not appear to be published on the spur of the occasion.' Wilson declared, however, that he did not want to see this book through the press in Bentham's absence. He went on to comment on signs of progress such as reform of ecclesiastical courts, consolidation of the customs, and the opening of ports to the French, linking the reception of WN to the changing times: 'Indeed, on all points of political economy, there is an evident change in public opinion within these ten years, which may be in some degree owing to the circulation of Smith's book, but still more to the events which have happened in our political and commercial connexion with America, to the utter disgrace of the old thrones.'

As is evident in Letter XIII of the *Defence of Usury*, Bentham controverted Smith's arguments about a high rate of interest and the role of projectors as expressed in WN I.ix, I.x.b, and II.iv, but in general Bentham and his circle saw Smith as an ally. The Austrian medical scientist F. X. Schwediauer wrote from Edinburgh as follows on 15 July 1784: 'Dr Smith with whom I am intimately acquainted, is quite our man, He is busy about a new edition of his wealth of nations.' The edition is question was the third, published towards the end of 1784: see Letters 222, 223, 227, 228, 231, and 232 for an account of the considerable revisions involved. This was the edition that Bentham had with him in Russia, for his citations in the *Defence of Usury*.

Another book in Bentham's mind during the writing of the *Defence of Usury* was probably one by William Playfair: *The Increase of manufactures, commerce and finance, with the extension of civil liberty, proposed in regulations for the interest of money* (1785). It took the position adopted by Bentham, but as he made clear to Wilson on 4/15 May 1787, it did so without the intellectual toughness that he sought: 'Nine-tenths of it is bad writation about the origin of society, and so forth: the other tenth is a perfectly vague and shapeless proposal for relaxing the rigour of the anti-usurious laws in favour of projectors; yet without any argument in it, or any other idea, but that vague one thrown out in almost as general and vague a way as I have stated it. I understand it has been well enough spoken of by several people.'

Bentham finished the *Defence* towards the beginning of May 1787 and forwarded it to Wilson via St. Petersburg, through the hands of Sergey Ivanovich Pleshcheyev who corrected some references to Russian rates of interest. In the event, Wilson did see the book through the press at the end of 1787, and on 6 June 1788 he sent to Bentham, who had been back in England some four months, an appreciative article in the *Monthly Review* (lxxviii. 361–70) which described the *Defence* as a 'political gem of the finest water'.[1] Apparently Adam Smith agreed in the main. Wilson wrote again to Bentham about his book on 4 December 1789: 'Did we ever tell you what Dr Adam Smith said to Mr William Adam, the Council M.P., last summer in Scotland. The Doctor's expressions were that 'the *Defence of Usury* was the work of a very superior man, and that tho' he had given [Smith] some hard knocks, it was done in so handsome a way that he could not complain,' and seemed to admit that you were right.'[2] Bentham took note of this report in the opening paragraph of the 'Letter to Dr Smith' which he added to the second edition of the *Defence of Usury* (1790), printed below, but he was careful to state that the conversion of Smith had not been reported to him directly from the author of WN himself. In view of Wilson's letter about the conversion, it is interesting to speculate, as Rae did, that if Smith had lived he might have altered his stand on the rate of interest and his inclination to equate projectors with prodigals.

[1] [*Bentham Corr.* iii. xxv–xxviii; 294–5; 518; 524; 532; 533; 543; 546.]
[2] [Rae 423–4.]

I. *Defence of Usury*, Letter XIII, 'To Dr. Smith, on Projects in Arts, &c.[3]

Crichoff, in White Russia, March 1787

Sir,

I forget what son of controversy it was, among the Greeks, who having put himself to school to a professor of eminence, to learn what, in those days, went by the name of wisdom, chose an attack upon his master for the first public specimen of his proficiency. This specimen, whatever entertainment it might have afforded to the audience, afforded, it may be supposed, no great satisfaction to the master: for the thesis was, that the pupil owed him nothing for his pains. For my part, being about to shew myself in one respect as ungrateful as the Greek, it may be a matter of prudence for me to look out for something like candour by way of covering to my ingratitude: instead therefore of pretending to owe you nothing, I shall begin with acknowledging, that, as far as your track coincides with mine, I should come much nearer the truth, were I to say I owed you every thing. Should it be my fortune to gain any advantage over you, it must be with weapons which you have taught me to wield, and with which you yourself have furnished me: for, as all the great standards of truth, which can be appealed to in this line, owe, as far as I can understand, their establishment to you, I can see scarce any other way of convicting you of any error or oversight, than by judging you out of your own mouth.

In the series of letters to which this will form a sequel, I had travelled nearly thus far in my researches into the policy of the laws fixing the rate of interest, combating such arguments as fancy rather than observation had suggested to my view, when, on a sudden, recollection presented me with your formidable image, bestriding the ground over which I was travelling pretty much at my ease, and opposing the shield of your authority to any arguments I could produce.

It was a reflection mentioned by Cicero as affording him some comfort, that the employment his talents till that time had met with, had been chiefly on the defending side. How little soever blest, on any occasion, with any portion of his eloquence, I may, on the present occasion, however, indulge myself with a portion of what constituted his comfort: for, if I presume to contend with you, it is only in defence of what I look upon as, not only an innocent, but a most meritorious race of men, who are so unfortunate as to have fallen under the rod of your displeasure. I mean *projectors*: under which invidious name I understand you to comprehend, in particular, all such persons as, in the pursuit of wealth, strike out into any new channel, and more especially into any channel of invention.

It is with the professed view of checking, or rather of crushing, these adventurous spirits, whom you rank with 'prodigals', that you approve of the laws which limit the rate of interest, grounding yourself on the tendency, they appear to you to have, to keep the capital of the country out of two such different sets of hands.

[3] See Letter 268. The copy-text for Letter XIII is that of the second edition (1790) as presented in *Jeremy Bentham's Economic Writings*, ed. Werner Stark (London, 1952), i. 167–87. Our editorial notes to the text are placed within square brackets. Bentham's citations of WN are from ed. 3, 1784; his footnote references have been converted to vol. and page references to ed. 3, and each is followed by the Glasgow Edition form.

The passage, I am speaking of, is in the fourth chapter of your second book, volume the second of the 8vo edition of 1784. 'The legal rate' (you say) 'it is to be observed, though it ought to be somewhat above, ought not to be much above, the lowest market rate. If the legal rate of interest in Great Britain, for example, was fixed so high as eight or ten per cent. the greater part of the money which was to be lent, would be lent to prodigals and projectors, who alone would be willing to give this high interest. Sober people, who will give for the use of money no more than a part of what they are likely to make by the use of it, would not venture into the competition. A great part of the capital of the country would thus be kept out of the hands which were most likely to make a profitable and advantageous use of it, and thrown into those which were most likely to waste and destroy it. Where the legal interest, on the contrary, is fixed but a very little above the lowest market rate, sober people are universally preferred as borrowers, to prodigals and projectors. The person who lends money, gets nearly as much interest from the former, as he dares to take from the latter, and his money is much safer in the hands of the one set of people than in those of the other. A great part of the capital of the country is thus thrown into the hands in which it is most likely to be employed with advantage.'[4]

It happens fortunately for the side you appear to have taken, and as unfortunately for mine, that the appellative, which the custom of the language has authorized you, and which the poverty and perversity of the language has in a manner forced you, to make use of, is one, which, along with the idea of the sort of persons in question, conveys the idea of reprobation, as indiscriminately and deservedly applied to them. With what justice or consistency, or by the influence of what causes, this stamp of indiscriminate reprobation has been thus affixed, it is not immediately necessary to enquire. But, that it does stand thus affixed, you and every body else, I imagine, will be ready enough to allow. This being the case, the question stands already decided, in the first instance at least, if not irrevocably, in the judgments of all those, who, unable or unwilling to be at the pains of analysing their ideas, suffer their minds to be led captive by the tyranny of sounds; that is, I doubt, of by far the greater proportion of those whom we are likely to have to judge us. In the conceptions of all such persons, to ask whether it be fit to restrain projects and projectors, will be as much as to ask, whether it be fit to restrain rashness, and folly, and absurdity, and knavery, and waste.

Of prodigals I shall say no more at present. I have already stated my reasons for thinking, that it is not among them that we are to look for the natural customers for money at high rates of interest. As far as those reasons are conclusive, it will follow, that, of the two sorts of men you mention as proper objects of the burthen of these restraints, prodigals and projectors, that burthen falls exclusively on the latter. As to these, what your definition is of projectors, and what descriptions of persons you meant to include under the censure conveyed by that name, might be material for the purpose of judging of the propriety of that censure, but makes no difference in judging of the propriety of the law, which that censure is employed to justify. Whether you yourself, were the several classes of persons made to pass before you in review, would be disposed to pick out this or that

[4] [ii. 44–5; II.iv.15.]

class, or this and that individual, in order to exempt them from such censure, is what for that purpose we have no need to enquire. The law, it is certain, makes no such distinctions: it falls with equal weight, and with all its weight, upon all those persons, without distinction to whom the term *projectors*, in the most unpartial and extensive signification of which it is capable, can be applied. It falls at any rate (to repeat some of the words of my former definition), upon all such persons, as, in the pursuit of wealth, or even of any other object, endeavour, by the assistance of wealth, to strike into any channel of invention. It falls upon all such persons, as, in the cultivation of any of those arts which have been by way of eminence termed *useful*, direct their endeavours to any of those departments in which their utility shines most conspicuous and indubitable; upon all such persons as, in the line of any of their pursuits, aim at any thing that can be called *improvement*; whether it consist in the production of any new article adapted to man's use, or in the meliorating the quality, or diminishing the expence, of any of those which are already known to us. It falls, in short, upon every application of the human powers, in which ingenuity stands in need of wealth for its assistant.

High and extraordinary rates of interest, how little soever adapted to the situation of the prodigal, are certainly, as you very justly observe, particularly adapted to the situation of the projector: not however to that of the imprudent projector only, nor even to his case more than another's, but to that of the prudent and well-grounded projector, if the existence of such a being were to be supposed. Whatever be the prudence or other qualities of the project, in whatever circumstance the novelty of it may lie, it has this circumstance against it, viz. that it is new. But the rates of interest, the highest rates allowed, are, as you expressly say they are, and as you would have them to be, adjusted to the situation which the sort of trader is in, whose trade runs in the old channels, and to the best security which such channels can afford. But in the nature of things, no new trade, no trade carried on in any new channel, can afford a security equal to that which may be afforded by a trade carried on in any of the old ones: in whatever light the matter might appear to perfect intelligence, in the eye of every prudent person, exerting the best powers of judging which the fallible condition of the human faculties affords, the novelty of any commercial adventure will oppose a chance of ill success, superadded to every one which could attend the same, or any other, adventure, already tried, and proved to be profitable by experience.

The limitation of the profit that is to be made, by lending money to persons embarked in trade, will render the monied man more anxious, you may say, about the goodness of his security, and accordingly more anxious to satisfy himself respecting the prudence of a project in the carrying on of which the money is to be employed than he would be otherwise: and in this way it may be thought that these laws *have* a tendency to pick out the good projects from the bad, and favour the former at the expence of the latter. The first of these positions I admit: but I can never admit the consequence to follow. A prudent man, (I mean nothing more than a man of ordinary prudence) a prudent man acting under the sole governance of prudential motives, I still say will not, in these circumstances, pick out the good projects from the bad, for he will not meddle with projects at all. He will pick out old-established trades from all sorts of projects, good and bad; for with a new project, be it ever so promising, he never will have any thing to do. By every man that has money, five per cent. or what-ever be the highest legal rate, is at all times, and always will be, to be had upon the very best security, that the best and most prosperous old-established trade can afford. Traders in general, I believe, it is commonly understood, are well enough inclined to enlarge their capital as far as all the money they can borrow at the highest legal rate, while that rate is so low as 5 per cent.[,] will enlarge it. How it is possible therefore for a project, be it ever so promising, to afford, to a lender at any such rate of interest, terms equally advantageous, upon the whole, with those he might be sure of obtaining from an old-established business, is more than I can conceive. Loans of money may certainly chance, now and then, to find their way into the pockets of projectors as well as of other men: but when this happens it must be through incautiousness, or friendship, or the expectation of some collateral benefit, and not through any idea of the advantageousness of the transaction, in the light of a pecuniary bargain.

I should not expect to see it alledged, that there is any thing, that should render the number of well-grounded projects, in comparison of the ill-grounded, less in time future, than it has been in time past. I am sure at least that I know of no reasons why it should be so, though I know of some reasons, which I shall beg leave to submit to you by and by, which appear to me pretty good ones, why the advantage should be on the side of futurity. But, unless the stock of well-grounded projects is already spent, and the whole stock of ill-grounded projects that ever were possible, are to be looked for exclusively in the time to come, the censure you have passed on projectors, measuring still the extent of it by that of the operation of the laws in the defence of which it is employed, looks as far backward as forward: it condemns as rash and ill-grounded, all those projects, by which our species have been successively advanced from that state in which acorns were their food, and raw hides their cloathing, to the state in which it stands at present: for think, Sir, let me beg of you, whether whatever is now the *routine* of trade was not, at its commencement, *project*? whether whatever is now *establishment*, was not at one time, innovation?

How it is that the tribe of well-grounded projects, and of prudent projectors (if by this time I may have your leave for applying this epithet to some at least among the projectors of time past), have managed to struggle through the obstacles which the laws in question have been holding in their way, it is neither easy to know, nor necessary to enquire. Manifest enough, I think, it must be by this time, that difficulties, and those not inconsiderable ones, those laws must have been holding up, in the way of projects of all sorts, of improvement (if I may say so) in every line, so long as they have had existence: reasonable therefore it must be to conclude, that, had it not been for these discouragements, projects of all sorts, well-grounded and successful ones, as well as others, would have been more numerous than they have been: and that accordingly, on the other hand, as soon, if ever, as these discouragements shall be removed, projects of all sorts, and among the rest, well-grounded and successful ones, will be more numerous than they would otherwise have been: in short, that, as, without these discourage-ments, the progress of mankind in the career of prosperity, would have been greater than it has been under them in time past, so, were they to be removed, it would be at least proportionably greater in time future.

That I have done you no injustice, in assigning to your idea of projectors so great a latitude, and that the unfavourable opinion you have professed to entertain of them is not confined to the above passage, might be made, I think, pretty apparent, if it be material, by another passage in the tenth chapter of your first book.[5] 'The establishment of any new manufacture, of any new branch of commerce, or of any new practice in agriculture,' all these you comprehend by name under the list of '*projects*': of every one of them you observe, that 'it is a speculation from which the *projector* promises himself extraordinary profits. These profits (you add) are sometimes *very great*, and sometimes, *more frequently perhaps*, they are *quite otherwise*: but in general they bear no regular proportion to those of other old trades in the neighbourhood. If the project succeeds, they are commonly at first very high. When the trade or practice becomes thoroughly established and well known, the competition reduces them to the level of other trades.' But on this head I forbear to insist: nor should I have taken this liberty of giving you back your own words, but in the hope of seeing some alteration made in them in your next edition, should I be fortunate enough to find my sentiments confirmed by your's. In other respects, what is essential to the publick, is, what the error is in the sentiments entertained, not who it is that entertains them.

I know not whether the observations which I have been troubling you with, will be thought to need, or whether they will be thought to receive, any additional support from those comfortable positions, of which you have made such good and such frequent use, concerning the constant tendency of mankind to get forward in the career of prosperity, the prevalence of prudence over imprudence, in the sum of private conduct at least, and the superior fitness of individuals for managing their own pecuniary concerns, of which they know the particulars and the circumstances, in comparison of the legislator, who can have no such knowledge. I will make the experiment: for, so long as I have the mortification to see you on the opposite side, I can never think the ground I have taken strong enough, while any thing remains that appears capable of rendering it still stronger.

'With regard to misconduct, the number of prudent and successful undertakings' (you observe[6]) 'is every where much greater than that of injudicious and unsuccessful ones. After all our complaints of the frequency of bankruptcies, the unhappy men who fall into this misfortune make but a very small part of the whole number engaged in trade, and all other sorts of business; not much more perhaps than one in a thousand.'

'Tis in support of this position that you appeal to history for the constant and uninterrupted progress of mankind, in our island at least, in the career of prosperity: calling upon any one who should entertain a doubt of the fact, to divide the history into any number of periods, from the time of Cæsar's visit down to the present: proposing for instance the respective æras of the Restoration, the Accession of Elizabeth, that of Henry VII, the Norman Conquest, and the Heptarchy, and putting it to the sceptic to find out, if he can, among all these periods, any one at which the condition of the country was not more prosperous than at the period immediately preceding it; spite of so many wars, and fires, and plagues, and all other public calamities, with which it has been at different times

[5] [i. 177; I.x.a.43.]   [6] [ii. 20; II.iii.29.]

afflicted, whether by the hand of God, or by the misconduct of the sovereign. No very easy task, I believe: the fact is too manifest for the most jaundiced eye to escape seeing it:—But what and whom are we to thank for it, but projects, and projectors?

'No', I think I hear you saying, 'I will not thank projectors for it, I will rather thank the laws, which by fixing the rates of interest have been exercising their vigilance in repressing the temerity of projectors, and preventing their imprudence from making those defalcations from the sum of national prosperity which it would not have failed to make, had it been left free. If, during all these periods, that adventurous race of men had been left at liberty by the laws to give full scope to their rash enterprizes, the increase of national prosperity during these periods might have afforded some ground for regarding them in a more favourable point of view. But the fact is, that their activity has had these laws to check it; without which checks you must give me leave to suppose, that the current of prosperity, if not totally stopt, or turned the other way, would at any rate have been more or less retarded. Here then' (you conclude) 'lies the difference between us: what you look upon as the cause of the increase about which we are both agreed, I look upon as an obstacle to it: and what you look upon as the obstacle, I look upon as the cause.'

Instead of starting this as a sort of plea that might be urged by you, I ought, perhaps, rather to have mentioned it as what might be urged by some people in your place: for as I do not imagine your penetration would suffer you to rest satisfied with it, still less can I suppose that, if you were not, your candour would allow you to make use of it as if you were.

To prevent your resting satisfied with it, the following considerations would I think be sufficient.

In the first place, of the seven periods which you have pitched upon, as so many stages for the eye to rest at in viewing the progress of prosperity, it is only during the three last, that the country has had the benefit, if such we are to call it, of these laws: for it is to the reign of Henry VIII. that we owe the first of them.

Here a multitude of questions might be started: Whether the curbing of projectors formed any part of the design of that first statute, or whether the views of it were not wholly confined to the reducing the gains of that obnoxious and envied class of men, the money-lenders? Whether projectors have been most abundant before that statute, or since that statute? And whether the nation has suffered as you might say—benefited, as I should say, most by them, upon the whole, during the former period or the latter? All these discussions, and many more that might be started, I decline engaging in, as more likely to retard, than to forward, our coming to any agreement concerning the main question.

In the next place, I must here take the liberty of referring you to the proof, which I think I have already given, of the proposition, that the restraints in question could never have had the effect, in any degree, of lessening the proportion of bad projects to good ones, but only of diminishing, as far as their influence may have extended, the total number of projects, good and bad together. Whatever therefore was the general tendency of the projecting spirit previously to the first of these laws, such it must have remained ever since, for any effect which they could have had in purifying and correcting it.

But what may appear more satisfactory perhaps than both the above considerations, and may afford us the best help towards extricating ourselves from the perplexity, which the plea I have been combating (and which I thought it necessary to bring to view, as the best that could be urged) seems much better calculated to plunge us into, than bring us out of, is, the consideration of the small effect which the greatest waste that can be conceived to have been made within any compass of time, by injudicious projects, can have had on the sum of prosperity, even in the estimation of those whose opinion is most unfavourable to projectors, in comparison of the effect which within the same compass of time must have been produced by *prodigality*.

Of the two causes, and only two causes, which you mention, as contributing to retard the accumulation of national wealth, as far as the conduct of individuals is concerned, projecting, as I observed before, is the one, and prodigality is the other: but the detriment, which society can receive even from the concurrent efficacy of both these causes, you represent, on several occasions, as inconsiderable; and, if I do not misapprehend you, too inconsiderable, either to need, or to warrant, the interposition of government to oppose it. Be this as it may with regard to projecting and prodigality taken together, with regard to prodigality at least, I am certain I do not misapprehend you. On this subject you ride triumphant, and chastise the 'impertinence and presumption of kings and ministers,' with a tone of authority, which it required a courage like your's to venture upon, and a genius like your's to warrant a man to assume[7]. After drawing the parallel between private thrift and public profusion, 'It is' (you conclude) 'the highest impertinence and presumption therefore in kings and ministers *to pretend to watch over the economy of private people*, and to restrain their expence, either by sumptuary laws, or by prohibiting the importation of foreign luxuries. They are themselves always, and without exception, the greatest spendthrifts in the society. Let them look well after their own expence, and they may safely trust private people with theirs. If their own extravagance does not ruin the state, that of their subjects never will.'

That the employing the expedients you mention for restraining prodigality, is indeed generally, perhaps even without exception, improper, and in many cases even ridiculous, I agree with you; nor will I here step aside from my subject to defend from that imputation another mode suggested in a former part of these papers. But however presumptuous and impertinent it may be for the sovereign to attempt in any way to check by legal restraints the *prodigality* of individuals, to attempt to check their *bad management* by such restraints seems abundantly more so. To err in the way of prodigality is the lot, though, as you well observe, not of *many* men, in comparison of the whole mass of mankind, yet at least of *any* man: the stuff fit to make a prodigal of is to be found in every alehouse, and under every hedge. But even to *err* in the way, of projecting is the lot only of the privileged few. Prodigality, though not so common as to make any very material drain from the general mass of wealth, is however too common to be regarded as a mark of distinction or as a singularity. But the stepping aside from any of the beaten paths of traffic, *is* regarded as a singularity, as serving to distinguish a man from other men. Even where it requires no genius, no peculiarity of talent, as where it

[7] [ii. 27; II.iii.36.]

consists in nothing more than the finding out a new market to buy or sell in, it requires however at least a degree of courage, which is not to be found in the common herd of men. What shall we say of it, where, in addition to the vulgar quality of courage, it requires the rare endowment of genius, as in the instance of all those successive enterprizes by which arts and manufactures have been brought from their original nothing to their present splendor? Think how small a part of the community these must make, in comparison of the race of prodigals; of that very race, which, were it only on account of the smallness of its number, would appear too inconsiderable to you to deserve attention. Yet prodigality is essentially and necessarily hurtful, as far as it goes, to the opulence of the state: projecting, only by accident. Every prodigal, without exception, impairs, by the very supposition impairs, if he does not annihilate, his fortune. But it certainly is not every projector that impairs his: it is not every projector that would have done so, had there been none of those wise laws to hinder him: for the fabric of national opulence, that fabric of which you proclaim, with so generous an exulta-tion, the continual increase, that fabric, in every apartment of which, innumerable as they are, it required the reprobated hand of a projector to lay the first stone, has required some hands at least to be employed, and successfully employed. When in comparison of the number of prodigals, which is too inconsiderable to deserve notice, the number of projectors of all kinds is so much more incon-siderable—and when from this inconsiderable number, must be deducted, the not inconsiderable proportion of successful projectors—and from this remainder again, all those who can carry on their projects without need of borrowing—think whether it be possible that this last remainder could afford a multitude, the reducing of which would be an object, deserving the interposition of govern-ment by its magnitude, even taking for granted that it were an object proper in its nature?

If it be still a question, whether it be worth while for government, by its *reason*, to attempt to controul the conduct of men visibly and undeniably under the dominion of *passion*, and acting, under that dominion, contrary to the dictates of their own reason; in short, to effect what is acknowledged to be their better judgment, against what every body, even themselves, would acknowledge to be their worse; is it endurable that the legislator should by violence substitute his own pretended reason, the result of a momentary and scornful glance, the off-spring of wantonness and arrogance, much rather than of social anxiety and study, in the place of the humble reason of individuals, binding itself down with all its force to that very object which he pretends to have in view?—Nor let it be forgotten, that, on the side of the individual in this strange competition, there is the most perfect and minute knowledge and information, which interest, the whole interest of a man's reputation and fortune, can ensure: on the side of the legislator, the most perfect ignorance. All that he knows, all that he can know, is, that the enterprize is a *project*, which, merely because it is susceptible of that obnoxious name, he looks upon as a sort of cock, for him, in childish wantonness, to shie at.—Shall the blind lead the blind? is a question that has been put of old to indicate the height of folly: but what then shall we say of him who, being necessarily blind, insists on leading, in paths he never trod in, those who can see?

It must be by some distinction too fine for my conception, if you clear yourself from the having taken, on another occasion, but on the very point in question, the side, on which it would be my ambition to see you fix.

'What is the species of domestic industry which his capital can employ, and of which the produce is likely to be of the greatest value, every individual' (you say[8]), 'it is evident, can, in his local situation, judge much better than any statesman or lawgiver can do for him. The statesman, who should attempt to direct private people in what manner they ought to employ their capitals, would not only load himself with a most unnecessary attention, but assume an authority which could safely be trusted, not only to no single person, but to no council or senate whatsoever, and which would no where be so dangerous as in the hands of a man who had folly and presumption enough to fancy himself fit to exercise it.

'To give the monopoly of the home market to the produce of domestic industry, in any particular art or manufacture, is in some measure to direct private people in what manner they ought to employ their capitals, and must in almost all cases be either a useless or a hurtful regulation.' Thus far you: and I add, to limit the legal interest to a rate at which the carriers on of the oldest and best-established and least hazardous trades are always glad to borrow, is to give the monopoly of the money-market to those traders, as against the projectors of new-imagined trades, not one of which but, were it only from the circumstance of its novelty, must, as I have already observed, appear more hazardous than the old.

These, in comparison, are but inconclusive topics. I touched upon them merely as affording, what appeared to me the only shadow of a plea, that could be brought in defence of the policy I am contending against. I come back therefore to my first ground, and beg you once more to consider, whether, of all that host of manufactures, which we both exult in as the causes and ingredients of national prosperity, there be a single one, that could have existed at first but in the shape of a project. But, if a regulation, the tendency and effect of which is merely to check projects, in as far as they are projects, without any sort of tendency, as I have shewn, to weed out the bad ones, is defensible in its present state of imperfect efficacy, it should not only have been defensible, but much more worthy of our approbation, could the efficacy of it have been so far strengthened and compleated as to have opposed, from the beginning, an unsurmountable bar to all sorts of projects whatsoever: that is to say, if, stretching forth its hand over the first rudiments of society, it had confined us, from the beginning, to mud for our habitations, to skins for our cloathing, and to acorns for our food.

I hope you may by this time be disposed to allow me, that we have not been ill served by the projects of time past. I have already intimated, that I could not see any reason why we should apprehend our being worse served by the projects of time future. I will now venture to add, that I think I do see reason, why we should expect to be still better and better served by these projects, than by those. I mean better upon the whole, in virtue of the reduction which experience, if experience be worth any thing, should make in the proportion of the number of the ill-grounded and unsuccessful, to that of the well-grounded and successful ones.

The career of art, the great road which receives the footsteps of projectors, may be considered as a vast, and perhaps unbounded, plain, bestrewed with gulphs,

[8] [ii. 182; IV.ii.10–11.]

such as Curtius was swallowed up in. Each requires an human victim to fall into it ere it can close, but when it once closes, it closes to open no more, and so much of the path is safe to those who follow. If the want of perfect information of former miscarriages renders the reality of human life less happy than this picture, still the similitude must be acknowledged: and we see at once the only plain and effectual method for bringing that similitude still nearer to perfection; I mean, the framing the history of the projects of time past, and (what may be executed in much greater perfection were but a finger held up by the hand of government) the making provision for recording, and collecting and publishing as they are brought forth, the race of those with which the womb of futurity is still pregnant. But to pursue this idea, the execution of which is not within my competence, would lead me too far from the purpose.

Comfortable it is to reflect, that this state of continually-improving security, is the natural state not only of the road to opulence, but of every other track of human life. In the war which industry and ingenuity maintain with fortune, past ages of ignorance and barbarism form the forlorn hope, which has been detached in advance, and made a sacrifice of for the sake of future. The golden age, it is but too true, is not the lot of the generation in which we live: but, if it is to be found in any part of the track marked out for human existence, it will be found, I trust, not in any part which is past, but in some part which is to come.

But to return to the laws against usury, and their restraining influence on projectors. I have made it, I hope, pretty apparent, that these restraints have no power or tendency to pick out bad projects from the good. It is worth while to add, which I think I may do with some truth, that the tendency of them is rather to pick the good out from the bad? Thus much at least may be said, and it comes to the same thing, that there is one case in which, be the project what it may, they may have the effect of checking it, and another in which they can have no such effect, and that the first has for its accompaniment, and that a necessary one, a circumstance which has a strong tendency to separate and discard every project of the injudicious stamp, but which is wanting in the other case. I moan, in a word, the *benefit of discussion*.

It is evident enough, that upon all such projects, whatever be their nature, as find funds sufficient to carry them on, in the hands of him whose invention gave them birth, these laws are perfectly, and if by this time you will allow me to say so, very happily, without power. But for these there has not necessarily been any other judge, prior to experience, than the inventor's own partial affection. It is not only not necessary that they should have had, but it is natural enough that they should not have had, any such judge: since in most cases the advantage to be expected from the project depends upon the exclusive property in it, and consequently upon the concealment of the principle. Think, on the other hand, how different is the lot of that enterprize which depends upon the good opinion of another man, that other, a man possessed of the wealth which the projector wants, and before whom necessity forces him to appear in the character of a suppliant at least: happy if, in the imagination of his judge, he adds not to that degrading character, that of a visionary enthusiast or an impostor! At any rate, there are, in this case, two wits, set to sift into the merits of the project, for one, which was employed upon that same task in the other case: and of these two there is one, whose prejudices are certainly not most likely to be on the favourable side. True it is, that in the jumble of occurrences, an over-sanguine projector may stumble upon a patron as over-sanguine as himself; and the wishes may bribe the judgment of the one, as they did of the other. The opposite case, however, you will allow, I think, to be by much the more natural. Whatever a man's wishes may be for the success of an enterprize not yet his own, his fears are likely to be still stronger. That same pretty generally implanted principle of vanity and self-conceit, which disposes most of us to over-value each of us his own conceptions, disposes us, in a proportionable degree, to undervalue those of other men.

Is it worth adding, though it be undeniably true, that could it even be proved, by ever so uncontrovertible evidence, that, from the beginning of time to the present day, there never was a project that did not terminate in the ruin of its author, not even from such a fact as this could the legislator derive any sufficient warrant, so much as for wishing to see the spirit of projects in any degree repressed?—The discouraging motto, *Sic vos non vobis*, may be matter of serious consideration to the individual, but what is it to the legislator? What general, let him attack with ever so superior an army, but knows that hundreds, or perhaps thousands, must perish at the first onset? Shall he, for that consideration alone, lie inactive in his lines? 'Every man for himself—but God,' adds the proverb (and it might have added the general, and the legislator, and all other public servants), 'for us all.' Those sacrifices of individual to general welfare, which, on so many occasions, are made by third persons against men's wills, shall the parties themselves be restrained from making, when they do it of their own choice? To tie men neck and heels, and throw them into the gulphs I have been speaking of, is altogether out of the question: but if at every gulph a Curtius stands mounted and caparisoned, ready to take the leap, is it for the legislator, in a fit of old-womanish tenderness, to pull him away? Laying even public interest out of the question, and considering nothing but the feelings of the individuals immediately concerned, a legislator would scarcely do so, who knew the value of hope, 'the most precious gift of heaven.'

Consider, Sir, that it is not with the invention-lottery (that great branch of the project-lottery, for the sake of which I am defending the whole, and must continue so to do until you or somebody else can shew me how to defend it on better terms), it is not I say with the invention-lottery, as with the mine-lottery, the privateering-lottery, and so many other lotteries, which you speak of, and in no instance, I think, very much to their advantage.[9] In these lines, success does not, as in this, arise out of the embers of ill success, and thence propagate itself, by a happy contagion, perhaps to all eternity. Let Titius have found a mine, it is not the more easy, but by so much the less easy, for Sempronius to find one too: let Titius have made a capture, it is not the more easy, but by so much the less easy, for Sempronius to do the like. But let Titius have found out a new dye, more brilliant or more durable than those in use, let him have invented a new and more convenient machine, or a new and more profitable mode of husbandry, a thousand dyers, ten thousand mechanics, a hundred thousand husbandmen, may repeat and multiply his success: and then, what is it to the public, though the fortune of Titius, or of his usurer, should have sunk under the experiment?

[9] [i. 164–9; I.x.b. 27–31.]

Birmingham and Sheffield are pitched upon by you as examples, the one of a projecting town, the other of an unprojecting one.[10] Can you forgive my saying, I rather wonder that this comparison of your own chosing, did not suggest some suspicions of the justice of the conceptions you had taken up, to the disadvantage of projectors. Sheffield is an old oak: Birmingham, but a mushroom. What if we should find the mushroom still vaster and more vigorous than the oak? Not but the one as well as the other, at what time soever planted, must equally have been planted by projectors: for though Tubal Cain himself were to be brought post from Armenia to plant Sheffield, Tubal Cain himself was as arrant a projector in his day, as ever Sir Thomas Lombe[11] was, or bishop Blaise.[12] but Birmingham, it seems, claims in common parlance the title of a projecting town, to the exclusion of the other, because, being but of yesterday, the spirit of project smells fresher and stronger there than elsewhere.

When the odious sound of the word *projector* no longer tingles in your ears, the race of men thus stigmatized do not always find you their enemy. Projects, even under the name of 'dangerous and expensive experiments,' are represented as not unfit to be encouraged, even though monopoly be the means: and the monopoly is defended in that instance, by its similarity to other instances in which the like means are employed to the like purpose.

'When a company of merchants undertake at their own risk and expence to establish a new trade, with some remote and barbarous nation, it may not be unreasonable' (you observe) 'to incorporate them into a joint-stock company, and to grant them, in case of their success, a monopoly of the trade for a certain number of years. It is the easiest and most natural way, in which the state can recompense them, for hazarding a dangerous and expensive experiment, of which the public is afterwards to reap the benefit. A temporary monopoly of this kind may be vindicated, upon the same principles, upon which a like monopoly of a new machine is granted to its inventor, and that of a new book to its author.'[13]

Private respect must not stop me from embracing this occasion of giving a warning, which is so much needed by mankind. If so original and independent a spirit has not been always able to save itself from being drawn aside by the fascination of sounds, into the paths of vulgar prejudice, how strict a watch ought not men of common mould to set over their judgments, to save themselves from being led astray by similar delusions?

I have sometimes been tempted to think, that were it in the power of laws to put *words* under proscription, as it is to put *men*, the cause of inventive industry might perhaps derive scarcely less assistance from a bill of attainder against the words *project* and *projectors*, than it has derived from the act authorizing the grant

---

[10] [i. 176; I.x.b.42.]

[11] [Sir Thomas Lombe (1685–1739) inventor; Sheriff of London, Knighted 1727; set up silk-throwing machines on the Derwent in 1718, from designs which his half-brother John smuggled out of Italy two years before. In fifteen years Lombe made a fortune of £120,000, and Parliament voted him £14,000 in 1732 for the surrender of his patent, which made it available to his rivals, mainly at Spitalfields and Macclesfield.]

[12] [Saint Blaise was an Armenian Bishop and martyr of uncertain date, applied to by sufferers from diseases of the throat. He is said to have saved a boy's life by extracting a fishbone from his throat.]

[13] [iii. 143–4; V.i.e.30.

of patents. I should add, however, for a time: for even then the envy, and vanity, and wounded pride, of the uningenious herd, would sooner or later infuse their venom into some other word, and set it up as a new tyrant, to hover, like its predecessor, over the birth of infant genius, and crush it in its cradle.

Will not you accuse me of pushing malice beyond all bounds, if I bring down against you so numerous and respectable a body of men, as the members of the *Society for the Encouragement of Arts*?[14] I do not, must not, care: for you command too much respect to have any claim to mercy. At least you will not accuse me of spiriting up against you barbarian enemies, and devoting you to the vengeance of Cherokees and Chicasaws.

Of that popular institution, the very professed and capital object is the encouragement of projects, and the propagating of that obnoxious breed, the crushing of which you commend as a fit exercise for the arm of power. But if it be right to crush the acting malefactors, it would be downright inconsistency not to crush, at the same time, or rather not to begin with crushing, these their hirers and abettors. Thank then their inadvertence, or their generosity, or their prudence, if their beadle has not yet received orders to burn in ceremony, as a libel on the society, a book that does honour to the age.

After having had the boldness to accuse so great a master of having fallen unawares into an error, may I take the still farther liberty, of setting conjecture to work to account for it? Scarce any man, perhaps no man, can push the work of creation, in any line, to such a pitch of compleatness, as to have gone through the task of examining with his own eyes into the grounds of every position, without exception, which he has occasion to employ. You heard the public voice, strengthened by that of law, proclaiming all round you, that usury was a sad thing, and usurers a wicked and pernicious set of men: you heard from one at least of those quarters, that projectors were either a foolish and contemptible race, or a knavish and destructive one: Hurried away by the throng, and taking very naturally for granted, that what every body said must have some ground for it, you have joined the cry, and added your suffrage to the rest. Possibly too, among the crowd of projectors which the lottery of occurrences happened to present to your observation, the prejudicial sort may have borne such a proportion to the beneficial, or shewn themselves in so much stronger colours, as to have given the popular notion a firmer hold in your judgement, than it would have had, had the contrary proportion happened to present itself to your notice. To allow no more weight to examples that fall close under our eyes, than to those which have fallen at ever so great a distance—to suffer the judgement on no occasion to indulge itself in the licence of a too hasty and extensive generalisation—not to give any proposition footing there, till after all such defalcations have been made, as are necessary to reduce it within the limits of rigid truth—these are laws, the compleat observance whereof forms the ultimate, and hitherto, perhaps for ever, ideal term of human wisdom.

You have defended against unmerited obloquy two classes of men, the one innocent at least, the other highly useful; the spreaders of English arts in foreign

[14] [The Society for Encouragement of Arts, Manufacture, and Commerce, founded in 1754; together with the Royal Society, actively encouraged men with new scientific ideas.]

climes,[15] and those whose industry exerts itself in distributing that necessary commodity which is called by the way of eminence the staff of life.[16] May I flatter myself with having succeeded at last in my endeavours, to recommend to the same powerful protection, two other highly useful and equally persecuted sets of men, usurers and projectors.—Yes—I will, for the moment at least, indulge so flattering an idea: and, in pursuance of it, leaving usurers, for whom I have said enough already, I will consider myself as joined now with you in the same commission, and thinking with you of the best means of relieving the projector from the load of discouragement laid on him by these laws, in so far as the pressure of them falls particularly upon him. In my own view of the matter, indeed, no temperament, no middle course, is either necessary or proper: the only perfectly effectual, is the only perfectly proper remedy,—a spunge. But, as nothing is more common with mankind, than to give opposite receptions, to conclusions flowing with equal necessity from the same principle, let us accommodate our views to the contingency.

According to this idea, the object, as far as confined to the present case, should be, to provide in favour of projectors only, a dispensation from the rigour of the anti-usurious laws: such, for instance, as is enjoyed by persons engaged in the carrying trade, in virtue of the indulgence given to loans made on the footing of *respondentia* or bottomry. As to abuse, I see not why the danger of it should be greater in this case than in those. Whether a sum of money be embarked, or not embarked, in such or such a new manufacture on land, should not, in its own nature, be a fact much more difficult to ascertain, than whether it be embarked, or not embarked, in such or such a trading adventure by sea: and, in the one case as in the other, the payment of the interest, as well as the repayment of the principal, might be made to depend upon the success of the adventure. To confine the indulgence to new undertakings, the having obtained a patent for some invention, and the continuance of the term of the patent, might be made conditions of the allowance given to the bargain: to this might be added affidavits, expressive of the intended application, and bonds, with sureties, conditioned for the performance of the intention so declared; to be registered in one of the patent-offices or elsewhere. After this, affidavits once a year, or oftener, during the subsistence of the contract, declaring what has been done in execution of it.

If the leading-string is not yet thought tight enough, boards of controul might be instituted to draw it tighter. Then opens a scene of vexation and intrigue: waste of time consumed in courting the favour of the members of the board: waste of time, in opening their understandings, clenched perhaps by ignorance, at any rate by disdain, and self-sufficiency, and vanity, and pride: the favour (for pride will make it a favour) granted to skill in the arts of self-recommendation and cabal, devoid of inventive merit, and refused to naked merit unadorned by practice in those arts: waste of time on the part of the persons themselves engaged in this impertinent inquiry: waste of somebody's money in paying them for this waste of time. All these may be necessary evils, where the money to be bestowed is public money: how idle where it is the party's own! I will not plague you, nor myself, with enquiring of whom shall be composed this board of nurses to grown gentlemen: were it only to cut the matter short, one might name

[15] [ii. 514 *et alibi*; IV.viii.44–8.]   [16] [WN IV.v.b.]

at once the committees of the Society of Arts. There you have a body of men
ready trained in the conduct of enquiries, which resemble that in question, in
every circumstance, but that which renders it ridiculous: the members or
representatives of this democratic body would be as likely, I take it: to discharge
such a trust with fidelity and skill, as any aristocracy that could be substituted in
their room.

II. *Defence of Usury*, 'To Dr Smith' [1790][17]

A little tract of mine in the latter part of which I took the liberty of making use
of your name, (the Defence of Usury) having been some time out of print, I am
about publishing a new edition of it. Now then is the time when /I am now therefore at a period at which/ if I have done you /or any body/ any injustice, I too shall
have the opportunity, and assuredly I do not want the inclination, to repair it:
or if in any other respect I have fallen into an error I could give myself and the
public the benefit of its being set right. I have been flattered by the assurance
/with the intelligence/ that upon the whole your sentiments with respect to the
points of difference are at present the same as mine: but as the information did
not come directly from you, nor has the communication of it received the sanction of your authority, I shall not without that sanction give any hint, honourable
as it would be to me, and great as the service is which it could not but render to
my cause.

   I have been favoured with the communication of a paper from Dr Reid of
Glasgow[18] of a /an inedited/ paper of his written /on the same subject/ a good
many years ago. He declares himself now fully of my way of thinking /opinion/
on the question of expediency and had gone a great /considerable/ length
towards it at that time. The only ground on which he differs from me is that of
the history /origination/ of the prejudice, of which his paper gives as might be
expected an account more ecclesiastical than mine. Anxious to do my cause as
much service as it is capable of receiving, I write to him to persuade him to give
his paper to the world, or if he looks upon so much of it as concerns the question
of utility superseded by mine, that he will either consign /communicate/ the
historical part that part which he prefers to mine to some general repository for
short publications, or allow me the honour of forwarding it to the world in company with mine. The account that has been given by the Marquis de Condorcet
of the sentiments of Turgot on the same subject is /already/ every bodys
without leave:[19] I shall therefore /accordingly publish/ annex by way of appendix

---

[17] [See Letter 296 and *Bentham's Economic Writings*, ed. Stark, i. 188–90. This ostensible
letter was the second of two prefaces Bentham wrote for the second edition of the *Defence
of Usury* (1790). The first draft is abstract and inconclusive (University College, London,
Bentham MSS. 169. 173). The second draft, the one printed here, was composed with
Adam Smith in mind, together with contemporary debates on the issue of the reduction
of interest by the Irish Parliament. Our copy-text is that of the manuscript (University
College, London, Bentham MSS. 169. 174–5). Bentham's spelling and punctuation are
retained, also his second thoughts and in one case a third thought, but rejected wording
is omitted. Second thoughts are presented within oblique strokes, and the third thought
between two oblique strokes.]

[18] [Thomas Reid; see Stewart, 'Account of Smith', Note K, subnote.]

[19] [Antoine-Nicolas Caritat de Condorcet, *Vie de Turgot* (London, 1786), 53–6, 228.]

to my new edition the original as well as a translation of the short passage. I am the more anxious to collect all the force I can muster, in as far as I find from the /printed/ debates as well as from private intelligence that the project of reducing the rate of interest in Ireland is not yet given up: though this perseverence is hardly consistent /reconcilable/ with the account I receive from the same quarter of the impression made /in that country/ by the Defence of Usury.[20] Yet the subjecting rate of interest to a further reduction by a new law is a much more mischievous and less defensible measure than the continuing of the restraint upon the old footing: and pregnant with mischief of a different and independent nature /adds to the mischief of the old established regimen others of a new and much more serious mature/. It would be a tax upon the owners of money much heavier than ever was based upon the proprietors of land: with this circumstance to distinguish it from all other taxes that instead of being brought into the treasury for the public service it is made a present of to the collectors in expectation of the good they are to do the nation by the spending of it. If this be good thrift in the name of consistency and equality let them impose a land-tax to the same amount and dispose of the produce in the same manner. What makes my anxiety the greater is the uncertainty whether this project of plunder without profit is not /may not be/ still hovering over this island. Last year it was roundly and positively asserted in the Irish H[ouse] of Commons /as if upon personal knowledge/ to be determined upon in the Cabinet here: and the administration being appealed to though they of course would not acknowledge would not contradict it. Its suspension hitherto may have resulted from nothing more than a doubt whether the nation were yet ripe, according to the Irish phrase for this mode of enrichment: as if there were a time when /at which/ a nation were riper for plunder and waste than at another. I am truly sorry I can not find time to make one effort more for the express purpose of stemming the torrent of delusion in the channel. The straw I have bestowed /planted/ already for that purpose has done something: what might not be looked for, if your oak-stick were added to /linked with/ it?

As the world judges, one upon examination, and nine hundred /and ninety-nine upon authority //trust// /, the declaration of your opinion upon any point /of legislation/ would be worth I won't pretend to guess /say/ how many votes: but the declaration of your opinion in favour of a side to which conviction and candour had brought you over from the opposite one, would be worth at least twice or thrice as many: in /under/ such circumstances the authority of the converter would tell for little in comparison of that of the proselyte, especially such

[20] [Bentham's father docketed a letter to his son from George Wislon dated 5 June with the note: 'The Defense of Usury had been reprinted at Dublin. Together with a Paper The World dated Fryday Feb. 22 1788 containing an Account of the Debates in the Irish Parliament upon a Proposal for reducing Public Interest.' Bentham told his brother Samuel on 2 May 1788, '[The *Defence*] has had some little sale in Ireland, and I hope it may do something towards preventing the success of the measure of reducing the rate of interest there—a measure which, after having been thrown out of the House of Lords there this winter, is to be brought on by administration the next it is said.' In Ireland the legal maximum interest was 6 per cent. In 1788 there was a successful movement to reduce it to 5 per cent in line with the English maximum: *Bentham Corr.* iii. 618; 620; W. E. H. Lecky, *A History of Ireland in the Eighteenth Century* (1913), ii. 492.]

a proselyte. We should have the Irish Chancellor of the Exchequer[21] abjuring his annual motion in the face of the House, and L[or]d Hawkesbury[22] who they say /it has been said/ is Mr Pitt's tutor in this wise business, quietly and silently putting his papers and calculations in the fire.

If then you agree with me in looking upon this as a most pernicious measure you would like me be glad to see it foiled /put an end to/, and the declaration /for that purpose the acknowledgment/ of your opinion on a subject which you have made so much and so honourably your own, is an expedient to the use of which I should hope you would not see any objection: the less as you would hardly I suppose let another edition of your great work go abroad with opinions in it that were yours no longer.[23] If then you proper to honour me with your allowance /permission/ for that purpose, then and not otherwise I will make it known to the public, in such words as you give me, that you no longer look upon the rate of interest as fit subject for restraint: and then, thanks to you and Turgot and Dr Reid, the Defence of Usury may be pronounced, in its outworks at least, a strong-hold.

[21] [John Foster (1740–1838), lawyer and politician; entered the Irish House of Commons 1761; Chancellor of the Exchequer in Ireland from 1784; protested against the union of the Irish and British Parliaments; opposed relief of Roman Catholics; cr. Baron Oriel 1821.]

[22] Charles Jenkinson, 1st Earl of Liverpool (1729–1808) protégé of Burke; Secretary-at-War under North 1778; President of the Board of Trade under Pitt 1786–1802, and Chancellor of the Duchy of Lancaster at the same time; cr. Baron Hawkesbury 1786; cr. Earl of Liverpool 1796; a born bureaucrat whose chief passion was for the details of office.]

[23] [WN ed. 5 was published in 1789, and Smith's last thoughts were apparently about TMS ed. 6 (1790): see Letters 294 and 295.]

Custom-house Documents

Adam Smith's father (1679–1723) became Comptroller of Customs at Kirkcaldy in 1714, at the same time as his cousin Hercules Scott Smith (d. 1738) became Collector. Smith's 'tutor' or guardian, also Adam Smith, became Collector at Kirkcaldy at a later date, as well as Inspector of Customs for the outports (Scott 16–17, 134). Yet another Adam Smith, cousin to the man of letters, was Collector at Alloa in 1754 (Letter 16). With this family background, it is not surprising that Smith was both revenue-minded and an acute critic of the revenue practices of his time, as is revealed in WN (e.g. IV.ii–v; V.ii.), also that he took readily to a post as Commissioner of Customs from 1778 until his death.

Letters 184–8 and 190–3 deal with his appointment; 208 and 274 have references to his attentiveness to duty; and 196 and 197 reflect his reading in a comparative European source on customs, as well as the interest his ideas aroused in politicians. Letter 235 is concerned with the management of funds under the Customs Board which were applied to the civil list. Special problems connected with the revenue service such as smuggling and trading patterns are discussed in 203, 233, 234, and the issue of free trade for Ireland in 200–2. Smith's work as a Commissioner and his access to official returns probably influenced the important revisions for WN ed. 3 of 1784, as indicated by Letters 222 and 227. He was also prepared to make revenue data available to George Chalmers, a contemporary analyst of economic conditions: 249–52.

Smith's colleagues as the other four members of the Customs Board at different periods were as follows: Mansfeldt de Cardonnel, grandson of the Duke of Monmouth and reputed to be as good a raconteur as his great-grandfather Charles II (Carlyle 228–9); Basil Cochrane (1701–88), relative of James Boswell and a former soldier, who was made Commissioner of Excise in 1761 and of Customs in 1763; James Edgar (d. 1799), old soldier and former Collector at Leith, who shared with Smith an interest in the Greek classics (John Kay, *Original Portraits*, 1842, i. 384–8); George Clerk Maxwell; David Reid; James Buchanan; John Henry Cochrane; and Robert Hepburn. The Solicitor to the Board and Inspector-General of Customs was the giant-like Alexander Osborne (Kay, *Portraits*, i. 344), and the Secretary was R. E. Phillips, who lived to be 104 and was buried in the same grave as Adam Smith in the Canongate kirkyard (Rae 330).

The bulk of the documents connected with Smith's service on the Customs Board are now in SRO, e.g. the minutes of the Board, from which a representative sample is drawn below. Other examples in the same repository are original letters and orders bound in volumes containing a large number of items signed by Smith and his colleagues: CE56/2/5A–5D, 5F (Dunbar), and CE62/2/1–4 (Inverness). There are a few documents with Smith signatures in CE67/2/1 (Alloa), CE71/2/1 (Irvine), and CE77/2/1 (Stranraer). Copy documents with copy Smith signatures are to be found in CE52/2/2–4 (Perth), CE60/2/271–6 (Port Glasgow and Greenock), and CE82/2/1–4, 83–6 (Campbeltown). Copies with copy Smith initials only are to be found in CE51/2/3–4 (Dumfries), CE53/2/1–2 (Montrose), CE60/2/319–27 (Port Glasgow and Greenock), CE73/2/1–2 (Rothesay), and CE76/1/10–6 (Ayr). The places listed in the parentheses were outports.

It is possible that some documents connected with Smith are in the library of H.M. Customs and Excise, King's Beam House, Mark Lane, London EC4, where is to be found his copy of Henry Crouch, *A Complete View of the British Customs* (London, 1727). Another likely source is the collection of Treasury papers in the Public Records Office, Chancery Lane, London WC2. In particular, for the relevant period there are Treasury in-letters, Treasury Board Papers (T.1), the Treasury out-letters, Customs (T.11), and the Treasury Minute Book (T.29). There are, in addition, important Customs documents among the Chatham papers (G.D.8), which have a bearing on the revenue service in Smith's time e.g. Bundle 231 (including an MS. booklet describing the business of various branches of the Treasury in 1782), and Bundle 283 containing letters and reports of the Customs Commissioners to the Treasury, and Customs accounts for the later part of the eighteenth century. These items at the PRO have been picked out from the useful bibliography in Elizabeth E. Hoon, *The Organization of the English Customs Systems, 1696–1786* (New York and London, 1938), 294–5.

Some notable figures have been connected with the revenue service or supported by it: Chaucer, William Prynne the Puritan pamphleteer, Elias Ashmole the antiquary, William Congreve, John Dennis the critic, and Tom Paine, to say nothing of Nell Gwynne, Charles II's mistress, who was maintained at the rate of £6,000 per annum out of the yield of the Excise duties. It is said that Smith recommended that Robert Burns be given a post as a Salt Officer in the Customs service, to assure him of a permanent income (F. B. Snyder, *The Life of Robert Burns*, New York, 1932, 232, n. 8). Among this company, perhaps the fullest record of service is available for Adam Smith, and it is proposed to illustrate this by presenting an extract from the Customs Board minutes, followed by a calendar of official letters, both handwritten and printed.

I. CUSTOMS BOARD MINUTES, SRO

Thursday the 31st December 1778
Adam Smith Esqr. in the Chair
Present
George Clerk Maxwell Esqr. and
Basil Cochrane Esqr.

Copy received for the
Solicitor A. Osborn

Read the Memorial of the Solicitor of the 24th Instant, laying before the Board a Letter from Mr David Rymer Tide Surveyor at Borrowstoness, submitting that he be indemnified in his Expences amounting to Two Pounds ten Shillings, incurred in coming twice to Edinburgh to be interrogated by the Solicitor relative to a Seizure of Aquavitae made by him in October 1777, and claimed by Andrew Stein, who having since withdrawn his Claim the said Seizure has gone into condemnation: And the Charge abovementioned appearing reasonable as Mr Rymer from lameness being unable to ride on Horseback must have taken a Chaise; the Board agree to the same being placed to the Seizure, of which the Solicitor and Register of Seizures are to have Notice.

Mr Robert Ferguson Collector at Air has leave to attend his Private Affairs for One Month, on his appointing a proper Person to carry on the Business for whom he will be answerable; which is to be Signified to the Port.

Vide Minute
20 Jan. 1779

Robert Cheshire Officer of the Salt Duty acting as a Riding Officer at Air has Three days Leave to attend to his private Affairs, in addition to the like Period granted by the Collector, which is to be signified to the Port.

Considered a Letter from the Collector and Comptroller at Leith of the 24th Instant, respecting the discharge of Coals at that Port out of the Sloops Janet John Halket Master, and Smart John Wilson Master, which Sloops Sailed with the said Cargoes from the District of Borrowstoness without reporting; And it appearing that the Cargo of the Smart and the greatest part of the Cargo of Janet were discharged for the Glasshouse at Leith, without being checked by the Coastwaiters, who upon being called before the Collector and Comptroller offer as an excuse the quick despatch made in discharging Coals for the Glasshouse, which allowed of little time for observation, and the nonsuspicion of Fraud in that part of the Business; Resolved that the Collector and Comptroller be directed to reprimand the Coastwaiters severely, acquainting them that if the like neglect should appear again they will be forthwith suspended, as they have already been informed that the Coast Trade is a common Channel for Smuggling, and therefore requires the strictest attention being paid to it.*

The Board adjourn till Tuesday next, on account of Handsel Monday.

Adam Smith

Copy received for the   *Considered a Letter from the Collector and Comp-
Solr. A. Osborn   troller at Kirkwall in Orkney of the 5th Instant signifying their Opinion that Thirty Pounds is a reasonable Allowance of rent for Mr Gordon's Warehouse at Stromness in which the Cargo of the Brigantine Three Brothers was secured for upwards of Eight Months in consequence of the Boards Order. Resolved that the Collector and the Comptroller be authorized to draw on the Solicitor for the Sum of Thirty Pounds the same appearing a reasonable Allowance for the use of the Warehouse abovementioned, and to discharge the Rent accordingly: Of which the Solicitor is to have notice.

II. OFFICIAL LETTERS

1. Kirkcaldy Museum

   1779, 8 Feb. Rejection of claim by the commander of the King's boat at Eyemouth and two of his crew for a share of a seizure. Sgd. Adam Smith, Basil Cochrane, George Clerk Maxwell.

2. Library, H.M. Customs and Excise, King's Beam House, Mark Lane, London EC4

   [Addressed to the Collector and Comptroller, Dunbar]

Custom-house, Edinburgh
[16] September 1779

Number One hundred

Gentlemen

We have received yours of the 14th inst. by express relative to three Privateers and a Frigate Supposed to be French, being off the Coast of Dunbar and Eyemouth, and also your Letter dated the 15th at one o'Clock noon signifying that four Vessels were then standing with their heads to the Northwards about twenty four Miles off Dunbar which it is beleived are Enemies Ships; And we command your Attention herein; and have communicated the Intelligence to the Commander in Chief, and to the Commanders of His Majesty's Ships in the Firth. We are,

Your Loving Friends
Adam Smith
George Clerk Maxwell
Basil Cochrane

[The story associated with this letter is the most stirring one of the period of Smith's commissionership. The squadron seen off Dunbar was commanded by

John Paul Jones (1747–92) in *Le Bonne Homme Richard*, and it appeared off the Isle of May on 16 September. A revenue cutter was ordered to reconnoitre, and her captain made a deposition the following day in the presence of the regulating officer and Commissioners George Clerk Maxwell and Adam Smith: 'at Daybreak, [he] found himself within Pistol Shot of a fifty Gun French Ship, upon which he tacked about and afterwards retook a prize they had taken in the Mouth of the Firth but a French twenty four Gun Frigate immediately made up, and obliged him to abandon the Prize, they brought on Shore a Boy from the Prize who says they put four Soldiers, four Men and two Officers on board him. The French Squadron consists of a fifty Gun Ship, a twenty four Gun Frigate and a Brig mounting ten Guns. The Ships sail ill, and they say they are determined to come up to Leith Road. The Commander of the fifty Gun Ship is said to be acquainted with the Coast. Both the fifty Gun Ship and Frigate are painted Black. The fifty Gun Ship has a White Bottom and very clumsy mast head. The Boy says seven Sail of them sailed in Company they went north the length of Shetland, and returned Separated in a Gale of Wind some Days ago from the rest of the Squadron. 17 September 1779' (Customs Board Minutes, 21 Dec. 1778–17 Jan. 1781, 197, SRO). The Commissioners transmitted this deposition by express to the Treasury in London the same day, and gave orders for the three revenue cutters on the East coast to be placed under the direction of the Commander-in-Chief in Scotland. It appears that the British Government had prompt information about Jones's movements from the time of his leaving France, and the revenue cutters were accordingly manned and armed 'to the fullest extent' (Henry Atton and Henry Hurst Holland, *The King's Customs*, London, 1910, ii. 490–1). For all that, John Paul Jones gained a famous victory on 23 September, when he closed with the *Serapis* convoying merchantmen returning from the Baltic, and fought with her from sunset until she surrendered three hours later under moonlight. Jones and his men then boarded her, leaving the burning *Le Bonne Homme Richard* to sink, and returned to France to be lionized.]

3. SRO, GD24/1/591

   1780, 19 Dec. Appreciation expressed to Lord Kames for his interest in improving legal procedures before the justiciary court involving revenue officers. Enclosed is a circular letter of 24 Jan. 1776 describing the Board's practice which coincides with Kames's ideas. Sgd. Adam Smith, George Clerk Maxwell, Basil Cochrane.

4. EUL, Dh. 6. 58*

   To Collectors and Comptrollers of the Custom-houses

   1782, 2 Sept. Instructions concerning the movement of goods and coal by transire, i.e. Custom-house permit, within the firths of Forth, Clyde, and Tay, and 'the River extending up the Country within the Heads of Cromarty'. Sgd. David Reid, Adam Smith, James Edgar.

5. Vanderblue Collection of Smithiana, Kress Library, Harvard: see Letter 220

   To George Rose, Esq., [Secretary to the Treasury]

   1782, 3 Sept. Encloses a report (31 Aug.) from the tide surveyor at

Newburgh as to the unfitness of John Greig to be an 'Extraordinary Boatman' there. The reasons given are that he was 'quite unacquainted with
Handling the Oar, Sails or any Article belonging to the Duty of a Boatman, aside so Extremely short sighted, that . . . he is very unqualified for
this Employment'. Sgd. James Buchanan, Adam Smith, Basil Cochrane.

To Rose, 19 Sept. Board interviewed Greig and arranged to have him tried
out by the Tide Surveyor at Leith, then directed that further trial was to
be made of him at Newburgh. Sgd. Basil Cochrane, Adam Smith, James
Buchanan.

To Rose, 24 Oct. Encloses a further report (21 Oct.) from the Newburgh
officer to the effect that Greig being a countryman did not take well to
handling a boat and that his shortsightedness was a 'Deficiency for day
Duty, and . . . much more so for Night'. The Board recommended that
Greig's appointment be stopped and that someone formerly employed as
boatman be taken on again. Sgd. James Buchanan, James Edgar, Adam
Smith.

6. University of Illinois

   To the Commander of the Cumbraes Cutter

   1783, 28 May. Concerns information about seizures by this officer. Sgd.
   Adam Smith, James Buchanan, James Edgar.

7. EUL, Dh. 6. 58*

   To [Collectors and Comptrollers of Custom-houses]

   1783, 8 Sept. Deals with a plan to prosecute the masters of fishing boats and
   to burn the boats if it could be proved they were engaged in bringing ashore
   cargoes from smuggling vessels lying twenty, thirty, or even forty miles
   offshore. Sgd. James Edgar, Adam Smith, George Clerk [? Maxwell].

8. EUL, Dh. 6. 58,* printed

   To the Collector and Comptroller of the Customs Dundee

   1784, 2 Sept. Concerns arrangements for the administration of the transire
   and the collection of fees. Instructs the officers to double their diligence in
   preventing frauds in the shipping and discharge of coals by transire. Sgd.
   David Reid, Adam Smith, James Edgar.

9. GUL, printed

   1786, 20 Dec. An Account of What Number of Ships from Scotland have
   been employed in the Whale Fishery to Davis's Streights, and the Green-
   land Seas. . . . From the 10th of October 1784 to the 10th October 1785.
   Sgd. Adam Smith, David Reid, Basil Cochrane.

10. University of Illinois, printed

    To [Collector and Comptroller of Customs Thurso]

    1789, 2 Dec. Notice of the dismissal of two land waiters at Alloa for taking
    unofficial fees and granting undue allowances to merchants: this to made
    known to all officers 'that they see what will be their Fate if they do not

discharge their Duty honestly and fairly in all Cases'. Sgd. Adam Smith, James Edgar, J.H. Cochrane.

11. Kirkcaldy Museum

Custom-house, Edinburgh
6 Aug. 1789

Gentlemen,

We have received your Letter of the 4th instant stating the proceedings of Mr Oliphant Tide Surveyor; Mr Stewart Commander of the Justice Hulk and the officers under their Survey, in watching a Lugger commanded by . . . Yawkins, so as to prevent her from landing any part of Her Cargo on the Coast, which Vessel has been captured and carried into Liverpool by Capt. Burges of His Majesty's Sloop Savage, who sailed in quest of her, in consequence of information from the Collector; and submitting, on account of the severe duty the officers and military were subjected to on this occasion, that they may be allowed a Gratuity out of the Service; We acquaint you that tho' the Services stated are very commendable, and what we much approve of, they are only such as come within the Line of their duty. We are,

Your Loving Friends
Robert Hepburn
Adam Smith
J. H. Cochrane

[The smuggler Yawkins was the prototype of Dirk Hatteraick in *Guy Mannering*. Scott provided some details about his career in an additional note printed at the end of the novel, 'Galwegian Localities and Personages . . . Alluded To': 'This man was well known on the coast of Galloway and Dumfriesshire, as sole proprietor and master of a *Buckkar*, or smuggling lugger, called The Black Prince. Being distinguished by his nautical skill and intrepidity, his vessel was frequently freighted, and his own services employed, by French, Dutch, Manx, and Scottish smuggling companies. . . . In those halcyon days of the free trade, the fixed price for carrying a box of tea, or bale of tobacco, from the coast of Galloway to Edinburgh, was fifteen shillings, and a man with two horses carried four such packages. The trade was entirely destroyed by Mr Pitt's celebrated commutation law, which, by reducing the duties upon excisable articles, enabled the lawful dealer to compete with the smuggler. The statute was called in Galloway and Dumfriesshire, by those who had thriven upon the contraband trade, "the burning and starving act".' In WN V.ii.k.35, Smith had argued that 'the temptation to smuggle can be diminished only by the lowering of the tax; and the difficulty of smuggling can be increased only by establishing that system of administration which is most proper for preventing it'. This theme was taken up by the House of Commons Committee appointed in 1783 to inquire into 'smuggling and other illicit practices' (see Letter 234 and the Parliamentary Papers cited below in the bibliography). Acting on the reports of the Committee, Pitt settled on tea for the experiment of lowering duty and brought in the Commutation Act of 1784. The smugglers took to the auction rooms to force up the price of tea but were outsmarted by Government-supported buying, and by 1789 it was reckoned that the contraband trade had been dealt a severe blow (Ehrman, *The Younger Pitt*, 1969, i. 242–5).]

12. Kirkcaldy Museum, copy

> 1790, 21 Jan. Query concerning the seizure of a box of tea in a swine house and two ankers of rum found among whins. Sgd. Adam Smith, James Edgar, Robert Hepburn.

III. SELECT BIBLIOGRAPHY DEALING WITH THE CUSTOMS SERVICE

A. Parliamentary Papers

XXXVI, *Reports*, VI, H.C. No. 58 (1783): 'First Report from the Committee appointed to Enquire into the Illicit Practices used in Defrauding the Revenue'; No. 59 (1784) 'Second Report'; No. 60 (1784) 'Third Report'.

The Reports of the Commissioners Appointed to Examine, Take, and State the Public Accounts of the Kingdom, by John Lane, Secretary to the Commissioners (London, 1787), iii, 'Thirteenth Report Relative to the Manner of Passing the Accounts of the Customs, in the Office of the Auditors of the Imprest', 1785; 'Fourteenth Report, Relative to the Charges of Management of the Customs Duties in the Port of London for the Year 1784', 1785; 'Fifteenth Report, Relative to the Payment to the Officers of the Customs at the Out Ports, etc. for the Year 1784', 1786.

B. Books

ATTON, HENRY, AND HENRY HURST HOLLAND, *The King's Customs*, 2 vols. (London, 1908–10).

BALDWIN, SAMUEL, *A Survey of the British Customs; containing the Rates of Merchandise* (London, 1770). [In Smith's Library: Mizuta 4.]

CARSON, EDWARD, *The Ancient and Rightful Customs: A History of the English Customs Service* (London, 1972).

CHESTER, W. D., *Chronicles of the Customs Service*, priv. ptd. (London, 1885).

CROUCH, HENRY, *A Complete Guide to the Officers of His Majesty's Customs in the Out-ports* (London, 1732).

——, ——, *A Complete View of the British Customs* (London, 1727). [Crouch was regarded as an official guide until late in the eighteenth century when errors were found in his statements. Smith's copy of this second book by him is in the library of H.M. Customs and Excise, King's Beam House, London EC4.]

DOWELL, STEPHEN, *A History of Taxation and Taxes in England from the Earliest Times to the Year 1885*, 4 vols. (London, 1888).

HALL, H., *A History of the Customs Revenues in England from the Earliest Times to the Year 1827*, 2 vols. (London, 1885).

HOON, ELIZABETH EVELYNOLA, *The Organization of the English Customs Systems, 1696–1786* (New York and London, 1938).

SAXBY, HENRY, *The British Customs, containing an Historical and Practical Account of each Branch of that part of the Revenue* (London, 1757). [In Smith's Library: Mizuta 54.]

Index of Persons

The first numeral after each name indicates the page on which a biographical note about the person may be found. An italic numeral in bold face indicates the first page of a letter from Adam Smith to the person named, and an ordinary italic numeral the first page of a letter from the person named to Smith. The following abbreviations have been used: AS for Adam Smith, DH for David Hume, GU for Glasgow University, and EU for Edinburgh University; also those cited on p. xv for Smith's writings. Numerals following * indicate mere mentions of the name.

Abercromby, George, 24 & n.

Adair, Surgeon-Gen. Robert, 307 & n.

Adam brothers: Robert, M.P., James, William, 125 & n.; failure of Adelphi scheme, 162 & n.; John's failure, 163 & n.

Adam, William, M.P., 387

Adams, Samuel, 183 n.

Adélaide, Princesse de France (Louis XV's dau.), 128

Ailesbury, Lady, 156 n.

Alembert, Jean le Rond d', & the Hume–Rousseau quarrel, 113 & n., 118, 135; *295

Alexander, Bishop of Murray (Moray), 147

Alexander, John, 84 & n.

Alexander, Robert or William, 79 & n.

Anderson, Adam, 124 & n., 248

Anderson, James, 251 & n.

Anderson, John, 18 & n., 19, 23

Angier, Mr. —, 317, 320, 321

Anker, Karsten, 247 n.

Anker, Peter, 247 & n.; AS acknowledges receiving Danish translation of WN, discusses armed neutrality, 253–4

Annand, William, 285

Anstruther, John, M.P., 235 n.

Anville (La Rochefoucauld d'Enville), Marie-Louise-Nicole, Duchesse d', 111 & n., 127, 128; her circle, 155 n.; complained of AS's French, 173; *228, 233, 239, 255, 287

Arbuthnot, Robert, of Kirkbraehead, 166 & n.

Argyll: Archibald Campbell, 3rd Duke of, AS meets, 6 & n.; 23; & TMS, 33, 35, 39; & management of Scotland, 50 & n.; AS visits at Inveraray, 59 & n.; & Church patronage in Scotland, 76 n.; & AS's professorship, 335;
John Campbell, 2nd Duke of, his London house, 1 & n.; AS visits his Oxfordshire house, 2 & n.;
John Campbell, 4th Duke of, 156 n.;
John Campbell, 5th Duke of, 184 n.

Arnold, Revd. William, 202 & n.

Arringask, Chaplain of, 149

Ashmole, Elias, 406

Baert, Alexandre Balthazar François de Paul de, 303 & n.

Bagwell, Mr. —, 16

Baird, George, AS expresses views to, on 'Rational Grammar', 87 & n.

Balfour, John, 99 & n., *139, 202, 248

Banks, Sir Joseph, AS introduces John Leslie to, 309 & n.

Barnard, Sir John, M.P., 333 & n.

Barré, Col. Isaac, M.P., 90 & n.

Barrett, Messrs., & Townshend's MS. 'History of the Sinking Fund', 328 n.

Barrington, Hon. Daines, 140 & n.

Bazinghen, François André, Abot de, 186 n., 187 n.

Beatson, Robert, 301 & n.

Beattie, James, 169 & n.; Hurd advises not to engage in controversy with Priestley, 182 & n.

Beauchamp, Francis Seymour Conway, Lord, 93 & n., 97, 102, 106

Beauclerk, Topham, 229 & n.

Bell, John, 40 & n.

Bentham: Jeremiah (Jeremy's fa.), 403 n.; Jeremy, 303 & n.; and Shelburne, 235 n.; 325; his circle regards AS as 'our man', 386–7; AS's opinion of, 387; (see Appendix C, 386–404); Samuel (Jeremy's bro.), 386, 403 n.

Bernard, Abbot of Aberbrothock (Arbroath), 146

Betham, Mr. & Mrs. 11 & n., 17

Bingham: Mrs. L. M., & reconciliation with her father, AS's cousin, 318
— Revd. Richard, 318 & n.

Birch, Thomas, 39 & n.

Black, Joseph, 23 & n.; as Smith's executor, burns papers, viii, 168 n., makes selection for EPS, 287 n.; attends AS's student, 63; GU Clerk of Senate, 86;

Index of Books and Subjects

The abbreviations for Adam Smith's writings cited on p. xv are used. He is referred to as AS and David Hume as DH. Titles of books in Smith's library as indicated by Bonar or Mizuta are identified by †. Editions, etc., in the library which contain titles that are cited are similarly identified, though within square brackets.

DATE DUE

SEP 1 5 1983			
APR 1 8 1985			
ILL: 4976375			
Due: 4/23/03			